STUDIES IN BAPTIST HISTORY AN
VOLUME 30.1

'Seditious Sectaryes

The Baptist Conventiclers of Oxford
1641-1691

STUDIES IN BAPTIST HISTORY AND THOUGHT
VOLUME 30.1

A full listing of all titles in this series
appears at the close of this book

STUDIES IN BAPTIST HISTORY AND THOUGHT
VOLUME 30.1

'Seditious Sectaryes'

The Baptist Conventiclers of Oxford
1641-1691

Larry J. Kreitzer

Foreword by Diarmaid MacCulloch

Paternoster:
thinking faith

First published 2006 by Paternoster

Paternoster is an imprint of Authentic Media
9 Holdom Avenue, Bletchley, Milton Keynes, MK1 1QR, UK
and
P O Box 1047, Waynesboro, GA 30830–2047, USA

12 11 10 09 08 07 06   7 6 5 4 3 2 1

British Library Cataloguing in Publication Data
A catalogue record for this book is available from the British Library

ISBN- 13: 978-1-84227-516-0
ISBN- 10: 1-84227-516-X

ISBN-13: 978-1-84227-518-4 (2 vol. set)
ISBN-10: 1-84227-518-6 (2 vol. set)

Typeset by Larry J. Kreitzer
Printed and bound in Great Britain
by Nottingham Alpha Graphics

STUDIES IN BAPTIST HISTORY AND THOUGHT

Series Preface

Baptists form one of the largest Christian communities in the world, and while they hold the historic faith in common with other mainstream Christian traditions, they nevertheless have important insights which they can offer to the worldwide church. *Studies in Baptist History and Thought* will be one means towards this end. It is an international series of academic studies which includes original monographs, revised dissertations, collections of essays and conference papers, and aims to cover any aspect of Baptist history and thought. While not all the authors are themselves Baptists, they nevertheless share an interest in relating Baptist history and thought to the other branches of the Christian church and to the wider life of the world.

The series includes studies in various aspects of Baptist history from the seventeenth century down to the present day, including biographical works, and Baptist thought is understood as covering the subject-matter of theology (including interdisciplinary studies embracing biblical studies, philosophy, sociology, practical theology, liturgy and women's studies). The diverse streams of Baptist life throughout the world are all within the scope of these volumes.

The series editors and consultants believe that the academic disciplines of history and theology are of vital importance to the spiritual vitality of the churches of the Baptist faith and order. The series sets out to discuss, examine and explore the many dimensions of their tradition and so to contribute to their on-going intellectual vigour.

A brief word of explanation is due for the series identifier on the front cover. The fountains, taken from heraldry, represent the Baptist distinctive of believer's baptism and, at the same time, the source of the water of life. There are three of them because they symbolize the Trinitarian basis of Baptist life and faith. Those who are redeemed by the Lamb, the book of Revelation reminds us, will be led to 'fountains of living waters' (Rev. 7.17).

Series Editors

Anthony R. Cross, Fellow of the Centre for Baptist History and Heritage, Regent's Park College, Oxford, UK

Curtis W. Freeman, Research Professor of Theology and Director of the Baptist House of Studies, Duke University, North Carolina, USA

Stephen R. Holmes, Lecturer in Theology, University of St Andrews, Scotland, UK

Elizabeth Newman, Professor of Theology and Ethics, Baptist Theological Seminary at Richmond, Virginia, USA

Philip E. Thompson, Assistant Professor of Systematic Theology and Christian Heritage, North American Baptist Seminary, Sioux Falls, South Dakota, USA

Series Consultant Editors

David Bebbington, Professor of History, University of Stirling, Scotland, UK

Paul S. Fiddes, Professor of Systematic Theology, University of Oxford, and Principal of Regent's Park College, Oxford, UK

† Stanley J. Grenz, Pioneer McDonald Professor of Theology, Carey Theological College, Vancouver, British Columbia, Canada

Ken R. Manley, Distinguished Professor of Church History, Whitley College, The University of Melbourne, Australia

Stanley E. Porter, President and Professor of New Testament, McMaster Divinity College, Hamilton, Ontario, Canada

To the members of
New Road Baptist Church, Oxford

Contents

Volume One: People and Places

Contents

Volume One: People and Places

Volume Two: Sources

FOREWORD

University-dominated, Tory, High Church Anglican Oxford: one might think that in relation to that well-known stereotype, the story of the foundation and development of Oxford's Baptist congregation might have the same sort of minor supporting role as Rosencrantz and Guildenstern in Shakespeare's *Hamlet*. Yet Tom Stoppard managed to send Hamlet backstage, and turn Rosencrantz and Guildenstern into the heroes of one of the twentieth century's most memorable comedies: it is all a matter of perspective. In this book, Dr Kreitzer's formidable research reverses roles with equally dramatic effect: in his tale, it is the world of the Anglican University which fades into the background, giving way to the determined, independent-minded people of the city and its surrounding countryside who defied the conventions of their day to worship God as they thought most fitting. Their moment came when the structures of church and kingdom had been shattered by civil war, when the breakdown of authority made it possible to say in public what had only been possible in quiet thoughts or in deep secrecy in earlier years. By 1656, amid the rather grudging experiment in religious toleration that was Oliver Cromwell's finest achievement, the Baptists of Oxford who became the New Road congregation, made their appearance on the historical stage. It is a mark of Dr Kreitzer's careful scholarship that we can now be certain about this date, rather than accepting previous inaccurate guesses blindly repeated from one book to another. This study is a labour of love on Dr Kreitzer's part, a significant contribution to local and Baptist historical scholarship, with an impressively exhaustive sweep through the primary sources. The research has been beautifully done with great enthusiasm, and it fits well with all that is being done at the moment to reassess the social and political position of early Dissent. This is the overview which will always be definitive on this important story, and it goes where previous scholars have not. It is also a tribute to a remarkable saga of continuity in one congregation from the mid-seventeenth-century to the present day: an English story, but an essential part of the jigsaw of worldwide Baptist history.

Diarmaid MacCulloch
St Cross College,
Oxford
August 2006

ACKNOWLEDGEMENTS

The initial impetus for this exploration into the origins of Baptists in Oxford was the celebration of the 350th anniversary of New Road Baptist Church, Oxford, an event that was officially marked in November of 2003. I was part of a church working-party which helped plan a public exhibition at the Museum of Oxford entitled 'Dissenting Voices'. My particular assignment within this group was the 17th century and the murky origins of Dissenters in Oxford, a matter which had been largely unexplored. The project gradually took over my research interests, and has culminated in this present study. Throughout I have deliberately concentrated on the importance of original sources, attempting, as much as is possible, to reconstruct the lives of the early Dissenters based on the surviving documents. An historical study of this type by its very nature involves engagement with primary source materials. A number of institutions and their libraries have proven invaluable in this regard, notably the Oxfordshire Records Office in Cowley, Oxford, The Bodleian Library, Oxford, the Angus Library, Regent's Park College, and the National Archives at Kew, London.

A special word of thanks is due to Jennifer Thorp, former archivist of the Angus Library at Regent's Park College, Oxford, now similarly employed at New College, Oxford; without her help this task would have been very much more difficult, if not impossible. She cheerfully introduced me into the world of 17th-century manuscripts, approaching each document or inscription I presented to her as if it was a personal challenge, a puzzle from the past which needed to be solved. I also would like to record my indebtedness to my wife, Deborah Rooke, for help with many of the Latin documents herein discussed, particularly the *Oxford Charter of 1688*. She managed amiably to incorporate my regular calls upon her expertise within her own demanding schedule at King's College London. Far too many more evening meals than we would care to admit were spent poring over Latin grammars with dinner plates balanced precariously on our knees.

Finally, a word is in order about the eleven illustrations scattered throughout the volume. The portrait of William Kiffen (Illustration #3) is reproduced with the kind permission of my college. I am grateful for the permission of both the Oxfordshire Records Office and the Bodleian Library, University of Oxford, to reproduce illustrations from documents within their collections (Illustrations #1, #2 and #10 are from Oxford City Council documents housed at the Records Office; #4, #6 and #8 are from the Bodleian Library). The remaining four illustrations are from items in my own collection.

Larry J Kreitzer
Regent's Park College, Oxford
 2006

ILLUSTRATIONS

ABBREVIATIONS

AARB	*The Abingdon Association Record Book*, Angus Library, Regent's Park College, Oxford, (D/AA/1)
AdWPR	*Adlestrop Wills and Probate Records*
AWPR	*Abingdon Wills and Probate Records*
CSC	Chronological Source Catalogue
DPWPR	*Dorchester Peculiar Wills and Probate Records*
GL MS	Guildhall Library Manuscript (London)
JHC	*Journal of the House of Commons*
OAR	*Oxford Archdeaconry Records*
ODR	*Oxford Diocesan Records*
OWPR	*Oxford Will and Probate Records*
SP	State Papers Domestic
TBCR	*Tiverton Baptist Church Records*

Introduction

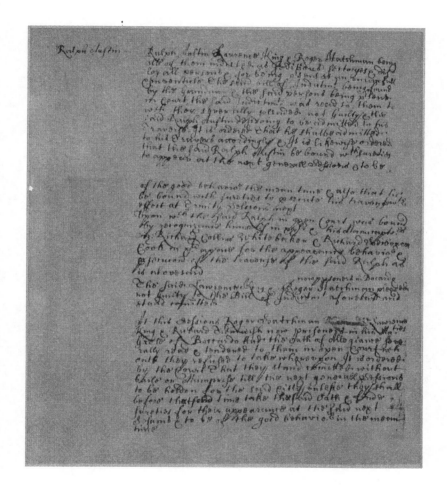

Illustration #1: Record from the Oxford Petty Sessions Court of January 1662 giving details of the indictment of Ralph Austen, Lawrence King, Roger Hatchman, and Richard Tidmarsh (*Oxford Petty Sessions Roll – 1656-1678* (O.5.11), folios 45 verso–46 recto.

Introduction

When attempting to trace the Baptist beginnings within 17th-century Oxford, one thing needs to be made clear at the outset: it is foolhardy to make hard and fast distinctions between Baptists, Independents, Presbyterians, and even Quakers, as denominational groups or religious bodies within the city.[1] The religious and theological boundaries between the dissenting groups blur and overlap, making it virtually impossible to distinguish absolutely one from the other with any degree of certainty.[2] This is partly because many of the historical sources which discuss them represent the viewpoint of the established Church of England at the time, and those sources tend to lump all the various groups together under the heading of 'Sectaryes' or 'Dissenters'. At the same time, all of the available evidence suggests that most of those who were disparagingly described as 'Sectaryes' or 'Dissenters' or, after 1672 (when the legal definition was established by *The Declaration of Indulgence*), as 'Nonconformists', should not be regarded as 'Separatists' as such, given that they did *not* by their religious meetings and practices originally intend to set up churches and congregations which were rivals to their local parish churches. It is true that there were some churches, notably the handful of congregations associated with the so-called Jacob-Lathrop-Jessey circle in London, which did self-consciously see themselves in this way, but they were the exception rather than the rule. For this reason, Murray Tolmie, in his important study entitled *The Triumph of the Saints: The Separate Churches of London 1616-1649* (1977) suggests that it is more correct to describe most of those involved in religious meetings and attending illegal conventicles during the 1630s and 1640s as 'semi-separatists' or 'quasi-separatists'.[3] An oft-cited passage from the warrant issued by the Court of High Commission in 1636 gives insight into how the conventiclers were commonly perceived by the ecclesiastical authorities:

---

[1] Failure to appreciate this remains one of the methodological weaknesses of Whiteman's seminal study *The Compton Census of 1676* (1986); the point is addressed somewhat in her follow-up article (Whiteman (1992): 91-96). Whiteman (1986): 425-426, gives a total population of 4351 for the fourteen parishes of the city of Oxford in 1676, including 34 Catholic Recusants and 79 Nonconformists.

[2] Spurr (1997): 90-124, offers a good survey for the second half of the century.

[3] Tolmie (1977): 28-34.

Whereas credible information hath bin given unto us of his Ma[jes]^{ties} Commission for causes ecclessiasticall that there are at this present remaining in areas of the Cittie of London, or suburbs thereof, and in many other parts within this kingdome of England, sundrie sorts of Separatists and sectaries ... who refuse upon Sondaies and other festivall daies to come unto their parish churches, there to joyne and participate with the parochiall Congregations in divine services, sacraments, and hearing of Gods word preached, but have and doe ordinarily use to meete together in great numbers on such daies and at other times in privat houses and places, and there keepe and maintaine privat Conventicles and exercises of Religion by the Lawes of this Realme prohibited, to the corrupting and perverting of sundrie his Ma[jes]^{ties} good subjects and the manifest contempt of his Highnes lawes and the disturbance of the peace of the Church.[1]

It is reasonable to assume that Oxford is among those places included in the pregnant phrase 'and in many other parts within this kingdome of England'. Two factors make such an assumption highly probable: Oxford's geographical proximity to London, and its prominence as the site of one of England's two universities, which effectively served to make it an intellectual crossroads cultivating new ideas and alternative conceptions about religious life. In this sense, we can expect that Oxford would have had its share of such 'sectaryes', and that they met in private homes and held illegal conventicles within the city just as was happening in the capital London a mere fifty miles away. Given the fact that conventicles were illegal, and attendance at them politically unwise, not to say potentially financially costly, it is hardly surprising that documentary evidence about them is scarce. At the same time, we know for certain that a Baptist church was functioning in Oxford by the mid-1650s, and a fair amount of evidence survives to help reconstruct its early life. What has not been explored by historians in any depth thus far is the extent to which the Baptist church which came to flourish in the city in the second half of the 17th century, can be said to trace its roots to the unlawful conventicles of the 1640s and the political moves made against supporters of the Parliamentary cause.

A. The Development of Baptist Self-Identity

It is widely agreed by historians that religion was one of the dominant forces within English society as a whole throughout the reign of the Stuart kings, and the rise of various dissenting groups is a primary expression of this fact.[2] In this regard Baptists were slowly, but certainly, beginning to carve out their own distinctive identity throughout England and Wales during this period, particularly wishing to distance themselves from the pejorative label of 'Anabaptists'. As Christopher Hill has noted: 'The name came to be used in a

---

[1] SP 16/314, folio 79 recto.
[2] See Seaward (1991); Harris (1990; 1993).

general pejorative sense to describe those who were believed to oppose the existing social and political order.'[1]

As a term, 'Anabaptist' had too many uncomfortable associations with radical revolutionaries on the continent, men such as Thomas Müntzer who, inspired by an apocalyptic zeal, became associated with the violent clashes of the 1520s. This was the popular understanding of what Anabaptists stood for, and many alarmist tracts and pamphlets were produced in the 1640s which capitalized on such associations. Images of Anabaptists in the popular press were universally negative, and the association with violence and murder was frequently highlighted. A good example is the pamphlet entitled *Bloody Newes from Dover* (1647), which purported to relate the story of a murder committed by Mary Champion, who decapitated her seven-week old child and gave the head to her husband in order that he might baptize it, presumably by sprinkling. What is intriguing about this particular pamphlet is the fact that Mary Champion has the word 'Anabaptist' prominently displayed next to her image on the cover of the tract, whereas her husband, as a respectable member of the party in the ascendancy at the time, is described as a 'Presbyterian' as he hold up his hands in disgust at her actions.

Another classic example of popular feeling about Anabaptists is an anonymous tract published in London in 1642 entitled *A Short History of the Anabaptists of High and Low Germany*.[2] The final words of the pamphlet argue for 'suppressing the growth of Anabaptisme, which is the canker of Religion and the gangrene of the State'. Another published in London in 1642 was entitled *A* Warning for England, *Especially for London in the Famous History of the Frantick Anabaptists, Their Wild Preachings and Practices in Germany*. The little book published by W Hughes entitled *Munster and Abingdon* (1657) is another case in point. This book, published in the aftermath of the upheaval surrounding the funeral of the Baptist leader John Pendarves on 30 September 1656, offered a short history of the violent revolution in Munster and suggested comparisons be drawn between the revolutionaries there and those in Abingdon. An association in the popular mind between Anabaptists and the Fifth Monarchy movement was commonplace, particularly in the period of uncertainty and upheaval following the death of Oliver Cromwell in September of 1658 and the Restoration of the monarchy in 1660. An anonymous tract, published in March of 1660, put the key point in the form of a satirical query, aimed at highlighting the threat to good government of the nation posed by both groups. It queries:

---

[1] Hill (1975): 26.

[2] Anthony Wood records in his diaries that he bought a copy of this in Oxford on 1 July 1661 (*MS Wood Diaries 5*, folio 22 recto).

> Whether the *Anabaptists*, or *Fift Monarchy-men* be the better Common-wealths men, since the second are resolv'd against all governments, and the first are content with none?[1]

Such dangerous associations with the Fifth Monarchists demanded that Baptists somehow distanced themselves from the perceived extremes of Anabaptism (as it was popularly conceived), and offered instead a re-definition of their own identity. We see something of this tension coming to a head in March of 1660, when the General Baptist Assembly in London published their *A Brief Confession or Declaration of Faith set forth by many of us who are (falsely) called Ana-Baptists* (1660) in order

> to inform all men (in these days of scandal and reproach) of an innocent belief and practice, for which we are not only resolved to suffer persecution, to the loss of our goods, but also life itself, rather than to decline the same.[2]

Nor should we overlook the fact that the seven Baptist congregations in London who published *The Confession of Faith* in 1644 did so as 'Churches which are commonly (though falsely) called Anabaptists'. Similarly, the General Baptist tract by Thomas Nutt entitled *The Humble Request of Certain Christians, reproachfully called Anabaptists* (1643) is another illustration of the point. So too is the General Baptist pamphlet entitled *The Fountain of Free Grace Opened*, published in 1645 and probably authored by Thomas Lamb;[3] it was issued in the name of 'the congregation of Christ in London, constituted by baptism upon the profession of faith, falsely called Anabaptists'.[4]

Other developments taking place at the time also need to be noted, for they too helped contribute to Baptists discovering a sense of independence and ecclesiastical identity. Thus, beginning in 1641 in the village of Westerleigh near Bristol, many Baptist leaders took part in the so-called 'disputations'; these were meetings at which religious and theological ideas were openly expressed and denominational identities forged in the cut-and-thrust of public debate. Perhaps the best known of these disputations was between William Kiffen and Daniel Featley in the borough of Southwark in Surrey on 17 October 1642. Featley's account of the disputation was published in the form of his *The Dippers Dipt, or, the Anabaptists duck'd and plung'd over head and eares* (1645), prompted by the issuing of *The Baptist Confession* (1644) under the guiding hand of Kiffen. Not surprisingly, Oxford was one of the geographical focal points for these public disputations. One of the most

---

[1] *Fanatique Queries, Propos'd for the present Assertors of the Good Old Cause* (1660): 3.
[2] *A Brief Confession or Declaration of Faith set forth by many of us who are (falsely) called Ana-Baptists* (1660): 1.
[3] So Crosby (1740): 3.56, states.
[4] Tolmie (1977): 55-65, 72-4, discusses these publications. Also see McGregor (1984): 23-39.

prominent figures in these disputations was John Tombes (1603-1676), a scholar from Magdalen Hall in Oxford, who is known to have participated in nine disputations from 1642-1676, including one in 1652 in Oxford.[1] In addition, the charismatic John Pendarves, a former student of Exeter College, Oxford, took part in a disputation on 11 September 1652 in the parish church at Watlington, Oxfordshire.[2] There was also a celebrated debate between William Erbery and Francis Cheynell which took place in St Mary the Virgin Church, Oxford on 11 January 1647.[3]

B. Sources for Study of Oxford Baptists

The aim of this study is to sketch out the details of the lives of some of the early Oxford conventiclers who eventually came to identify themselves with the Baptist cause of dissent in Oxford. In so doing one is immediately confronted with the question of what primary sources to use as the basis for any historical reconstruction. As I have hinted, many of the most important sources for an investigation into Oxford life in the 17th century are avowedly Anglican in sentiment, and thus not favourably disposed to 'Dissent' in general, nor '(Ana)Baptists' in particular. Nevertheless, there is ample material at hand, much of it never before used in attempting to explore the Baptist beginnings in Oxford. Sifting through the primary sources is not an easy task, for little of it is indexed or catalogued, but the dividends more than justify the effort.

I shall make frequent use of the writings of the 17th-century Oxonian Anthony Wood, whose first-hand, eyewitness accounts of much of what happened in the city are invaluable, even if biased against the Dissenters' cause. I shall also cite primary source materials from various Oxford City Council records and the Oxford City Archives, many of which have now been published and are available as volumes in the *Oxford Historical Society* series. Special attention will also be given to relevant documents from the Oxford Diocesan Records and the Oxford Archdeaconry Records, most of which have not been published. Many of these records are a mixture of Latin and a highly formulaic English; they are heavily abbreviated, highly idiosyncratic, and at times are extremely difficult to decipher paleographically. Their neglect is one of the great oversights in the study of 17th-century Nonconformity, and is a matter which seriously needs to be addressed if we are to entertain any hope of

---

[1] Langley (1918-9): 222-39, lists these as taking place in 1642 (Bristol); January 1643 (London); 1 January 1650 (Bewdley, Worcestershire); 1652 (Oxford); 5 September 1653 (Abergavenny); 1657 (Leominster, Herefordshire); 27 November 1660 (Leominster, Herefordshire)); and a debate in Hereford the date of which is uncertain. John Tombes was known to have been particularly interested in public controversies in Leominster as early as 1642 (see Whitley (1920-21): 13-18, for details).

[2] Langley (1918-19): 227.

[3] Langley (1918-19): 225. For more on Erbery, see White (1969-70): 114-125; Hill (1975): 192-197; Roberts (2004).

providing a faithful picture of the time. The words of E R Brinkworth, published over 60 years ago, remain as true today as then:

> There can be no doubt that the records of archdeacons' courts, and indeed, of all ecclesiastical courts, have been very generally neglected by both custodians and students .... And but an infinitesimal fraction of what is known to exist has ever been published in any form. In short, the field is almost untouched.[1]

Within the discussion that follows I have attempted a first step in correcting this oversight concerning the use of ecclesiastical documents. Wherever possible I have provided a reconstructed text and, in the case of the Latin entries, a translation of the entry; at times the translation offered is a paraphrase communicating the general *sense* of the entry since a literal, word-for-word translation of the Latin terms is incomprehensible.

Another important, and often overlooked, source of information about the life of Dissenters, are the wills and testaments which have survived. The interpretation of such documents presents special problems, one which arises out of their complex nature. Wills were often produced through the agency of professional clerks, scribes, and copyists, who, in the course of producing them, combined formulaic forms and expressions with the genuinely-held religious convictions and beliefs of the person for whom they were prepared. In this regard they represent an indispensable, if problematic, source of information. As Christopher Marsh has noted:

> Wills are not a source into which historians can dip for swift and reliable results. When studied with care, however, they can tell us much of lay faith ... The witness lists can also yield invaluable information enabling the historian to reconstruct local religious networks, albeit imperfectly.[2]

As shall be seen, the dozen or so wills relating to known Baptist Dissenters provide important insights into the web of connections between family, friends and colleagues. They also allow us to reconstruct, however imperfectly, the family trees of some of these early Baptists. Other relevant financial documents relating to Oxford, such as the various collections of the infamous Hearth Tax of 19 May 1662,[3] collections of various Lay Subsidies granted by

---

[1] Brinkworth (1943): 93.

[2] Marsh (1990): 248.

[3] Parliament passed a bill for 'laying an imposition upon chimney hearths' which received the assent of Charles I on 19 May 1662. Within the National Archives in London there are four documents relating to the collection of this tax in Oxford and its suburbs. In this study the four are delineated by the date (as best can be determined) when the tax was collected: *Hearth Tax for Michaelmas 1662* (E 179/255/3); *Hearth Tax of August-November 1662* (E 179/255/4); *Hearth Tax of Michaelmas 1665* (E 179/164/513); and *Hearth Tax of 24 April 1666* (E 179/164/514). For more on the Hearth Tax, see Marshall (1936): 628-646; Weinstock (1940); Geere (1985); and Jurkowski, Smith and Crook (1998): 261-165.

Parliament from 1640-1664,[1] the Poll Tax of 1667,[2] the War Taxes of 1667-1668,[3] and a variety of other taxes from 1692-1696,[4] will also be consulted in

---

[1] Within the National Archives in London there are nine documents relating to the collection of a number of Lay Subsidies in Oxford and its suburbs. In this study these nine documents and the date (as best can be determined) when the tax was collected are as follows: *Lay Subsidy of 10-23 December 1640* (E 179/164/477) – collected 20 March 1641; *Lay Subsidy of 10-23 December 1640* (E 179/164/495) – collected 30 April 1641; *Lay Subsidy of 23 June 1647* (E 179/164/497) – collected 27 December 1647; *Lay Subsidy of 23 June 1647* (E 179/164/498) – collected in 1648; *Lay Subsidy of 23 June 1647* (E 179/164/498a) – collected in 1648; *Lay Subsidy of 17 March 1648* (E 179/164/499) – collected in 1648; *Lay Subsidy of 29 December 1660* (E 179/164/501a) – collected 12 July 1661; *Free and Voluntary Present of 8 July 1661* (E 179/255/5/4) – collected on 13 October 1661; *Lay Subsidy of 27 July 1663* (E 179/164/503) – collected on 17 October 1663. Three Oxford City Council documents entitled *Subsidies granted to the King by Parliament* (B.1.4) also belong to this category of taxation records, and are here designated by the date of their collection. These are: *Lay Subsidy of 20 March 1641* (B.1.4c), *Lay Subsidy of 6 December 1641* (B.1.4d), *Lay Subsidy of 11 April 1664* (B.1.4f). The *Lay Subsidy of 23 June 1647* was intended to raise £60,000 per month to help maintain the armies under the command of Sir Thomas Fairfax and to help finance the cost of the war in Ireland (see Jurkowski, Smith and Crook (1998): 237, for details). The *Lay Subsidy of 17 March 1648* was intended to raise £60,000 per month for six months; the tax was extended a further six months by Parliament on 6 October 1648 (see Jurkowski, Smith and Crook (1998): 240, for details).

[2] *Poll Tax of 1667* (P.5.7). This was a graduated poll tax granted by Parliament on 18 January 1667 and collected on 8 April 1667. See Jurkowski, Smith and Crook (1998): 267-269, for details of this tax.

[3] These are recorded in *War Taxes – 1667-1668* (P.5.8), which contains records for seven assessments for the years 1667-1668. The seven assessments are: *Collection of 24 June 1667* – for the 10th of 12 quarterly assessments of the 'Royal Ayde Act' passed on 9 February 1665, and for the 6th of 8 quarterly assessments of the 'Additional Act' passed on 31 October 1665; *Collection of 29 September 1667* – for the 11th of 12 quarterly assessments of the 'Royal Ayde' Tax, and for the 7th of 8 quarterly assessments of the 'Additional Act'; *Collection of 21 December 1667* – for the 12th of 12 quarterly assessments of the 'Royal Ayde' Tax, and for the 8th of 8 quarterly assessments of the 'Additional Act'; *Collection of 26 March 1668* – for the so-called 'Act for Assessment to the Duke of York', passed by the Cavalier Parliament on 31 October 1665, which was collected together with the taxes levied under the 'Act for Granting £1,256,347 13s for the War against the Dutch', passed on 8 February 1668; *Collection of 26 June 1668* – a quarterly tax assessment records relating to the 'Act for Granting £1,256,347 13s for the War against the Dutch'; *Collection of 26 September 1668* – a quarterly tax assessment records relating to the 'Act for Granting £1,256,347 13s for the War against the Dutch'; and *Collection of 26 December 1668* – a quarterly tax assessment records relating to the 'Act for Granting £1,256,347 13s for the War against the Dutch'. See Jurkowski, Smith and Crook (1998): 266-269, for details of these taxes. A record of the *Collection of 24 June 1667* was published in Salter (1923): 337-353.

[4] These are recorded in two Oxford City Council manuscripts: *Taxes – 1691-1694* (P.5.9), which contains the rather garbled records for six assessments for the years 1692-1695, notably poll taxes which were granted by Parliament in order to raise money for

this regard. Oxford is particularly fortunate in having a large number of surviving taxation records, although these have not yet been explored for the light they may shed on Baptists within the city. Similarly, the city records relating to the municipal careers of these Baptists, as well as their professional lives as tradesmen working in and around Oxford, are well worth consulting for they significantly help to fill out our picture of them. Several Baptists conventiclers were cordwainers, two were mercers, and another a weaver, and the surviving guild records are invaluable for reconstructing their lives.

However, the starting point for identifying those who associated themselves with the Baptist cause in Oxford will be the records of the churches themselves, notably the records of the Abingdon Association. This consists of two important seventeenth-century manuscripts, both of which are contained in the Angus Library at Regent's Park College, Oxford. The first is commonly known as the *Longworth Churchbook* (the Angus catalogue designation of which is Longworth 1/1); the second is known as the *Abingdon Association Records Book* (the Angus catalogue designation of which is D/AA/1).[1] The *Longworth Churchbook* is significant in that it contains several references to the Baptist church from Oxford as a constituent member of the Abingdon Association, and figures in the debate about when the church was officially welcomed into it.[2] Unfortunately, the *Longworth Churchbook* gives no further details about the church, and it does not name any of the Oxford messengers. The *Abingdon Association Records Book* is more forthcoming in this regard, and as such is more important as a result. The full text of the *Abingdon Association Records Book* was published in 1974 by my colleague Dr B R White, Principal Emeritus of Regent's Park College, although there are some minor corrections and additional considerations which need to be made to his seminal work.[3] In addition, other Baptist tracts, pamphlets and broadsheets were occasionally issued which specifically identified representatives of the Baptist church in Oxford as signatories. These include *The Complaining Testimony of Some ... of Sions Children* (1656); *The Testimony to Truth,*

---

the war against France; and *Taxes – 1694-1746* (P.5.10), which contains incomplete records of a number of additional assessments, including the *Poll Tax of 1694,* the *Poll Tax of 1695,* the *Marriage, Birth and Burial Tax of 1695,* the *Poll Tax of 1696,* the *Window Tax of 1696,* the *Window Tax of 1697,* and *Marriage, Birth and Burial Tax of 1696.* The *Window Tax for 1696* was published in Hobson (1939): 340-372.

[1] *The Abingdon Association Records Book* was purchased by Dr Ernest A Payne, then General Secretary of the Baptist Union of Great Britain & Ireland, from Guntrips Bookshops Ltd., of 115, Week Street, Maidstone, Kent in June 1954 for £5 5s 0d. It contains 47 foliated pages.

[2] Oxford probably joined in March of 1656, although some have argued for an earlier date in 1653. See Kreitzer (2005): 207-219, for details of this debate.

[3] Unfortunately White's published version does not include a cross-referencing of the pagination of the manuscripts themselves, which has made for some difficulties in accurate referencing for interested scholars. I have attempted to correct this shortcoming by including the manuscript page numbers alongside references to White's work.

Agreeing with an Essay for Settlement (1659);[1] *Innocency Vindicated: or, Reproach Wip'd Off* (1689), and *A Narrative of the Proceedings of the General Assembly* (1689). The full text of these documents is given below as Appendices A-D. Finally, records of other 17th-century Baptist congregations occasionally shed some light on the congregation in Oxford. Two good examples from London are William Kiffen's church in Devonshire Square, and the church which met in Petty France, both of whose records are now in the Guildhall Library, London.[2]

C. Thé Social Network of Oxford's Early Baptists

Daniel Featley, in his vituperative tract *The Dippers Dipt, or, the Anabaptists duck'd and plung'd over head and eares* (1645), described Baptists as crude and uneducated, suggesting that they were mainly made up of barely literate tradesman and artisans. Sarcastically, he says they were 'Russet Rabbies, and Mechanic Enthusiasts, and profound Watermen, and Sublime Coachmen, and Illuminated Tradesmen.'[3] In the main, the members of the Oxford Baptist conventicle were not academics, and rarely were any of them associated directly with the University of Oxford as such.[4] On the other hand, neither were they from the lowest social strata, as has often been suggested, particularly by those who insist on associating the rise of a Baptist presence in Oxford with the arrival of the Parliamentary army under Lord Fairfax in June of 1646.[5] At the same time, the army connection is not an unreasonable one to

---

[1] Reprinted in *A Warning-Piece to the General Council of the Army, Being Sundry Concurrent Essaies Towards a Righteous Settlement* (1659): 11-13.

[2] *Devonshire Square (Particular) Baptist Church* (MS 20 228 1A); *Petty France (Particular) Baptist Church* (MS 20 228 1B).

[3] Featley (1645): C3. See McGregor (1984): 36-39, on this point.

[4] Rarely, some of the Baptists who were initially educated at Oxford as members of the Church of England, wrote tracts and pamphlets individually. Examples include John Pendarves's *Arrows Against Babylon* (1656), and the eccentric Francis Bampfield, whose publications on such eclectic topics as sabbatarianism, the theological importance of biblical Hebrew as a language, and his own prison experiences included *The Judgment of Mr. Francis Bamfield ... for the Observation of the Jewish ... Sabboth* (1672); *All in One* (1677); *The House of Wisdom* (1681); *A Name, An After-One* (1681); *The Holy Scriptures* (1684); *A Just Appeal from Lower Courts on Earth* (1683); and *The Lord's Free Prisoner* (1683). Greaves (1985): 179-210, offers a study of Bampfield's life. For more on the University of Oxford as an important contributor to the shaping of the religious and theological thought in England immediately prior to the civil wars, see Curtis (1959): 165-226.

[5] Thus, Stevens (1948): 3, states: 'The year in which distinctively Baptist principles first began to be actively canvassed in Oxford can be determined with a fair degree of assurance as 1646, when the city surrendered to the besieging Parliamentary army.' Payne (1951): 32, similarly remarks: 'There was probably a Baptist Church in the University town from shortly after its surrender to the parliamentary forces in 1646.' Also see Colvin (1979): 417: 'A Baptist group was probably established in Oxford shortly after the surrender of the royalist garrison in 1646'. The suggestion that Baptists

highlight, given the fact that many Baptists served in the military and viewed their participation in the Parliamentary cause as part and parcel of their fight for religious liberty against an oppressive king. This became even more significant with the rise of Oliver Cromwell to political prominence and the establishment of the New Model Army.[1] Certainly, there is ample evidence of Baptists functioning as chaplains in the army, as well as serving as regular troops within the military ranks.[2] We also know that many leading Baptists, notably the wealthy merchant William Kiffen (1616-1701), were broadly supportive of Cromwell's religious and political ideals and threw their not inconsiderable influence behind him, even taking up military commands when needed.[3] However, it is wholly misleading to suggest that Baptists only came to the city of Oxford when the Parliamentary army arrived in the summer of 1646.

Instead, there is good evidence to suggest that Baptists, or to be more precise, Dissenters who later identified themselves with the Baptist cause, were active in the city *prior* to the arrival of the Parliamentary army. All the evidence suggests that these early Baptists Dissenters were an indigenous group largely made up of local residents and citizens, often from well-

---

were present in Oxford as early as 1618 (such as is stated in Alden (1904): 7; (1910): 87) is sheer fantasy. For one thing, this seems to be based on the idea that Vavasor Powell, the Baptist preacher from Wales, was responsible for founding the first Baptist society in Oxford (see Moore (1875): 11). Powell was only born in 1617 and his arrival as a student in Oxford (a fact which is disputed by some historians altogether) is generally dated to 1634.

[1] As Underwood (1947): 64, put it: 'Independents and Baptists formed the backbone of the New Model Army.' Robinson (1927): 153, similarly remarked that 'the New Model Army was largely recruited and officered from Baptists'. Indeed, Southern's recent study *Forlorn Hope: Soldier Radicals of the Seventeenth Century* (2001) concentrates on five soldiers who served in Cromwell's New Model Army, two of whom were Baptists, namely Robert Lockyer (c.1626-1649) and Richard Rumbold (c.1622-1685). Both of these Baptist soldiers had fascinating military careers. Lockyer fought at the battle of Naseby on 14 June 1645, before falling foul of his military superiors who tried him for mutiny and eventually had him executed; Rumbold was sufficiently trusted as a military leader to be among the soldiers serving as military escorts on the scaffolding when King Charles I was beheaded in London. Gentles (1992) is the latest full-bodied treatment of the New Model Army; also see Firth (1905): 341-345; Kishlansky (1978): 51-74; (1979). For more on the social make-up and motivation within Cromwell's army, see Hill (1970): 76-78. The study of Carlton (1992) is also important as a record of the experiences of soldiers who fought in the Civil War. Hibbert and Hibbert (1993) and Adair (1998) are among the most readable histories of the period.

[2] Laurence (1990); Herspring (2001): 55-77. On this general point, also see Whitley (1932): 73-5; (1938-39): 307-10; Torbert (1963): 46-8. Robinson (1927): 28-34, 154-5); Underwood (1947): 74-7; Hardacre (1961-62): 292-308; Tolmie (1977); and, Capp (1989): 295, 298, 305-6, 316, 319, 322, give details of some notable Baptist soldiers and sailors.

[3] White (1983): 70-1.

established families with long-standing connections in Oxford. Most of the people discussed within the chapters which follow are from a socio-economic middle ground, drawn mainly from the world of trade and commerce.[1] As Nigel Smith, in his important study *Perfection Proclaimed: Language and Literature in English Radical Religion 1640-1660* (1989), has noted:

> While it is true that some servants and rural labourers did become sectarians, … recent research suggests that the bulk of sectarian membership remained among the lower professions and merchants, the artisanal groups in the cities, and the yeomanry in the country.[2]

Not surprisingly, most of the Baptists in Oxford who emerge from the pages of the documents here offered are prominent trades-people and merchants, and *not* intellectuals from the University of Oxford. Equally as unsurprising, given the social conventions of the 17th century, is the fact that most of them are men. Having said that, the wives of many of the prominent Baptists did have an important role to play, as the study here presented demonstrates. Speaking of the period 1640-1660, Christopher Hill once remarked that

> women gained immeasurably in status during this period, not only to the greater equality they enjoyed in sectarian congregations but also to economic activities forced on them by the absence of husbands on military service or in exile.[3]

This study helps demonstrate the wisdom and insight of Hill's statement. This can readily be seen, not least by the frequency with which Dissenter's wives' names appear alongside their husbands, particularly within indictments recorded in the ecclesiastical court documents. True, social conventions being what they were, the names of the wives are sometimes not recorded in the ecclesiastical documents, but nonetheless, the women are there, facing the court officials.

Dissenters have sometimes been seen as independent, self-contained groups who were largely detached from the social fabric of the communities in which they lived. Certain ecclesiastical records, such as churchwarden presentments and formal excommunications, have frequently contributed to such an

---

[1] A possible exception to this is Ralph Austen, who styles himself in some documents (notably his will) as a 'Gentleman', thus asserting that he belonged to the lesser landed gentry on the fringe of the ruling class. It has been estimated that there were between 10,000-14,000 'gentlemen' out of a national population of 4,5000,000. See Woolrych (1968): 4-5.

[2] Smith (1989): 10-1. Wykes (1990): 39-62, also offers a valuable discussion, challenging the frequent assertion that Dissenters were driven to careers as tradesmen and craftsmen by the legal and religious penalties imposed upon them as Nonconformists. However, his assertion that Baptists were from 'the lower social groups' (page 40) needs some qualification, at least as far as the city of Oxford is concerned.

[3] Hill (1978): 149.

assessment, This is understandable, given the fact that such documents arise out of a situation of conflict in which the prevailing power structures were attempting to maintain the status quo by suppressing 'sectaryes' or fanatics' who were thought to pose a threat.   Records from the various levels of ecclesiastical hierarchy certainly do shed light on the lives of the Oxford Dissenters, although care must be taken in determining their significance. We now know the situation in most 17th-century communities was much more complex than was once believed the case, and that, as Bill Stevenson suggests, 'cooperation, not conflict, was the order of the day'.[1] The evidence relating to the Baptist Dissenters in Oxford reveals just how well integrated they were into the life of the city, including the administration of the parish churches. This is not to say that there were no points of friction or disagreement – certainly there were, particularly at the upper levels of the Anglican ecclesiastical establishment. For example, in an attempt to ascertain the state of health of the Church of England, the Bishop of Oxford, John Fell, had a list of recusants and Dissenters within the diocese compiled.[2]   The list is geographically arranged by parishes and dates to early 1679, no doubt in preparation for his triennial visitation which took place in June of that year.[3] A number of individuals included within this list were long known to have belonged to Dissenting conventicles in the city of Oxford, some of them attending conventicles as early as the 1640s. Some of these people are later specifically identified as Baptists (or Anabaptists) and thus form the first generation of Baptist witness within the city.

D. 1641 and 1691: Establishing Chronological Parameters and Identifying Individuals

The chronological parameters stated in the subtitle of this book are somewhat artificially imposed, but they do represent key dates in the lives of Baptist Dissenters: 1641 was the year in which the shop of one of the 'religious brothers' along the High Street caught fire and burned, giving rise to the publication of a controversial pamphlet about him, and 1691 was the year in which one of the leaders of the Baptist meeting-house left Oxford for a ministry in Devon. It is during the fifty year interval between these two events that a number of conventiclers first began to meet, formed themselves into a

---

[1] Stevenson (1995): 387. Stevenson concentrates on Quakers and Baptists in rural communities in Huntingdonshire, Cambridgeshire and Bedfordshire within his study, but the essential point about the participation and social integration of Dissenters within their communities also holds for the city of Oxford.

[2] *OAR: Returns of Recusants – 1679-1706* (c. 430), folios 41 recto and verso = CSC #588 and CSC #589 . *ODR: Memorandum from Diocesan Books – 1679-1814* (b. 68), folio 6 recto and verso, also dates from this visitation.

[3] To prepare for this visit Fell published *Articles of Visitation & Enquiry Exhibited to the Ministers, Churchwardens, and Sidemen of every Parish in the primary Episcopal Visitation of the Right Reverend Father in God John* (1679).

Baptist congregation which associated with like-minded Dissenters in neighbouring towns and villages, and eventually came to be recognized and licensed by the state authorities. This study proposes that a total of thirty-seven named individuals can confidently be described as Baptists living and worshipping in conventicles in Oxford between 1641-1691. These include eleven whose names can be gleaned from Baptist publications of the period and from records of the Abingdon Association of Baptist churches (of which Oxford was a member). These are Richard Tidmarsh, Thomas Tisdale, Lawrence King, Roger Hatchman, Thomas Hatchman, Richard Quelch junior, Ralph Austen, John Higgins, George Astin, John Edwards, and Humphrey Gillet. A further twenty-one names can reasonably be deduced from various documents contained within the Oxford city and Oxfordshire county archives, namely Thomas Williams, Alice Williams, Anne King, Edward Wyans senior, Edward Wyans junior, Abraham Ward, Thomas Mason, Emma Mason, Thomas King, James Jennings, Edward Jennings, John Toms, Frances Toms, Jeane Tidmarsh, Joan Tisdale, Hannah Jennings, Edith Jennings, Anne Jennings, Elizabeth Higgins, Katharine Gillet, and Ellinor Seale. A further three names can be gleaned from the records of the Baptist church in Petty France, London, namely Francis Gibbes, a Sister Hall, and William Rogers. In addition, a Mrs Davies, is mentioned in passing in the *State Papers* of Charles II, and there is some evidence to suggest that she and her husband Abraham attended the Baptist conventicles within the city.

For several of these figures, few concrete facts about their lives are certain, so infrequently do they appear in surviving records. For example, John Edwards and George Astin[1] were two of the eight Baptists from Oxford who signed the broadsheet entitled *A Testimony to Truth, Agreeing with an Essay for Settlement* (1659), but beyond that brief appearance in a printed document little else is known about them.[2] There is record of Edwards and his wife

---

[1] This George Astin is not to be confused with *Captain* George Austen who served as an officer in the Parliamentary army during the Civil War and who was incarcerated for a period in the castle gaol in Oxford. This Captain Austen is mentioned in an anonymous tract entitled *A True and Most Sad Relation of the Hard Usage and Extreme Cruelty Used on Captaine Wingate, Captaine Vivers, Captaine Austin etc.*, (1643). Captaine Austen also appears in Edmund Chillenden's *The Inhumanity of the King's Prison Keeper at Oxford* (1643). Given that Captain Austen was one of the officers imprisoned in Oxford in early 1643, we can reasonably infer that he participated in the battle of Edgehill and was captured by royalist forces there. Varley (1932-34): 420-422, discusses the imprisonment of soldiers in the Oxford gaol.

[2] There is record of George Astin being given his 'Freedom of the City' on 11 April 1656 (*City Council Proceedings – 1629-1663* (A.5.7), folio 231 recto) = CSC #235. He is described within this record as a former soldier who was trading in Oxford as a chandler. He married Margaret Stibbes of Cumnor on 22 November 1655 (*Parish Register of St Michael-at-the-Northgate – 1654-1683* (Par 211/R1/1/2), folio 34 recto) = CSC #228. Interestingly, Margaret Stibbes's sister Joan married the Baptist conventicler Thomas Tisdale on 11 March 1658 (*Parish Register of St Michael-at-the-Northgate – 1654-1683* (Par 211/R1/1/2), folio 41 verso) = CSC #256.

Phillipa, who were from the parish of Mary Magdalen, being cited to appear before the ecclesiastical courts on 8 and 15 March 1662,[1] but he appears to have died shortly thereafter and his widow relocated to Burchester (Bicester).[2] Similarly, the records of the three people from the Baptist church in Petty France, London have to do with their transferral of membership to and from the church in Oxford, and there is little additional information about them beyond that administrative action.[3] For others, however, some sketchy details are forthcoming, particularly within the civic and ecclesiastical records associated with the city of Oxford. A case in point is Humphrey Gillet (or Gillett), another of the signatories to *A Testimony to Truth, Agreeing with an Essay for Settlement* (1659), who does appear in some of these city documents. There is a record in the parish register of the church of St Michael-at-the-Northgate of Gillet's marriage to Katharine Nicholls on 7 July 1656, and of the birth of their daughter Rebeckah on 31 March 1657.[4] It appears that the Gillet family moved from Oxford to the village of Swerford outside Hook Norton sometime after 1659 and soon became involved with the Baptists in the area. There are excommunication orders relating to several members of the Gillet family over the years. An excommunication order for Humphrey was issued 11 April 1663,[5] and within one record the reason for his excommunication is said to be 'for withdrawing from all solemnities of publiq[ue] services of God'.[6] Similarly, an excommunication order for Katharine was issued on 10 December 1664 and was published in the parish church of Swerford on 19 February 1665.[7] Interestingly, the reason for Katharine's excommunication in another record is simply said to be because she is 'an Anabaptist', one of the very few times that any Dissenter associated with the Baptists in Oxford is ever so described within ecclesiastical records.[8]

---

[1] *ODR: 1 February 1660 – 4 October 1662* (c. 3) folios 10 verso and 12 verso.

[2] She is cited in records from 22 March, 19 and 26 April, 3 and 10 May 1662 (*OAR: 1 February 1660 – 4 October 1662* (c. 3) folios 15 recto, 17 verso, 18 recto, 19 verso and 20 verso). There is considerable confusion over Phillipa's name in these records: in the first she is called Martha, and in the last four she is called Mary.

[3] Francis Gibbes was received into membership at Petty France on 29 April 1677 and Sister Hall on 16 December 1677; both had letters of recommendation sent from Oxford to London to facilitate this (*Petty France (Particular) Baptist Church* (MS 20 228 1B), pages 5 and 7 = CSC #563a and CSC #571a). On the other hand, Brother William Rogers was recommended to the church in Oxford by the church in London on 7 April 1695 (*Petty France (Particular) Baptist Church* (MS 20 228 1B), page 39).

[4] *Parish Register of St Michael-at-the-Northgate – 1654-1683* (Par 211/1/R1/2), folios 36 verso and 1 verso.

[5] *ODR: Excommunication Schedules – 1662-1667* (c. 100), folio 50 recto = CSC #373.

[6] *ODR: Excommunications: 1633-1791* (c. 99), folio 239 verso.

[7] *ODR: Excommunication Schedules – 1662-1667* (c. 100), folio 119 recto = CSC #400.

[8] *ODR: Excommunications: 1633-1791* (c. 99), folio 243 recto. There is also record of the excommunication order for Sarah Green, the daughter of Humphry Gillet, from

As far as the civic and ecclesiastical documents are concerned, the textual starting point for the discussion of Oxford Baptists within this study will be the records for the Petty Sessions court. This court met in the Town Hall four times a year in order to deal with serious breaches of the law, including offences against the established religious conventions of the day. The records for the session of this court convened on 9 January 1662 give the names of four Baptist conventiclers: Richard Tidmarsh, Lawrence King, Roger Hatchman, and Ralph Austen (sometimes spelled *Austin*).[1] The officials presiding over the proceedings were Leonard Bowman, the Mayor of Oxford, Richard Croke, the recorder of the City Council, Francis Harris and Martin Wright, city aldermen, and Dr John Fell of Christ Church. The four Baptists were indicted by the court, and all save Austen were detained in the Bocardo prison. The full text of this court record (see Illustration #1) reads:

[folio 45 verso]

Ralph Austin – Ralph Austin Lawrence King and Roger Hatchman being all of them indicted as Seditious sectaryes & dis loyal persons & for being present at an unlawfull Conventicle The said bill of Indictm[en]t being found by the Grandiury & the said persons being p[re]sent in Court: the said Indictm[en]t was read to them to w[hi]ch they severally pleaded not Guilty & the said Ralph Austin desireing to be admitted to his Traverse. It is ordered That he shalbe admitted to his Traverse accordingly & It is likewise ordered that the said Ralph Austin be bound w[i]th sureties to appear at the next generall Sessions and to be

[folio 46 recto]

of the good behavio[ur] the mean time & also that he be bound with sureties to p[re]sente his traverse w[i]th effect at Trinity Sessions next.
Upon w[hi]ch the said Ralph in open Court was bound by recognizance himself in xx [li[bras]] & his Manucapto[ur][s] viz: Richard Collins Whitebaker & Richard Heibourn[2]

Hook Norton which was issued on 17 April 1684 (*OAR: Excommunications: 1610-1783* (c. 121), folio 28 recto and verso).

[1] The manuscript reference is *Oxford Petty Sessions Roll – 1656-1678* (O.5.11), folios 45 verso – 46 recto).

[2] Heibourne's name is variously spelled in surviving documents. He and his wife Elizabeth were indicted to appear before the ecclesiastical court on 28 June 1662, charged with not attending their parish services (*ODR: 1 February 1660 – 4 October 1662* (c. 3) folio 29 recto). Heibourne responded by saying that 'his imployment hinders him from going to church'. Elizabeth must have died soon after, for there is record of a marriage bond between Richard Heyborne, who is described as a widower, and Jane Wale, which is dated 8 December 1669 (*OAR: Marriage Bonds – 1669* (c. 459), folio 30). Later Heibourne is known to have served as one of the two 'Overseers of the Poor' within the parish of St Michael-at-the-Northgate. Records of him serving alongside Matthew Jellyman in this regard in September of 1677 have survived,

Cook in x [li[bras]] apiece for the appearance behaviour &
p[er]secuc[i]on of the traverse of the said Ralph as
is aforesaid.   now prisoners in Bocardo
The said Lawrence King & Roger Hatchman ^ pleaded
not Guilty to the Bill of Indictm[en]t aforesaid and
stand committed.

At this Sessions Roger Hatchman ~~Richard~~[1] Lawrence
King & Richard Tidmarsh now prisoners in his Ma[jes][ties]
Gaole of Boccardo had the Oath of Allegiance severally read & tendered to them in open Court w[hi]ch
oath they refused to take where upon It is ordered
by the Court That they stand com[m]itted without
baile or Manuprise till the next generall Sessions
to be holden for the said Citty unlesse they shall
before that said time take the said Oath & finde
Sureties for their appearance at the said next
Sessions & be of the good behaviour in the mean
time.[2]

The court appearance of Richard Tidmarsh, Lawrence King, Roger
Hatchman, and Ralph Austen, seems to focus, at least initially, on them all
attending a religious service together. This is described in the record as 'an
unlawfull Conventicle', and probably was a meeting of the Baptists of Oxford
at the house of either Tidmarsh or King (both were known to have held
religious meetings in their homes). However, there are also political overtones
within the court's indictment: Hatchman, King and Tidmarsh all refused to
swear an oath of allegiance to Charles II.   Oath-taking was to remain a
defining issue of many Dissenting movements of the time and stands as an
indication of how intertwined religious and political convictions were for many
people attending such illegal conventicles.   At the same time, the socio-
economic dimensions also need to be kept in mind, for it is not without
significance that all of these men were either well-known merchants and
tradesmen in Oxford, or came from established families of tradesmen within
the city.
It is this particular court record which provides the phrase used as the title of
this study: here Ralph Austen, Lawrence King, and Roger Hatchman were all
brought before the court and indicted as 'seditious Sectaryes & disloyal
persons and for being present at an unlawfull Conventicle'.   Austen was

---

although he signs his name as *Heboarne* within these documents (*Oxford Petty Sessions Roll – 1656-1678* (O.5.11), folio 177 recto).

[1] An error in writing the first name of Lawrence King is corrected within the document. The first name is originally given as *Richard*, but this is then erased, although it can still be made out. The error is probably due to the anticipation of the first name of Richard Tidmarsh which follows.

[2] *Oxford Petty Sessions Roll – 1656-1678* (O.5.11), folios 45 verso–46 recto = CSC #339.

released on bail, but King and Hatchman joined Richard Tidmarsh in the Bocardo prison where, as noted, they were committed for refusing to take the oath of allegiance. Interestingly, this is the only time that all four of these Dissenters appear together in a single document, although they appear in a variety of different combinations elsewhere. These four men, each of whom established himself in some way as a leading citizen within the city, are treated in turn within the first four chapters of the book. The studies of these four figures will also provide opportunity for discussion of other members of the Baptist conventicle along the way. Thus, Thomas Tisdale, a well-established mercer within the city of Oxford, will be briefly discussed within the chapter on Richard Tidmarsh. The chapter will also contain a brief discussion of the cordwainers Edward Wyans senior and Edward Wyans junior, which seems appropriate given that the two families were related by marriage (Tidmarsh's son married into the Wyans family). Meanwhile, the cordwainer John Toms and his wife Frances will be contained within the chapter on Lawrence King; this is sensible given that all were residents of the parish of All Saints' in the city. Thomas Hatchman, a butcher who served as a messenger of the church in Oxford to the wider Abingdon Association and is named as such in the *Abingdon Association Records Book*, will be treated in chapter 3 alongside his father Roger. This chapter will also contain a brief discussion of the weaver John Higgins, which seems appropriate given that Thomas Hatchman married into the Higgins family. Richard Quelch junior, a watchmaker who became embroiled in the Fifth Monarchy movement, and James Jennings, a button-maker whose family were prominent tailors within Oxford, will be treated within the chapter on Ralph Austen. This is appropriate since both Quelch and Jennings were given preferments to college positions by the Parliamentary visitors during the commonwealth period, appointments which would have brought them into direct contact with Austen, the *Registrarius Commissionariorum*. The milliner Thomas Williams, another important figure within the civic life of the city of Oxford, who is implicated as an Anabaptist and conventicler within some 17th-century sources, is briefly discussed in chapter 5. The final chapter addresses the vexed question of where physically the early Baptists might have held their meetings, as well as offering some suggestions about the relationship between the Baptist conventicle in Oxford and its sister church in Abingdon.

Finally, in addition to the tracts and broadsheets issued by the Baptists themselves (mentioned above as Appendices A-D), there are a number of official documents issued by the king and Parliament which are of special note with regard to the Oxford conventiclers. The full text of several of these is supplied as additional appendices. These include: Charles II's *The Conventicle Act* (1664) (Appendix E); Charles II's *The Declaration of Indulgence* (1672) (Appendix F); William and Mary's *The Act of Toleration* (1689) (Appendix G); and James II's *Royal Charter of Oxford* (1688) (Appendix H). In addition, I have also included reconstructed charts of 'Family Trees' of eleven of the key figures discussed within the book (Appendix I). Most importantly, I have gathered together approximately 700 of the key primary sources into the accompanying Chronological Source Catalogue (CSC) in the second volume of this study, giving the full text and a translation, whenever possible. The intention is that readers who do not have easy access to the wide variety of documents pertaining to the Baptist Conventiclers of Oxford will be able to read them and enter into the world of these 'Seditious Sectaryes' for themselves.

1. The Tanner:

Richard Tidmarsh

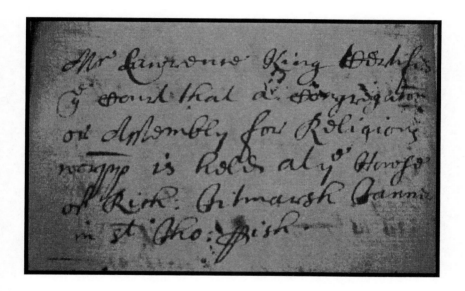

Illustration #2: Record from a court clerk's notebook in which it is recorded that Lawrence King certifies that 'a Congregation or Assembly for Religious worship is held at the Howse of Rich. Titmarsh, Tanner in St Thomas's parish' (*Oxford Petty Sessions Clerk's Notebook, 1687-1701* (O.2.1), folio 18 verso). The record is dated 15 April 1689.

1. The Tanner:
Richard Tidmarsh

Within this chapter I shall consider the life and career of Richard Tidmarsh, a tanner by trade, who became a controversial civic leader within the city of Oxford. By all accounts Richard Tidmarsh was extremely influential in helping to establish the Baptist cause within the city, and remained at the forefront of much that was taking place among the Dissenters in Oxford for over thirty years. Tidmarsh is consistently acknowledged within the contemporary sources as *the* primary leader of the Baptist congregation in Oxford for most of his adult life. Unfortunately, he has not received the attention that is due, and consequently he remains something of an underrated figure within 17th-century Oxford history. The chapter will conclude with a brief discussion of another important Baptist Dissenter with whom Tidmarsh had contact, namely Thomas Tisdale, an Oxford mercer and a fellow signatory of *A Testimony to Truth, Agreeing with an Essay for Settlement* (1659).

A. Family Background and Apprenticeship

1. Family in Adlestrop, Gloucestershire

Richard Tidmarsh[1] was not a native Oxonian, but came from the village of Adlestrop in the adjoining county of Gloucestershire. His baptism is noted in the village's parish church register from 1626: 'Richard Tydmashe the son of Oswald Tydmarshe was baptised the xiii day of March.'[2] From the surviving local parish records and probate records a fairly full picture of the wider Tidmarsh family, stretching over several generations and made up predominantly of farmers, can be reconstructed. The parish records in Adlestrop indicate that Richard Tidmarsh had at least two brothers and three sisters (see the accompanying chart on 'The Family Tree of Richard Tidmarsh' for some details of the larger family connections). Most of his immediate family appear to have remained in Adlestrop, although all indications are that

---

[1] The surname is variously spelled, frequently appearing as Titchmarsh, Titmarch, and even Titmouse.

[2] *Adlestrop Parish Register 1598-1673* (P5/IN/1/2), folio 36 verso.

his older brother Thomas sent at least three of his sons to London to make their fortune. All three sons (Thomas junior,[1] James,[2] and Samuel[3]) were apprenticed to master pewterers and soon a thriving family business was established; it extended over several generations and lasted well into the 1760s.[4]

It does not appear that Richard Tidmarsh inherited a tradition of religious nonconformity. There is little direct evidence that many of the family members living in Adlestrop were Baptists, or even Dissenters of any description. Few records of the Tidmarshes survive beyond those of the village of Adlestrop, although it is worth noting that James II issued a warrant on 17 December 1686 to prevent any legal process being brought against a Thomas Tidmarsh of Adlestrop for his Dissenting activity.[5] It is possible that this was a relative of Richard Tidmarsh, perhaps even his own brother, although this is not entirely

---

[1] There are records of Thomas taking on twelve apprentices between 1680-1727; he died in 1728 (*PCC – Will of Thomas Tidmarsh* (PROB 11/622), folio 469 verso–470 recto). Three of Thomas's sons (Thomas, John and Richard), and one grand-daughter (Ann, the daughter of Thomas) followed him into the profession. There is record of a marriage allegation between the son John and a Mary Knight (*Lambeth Palace Library: Vicar General Marriage Allegation* – 2 November 1715); also see her will (*PCC – Will of Mary Tidmarsh* (PROB 11/813), folio 217 verso–218 recto), and her father's will (*PCC – Will of William Knight* (PROB 11/647), folios 285 recto-287 verso).

[2] James was apprenticed to William Warters on 14 December 1693 (*Pewterers' Company Apprenticeships – 1675-1691* (GL MS 7090/8), folio 34 verso). There is a marriage allegation dated 21 July 1709 for a marriage between James and a Phyllis Harrison from the parish of St Peter, Cornhill in London (*London Diocese Marriage Allegation – June-December 1709* (MS 10,091/45); the marriage took place in the parish church of Allhallows London Wall, London on the same day (*Parish Register of Allhallows London Wall, London* (GL MS 5087). There are records of James taking on two apprentices in 1716 and 1724, before suffering an early death in 1731. His wife Phyllis carried on his trade, taking on an apprentice named John Hawkins on 14 July 1731 (*Pewterers' Company Apprenticeships – 1711-1740* (GL MS 7090/9), folio 220 recto). However, this apprenticeship was not completed, but was transferred to her son, the pewterer James Tidmarsh junior, on 20 December 1734 (*Pewterers' Company Apprenticeships – 1711-1740* (GL MS 7090/9), folio 259 recto). The records indicate that this son took over his father's business; he took on seven apprentices between 1734-1753. There is a marriage allegation and bond dated 24 July 1737 signed by him. Within it he is described as a twenty-seven year-old bachelor and pewterer from the parish of St George in Middlesex (*Marriage License Record – St Katherine-by-the-Tower – 1720-1802* (GL (9772/16), folio 100). The allegation gives his bride's maiden name as Mary Cope, describing her as a twenty-two year-old spinster from the same parish.

[3] The third son, Samuel, was apprenticed to John Kenton on 26 April 1683 (*Pewterers' Company Apprenticeships – 1675-1691* (GL MS 7090/7), folio 153 verso).

[4] See Ricketts (2001): 213-214, for details of the Tidmarsh family's involvement in the pewterers' trade in London.

[5] SP 44/337, pages 160-161. The warrant specifically protect him against charges being brought for not taking the Oath of Allegiance, or for failing to attend his local parish church, or not receiving the sacrament of the Lord's Supper.

clear. It appears that this Thomas Tidmarsh became a Quaker and raised his family as Quakers; the will of his son, whose name was named John, is signed '*John Tidmarsh, secundum ordinem Quakeriorum* (John Tidmarsh, in accordance with the rule of the Quakers)'.[1]

2. Family in Oxford

A number of records from Oxford allow us to piece together a picture of Tidmarsh's own children and grand-children within the city. The surviving records relating to Richard Tidmarsh in Oxford generally describe him as living in the parish of St Thomas, near the castle and next to the Castle Mill stream.[2] According to the Poll Tax records of 1 March 1667, his household consisted of himself, his wife, one son and three daughters, a servant named Elizabeth Cantwell, and one unnamed apprentice.[3] Although, the Poll Tax records do not give us the first name of Tidmarsh's wife, a later burial notice within the register of St Thomas parish church indicates that her name was Jeane (Jane): 'Jeane, the wife of Richard Titmarsh: Buried Sep[tember] 6 [1673]'.[4] As best can be determined, the son mentioned in the Poll Tax was named Samuel, who was apprenticed to the London stationer John Syms on 7 November 1670[5], and upon successful completion of an eight year apprenticeship, was made a

---

[1] *John Tidmarsh* (AdWPR 1698/226). The will was probated 29 November 1698.

[2] Richard Tidmarsh's house on the south side of High Bridge near the castle; see CSC #539 for the probable location of this property in David Loggan's *Oxonia Illustrata* (1675). The property is mentioned in a number of Christ Church leases for an adjoining property known as Alley Meads. These are dated 22 March 1670 (*II. St Thomas – Alley Meads #7*), 11 July 1672 (*II. St Thomas – Alley Meads #8 and #9*); 28 January 1682 (*II. St Thomas – Alley Meads #10 and #11*); 22 December 1692 (*II. St Thomas – Alley Meads #12 and #13*); 6 December 1700 (*II. St Thomas – Alley Meads #14 and #15*); and 1 June 1708 (*II. St Thomas – Alley Meads #16*). This does not necessarily mean that Tidmarsh lived there as late as 1708, however. Rather, it probably is simply an indication that details of boundaries of the adjoining properties, including the names of the lease-holders, were mechanically copied in from previous leases without checking if they were still accurate. The first leases which show that Tidmarsh's property had been taken over by someone else are dated 20 August 1715, where a 'John Francklyn, Tanner' is listed as the occupier (*II. St Thomas – Alley Meads # 17, #18 and #19*). Francklyn was the lease-holder of the property when the old Tidmarsh house it was attacked by a Jacobite mob on 29 May 1715 (see page 307 below).

[3] *Poll Tax of 1667* (P.5.7), folio 24 verso. Tidmarsh payment is for 9*s*, which includes tax on the servant Elizabeth Cantwell's wages of 20*s*.

[4] *Parish Register of St Thomas – 1655-1755* (Par 217/1/R1/1), 62 verso. Elsewhere her name is given as Jane. It should be kept in mind, regardless, that 17th-century spelling was not standardized and the spellings of the two names were often interchanged.

[5] *Stationers' Company Archives: Apprenticeship Register – 7 August 1666-6 March 1727*, folio 23 recto = CSC #492a; *Stationers' Company Archives: Master and Apprenticeship Calendar – 5 March 1654-7 September 1685*, folio 32 verso.

freeman of the company on 2 December 1678.[1] He went on to become a successful bookseller in London with a shop at the King's Head in Cornhill, next to the Royal Exchange.[2] There is a marriage allegation pertaining to Samuel's marriage to a Sarah Wall dated 20 January 1681.[3] Unfortunately, there is no record of the marriage within the parish church of St Michael, Cornhill, although the baptisms and deaths of several of their children are recorded in the parish register.[4] The names of the three daughters of Richard and Jeane Tidmarsh are more difficult to determine. It is possible that the name of one daughter was Jane; there is a record of her baptism in the register of the parish of St Thomas, probably dated to 22 October 1669.[5] The second daughter was probably named Mary; there is record of her marriage to Thomas Sansbury

---

[1] *Stationers' Company Archives: The Register of Freemen – 2 July 1605-6 March 1703*, folio 122 recto.

[2] Interestingly, there is also record of Samuel Tidmarsh taking on Richard Carter (the son of the Oxford carrier Richard Carter) for a seven year apprenticeship which is dated 1 March 1680 (*Stationers' Company Archives: Apprenticeship Register – 7 August 1666-6 March 1727*, folio 68 recto; *Stationers' Company Archives: Master and Apprenticeship Calendar – 2 May 1670-17 July 1690*, folio 34 verso).   The elder Richard Carter was a controversial member of the Oxford City Council who, along with the Baptist mercer Thomas Tisdale and several others, was censured in 1677 for failing to meet his civic responsibilities (see page 90 below).

[3] *Lambeth Palace Library: Faculty Office Marriage Allegation – 20* January 1681 = CSC #601a.

[4] The records are as follows: a son named Samuel who was baptized on 11 March 1683 but died and was buried less than a month later on 6 April 1683 (*Parish Register of St Michael, Cornhill – 1653-1736* (GL MS 4063/1), folios 28 recto and 168 recto); twins named Judah and Anne were baptized on 5 June 1684 but died and were buried on 24 July 1684 (*Parish Register of St Michael, Cornhill – 1653-1736* (GL MS 4063/1), folios 29 recto and 169 verso; an unnamed son (other records indicate that he was probably named John) was baptized on 17 May 1685 (*Parish Register of St Michael, Cornhill – 1653-1736* (GL MS 4063/1), folio 30 recto); a son named Samuel was baptized on 1 March 1687 (*Parish Register of St Michael, Cornhill – 1653-1736* (GL MS 4063/1), folio 31 verso); and a daughter named Sarah was baptized on 17 June 1688 – *Parish Register of St Michael, Cornhill – 1653-1736* (GL MS 4063/1), folio 33 recto). There is something of a mystery surrounding the name of Samuel Tidmarsh's wife in these records. In the records pertaining to the first four children, the name of his wife Sarah is not given - a blank space is left where her name ought to be. However, in the records pertaining to the last two children her name is given as *Elizabeth*. Why this is so is unknown. It is possible that the parish clerk was uncertain about her name, or that she used a middle name (Elizabeth) instead of the name on her marriage allegation record (Sarah).

[5] *Parish Register of St Thomas – 1655-1755* (Par 217/1/R1/1), folio 2 recto. I am assuming, of course, that there was a considerable delay between Jane Tidmarsh's birth and her baptism. Indeed, the year of her baptism is very indistinct in the relevant parish register; it may be 1670, rather than 1669. The reference to her baptism is somewhat unusual for a Baptist minister at this time (more on this below on page 50).

on 15 November 1685.[1] The name of the third daughter was probably Anne; there is record of her making two quarterly installments of the Poll Tax of 1692 while living in the parish of St Thomas.[2]

In addition to the *Poll Tax* entry of 1667 which mentions four children, there are other records that show that Richard and Jeane Tidmarsh had at least three, and possibly four, other children. The first of these is a first-born son named John, who probably did not live with his parents at the time of the Poll Tax.[3] Second, there are records of a son named James and a daughter named Hannah, both of whom apparently were born after the Poll Tax was collected.[4] Third, there is a record of a Judith Tidmarsh (Titmarsh) paying the Poll Tax in 1667.[5] She is listed as receiving wages from Robert Sadler and his wife Mary who lived at what is now 5 Queen Street; it is possible that she is an additional daughter who, like her older brother John, did not live with her parents when the Poll Tax was collected.

There are records of Tidmarsh paying a number of other taxes during 1662-1668 which provide evidence of the longevity of his residence within the parish of St Thomas, as well as giving an indication of his socio-economic status as a well-established artisan living comfortably in a medium-sized property there. There is record of him paying 4*s* on a four-hearth property in the Hearth Taxes of Michaelmas 1662,[6] Michaelmas 1665,[7] and Lady Day 1665.[8] In addition, Tidmarsh is listed as paying a number of the War Taxes of 1667-1668,[9] commencing with a quarterly contribution of 4*s* 5*d* for the collection dated 24 June 1667.[10] Two further such quarterly payments, assessed at the rate of 4*s*

---

[1] *Parish Register of St Aldate's – 1678-1813* (MS DD Par Oxford - St Aldate's b.1), folio 110 verso. The couple had a son named Thomas who died and was buried on 31 May 1694; he was soon followed in death by Thomas Sansbury senior, who was buried on 24 December 1694 (*Parish Register of St Aldate's – 1678-1813* (MS DD Par Oxford - St Aldate's b.1), folio 63 verso).

[2] *Taxes – 1691-1694* (P.5.9), folios 6 verso, 41 recto. Anne Tidmarsh's entry is listed together with that of a John Franklin, his wife, one child, and a servant named Robert Kemp. Apparently Anne continued to live in the Tidmarsh family home for a while after her father moved to Tiverton and his lease for the property was taken over by John Franklin. However, the Poll Tax entries for Franklin dated 2 May and 27 August 1694 and 25 February 1695 do *not* mention Anne Tidmarsh (*Taxes – 1691-1694* (P.5.9), folios 141 recto, 162 recto and 185 verso).

[3] John Tidmarsh is identified as the eldest son of Richard Tidmarsh in *Civic Enrolments – 1662-1699* (L.5.4), page 629.

[4] The date of the birth of the son James is unknown. The daughter Hannah was born on 17 December 1670; she died on 3 August 1672 (*Parish Register of St Thomas – 1655-1755* (Par 217/1/R1/1), folios 2 recto and 62 verso).

[5] *Poll Tax of 1667* (P.5.7), folio 7 verso.

[6] *Hearth Tax of August-November 1662* (E 179/255/4), Part 2, page 68.

[7] *Hearth Tax of Michaelmas 1665* (E 179/164/513), membrane 28 verso.

[8] *Hearth Tax of 24 April 1666* (E 179/164/514), membrane 24 verso.

[9] See pages 8-10 above for an explanation of these taxes.

[10] *War Taxes – 1667-1668* (P.5.8), folio 16 recto.

4*d*, were made by Tidmarsh on 29 September 1667[1] and 21 December 1667.[2] There is also a quarterly tax record dated 26 March 1668 in which Tidmarsh paid 4*s* 2*d* in tax.[3] There are also three further quarterly tax records dated 26 June 1668, 26 September 1668, and 26 December 1668; within all three collections Tidmarsh was again assessed at 4*s* 2*d* for his contribution to the taxes.[4]

Finally, it is worth noting that there is record of a 'Mrs Tittmarsh' paying 4*s* in Poll Tax in 1694 and 1696 while living in the parish of St Thomas.[5] Similarly, there are records of a 'Widow Tidmarsh' paying 6*s* 2*d* in Window Tax on six windows for a property in the parish of St Thomas in 1696 and 1697.[6] Unfortunately, the address of the property is not given, nor are any other people with the surname of Tidmarsh listed among the 132 names paying the window tax in that district of the city. It is clear that these tax records cannot refer to Richard Tidmarsh's wife Jeane, for, as we noted above, there is record of her burial on 6 September 1673. It is likely that these tax records from 1694-1697 refer to the wife/widow of one of Richard and Jeane's sons, possibly the first-born son John, who, as I suggested above, had left home by 1667. There is record of a John Tidmarsh being buried on 2 May 1696 within the adjoining parish of St Ebbe's,[7] apparently leaving his widow to pay the taxes concerned. The couple apparently had at least two children, a daughter and a son, probably named Richard after his Baptist grandfather. Thus, there is also record of the marriage of an Elizabeth Tidmarsh to Richard Mitchell on 22 June 1696 in the parish of St Peter-in-the-East.[8] In addition there is record of a Richard Tidmarsh who married Mary Turner, a widow, on 24 April 1692.[9] It is likely that this was the grandson Richard Tidmarsh's second marriage, for there is record of the burial of 'the wife of Richard Tidmarsh' on 2 November 1689,[10] and of the burial of 'a childe of Rich[ard] Tidmarsh' on 29 July 1681.[11]

---

[1] *War Taxes – 1667-1668* (P.5.8), folio 38 recto.

[2] *War Taxes – 1667-1668* (P.5.8), folio 63 recto.

[3] *War Taxes – 1667-1668* (P.5.8), folio 59 recto.

[4] *War Taxes – 1667-1668* (P.5.8), folios 74 verso, 100 verso and 116 recto.

[5] *Taxes – 1694-1746* (P.5.10), folios 14 verso and 38 recto.

[6] *Taxes – 1694-1746* (P.5.10), folio 49 verso and 62 recto.

[7] *Parish Register of St Ebbe's – 1678-1812* (MS DD Par Oxford – St Ebbe's b. 35), folio 54 recto.

[8] *Parish Register of St Peter-in-the-East – 1653-1807* (Par 213/1/R1/3), folio 43 recto.

[9] *Parish Register of St Thomas – 1655-1755* (Par 217/1/R1/1), folio 43 recto. Richard is said to be 'of St Peters in ye East' within the registry entry. There was an Archdeaconry marriage bond for this marriage which was noted in a catalogue list compiled in 1850, but it was lost sometime between then and 1920 when the records were deposited in the Bodleian Library.

[10] *Parish Register of St Thomas – 1655-1755* (Par 217/1/R1/1), folio 69 recto.

[11] *Parish Register of St Thomas – 1655-1755* (Par 217/1/R1/1), folio 66 recto.

3. Apprenticeship as a Tanner

On 25 March 1644, at the age of eighteen, the future Baptist Richard Tidmarsh, was apprenticed to the Oxford tanner John Walter. He was several years older than the age at which most young men entered into such apprenticeships; this unusual course of events may have been due to the fact that the Civil War was raging at the time. It may be a classic case of a young man leaving the family farm to seek fame and fortune in the city. There must have been a certain amount of danger involved with Oxford's position as the royalist stronghold under threat by Parliamentary forces. Indeed, this may have added to the attraction of the place for Tidmarsh. It is possible that he had a relative living within the city who served as a contact, for in the parish register of St Ebbe's there is mention of a 'W[illia]m Titmus' which dates to 1644.[1]

The seven-year apprenticeship contract with John Walter was duly entered in the book of *Civic Enrolments* (sometimes described as the *Hanister's Lists*), and the young man formally began his vocational training. However, Tidmarsh's master died within nine months, leaving the apprenticeship contract unfinished. Fortunately, a satisfactory arrangement was struck with another Oxford tanner, Matthew Langley junior, an influential man who also happened to be one of the city Bailiffs. Thus, on 27 January 1645 an amendment was added to the contract which set out modified arrangements for the completion of Tidmarsh's apprenticeship.[2]

B. Master Tanner and Oxford Citizen

1. 'Freedom of the City'

Once Tidmarsh had completed his apprenticeship the stage was set for him to become a citizen of the city of Oxford and begin his career as a master craftsman. It is perhaps not without significance that his own apprenticeship master, Matthew Langley junior, had been elected Mayor of the city in September of 1651, and no doubt helped facilitate Tidmarsh's citizenship. In any event, Tidmarsh was granted his 'Freedom of the City' on 19 January 1652, after swearing the requisite oaths and paying the customary fees to seal the

---

[1] The register records the burial of William Titmus's daughter Joane on 26 June 1644 (*Parish Register of St Ebbe's – 1557-1672* (MS DD Par Oxford - St Ebbe's b. 33), folio 72 recto). She probably died from the plague, since her entry is the first of three in as many days and the third specifically states 'suspected to die of ye plague'. William Titmus was from Chadlington in Oxfordshire and was a mercer by trade (*Enrolment Book of Statute Merchants – 1637-1675* (F.4.1), folio 92 verso). Unfortunately, there are no further records relating to William Titmus, or his daughter, which might help to clarify the possible connection to Richard in Oxford. However, there is record of a William Titmouse from Islip whose wife Joyce was cited in a court case of defamation on 20 February 1664 (*ODR: Citations – 1662-1664* (c. 39), folio 34).

[2] *Civic Enrolments – 1639-1662* (L.5.3), folio 39 verso = CSC #45.

transaction.[1] Following the grant of his Oxford citizenship Tidmarsh was awarded £25 from a charity established in the name of Sir Thomas White.[2] The money was probably awarded to help the young man start up his business as a tanner. [3] The award, which was duly repaid in 1660, proved to be a wise and sound investment.[4]

2. Apprenticeship Contracts

Tidmarsh soon began to establish himself as a master tanner within the city, taking on his first apprentice a year after being granted his citizenship. There are records of Tidmarsh's involvement in five apprenticeships extending over approximately twenty-four years. The details of the apprenticeships are as follows:

Name of Apprentice	Date of Contract	Duration	Citizenship Granted
John Terrell	21 January 1653[5]	Seven years	
Thomas Walter	19 April 1658[6]	Seven years	
John Haines	13 January 1664[7]	Seven years	

---

[1] *Civic Enrolments – 1639-1662* (L.5.3), folio 241 verso = CSC #105. Salter (1928): vi-ix, explains the procedure in for a person being accepted as a freeman of the city. He explains that the officers' fees were an administrative charge for the process and notes (p. viii) that everyone 'had to pay 4s. 6d. for the officers' fees, of which the Mayor received 16d. for sealing "the copy", the Town Clerk 16d. for writing it, the Chamberlains, the Bailiffs and the Mayor's serjeant each received 4d., and the Crier 2d.'

[2] *Audit Book – 1592-1682* (P.5.2), folio 286 verso.

[3] *Civil War, Charities & General Minutes – 1645-1695* (E.4.6), folios 64 recto and 72 verso. The money was apparently lent to Tidmarsh when an earlier loan to another tradesman named Roger Payne was repaid before it was due.

[4] Tidmarsh was evidently very successful financially, for he was able to stand securities for others even before he finished paying back the loan. There is record of him standing as one of two persons offering securities on a loan of £10 which was made to Edward Lloyd from the charity of Dr Kilby. This loan was scheduled to be repaid on 20 January 1658 (*Civil War, Charities & General Minutes – 1645-1695* (E.4.6), folios 71 recto). Tidmarsh was also subsequently one of three people who offered security on a loan of £25 made to William Parkes from the charity of Sir Thomas White. This loan was due 29 September 1668 (*Civil War, Charities & General Minutes – 1645-1695* (E.4.6), folios 77 recto).

[5] *Civic Enrolments – 1639-1662* (L.5.3), folio 117 verso = CSC #131; the apprenticeship contract is backdated to 29 September 1652.

[6] *Civic Enrolments – 1639-1662* (L.5.3), folio 164 verso = CSC #258; the apprenticeship contract is backdated to 25 March 1658. Thomas Walter was the son of John Walter, the person with whom Tidmarsh's original apprenticeship contract was made (see page 29 above).

[7] *Civic Enrolments – 1662-1699* (L.5.4), page 27 = CSC #389; the apprenticeship contract is backdated to 2 November 1663. John Haines was probably the unnamed apprentice listed as living with the Tidmarsh family in the Poll Tax of 1 March 1667

| William Stibbs | 17 January 1671[1] | Seven years | 31 May 1678[2] |
| John Tidmarsh | | | 7 February 1678[3] |

The last of these apprenticeships is in some ways the most interesting in that it was made with Richard Tidmarsh's eldest son, John. Although no formal contract of the apprenticeship is included within the book of *Civic Enrolments*, John was granted his 'Freedom of the City' on the basis of him being the eldest son of a citizen, which generally is an indication that the son has followed his father in a chosen trade or profession and learned his trade as an apprentice to his father.

3. Civic Offices and Responsibilities

The successful launch of a career as a craftsman generally brought with it civic responsibility, and Richard Tidmarsh was no exception to the rule, although his career in civic government was rather chequered. On 30 September 1653, two years after he was given his 'Freedom of the City', Tidmarsh was appointed to be one of the twenty-four members of the Common Council of the city of Oxford.[4] However, the council minutes for the next year record that Tidmarsh did not take up his place; he was eventually relieved of his position and another man chosen instead. Two consecutive entries within the minutes of the City Council proceedings, both dated 30 September 1654, provide details of this removal from office.[5] They show that, in addition to swearing a customary oath of office, election to a place within the Common Council carried with it the obligation of making a payment of £4, 'in Lieue of a customary Enterteynm[en]t to the use of the Citty'. This payment Tidmarsh refused point-blank to make. However, it is possible that the sticking point for Tidmarsh was not, strictly speaking, the payment of £4, as the council record suggests, but the swearing of an oath as condition of admission to the position (more on this below).

The saga over Tidmarsh's election to the Common Council rumbled on for some years. He apparently did not hold any City Council post from 1654 until 1659, although there was clearly a feeling among some of the citizens of Oxford that he should have such a place within their civic government. Matters

---

(*Poll Tax of 1667* (P.5.7), folio 8 recto. His father Richard Haines was a cordwainer from Burford.

[1] *Civic Enrolments – 1662-1699* (L.5.4), page 171 = CSC #493; the apprenticeship contract is backdated to 29 September 1670. William Stibbs as the son of Thomas Stibbs from Eastgaston in Berkshire.

[2] *Civic Enrolments – 1662-1699* (L.5.4), page 637 = CSC #578.

[3] *Civic Enrolments – 1662-1699* (L.5.4), page 629 = CSC #573. Payment of 3d for his admission is also recorded in *Audit Book – 1592-1682* (P.5.2), folio 370 recto.

[4] *City Council Proceedings – 1629-1663* (A.5.7), folio 217 verso = CSC #153. His name is the 23rd in the list of the 24 Common Council members (*City Council Proceedings – 1629-1663* (A.5.7), folio 218 recto).

[5] *City Council Proceedings – 1629-1663* (A.5.7), folio 223 verso = CSC #193.

came to a head during the political crisis that followed the collapse of Richard Cromwell's Protectorate and the recall of the Rump Parliament. The City Council minutes for the meeting held on 30 September 1659 record that Tidmarsh's name was again brought forward, and the suggestion was made that he 'might Yett be admitted into this house into which he was Elected'. The matter was publicly debated, and it was decided that he could not be offered a place within the Common Council without there being a new election, but that they could offer him a position as a chamberlain instead.[1]

What is interesting about this particular compromise arrangement is not that Tidmarsh was given a place within the lesser body of city chamberlains, but that his name was being put forward at all. Clearly the 'several freeman' who did so considered him a person of such trust and importance that they were willing to bring up old disputes, and they succeeded, in some measure, to carry the day. It is not hard to see why this was so. The Protectorate of Richard Cromwell had collapsed in May of 1659 and the country was effectively in the control of the Rump Parliament which was increasingly under pressure by disaffected factions, some of which were committed to the overthrow of the government. There was a strong feeling amongst many that the militia of the city of London and the nation should be placed 'into the hands of religious men, and friends to the Common Cause'.[2] It was generally believed up and down the country that radical groups such as the Quakers and the Anabaptists were again in the ascendancy, and the putting forward of Tidmarsh, by this time an acknowledged leader of the Baptists, is best viewed against this backdrop. Indeed, it appears Tidmarsh became involved with the Oxfordshire militia at precisely this juncture, for he was commissioned by the Council of State as a cornet in a troop of horse under the command of Major Robert Huntington on 9 August 1659.[3] As it turned out, the proposed compromise within the Oxford City Council over Tidmarsh's position proved to be irrelevant, since Charles II arrived the next year to take control and return the country to some sort of monarchial 'normality'.

Indeed, it is against the backdrop of the restoration of the monarchy that we see Tidmarsh once again coming into the firing line amidst the political

---

[1] *City Council Proceedings – 1629-1663* (A.5.7), folio 265 recto = CSC #294; *Council Minutes – 1657-1668* (A.4.4), folio 48 recto. Tidmarsh's name appears elsewhere among the list of chamberlains (*City Council Proceedings – 1629-1663* (A.5.7), folio 266 recto; *Council Minutes – 1657-1668* (A.4.4), folio 49 verso).

[2] *The Weekly Intelligencer of the Common-Wealth*, No. 5 (Tuesday, May 31 to Tuesday, June 7, 1659): page 38.

[3] *JHC* 7: 753 = CSC #291. This is the only evidence of Tidmarsh's direct involvement with the military. It is significant that other members of the Baptist congregation were also commissioned at the same time. Both Ralph Austen and Thomas Tisdale served in the Oxfordshire militia in the regiment of foot which was commanded by the regicide Colonel Adrian Scroope (see pages 82 and 202 below). The establishment of an Oxfordshire militia had been ordered by the Council of State on 31 July, and the commissions for the officers were approved on 11 August (SP 25/98), pages 52 and 105 = CSC #292).

manoeuvrings going on within the City Council. Not surprisingly, it is the matter of oaths, and in particular, oaths of allegiance, which becomes one of the focal points of debate.[1] The best indication of this is contained within the City Council records from May-June 1660, shortly after news of Charles II's return from exile had reached the city and the restoration of the monarch seemed imminent.[2] Like much of the rest of the country, Oxford had been overtaken by the return of Charles II to Dover in May of 1660. The restoration had particular impact in Oxford, and the city became obsessed with making elaborate preparations for a public celebration of the event. These included public fountains filled with claret, the distribution of free wine, cakes, bread and beer, and a colourful parade of public officials bedecked in scarlet gowns and riding in an orderly procession. It was even decided that the city's Commonwealth seal was to be ceremonially broken and that a new mace was to be made with the king's name on it.[3] There is a note of irony in all of this, given the fact that the person commissioned to write the declaration which was to be given to the king along with the mace, the deputy-recorder named Richard Croke, had been assigned the same task for the mace that was to be given to Richard Cromwell just eighteen months before in October of 1658.[4] Anthony Wood's incisive comment sums up Croke's chameleonic character well: 'he alwaies ran with the times'.[5]

On 15 May Croke, as deputy-recorder for the council, drew up a delicately phrased document expressing the city's hearty congratulations to the king.[6] This petition met with the approval of the house and was duly sent to Charles II. Soon thereafter moves were made to require City Councilmen to swear the Oath of Supremacy to Charles II, and a list of those who did so was compiled on 1 June 1660. It contains 71 names, but Tidmarsh's is not among them.[7]

Tidmarsh was by no means alone in his stance against the taking of oaths.[8] Indeed, many prominent figures in the city of Oxford disapproved of the taking of oaths on religious grounds. Perhaps the most celebrated is the scientist Robert Boyle, who even wrote a tract entitled *Free Discourse Against*

---

[1] See Hill (1962a): 382-419, for a general discussion on oath-taking in the period.

[2] *City Council Proceedings – 1629-1663* (A.5.7), folio 273 recto.

[3] *City Council Proceedings – 1629-1663* (A.5.7), folio 272 recto.

[4] Toynbee (1960): 73-95, gives details. The article includes photographs of the mace and its accompanying coronation cup.

[5] *MS Wood D 4*, folio 297b. Croke died on 15 September 1683.

[6] *City Council Proceedings – 1629-1663* (A.5.7), folio 273 recto.

[7] *City Council Proceedings – 1629-1663* (A.5.7), folio 274 recto.

[8] In his *Folly and Madnesse Made Manifest* (1659), William Fiennes, Viscount Say and Sele of Oxford, mentions that Anabaptists of Bloxham were given to such a position. He suggests that the delusion 'commeth from the Anabaptists of Germany' (page 10). However, Richard Tidmarsh does not seem to have been followed in his convictions by his son James. There is record of James Tidmarsh voluntarily taking the oath of allegiance to Charles II on 10 June 1682 (*Oxford Petty Sessions Roll – 1679-1712* (O.5.12), folio 42 verso).

Swearing, published posthumously in 1695.[1] Boyle certainly subjected his own career and reputation to the scruples he had over oath taking, and attempted to live his life by the principles he had adopted in this matter. Thus, although elected President of the Royal Society in London on 30 November 1680, Boyle declined to take up the post because it would involve the swearing of an oath. Although no record of any direct contact between Richard Tidmarsh and Robert Boyle is extant, the two men had a mutual friend in the person of Ralph Austen (see chapter 4). It is not beyond the bounds of possibility that Boyle and Tidmarsh did meet, or at least knew of each other's stance on oath-taking. According to John Williams, who edited Boyle's tract and arranged to have it published, the great scientist was aware of how oath-taking was viewed by some Anabaptists, but sought to distance himself somewhat from them. Williams writes:

> In order to ensure that his ideas do not get misunderstood he writes that at no point of this Discourse my intention was to justify that Plausible Error of our modern Anabaptists, that indiscriminately condemn all Oaths as absolutely and indispensibly prohibited and abolished by the Gospel.[2]

In the end, Tidmarsh held his place as a chamberlain on the City Council for less than a year. The political landscape was changing dramatically, and the star of Charles II was in the ascendancy. The traditionalists who supported the restoration held sway within the Oxford City Council, and Tidmarsh, the avowed Baptist, was viewed with suspicion by many. The City Council minutes for 28 September 1660 record that the previous decision to grant Tidmarsh a place as a chamberlain was revoked. It was made void, so the minute relates, 'because Mr Tidmarsh did never offer himself to take his oath nor to come to the Councells'.[3]   In short, it seems clear that Tidmarsh's involvement in city government (or the lack of it!), was very much conditioned by his stance on the question of oaths, and in particular, oaths of allegiance to a ing. No doubt he saw this as part and parcel of his religious convictions and republican ideals.[4]

---

[1] However, there is some debate about whether the tract was even written by Boyle himself. See Fulton (1961): 137, for details.

[2] Boyle (1695): 129.

[3] *City Council Proceedings – 1629-1663* (A.5.7), folio 279 verso = CSC #315. At the same council meeting the out-going Mayor John Lambe gave an account of money collected during the past year to pay for the so-called 'Carfax lectures', a programme of public preaching at the Carfax church supported by the City Council. Tidmarsh is listed as one of eight people 'who are behind on what is due from them'. The Carfax lecturers from 1647-1661 were the Presbyterian divines Henry Wilkinson and Henry Cornish; they were paid £20 per year. Tidmarsh's contribution as a chamberlain would have been 10*d* collected quarterly.

[4] Underwood (1947): 91-92, discusses the theological difficulties that some Baptists in the early 1660s had in swearing the oaths of allegiance which were being demanded by Charles II.

There are other glimpses of Tidmarsh's activity as an Oxford citizen after the restoration of the monarchy, however. One of his more unusual appearances in the Oxford Petty Sessions court records occurs in connection with a local parish matter. In an entry dated 6 October 1664 there is record of a complaint made by Tidmarsh against the inhabitants of the parish of St Thomas for money that was owed him.[1] Tidmarsh had been appointed as an 'Overseer of the Poor' within the parish of St Thomas in the spring of 1663,[2] and it appears that while serving in this capacity he had distributed 47s 7d to the poor. The parish churchwardens refused to reimburse him for this, and Tidmarsh pursued the matter within the courts. In the end, the Petty Sessions court upheld Tidmarsh's complaint and reimbursement was ordered.

However, this was not the only time that Tidmarsh clashed with authorities over local political matters within the parish of St Thomas. Another interesting contest concerned a long-running battle between the inhabitants of St Thomas parish and the Oxford City Council. An entry within the City Council records of 6 August 1666 records a payment of £3 that is made to Tidmarsh, to go 'toward the erecting of the Arch neere his doore'.[3] It is not difficult to guess what is meant by 'an arch' here.[4] It refers to a bridge, or a pedestrian walkway, over the river, which makes sense when we remember that Tidmarsh lived in the parish of St Thomas in what is now Tidmarsh Lane. His house was near the river Thames (Isis), and he conducted his business as a tanner from there, conveniently located as it was by the old castle mills. But why is Tidmarsh erecting a bridge over the river near his home, and when did he do so? Part of the answer comes in the records of two City Council meetings held several years previously, one on 21 September 1657, and the other on 4 February 1659. The first of these entries makes reference to the decaying state of the 'Bridge neere the Cyttie Mills', and hints that part of the problem is the number of carts that are passing over it. To help control the passage of carts, four of the inhabitants of St Thomas parish petitioned that a post and chain be set up on the west end of the bridge (in accordance with an earlier decree set down in the days of James I).[5] This seemed sensible and was agreed by the City Council. The second entry from 1659 notes the continuing controversy between the city and the inhabitants of St Thomas parish over the repairing of

---

[1] *Oxford Petty Sessions Roll – 1656-1678* (O.5.11), folio 72 verso = CSC #399.

[2] *Husting and Mayor's Court 1662; Licenses and Overseers* (N.4.3), folio 15 recto = CSC #372.

[3] *City Council Proceedings – 1663-1701* (B.5.1), folio 39 verso = CSC #432.

[4] There is mention in the records of 15 July 1659 of an arch at High Bridge being filled with dirt and mud and being cleaned at the city's expense (see *City Council Proceedings – 1629-1663* (A.5.7), folio 262 verso. Similarly, it is recorded on 21 August 1660 that the city mills around the castle are 'flundered upp w[i]th Mudd and Filth by w[hi]ch meanes the Mills is like to bee stopt upp and made uselesse unlesse it bee speedyly cleansed' (*City Council Proceedings – 1629-1663* (A.5.7), folio 277 verso).

[5] *City Council Proceedings – 1629-1663* (A.5.7), folio 243 recto = CSC #254.

this Castle Mill bridge.[1] The minute records an agreement whereby the city should pay annually 6s 8d toward the costs, provided that the parishioners of St Thomas be responsible for the actual repairs and maintenance of the bridge. Hence, in the City Council minute from 6 August 1666 it looks as if Tidmarsh is being reimbursed for his personal expenditure on either the Castle Mill bridge to the south of his house (an expenditure which strictly speaking was the responsibility of the city), or on another bridge between the Castle Mill bridge and the High bridge, probably either what is now known as Quaking bridge to the west of the castle, or Pacey's bridge on Park End road.

All of the debate about the repair of the Castle Mill bridge needs to be set against similar discussions about the state of the main bridge across the river, the High bridge. For example, mention is made in the records for 25 October 1660 of the city being officially accused of not meeting its obligations in 'repayreing the high wayes leading from the George Lane to High Bridge'. The matter is said to be referred to the Mayor and his council, and they are instructed to try and put a stop to any further accusations of default being made along these lines, with all of the attendant costs being paid for by the city.[2] The issue dragged on for some further months, for there is another mention of it in the records for 6 December 1660. Here the City Council agreed to repair the cartway on High Bridge, albeit with a careful eye to the types of repairs made and the costs involved.[3] Mention is then made of the High Bridge again some five months later, in the records for 19 March 1661, when it is recorded that the city chamberlains are requested (again!) to repair and paint the bridge at the city's expense.[4]

How does this long saga over the state of the High Bridge affect the petition made by Tidmarsh that he be reimbursed £3 for his expenditure on the 'arch' near his house? Perhaps what we detect within the record from 6 August 1666 is a long-standing grievance on the part of Tidmarsh and others living in the parish of St Thomas over the state of the pathways and bridges westwards across the river into their area of the city. The state of disrepair of the High Bridge meant that people were forced to cross the river using alternative footpaths and bridges. The increase of traffic caused inevitable pressure on existing bridges and the need for new ones arose. It looks as if Tidmarsh was spear-heading a local campaign in 1666 to maintain 'an arch neere his door' as a viable path over the river and was getting reimbursed for his efforts. The matter of responsibility for the western bridges continued to be a point of controversy for years afterward, if the passing mention contained in Anthony

---

[1] *City Council Proceedings – 1629-1663* (A.5.7), folio 257 recto = CSC #277. There is also an account of this debate which lists the names of the various representatives of the parish of St Thomas, including Tidmarsh's fellow conventicler Ralph Austen (see *Civil War Charities and General Minutes – 1645-1695* (E.4.6), folio 23 verso) = CSC #278.

[2] *City Council Proceedings – 1629-1663* (A.5.7), folio 282 verso.

[3] *City Council Proceedings – 1629-1663* (A.5.7), folio 282 verso = CSC #317.

[4] *City Council Proceedings – 1629-1663* (A.5.7), folio 286 verso.

Wood's diary entry for 30 October 1685 is anything to go by. As Wood records in connection with the Castle Mill bridge, it became a classic example of 'passing the buck':

> In this month of Oct[ober] was the bridge at Castle-mill tayle repaired at ye charg of the city of Ox[ford] after it had laid ruinous neare an yeare. The parishioners of St. Tho[mas] they refused to repaire it and alledged that it was to be don by ye miller; the miller alledged it was to be don by ye pa[rishioners]. Whereupon a meeting of ye matter being made at the assize in July going before, it was adjudged to be done by the city.[1]

One further indication of Tidmarsh's involvement in parish matters during the reign of Charles II is also worth highlighting. As noted above (page 9), in 1668 a tax was levied relating to the 'Act for Granting £1,256,347 13s for the War against the Dutch'. Ironically, given the fact that Dissenters were under persecution at the time, there are three records which show that Tidmarsh served as one of the two assessors responsible for facilitating the collection of these war taxes within the parish of St Thomas.[2] In effect, he was helping to collect taxes for the king in whose name he was being prosecuted as a 'seditious sectarye', and at exactly the same time that moves were under way to have him excommunicated from the Anglican church (more on this below).

Tidmarsh's most controversial engagement with Oxford politics takes place some years later during the reign of James II. Along with other prominent Dissenters, Tidmarsh becomes a political pawn in James II's struggle to maintain control during the final year of his troubled reign.[3] On 16 February 1688 the Mayor of Oxford, John Payne, produced in the City Council two letters from James II, written on 20 and 21 January 1688, the first of which demanded the removal of a number of City Councilmen, and the second of which named acceptable replacements. The City Council records give details of the king's new appointees, naming Richard Tidmarsh as one of the eight Bailiffs.[4] Significantly, the record states that the conditions about the swearing of oaths were dispensed with by the king in his letter: only oaths pertaining to the execution of the office concerned needed to be sworn. This meant that Tidmarsh was free to accept the appointment without swearing an oath of allegiance to the king. As the entry states: 'And thafores[ai]d Richard Tidmarsh came into this House & tooke the Oath of a member of this House.'

---

[1] *MS Wood Diaries 29*, folio 60 verso = CSC #615. Also see *City Council Proceedings – 1663-1701* (B.5.1), folio 235 recto and verso, where the matter is discussed.

[2] *War Taxes – 1667-1668* (P.5.8), folios 125 verso, 126 recto, and 127 verso. His fellow assessor in each instance was a gardener named John Lucas.

[3] Lacey (1969): 175-208, discusses James II's attempts to entice the Dissenters to support his challenge to the Anglican establishment. Also see Miller (1989): 8-27, for more on the complexities of the situation facing James II. Kreitzer (2004b): 430-435, discusses Egbert van Heemskerk's painting of the City Council elections of 1688.

[4] *City Council Proceedings - 1663-1701* (B.5.1), folio 261 recto = CSC #624.

All of this political manoeuvring and reshuffling of the council 'pack' was in anticipation of the new Oxford charter, the granting of which was drawn up in a warrant dated 9 August 1688.[1] The charter itself was formally issued by James II on 15 September 1688[2] and it named a number of prominent Dissenters to key positions. One of those Dissenters was Tidmarsh, who is named in the charter as an 'Assistant'.[3] According to the City Council records, Tidmarsh swore his oath of office before the Mayor, Richard Carter, on 25 September 1688.[4] On the strength of his place as an 'Assistant', Tidmarsh was also nominated to be one of the five Keykeepers of the City. The City Council records show that he swore the oath relevant to that office on 28 September 1688.[5]

The Oxford charter was revoked less than a month later on 22 October 1688, and Tidmarsh lost his position as a City Councilman. He never again appears within the surviving City Council records, and effectively disappears from city politics altogether. The only vestige of this bizarre period of his life was his signature on a single-page document entitled *Innocency Vindicated: or, Reproach Wip'd Off* (1689) (see Appendix C).[6] It was signed by 24 Baptist pastors from England and Wales and was published to challenge the suggestion that they had compromised the cause of civil and religious liberty by accepting municipal offices from the devious James II as part of his scheme to disrupt the Anglican establishment. Whatever the rights or wrongs of the charge, the accusation clearly bit deep and a public response by those accused of complicity was thought necessary.

Certainly many high-church Anglicans felt that the Baptists were deeply implicated in James II's attempts to impose Roman Catholicism upon the country. In 1690 one anonymous author, obviously an Anglican, went so far as to describe the Anabaptists as the first of 'Six Popish Pillars', meaning the six dissenting sects or interested parties who fell for the false promises made by James II when he issued his *Declaration of Indulgence concerning Liberty of Conscience* on 4 April 1687. The anonymous author of this tract from 1690 argues that these six sectarian groups (which included the Anabaptists,

---

[1] SP 44/338, pages 47-49 = CSC #628.

[2] Anthony Wood states that the charter was received in Oxford on St Matthew's day, 20 September (*MS Wood Diaries 32*, page 49.

[3] *James II's Charter for Oxford – 15 September 1688* (I. 43). The charter consists of four vellum sheets; Tidmarsh's name appears in line 58 on sheet two, and in line 180 on sheet four.

[4] *City Council Proceedings - 1663-1701* (B.5.1), folio 266 recto. Carter was probably a Roman Catholic. There is record of his excommunication on 23 July 1664 (*ODR: Excommunication Schedules – 1662-1667* (c. 100), folio 88 recto; *ODR: Excommunications – 1633-1791* (c. 99), folio 242 recto).

[5] *City Council Proceedings - 1663-1701* (B.5.1), folio 266 verso.

[6] It appears that only a few copies of the document have survived, one of which is now contained in the Bodleian Library in Oxford, and another in the Congregational Library in London (84.2.5 (96)). Baines (1955-6): 164-170, offers an interesting study of it.

Presbyterians, Quakers and Independents) ended up unwitting dupes in James II's long-term aim of promoting Roman Catholicism. More to the point, the author of this tract notes that Oxford Baptists joined with Baptists from Abingdon (in Berkshire) and Wantage (in Berkshire) in presenting the king with an additional letter of support which was over and above those offered previously by the counties of Oxfordshire and Berkshire.[1] The anonymous pamphlet explains that the counties had presented the king with their address on 29 June 1687:

> And after these were presented, yet one more Humble Address of the *Anabaptists* of *Oxford, Abbington* and *Wantage*, with the same Flatteries and Warranties as their Fellows. They had once afore Addressed in that of the Counties of *Oxon* and *Berks*: But it seems these *Anabaptisto-Papists* could not rest so without a peculiar application, so proud it seems they were of their Interest in a Popish Prince.[2]

According to Narcissus Luttrell the address from the Baptists of Oxford, Abingdon and Wantage was presented to the king on 24 October 1687; he does not record the king's reaction.[3] The text of the address was printed in the *London Gazette* in the second week of November 1687.[4] Although the published version of the address did not include the names of the signatories, it is virtually certain that Tidmarsh would have been one of the people who put his name to the document. It is difficult to imagine Baptists from Oxford making such a move without his lead.

The revocation of the Oxford charter in October of 1688 effectively marks the end of Tidmarsh's activity within the political arena. However, the flight of James II to France on Christmas Day 1688, coupled with the eventual triumph of William of Orange on the English throne,[5] brought new opportunities of religious freedom for Dissenters, as exemplified in the issuing of the *Act of Toleration* in 1689. The fresh atmosphere of religious liberty meant that the Baptist church in Oxford could meet openly in a way not permitted before. The transition from illegal conventicle to licensed congregation was under way, and it was into the Baptist congregation, with its new legal identity, that the sixty-two year old Tidmarsh seems henceforth to have concentrated all his

---

[1] *The London Gazette* #2255 (Monday, 27 June to Thursday, 30 June 1687), page 1.

[2] *A Brief History of the Rise, Growth, Reign, Supports, and sodain fatal Foyl of Popery during the three Years and an half of James the Second, King of England, Scotland, France and Ireland, together with a description of the Six Popish Pillars* (1690): 9-10.

[3] Luttrell (1857): 418. See Ashley (1966): 115, for more on the addresses sent to James II by Dissenters.

[4] *The London Gazette* #2294 (Thursday 10 November to Monday 14 November 1687), page 1 = CSC #621.

[5] Childs (1988): 398, describes the so-called 'Glorious Revolution' as 'a bizarre event in a bizarre decade'.

considerable energy and interest. I turn now to consider more closely his long involvement with the Baptist church in Oxford.

C. Leader of the Baptist Conventicle in Oxford (1656-1691)

One of the earliest records of a Baptist meeting house in Oxford is a passing reference contained in an account of the visit of the Quakers John Camm and John Audland to the city in 1654. The record describes how the two men spoke at the Baptist meeting house, to the great satisfaction of the congregation there. Although it does not specify Richard Tidmarsh by name, it does note that 'y man in whose house y Meeting was kept received John Audland & John Camm into theire house with Rich[ard] Bettris & Lawrence Willier who accompanyd ym.'[1] In all probability, this was the home of Richard Tidmarsh, who is specifically identified in other records of the 1650s.

1. Abingdon Association Records

Tidmarsh is commonly regarded as the most important figure in the earliest days of Baptist witness within the city of Oxford. The records of the Abingdon Association of Baptist churches show that he twice served as a delegate from Oxford at the association meetings held at Tetsworth, a village south of Oxford on the London road. In the meetings beginning 11 March 1656 he is mentioned alongside Thomas Tisdale as one of the two Oxford delegates,[2] and in the meetings commencing 5 April 1659 Tidmarsh is listed as the sole delegate from Oxford.[3] In the 1659 meetings Tidmarsh offered a brief account of the state of the church, reporting on the addition of four new members to the congregation, and that there were several matters of discipline and concern, namely that 'two among them do observe the seventh-day sabbath, yet forsake not y church'.[4] It was perhaps on the strength of this experience that Tidmarsh was delegated by the messengers of the Association to assist in a matter of some delicacy involving some of the member churches. It seems that the churches in Kingston, Watlington and Haddenham had been approached by the 'baptized people of Bledlow, most of which doe now hold the 7th-day sabbath'. Sabbatarianism was a doctrinal difference apparently severe enough to have caused the three named Association churches to break fellowship with the church at Bledlow. The members of the church in Bledlow had now contacted the three churches 'which did formerly hold com[m]union with them' and

---

[1] *Manuscripts – First Publishers of Truth: Portfolio 7*, folio 64a recto = CSC #199. Bettris (sometimes spelled *Betteris* or *Betterice*) and Willier were well-known Oxford Quakers. This record of Quaker activity in Oxford during 1654 was probably compiled in the early 1700s; it is not specifically dated, although the covering page of the manuscript does mention the year 1706.

[2] *AARB*, folio 13 verso = White (1974): 145.

[3] *AARB*, folio 36 verso = White (1974): 189.

[4] *AARB*, folio 38 recto = White (1974): 191 = CSC #279.

petitioned for a meeting, 'to the end that they might [decide how] far they can all walke together'. The Abingdon Association messengers advised that contact with the sabbatarians at Bledlow was desirable, and a meeting was set up to take place at Kingston on 20 April 1659. Tidmarsh was one of those who was asked to attend and offer advice and assistance in the matter.[1] This was not the only time that Tidmarsh was called upon to exercise a ministry of diplomacy among the wider Baptist denomination, nor was it the only time that he had to deal with Baptists who became involved in the sabbatarian controversy. Indeed, later in his life Tidmarsh became involved in helping to settle a dispute between the sabbatarian congregations of John Belcher and Francis Bampfield in London (see page 72 below). It is possible that Tidmarsh and Belcher were friends, and the two men certainly knew each other as early as 1656; Belcher was one of the messengers sent by the church at Kingston to the Abingdon Association meetings held on 11-14 March 1656, at which Tidmarsh was present. Indeed, it is possible that Tidmarsh was also involved in inviting the controversial Belcher to visit Oxford in January of 1660, where he preached at the parish church of St Peter-in-the-Bailey (see pages 179-80 below). Although it was not Tidmarsh, but his fellow Baptist conventiclers Roger Hatchman and Ralph Austen who were named by Anthony Wood as having engineered the preaching engagement, this is probably because Hatchman and Austen both lived near St Peter-in-the-Bailey. Tidmarsh may not be specifically named, but it is difficult to imagine that he, as the leader of the Baptists in Oxford, was not involved somehow in the affair.

The Abingdon Association records are the earliest evidence of Tidmarsh's involvement with the Baptist cause in Oxford, and in fact represent the earliest confirmation of the existence of a Baptist church in the city. Clearly Baptists had been meeting for some time prior to 1656, but by the time of this Abingdon Association meeting it appears that the thirty-year-old Tidmarsh had risen to a position of leadership and responsibility within the congregation. Later in the year we find Tidmarsh implicated in what was one of the most significant developments within the life of the Abingdon Association, an event which was to propel Oxfordshire Baptists onto the national stage and embroil them in the complexities of Cromwellian power politics. This was the funeral of John Pendarves, the pastor of the Baptist church in Abingdon, who died suddenly in September of 1656.[2] Pendarves was an extremely influential figure, a charismatic leader reputed to have had associations with the Fifth Monarchy movement. His funeral in Abingdon on 30 September 1656 was attended by a

---

[1] *AARB*, folios 40 recto and 40 verso = White (1974): 195 = CSC #280.

[2] See White (1973-74): 251-71, for an in-depth study of Pendarves. Also see Hambleton (2000): 1-10, for an imaginative reconstruction of the tumultuous events which took place at his funeral on 30 September 1656. According to one anonymous 17th-century source, 'About the beginning of September 1656: The famous preacher Mr. Pendarvis of Abington died at London of the plague in the guts' (*MS Rawlinson D 859*, folio 162). It is likely that Pendarves suffered with tuberculosis, although it is unclear if this contributed directly to his early death (see Kreitzer (2004a): 281-289, for details).

number of Baptists from around the country, including Richard Tidmarsh and Richard Quelch junior from Oxford. The funeral became a point of conflict as government troops clashed with the mourners, wounding some and briefly imprisoning others. The incident led to the publication of a tract by the Baptist mourners decrying their treatment by the soldiers. The pamphlet was entitled *The Complaining Testimony of Some ... of Sions Children* (1656); Richard Tidmarsh and Richard Quelch junior were among its signatories (see Appendix A for the full text of this important document).

2. State Papers of Charles II (1661)

With the restoration of the monarchy under Charles II the Dissenters in Oxford once again found themselves the objects of hatred and the victims of persecution. Tidmarsh was in trouble with the authorities several times during the early 1660s, and one or two stories about the difficulties he endured have come down to us through Baptist historians. Thus, Thomas Crosby's *The History of the English Baptists* (1740) has one brief paragraph about Richard Tidmarsh:

> Mr. Tidmarsh was minister several years to the congregation of Baptists at Oxford; a man greatly esteemed, and of good reputation; one that suffered much in the time of persecution for his nonconformity.[1]

Other official state records from the 1660s recount the difficulties that the church in Oxford experienced, particularly in the wake of the oppressive policies adopted by Charles II toward religious dissent. For example, there is a letter within the *State Papers* of Charles II which records how the violence of the so-called Venner uprising in London had heightened public fear about Anabaptists.[2] The Venner rebellion commenced on 6 January 1661 and this letter was written in the wake of that rebellion; it is dated 15 January 1661. It was penned by Thomas Lamplugh, a fellow of Queen's College, Oxford, to Joseph Williamson, who served in the office of Charles II's Secretary of State, and was a former student of Lamplugh's at Queen's.[3] Lamplugh was in regular

---

[1] Crosby (1740): 3.125-126. The paragraph is taken over in its entirety by Ivimey (1814): 2.521, who adds two extra sentences: 'Richard Tidmarsh was the minister of Particular baptists at Oxford in 1688. He attended the meetings of the general Assembly in London.'

[2] Baptists in London published a pamphlet entitled *The Humble Apology of some commonly called Anabaptists* (1661) which denounced the uprising. Thomason dated the pamphlet to 28 January 1661.

[3] Thomas Lamplugh was one of Charles II's commissioners to the University in 1660. Anthony Wood describes him in uncomplimentary terms: 'Dr. Thom[as] Lamplugh another y^t kept his fellowship in Queens College after 1648 & y^t he might shew himself a true Royallist, got to be one of the kings Com[m]issioners this year, & at length by flatteries & rewards shiffled himself into consid[er]able spiritualities. A great cringer form[er]ly to p[re]sbyterians & Independents, now to ye prelates & those in

correspondence with Williamson, and although his letters are often filled with college gossip, they do occasionally offer insight into what is happening elsewhere within the city of Oxford.[1] Thus, the letter of 15 January describes an incident involving the Baptist meeting house, almost certainly the home of Richard Tidmarsh. Lamplugh describes how the meeting houses of Dissenters, including Baptists, 'were beset by 'them of ye Militia, their quarters bit up & some dismissed and others secured'.[2]

Tidmarsh was also implicated in another incident later in the year, one which serves to illustrate the fear and paranoia about insurrection that persisted long after Venner's revolt was crushed. The primary source for this particular episode is an obscure pamphlet by Andrew Yarranton entitled *A Full Discovery of the First Presbyterian Sham-Plot* (1681). Yarranton concentrated on Worcestershire in his pamphlet, providing details of a plotted insurrection against Charles II that took place in the county in November of 1661. In passing, however, details of a similar plot in Oxfordshire are also recounted and through these we catch further glimpses of Tidmarsh and his fellow Baptist Dissenters. It seems that in early November of 1661 a letter was delivered under mysterious circumstances to a Mr Martin, the Town-Clerk of Oxford. The letter purported to contain instructions for Martin to alert a number of Oxford citizens to arm themselves and gather together at an prearranged place and time; a total of 111 names were included in a list which accompanied the letter. These Oxford citizens were thus to join 200 armed men who were to enter Oxford, and participate in an organized revolt which was to extend across six counties and bring down the monarchy. Martin was unsure whether the letter represented an actual threat or not. He immediately contacted the Mayor of Oxford, Leonard Bowman, who in turn wrote to Lord Falkland, one of Oxford's MPs and the Lord Lieutenant of the county;[3] a further copy was later sent to the city recorder Richard Croke, who was responsible for conveying its contents to one of the secretaries in the Privy Council of Charles II. The credibility of the alleged plot is difficult to judge, although Martin and Bowman

---

authoritie, to raise himselfe & settle a familie' (*MS Wood F 31*, folio 14 verso). Similarly, Wood relates Lamplugh's treachery in supporting and then betraying James II in the face of the arrival of William of Orange in November 1688 (*MS Wood Diaries 32*, page 60). Fletcher (1896): 76-77, summarizes his career.

[1] Jabez-Smith (1986): 145-161, discusses the longstanding friendship between Williamson and Lamplugh. Williamson's career as an administrator in Charles II's court is treated in Marshall (1996): 18-41.

[2] SP 29/28, page 109 = CSC #320. Greaves (1986): 54, alludes to this letter but does not discuss Tidmarsh or the Baptists themselves.

[3] Henry Carey, 4th Viscount Falkland (1634-1663), was MP for Oxfordshire from January to April 1659, for Oxford City from April 1660 to December 1660, and then again for Oxfordshire from March 1661 until his death on 2 April 1663. He was appointed Oxfordshire's Lord Lieutenant (and *Custos Rotulorum*) on 10 December 1660 and served in that capacity until his death. He died in London, but was buried in Great Tew. He was the only son of Lucius 2nd Viscount Falkland, Secretary of State to Charles I, who was killed at the first battle of Newbury on 20 September 1643.

together came to the conclusion that it was probably 'at the worst, but a design to try or to intrap the Town-Clark' (Martin had himself been a member of the Oxfordshire militia commissioned by Parliament in August of 1659).[1] What is most interesting about the incident is the fact that the list of the 111 alleged conspirators includes the names of many of the Baptist Dissenters in Oxford, notably that of a 'Mr Titmons'.[2] This almost certainly means Richard *Tidmarsh*, whose surname is sometimes given in documents as *Titmus* (the confusion between the letters *u* and *n* in hand-written documents is not uncommon).[3] Even more suggestive is a tantalyzing connection between Tidmarsh and Lord Falkland himself, one involving an incident which took place two years before in the summer of 1659 when it it looked as if the dreams of a true republic might still be realized.

There is good evidence to suggest that there was a bit of bad blood between Lord Falkland and supporters of the republican cause within Parliament. A case in point took place in August of 1659 when Falkland was suspected of being involved in Sir George Booth's Cheshire insurrection.[4] Orders went out for Falkland's arrest, and by 5 August he was in custody in Oxford. He was sent to London and placed in the Tower on 12 August, charged with 'high Treason in raiseing Warre ag[ain]st P[arl[iamen]t'; he was ordered to be detained in prison for 'further examination and his tryall at law'.[5] Examination of Falkland in prison raised concerns about his storage of secret arms and on 29 August an order was sent by the Council of State to Major Huntington, the commander of the very unit of horse within the Oxfordshire militia of which Tidmarsh was commissioned a cornet (see above). The soldiers were ordered to search Lord Falkland's home in Great Tew and 'to demand the thirty Case of

---

[1] *JHC* 7: 752-3. Interestingly, the Baptist Dissenter Thomas Tisdale was Martin's ensign. Both Bowman and Martin were among the Oxford citizens who attended the coronation of Charles II on 23 April 1661; they apparently agreed to serve in the royal kitchens in order to be included in the ceremonies (*Suits with the University – 1634-1680* (F.4.3), folios 170-173).

[2] *A Full Discovery of the First Presbyterian Sham-Plot* (1681) = CSC #336. Greaves (1986): 75-76, discusses the incident, but again does not mention Tidmarsh by name.

[3] Several other Baptist Dissenters in the list have slightly unusual spellings, probably indicative of the nature of the list as a hand-written copy of names as they were spoken. Thus, the list includes a Mr Achman (Roger *Hatchman*), a Mr Tindall (Thomas *Tisdale*), a Mr Wiance (Edward *Wyans*), a Mr Tomes (John *Toms*), and a Mr Asting (Ralph *Austen*). More easily recognizable are the names of a Mr King (Lawrence King), two Mr Jennings (James and Edward Jennings), a Mr Quelch (Richard Quelch junior), and a Mr Williams (Thomas Williams).

[4] Jones (1956-57): 413-443; Underdown (1960): 254-313, discuss Booth's rising.

[5] SP 25/79, pages 428 and 431. His arrest and detention were reported in *Mercurius Politicus* #583 (11-18 August 1659), pages 664-665. Also see Clarendon (1786): 3.544, where it is mentioned in a letter from John Greenville to Lord Chancellor Hyde dated 19 August 1659.

pistolls w[hi]ch the said Lord acknowledged to be in his house'.[1] Lord Falkland petitioned against his imprisonment, and on 2 September the Council of State ordered that he was to be re-examined; apparently the cache of pistols had not been yet been found and they wanted more information about their location.[2] It was a tense time and the Oxfordshire militia was diligent, capturing documents from a Scotsman which appear to have further implicated Falkland.[3] On 5 October the Commissioners of the Oxfordshire militia sent a letter to the Council of State and included within it a number of statements taken down in evidence at an investigation they conducted into the matter.[4] The same day the Council of State discussed a report by Huntington, written two days earlier, about the search of Lord Falkland's house. They also heard the sworn testimony of a Symon Paget, one of the soldiers from Huntington's troop, who related how a cache of weapons had been discovered hidden in a wall in the uppermost room of the house. Paget also recounted that 'in another place of the said House being a low Roome near the Cellar under a parcell of Faggotts, they found a Barrell of powder and eighteene Case of pistolls with Holsters'.[5] This was no doubt taken as proof of Lord Falkland's hostility to the Commonwealth, and justification of his imprisonment in the Tower.

On 10 October the Council of State agreed to send a letter to the Commissioners of the Oxfordshire militia thanking them for their action in the Falkland affair, saying that they 'looke upon this Service as a further testimony of your good affect[i]ons to y[e] good old Cause'.[6] Huntington was further rewarded when the City Council granted him the 'Freedom of the City' and a Bailiff's place on 30 December 1659.[7] In short, Tidmarsh was one of the officers of the troop of militia which searched Lord Falkland's house and uncovered hidden weapons, a discovery that no doubt prolonged Falkland's inconvenient imprisonment in the Tower. Once he was released from prison Falkland remained active in the political scene in Oxfordshire. Most significantly he served as one of the delegates who delivered a petition signed by 5,000 inhabitants of the county to General Monck at his quarters in Broadstreet in London on 13 February 1660.[8] The petition outlined the grievances of the signatories, as well as their expectations for the future,

---

[1] SP 25/79, page 501.

[2] SP 25/79, page 513.

[3] SP 25/79, pages 609 and 620. These are discussed in council meetings held on 21 and 26 September.

[4] *MS Clarendon 65*, folios 139-140 = CSC #296.

[5] SP 25/79, page 650 = CSC #297.

[6] SP 25/79, page 661; SP 25/98, page 217. *Mercurius Politicus* #582, page 647, gives the names of the Commissioners appointed on 5 August as John Cox, Edward Vivers of Banbury, John Eles and Adam Berry.

[7] *City Council Proceedings – 1629-1663* (A.5.7), folio 268 recto. Huntington swore the required oaths and took up his place in the council on 11 September 1660 (*City Council Proceedings – 1629-1663* (A.5.7), folio 279 recto).

[8] *The Declaration of the County of Oxon to His Excellency the Lord General Monck* (1660). A copy is contained in SP 18/279, folio 76.

although it remained staunchly republican in spirit and mentions nothing about the return of Charles II to the throne.

The incident with the militia provides a backdrop against which to to understand Lord Falkland's antipathy towards Tidmarsh and the Baptists once the tables were turned and he returned to a position of power in the Restoration. Not wishing to play favourites in turbulent and unpredictable times, the City Council treated Falkland just as they had Huntington in December, awarding him the 'Freedom of the City' and a Bailiff's place on 14 March 1660.[1] Three weeks later Falkland was elected one of Oxford's two MPs, polling 450 out of the 1586 votes cast.[2] Two months after that, on 18 May, Parliament appointed him one of the Commissioners sent to meet and welcome Charles II at the Restoration.[3]

The story of the Baptist alleged insurrectionists is continued in another letter within the *State Papers* of Charles II dated 25 November 1661.[4] Here Roger Griffin, a City Councilman and one of the Keykeepers of the City, wrote a letter of report to the Oxford MP Lord Falkland and enclosed some documents as supporting evidence for his suggestions about the political threat that Baptists presented to the crown. One of these supporting documents was a letter from George Howe which gave details of the mortal wounding of a lieutenant in Barwick in Wiltshire, an incident which took place four days earlier on 21 November. Griffin's letter mentions Tidmarsh by name, noting 'a very great meeting of the Anabaptists' at his house in Oxford the previous Sunday (17 November).[5] It is there, Griffin says, that the Baptists 'held forth in as seditious words as their capacities could well find'. Griffin also describes how he and the Mayor of the city sent for the constables and had them all arrested. When the Baptists were brought before the court officials they refused to take the oath of allegiance, or to offer securities for their conduct; not surprisingly, they were all jailed.

3. Petty Sessions court records

The records of the Oxford Petty Sessions court first mention Richard Tidmarsh in connection with an incident involving a man named William Robins. Robins was indicted for refusing to take the oath of allegiance and for failing to turn

---

[1] *City Council Proceedings – 1629-1663* (A.5.7), folio 270 recto.
[2] *City Council Proceedings – 1629-1663* (A.5.7), folio 271 recto. ⸱
[3] Falkland was back in Oxford in June and the City Council agreed to entertain him during his visit (*City Council Proceedings – 1629-1663* (A.5.7), folio 274 verso).
[4] SP 29/44, page 194 = CSC #334.
[5] SP 29/44, page 195 = CSC #334. The letter states: 'The last night a Lieutenant of mine was bid stand by two men very well mounted & they demanded of him whom hee was for; hee said he was for God & king Charles, one of them replyed hee was for God and Greene Sleeves & imediately drew a pistoll out of his pocket & shot my Lieut[enant] & I fear his wound is mortall.' Greaves (1986): 82, discusses this letter, but does not mention Tidmarsh by name.

over some arms that he was accused of possessing. The court record for 4 October 1660 states that Richard Tidmarsh and Lawrence King both offered financial securities of £20 each on behalf of the said Robins, who, it was claimed, was ill and unable to attend the court.[1] As arranged, the case of William Robins was brought up again in the next court sessions, and there is a record of it being dealt with on 10 January 1661. However, Robins did not appear in court to answer the charges against him.[2] We can only presume that the hefty financial sureties that Lawrence King and Richard Tidmarsh laid down for William Robins were forfeited as a result of his failure to appear.

There are several other Petty Sessions court records which detail Tidmarsh's own clash with the political and ecclesiastical authorities, occasionally resulting in his incarceration within the infamous Bocardo prison in Oxford. We have already noted above that the Petty Sessions court records for 9 January 1662 relate that Tidmarsh, together with Lawrence King and Roger Hatchman, were detained in the Bocardo (see pages 17-18 above). Given what we have already noted about Tidmarsh's refusal to swear oaths, it is not surprising to find that he was indicted to appear before the Petty Sessions court on 15 January 1663 in connection with such a refusal. The Petty Sessions court record notes that on this occasion Tidmarsh 'was fyned 30s to the use of the poor'.[3]

Similarly, on 9 June 1664 Tidmarsh was indicted along with three others, John Day, William Nicholls, and William Heycock for not attending his local parish church.[4] Tidmarsh also appears in the Petty Sessions court records dated 18 April 1667. This record is frustratingly vague, simply noting that Tidmarsh (along with five others) was 'presented for several offences', but was discharged after submitting to the court and paying a fine.[5] In addition, Tidmarsh is one of a group of five people mentioned in the records for 13 January 1670, charged with being at an unlawfull conventicle;[6] this group almost certainly constitutes a meeting of the Baptist conventiclers at the house of Lawrence King in the High Street (see page 120 below for more on this).

4. Ecclesiastical court records

Tidmarsh's name appears regularly in the ecclesiastical court records from 1666-1686. Some of these records from the 1660s include his wife Jeane within the indictment, although her first name is never given within the various entries - she is simply described as 'the wife of Richard Tidmarsh', or as '[blank] Tidmarsh'. The last entry mentioning her is dated 15 February 1668, five years before her death in September of 1673. A brief discussion of some of the more important records is in order, for they help build up a picture of

---

[1] *Oxford Petty Sessions Roll – 1656-1678* (O.5.11), folio 36 verso = CSC #316.
[2] *Oxford Petty Sessions Roll – 1656-1678* (O.5.11), folio 37 verso.
[3] *Oxford Petty Sessions Roll – 1656-1678* (O.5.11), folio 49 recto = CSC #365.
[4] *Oxford Petty Sessions Roll – 1656-1678* (O.5.11), folio 68 recto = CSC #393.
[5] *Oxford Petty Sessions Roll – 1656-1678* (O.5.11), folio 93 verso = CSC #442.
[6] *Oxford Petty Sessions Roll – 1656-1678* (O.5.11), folio 114 recto = CSC #480.

Tidmarsh's continuing struggle as a Dissenter facing opposition from the established church.

In 1666 Tidmarsh is cited in Diocesan records three times (on 7, 14 and 21 July).[1]   The third of these entries is the fullest and most interesting, summarizing the case being made against him for not attending his local parish church. Tidmarsh freely admitted that he did not attend services on Sundays, and that he had not received communion at Easter (15 April). He petitioned the court that he might be given some time 'to Informe himself better of some things w[hi]ch hee at p[re]sent scruples at'.   The court allowed this and admonished Tidmarsh 'to Conferre w[i]th Some learned Divine of the Church of England and better to Informe himself' before the following feastday of St Michael (29 September). He was also required to prove that he had done so at the next court sessions.[2]

In 1667 Tidmarsh is cited on his own three times (on 10 January; 30 March; and 27 July);[3] with his wife Jeane eight times (18 May; 8, 15 and 22 June; 6, 13, 20, and 27 July);[4] and Jeane is cited on her own five times (9, 16 and 23 November; 7 and 14 December).[5] Within the first of these entries, the record dated 10 January 1667, it is clear that pressure was being placed upon Tidmarsh to explain his continued absence from local parish services. According to the entry Tidmarsh admitted that he still did not attend his local parish church, but explained that 'hee doth not refrayne through obstinacy or contempt, but merely through tendernes of conscience being not satisfied in some p[ar]ticulars concerning the same'. He further explained that, in accordance with the court's earlier requirements, he had indeed conferred with the minister of the local parish, a Mr Martin. However, Tidmarsh went on to explain, these discussions with Martin did not persuade him to alter his stance on matters of his religious belief. He therefore petitioned the court for yet more time to continue the conversations with Martin, or some other suitable representative of the established church. The court again agreed, granting him more time to inform himself about the need to conform to the ecclesiastical laws.   In addition, Tidmarsh was once again told that he was to go to his local Anglican church in St Thomas parish before the next Easter (7 April), and to appear at

---

[1] *ODR: 23 June 1666-22 January 1670* (c. 9), folios 13 recto, 21 verso, 39 verso. The entry for 7 July states that Tidmarsh was personally cited before the Oxford townhall on 4 July by John Brees, the apparitor of the Diocesan court. By all accounts Brees was a man who prosecuted Dissenters vigorously. Brees was given the 'Freedom of the City' on 18 March 1653 (*City Council Proceedings – 1629-1663* (A.5.7), folio 213 verso.

[2] *ODR: 23 June 1666-22 January 1670* (c. 9), folio 39 verso = CSC #429.   The record also notes that Tidmarsh had a fine of 3s 6d levied against him.

[3] *ODR: 7 October 1665-7 March 1668* (c. 5), folios 166 verso-167 recto, 226 recto; *OAR: 11 May 1667-21 July 1669* (c. 17), folio 56 recto.

[4] *OAR: 11 May 1667-21 July 1669* (c. 17), folios 9 verso, 14 verso, 21 verso, 27 verso; 36 recto, 42 verso, 47 verso, 54 recto.

[5] *OAR: 11 May 1667-21 July 1669* (c. 17), folios 58 verso, 62 verso, 65 verso, 68 verso, 71 verso.

the next court sessions.[1] The entry concludes with the comment, 'See it is certified'. The note about certification at the end of the entry gets picked up in a further record of the Diocesan court which is dated 30 March 1667. This particular record is the concluding entry of the Diocesan court sessions in the run-up to Easter, and it is perhaps most interesting because it brings together Lawrence King, John Toms senior, and Richard Tidmarsh, all Baptist conventiclers. All three men were required to certify that they had attended their local parish churches at the next court day after Easter.[2]

There is a companion record within the Archdeaconry court sessions to the entry from the Diocesan court dated 10 January cited above. The Archdeaconry record, which is dated 2 September 1667, mistakenly gives Tidmarsh's first name as *Thomas* - a simple confusion with the name of the parish in which he lived (the contents of the record clearly demonstrate that it refers to Richard Tidmarsh). The record demonstrates that Tidmarsh's failure to heed the warnings issued against him means his case is being referred to another level of ecclesiastical discipline. The court here reiterated the stipulations laid down within the Diocesan court and agreed to suspend proceedings for Tidmarsh's excommunication in the meantime.[3]

A similar pattern of Dissenting activity appears in 1668, although there are no records of Richard and Jeane Tidmarsh being cited together as a couple. However, Tidmarsh is cited on his own sixteen times (29 February; 7 and 14 March; 4, 11 and 18 July; 10, 17, 24 and 31 October; 7, 14, 21 and 28 November; 5 and 12 December),[4] and Jeane Tidmarsh is cited on her own three times (1, 8, and 15 February).[5] Of these nineteen records, the entry dated 12 December is the most interesting, for here Tidmarsh's failure to appear before the court after three public callings by the court cryer[6] results in him being

---

[1] *ODR: 7 October 1665-7 March 1668* (c. 5), folios 166 verso-167 recto = CSC #435.

[2] *ODR: 7 October 1665-7 March 1668* (c. 5), folio 226 recto = CSC #441. The entry lists fourteen Dissenters from Oxfordshire, but only the four Baptist conventiclers are said to be from the city of Oxford itself. Of the remaining ten, seven are said to be from Sommertown and three from Burchester (Bicester).

[3] *OAR: 11 May 1667-21 July 1669* (c. 17), folio 56 recto = CSC #445. Tidmarsh appeared before Nicholas Horsman, the Registrar of the Diocese of Oxford. Horsman was a student of Corpus Christi College, having received his BA on 21 January 1656, his MA on 17 March 1659, and been awarded a Bachelor of Divinity degree on 31 October 1667. Anthony Wood records in *Athenae Oxonienses* that he had a mental breakdown in 1669 (see Bliss (1820): 4: 616-617).

[4] *ODR: 7 October 1665-7 March 1668* (c. 5), folios 280 verso; *OAR: 11 May 1667-21 July 1669* (c. 17), folios ii and vii verso; 158 recto, 160 verso, 171 verso, 181 recto, 187 recto, 194 recto, 201 recto, 207 verso, 214 recto, 221 verso, 227 verso, 234 recto, and 240 recto.

[5] *OAR: 11 May 1667-21 July 1669* (c. 17), folios 74 verso, 77 recto, 79 verso.

[6] The formal procedures involved in court sessions, including the three public callings made by the court cryer (a standard feature in many court records), are discussed in *The Office of the Clerk of Assize* (1682).

pronounced contumacious by the court. Matters had come to a head and procedures were put into motion to excommunicate him from the Church of England.[1] A formal declaration of his excommunication was issued by the ecclesiastical authorities on 7 January 1669,[2] and the notice of his formal excommunication was publicly read out, as required by law, in the parish church of St Thomas on 5 June 1670.[3]

What was Tidmarsh's reaction to this formal excommunication? Unfortunately, there is little direct evidence to give us an answer, although the seventeen-month gap between the issuing of the excommunication decree and its public reading seems unusually long and invites speculation. Fortunately, the parish records of the church of St Thomas do offer one intriguing bit of information which may be of relevance. We noted above (page 26) that there is an entry within the register concerning two children of Richard and Jeane Tidmarsh, named Jane and Hannah.[4] Interestingly, the entry records the *baptism* of the daughter Jane on 22 October 1669. The reference to the baptism is not unusual in and of itself, although why a Baptist minister known for his Dissenting views would allow his child to be baptized within his local parish church certainly does require some explanation. Clearly there is evidence as early as 1647 that other Baptist Dissenters in Oxford were not having their children baptized in local parish churches, as the case of two of the sons of Edward Wyans senior illustrates. The parish records relating to Edward Wyans junior and his younger brother Thomas, similarly record their *birth*, rather than their baptism, on 28 August 1647 and 1 December 1652 respectively.[5] Thus, Jane Tidmarsh's baptism, coupled with the accompanying entry which registers Richard and Jeanne Tidmarsh's daughter Hannah as 'born' and not 'baptized', is odd to say the least (there are 20 other entries on this page of the register and all of them clearly record baptisms, not births).[6] Why is one Tidmarsh daughter

---

[1] *OAR: 11 May 1667-21 July 1669* (c. 17), folio 240 recto = CSC #460. The clerk appears to have entered Tidmarsh's case as normal in the court records for 12 December 1668, and then later recorded that the official excommunication order was issued to him on 7 January 1669.

[2] This is the very same day that Lawrence King was excommunicated (see below page 95). The two excommunication orders were written by the same hand and are virtually identical in appearance, with wax seals similarly placed in the upper left corner of the document. Clearly the two Baptist conventiclers men were being handled together by the church officials.

[3] *OAR: Excommunications – 1610-1783* (c. 121), folio 327 recto = CSC #462.

[4] *Parish Register of St Thomas – 1655-1755* (Par 217/1/R1/1), folio 2 recto. The year of Jane's baptism is very indistinct and the ink faded. It is possible, though I think unlikely, that it may be *1670*, rather than 1669.

[5] *Parish Register of St Martin's – 1569-1705* (Par 207/1/R1/2), folios 28 recto and 29 recto. For more on Wyans see pages 59-72 below.

[6] The reverse of the folio records entries for 21 children – 18 are straightforwardly listed as 'baptized', two are registered as 'born' (both of which have the word 'baptized' crossed out), and one is described as 'born & baptized'. The two entries recorded as

baptized and the other not? The answer may be found in a careful consideration of the overall chronology of Tidmarsh's own clash with ecclesiastical authorities and his relationship with the parish church of St Thomas. The key here is that the baptism of Jane comes chronologically *after* the excommunication order against him was issued by the Archdeaconry court on 7 January 1669, but *before* that order was read out, and locally implemented, in the parish church on 5 June 1670. The baptism may have been a gesture of reconciliation on the part of Tidmarsh toward his local church, perhaps based on a friendship he established with its previous minister, the Reverend Mr Martin (Martyn). However, once the local implementation of that excommunication process took place, and the excommunication order was read out in public by the new vicar John Harris, the situation changed. It looks as if Tidmarsh refused to compromise further, and did not bring his daughter Hannah forward to be similarly baptized; as a result, it is merely her birth that is recorded within the parish register.

If this is a correct interpretation of the entries in the parish register, it suggests that some Baptists within the city may have adopted a practice of 'occasional conformity' when it came to the question of infant-baptism.[1] It also establishes an historical precedent for the practice of later generations of Baptists in the 18th century who refused to allow the question of baptism to be a divisive factor in their congregational life together. Rather than be divided on the matter, they established a covenant incorporating both standpoints: both those holding to believers' baptism and those holding to the baptism of infants were accepted.[2]

Richard Tidmarsh continued to be active as a Dissenter throughout the 1670s and 1680s and his name appears in several interesting ecclesiastical documents. Thus, he is named in a further excommunication order dated 29 January 1679.[3] This document lists 104 people from various places throughout Oxfordshire and Tidmarsh is described as one of two people from the parish of St Thomas who were so punished. He is cited for 'not comeing to Church to hear divine service' in an ecclesiastical court citation dated 9 June 1680,[4] and he is also included among a group of 17 people from various parishes in Oxford who

---

'births' are dated 15 July 1669 and 10 March 1670. The entry which reads 'born and baptized' is dated 1 September 1670.

[1] Similarly, there is also record of a John Toms senior having his daughter Abigail baptized in the parish church of All Saints' on 9 June 1662 (*Parish Register of All Saints' – 1559-1810* (Par 189/1/R1/1), folio 25 verso). In addition, there is some evidence to suggest that John Bunyan had a son christened in the parish church of St Cuthbert's in Bedford on 16 November 1672 (so Brown (1928): 221-223, argues). In contrast, Whitley (1910-11): 255-263, and Greaves (2002): 275, insist that this refers to Bunyan's son rather than the famous author himself. The evidence is Bunyan's involvement in the controversy over baptism is a complicated matter; see Greaves (2002): 293-300, for a helpful recent discussion.

[2] See Fiddes (2003): 65-105.

[3] *ODR: Excommunications: 1633-1791* (c. 99), folios 226 recto and 227 recto = CSC #586.

[4] *ODR: Miscellaneous Citations* (c. 62), folio 39 recto = CSC #592.

were cited on 6 July 1680 to appear before the court.[1] This lead to yet another excommunication order which is dated 30 August 1680.[2] This document lists 35 people from various places throughout Oxfordshire; Tidmarsh is listed as one of five people from the parish of St Thomas in Oxford who were so chastised by the ecclesiastical court.

5. Licensing under the Declaration of Indulgence (1672) and the Act of Toleration (1689)

Following Tidmarsh's excommunication from the Church of England he drops out of the ecclesiastical court records, for a while at least. The fact that Charles II issued the *Declaration of Indulgence* in 1672 also gave Tidmarsh and the other Baptist conventiclers some breathing space and religious freedom. In fact the next time we encounter Richard Tidmarsh within the ecclesiastical court records is in December of 1673.

Tidmarsh is cited in twenty-four ecclesiastical court records covering 1673-1683: two in 1673 (6 and 13 December);[3] ten in 1674 (17, 24 and 31 January; 7, 14 and 21 February; 7, 14, 21 and 28 March);[4] four in 1678 (7 and 14 December);[5] seven in 1680 (17, 19 and 26 June).[6] and one dated 2 December 1683 which is contained in a style manual apparently designed to help court clerks know how to compose the phrasing of official records.[7] Unfortunately most of these records do not offer much in terms of additional information about Tidmarsh, although they do consistently list him as a resident of St Thomas parish. Generally they either state that he has been cited to appear, or that he appeared and was questioned, or (most often) simply that his case was to be reserved to the next court session. The nature of the charges against him is rarely explained. The only significant information in many of the entries is that Tidmarsh is 'to be excommunicated' (*exc[ommunicandum]*), or that he 'is declared excommunicated' (*dec[ernitu]r exco[mmun]icari*). However, the record from 1683, one of the last documents illustrating Tidmarsh's clash with the Anglican establishment, is slightly more forthcoming about details. It

---

[1] *ODR: Citations 1678-1681* (c. 46), folio 131 = CSC #594.
[2] *ODR: Excommunications – 1633-1791* (c. 99), folio 60 recto and verso = CSC #598.
[3] *OAR: 29 November 1673-20 February 1675* (c. 21), folios 5 verso and 9 recto.
[4] *OAR: 29 November 1673-20 February 1675* (c. 21), folios 13 recto, 17 recto, 22 recto, 27 recto, 32 recto, 37 recto, 45 verso, 49 recto, 52 verso, and 56 recto.
[5] *ODR: 1 June 1678–27 November 1680* (c. 2134), folios 40 verso and 43 recto; *OAR: 1 June 1678-30 July 1681 and 4 July 1674-17 October 1674* (c. 22), folios 64 verso and 69 recto. The Diocesan and Archdeaconry court records overlap for both dates.
[6] *ODR: 1 June 1678–27 November 1680* (c. 2134), folios 98 verso, 102 verso and 107 recto; *OAR: 1 June 1678-30 July 1681 and 4 July 1674-17 October 1674* (c. 22), folios 124 recto, 125 recto, 128 verso, and 130 verso. The Diocesan and Archdeaconry court records overlap for 3 and 17 July 1680.
[7] *Precedents – 1660-1710* (N.4.6), folio 197 verso = CSC #612.

specifically gives the age of the Baptist leader, noting that he 'was of the age of sixty years or more (*fuit etatis sexdecem Annor[um] & amplius*)'. It also records that Tidmarsh was fined £20 for failing to attend his local parish church during the last month, action which was construed to be in contempt of the 'crown and dignity' of the king.

As noted, King Charles II issued the *Declaration of Indulgence* on 15 March 1672, which allowed Dissenters to worship freely, provided that their place of worship was licensed, and the ministers who were to conduct services were also licensed, either as itinerant preachers or linked to specific congregations. Under the provisions of the Act, Tidmarsh licensed his own home in Oxford as a Baptist place of worship, and both he and Lawrence King were licensed as ministers for the Baptists meeting in Oxford in April of 1672. Within the *State Papers* of Charles II there are three documents which relate to this matter. The first is an undated record of the license application which is signed by the processing clerk Owen Davies.[1]   The second is a record of the application in the official list of *Indulgences* and is specifically dated 19 April 1672.[2] Three days later, on 22 April, Owen Davies signs to confirm receipt of the two licenses for King and Tidmarsh; this comes within a batch of five licenses, two for the Oxford Baptists, and three for Congregationalists in London.[3]

The *Declaration of Indulgence* was cancelled on 7 March 1673, less than a year after it was issued, although there is evidence to confirm the continued use of Tidmarsh's house in the parish of St Thomas as a Baptist meeting place for a number of years.[4] There are one or two records which point in precisely this direction. *The Compton Census*, an ecclesiastical survey initiated by and named after Henry Compton, the Bishop of London, reported in 1676 that within the parish of St Thomas in Oxford there were 462 Conformists, 3 Papists and 5 Nonconformists.[5] There is also an order for the excommunication of a number of Dissenters throughout Oxfordshire which is dated 30 August 1680. This includes five Dissenters from the parish of St Thomas, and Richard

---

[1] SP/29 320, page 118 = CSC #505. See Turner (1911): 1.243.

[2] SP/44 38A, page 33 = CSC #506. See Turner (1911): 1.440.

[3] SP/29 320, page 146 = CSC #507. See Turner (1911): 1.258. Bate (1908): xv, has examples of the various licenses themselves. There were five Baptist licenses granted to ministers within the county of Oxfordshire; in addition to the licenses granted to Tidmarsh and King in Oxford, there was a license granted to John Carpenter of Witney, John Harper of Watlington, and Thomas Packford of Finstock. In addition, there were four licenses granted to Baptist places of worship within Oxfordshire: the house of Thomas Crasse in Finstock, the house of Jane Tuckwell in Longworth, the house of James Beckford in Wolvercote, and the house of Widow Collier in Witney (see Turner (1911): 2.830-1). It is probable that there were many other Baptists conventicles within the county which did not apply for a license, viewing the whole application procedure as an unwarranted infringement on their religious liberty (see Lacey (1969): 66, on this point).

[4] Greaves (1990): 226, suggests that the cancellation of the *Declaration of Indulgence* had 'relatively little impact on dissenting meetings'.

[5] *The Compton Census* (1676), page 361 = Whiteman (1986): 426.

Tidmarsh is listed as one of the five.[1] Meanwhile, the list of Dissenters presented to Archdeacon Timothy Halton during his visitation to Oxford in 1683 records that the parish of St Thomas had 6 Dissenters.[2] Confirmation that Richard Tidmarsh was one of these Dissenters comes in the form of Bishop John Fell's notes on Dissenters within the various parishes of the city, notes which were written in circa 1679. Fell's note for the parish of St Thomas list Abraham Badger, *Thomas* Tidmarsh, and William Nicholls as Dissenters.[3] The substitution of the name 'Thomas' for 'Richard' here is probably just an error of record-keeping, perhaps a duplication of the word because the three men are from the parish of St Thomas. The size of the congregation which met at Tidmarsh's house is very difficult to determine, although it was not very large if these records are anything to go by. However, it must be remembered that Dissenters from other parishes in the city would have attended the Baptist conventicle meeting at Tidmarsh's house in St Thomas parish, so it would have consisted of more than just the five or six people identified as Dissenters in St Thomas parish.

There is a private letter dated Tuesday, 18 June 1672 which has an important bearing on our knowledge of Tidmarsh's ministry in Oxford following his licensing under the *Declaration of Indulgence* (1672). The letter, which is part of the collection of the Dr Williams's Library in London,[4] is written by a Mr James Penny from Christ Church to his friend William Norton.[5] Within this letter Penny describes what he feels is the deplorable situation in Oxford in the aftermath of the Charles II's issuing that *Declaration*. He writes:

> Now I think on't, I can tell
> you that there are two meetings in this Town, one of the Presbyters, and
> another of Independents and Anabaptists (the latter being both joyned into one Con-
> gregation), the teacher to the Former is Dr Langley formerly head of Pembroke
> Colledge who began here the first time last Sunday, and held forth two houres,
> (possibly he was to eate roast-meat after, and so needed not to spare his breath to
> cool pottage) upon the Spirit, of which subject they say he preacht in the
> late times neare two yeares, and they say he was all the while so unintelligible
> from that time to this, no body could tell whence sound thereof
> came, or whither 'tis goeing. The Teacher of the other Assembly is a Tanner

---

[1] *ODR: Excommunications – 1633-1791* (c. 99), folio 60 verso. The other four excommunicated from the parish were Thomas Fletcher, William Nicholls, Thomas Browton, and Michael Rose.

[2] *ODR: Memorandum from Diocesan Books – 1679-1814* (b. 68), folio 6 verso. Clapinson (1980): 68, note 322, states that there were 9 inhabitants, including one Papist, excommunicated from the parish during 1662-65; this is based on *ODR: Excommunications – 1633-1791* (c. 99), folio 238-243.

[3] *ODR: Bishop Fell's Notes on Dissenters – 1679-1685* (d. 708), folio 60 recto.

[4] Dr Williams's Library, Richard Baxter's *Letters*, Volume 2, No. 51, folio 3 = CSC #508.

[5] James Penny was from Bruton near Chesterfield in Somerset and matriculated in the University on 14 July 1665 at the age of fifteen. He took his BA in 1669, his MA in 1672 and died in 1694. Bate (1908): 97, mistakenly gives his surname as 'Penry'.

with the name Titmarsh, who is cryed up much above Langley even
by his own party, and doubtfull would spoile the credit of any other pretender
of <u>Gifts</u> in this county did not his Assistant, a Miller of Abingdon, carry
(I would say) The <u>Bell</u>, were not that a profane thing. The Junior Schollers
have been something rude to these <u>Parlour Preachers</u>, as you know they
usually are, but the Vice Chancellor is putting out a Programme against
any disorders that may happen by the Scholars, to whom It could make
you laugh to heare the <u>Mouth that speakes from the Joynt-stool[1]</u>
<u>pronouncing his Anathema's Maranatha's</u>, in the very express termes.

There is an element of irony within Penny's underlined remark about 'the
Mouth that speakes from the Joynt-stool pronouncing his Anathema's
Maranatha's'. Almost certainly this is a reference to Tidmarsh, as the 'Mouth'
of the joint congregation of Independents and Baptists, making a
pronouncement about Peter Mews, the Vice-Chancellor of the University of
Oxford. Generally, Mews was renowned for his strong stance in opposition to
the activity of Dissenters, but the issue of the *Declaration of Indulgence* in
March of 1672 altered the situation considerably. Prior to the issuing of that
document Mews would have been the last person with whom Tidmarsh wanted
any dealings – his 'Anathema', so to speak. There is good evidence of Mews
persecuting Baptists, notably Lawrence King, within the city (see pages 128-9
below for details).   Now, however, the Dissenters look forward to the
'presence' of the said Vice-Chancellor in helping to calm any disturbance
between them and the students of the University.   In this respect, any dealings
with the antagonist formerly regarded as 'Anathema' were tempered with new
expectations of his (the Lord Vice-Chancellor's!) arrival – his 'Maranatha'.[2]

Perhaps the most important piece of information contained within this letter is
the reference to Baptists and Independents worshipping together in one place,
namely the house which Tidmarsh had officially registered in compliance with
the demands of the *Declaration of Indulgence*.   Positive identification of
Tidmarsh's companion, the 'Miller from Abingdon', is uncertain. One possible
candidate is Lawrence King, who, as we noted, had been licensed alongside
Tidmarsh as Baptist ministers for the religious meetings that took place in
Tidmarsh's house.   A more likely possibility is that this is a reference to
Thomas Tisdale (or Tesdale) who was originally from Abingdon and is known
to have served with Tidmarsh at Abingdon Association meetings (more on
Tisdale below). A third possibility, perhaps the most likely, is that it refers to a
Mr Combes who is described in Bishop Walter Blandford's report about

---

[1] A 'joynt-stool' originally was a wooden piece of furniture built by a joiner rather
than a more-skilled wood craftsman. It also became a proverbial term expressing
disparagement or ridicule. Here it may be a reference to Tidmarsh speaking from the
pulpit in the Assembly which effectively is a 'join-ing' of two congregations, the
Anabaptist and the Independent.

[2] Penny is here alluding to 1 Corinthians 16:22, an Aramaic invocation best
translated 'Our Lord, come!'.

conventicles in the Oxford diocese compiled in 1669.[1] There Combes is said to be 'a miller from Abingdon' who serves as the teacher of a group of upwards of 100 Anabaptists meeting in the home of Francis Ambrose in Willcot within the North Leigh parish.[2]

As noted above, William of Orange brought a change in the religious climate of the country when he was crowned William III, for he enacted the *Act of Toleration* in May of 1689 (see Appendix G).[3] Richard Tidmarsh and Lawrence King quickly took advantage of this anticipated relaxation of laws governing religious worship and registered Tidmarsh's house as a 'Congregation or Assembly for religious worship' in April of 1689. Two documents attesting to this registration survive among the Oxford Petty Sessions court records. The first is from the *Petty Sessions Clerk's Notebook* and is dated 15 April 1689;[4] the second is the official record of the Petty Sessions court for the session held on 15 July 1689.[5]

6. The Case of Stephen College - 'the Protestant Joyner' executed for treason (1681)

Tidmarsh continued his ministry among the Baptists in Oxford for many years, but only occasionally do we get any external evidence of its impact within the city. One very interesting example of this comes in 1681 in connection with a man named Stephen College (or Colledge), commonly described in contemporary sources as 'the Protestant Joyner'.[6] College was one of those poor unfortunates who got caught up in the frenzied reaction to the 'Popish plot' against King Charles II.[7] Foolishly, in March of 1681 College, a Whig

---

[1] *Lambeth MS 951/1*, folio 113 verso.

[2] Clapinson (1980): 47.

[3] A facsimile of the printed text of *The Act of Toleration* is contained in Grell, Israel and Tyacke (1991): 411-428.

[4] *Oxford Petty Sessions Clerk's Notebook – 1687-1701* (O.2.1), folio 18 verso = CSC #630.

[5] *Oxford Petty Sessions Roll – 1679-1712* (O.5.12), folio 66 verso = CSC #633.

[6] The case of Stephen College was the subject of a number of contemporary songs, poems, and pamphlets about 'the Protestant Joyner'. These include *A Letter from the Grand-Jury of Oxford to the London Grand-Jury relating to the Case of the Protestant Joyner* (1681); *The Whiggs Lamentation for the Death of their Dear Brother Colledge, The Protestant Joyner* (1681); *A Letter from Mr. Edward Whitaker to the Protestant Joyner upon his being sent to Oxford* (1681); *A Congratulation of the Protestant Joyner to Anthony King of Poland upon his Arrival in the Lower World* (1681); *A Poem (by way of Elegie) upon Mr. Stephen Colledge, Vulgarly known by the Name of the Protestant Joyner* (1681); *A Letter from A Gentlemen in London to his Friend in the Countrey on the Occasion of the late Tryal of Stephen Colledge* (1681); *The Protestant Joyners Ghost to Hone the Protestant Carpenter in Newgate* (1683).

[7] For more on Stephen College, see Kenyon (2000): 276-7.

sympathizer, had appeared brandishing arms before the Oxford Parliament.[1] There he denounced King Charles II's support of his brother James, an act which was interpreted as high treason against the crown. He was later arrested in London and sent to the Tower, but a grand-jury for Middlesex threw the case out of court. The case was ordered retried and was moved to Oxford because it was feared that a 'fair hearing' (i.e. a conviction for treason) would be not be possible in the capital. Not surprisingly, in royalist Oxford Stephen College was convicted on 18 August and sentenced to death; the sentence was carried out on Wednesday 31 August with his execution taking place over against the gate of the castle.[2] Full details of the incident were published in 1681 with the imprimatur of Sir Francis North, the Lord Chief Justice of the Court of Common Appeals, who had presided over the trial in Oxford. This 140-page booklet was entitled *The Arraignment, Tryal and Condemnation of Stephen Colledge for High Treason* (1681).[3]

The connection with Richard Tidmarsh came about while College was in gaol in the Oxford castle awaiting execution. As a condemned prisoner College received a number of visitations from prominent clergymen of the city and University, mostly arranged through the Bishop of Oxford, John Fell. It also appears that he was also visited by an unnamed Quaker on the Monday before his death; probably this was Richard Betteris (frequently spelled *Betterice*), the well-known Quaker surgeon who lived in the parish of St Peter-in-the-Bailey.[4] Interestingly, the Tory pamphleteer Roger L'Estrange reports that College himself asked to be visited by Richard Tidmarsh, but that this request was refused. L'Estrange's comment states:

> He (Colledge) press'd very earnestly that *Titmarsh, the Preaching-Anabaptist-Tanner*, might come and Pray with him; and he was privately sent for, but not suffer'd to come at him.[5]

Tidmarsh is also mentioned by name in some of the official government documents relating to the Stephen College case. Thus, Thomas Hyde, the

---

[1] Fearful of public reaction, Charles II arrived in Oxford on 14 March 1681, surrounded by a protective bodyguard of troops. See Childs (1979): 381-387, for details.

[2] College's final words from the allows were published as *The Speech and Carriage of Stephen Colledge at Oxford before the Castle on Wednesday, August 31, 1681* (1681).

[3] See North (1681b).

[4] Betteris was the neighbour of Roger Hatchman, another Oxford Baptist (see page 126 below). There are many records of his being cited for his Dissenting activities within the ecclesiastical records, including an excommunication order which is dated 26 July 1662 (*ODR: Excommunication Schedules – 1662-1667* (c. 100), folio 2 = CSC #350. Betteris's son appears to have followed in his father's footsteps as a Dissenter; there is record of a Richard Betterice junior being excommunicated from his parish church of St Michael's in Oxford on 26 November 1681 (*OAR: Excommunications – 1610-1783* (c. 121), folio 300 recto = CSC #610.

[5] L'Estrange (1681): 8.

Archdeacon of Gloucester, reports on 27 August to Sir Leoline Jenkins, the Secretary of State, about College's imprisonment:

> He had the Sacraments administered to him last Sunday and has sometimes endured the prayers of our Church to be prayed with him, but somewhat unwillingly, and he has often refused it and professes he does not benefit by them. But he is of very fanatical principles and a great admirer of Quakers and says they are godly men and (if it might be) desires their company, especially that of one Titmarsh, who keeps a conventicle in Oxford, as does Butress [Betteris] also.[1]

The trial and execution of Stephen College created quite a stir among Oxford residents. It is mentioned in three letters written by Reverend Thomas Dixon to his friend Sir Daniel Fleming in July-September of 1681, for example.[2] Passing mention is also made of it in a letter from Henry Fleming to Sir Daniel Fleming dated 28 August; Henry Fleming adds the detail that College 'was condemned to be hanged, drawn and quartered'.[3] Neither Thomas Dixon or Henry Fleming mention Tidmarsh by name within their letters, although Dixon does state that College 'complain'd much of being debarr'd ye liberty of having Gifted men to cant & pray wth him.' The court's refusal to allow 'neither friend or relation' to visit him in prison was even noted by John Hawles, a barrister of Lincoln's Inn, in his *Remarks upon the Tryal of Stephen Colledge* (1689), although again Tidmarsh is not mentioned by name within the pamphlet.[4]

The Stephen College affair is also discussed in several of Anthony Wood's diaries and papers.[5] Although Wood gives numerous details about the various Church of England clergymen who visited College in gaol, no mention is made of Tidmarsh.[6] Despite the fact that published accounts of College's last speech before his execution record his admission that for more than twenty years he was 'under the Presbyterian Ministry',[7] some newspapers reported College's faithfulness to the Church of England and downplayed his interest in Dissenters

---

[1] SP 29/416, Part 2, page 52 = CSC #607. A similar anonymous report about the progress of the trial, perhaps written by Lord Chief Justice North to Jenkins, does not make reference to any visit of College by Tidmarsh (North (1681a)). Similarly, the official published transcript of the proceedings of the trial, issued with the imprimatur of Sir Francis North, does not mention the request by College to have Tidmarsh visit him (North (1681b)).

[2] Magrath (1913): 2.21, 25-6, 29-32.

[3] Magrath (1913): 2.27.

[4] Hawles (1689): 31.

[5] Especially *MS Wood Diaries 25,* folios 38 recto–39 recto. Luttrell (1857): 118, says that College was 'visited daily by Dr. Marshall and Dr. Hall, two able divines of the University'.

[6] This is precisely the line taken in the *DNB* article on College. See Ebsworth (1908): 788-9. Greaves (1982): 1.161-2, also fails to make any mention of Tidmarsh in his discussion of Stephen College.

[7] College (1681): 6.

altogether.[1] A somewhat contradictory account of Tidmarsh's involvement is given by Humphrey Prideaux in a letter written from Oxford to John Ellis, a Secretary to the Earl of Ossory, and dated 22 September 1681, three weeks after College's public execution. Prideaux, an academic from Christ Church, Oxford who later became the Dean of Norwich, sent news of college gossip to Ellis, and in the course of it made passing reference to Tidmarsh's involvement with College:

> It seems it
> was one Titmarsh, an Anabaptist preacher, that made Colledge
> dy without confesseing; for till he came to him, which was the
> Munday before his Execution, he owned all y[t] was sworn against
> him, except Haynes depositions (whom I really beleive a raskal),
> & seemed very penitent for it; but after this fellow had been
> with him some hours he grew sullen, would admit none of
> his former confesson & soe dyed without confesseing any thing
> further.[2]

How can we account for this assertion that Tidmarsh *did* visit Stephen College while he was languishing in gaol in Oxford awaiting execution when all other sources suggest he did not? The simplest solution seems to be to suggest that Humphrey Prideaux has confused the visit of the unnamed Quaker (presumably the surgeon Richard Betteris) on Monday 29 August with College's specific request that Tidmarsh be allowed to visit him, and conflated the two matters. Perhaps the distinction between a Quaker and an Anabaptist would have been too subtle for someone like Humphrey Prideaux to appreciate – both categories of dissent were simply beyond the bounds of his experience and understanding. In short, it looks as if the condemned man Stephen College requested that Tidmarsh, the leader of the Baptists in Oxford be allowed to visit him. The request, as best can be determined, was denied, although news of College's petition eventually leaked out and was remembered by some who were involved in the case.

7. The relationship with Edward Wyans senior, a cordwainer of Oxford

It is safe to assume that in the midst of his busy life as a tradesman and a leading Baptist conventicler, Richard Tidmarsh did attend to the range of normal responsibilities to his family and friends. Such activities inevitably produce a 'paper trail' of documents actually signed by the person concerned, and this is so with Tidmarsh, although in his case it is a rather flimsy trail. To

---

[1] A good example is *The Impartial Protestant Mercury* (No. 37 - 26-30 August 1681), which reported: 'But whereas *Thompson* maliciously says he was *Reconciled to the Church of England* (thereby insinuating as if he had been before a *Papist* or *Presbyterian*) 'tis well known that h never made any other Profession, nor ever was joyned to any Sect, or other Congregation in his life.'
[2] *BL Additional MS 28,929*, folio 60 recto = Thompson (1875): 95 = CSC #608.

date, I have found *five* documents which bear the actual signature of Richard Tidmarsh: four of which are associated with the last will and testaments of two of his fellow Baptist conventiclers, Ralph Austen and Edward Wyans senior, and the fifth is an Association Oath roll from 1696 (more on this below). I shall discuss Ralph Austen more fully in chapter 4 below, but the case of Edward Wyans senior is worth considering in more detail here for his life intertwines with that of Richard Tidmarsh at several points.

The earliest document bearing Tidmarsh's signature is the will of the cordwainer Edward Wyans senior. Tidmarsh was one of the two legally required witnesses to this document, which was produced in March of 1668.[1] The will is of interest not only because it is one of the few documents actually bearing Tidmarsh's signature, but also because of the information that it provides about the family and circumstances of Edward Wyans senior. We learn through it of his wife Alice, and their two children Edward junior, and Alice (see the accompanying chart on 'The Family Tree of Edward Wyans senior' for details of his family). The will helps explain the connection between the Tidmarsh family and the Wyans family, a connection which is most clearly set forth in the will of Edward Wyans junior where it is revealed that his sister Alice was married to James Tidmarsh (more on this below). There is ample evidence that Edward Wyans senior was a prominent tradesman within Oxford, and that he made his living as a cordwainer. No doubt the relationships between the Tidmarsh family and the Wyans family were reinforced by other business connections; cordwainers would have natural links with tanners for their supply of leather.

In some respects the making of a will in March of 1668 was somewhat premature, for Edward Wyans senior was to live several more years. It is likely that at the time of the writing of the will he was ill and thought to be near death. As it turns out, he died in St Martin's parish four years later on 6 February 1672, was buried on 8 February 1672, and an inventory of his goods was compiled a few weeks later on 28 February 1672.[2] The inventory lists property and goods valued at £150 14*s* 6*d*, a modest sum for the time. The two appraisers of the goods who signed the document were Richard Phillips and Richard Tidmarsh; the inventory is thus the second example of Tidmarsh's signature on primary sources.

The life and career of Edward Wyans senior is worth considering in more depth. He was one of the most prominent conventiclers in Oxford, and was well-connected with several of the known Baptists in the city. Wyans and his wife Alice lived in the parish of St Martin, and there are many documents which establish his residency there. For example, he is known to have paid 1*s* 6*d* and 1*s* in two collections of the Lay Subsidy of 23 June 1647,[3] and 1*s* in the

---

[1] *Edward Wyans senior* (OWPR 72/1/9) = CSC #448.

[2] *Parish Register of St Martin's – 1569-1705* (Par 207/1/R1/2), folio 60 verso; *Edward Wyans senior* (OWPR 72/1/9) = CSC #502.

[3] *Lay Subsidy of 23 June 1647* (E 179/164/498a), membrane 1, and *Lay Subsidy of 23 June 1647* (E 179/164/498), membrane 2.

Lay Subsidy of 17 March 1648,[1] and made a contribution of 4*s* in the Free and Voluntary Present granted by Parliament on 8 July 1661.[2] He also paid tax on a house containing two hearths in the Lady Day Hearth Tax of 1665, almost certainly on the property now designated 140 High Street.[3] An earlier collection for the Michaelmas Hearth Tax of 1665 lists him as having two hearths on his property, but he is discharged from having to pay any tax due to his poverty.[4] There is also an entry for Edward Wyans and his wife Alice paying 2*s* in the Poll Tax of 1 March 1667; the same entry includes a payment for their son, Edward junior,[5] and daughter named Alice, two apprentices, and one lodger.[6] As a resident of St Martin's parish, Wyans also made regular payments of the War Taxes during the years 1667-1668.[7] He was even appointed as one of the 'Overseers of the Poor' for the parish in the spring of 1668.[8]

Edward Wyans was born into a family for whom cordwaining was a way of life. There are records suggesting that his father Thomas Wyans made his living as a cordwainer, although he does not appear to have ever been a

[1] *Lay Subsidy of 17 March 1648* (E 179/164/499), membrane 1 = Salter (1923): 164.

[2] *Free and Voluntary Present of 8 July 1661* (E 179/255/5/4), membrane 4. Wyans made his contribution on 4 November 1661.

[3] *Hearth Tax of 24 April 1666* (E 179/164/514), membrane 24 verso. The surname is spelled 'Wiance' within this entry and is recorded under the heading of the 'Southeast Ward' of the city. See CSC #542 for the location of this property in David Loggan's *Oxonia Illustrata* (1675). In leases from 1657, 1670 and 1687 pertaining to the adjoining property at 141-142 High Street, Wyans is named as the occupier of the property to the east (*Oxford City Ledgers – 1636-1675* (D.5.6), folios 249 recto – 249 verso, 448 recto – 449 verso; and *Oxford City Ledgers – 1675-1696* (D.5.7), folios 19 recto – 21 recto). Also see Salter (1960): 1.165 for details of the leases on this property. A dispute with a neighbour over responsibility for the repair of a gutter was resolved in the Mayor's court on 3 November 1673 (*Husting and Mayors Courts – 1672-1677* (M.4.7), folio 21 recto) = CSC #521.

[4] *Hearth Tax of Michaelmas 1665* (E 179/164/513), membrane 30 = Weinstock (1940): 89. Weinstock lists this entry as pertaining to 'Edward Wyam' but this is a misreading of the spelling.

[5] He was born on 28 August 1647 (*Parish Register of St Martin's – 1569-1705* (Par 207/1/R1/2), folio 28 recto).

[6] *Poll Tax of 1667* (P.5.7), folio 8 recto.

[7] He paid 3*s* 2*d* in the tax of 24 June 1667 (*War Taxes – 1667-1668* (P.5.8), folio 9 verso); 3*s* in the tax of 29 September 1667 (*War Taxes – 1667-1668* (P.5.8), folio 34 recto); 3*s* in the tax of 21 December 1667 (*War Taxes – 1667-1668* (P.5.8), folio 53 verso); 3*s* 2*d* in the tax of 26 March 1668 (*War Taxes – 1667-1668* (P.5.8), folio 60 verso); 3*s* 2*d* in the tax of 26 June 1668 (*War Taxes – 1667-1668* (P.5.8), folio 81 recto); 3*s* 4*d* in the tax of 26 September 1668 (*War Taxes – 1667-1668* (P.5.8), folio 94 recto); and 3*s* 2*d* in the tax of 26 December 1668 (*War Taxes – 1667-1668* (P.5.8), folio 106 recto).

[8] *Husting and Mayor's Court 1662; Licenses and Overseers* (N.4.3), folio 57 recto = CSC #451.

member of the official guild within the city of Oxford.[1] Nevertheless, he was granted his 'Freedom of the City' on 1 September 1620, not on the basis of having completed an apprenticeship with an approved master, but on the basis of being the son of his father John Wyans, a wealthy Oxford citizen who had recently died.[2] Indeed, in his own will dated 14 April 1664 Thomas Wyans is described as 'of ye Citty of Oxford, cordwainer'.[3] In terms of a trade, Thomas Wyans's son Edward followed in his father's footsteps. His apprenticeship contract to the cordwainer Robert White is recorded in the city's *Civic Enrolments*, where it was dated to 1 November 1631.[4] His apprenticeship contract is also recorded in a 17th-century manuscript in the Bodleian Library, namely *MS Morrell 23*, an official minutes and order book of the guild of cordwainers in the city of Oxford. This manuscript was one of several relating to the guild deposited in the Bodleian Library in March 1925 by Frederick Joseph Morrell, the Solicitor to the University, who collected and preserved many such documents for posterity. Wyans's apprenticeship under Robert White is entered within this manuscript and dated 22 October 1632, the end of the administrative year, and notes that the master White paid the requisite fee of 1*s* 8*d*.[5] The records reveal that Robert White died before the apprenticeship was complete and Wyans finished it under the cordwainer Richard Phillips in 1640. Thus, there is record within the City Council records of a *Robert* Wyans being granted his 'Freedom of the City' on 10 November 1640; this is a clerical error in writing down the abbreviated Latin first name of the apprentice ('Rob[er]tus' is substituted for 'Ed[wa]r[d]us'.[6] According to another record book of the cordwainers' guild, *MS Morrell 14*, Wyans was admitted as a guild member on 30 November 1640, having paid the usual fee of 3*s* 4*d* for the privilege.[7] At the time Wyans's apprenticeship master, Richard Phillips, held

---

[1] There are records of two apprenticeship contracts involving Thomas Wyans: one with William Thompson dated 7 August 1643 (*Civic Enrolments – 1639-1662* (L.5.3), folio 32 verso = CSC #41), and one with William Ford dated 16 September 1651; the apprenticeship contract is backdated to commence on 25 March 1651 (*Civic Enrolments – 1639-1662* (L.5.3), folio 104 verso = CSC #98). Thomas Wyans lived in the parish of St Mary Magdalen and paid 2*s* and 1*s* in the two collections of the Lay Subsidy of 23 June 1647 (*Lay Subsidy of 23 June 1648* (E 179/164/498a), membrane 2; *Lay Subsidy of 23 June 1648* (E 179/164/498), membrane 4), and 6*d* in the Lay Subsidy of 17 March 1648 (*Lay Subsidy of 17 March 1648* (E 179/164/499), membrane 6.

[2] *Civic Enrolments – 1613-1640* (L.5.2), folio 347 verso) = CSC #4. John Wyans is here described as a taylor.

[3] *Thomas Wyans* (OWPR 71/4/2) = CSC #362.

[4] *Civic Enrolments – 1613-1640* (L.5.2), folio 214 verso) = CSC #6.

[5] *MS Morrell 23 – List of Cordwainers' Apprentices (1590-1660)*, folio 72 verso = CSC #10.

[6] *Civic Enrolments – 1639-1662* (L.5.3), folio 275 verso = CSC #21.

[7] *MS Morrell 14 – Minutes of Meetings of the Guild of Cordwayners (1614-1711)*, folio 39 verso = CSC #22. His payment is also recorded in the accounts submitted by Richard Phillips at the end of his year of office as 'Master' of the guild on 12 November 1641 (*MS Morrell 20 – Annual Meetings & Accounts (1534-1645)*, folio 91 recto).

the top administrative position within the guild, the 'Master of the Guild', and he may have helped facilitate Wyans's entrance into the corporation. However, there appears to have been something of a dispute about Wyans's acceptance by other cordwainers, for an intriguing entry from *MS Morrell 14* dated 4 December 1640 relates how six guild members publicly spurned Phillips by not attending a ceremonial breakfast paid for by Wyans as part of his celebrations for having joined the company of cordwainers.[1] The matter was brought to a tribunal convened by the city Mayor, Humphrey Whistler, who rebuked the six men, pointing out that their actions in this regard were 'to the discreditt and to the Lessinge of the' reputation and esteeme of the same Company'. The six admitted manifest disrespect toward Phillips and declared that they 'doe promise in time to come to be conformable to the orders of the said Company, and to have the Maister thereof in better Estimat[i]on'. It is probable that the six objected to Phillips because of his stance on matters of politics and religion.[2]

Although Wyans had completed his apprenticeship and had been enlisted in the guild of cordwainers, it may have taken some time before he was able to establish himself as a tradesman. Indeed, it looks as if he worked briefly as a labourer in 1641 helping to construct the great quadrangle in Christ Church.[3] If this is correct, then he worked alongside the stonemason Roger Hatchman and struck up a friendship with him, which helps explain why 'Edward Wyans, of the parish of Saint Martin's, Carfax, Cordwainer' is later named in a caveat on the probate records of John Hatchman which is dated 8 November 1661 (see page 163 below for more on this).[4] What is certain is that Edward Wyans senior eventually went on to have a highly successful career as a cordwainer within the city of Oxford. His name appears regularly within the minutes recorded in *MS Morrell 14*, commencing in 1641 where he is listed among those cordwainers of the 'Com[m]onalitie of Oxford'.[5] Wyans is also named

---

[1] *MS Morrell 14 – Minutes of Meetings of the Guild of Cordwayners (1614-1711)*, folio 40 recto = CSC #23.

[2] Not only did Phillips serve as the master for the apprenticeships of two cordwainers who went on to become prominent Baptists within the city (i.e. Edward Wyans senior and John Toms senior), but his republican views can also be inferred by his involvement with acknowledged Parliamentarians such as Ralph Austen, Richard Quelch senior and Thomas Williams, notably in 1648 when a dispute arose over the election of the Mayor and Bailiffs of the city (see page 244 below).

[3] *Disbursements Book 1641-2* (Ch. Ch. MS xii b 85), folios 11 recto and verso.

[4] *Oxford Caveats – 1643-1677* (MS Wills 307), folio 47 recto.

[5] *MS Morrell 14 – Minutes of Meetings of the Guild of Cordwayners (1614-1711)*, folio 41 verso. His name appears in the lists for 24 October 1642 (folio 42 recto); 19 October 1646 (folio 46 recto); 25 October 1647 (folio 48 verso); 24 October 1648 (folio 50 recto); 22 October 1649 (folio 53 recto); 21 October 1650 (folio 54 recto); 20 October 1651 (folio 55 recto); 20 October 1652 (folio 56 recto); 24 October 1653 (folio 57 verso); 23 October 1654 (folio 60 verso); 22 October 1655 (folio 61 verso); 20 October 1656 (folio 62 verso); 29 October 1657 (folio 64 recto); 25 October 1658 (folio 66 recto); 24 October 1659 (folio 67 verso); 22 October 1660 (folio 69 recto); 21

four times within the Bodleian manuscript *MS Morrell 12*, another official record of the early years of the cordwainers' guild, the so-called 'Oncorporacion [*sic*] of Cordwayners'. It gives details of the election of officers,[1] as well as a full account of financial receipts and expenditures, including the itemized account of what was spent in preparing for the annual dinner celebrated by members of the guild.[2] Within the manuscript Wyans's involvement at the highest level of his chosen profession can readily be seen. His name first appears in the itemized accounts dated 7 November 1651 where it is noted, 'Rec'd of Edw[ar]d Wyans for his warden's place – £ 1. 10. 00'.[3] The second reference to him occurs in the records dated 24 October 1653, where the results of the yearly elections for officeholders are detailed.[4] Here Wyans is listed as one of the four 'Keykeepers' of the cordwayners' guild. However, he rose to the top of his profession eleven years later when he was elected to the senior post within the cordwayners' guild. The record for elections held on 24 October 1664 relates that Wyans was 'Elected Master of the Incorpora[t]ion of Cordwayners infranchized in the Cittie of Oxford for the yeare & is sworne.'[5] Entries from the year 1665 record financial payments being made to Wyans as a result of his year in office as Master of the Guild. There is an entry dated 10 November 1665 which records a payment of £1 to Wyans, 'for his first time being Master'.[6] Apparently the payment of this money was not made promptly, for there is a subsequent description of the summary accounts which records 4*s* 'paid to Mr Wyans the old Master as was forgotten in his Accompts'.[7] There are two records of Wyans being involved

---

October 1661 (folio 71 verso); 21 October 1662 (folio 74 recto); 19 October 1663 (folio 75 recto); 24 October 1664 (folio 77 recto); 23 October 1665 (folio 79 recto); 28 October 1666 (folio 81 recto); 20 October 1667 (folio 83 recto); 19 October 1668 (folio 85 recto); 25 October 1669 (folio 87 recto); 24 October 1670 (folio 88 verso); and 23 October 1671 (folio 90 verso).

Not surprisingly his name is absent from lists for the years 1643-45, which suggests that he may have relocated to Abingdon along with Roger Hatchman and others when Charles I issued orders about the disenfranchisement of disaffected citizens (see pages 128-131 below). Wyans's name is also absent from several minutes from 1646-1649 detailing arrangements of how the guild was to operate. However, he does sign an extended revision of the guild's rules which were agreed at a meeting on 26 December 1653 (*MS Morrell 14 – Minutes of Meetings of the Guild of Cordwayners (1614-1711)*, folio 58 verso–59 verso = CSC #161).

[1] The listed officers of the guild were the Master, the Warden, four Keykeepers, and two Searchers; all officers were elected annually in the third week of October.

[2] The dinner was by all accounts an extravagant affair, often costing between £7-£9 per year.

[3] *MS Morrell 12 - Gylde of Cordwayners (1648-1758)*, folio 12 verso. A similar entry dated 8 April 1651 is found in *MS Morrell 14 – Minutes of Meetings of the Guild of Cordwayners (1614-1711)*, folio 53 verso = CSC #90.

[4] *MS Morrell 12 - Gylde of Cordwayners (1648-1758)*, folio 16 recto.

[5] *MS Morrell 12 - Gylde of Cordwayners (1648-1758)*, folio 43 recto.

[6] *MS Morrell 12 - Gylde of Cordwayners (1648-1758)*, folio 45 verso.

[7] *MS Morrell 12 - Gylde of Cordwayners (1648-1758)*, folio 46 recto.

with various charities that were set up by wealthy benefactors of the city. The first of these concerns the legacy fund established by Sir Thomas White; Wyans receives a payment of £25 from the fund which was due to be re-paid in September 1660.[1] Interestingly, the three people offering securities for this loan are named as Matthew Langley junior, Richard Phillips and John Ryland; each appears to have had some sort of personal or business association with Wyans.[2] The second record associating Wyans with a city charity concerns the legacy fund set up by Mrs. Wickham. In this instance, the roles are reversed and Wyans offers securities on a loan of £10 made from the fund to Thomas Hartley, repayment of which was due in March of 1665.[3] Further evidence of his position within the cordwainers' guild can be seen by the fact that he, along with his fellow Baptist John Toms senior, Wyans, assisted in the renewal of the guild's orders on 20 April 1666, helping to ensure that they were appropriately presented to the judges at the Oxford assizes.[4] Wyans also served on a number of occasions as an elected official within Oxford's civic government. He was elected a 'Constable' for the north-west ward of the city on 30 September 1648,[5] and was appointed one of the city's four 'Leathersearchers' on 30 September 1651.[6] He was appointed again as a city 'Leathersearcher' on 30 September 1659, this time serving with his fellow Baptist John Toms.[7] His name appears in the lists of 'suitors' ('*sectatores*') for the Hustings Court of Oxford during the years 1661-1672.[8]

Wyans was clearly well-established as a respectable tradesman within the city of Oxford. He was followed in his chosen profession by his son Edward Wyans junior, who was admitted into the guild of cordwainers on 28 June

---

[1] *Civil War, Charities & General Minutes – 1645-1695* (E.4.6), folio 64 recto. The details of the loan are given again on folio 72 verso.

[2] Matthew Langley junior was a tanner under whom Richard Tidmarsh had served his apprenticeship; Richard Phillips was a fellow cordwainer, a member of the guild in the city, and Wyans's own master (see page 45 above); John Ryland was a whitebaker whose son George served an apprenticeship with Wyans. John Ryland was also a friend of Edward Wyans's father Thomas Wyans, who appointed him to be the overseer of his will (see *Thomas Wyans* (OWPR 71/4/2) = CSC #362).

[3] *Civil War, Charities & General Minutes – 1645-1695* (E.4.6), folio 74 verso.

[4] *MS Morrell 14 – Minutes of Meetings of the Guild of Cordwayners (1614-1711)*, folio 80 verso = CSC #426.

[5] *City Council Proceedings – 1629-1663* (A.5.7), folio 170 verso.

[6] *City Council Proceedings – 1629-1663* (A.5.7), folio 201 verso.

[7] *City Council Proceedings – 1629-1663* (A.5.7), folio 265 recto; *Council Minutes – 1657-1668* (A.4.4), folio 47 verso.

[8] *Civic Enrolments – 1639-1662* (L.5.3), folios 215 recto and 212 verso; *Civic Enrolments – 1662-1699* (L.5.4), pages 742, 731, 725, 720, 715, 709, 703, 696, 688 and 682. The entry for 1661 shows that Wyans paid 3s 4d to assume the place of Sergeant Croke. The entry for 1672 lists both Edward Wyans senior and his wife Alice, who is described as 'widow (*vidua*)'; she takes over his suitor's place within the court until her death (see below). According to Salter (1928): xiii, the *sectatores* of the Hustings Court of Oxford were 'all those freeholders who were not freemen of the city'.

1672, upon the death of his father,[1] and was granted his 'Freedom of the City' on 25 September 1668.[2] Edward Wyans junior appears regularly in the lists of the guild of cordwainers for the years 1672 to 1686 (where his death is noted ('Ed[wa]r[d]us Wyans mort[uus] est').[3] There are also several records of Wyans junior within *MS Morrell 12*. The first of these is dated to 8 November 1672 and records his entry into the guild: 'Rec'd of Edw[ard] Wyans for his entry into the Company 3s 4d & his gift £1'.[4] Another entry is dated 8 November 1677. This records the receipt of 15s from Wyans who had compounded for a warden's place;[5] he was granted the place the next day.[6]

Like his father, Wyans junior also served on a number of occasions as an elected official within Oxford's civic government. He was elected a 'Constable' for the north-west ward of the city on 30 September 1675,[7] and was appointed one of the city's four 'Leathersearchers' on 29 September 1679.[8] As a Constable within the city he is recorded as receiving money on two occasions: once on 7 March 1678[9] when he receives £25, and once on 13 September 1680 when he again receives £25.[10] Also like his father, Wyans junior appears in two records involving city charities. Thus, he offers securities on a loan of £25 given to Samuel Westbrook from Mr Whistler's money; the loan is due to be repaid on 20 August 1680. The roles are reversed later as Westbrook offers

---

[1] *MS Morrell 14 – Minutes of Meetings of the Guild of Cordwayners (1614-1711)*, folio 91 verso = CSC #510.
[2] *Civic Enrolments – 1662-1699* (L.5.4), page 704 = CSC #457; *Husting and Mayors Courts – 1666-1672* (M.4.6), folio 81 verso (Mayors). Edward Wyans junior lived in the parish of St Thomas together with his wife and son and daughter. He paid 4s in the Poll Tax of 1667 as a resident there (*Poll Tax of 1667* (P.5.7), folio 22 recto), and also made regular contributions of between 6s-£1 to the so-called War Taxes of 1667-68 as a resident of the parish (*War Taxes – 1667-1668* (P.5.8), folios 16 recto, 38 recto, 63 recto, 74 verso, 100 verso, and 106 recto).
[3] *MS Morrell 14 – Minutes of Meetings of the Guild of Cordwayners (1614-1711)*, folio 118 recto. Wyans's name also appears as a member of the guild within the lists dated 23 October 1671 (folio 91 recto); 20 October 1673 (folio 93 verso); 19 October 1674 (folio 96 recto); 25 October 1675 (folio 98 recto); 23 October 1676 (folio 100 recto); 22 October 1677 (folio 101 verso); 21 October 1678 (folio 103 recto); 20 October 1679 (folio 104 verso); 25 October 1680 (folio 105 verso); 24 October 1681 (folio 107 recto); 23 October 1682 (folio 108 recto); 22 October 1683 (folio 110 verso); 20 October 1684 (folio 113 recto); and 19 October 1685 (folio 115 recto).
[4] *MS Morrell 12 - Gylde of Cordwayners (1648-1758)*, folio 60 verso. The same page records that 5s was spent 'at the admittance of Edward Wyans'.
[5] *MS Morrell 12 - Gylde of Cordwayners (1648-1758)*, folio 71 verso.
[6] *MS Morrell 14 – Minutes of Meetings of the Guild of Cordwayners (1614-1711)*, folio 102 recto = CSC #571.
[7] *City Council Proceedings – 1663-1701* (B.5.1), folio 142 verso.
[8] *City Council Proceedings – 1663-1701* (B.5.1), folio 178 recto.
[9] *City Council Proceedings – 1663-1701* (B.5.1), folio 165 verso.
[10] *City Council Proceedings – 1663-1701* (B.5.1), folio 185 recto.

securities on a loan of £25 Wyans receives from the same charity; this loan is due to be repaid on 21 December 1685.[1]

There are a number of records of both Edwards Wyans senior and Edward Wyans junior serving as masters for several apprentices, some of whom went on to become citizens of the city of Oxford. The apprenticeship contracts associated with the name Edward Wyans (occasionally it is not clear whether father or son is meant) are as follows:

Name	Date of Contract	Duration	Citizenship Granted
William Bourne	24 December 1646[2]	Seven years	
George Ryland	23 September 1647[3]	Seven years	
William Wilder	11 July 1651[4]	Eight years	
Richard Bignell	17 December 1656[5]	Seven years	18 August 1664[6]
John Bignell	11 October 1658[7]	Seven years	
Edward Rawlins	23 December 1661[8]	Eight years	10 March 1671[9]
Joshua Jellyman	7 May 1666[10]	Seven years	

---

[1] *Civil War, Charities & General Minutes – 1645-1695* (E.4.6), folio 101 recto. A second copy of these details is contained on page 107 verso, although it wrongly gives the second date as 21 December 1680.

[2] *Civic Enrolments – 1639-1662* (L.5.3), folio 60 recto = CSC #49; the apprenticeship contract was originally made with John Teagle and was backdated to begin on the Feast day of St Thomas (21 December). It was amended to a contract with Edward Wyans senior on 30 June 1651.

[3] *Civic Enrolments – 1639-1662* (L.5.3), folio 68 verso = CSC #54; the apprenticeship contract is backdated to 25 March 1647. Also see *MS Morrell 23 – List of Cordwainers' Apprentices (1590-1660)*, folio 85 verso.

[4] *Civic Enrolments – 1639-1662* (L.5.3), folio 103 verso = CSC #93; the apprenticeship contract is backdated to 24 June 1651. Also see *MS Morrell 23 – List of Cordwainers' Apprentices (1590-1660)*, folio 87 verso.

[5] *Civic Enrolments – 1639-1662* (L.5.3), folio 151 verso = CSC #245; the apprenticeship contract is backdated to 20 November 1656. Also see *MS Morrell 23 – List of Cordwainers' Apprentices (1590-1660)*, folio 91 verso. Richard Bignell is named as a lodger living with Edward Wyans senior in the Poll Tax of 1667 (*Poll Tax of 1667* (P.5.7), folio 8 recto). He was admitted to the guild of cordwainers on 18 August 1676 (*MS Morrell 14 – Minutes of Meetings of the Guild of Cordwayners (1614-1711)*, folio 98 verso = CSC #555).

[6] *City Council Proceedings - 1663-1701* (B.5.1), folio 12 recto = CSC #397.

[7] *Civic Enrolments – 1639-1662* (L.5.3), folio 169 verso = CSC #269; the apprenticeship contract is backdated to 29 September 1658. Also see *MS Morrell 23 – List of Cordwainers' Apprentices (1590-1660)*, folio 92 verso.

[8] *Civic Enrolments – 1639-1662* (L.5.3), folio 196 recto = CSC #337; the apprenticeship contract is backdated to 24 June 1661.

[9] *Husting and Mayors Courts – 1666-1672* (M.4.6), folio 161 recto (Mayors).

[10] *Civic Enrolments – 1662-1699* (L.5.4), page 71 = CSC #427; the apprenticeship contract is backdated to 6 March 1666. Joshua (Josiah!) Jellyman is named as an apprentice living with Edward Wyans senior in the Poll Tax of 1667 (*Poll Tax of 1667* (P.5.7), folio 8 recto).

Edward Billingsley	Unknown[1]	Unknown	
John Hardwell	2 July 1672[2]	Seven years	24 August 1679[3]
William Beck	27 May 1678[4]	Seven years	
Daniel Wildgoose	26 April 1669[5]	Seven years	21 September 1677[6]
Timothy Bignell	9 November 1680[7]	Seven years	

Many records of Wyans senior and his wife Alice being hauled before the civil and ecclesiastical courts are extant. The very first record of Wyans appearing before the civil courts is dated 16 April 1659 when he, along with six others, was fined 5*s* in connection with his failure to appear and serve upon a grand jury inquest when required to do so.[8] We can only guess as to the nature of the case upon which Wyans refused to sit in judgment, although it may have involved contentious religious matters.[9] Wyans developed a reputation as a Dissenter and, like his fellow Baptist Richard Tidmarsh, he was named as one of the insurrectionists in the so-called 'Presbyterian Sham-plot' of 1661 (see pages 43-44 above). More significantly, Edward and Alice Wyans are named regularly in the records of the Saturday court sessions during the 1660s and 1670s, a period of intense hostility toward Dissenters. As usual, Alice Wyans is never herself named herself within these documents; she always appears either as 'the wife of Edward Wyans' or simply as '[blank] Wyans'.

In 1662 Wyans and his wife are mentioned five times in the court sessions (28 June; 5, 12, 19, and 26 July) charged with not attending their parish church.[10] The record from 12 July shows that Wyans appeared in person before

---

[1] Edward Billingsley is named as an apprentice living with Edward Wyans senior in the Poll Tax of 1667 (*Poll Tax of 1667* (P.5.7), folio 8 recto).

[2] *Civic Enrolments – 1662-1699* (L.5.4), page 199 = CSC #511; the apprenticeship contract is backdated to 1 May 1672.

[3] *City Council Proceedings – 1663-1701* (B.5.1), folio 176 recto = CSC #587. He was admitted to the guild of cordwainers on 1 May 1685 (*MS Morrell 14 – Minutes of Meetings of the Guild of Cordwayners (1614-1711)*, folio 114 recto = CSC #614).

[4] *Civic Enrolments – 1662-1699* (L.5.4), page 287 = CSC #577; the apprenticeship contract is backdated to 1 May 1678.

[5] *Civic Enrolments – 1662-1699* (L.5.4), folio 137 = CSC #468. Although it was originally made with Edward Wyans senior, after his death the apprenticeship was transferred to Edward Wyans junior on 28 October 1672.

[6] *Civic Enrolments – 1662-1699* (L.5.4), page 643 = CSC #569. He was admitted to the guild of cordwainers on 14 January 1679 (*MS Morrell 14 – Minutes of Meetings of the Guild of Cordwayners (1614-1711)*, folio 103 verso = CSC #584).

[7] *Civic Enrolments – 1662-1699* (L.5.4), folio 321 = CSC #600; the apprenticeship contract is backdated to 29 September 1680. Although it was originally made with Edward Wyans junior as the master, the apprenticeship was transferred to Charles Prince on 11 May 1685, probably because of Wyans's ill health.

[8] *Oxford Petty Sessions Roll – 1656-1678* (O.5.11), folio 24 recto.

[9] At least one of the other six people fined, Robert Pawling, was later embroiled in political in-fighting during the reign of James II.

[10] *ODR: 1 February 1660-4 October 1662* (c. 3), folios 30 recto = CSC #346, 32 recto, 33 verso, 34 verso, and 39 recto.

the court, but refused to answer the charge.[1] The court ordered the presenting church wardens to justify their accusation at a further court session. This was done on 26 July, and when neither Wyans nor his wife appeared before the court, they were pronounced contumacious and excommunicated.[2] Although an excommunication order itself does not appear to have survived, their names appear on a list composed in about 1665 which gives the reason as 'for not goeing to divine service for ye last yeare'.[3] At some point Edward and Alice Wyans may have petitioned the court that the excommunication order of 26 July 1662 be lifted, for Edward was excommunicated again the next year.

In 1663 there were several other court citations for Wyans independently of his wife Alice. He was indicted before the Petty Sessions court on 15 January 1663 along with Lawrence King, John Toms senior, Richard Quelch junior, and James Jennings for attending an illegal conventicle.[4] The conventiclers all threw themselves on the mercy of the court and were fined 10s apiece. In addition, Wyans is mentioned six times in the ecclesiastical court sessions for 1663 (23 and 30 May; 20 and 27 June; 4 and 8 July).[5] These court indictments are particularly interesting in that they concern an allegation made against Wyans that he has not paid his share of taxes due for the repair of the local parish church; the amount concerned was 4s. Matters soon reached a crisis point for Wyans as formal proceedings were instituted to excommunicate him once again from the Church of England on 18 July 1663.[6]

Prosecution did not cease with the excommunication, although the couple are absent from ecclesiastical court records between the summer of 1663 and the summer of 1668. However, there is record of an appearance of Wyans before the Petty Sessions court on 14 April 1664. This is in connection with a charge that he and two fellow Baptists, namely Lawrence King and Richard Quelch junior, had failed to attend their local parish churches for four consecutive Sundays. The trio did not contest the charge and were fined 4s each.[7] Indictments against Edward and Alice Wyans as a couple pick up again a few years later. There are eleven records of them being cited in the ecclesiastical

---

[1] *ODR: 1 February 1660-4 October 1662* (c. 3), folio 33 verso = CSC #347.

[2] *ODR: 1 February 1660-4 October 1662* (c. 3), folio 39 recto = CSC #349.

[3] *ODR: Excommunications – 1633-1791* (c. 99), folio 238 recto = CSC #423.

[4] *Oxford Petty Sessions Roll – 1656-1678* (O.5.11), folio 49 verso = CSC #366.

[5] *ODR: 4 April 1663-12 December 1663* (c. 6), folios 14 verso and 19 recto = CSC #377 and CSC 378#; *ODR: 27 September 1662-15 April 1665* (c. 4), folios 120 verso, 123 recto, 124 verso, and 127 recto = CSC #380 and CSC #381.

[6] *ODR: Excommunication Schedules – 1662-1667* (c. 100), folio 58 = CSC #382; *ODR: Excommunications – 1633-1791* (c. 99), folio 239 verso = CSC #423. The excommunication order covers both Edward Wyans and William Boddely, who also contested the tax imposed upon him by the churchwardens. It appears that the excommunication order was publicly read out in the parish church some months later, probably on 21 February 1664 (unfortunately the reverse of the folio is torn and the name of the month is missing, but this is the first subsequent Sunday that falls on the twenty-first day of the month).

[7] *Oxford Petty Sessions Roll – 1656-1678* (O.5.11), folio 66 verso.

court proceedings for 1668 (18 July; 10, 17, 24 and 31 October, 7; 14, 21 and 28 November; and 5 and 12 December).[1] Similarly, there are nineteen such records for them from 1669 (16 and 23 January; 6, 13 and 27 February; 13, 20 and 27 March; 3 April; 8 and 15 May; 12, 19 and 26 June; and 3, 17, 24 (twice) and 31 July).[2]

As noted above, Edward Wyans senior died on 6 February 1672, but there are further court records in the name of 'Weyance' (or a variant spelling) with no first name given. There are two such records for the year 1673 (6 and 13 December),[3] and eleven such records for the year 1674 (17, 24 and 31 January; 7, 14, 21 and 28 February; 7 14, 21 and 28 March).[4] These almost certainly refer to Alice Wyans (it is unlikely that a man would have been subjected to the indignity of having his identity being reduced to a surname), and it seems clear that the widow carried on her husband's activities as a Dissenter, or at least was regarded as such by the court authorities. Thus, she may well be reckoned among the three Dissenters listed for the parish of St Martin's parish in the list presented to Archdeacon Timothy Halton during his visitation to Oxford in 1683.[5]

Alice Wyans apparently lived on her own following her husband's death, although where is not clear. She was still alive when her son Edward made his will on 21 December 1686.[6] It appears that Alice Wyans died early in 1705; she is almost certainly the 'widow Wyans' who was buried on 9 January 1705.[7]

---

[1] *OAR: 11 May 1667–21 July 1669* (c. 17), folios 172 verso, 181 verso, 187 verso, 194 verso, 201 verso, 208 recto, 214 verso, 222 recto, 228 recto, 234 verso, 240 verso.

[2] *Archdeaconry Records – 11 May 1667–21 July 1669* (c. 17), folios 246 verso, 250 recto, 253 recto, 256 recto, 259 recto, 261 verso, 263 verso, 266 recto, 268 verso, 271 recto, 273 verso, 276 verso, 280 recto, 283 verso, 287 recto, and 291 verso; *OAR: 24 July 1669–July 1672* (c. 19), folios 4 verso, 5 recto and 10 recto.

[3] *OAR: 29 November 1673–20 February 1675* (c. 21), folios 4 verso and 8 verso.

[4] *OAR: 29 November 1673–20 February 1675* (c. 21), folios 12 verso, 15 verso, 20 verso, 25 verso, 30 verso, 36 recto, 40 verso, 44 verso, 48 recto, 51 verso, and 55 recto.

[5] *ODR: Memorandum from Diocesan Books: 1679-1814* (b. 68), folio 6 verso.

[6] *Edward Wyans junior* (OWPR 73/2/3) = CSC #617. At some point Edward Wyans junior moved to the parish of St Mary Magdalen; he is specifically said to be a resident of the parish within both the will and inventory of his goods. Notice of his burial on 22 December 1687 is recorded within the records of St Martin's parish, although the entry specifically notes that he was from the parish of St Mary Magdalen (*Parish Register of St Martin's – 1678-1789* (Par 207/1/R1/4), folio 3 recto). Richard Heathfeild & William Fowler were named overseers of his will. Heathfield was a fellow cordwainer, having served an apprenticeship with Thomas Bartlett which commenced on 10 June 1652 (*Civic Enrolments 1639-1662* (L.5.3), folio 111 recto). He was given his citizenship on 28 March 1659 (*Civic Enrolments 1639-1662* (L.5.3), folio 221 verso)

[7] *Parish Register of St Peter-in-the-Bailey – 1684-1742* (Par 214/1/R1/3), folio 62 recto. Her name is crossed out in the list of the 'suitors' ('*sectatores*)' of the Hustings Court of Oxford for that year and the place taken by Henry Lay (*Civic Enrolments – 1697-1780* (L.5.5), folio 19 recto). Her name appears regularly in a list of the 'suitors' of the Hustings Court of Oxford for the years 1672-1704 (see *Civic Enrolments – 1662-1699* (L.5.4), pages 682, 676, 670, 663, 656, 651, 640, 632, 616, 612, 604, 601, 594,

Apparently Wyans junior never married, for within the will he does not mention a wife or any children. Instead he leaves his mother the money remaining in his accounts once debts and funeral costs are paid.[1] Alice Wyans leaves her mark, a scraggly 'A W' on the official probate documents pertaining to the property of her son which are dated 23 May 1687. However, the courts had to intervene in the matter because, although Wyans junior left a will which was properly witnessed and signed, he neglected to name an executor within it.

The will is also significant because it helps confirm precisely what the marital relationship was between the Tidmarsh family and the Wyans family. Within the will Wyans specifically mentions 'my Syster, Mrs Tidmarsh'; this sister was named Alice and there are records of her marriage to James Tidmarsh dated 31 March 1684.[2] The will also names both James Tidmarsh and his father Richard, leaving Richard 'Twenty shillings to be paide within the yeare after my decease.' Most prominently in the will, Wyans mentions, apparently with great affection, his niece, Jane Tidmarsh, the daughter of James and Alice Tidmarsh. The exact date of her birth is unrecorded, although it was probably some time in 1685 or 1686, certainly before Edward Wyans junior dictated his will in December of 1686. Thus, the little girl was probably less than two years old when her well-intentioned uncle died. Sadly, it appears that the beloved niece Jane Tidmarsh herself died and was buried a year later on 16 December 1687.[3] However, James and Alice Wyans went on to have several other children. Thus, there are two records of James Tidmarsh making quarterly payments of 5s in the Poll Taxes of 10 March and 27 June 1692 to cover himself, his wife and three children while living in the parish of St Thomas.[4] In the Poll Tax of 1693 this was reduced to quarterly payments of 3s, probably indicating the death of two of the children.[5]

The names of two of the sons of James and Alice Tidmarsh can be gleaned from apprenticeship records in London. There is record of a Wyans Tidmarsh being apprenticed to the feltmaker Humphrey Mason on 18 December 1704. He is here described as the son of James, a tanner from the parish of St Botolph-without-Aldgate in London, which suggests that at some stage James Tidmarsh and his family had moved to the capital.[6] Similarly, there is record of

---

589, 583, 575, 568, 516, 518, 520, 527, 533, 537, 542, 547, 557, 563, 565; *The Enrolments of Apprentices – 1697-1800* (F.4.9), folio 150 recto; *Civic Enrolments – 1697-1780* (L.5.5), folios 6 recto, 7 recto, 10 recto, 12 recto, 14 recto, 16 recto and 19 recto).

[1] His estate is valued by the appraisers to be worth £138 5s 7d.

[2] *Parish Register of St Thomas – 1655-1755* (Par 217/1/R1/1), 41 verso.

[3] There is record of the burial of 'A childe of James Tidmarsh, of st. peters' (see *Parish Register of St Thomas – 1655-1755* (Par 217/1/R1/1), 68 recto).

[4] *Taxes – 1691-1694* (P.5.9), folios 5 verso and 40 verso.

[5] *Taxes – 1691-1694* (P.5.9), folios 89 recto and 115 recto. The second entry is given as 'Mr Tidmarshes void Tenem[en]t'.

[6] *Feltmakers' Company Apprentices, Volume 1 – 1694-1731* (GL MS 1573/1), folio 11 verso; *Feltmakers' Company Apprenticeships – 1692-1708* (GL MS 1570/2), page 424. For some reason the apprenticeship was transferred to John Grumball on 7 April

a Richard Tidmarsh being apprenticed to the vintner John Tidmarsh, a cousin, on 6 December 1721.[1] Here the young apprentice's father is described as 'James Tidmarsh, tanner of Oxford, deceased'. James and Alice Tidmarsh also had another son, named James, but what his profession was is unclear. However, his last will and testament has survived and it does provide some additional details about his family (the will was probated on 4 January 1740). From it we learn that James's wife's name was Ann,[2] and that the couple had four sons and three daughters.[3]   It is uncertain what happened to Alice Tidmarsh, the wife of James Tidmarsh, following their move to London.

8. Tidmarsh as a Denominational Figure – Arbitrator in Disputes and Signatory of Baptist Publications

It is perhaps inevitable that Tidmarsh's years of faithful ministry in Oxford meant that he became a respected leader within the larger Baptist world. One of the ways that this can be illustrated is the fact that his name appears on several important publications which were issued by and on behalf of Baptist churches.   Another index into Tidmarsh's respectability within the denomination is the fact that he was called upon to serve as an arbitrator in a controversy between two influential churches.   The controversy concerned arose between two London churches: the congregation of John Belcher in Bell Lane in Spitalfields and the congregation associated with the ministry of Francis Bampfield in Pinners' Hall in Broad Street. The relevant records of the dispute survive in a manuscript which is now located with the Seventh Day Congregation of Plainfield, New Jersey, although a photograph copy of the

---

1707 (*Feltmakers' Company Apprentices – 1692-1708* (GL MS 1570/2), page 484). Wyans Tidmarsh took an apprentice of his own named Spelman Simmons on 1 July 1728 (*Feltmakers' Company Apprentices, Volume 1 – 1694-1731* (GL MS 1573/1), folio 31 verso).

[1] *Vintners' Company Apprenticeships – 1666-1736* (GL MS 15, 220/2), page 667. John Tidmarsh was a cousin.   His father was Samuel Tidmarsh, one of Richard Tidmarsh's sons.   The grandson John Tidmarsh successfully completed his apprenticeship and became a master vintner in the city, taking on twelve apprentices between 1715-1732, including his own son William on 7 June 1732 (*Vintners' Company Apprenticeships – 1666-1736* (GL MS 15, 220/2), page 759).   Unfortunately, he died soon thereafter; his will was proven on 10 April 1735 (*PCC – Will of John Tidmarsh* (PROB 11/670), folios 341 verso-342 recto).

[2] There is a marriage bond dated 27 October 1727 signed by James Tidmarsh. Within it he is described as being from the parish of St Mary in Whitechapel (*Marriage License Record – St Katherine-by-the-Tower – 1720-1802* (GL (9772/6), folio 80). The bond also gives the bride's maiden name as Anne Preston.

[3] *PCC – Will of James Tidmarsh* (PROB 11/700), folios 205 verso-206 recto = CSC #687a. James made generous, if unusual, provision for his family, bequeathing to them four lottery tickets. If any of these proved to be a winning ticket, he stipulated that the proceeds were to be divided into equal parts, including one share 'to be given away to charitable uses.' Seven children are named within the will.

manuscript, which is entitled *Church Book of the Francis Bampfield Congregation 1686-1843*, was presented to Dr Williams's Library in London in 1952. Relations between the two London churches were strained, and had been for many years – perhaps even as far back as Francis Bampfield's own ministry (he died in 1683). The root cause of the tension appears to have been the delicate matter of the acceptance into church membership of a person who was under discipline by the sister church. Thus, the minutes of the Bampfield church, dated 13 February 1688, record an attempt to resolve the disagreement by selecting a panel of mutually-agreed adjudicators drawn from elders of several Baptist churches in London.[1]

The conflict between the two churches was not so easily laid to rest, however. Late in 1689 Tidmarsh, as one of a panel of five Baptist leaders, was called upon to adjudicate another bitter dispute between the two congregations. Apparently this concerned the irregular transfer of membership of a man named John Jones, who had joined Bampfield's congregation while still being under church-discipline at Belcher's church. The minutes for the resolution of the matter reveal the delicate and sensitive way in which Tidmarsh and his fellow elders, including William Kiffen (1616-1701), dealt with the matter.[2] Kiffen, a wealthy London-based merchant, was clearly a man of considerable wealth and influence, as can be readily seen in the contemporary oil portrait of him which is dated to 1667 (see Illustration #3).[3]

The handling of the controversial dispute between the two London congregations certainly did Tidmarsh's reputation no harm, but it was probably his involvement with denominational publications that got his name more widely circulated among Baptists throughout the country. It does not appear that Tidmarsh was one given to writing and publishing his own sermons or ideas, for there are no books or pamphlets that he authored individually. However, his name does appear in several important Baptist publications over the years. As noted above (page 10), Tidmarsh is listed as one of the signatories of the pamphlet entitled *The Complaining Testimony of Some ... of Sions Children* (1656) published in response to the uproar at the funeral of John Pendarves which Tidmarsh attended (see Appendix A). In addition to that influential tract, Tidmarsh was one of eight signatories from Oxford who signed *A Testimony to Truth, Agreeing with an Essay for Settlement* (1659). This broadsheet was probably issued in Oxford in November or December of the year, in the wake of the expulsion of the Rump Parliament by Major-General Lambert and the army (see Appendix B for the full text). In addition to the eight signatories from Oxford, it contains the names of 24 other signatories from five other churches in and around Abingdon (Abingdon, Wantage, Longworth), Farringdon), and Wallingford), and was produced as a deliberate

---

[1] *Church Book of the Francis Bampfield Congregation 1686-1843*, page 11 = CSC #625.

[2] *Church Book of the Francis Bampfield Congregation 1686-1843*, page 16 = CSC #639.

[3] The portrait hangs in the Senior Common Room of Regent's Park College, Oxford.

Illustration #3: Painting of William Kiffen (1616-1701). The painting hangs in the Senior Common Room of Regent's Park College, Oxford.

re-working of an earlier broadsheet, namely *An Essay Toward Settlement upon a Sure Foundation*. This earlier document was published in September of 1659[1] as a reaction to what was seen as the failure of the Protectorates of both Oliver and Richard Cromwell. It was a protest against any form of government which relied upon a single human ruler, whether that be a King or a Protector, and offered an alternative vision of society. It called for the three nations to be ruled by the Lord Jesus Christ himself, and asserted that 'a certaine number of men qualified and limited according to his Word, ought to be sett apart to the Office of chief *Rule and Government* over these *Nations*'. In short, *An Essay Toward Settlement upon a Sure Foundation* was a call for the rule of the saints, narrowly defined and scrupulously vetted. Effectively it wanted to roll back the clock to 1653 and the rule of the Barebones Parliament – an idealistic, but ultimately hopeless dream.[2] In this respect *A Testimony to Truth, Agreeing with an Essay for Settlement* (1659) shows how wedded to the idealistic dreams of the Commonwealth the Baptists of the Abingdon Association were in late 1659, and it makes sense that the two documents were re-issued together, along with two other like-minded declarations, under the provocative title *A Warning-Piece to the General Council of the Army, Being Sundry Concurrent Essaies Towards a Righteous Settlement* (1659).

However, there are two other publications issued by the Particular Baptists under the leadership of William Kiffen which also bear Tidmarsh's name as a signatory from the church in Oxford. The first of these publications is the single-page document entitled *Innocency Vindicated: or, Reproach Wip'd Off* (1689) which was issued as a public response to accusations that Baptists had compromised their integrity by accepting municipal offices under James II (this was discussed above on page 38). The second, and more important, publication Tidmarsh signed is *A Narrative of the Proceedings of the General Assembly* (1689), where his name appears at three points: once as a signatory to the 'General Epistle' at the beginning of the document, once as the pastor of the church in 'Oxford City' within the list of constituent churches, and once as a signatory to the 'Epistle' with which the document concludes (see Appendix D). Both of these documents were issued in light of the meetings of the General Assembly of Particular Baptists in London which Tidmarsh had attended. The General Assembly had been convened by the London Baptists under the leadership of William Kiffen and Hanserd Knollys. They issued a circular letter dated 28 July 1689 to Baptist churches throughout the land, inviting them to send two messengers each to the meetings in London.[3] The

---

[1] The date given in the Thomason copy of the broadsheet is 19 September. Woolrych (1957): 133-161, provides a helpful background discussion.

[2] The broadsheet prompted two published reactions, both of them critical: the anonymous *A Word to the Twenty Essayes towards a Settlement* (1659), and Edward Johnson *An Examination of the Essay, Or, An Answer to the Fifth Monarchy* (1659). Mayers (2004): 65-67, offers a brief discussion of the documents.

[3] According to *A Narrative of the Proceedings of the General Assembly* (1689): 9, this letter of invitation was dated 28 July 1689. The alteration to 22 July 1689 is

Baptist church in Oxford is also listed as a constituent member of the Abingdon Association in the published proceedings of the General Assembly of the Particular Baptists in the two succeeding years, namely *A Narrative of the Proceedings of the General Assembly* (1690) and *A Narrative of the Proceedings of the General Assembly* (1691). However, Tidmarsh's name is absent from the signatories to the 'General Epistle' which introduces each of these publications, and it is not contained in the account of constituent churches, which is understandable given that only the names of the churches, not the names of their delegates, are provided. In short, Tidmarsh's name does not appear in either of the publications dating from 1690 and 1691.

However, the published proceedings of the General Assembly of Baptists held in London on 3-12 September 1689 give details of the decision to send ordained ministers to those parts of the country where there was not a Baptist presence. The so-called *A Narrative of the Proceedings of the General Assembly* issued in 1690 describes the mission and gives some details of its difficulties and successes, noting that 'great Good that hath been effected by it, especially in *Essex* and *Suffolk*', and explaining that some ministers 'at the cost of the Fund were sent out to preach the Gospel'.[1] In this regard details of an extended preaching tour that Tidmarsh made through Essex, Suffolk and Norfolk have been preserved in the records of the Baptist church at Eld Lane in Colchester. In 1797 the Reverend Joshua Thomas, minister of Leominster, made a manuscript copy of the history of the church in Colchester which covered its first 100 years, and specific mention is made of Tidmarsh's role in establishing the church. Unfortunately the original manuscript of this history (upon which Thomas's copy was based) is now lost, although the manuscript copy was available for consultation when the church at Eld Lane in Colchester celebrated its bi-centenary in 1889. This manuscript copy contains a couple of paragraphs, ostensibly written by Tidmarsh himself, in which the preaching tour through the area is described. The manuscript was prefaced 'An account of Brother Tidmarsh's journey into the country, by order of the Elders and Trustees in London in pursuance of the conclusion of the first General Assembly of the Messengers of the Churches, for visiting the churches in the country'. In particular, it gives details of Tidmarsh preaching in (among other places) Colchester, Wivenhoe, and Norfolk.[2]

We also have evidence of a mission that Tidmarsh made to Devon. This comes in part through a record of a financial gift awarded to him on 17 March 1690. This is recorded within an account book covering the financial records

---

probably due to an error by a copyist somewhere along the line. Ivimey (1811): 1.279-280, gives 22 July for the date and may be ultimately responsible for the error. For a copy of one of these letters, see *Baptist Missionary Society – Home Papers: Underhill's Copies of Three Seventeenth-Century Letters* (H/13/5/iii), pages 1-2 = CSC #633a. Also see Ivimey (1811): 1.479-480.

[1] *A Narrative of the Proceedings of the General Assembly, A* (1690)): 4-5 = CSC #634.

[2] Spurrier (1899): 10-11 = CSC #638; Klaiber (1928-29): 119-20; (1931): 40-41.

of the central fund of the General Assembly during 1689-1690. The account book records a gift of £20, given in recognition of 'the service, sufferings and present circumstances of our honored and Well beloved Bro^ther Tidmarsh'.[1] No doubt this visit to Devon helped pave the way for Tidmarsh's move to Tiverton shortly afterward; it was there that he was to spend the last years of his life, serving the Baptist church in the town. The circumstances of his departure from the church in Oxford, which had met at his house and which he had served for so long, are unknown. In fact, very little is known about the fate of the congregation once Tidmarsh departed in 1691; the next major incident in the life of the church was its getting caught up in the Oxford riots of 1715. The one indication of what *might* have happened to the congregation in the immediate aftermath of Tidmarsh's departure is found in a diary entry made by Anthony Wood. This dates to 6 July 1692 and reads:

> Wedn[esday]. Rich[ard] Claridg, somti[m]es of St. Mar[y] Hall,
> afterwards a zealous Independent, opened his meeting-place at the
> house, somtimes Tydmersh, near the Castle. He spoke, or at least
> reflected, on the ceremonies of the church of England, and
> Oldfi[el]d, sometimes a scholar of Camb[ridge], a presbyterian
> preacher among them in St. Ebbs parish, did then oppose him.[2]

A similar possibility is contained in Thomas Crosby's *The History of the English Baptists* (1740). Crosby makes passing reference to a John Toms, who preached to the Baptist congregation which met at Richard Tidmarsh's house near the castle after he (Tidmarsh) had moved to Tiverton.[3] Almost certainly this refers to the cordwainer John Toms junior, who moved to London in 1696 (see page 152 below for details).

One final glimpse of the Baptist meeting house in the parish of St Thomas can be seen from an intriguing tax record from 1693 involving a Mr Warberton.[4] The entry states 'Mr Warberton teacher to the Baptise meeting for his pol[l] & preaching _____ £4 04 00'. Unfortunately, no other information about Warberton or his association with the Baptist cause in

---

[1] *Letter of Joshua Thomas to John Rippon* (D/RPN 4/1), page 2 = CSC #643. The accounts record also records that Tidmarsh was paid £15.0.0 'for his journey to visit the churches', and, reciprocally, that John Tomkins was similarly given £10.0.0 for 'Oxford ministry' on 13 June 1690. The letter from Joshua Thomas to John Rippon is appended to the account of payments; it was transcribed from a book originally belonging to Isaac Marlow. The letter itself is dated 6 February 1695. Hayden (1981-82): 133-4, mentions the entry about Tidmarsh in a footnote, but does not provide full bibliographical reference to it.

[2] *MS Wood Diaries 36*, folio 38 recto. Claridge is also mentioned in *Athenae Oxonienses*: 'He ... turned an independent and in 1692 open'd a meeting house in Oxford for persons of that persuasion' (see Bliss (1820): 4.476).

[3] Crosby (1740): 4.138-9.

[4] *Taxes – 1691-1694* (P.5.9), folio 93 recto. The record itself is undated, but entries from the previous page are dated 12 and 19 May 1693.

Oxford is known; he is not mentioned in any other records pertaining to them. It appears that Warberton was a Dissenting preacher and teacher who offered his services wherever he was needed, [1] and in this regard he helped the Baptists who continued to meet together after Richard Tidmarsh had departed for Tiverton.

D. Final Years of Ministry in Tiverton, Devon (1691-1708)

Few details have survived about Tidmarsh's ministry at Tiverton, although one or two intriguing records do offer brief glimpses into his presence and activities there. The most important of these is the minute book of the Baptist church in Tiverton, the opening paragraph of which declares it to be: 'A Record or Register of the Church of Christ in Tiverton, And of the afairs and proceedings thereof: since by the Mercy and providence of god we have the injoyment of liberty and peace in the year 1687. Our former book Containing matters of this Nature being lost in the late times of trouble'. [2] Within the minute book there is an entry pertaining to the commencement of Richard Tidmarsh's ministry in the church which is dated 12 November 1691. It notes that Tidmarsh was ordained 'to the work of Eldership or pastorship' by Brother Thomas Whinnell, a Baptist minister from the nearby town of Taunton. [3] This official role is confirmed by one of the most interesting supplementary documents among the records of the Baptist church in Tiverton, namely a license which was granted by William III in 1697. The document is dated 18 May 1697 and it lists Richard Tidmarsh as one of the teachers or ministers of a house 'Intended and designed for a publicke place of Divine worshipp therein from henceforth for Protestants dissenting from the Church of England comonly Called Anabaptists'. [4]

The Tiverton church minute book also contains several lists giving all the names of the congregation members; two of these give 'Richard Tidmarsh Pastor' as the first name in the list. The first is dated 19 March 1702 and contains 156 names in total. [5] The second is dated 8 May 1708 and contains 99 names. [6] The minute book also helps us determine the length of Tidmarsh's

---

[1] There is a similar entry on the same page under the heading of All Saints' parish which reads: 'Warberton for being a Preacher for one yeare & his head _____ £4 04 00'.

[2] *TBCR: Church Minute Meeting Book – 1687-1845 – #3958D #1*, folio 1 recto.

[3] *TBCR: Church Minute Meeting Book – 1687-1845 – #3958D #1*, folio 3 verso = CSC #649. The entry is cited in Ivimey (1814): 2.138.

[4] *TBCR: License for the Baptist Meeting House – 18 May 1697 – #3958D #4* = CSC #670. Case (1907): 24, discusses this, but again he does so imperfectly.

[5] *TBCR: Church Minute Meeting Book – 1687-1845 – #3958D #1*, folios 10 verso-11 recto. The list contains the names of 67 men and 89 women, including some who had died, some who had moved away, and some who were under discipline and not in full communion with the church.

[6] *TBCR: Church Minute Meeting Book – 1687-1845 – #3958D #1*, folio 17 recto. The list contains the names of 47 men and 52 women, including four men who were 'rejected' and two women who had 'died'.

ministry in Tiverton, and by implication, when he died. In this regard there is another list of the names of the congregation members which is dated 20 July 1713; Tidmarsh's name is *not* included at the head of the list, suggesting he had died by this time. There are some suggestions that Tidmarsh was not in the best of health during these twilight years of his ministry. Thus, the minute book contains an entry dated 5 November 1701 which relates that the church decided to appoint an additional minister to help and support Richard Tidmarsh, who 'by Reason of old age is grown very weak and infirm'.[1] However, this does not mean that Tidmarsh ceased to be an honored and respected spiritual leader of the church. Indeed, there are other glimpses of him within the surviving records which show that he continued to serve not only as a pastor, but as a messenger of Tiverton to wider denominational meetings. According to Ivimey Tidmarsh attended a meeting of the so-called Western Association of Baptist churches which took place at Exeter on Easter Tuesday of 1700. Tidmarsh is listed as one of eighteen signatories of the letter issued following this meeting.[2]

Interestingly, the Tiverton church minute book gives details of the discipline imposed upon a number of congregation members for a variety of offences, including failure to attend services, public drunkenness, adultery, fornication, tax evasion, and misconduct on the part of the ministers. In five of these cases Tidmarsh was delegated to represent the church, or to communicate its disciplinary decisions to the offender concerned. The first of these involved a man named John Olliver, who was accused of neglecting his responsibilities as a church member and for associating with an evil and drunken crowd. After much deliberation a decision was made on 1 January 1699 to 'Withdraw thier Communion from him as a Disorderly p[er]son'.[3] Tidmarsh declared the church's decision to Olliver on 9 January 1699. The second case dates from April of 1669 and concerns a John Brewer, who was accused of 'frequently spending his time & Mony In Excessive drinking with Evill Company'.[4] Once again the church withdrew fellowship from the offender, and Tidmarsh was one of the messengers appointed 'to declare this Act of ye Ch[urch] to him w[i]th An admonition to Repentance'. The third case involved a man named James Mogeridge, who was accused of fornication with a young woman to whom he claimed to have been engaged. At a church meeting held on 5 May 1700 the church found him guilty of fornication and excommunicated him for this transgression, citing 1 Corinthians 5 as their scriptural warrant.[5] The entry

---

[1] *TBCR: Church Minute Meeting Book – 1687-1845 – #3958D #1*, folio 13 verso = CSC #676.

[2] Ivimey (1811): 1.541.

[3] *TBCR: Church Minute Meeting Book – 1687-1845 – #3958D #1*, folio 7 recto = CSC #671.

[4] *TBCR: Church Minute Meeting Book – 1687-1845 – #3958D #1*, folios 7 verso-8 recto = CSC #672.

[5] *TBCR: Church Minute Meeting Book – 1687-1845 – #3958D #1*, folios 9 recto-9 verso = CSC #673.

records that, in order to achieve Mogeridge's 'more Efectual Conviction', Tidmarsh and two other leaders 'were desired to Represent unto him his sin, w[i]th y^e Agravations thereof, & The Ch[urch']s proceeding against him'. The fourth case involved a Sarah Darby, who was first brought before the church in January of 1702 and made to answer charges of using 'Revileing Languages' against other members of the congregation.[1] The case dragged on for months, and on 12 July Tidmarsh, along with two others, was deputed 'In the Ch[urch']s name to admonish her of her wickedness that she stands charged with and to require her to appear before the Ch[urch]'. However, arguably the most serious damaging case involved a William Bower, one of the ministers of the church.[2] On 21 February 1703 Tidmarsh reported to the church that many members of the congregation were dissatisfied with Bower in several respects, so much so that some of them 'did refuse to hear him preach'. It was decided that call Bower before the church on 4 March so as to address these grievances, and Tidmarsh was deputed to communicate this decision to Bower. At the arranged meeting on 4 March several charges were brought against Bower, including lying about other members, and that 'he had preached up singing at Southmoulton'. At a subsequent meeting held on 21 March the church concluded that Bower was 'manifestly guilty of Railing and Lying', and the church withdrew fellowship from him. Bower was not present at the time and two members were delegated to come before the church the next week, but he did not appear. Therefore, on 28 March 1703 the church appointed Tidmarsh and another member to communicate the church's decision to him. This Tidmarsh did on 31 March 1703. This was a particularly acrimonious case in the life of the fellowship and it continued for some time. Bower was present at a further church meeting held on 4 July 1703, where he admitted some of the charges, but resolutely refused to acknowledge his guilt in others. Relationships had broken down to the point that Bower at this meeting 'declared that he did not Look on himself as a member under thier Care'.

Included among other surviving records of the Baptist church in Tiverton are two letters written by Thomas Whinnell of Taunton, who, as noted above, ordained Richard Tidmarsh to his ministry; both letters specifically mention Tidmarsh by name. The first of these letters, dated 9 February 1695, was written on a half sheet of foolscap paper to a Mr Tristram Trurin who lived in Tiverton and served as one of the Baptist ministers there. It refers to the death of a member of the Baptist church in Dunster in Somerset, a Sister Jane Prowse, and notes that she left as a legacy 'a Mourning Ring to Bro[the]^r Titmarsh'.[3] The letter also suggests that Tidmarsh might attend the funeral of the deceased Sister Prowse, and that he could receive the ring at that time (she was buried on 14 February). The second letter is dated 18 February 1695 and

---

[1] *TBCR: Church Minute Meeting Book – 1687-1845 – #3958D #1, folios 12 verso-13 recto = CSC #677.*

[2] *TBCR: Church Minute Meeting Book – 1687-1845 – #3958D #1, folio 15 recto =* CSC #678.

[3] *TBCR: Thomas Whinnell Letter – 9 February 1695 – #3958D #3 = CSC #662.*

was written to a Brother Stone after the funeral of Sister Prowse had taken place. Unfortunately, Tidmarsh had not been able to attend due to bad weather, so Whinnell suggested an alternative arrangement for the mourning ring to be delivered to him.[1] Tidmarsh also received money from a trust set up by Mrs Prowse the year before she died. On 3 January 1694 she established a deed of settlement specifically designed to assist the work of Baptists in the area.[2] On 9 December 1696 a payment of 12*s* was made to Richard Tidmarsh, 'as a Gosple Minister accordinge to the Donors will'.[3] Six other payments were made to Tidmarsh from the trust: he received £1 3*s* 6*d* on 27 December 1698, 17*s* on 15 July 1699, £1 4*s* 0*d* on 17 December 1700, £1 4*s* 0*d* on 28 February 1701, £1 10*s* 0*d* on 28 April 1703, and £3 0*s* 0*d* on 17 February 1704.[4]

Tidmarsh was also the recipient of a gift under the provisions of a donation made by Mrs Elizabeth Fursdon of Tiverton. She initially set out her intentions in her last will and testament dated 10 May 1687, designating three clothiers from the town as executors of the trust.[5] Further details of how the three executors of the trust carried out their responsibilities are found in a record dated 1 March 1705. It records that the legacy consisted of £20 lent out at interest, with the profits being given to Baptist ministers designated by the trustees 'for the maintenance of a gospell ministry in the Congregat[i]on of protestants known by the name of Anabaptist owning the Doctrines of p[er]sonall Election & final P[er]severance in Tiverton.'[6] From this trust Tidmarsh received 10*s* on 14 December 1701 and £1 14*s* 0*d* on 18 March 1703.[7]

Finally, one other document needs to be noted as another indication of Tidmarsh's time in Tiverton. As noted above, in 1696 Tidmarsh added his name to an Association Oath roll compiled by the citizens of the town.[8] This document was a gesture of support for King William III following the foiled plot to assassinate the monarch and re-establish the rule of the Stuarts on the

---

[1] *TBCR: Thomas Whinnell Letter – 18 February 1695 –* #3958D #2 = CSC #663. Case (1907): 22-23, discusses both letters, although his transcription of them contains a number of errors.

[2] *TBCR: Jane Prowse Trust Deed – 1694-1702 –* #3958D Add #5, folio 2 recto-2 verso = CSC #656.

[3] *TBCR: Jane Prowse Trust Deed – 1694-1702 –* #3958D Add #5, folio 4 recto.

[4] *TBCR: Jane Prowse Trust Deed – 1694-1702 –* #3958D Add #5, folios 4 recto and 5 recto; *TBCR: Jane Prowse Trust Payments – 1701-1717 –* #3958D Add #6, folios 3 recto.

[5] *TBCR: Will of Elizabeth Fursdon – 10 May 1687 –* #3958D Add #9 = CSC #618.

[6] *TBCR: Elizabeth Fursdon Donation for Baptist Ministry – 1687-1802 –* #3958D Add #1, folio 9 verso = CSC #681.

[7] *TBCR: Elizabeth Fursdon Donation for Baptist Ministry – 1687-1802 –* #3958D Add #1, folios 9 recto and 10 recto.

[8] *Association Oath Roll – Tiverton – 1696* (c. 213/86) = CSC #669.

throne.[1] The assassination attempt, originally planned to take place at Turnham Green on 15 February 1696 as William III returned from hunting in Richmond, was to be carried out by Sir George Barclay, one of the generals of the exiled James II. However, the plot was uncovered shortly before it could be carried out and those involved in this 'horrid and detestible Conspiracy' fled for their lives. William III declared that 16 April was appointed a day of public thanksgiving for his deliverance from such treachery. In the months that followed, groups of concerned citizens up and down the country, fearful of such a French-financed Catholic conspiracy, rallied together and signed parchment petitions and scrolls which were sent to the king. In all a total of 434 citizens and inhabitants from Tiverton signed the town's Association Oath roll, pledging themselves in no uncertain terms to William III, even to the point of promising revenge should he come to a violent death at the hands of his enemies.

Although he was infirm in health, Tidmarsh ministered in Tiverton until he was in his eighties. Details as to the date and place of his death are unknown,[2] although it is likely that he died in late 1708 or early 1709.

E. Thomas Tisdale: Mercer and Signatory of *A Testimony to Truth, Agreeing with an Essay for Settlement* (1659)

As noted above, Richard Tidmarsh served with Thomas Tisdale as one of the two Oxford representatives at the meetings of the Abingdon Association which began on 11 March 1656.[3] We may also deduce that Tisdale was present at the meetings which commenced on 16 September 1656. The Abingdon Association records do not contain a list of the names of the delegates for that particular meeting, but Tisdale's name does appear as one of the signatories of a letter sent by the Association to a number of other Baptist churches in different towns, including Warwick, Tewkesbury, and Darby.[4] Tisdale does not appear as one of the signatories for the pamphlet *The Complaining Testimony of Some ... of Sions Children* (1656), although it is also significant that he and Tidmarsh are the first two names of the eight Oxford signatories of *A Testimony to Truth, Agreeing with an Essay for Settlement* (1659). This illustrates something of their political beliefs and allegiances in the wake of the collapse of the Protectorate of Richard Cromwell. So too does the fact that both Tisdale and Tidmarsh, together with their fellow conventicler Ralph Austen, were commissioned as officers within the Oxfordshire militia on 9

---

[1] Garrett (1980) offers a comprehensive study of the plot. Also see Cruickshanks (1995): 7-13.

[2] In the Angus Library there is an 18th-century account entitled *The Records of Baptist Meetings in Devon* (D/DA/1). The Tiverton entry on page 2 of the document contains an appended note referring to the ministry of 'Tidmarsh from Oxford', but no clear dates of its duration are given.

[3] *AARB*, folio 13 verso = White (1974): 145.

[4] *AARB*, folio 25 recto = White (1974): 167 = CSC #240.

August 1659. In this case Tisdale was commissioned an Ensign under the command of Captain Matthew Martin.[1] Tidmarsh's association with Thomas Tisdale was forged over a number of years, possibly beginning as early as 1652 when the two men were granted their 'Freedom of the City' at the same council meeting upon completion of their respective apprenticeships.

There is some evidence to suggest that Tisdale was active as a Baptist as early as 1653. There is record of a Thomas Tisdale representing the Baptist church in Abingdon at the meeting of the Abingdon Association which commenced on 10 June 1653;[2] almost certainly this is the same person, for Tisdale was from Abingdon. Indeed, Tisdale's apprenticeship contract from 1644 describes him as the 'sonne of John Tesdale of Abington in the County of Berk[shire] gent[leman]' (his apprenticeship is discussed more fully below).[3] Thomas's older brother Richard also was sent to Oxford to serve out an apprenticeship as a mercer.[4] The brothers apparently remained close throughout their lives, although Richard died at a relatively early age; he named 'my deare Brother Thomas' as one of the overseers of his last will and testament dated 6 December 1665.[5]

---

[1] *JHC* 7: 752-3.

[2] *AARB*, folio 4 verso = White (1974): 131.

[3] *Civic Enrolments – 1639-1662* (L.5.3), folio 39 verso = CSC #44.

[4] He was apprenticed to Richard Yate on 4 July 1639 (*Civic Enrolments – 1613-1640* (L.5.2), folio 322 recto); upon successful completion of that apprenticeship he was granted his 'Freedom of the City' on 14 December 1646 (*Civic Enrolments – 1639-1662* (L.5.3), folio 259 recto). It appears that he married Elizabeth Stiles on 29 December 1654; the entry in the parish register for this marriage gives the groom's name as Thomas, but this is probably a clerical error confusing the two brothers (*Parish Register of St Michael-at-the-Northgate – 1653-1683* (Par 211/1/R1/2), folio 30 recto = CSC #198). Richard and Elizabeth returned to Abingdon and became active Dissenters within the Baptist church there; they appear in a number of records relating to Dissenters (including *Miscellaneous Quarter Sessions Papers Relating to Nonconformity in Abingdon – 1637-1704* (A/JQz 11), #13, #14, #15, #18, #20, and #59). Preston (1929): 119, 121 and 128, discusses their prosecutions in 1662-1664 under the stipulations of the *Conventicle Acts*).

[5] Richard died and was buried on 14 January 1666 (*Abingdon, St Helen Parish Registers – Baptisms 1538-1679 and Burials 1538-1678* (2001), page 201); his wife Elizabeth was pregnant at the time, but the child died and was buried on 22 May 1666 (*Abingdon, St Helen Parish Registers- Baptisms 1538-1679 and Burials 1538-1678* (2001), page 202). The couple had a number of children, five of whom are mentioned in his will (*Richard Tesdale* (AWPR D/A1/128/58) = CSC #422). Two of their sons, John and Joseph, were granted their 'Freedom of the City' of Oxford on 5 February 1685 (*Civic Enrolments – 1662-1699* (L.5.4), page 579). Another son, Joshua, became an active member of the Baptist church in Abingdon (see *Miscellaneous Quarter Sessions Paper Relating to Nonconformity in Abingdon – 1637-1704* (A/JQz 11), #59). He was one of the eight members of the church who signed the broadsheet entitled *A Testimony to Truth, Agreeing with an Essay for Settlement* (1659). Richard was quite successful as a trader of woolen products; his assets recorded in the probate inventory totaled £1314 4s 7d.

Some details of Tisdale's family and living circumstances in Oxford can be gleaned from the available sources (see the accompanying chart on 'The Family Tree of Thomas Tisdale' for details of the larger family connections). He married Joan (or Joanna) Stibbes of Cumnor in Berkshire on 11 March 1658, the wedding being performed by the Mayor of Abingdon.[1] The couple lived in the parish of St Martin's in what is now 65 Cornmarket,[2] and remained there for the whole of their married life together. It is known that Tisdale made a contribution of 10s in the Free and Voluntary Present granted by Parliament on 8 July 1661.[3] In June 1663 Tisdale was involved in a minor property dispute and city viewers were appointed to render an opinion about the boundaries.[4] While at this address Tisdale paid for two hearths in the Hearth Tax of Michaelmas 1662.[5] Tisdale also paid the Poll Tax of 1667 as a resident of St Martin's, and served as one of the two sub-collectors of the tax within the parish.[6] Tisdale's payment was for £3 9s, which included tax on £300 in money, polls on himself, his wife Joan, their two children Elizabeth and Hannah, two apprentices (Richard Harris and John Tompkins), and the servant Mary Brookes's wages of 40s. It is likely that Thomas and Joan also had at least two other children who were born after the Poll Tax was collected in 1667. There is record of a daughter named Frances, who died and was buried in Abingdon on 18 February 1697.[7] Interestingly, Frances is described in the parish register as a 'spinster', which suggests that she never married. More importantly, the entry goes on to note that she was 'buried in Ock St. Baptist Place', suggesting that she was active within the Baptist church in Abingdon. There is also record of a son Joseph, who married Mary Spencer on 2 March 1690.[8] Joseph and Mary had at least five children, although three of them died before adulthood and were buried in the church of St Helen's in Abingdon.[9] Joseph himself was also buried in the parish church on 23 March 1727; the burial notice within the parish register describes him as a'

---

[1] *Parish Register of St Michael-at-the-Northgate – 1653-1683* (Par 211/1/R1/2), folio 41 verso. The Mayor of Abingdon was John Boulter.

[2] See CSC #543 for the location of this property in David Loggan's *Oxonia Illustrata* (1675).

[3] *Free and Voluntary Present of 8 July 1661* (E 179/255/5/4), membrane 3.

[4] *Husting and Mayors Court 1660-1664* (M.4.4), folio 94 verso (Mayors) = CSC #379.

[5] *Hearth Tax of August-November 1662* (E 179/255/4), Part 2, folio 69.

[6] *Poll Tax of 1667* (P.5.7), folios 6 verso and 9 recto. The other sub-collector was John Wildgoose, the apprentice master of Tisdale's fellow Baptist Thomas King.

[7] *Abingdon, St Helen Parish Registers - Burials 1688-1812* (2003), page 240.

[8] *Parish Register of St Cross, Hollywell – 1654-1812* (Par 199/1/R1/1), page 173. Joseph Tisdale himself signed a bond for this marriage on 27 February 1690 (*OAR: Marriage Bonds – 1689* (c. 476), folio 133) = CSC #642. Within the bond he is described as a mercer from the parish of St Martin's, which suggests that he took over his father's business.

[9] On 14 February 1696, 8 March 1699, and 7 October 1703 respectively (*Abingdon, St Helen Parish Registers - Burials 1688-1812* (2003), pages 238, 243 and 250).

shopkeeper', indicating that he had carried on the family tradition as a mercer.[1]

Thomas Tisdale's wife Joan died and was buried on 22 July 1677.[2] It appears that Tisdale himself re-married following her death, probably during 1678 or 1679. His new wife was named Sarah,[3] and even though Tisdale was most likely in his fifties, it appears that the couple had a daughter who was named Anne. There is record of her baptism in the parish church of St Peter-in-the-Bailey on 22 February 1680.[4] There is also record of a Sarah Tesdale who died and was buried in St Ebbe's parish church on 17 May 1695; it is possible that she was another daughter of Thomas and Sarah Tisdale.[5]

The property in St Martin's parish was owned by Christ Church and Tisdale is named in leases dated 25 October 1658, where he is described as inhabiting a tenement leased to Richard Shurley,[6] and 10 December 1672, where he himself is named as the leaseholder for the forty-year lease.[7] The lease was renewed on 19 October 1687[8] and again on 23 October 1701;[9] in both of these lease renewals Tisdale is described as a 'Gentleman from Abingdon', suggesting that he had moved to the nearby market-town sometime before 1687. At the same time, there are surviving rental records which show Tisdale paying 9*s* in rent on the property in St Martin's parish over a number of years.[10] In addition, there is a lease for the Tisdale property in St Martin's which is dated 1 July 1719; this lease is significant in that it was clearly issued *after* Tisdale's death. Thus, it is in the name of 'James Stonhouse of Radleigh in the County of Berks[hire], Esq[uire], & Hannah his wife, who was the sole

---

[1] *Abingdon, St Helen Parish Registers - Burials 1688-1812* (2003), page 287.

[2] *Parish Register of St Martin's – 1569-1705* (Par 207/1/R1/2), folio 62 recto.

[3] Our knowledge of Sarah Tisdale comes mainly from a probate bond dated 21 February 1721 where a 'Hannah Stonehouse, alias Teasdale' is described as her daughter-in-law (*Sarah Teasdale* (OWPR 175/3/13) = CSC #686). This Hannah was the daughter of Thomas and Joan Tisdale who appears in the Poll Tax of 1667; she is named in several Christ Church property leases (see below).

[4] *Parish Register of St Peter-in-the-Bailey – 1659-1689* (Par 214/1/R1/2), folio 28 recto.

[5] *Parish Register of St Ebbe's – 1678-1812* (MS DD Par Oxford – St Ebbe's b. 35), folio 54 recto.

[6] *VIII. St Martin's – 1ˢᵗ Tenement – #7* (25 October 1658) = CSC #270. The copy belonging to Christ Church (*VIII. St Martin's – 1ˢᵗ Tenement – #6* (25 October 1658)) is signed by the Dean, the Puritan divine John Owen.

[7] *VIII. St Martin's – 1ˢᵗ Tenement – #9* (10 December 1672) with bond of £100 = CSC #515. This is the copy belonging to Christ Church signed by Tisdale. Tisdale's copy of this indenture (#8) is sealed by the Dean of Christ Church; it has an added note on the reverse which reads 'Tenement in St Martin's to Mr Tisdale cancelled 1687'.

[8] *VIII. St Martin's – 1ˢᵗ Tenement – #11* (19 October 1687) with bond of £40 = CSC #620. This is the copy belonging to Christ Church signed by Tisdale.

[9] *VIII. St Martin's – 1ˢᵗ Tenement – #13* (23 October 1701) with bond of £100 = CSC #675. This is the copy belonging to Christ Church signed by Tisdale.

[10] See Salter (1931): 320, 321, 325, 327, 328 and 330, for details of rental receipts for the years 1666, 1676, 1686, 1696, 1706 and 1716.

Executrix of the last Will & Testament of Thomas Tisdale, Gent[leman]'.[1] Tisdale's daughter Hannah Stonehouse also outlived her husband James.[2] She surrendered the lease on the St Martin's property on 25 May 1733 so that a new lease might be granted to William Scandrett, a haberdasher of Oxford, his wife Elizabeth, and Hannah Blower, a spinster.[3]

Thomas Tisdale, like his fellow Baptists Richard Tidmarsh, Edward Wyans senior and Ralph Austen, was named as one of the insurrectionists in the so-called 'Presbyterian Sham-plot' of 1661 (see above). Tisdale and his wife Joan were also amongst those Dissenters in Oxford who on were identified as not attending their local parish and were prosecuted for it. In this regard, there are a number of records pertaining to them being cited to appear in the ecclesiastical courts between 1662-65. These include thirteen records from records from 1662 (28 June, 5, 19 and 26 July, 4, 11 and 25 October, 8, 15, 22 and 29 November, 6 and 13 December),[4] one record from 1663 (10 January),[5] two records from 1664 (18 and 23 June),[6] and five records from 1665 (10, 17, 23 and 24 June, and 1 July).[7] Among the more interesting of these is the record dated 23 June 1664 in which the case against them came to a head and Thomas admitted that 'hee and his wife have not frequented theire p[ar]ish Church of late'.[8] The presiding judge warned them to attend their local parish church and to certify that they had done so before the ensuing Michaelmas court sessions. However, commitment to the local parish church was not forthcoming, for Tisdale and his wife were presented again the next year for the same offence. The record for 10 June 1665 notes that John Brees, the apparitor, issued a summons at the Tisdale home on the previous Wednesday (7 June), but neither Thomas nor Joan appeared in court in person to answer it. Tisdale did appear before the court on 24 June 1665 and admitted 'that hee and his wife have not duely and constantly Gone to their owne p[ar]ish Church to heare divine service and sermons'. His defence was that 'they sometimes goe to to their owne p[ar]ish and at other times to other parish Churches'.[9] Again

---

[1] *VIII. St Martin's – 1st Tenement* – #15 (1 July 1719) with bond of £40 = CSC #684.

[2] He died and was buried on 7 December 1730; Hannah died and was buried on 3 March 1738. Her will was signed and sealed on 3 August 1732 and was probated on 10 June 1740 (*PCC – Will of Hannah Stonhouse – 3 August 1732* (PROB 11/703), folios 190 recto – 191 recto).

[3] *VIII. St Martin's – 1st Tenement* – #16 (25 May 1733) = CSC #687.

[4] *ODR: 1 February 1660-4 October 1662* (c. 3), folios 30 recto, 32 recto, 36 recto, 39 recto, 42 recto; *ODR: 27 September 1662-15 April 1665* (c. 4), folios 12 recto, 20 recto, 28 recto, 36 recto, 42 recto, 47 recto, 51 recto and 57 recto.

[5] *ODR: 27 September 1662-15 April 1665* (c. 4), folio 63 verso.

[6] *ODR: 27 September 1662-15 April 1665* (c. 4), folios 186 verso and 186 recto.

[7] *OAR: 11 May 1667 – 21 July 1669* (c. 17), folios 208 recto and 211 verso; *ODR: 15 October 1664 – 30 September 1665* (d. 12), folio 185 verso = CSC #412, 195 verso and 220 recto.

[8] *ODR: 27 September 1662-15 April 1665* (c. 4), folio 186 recto = CSC #394.

[9] *OAR: 11 May 1667 – 21 July 1669* (c. 17), folio 211 verso = CSC #416.

they were ordered to attend their own parish church and to certify that they had done so at the Michaelmas court sessions. Apparently this court order was met by Tisdale and his wife, for they are dropped in further court records for the next year or so. In addition, unlike other Baptist Dissenters similarly cited, namely Thomas and Emma Mason, Edward and Alice Wyans, Edward and Edith Jennings, Roger and Alice Hatchman, Richard Quelch junior, Thomas Swan, and Thomas King, they are *not* included in the schedule of excommunications from 1662-1665. Instead, it appears that Tisdale conformed enough to keep the churchwardens at bay and concentrated on his life as a merchant and civic official within the city, although he did later fall foul of the ecclesiastical authorities in 1668 and again in 1673-4 in such a way that suggests he continued to subscribe to Dissenting ideas.

On 23 April 1668 Tisdale appeared before the ecclesiastical court on behalf of himself and his wife, again charged with not attending his local parish church and failing to receive the sacrament of the eucharist during Easter.[1] In the court, which was held in St John's College, Tisdale admitted the charge but asked for time to conform. The presiding judge, Francis Lownes, granted the request, warned them to attend their local parish church within a month of the ensuing Feast of Pentecost, and admonished them to receive the sacrament the next time it was administered there. He also required them to certify that they had done so at the next court sessions.

Tisdale's professional career continued apace despite these ecclesiastical disputes. He served an apprenticeship which was originally made with the Oxford mercer George Potter on 23 March 1644, and upon successful completion of it Tisdale was granted his 'Freedom of the City' on 19 January 1652.[2] He became a well established mercer in Oxford, joining the Guild of Mercers, Grovers and Linendrapers in 1654.[3] Tisdale rose steadily through the ranks of the guild: he was elected to a warden's place in 1664, a master's place in 1666, and was elected to be the ruling master for the year 1671-2.[4] As a successful mercer Tisdale agreed four apprenticeship contracts over the space of sixteen years (1662-78). All four of his apprentices went on to become Oxford citizens in their own right. The details of these apprenticeships are as follows:

---

[1] *OAR: 11 May 1667-21 July 1669* (c. 17), folio 84 verso = CSC #453.

[2] *Civic Enrolments – 1639-1662* (L.5.3), folio 242 recto = CSC #104.

[3] *Mercers, Grocers & Linendrapers Guild Book – 1572-1855* (G.5.4), folio 24 recto. It is probably not without significance that Thomas Williams, a fellow Dissenter, was the ruling Master of the Guild, as well as Mayor of Oxford, at the time (see chapter 5).

[4] *Mercers, Grocers & Linendrapers Guild Book – 1572-1855* (G.5.4), folios 32 verso, 34 verso and 40 recto. Elections for the officers of the guild took place in June of the year.

Name of Apprentice	Date of Contract	Duration	Citizenship Granted
Richard Harris	5 June 1662[1]	Seven years	27 November 1669[2]
John Tompkins	9 January 1666[3]	Seven years	2 May 1673[4]
Robert Stiles	22 May 1671[5]	Seven years	8 April 1678[6]
William Burrowes	17 January 1678[7]	Seven years	9 February 1690[8]

There are indications that he had good relations with other mercers in the city. For example, he was a witness to the last will and testament of John Hunt, which was signed and sealed on 5 January 1658.[9]

One of the most interesting features of Tisdale's life as a citizen of Oxford was his involvement with Alderman Nixon's Free School, a charity for educating underprivileged boys and preparing them to become apprentices to established tradesmen in the city. This charity was first set up by John Nixon in 1658, and, following his death in 1662,[10] was carried on by his widow Joane. In 1665 Mrs Nixon purchased some land in the village of Bletchington and established a trust whereby the rental income from the property was used to enable two boys per year who were attending the Free School to be bound as apprentices 'unto some honest Trade within the said Cittie [of Oxford]'.[11] On 19 July 1665 Tisdale was elected one of the nine original trustees of this Mrs Nixon's trust; it was obviously a position of great importance to him, for he

---

[1] *Civic Enrolments – 1639-1662* (L.5.3), folio 200 verso = CSC #341; the apprenticeship contract is backdated to 19 May 1662.

[2] *Civic Enrolments – 1662-1699* (L.5.4), page 694 = CSC #478; *Husting and Mayors Courts – 1666-1672* (M.4.6), folio 121 recto (Mayors).

[3] *Civic Enrolments – 1662-1699* (L.5.4), page 65 = CSC #424.

[4] *Civic Enrolments – 1662-1699* (L.5.4), page 672 = CSC #518.

[5] *Civic Enrolments – 1662-1699* (L.5.4), page 178 = CSC #495. It is likely that Robert Stiles was related by marriage. As noted above (page 60, note 314), there is record of an Elizabeth Stiles marrying a *Thomas* Tisdale on 29 December 1654, but this is probably a clerical error for his brother Richard Tisdale.

[6] *Civic Enrolments – 1662-1699* (L.5.4), page 638 = CSC #575.

[7] *Civic Enrolments – 1662-1699* (L.5.4), page 281 = CSC #572; the apprenticeship contract is backdated to 14 January 1671. It was transferred to John Tompkins, one of Tisdale's earlier apprentices, on 6 September 1680.

[8] *Civic Enrolments – 1662-1699* (L.5.4), page 545 = CSC #641.

[9] *PCC – Will of John Hunt* (PROB 11/288), folios 170 recto and verso = CSC # 255a. The will was probated on 17 February 1659.

[10] John Nixon's will was probated on 30 April 1662 (*PCC – Will of John Nixon* (PROB 11/307), folios 414 recto – 415 verso.

[11] *Alderman Nixon's Free School- 1658* (Q.5.1), pages 22-24 = CSC #420. Other trustees included the glover John Sheene (Lawrence King's apprenticeship master), and Richard Phillips (Edward Wyans' apprenticeship master).

continued as a trustee until at least 1691.[1] In the records relating to this trusteeship Tisdale is specifically identified as a mercer within the city of Oxford; clearly his role as an established tradesman was a qualification for the post.

Tisdale's career as a mercer also paved the way for civic advancement, although he had a chequered career in municipal government. He is first mentioned in City Council records for 30 September 1668 when he was appointed 'Constable' of the north-west ward of the city.[2] However, on 20 September 1669 he was fined 2s 6d for neglecting his duties as such during the annual city elections.[3] Ten days later the City Council agreed to formalize the imposition of fines upon those who refused to bear the responsibility for their elected offices.[4] Tisdale was next elected to a Bailiff's place ('one of the 24ty') on 30 September 1673,[5] but his involvement as a Bailiff in civic affairs remained controversial, largely because of his position on the contentious matter of oath-taking. He refused to take the oath of office on a council meeting held on 12 January 1674, which was interpreted by the house as 'A Refusal to Execute his s[ai]d Office'.[6] There were attempts to force him to do so in a council meeting which took place on 15 June 1674, at which it was decided to approach one of Oxford's Parliamentary representatives, Brome Whorwood, for assistance.[7] At a further meeting held on 25 August 1674 it was agreed that proceedings be initiated to bring Tisdale before Charles II over the matter.[8] Some sort of behind-the-scenes negotiation must have taken place and a compromise agreed upon, for a council minute for a meeting held three days later on 28 August 1674 records that Tisdale took up his Bailiff's place. Interestingly, he did so by paying a reduced fine of £15, the lesser sum being allowed 'in Regard of some eminent service formerly done by him for the Citty'.[9] What this service was, or when it was rendered by Tisdale to the city, are matters not recorded. The council's threat to take the matter before the king seems to have done the trick here, although there is no mention of Tisdale taking any oaths in connection with the assumption of his office,[10] nor is there any suggestion that he obtained a sacramental certificate to meet the legal

---

[1] *Alderman Nixon's Free School- 1658* (Q.5.1), page 25 = CSC #646. Joan Nixon signed her last will and testament on 28 July 1671 (*PCC – Will of Joan Nixon* (PROB 11/337), folios 103 recto – 104 recto. The will was probated on 20 September 1671.

[2] *City Council Proceedings – 1663-1701* (B.5.1), folio 67 verso.

[3] *City Council Proceedings – 1663-1701* (B.5.1), folio 78 verso = CSC #475.

[4] *City Council Proceedings – 1663-1701* (B.5.1), folio 81 recto = CSC #476.

[5] *City Council Proceedings – 1663-1701* (B.5.1), folio 123 recto = CSC #520.

[6] *City Council Proceedings – 1663-1701* (B.5.1), folio 126 recto = CSC #523.

[7] *City Council Proceedings – 1663-1701* (B.5.1), folio 128 verso = CSC #526.

[8] *City Council Proceedings – 1663-1701* (B.5.1), folio 129 verso = CSC #527.

[9] *City Council Proceedings – 1663-1701* (B.5.1), folio 130 verso = CSC #528.

[10] Tisdale is thus a case in point illustrating that the Corporation Act of 1661 and the Test Act of 1673 were not effective bars against Dissenters serving in municipal government (see Wykes (1990): 42-48, for more on this).

requirements.[1] Nonetheless, on 29 September 1674 he is named as one of the city Bailiffs in the list of council members published at the commencement of the municipal year.[2] One small measure of his involvement is the fact that on 25 June 1675 he was one of eighteen citizens who signed a subscription to support the erection of 'A noble Hall for ye publique use of all ye Companies in the Citty', pledging £4 towards the effort.[3]

However, although Tisdale was now officially a member of the City Council, his allegiance to it as an institution was another matter. The next mention of him in the City Council records is dated 8 June 1675 where he failed to attend a council meeting and was fined 2s 6d as a result.[4] Tisdale, and several other council members, continued to be the subject of censure for non-attendance in succeeding years. Thus, on 15 December 1676 the City Council took action against him and six others in an attempt to force them to come to council meetings.[5] A council meeting held on 26 February 1677 established a principle whereby failure to attend such meetings resulted in a fine of 10s for every session missed. Tisdale is one of seven offending members named within this particular record; they were accused of not shouldering their responsibilities and 'unworthily mindeing their owne private Ease and profitt more then the good and Benifitt of the said Citty whereof they are Members'.[6] Despite this rebuke, Tisdale did not attend a council meeting on 16 March 1677, and he was fined accordingly.[7] A further fine of 10s was levied against him for not attending a meeting on 12 April 1677, where it is noted that Tisdale was 'p[re]tending he is not of the howse'.[8] He was also fined and threatened with the distress of his goods for not attending the meeting held on 16 July 1677.[9] His absence from these meetings may be partly due to the fact that his wife Joan was seriously ill at the time. In any event, a reconciliation seems to have been effected between Tisdale and the City Council, for a record from the meeting of 27 August 1677 notes that the council unanimously decided to offer Tisdale a Bailiff's place, with all the outstanding fees remitted and all distressed goods returned.[10] In part this may have to do with the fact that Tisdale represented the City Council's interests in a particular episode of a long-running battle with the University over night patrols, the so-called

---

[1] A copy of such a certificate issued in 1680 is contained in *Sundry Documents – Hester's Collections I – 1549-1750* (F.5.2), folio 144.

[2] *City Council Proceedings – 1663-1701* (B.5.1), folio 134 recto.

[3] *Sundry Documents – Hester's Collections I – 1549-1750* (F.5.2), folio 140 = CSC #535.

[4] *City Council Proceedings – 1663-1701* (B.5.1), folio 139 recto = CSC #534.

[5] *City Council Proceedings – 1663-1701* (B.5.1), folio 152 recto = CSC #558.

[6] *City Council Proceedings – 1663-1701* (B.5.1), folios 152 verso–153 recto = CSC #560.

[7] *City Council Proceedings – 1663-1701* (B.5.1), folio 154 recto = CSC #562.

[8] *City Council Proceedings – 1663-1701* (B.5.1), folio 154 verso = CSC #563.

[9] *City Council Proceedings – 1663-1701* (B.5.1), folio 155 verso = CSC #565.

[10] *City Council Proceedings – 1663-1701* (B.5.1), folio 157 recto = CSC #566.

'noctivagation' controversy.[1] This involved a clash between George Barbour , a pro-proctor from Oriel College, and Philip Dodwell, a chandler and citizen of the city, which took place on 4 August 1677. It seems that Barbour, while on night patrol, met Dodwell at about 11:00 p.m. and confronted him, demanding to know who he was and what business he had being out that late (the University curfew ran from 9:00 p.m. to 4:00 a.m.).[2] The night patrol was particularly vigilant since the Duke of Ormond, the Chancellor of the University, was in Oxford at the time and there were fears that a public disturbance might be raised against him. Dodwell was dismissive of the right of Barbour to challenge him in this way, was verbally abusive, and eluded Barbour by running away into his house. Barbour subsequently fined him 40*s*, but Dodwell refused to pay and was threatened with a court action against him. Tisdale and William Cornish, representing the city, attempted to circumvent the legal suit and effect a compromise with Barbour. In Barbour's words, 'Tisdall was pleased to tell me "It was the sense of the towne, wee had nothing to do with them after nine at night."'[3] The matter eventually came to the Vice-Chancellor's court in January of 1678, with, predictably, the University supporting Barbour and the city supporting Dodwell. The suit was then taken to the Court of Common Pleas in London and a compromise agreed on 30 October 1678.[4] Tisdale, Cornish and Dodwell would have known each other well, all of them being members of the Guild of Mercers, Grocers and

---

[1] This was a point of conflict between the university and the city for many years. It became a particular point of conflict in 1649, when the officials of the city submitted a petition to Parliament outlining a number of their grievances with the University, including the imposition of 40*s* fines for noctivagation (see *The Humble Petition of the Mayor, Aldermen, Bayliffs and Commonalty of the City of Oxon* (1649). The matter also surfaced in 1690, when the university rehearsed its case by publishing *A Defence of the Rights and Privileges of the University of Oxford* (1690). Crossley (1997): 125-126, offers an overview.

[2] A similar clash between university and city officials occurred on 17 May 1647. It seems that a Bailiff attempted to break up a late-night gambling house in All Saints' parish, but was abused by a Christ Church proctor in the performance of his duties and accused of breaking the curfew himself. Interestingly, the cordwainer Martin Seale, whose wife was an active Dissenter (see page 124 below), became involved in the matter (see *Oxford City Records – 1605-1649* (D.5.2), folio 250).

[3] *MS Bodl 594*, folio 158 verso = CSC #567. This account of this incident (folios 157 recto–159 recto) is in the hand of Anthony Wood. The matter is also discussed in a letter from John Nicholls, the Vice-Chancellor, to Sir Joseph Williamson dated 6 February 1678. Nicholls, reflecting the university's perspective on the matter, declares, 'this Citty does endeavour to robb us of our Priviledges', and suggests that if the university's right to have night patrols is removed chaos will result: 'all disorders comitted will be layd to schollars charge & all schollars will free themselves from Proctors under the p[re]tence of being townsmen' (SP 29/401, folio 20).

[4] A copy of the proceedings of the case within the Vice-Chancellor's court is contained in *Suits with the University: Barbour v. Dodwell – 1979* (N.4.15).

Linendrapers. In fact, Tisdale and Dodwell were elected to be the two senior wardens of the guild for the year 1664-5.[1]

Tisdale was again elected to a Bailiff's place on 17 September 1677,[2] and took up the post of *Senior* Bailiff and this time swore the required oaths of office on 29 September 1677.[3] There are a few records relating to Tisdale discharging the responsibilities of his office. For example, there is a note appended to the apprenticeship contract of George White junior dated 11 February 1678 which records that 'Mr Nicholls's money p[ai]d by Tho[mas] Tesdale, sen[ior] Bayliffe'.[4] The next year Tisdale advanced to the position of 'One of the Eight Assistants'. On 13 September 1678 he paid the requisite fee of £5 for this position, swore the three oaths of office, and 'subscribed the declaration in the Act of Parliament for regulating Corporations' for the year ensuing.[5] On 29 September 1678, at the end of his year in office, he surrendered his responsibilities as Senior Bailiff and handed over the city treasury of £30 to a successor.[6] There is little evidence that he was very active as an 'Assistant' to the Mayor, although there are several relevant entries in the Accounts of Chamberlains for the municipal years 1678-9. Thus, from 1678 there is note of a payment of £8 4s 3d being made to Tisdale and John Crony (a Bailiff) 'for the Citty p[ar]te of his Ma[jes]ties Fee Farme due at Lady day last', and an unspecified payment of £1 made to Tisdale during the 'Franchizes'.[7] There are also records from 1679 of £4 12s 7d being paid to Tisdale 'for the expence att ye Franchize dinner', of Tisdale being reimbursed £12 7s 0d 'which he laid out for the Lord High Steward for A Supper at Esq[uire] Lowe's house', and another payment of £8 4s 3d being made to Tisdale and Crony, 'former Bayliffs for halfe A yeere in Arears for the Fee Farme'.[8]

On 11 June 1680 Tisdale was appointed by the council to be one of the viewers for a proposal put forward by a Mr Squire to renew his lease on a property near the east gate to the city.[9] In the end, Tisdale only served as an 'Assistant' for two years, and sent a letter of resignation to the council which was read out publicly in a council meeting held on 3 August 1680.[10] The council elected the brewer Richard Carter to take his place on 9 August 1680, but Carter refused to serve and proceedings were set in place to force him to do

---

[1] *Mercers, Grocers & Linendrapers Guild Book – 1572-1855* (G.5.4), folio 32 verso.

[2] *City Council Proceedings – 1663-1701* (B.5.1), folio 157 verso = CSC #568.

[3] *City Council Proceedings – 1663-1701* (B.5.1), folio 158 recto = CSC #570.

[4] *Civic Enrolments – 1662-1699* (L.5.4), page 283.

[5] *City Council Proceedings – 1663-1701* (B.5.1), folio 167 verso = CSC #582.

[6] *City Council Proceedings – 1663-1701* (B.5.1), folio 168 recto = CSC #583.

[7] *Audit Book – 1592-1682* (P.5.2), folios 368 verso and 371 verso. The entries come in accounts that were audited in December 1678.

[8] *Audit Book – 1592-1682* (P.5.2), folios 372 verso and 373 recto. The entries come in accounts that were audited in December 1679.

[9] *City Council Proceedings – 1663-1701* (B.5.1), folio 183 recto = CSC #593.

[10] *City Council Proceedings – 1663-1701* (B.5.1), folio 184 recto = CSC #596.

so, just as they had been for Tisdale.[1] As noted above (page 38), Carter went on to become a figure of prominence in the city in 1688 during the reign of James II, but Tisdale was *not* identified as one of the Dissenters chosen by the king for civic advancement in *The Charter of Oxford* (1688). This is somewhat unusual, especially since other Baptists in the city were so advanced, namely Richard Tidmarsh, Lawrence King and John Toms senior. However, there is a good explanation for this.

It appears that Tisdale either retired or moved away from Oxford by the end of 1680. One indication of this is the fact that he agreed to sign over his apprentice William Burrowes to John Tompkins, another former apprentice, on 6 September 1680. Tisdale disappears from further City Council records after this date. An even more suggestive indication is the fact that Tisdale's name does appear in the list of members of the Guild of Mercers, Grocers & Linendrapers for the year 1680, but his name is dropped for the year 1681.[2] All indications are that Tisdale moved in retirement to the nearby town of Abingdon, probably to the house owned by his parents which he inherited.[3] Certainly he was still in the Oxford area, and occasional glimpses of him can be found in a few surviving records. For example, he attended a meeting of the trustees of Mrs Nixon's Free School in Bletchington on 16 April 1691 and helped elect five additional trustee members.[4] In addition, it is known that Tisdale signed the Association Oath roll compiled by the citizens of Oxford in 1696 as a gesture of support for William III.[5]

Precisely where and when Tisdale the mercer died are unknown, although he may have been buried in Abingdon in Berkshire, the town of his father and mother. Thus, there is record of a 'Thomas Tesdale, gentleman', being buried in the church of St Helen's in Abingdon on 17 July 1702.[6]

---

[1] *City Council Proceedings – 1663-1701* (B.5.1), folio 184 verso = CSC #597.

[2] *Mercers, Grocers & Linendrapers Guild Book – 1572-1855* (G.5.4), folios 49 recto and 50 recto. The lists were compiled annually in June.

[3] Thomas Tisdale's father John died and was buried on 17 August 1665 (*Abingdon, St Helen Parish Registers- Baptisms 1538-1679 and Burials 1538-1678* (2001), page 201); his mother Elizabeth died in late 1671 and her will was probated on 26 March 1672 (*Elizabeth Tesdale* (AWPR D/A1/128/92) = CSC #494).) = CSC #494). John Tesdale's will specifies that the family house in Abingdon should go to Thomas after his mother's death (*John Tesdale* (AWPR D/A1/128/57) = CSC #114).

[4] *Alderman Nixon's Free School – 1658* (Q.5.1), page 25 = CSC #646.

[5] *Association Oath Roll – Oxford – 1696* (c. 213/208) = CSC #668.

[6] *Abingdon, St Helen Parish Registers - Burials 1688-1812* (2003), page 247. This fits well with the fact that Tisdale is *not* listed among the trustees of Mrs Nixon's Free School attending a meeting held on 8 November 1705.

2. The Glover:

Lawrence King

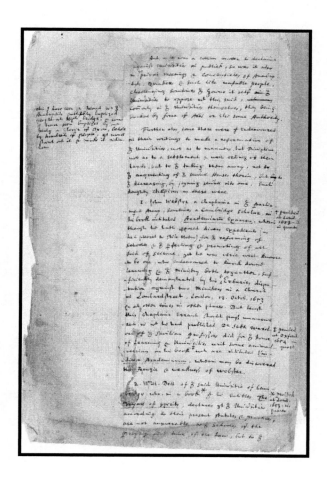

Illustration #4: Page from a manuscript of the Oxford antiquarian Anthony Wood (1632-1695). Wood here relates his witnessing of Lawrence King baptizing people in the river at High Bridge in Oxford in December of 1659. The manuscript is part of the collection in the Bodleian Library, Oxford (*MS Wood F 31,* folio 7 verso).

2. The Glover:

Lawrence King

Within this chapter I shall consider more fully the life and career of Lawrence King, a glover by trade, who became a prominent civic leader within Oxford, as well as being one of the first to commit himself openly to the Baptist cause. As noted above in the introduction (pages 17-18), Lawrence King, Richard Tidmarsh, Roger Hatchman and Ralph Austen appeared before the Oxford Petty Sessions court on 9 January 1662, charged with being 'seditious sectaryes & disloyal persons'. As a result King, Hatchman and Tidmarsh were jailed in the Bocardo prison at the North Gate of the city until such time as they would swear an oath of allegiance to Charles II and satisfy the court as to their behaviour and intentions.

This chapter will discuss Lawrence King's life, beginning with his family background and arrangements for his apprenticeship, proceed to consider his professional life as a citizen and tradesman within Oxford, and then move on to examine his role as a religious leader among the Baptists who met in the city. The chapter will conclude with a brief discussion of another important Baptist Dissenter with whom King had contact, namely John Toms senior an Oxford shoemaker and a royal appointee in James II's *The Charter of Oxford* (1688).

A. Family Background and Apprenticeship

1. Family in Oxford

Lawrence King was born and raised an Oxonian. He was baptized at All Saints' Church on the High Street in 1629. The parish register records the event, providing us with the name of his father: 'Laurence sonne to Robert King ————— Novemb[er] 18 [1629]'.[1] Further details about Robert King are sketchy, although there is a record of him marrying Margaret Higgs on 24 October 1624 in the parish church of St Mary the Virgin.[2] This may indicate that her family were residents of that parish, although this is not certain. Little else is known about Margaret King, since the only other time her actual name

---

[1] *Parish Register of All Saints' – 1559-1810* (Par 189/1/R1/1), folio 16 recto.
[2] *Parish Register of St Mary the Virgin – 1599-1694* (Par 209/1/R1/1), page 24.

appears in the primary sources is in connection with the death of her husband (see below).

The City Council records for 15 June 1638 note that Robert King was granted Oxford citizenship, the 'Freedom of the City', after paying the required fees.[1] His citizenship was duly entered in the *Civic Enrolments* for 12 December 1638.[2] There are also records of a Robert King who lived in the parish of St Peter-in-the-Bailey and paid 6*d* in the Lay Subsidy of 23 June 1647[3] and 8*d* in the Lay Subsidy of 17 March 1648.[4] It is probable that this tax-payer was Lawrence King's father, although when the family moved from the parish of All Saints' (where Lawrence was baptized) to the parish of St Peter-in-the-Bailey is unknown.

Two other fleeting glimpses into Robert King's working life are also extant. Together they confirm his residency within the parish of St Peter-in-the-Bailey, and present him as a person who hired himself out as a courier on horseback but later became an inn-keeper. The first record of King occurs in the financial account books of the Vice-Chancellor of the University of Oxford, for the academic year 1641-2. The account ledger lists a payment to him: 'Robert Kinge himselfe and his horse to carry a letter to ye Chancell^our - £1 00 00'.[5] The second is contained in the Oxford City Council's records relating to the licensing of inns; within Oxford such matters were dealt with by the Mayor of Oxford, who granted a license to display a sign advertising the name of the inn being registered. There is a record dated 30 July 1647, during the Mayoral year of John Nixon, granting to Robert King of the parish of St Peter-in-the-Bailey a license for the Flying Horse inn.[6]

Robert King died in late July or early August of 1651. Unfortunately, his death is not recorded within the parish registers of St Peter-in-the-Bailey, and no will has survived. However, there are two brief notes about him in connection with the settlement of his estate following his death. These are found in a register of caveats on wills and are both dated 4 August 1651; the second is the more interesting of the two in that it mentions the name of King's wife, describing her as 'Margarett his Relicte'.[7] She appears to have survived her husband by many years. It it probable that Margaret King died and was

---

[1] *City Council Proceedings – 1629-1663* (A.5.7), folio 83 recto = CSC #15.

[2] *Civic Enrolments – 1613-1640* (L.5.2), folio 340 verso) = CSC #16.

[3] *Lay Subsidy of 23 June 1647* (E 179/164/498), membrane 1. His name does not appear in the records of the other earlier collection of this tax (*Lay Subsidy of 23 June 1647* (E 179/164/498a), membrane 1), which suggests that he moved into the parish between the two collections.

[4] *Lay Subsidy of 17 March 1648* (E 179/164/499), membrane 4.

[5] *Liber Computus Vicecancellarii Oxon 1547-1666* (WPB/21/4), folio 130 recto.

[6] *Oxford City Ledgers – 1636-1675* (D.5.6), folio 555 verso = CSC #52. Salter (1969): 110, discusses several inns in the city which had the name of 'The Flying Horse'.

[7] *Oxford Caveats – 1643-1677* (MS Wills 307), folio 53 recto = CSC #96.

buried on 11 May 1680; a parish register entry records the burial of 'Mrs King, widow' on that date.[1]

Robert and Margaret King had several other children besides their son Lawrence (see the accompanying chart on 'The Family Tree of Lawrence King' for details of the larger family connections). There is an entry in the parish register of All Saints' recording the baptism of a child named William on 16 October 1627, two years before Lawrence.[2] In addition, there is a record of an Anne King, who is described as a 'mayd', being buried on 8 November 1630.[3] It is probable that this was a sister of Lawrence who died either as a child or a young girl.

At least one other son, named Thomas, was born to Robert and Margaret King; he was baptized in the parish of St Peter-in-the-Bailey on 16 May 1633.[4] Establishing the personal life and civic career of Thomas King are difficult matters since there are a number of different kinds of records bearing this name, and they come from different parishes, and stretch over many years. The name was a common one within the city of Oxford and relocation from one parish to another not unusual.[5] However, it is known that Robert King's son

---

[1] *Parish Register of St Peter-in-the-Bailey – 1659-1689* (Par 214/1/R1/2), folio 56 recto.

[2] *Parish Register of All Saints' – 1559-1810* (Par 189/1/R1/1), folio 15 verso. Unfortunately, the baptismal record does not give the name of his father. However, there is record of his apprenticeship to the glover John Browne dated 31 May 1641 which does; the apprenticeship was cancelled on 18 June 1645 and then the apprenticeship was assumed by Richard Saintsbury on 18 July 1645 (*Civic Enrolments – 1639-1662* (L.5.3), folio 12 verso = CSC #24). William King was granted citizenship of Oxford on 20 October 1652, having served his apprenticeship with Saintsbury (*MS Morrell 23 – List of Cordwainers' Apprentices (1590-1660)*, folio 71 recto; *Civic Enrolments – 1639-1662* (L.5.3), folio 238 verso). King then took on John Saintsbury, the son of his master, as an apprentice on 1 August 1653 (*Civic Enrolments – 1639-1662* (L.5.3), folio 121 recto); the apprenticeship did not succeed, however, and another master was chosen on 6 November 1653. King also took on John Hanns as an apprentice on 31 December 1655 (*Civic Enrolments – 1639-1662* (L.5.3), folio 141 verso). He was the son of Edward Hanns. There is record of the baptism of a Margaret King, the daughter of William King, on 27 July 1673 (*Parish Register of St Peter-in-the-Bailey – 1659-1689* (Par 214/1/R1/2), folio 17 verso). It is possible that she was the daughter of the glover.

[3] *Parish Register of All Saints' – 1559-1810* (Par 189/1/R1/1), folio 87 recto.

[4] *Parish Register of St Peter-in-the-Bailey – 1585-1646* (Par 214/1/R1/1), folio 45 recto.

[5] For example, there is record of a Thomas King from the parish of All Saints', a glasier, who agreed an apprenticeship with Joseph Tredwell on 15 March 1688 and, upon completion of it, was granted his 'Freedom of the City' on 16 April 1694 (*Civic Enrolments – 1662-1699* (L.5.4), pages 410 and 530). This Thomas King married Mary Stoker on 16 June 1694 (*ODR: Marriage Bonds* (d. 60), folio 49); she is described as a 'spinster' from Iffley in Oxfordshire. The couple made quarterly payments of the Poll Tax on 27 August and 17 December 1694 and 25 February 1695, and paid the Poll Tax of 1696 while living in the parish of All Saints' (*Taxes – 1691-1694* (P.5.9), folios 155

Thomas was enrolled in an apprenticeship contract to the tailor John Wildgoose on 23 March 1647,[1] although it is appears that the apprenticeship was transferred to Henry East at some point (the reason for the transferral is not clear).[2] In any event, Thomas was granted his 'Freedom of the City' on the successful completion of his apprenticeship on 1 April 1660.[3] It is likely that he married sometime in the late 1650s and he and his wife Mary began a family of their own. Unfortunately, parish records for the parish of St Peter-in-the-Bailey during the 1650s are incomplete, although it is virtually certain that the couple had a son who was also named Thomas.

There are no surviving records of the marriage of Lawrence King and his wife Anne, but it is likely they were married in Oxford in the early 1650s. Church records in Oxford are notoriously incomplete for the Commonwealth period, and this is probably the reason for the missing marriage records. Rental records show that the couple lived in a property along the High Street, opposite All Saints' parish church. The property was part of a complex known as Redcock's, comprising a number of shops and tenements, on several floors. As best can be determined, King and his family lived in the house now designated 119 High Street.[4] Lawrence and Anne King had a number of children, and details are known about some of their sons.

---

recto, 175 recto and 188 verso; *Taxes – 1694-1746* (P.5.10), folio 29 recto). Baptismal records from the parish of All Saints' show that four children were born to the couple between 1695 and 1705: a son Richard was baptized on 7 June 1695; a daughter Mary on 24 March 1697; a son Thomas on 10 April 1699, and a son Edward on 15 March 1705 (*Parish Register of All Saints' – 1559-1810* (Par 189/1/R1/1), folios 38 verso, 39 recto, 39 verso and 41 recto).

[1] *Civic Enrolments – 1639-1652* (L.5.3), folio 62 verso = CSC #51. The apprenticeship is also recorded in *Civil War, Charities & General Minutes – 1645-1695* (E.4.6), folio 6 verso = CSC #50. King's apprenticeship to Willgoose is also recorded in the Company of Taylors official register of Enrolments for 1646-7, where he is included among 'The names of those that were not Freemans sonnes of the Company of Taylors' (*MS Morrell 22 – The Company of Taylors: Enrolling Book (1604-1807)*, folio 46 recto).

[2] Whatever the reason, it was not because of Wildgoose's death or withdrawal from the Company of Taylors. He continued to serve as an active member of the guild, eventually rising to the rank of Master in 1652; his name appears regularly in records up to his death in late 1676 or early 1677 (*MS Morrell 6 – Election and Order Book of the Company of Taylors (1572-1711)*, folios 157 and 211 verso).

[3] *Civic Enrolments – 1639-1662* (L.5.3), folio 217 verso = CSC #309.

[4] See CSC #541 for the location of this property in David Loggan's *Oxonia Illustrata* (1675). Salter (1926): 126-127, gives details of the leases for the Redcock's property. In 1674 the lease for the property was granted to the goldsmith Daniel Porter, who took on one of Lawrence King's sons as an apprentice (*Old Leases and Counterparts: All Saints' Parish* (S 1.1d); *Oxford City Ledgers – 1636-1675* (D.5.6), folios 533 recto – 534 recto; *Oxford City Ledgers – 1675-1696* (D.5.7), folios 225 verso – 226 verso). According to the survey of Oxford completed by a Mr Blowfield in 1772, the property was measured to have a frontage of 4 yards 1 foot and 7 inches along the High Street. At present (2006), 119 High Street is occupied by the gowners Ede and

For example, it is known that two of Lawrence and Anne King's sons served as apprentices to their father. There is record of an apprenticeship with a son named Lawrence, probably the eldest of the sons, dated 7 November 1674.[1] No other record of Lawrence junior survives, which probably indicates that he died before the apprenticeship was completed, perhaps the victim of a smallpox epidemic which swept through Oxford in the summer of 1675. There is also a record of an apprenticeship contract with a son named Jonathan dated 9 March 1680.[2] Jonathan was granted his 'Freedom of the City' on the basis of the successful completion of his apprenticeship, and took over the family business when his father came to retirement age (more on this below). His citizenship is recorded in two documents, dated 13 September 1689[3] and 27 September 1689.[4]

Some taxation records relating to Jonathan King help fix his place of abode within the parish of St Michael during the years 1694-1719. There are records of him occupying a small tenement just outside the city walls along what is now Turl Street.[5] Thus, there are records of him paying 1*s* in the quarterly Poll Tax levies collected in 1694-5, including those on 2 May, 27 August and 17 December 1694, and 25 February 1695.[6] Similarly, he is known to have paid the Window Tax of 1696 while living in the property;[7] he also paid 6*d* as a 'Bachelor' under the provisions of the Marriage, Birth and Burial Tax of 1696 while living there.[8] He did not remain a bachelor long after this, however. In fact, Jonathan King was married twice: first to Elizabeth Mitchell in St John's Church in Holywell in 1699,[9] and then to Ann Rainsford of St Michael's parish in 1709.[10] His first wife Elizabeth died and was buried on 12 July 1706;[1] there

---

Ravenscroft. Interestingly, the adjoining property to the west, 120 High Street, was occupied by Thomas Williams, a milliner who was elected mayor of Oxford in 1653 (see chapter 6 below). Apparently Williams and Lawrence King were friends for many years, for King is named as one of the overseers of Williams's will (*PCC – Will of Thomas Williams* (PROB 11/345), folios 318 verso-319 recto) = CSC #523a).

[1] *Civic Enrolments – 1662-1699* (L.5.4), page 236 = CSC #531.

[2] *Civic Enrolments – 1662-1699* (L.5.4), page 311 = CSC #591.

[3] *Civic Enrolments – 1662-1699* (L.5.4), page 554 = CSC #635.

[4] *City Council Proceedings – 1663-1701* (B.5.1), folio 275 verso = CSC #636.

[5] *Oxford City Ledgers – 1697-1706* (D.5.9), folios 71 verso–72 verso. See Salter (1926): 278-281, for details of the leases pertaining to the property. The property no longer exists; it was demolished when Turl Street was widened in 1780. However, it is visible in David Loggan's *Oxonia Illustrata* (1675) = CSC #549.

[6] *Taxes – 1691-1694* (P.5.9), folios 117 verso, 133 verso, 152 recto 178 verso and 186 verso; *Taxes – 1694-1746* (P.5.10), folio 10 verso.

[7] *Taxes – 1694-1746* (P.5.10), folio 54 recto.

[8] *Taxes – 1694-1746* (P.5.10), folio 159 verso. This represents half of his annual levy as a 'Bachelor'. There is record of Jonathan King putting up money for a bond of recognizance for a Geoffrey Almont in a misdemeanour case of assault on 28 February 1701 (*Oxfordshire Quarter Sessions – Easter 1701* (QS/1701/EA), folio 76).

[9] *OAR: Marriage Bonds – 1699* (c. 485), folio 80. The bond is dated 8 July 1699.

[10] *OAR: Marriage Bonds – 1709* (c. 495), folio 97. The bond is dated 15 October 1709.

appears to have been no children from the marriage. Jonathan's second wife Ann was still living when he died in 1719. They had at least three children: a daughter named Mary, who was born on 16 September 1710 and baptized a few weeks later on 29 September 1710;[2] a son named Jonathan, who was born on 23 February 1712, but died and was buried on 26 September 1713;[3] and a daughter, named Anne, who was born on 3 November 1715, but died and was buried on 26 April 1719.[4] Jonathan King himself died on 19 January 1719 but he apparently did not leave a will, for his wife Ann signed the probate bond pertaining to his property on 10 November 1719. An inventory of his property was compiled on 9 November 1719; the goods and chattels in the six rooms of his house and shop were assessed to be worth a modest £36 19s 10d.[5] Ann did not marry again and lived for many more years within the parish of St Michael; she died and was buried there on 18 May 1742.[6]

In addition to Lawrence junior and Jonathan, Lawrence and Anne King also had a son named Ebennezar, a son named Lemuel, who became a goldsmith, a son named Elisha who was apprenticed to his brother Lemuel, a son named Samuel who became a painter-stainer, and perhaps even another son named Hezekiah. Some details of these sons survive, although the interpretation of some of the records concerned is difficult. However, a careful examination of the available documents often reveals fascinating details about these sons, both in terms of their family connections and their professional business contacts. First let us consider the records relating to Ebennezar.

Within the Bodleian Library there is a single vellum page from the register of All Saints' parish church in Oxford.[7] The page records the birth (as opposed to

---

[1] *Parish Register of St Michael-at-the-Northgate – 1683-1736* (Par 211/1/R1/3), page 48.

[2] *Parish Register of St Michael-at-the-Northgate – 1683-1736* (Par 211/1/R1/3), page 305.

[3] *Parish Register of St Michael-at-the-Northgate – 1683-1736* (Par 211/1/R1/3), pages 307 and 99.

[4] *Parish Register of St Michael-at-the-Northgate – 1683-1736* (Par 211/1/R1/3), pages 295 and 108.

[5] *Jonathan King* (OWPR 169/2/15) = CSC #685.

[6] *Parish Register of St Michael-at-the-Northgate – 1683-1736* (Par 211/1/R1/3), page 159.

[7] The manuscript is designated *MS Top Oxon* (b. 40). It is a leaf of a registry of births covering the period January 1653/4 to February 1659/60, probably part of the register which was originally composed by Matthew Jellyman, who had been appointed Registrar for the five contiguous parishes of All Saints', St Mary's, St Peter's-in-the-East, St Michael's and St John's in October 1653 (see *MS Rawlinson B 402a*), folio 1 recto). The page was donated to the Bodleian by W N Worren of Gobion's Hall, Great Leighs, Chelmsford in Essex on 17 November 1896, after having been in the Great Leighs parish chest. How and when the page became detached from Jellyman's register and eventually came to be in the parish church in Great Leighs is a mystery. Jellyman's appointment as Registrar was made in accordance with an Act of Parliament dated 24 August 1653 which was entitled *An Act Touching Marriages and the Registring thereof; and also touching Births and Burials* (see Firth and Rait (1911): 715-718, for

the baptism!) of a son named Ebennezar in 1655 ('Ebennezar ye sonn of Laurance King born March 15 1654'), as well as the birth of another son named Ebenezer in 1656 ('Ebenezer the sonne of Laurence Kinge borne July 24 1656').[1] How is this to be explained? One possible explanation is that this is simply a clerical error, but a more likely explanation is that Ebennezar (the child born in 1655) died in infancy, and when the next son was born fifteen months later he was given the same name as his recently deceased elder brother.[2] Since no other records mentioning Ebenezar (or Ebenezer) are extant, we may infer that the second son by that name also died sometime in childhood.

The birth of another son, Lemuel, in 1658 is also recorded on the same folio page from the register of All Saints' ('Lemmuell the son of Laurence King borne Dec[ember] 4 1658').[3] Unlike Ebenezar, Lemuel does appear in a few other records, and through them we can reconstruct something about his life. We know that he was apprenticed to Daniel Porter, a neighbour of Lawrence King, who ran a goldsmith's shop along the High Street. The apprenticeship contract is dated 23 August 1672 and was agreed for a standard eight year period.[4] Following his completion of the apprenticeship Lemuel was granted his 'Freeedom of the City' on 15 November 1680[5] and soon established himself as a goldsmith and engraver.[6]

We also know that Lemuel married Mary King (a distant relation?) in 1681, and the bond for their marriage was signed on 11 November 1681.[7] Within the marriage bond Lemuel King is described as a 'bachelor' from the parish of St Martin's and St Michael's in Oxford, while his bride is said to be a 'spinster' from the parish of St Ebbe's within the city, although the marriage was licensed to take place in the parish church of Forrest Hill in Oxfordshire. It looks as if Lemuel King and his new wife soon settled in the parish of All Saints' where

---

details).

[1] *MS Top Oxon* (b. 40), folio 1 recto.

[2] This is the suggestion offered by Clark in *MS Top Oxon* (d. 44), folio 20 recto.

[3] *MS Top Oxon* (b. 40), folio 1 verso.

[4] *Civic Enrolments – 1662-1699* (L.5.4), page 210 = CSC #512.

[5] *Civic Enrolments – 1662-1699* (L.5.4), page 610 = CSC #601.

[6] Several examples of his skill as an engraver have survived, notably three pieces of gilt silver at St John's College: a large ewer and basin from 1685-6, a porringer from 1688-9, and an undated tankard. The basin is of exceptional quality and bears his signature ('*L. King sculpsit*'), as does the porringer. See Moffatt (1906): 172-175 + plates LXXXIV and LXXXV; Clifford (2004): 106 and 143, for details.

[7] *OAR: Marriage Bonds – 1681* (c. 469), folio 68 = CSC #609. Interestingly, Lemuel King himself signed a marriage bond a few short weeks later on 30 November 1681, where he is described as an 'Aurifabr[ic]um' from the parish of Saint Martin. This was a marriage bond between Jane Darton of Walcott in Charlbury and John Williams, an upholsterer from the parish of Saint Mary the Virgin in Oxford (*ODR: Marriage Records – W 1634-1704* (d. 92/2), folio 120). It is possible that this John Williams was distantly related to Thomas Williams, an active Dissenter who was elected Mayor in 1653 (see chapter 5).

he began to take an active role within the life of the parish church there, since there is a record of his service as one of the 'Overseers of the Poor' for the parish. In this capacity he signs a document dated 1 August 1687 which acknowledges the transfer of Richard Souch and his wife and family from the parish of St Mary to the parish of All Saints'.[1] There is record of the burial of a Mary King within the register of All Saints' parish; this is dated 2 September 1690 and it *might* refer to the wife of Lemuel King, although she is not described as such within the brief entry.[2] However, Lemuel King is not listed in the records pertaining to the collection of the Marriage, Birth and Burial Tax of 1696 whereby 'Bachelors' and 'Widowers' were liable for an annual levy of 1s, although he does pay 16s in connection with the Poll Tax of the same year.[3] This suggests that he was married (re-married?) at the time of the collection of the 'Bachelor Tax'.

The most unusual record we have of Lemuel King concerns problems he had in working with an apprentice. There is an obscure notation contained within one of the notebooks of the clerk of the Petty Sessions court dated 17 October 1690 which alludes to an apprenticeship contract that Lemuel had with one Elisha King. It appears from the record of the dispute that the Elisha was Lemuel's younger brother, although this is not entirely clear and he may have been just a distant relative.[4] Apparently the apprenticeship was a wholly unsatisfactory arrangement, for Elisha King lodged a complaint with the court against his master. This led to the apprenticeship being cancelled, which meant that alternative arrangements with another master tradesman had to be negotiated. At one point in the court proceedings it was suggested that Lawrence King be consulted with regard to the appointment of a new master for Elisha, although the court clerk does later cross out the reference to Lawrence King. It is difficult to know precisely what the nature of the dispute was, although the court's attempt to involve Lawrence King in the resolution of the matter is intriguing. However, the fault might not lie with Lemuel King as the abusive master, if further apprenticeship records are anything to go by. There is some indication that Elisha King himself was something of an awkward customer, as can be seen within a court document from the Oxford Petty Sessions court dated 9 January 1696. Here Elisha King was indicted for

---

[1] *Oxford Petty Sessions Roll – 1679-1712* (O.5.12), folio 203 recto.

[2] *Parish Register of All Saints' – 1559-1810* (Par 189/1/R1/1), folio 13 verso.

[3] *Taxes – 1694-1746* (P.5.10), folio 34 verso.

[4] *Oxford Petty Sessions Clerk's Notebook – 1687-1701* (O.2.1), folios 39 verso–40 recto = CSC #644. The record describes Lawrence King as 'his father', but it is unclear if this means the father of Lemuel or Elisha. Moreover, there is an unusual court record from 8 October 1657 which refers to an Elisha King, 'a noted old Theife whoe was lately with a Turkey stolen from a man unknown' (*Oxford Petty Sessions Roll – 1656-1678* (O.5.11), folio 5 recto). The unusual name raises the possibility that Elisha King the apprentice was the namesake son of a turkey-stealing father, and *not* the son of Lawrence King. However, in the absence of any further information I take Elisha King to be the son of Lawrence King.

abuse of his own apprentice, whose name was Stephen Wells.[1] A further glimpse of Elisha King and his long-suffering apprentice can be found in the Poll Tax records of 1692-1695, where entries for 27 June 1692 and 2 May 1694 record payments of 2*s* to cover both men.[2] It seems that Elisha King never married, for he paid 6*s* as a 'Bachelor' under the provisions of the Marriage, Birth and Burial Tax of 1696.[3] He died and was buried 22 October 1697 in the parish of St Martin's.[4] On the other hand, his older brother Lemuel King apparently moved to London and continued his career as a goldsmith, There is record of his burial in the parish of St James, Clerkenwell in Middlesex on 21 June 1719.[5]

The records relating to another of the sons of Lawrence and Anne King, Samuel, are very minimal indeed, and have to do with his apprenticeship. Moreover, this apprenticeship is unusual in that Samuel was apprenticed to the London painter-stainer Leonard Cotes from on 14 October 1681,[6] the only example of such a King-family apprenticeship being set up outside of the city of Oxford where Lawrence had been born and worked all his life. Perhaps the fact that the apprenticeship was agreed less than a month before Anne King died had something to do with this arrangement. If her state of health was such that Lawrence King knew that her death was impending, he may have been trying to ensure that the son was well placed and provision was made for his future.

Finally, there is the case of Hezekiah who is known only through passing entries contained within the parish register of St Peter-in-the-Bailey. Like most of the other sons of Lawrence and Anne King, he was given the name of a biblical character from the Old Testament. There are no records of Hezekiah's birth, nor of his apprenticeship and professional career, or of his marriage. However, there are records of two of his children: a son named John who was born on 9 January 1691, and a son named Edward who was baptized on 18 May 1692.[7] There is also record of Hezekiah King's burial on 23 July 1713.[8]

---

[1] *Oxford Petty Sessions Roll – 1679-1712* (O.5.12), folio 86 verso = CSC #666.

[2] *Taxes – 1691-1694* (P.5.9), folios 61 verso and 138 recto. The first of these places the men in the parish of All Saints' and the second places them in the parish of St Martin's. Elisha King made an earlier quarterly payment on his own while living in the parish of St Martin's (*Taxes – 1691-1694* (P.5.9), folio 8 verso). This suggests that he had briefly relocated to the adjoining parish in the spring of 1692, perhaps in order to try and establish himself as a tradesman in his own right. Neither King nor Wells appear in the St Martin's records for the poll tax collection of 27 August 1694.

[3] *Taxes – 1694-1746* (P.5.10), folio 160 verso.

[4] *Parish Register of St Martin's – 1678-1789* (Par 207/1/R1/4), folio 6 verso.

[5] *Parish Register of St James, Clerkenwell, Middlesex – Burials 1666-1719.*

[6] *Painter-Stainers' Company Apprenticeships – 1666-1795* (GL MS 5669/1), folios 56 recto = CSC #608a and 63 verso (dated 8 July 1685).

[7] *Parish Register of St Peter-in-the-Bailey – 1684-1742* (Par 214/1/R1/3), folios 9 verso and 10 verso.

[8] *Parish Register of St Peter-in-the-Bailey – 1684-1742* (Par 214/1/R1/3), folio 53 verso.

In summary then, there are eight sons born to Lawrence and Anne King who can reasonably be deduced from the surviving records. This accords reasonably well with the entry in the Poll Tax of 1667 relating to King and his wife in the parish of All Saints', for on 1 March 1667 King paid 7s for himself, his wife and their five children (as noted, at least one child, Ebennezar, died in 1655). A picture of the wider King household can be gleaned from the other payments relating to the Poll Tax entry associated with the property. Thus, the entry records that King had an apprentice, Francis Carter, who, paid 1s in tax; a 'mayde', Elizabeth Cuberne, who paid 3s in tax on her wages of 40s; and a 'journyman', John Claydon, who paid 1s in tax.[1]

A number of other tax records from the 1660s are extant which relate to the Kings' residence along the High Street. The earliest of these shows that King paid for one hearth in the Hearth Tax of Michaelmas 1662 as part of the returns for All Saints' parish in the south-east ward of the City.[2] In addition, King is listed as paying a number of the War Taxes of 1667-1668,[3] commencing with a quarterly contribution of 2s 6d for the collection dated 24 June 1667.[4] Two further quarterly payments, assessed at the same rate, were made by King on 29 September 1667[5] and 21 December 1667.[6] There is also a quarterly tax record dated 26 March 1668 in which King paid 2s 6d in tax.[7] Finally, there are also three further quarterly tax records dated 26 June 1668, 26 September 1668, and 26 December 1668; within the first two collections King was assessed at 2s 6d for his contribution to the taxes, and within the third his contribution rises to 2s 8d.[8]

Later tax records from the 1690s also help to fill out the picture. A number of further tax payments were made by King, although in each instance the records are associated with Saint Mary's parish and *not* All Saints' parish. This suggests that King had relocated further along the High Street, probably moving in retirement.[9] The first of these are the Poll Taxes of 1692-1695, levied to help William III pay for the war against France. Interestingly, these

---

[1] *Poll Tax of 1667* (P.5.7), folio 10 recto = Salter (1923): 228. Salter gives the wages of the servant Elizabeth Cuberne here as £2. John Claydon went on to complete an apprenticeship with King (see page 82 below).

[2] *Hearth Tax of August-November 1662* (E 179/255/4), Part 2, page 8. For some reason Lawrence King's name does not appear in the surviving records for the Hearth Tax levied in 1665 and 1666 (E 179/164/513 and E 179 164/514). This should not overly concern us, however, since the Oxfordshire records for the Hearth Tax are notoriously incomplete.

[3] See pages 5-6 for an explanation of these taxes.

[4] *War Taxes – 1667-1668* (P.5.8), folio 3 verso.

[5] *War Taxes – 1667-1668* (P.5.8), 23 recto.

[6] *War Taxes – 1667-1668* (P.5.8), 41 verso.

[7] *War Taxes – 1667-1668* (P.5.8), 59 recto.

[8] *War Taxes – 1667-1668* (P.5.8), folios 79 verso, 97 verso and 107 recto.

[9] Speaking of the 'Window Tax of 1696', Hobson (1939): 366, states that the record relating to St Mary's parish 'begins at the boundary of All Saints' on the south side of the High St'. Lawrence King's name is the first listed under St Mary's parish records.

entries show regular quarterly payments of 5s, initially to cover 'Lawrence King, his wife and three children'.[1] The poll levied later drops in May 1694 to 4s, covering King, his wife and *two* children, suggesting that one of the children had moved away.[2] The final entry for this year is dated 25 February 1695 and shows King paying 6s to cover himself, his wife, two children, one lodger and one servant.[3] These are the only records that are extant which suggest that King remarried following the death of his first wife Anne in 1681; no record of the marriage itself appears to have survived. Indeed, even the names of his second wife and the children concerned are unknown, as are the precise details of the relationship between King and the children (it is possible that some of the children listed in the tax records were his new wife's children and that Lawrence King was their step-father). However, there is record of the burial of 'Joseph (an Infant) son of [*blank*] King, Glover' on 28 February 1687 in the parish of St Martin's.[4] It appears likely that this was a son of Lawrence King and his second (unnamed) wife.

The next of these tax records is dated to 1694 and concerns the Poll Tax granted by Parliament to assist in the prosecution of the war against France. In this instance Lawrence King paid £4 in tax based upon an assessment of his rent and trading stock.[5] The second tax record concerns the Poll Tax of 1696; here he paid £3 based on a subsequent assessment.[6] The third tax record is again from 1696 and concerns the so-called 'Window Tax'; here King paid 6s on ten windows contained in his High Street property.[7] The tax was levied annually upon the occupier of every house in the land; it was collected from 1696-1706, although in Oxford only the records for the collection in 1696 have survived.

---

[1] *Taxes – 1691-1694* (P.5.9), folios 22 recto and 43 verso. The first record from 10 March 1692 also notes that King was taxed an extra 10s on 'goods worth 300[li]'. King appealed against this assessment, stating that he was not worth £300, and a panel of assessors on 11 April 1692 relieved him of the additional 10s tax (*Taxes – 1691-1694* (P.5.9), folio 203 verso). King also appealed against a similar assessment of him for the second quarterly payment of the year; on 19 July 1692 the assessors relieved him of 10s in tax and accepted that he was 'not a trader' (*Taxes – 1691-1694* (P.5.9), folio 201 verso). Records from 1693 and 1694 similarly deal with tax levied on rents and stocks (*Taxes – 1691-1694* (P.5.9), folios 85 verso and 103 verso). Interestingly, King served as one of the two 'Assessors' for the parish of St Mary's in the year 1694; his fellow assessor was Arthur Tylliard (*Taxes – 1691-1694* (P.5.9), folio 104 recto).

[2] *Taxes – 1691-1694* (P.5.9), folios 141 verso and 154 recto. It is most likely that his son Jonathan moved to the parish of St Martin and established himself as a glover in his own right (see below).

[3] *Taxes – 1691-1694* (P.5.9), folio 190 verso.

[4] *Parish Register of St Martin's – 1678-1789* (Par 207/1/R1/4), folio 3 recto.

[5] *Taxes – 1694-1746* (P.5.10), folio 6 verso.

[6] *Taxes – 1694-1746* (P.5.10), folio 35 recto.

[7] *Taxes – 1694-1746* (P.5.10), folio 55 recto.

2. Apprenticeship as a Glover

Unfortunately, little is known about Lawrence King's early years. The one certain fact is that he was apprenticed to the glover Thomas Meares on 6 July 1641. The apprenticeship was for a standard eight-year contract; at the time Lawrence was not quite twelve years old. However, the record indicates that something went wrong with the arrangement, and the young apprentice was transferred to the glover John Sheene on 11 September 1646.[1] Precisely what happened to necessitate the amendment of the contract is difficult to determine; perhaps it was due to the general disruption caused by the Civil War.[2]

In any event, Lawrence King's apprenticeship record was amended to reflect a change in circumstance as his unfinished apprenticeship to Thomas Meares was re-negotiated in favour of a five-year contract with John Sheene. King would have been about seventeen years of age at the time; it was a tumultuous period with the city of Oxford recently having surrendered to the Parliamentary forces led by Sir Thomas Fairfax. There are some indications that John Sheene and Lawrence King shared a common outlook on religious matters For example, John Sheene was indicted, along with seven others including Ralph Austen (whom we will discuss more fully below in chapter 4), at the Oxford Petty Sessions court on 7 October 1669.[3] Other records of John Sheene, and his wife Elizabeth, appearing before the ecclesiastical courts are also extant. These include records for 22 June 1667 and 22 June 1668.[4] Within the first of these records it is stated that 'hee (Sheene) with his wife are p[rese]nted for not receiving y[e] Sacrament at Easter', and records that Sheene's response was that 'they are not fully satisfied touching the receiving of the same'. Later, in April of 1689, with William III promising a new era of religious toleration and freedom, John Sheene registered his home as a place of worship for Dissenters.[5] It is certainly not beyond the bounds of possibility that Lawrence

---

[1] *Civic Enrolments – 1639-1662* (L.5.3), folio 14 verso = CSC #25.

[2] The break in the apprenticeship contract does not appear to have caused an permanent rift between the two families for other members of the Meares family later take up apprenticeships with both Lawrence and Jonathan King (see pages 112 and 115 below).

[3] *Oxford Petty Sessions Roll – 1656-1678* (O.5.11), folio 112 recto.

[4] *OAR: 11 May 1667 – 21 July 1669* (c. 17), folios 29 recto and 136 recto.

[5] *Oxford Petty Sessions Clerk's Notebook – 1687-1701* (O.2.1), folio 21 recto. Another indication of Sheene's political and religious views is provided by the fact that the University of Oxford gave him the contract for making gloves to be presented to the judges and clerks of the assizes during the years 1652-8, the years of the Commonwealth and Protectorate. Prior to that time this lucrative contract was held by another unnamed glover, and after the Restoration it was awarded to another glover named William New, who held a city lease for the Bear Public House in All Saints' parish (*Ledger Book 1675-1696* (D.5.7), folio 12). See *Liber Computus Vicecancellarii Oxon 1547-1666* (WPB/21/4), folio 147 recto–162 verso, where a dozen or so payments to John Sheene for gloves made for the court officials are recorded.

King first become involved with Dissenters while serving as an apprentice to John Sheene.[1]

B. Master Glover and Oxford Citizen

1. *'Freedom of the City'*

The apprenticeship with John Sheene eventually proved successful and upon completion of it King was granted his citizenship, the 'Freedom of the City', on 22 September 1651.[2] The stage was thus set for Lawrence King to launch his professional career as a tradesman in Oxford, with all of the attendant duties and responsibilities within the city that followed.

Lawrence King was one of several prominent glovers operating within the city of Oxford during the second half of the 17th century. The trade had flourished there for centuries and a glover's guild had been established in the city since 1461. Gloves were often presented as gifts, particularly to royalty and noblemen by any well-wisher wanting to make a favourable impression. Interestingly, Anthony Wood records in a number of places within his *Diaries* the times and places where he purchased gloves. Although Wood never mentions Lawrence King in this regard, he does record an instance in August of 1659 when he purchased a pair of gloves from King's apprenticeship master John Sheene.[3] One contemporary of Wood's, and King's, writing in 1677, remarked that, 'Oxford had the reputation of the best gloves and knives, of any place in England.'[4]

Once Lawrence King had been granted his 'Freedom of the City', he quickly established himself as a master tradesman in his own right. All indications are that Lawrence King conducted his glover's business from the property at 119 High Street, probably living above his ground-floor shop. An intriguing artifact of the establishment of his trade as a High Street glover are the tokens which Lawrence King issued, most probably sometime between 1652-1660. These small farthing (1/4*d*) pieces boldly advertised the business. The obverse of the Lawrence King token has an inscription which reads LAWRANCE KING surrounding the letters L K in the centre. The reverse of the coin has a surrounding inscription which reads GLOVER IN OXON and the image of a glove in the centre (see Illustration #5). Both right hand and left hand varieties of the token are extant.[5]

---

[1] Sheene signed his last will and testament on 1 March 1690 (*PCC – Will of John Sheene* (PROB 11/412), folios 287 recto – 288 recto. The will was probated on 23 December 1692.

[2] *Civic Enrolments – 1639-1662* (L.5.3), folio 244 recto = CSC #99.

[3] *MS Wood Diaries 3*, folio 21 recto.

[4] Plot (1677): 280. For more on glove-making in Oxford, see Schulz (1938): 139-140; Crossley (1979): 325-326.

[5] Thompson and Dickinson (1993): Plate 30, #3700 and #3701. Also see Leeds (1923): 418; Dickinson (1986): 179, #150.

Illustration #5: Lawrence King Trade Token

Soon after he established himself as a citizen and tradesman in Oxford, King began to be awarded lucrative civic contracts; this involved making gloves which were presented to dignitaries on behalf of the municipality.   Some interesting records detailing these contracts have survived. Thus, the city of Oxford's *Audit Book – 1592-1682* records King twice being paid for gloves presented to the Judge at the Petty Sessions court assizes in 1654.[1]

2. Apprenticeship Contracts

Another indication of the success that King had as a glover is the number of apprentices that he supervised as a master craftsman.   The Oxford City Council's volumes of *Civic Enrolments* give details of seventeen such apprenticeships spanning nearly thirty years.   At least seven of these apprentices went on to become citizens of Oxford themselves. The names and dates for these apprenticeship contracts, and the dates when the apprentices were granted their 'Freedom of the City', are as follows:

Name	Date of Contract	Duration	Citizenship Granted
Francis Smith	11 December 1652[2]	Seven years	26 January 1663[3]
Moses Clark	15 August 1655[1]	Eight years	

---

[1] *Audit Book – 1592-1682* (P.5.2), folio 290 verso and verso = CSC #200.

[2] *Civic Enrolments – 1639-1662* (L.5.3), folio 116 verso = CSC #126.

[3] *Civic Enrolments – 1662-1699* (L.5.4), page 737 = CSC #368; *Husting and Mayors Court 1660-1664* (M.4.4), folio 93 verso (Husting).   There is also an incomplete entry for Francis Smith's citizenship in *Civic Enrolments – 1639-1662* (L.5.3), folio 211 recto. Francis Smith's successful completion of his apprenticeship (on 8 January 1663) and the granting of his citizenship is also recorded in *Precedents – 1660-1710* (N.4.6), folios 164 recto-163 verso = CSC #364; here it serves as a template for recording such matters in official court records.

John Claydon	7 September 1659[2]	Seven years	12 September 1670[3]
Francis Carter	4 August 1664[4]	Seven years	11 September 1671[5]
John Baker	24 August 1664[6]	Seven years	
Nathaniell Lloyd	26 February 1667[7]	Eight years	
Thomas Powell	11 March 1667[8]	Seven years	

---

[1] *Civic Enrolments – 1639-1662* (L.5.3), folio 138 verso = CSC #219.

[2] *Civic Enrolments – 1639-1662* (L.5.3), folio 177 verso = CSC #293; the apprenticeship contract is backdated to 24 June 1659. Claydon was listed as a 'journeyman' living with the King's and paying 1s in the Poll Tax of 1667 (see page 106 above).

[3] *Civic Enrolments – 1662-1699* (L.5.4), page 690 = CSC #488; *Husting and Mayors Courts – 1666-1672* (M.4.6), folio 144 verso (Mayors).

[4] *Civic Enrolments – 1662-1699* (L.5.4), page 39 = CSC #395; the apprenticeship contract is backdated to 29 September 1663.

[5] *Civic Enrolments – 1662-1699* (L.5.4), page 684 = CSC #499; *Husting and Mayors Courts – 1666-1672* (M.4.6), folio 187 verso (Hustings).

[6] *Civic Enrolments – 1662-1699* (L.5.4), page 40 = CSC #398; the apprenticeship contract is predated to begin on 1 March 1667.

[7] *Civic Enrolments – 1662-1699* (L.5.4), page 85 = CSC #438. Lloyd was originally apprenticed to the sadler Richard King, perhaps a distant relative of Lawrence, on 19 December 1665 (*Civic Enrolments – 1662-1699* (L.5.4), page 64). Richard King served as a sadler's apprentice to John Newman (*Civic Enrolments – 1613-1640* (L.5.2), folio 325 verso) and was granted his Oxford citizenship on 11 September 1647 (*Civic Enrolments – 1639-1652* (L.5.3), folio 252 recto). He had a successful career as a sadler and took on several apprenticeships in addition to the one with Nathaniell Lloyd. There is an apprenticeship contract between Richard King and Bezaliell Jellyman which is dated 16 October 1654 (*Civic Enrolments – 1639-1652* (L.5.3), folio 131 verso); one with Nathaniell Harding dated 8 June 1659 (*Civic Enrolments – 1639-1652* (L.5.3), folio 176 recto); one with Timothy Borne dated 2 July 1667 (*Civic Enrolments – 1662-1699* (L.5.4), page 97); one with Joseph Cadwallington which is dated 22 June 1672 (*Civic Enrolments – 1662-1699* (L.5.4), page 198); one with George Annesly which is dated 26 March 1677 (*Civic Enrolments – 1662-1699* (L.5.4), page 270); one with Richard Swell which is dated 30 May 1681 (*Civic Enrolments – 1662-1699* (L.5.4), page 327); and one with Thomas Martin dated 9 May 1685 (*Civic Enrolments – 1662-1699* (L.5.4), page 374). On 30 April 1663 King was indicted to appear before the Petty Sessions court for not attending his local parish, but he was deemed to have conformed and was discharged (*Oxford Petty Sessions Roll – 1656-1678* (O.5.11), folio 51 verso). A bond for the marriage between Richard King and Jane Peisley was signed on 10 September 1673 (*OAR: Marriage Bonds – 1673* (c. 462), folio 69). In this bond the sadler Richard King is described as a 'widower' from the St Martin's parish in Oxford; Jane Peisley is described as a 'spinster' from the same parish. Details of Richard King's previous marriage are unknown, although there is a record of the death of an Elizabeth, the wife of Richard King on 25 February 1659 (*Parish Register of St Peter-in-the-East – 1600-1673* (Par 213/1/R1/2), folio 66 verso). Richard King was buried in the parish of St Giles on 25 July 1699 (*Parish Register of St Giles – 1679-1768* (MS DD Par Oxford – St Giles c. 1), page 189). His will was probated on 27 September 1699 (*Richard King* (OWPR 138/2/35)).

[8] *Civic Enrolments – 1662-1699* (L.5.4), page 87 = CSC #440; the apprenticeship contract is backdated to 25 February 1667.

Jeffery Hands	16 March 1668[1]	Seven yeares	7 June 1675[2]
James Newman	14 April 1668[3]	Seven years	
Thomas Cooper	25 June 1670[4]	Eight years	10 February 1678[5]
Caleb Tomkins	11 April 1672[6]	Seven years	
James Leverett	16 April 1673[7]	Eight years	
Joseph Mason	4 September 1674[8]	Seven years	
Lawrence King	7 November 1674[9]	Eight years	
Thomas Meares	9 July 1675[10]	Seven years	13 September 1695[11]
Jonathan King	9 March 1680[12]	Seven years	13 September 1689[13]
Robert Tewson	5 May 1684[14]	Seven years	

The apprenticeship contract with Nathaniell Lloyd, dated to 26 February 1667, is of particular interest in that it was not completed with Lawrence King, but was transferred to another glover. It is the only one of Lawrence King's apprenticeship contracts to be so altered. The contract was originally made with King at a time during the reign of Charles II when the policy of

---

[1] *Civic Enrolments – 1662-1699* (L.5.4), page 112 = CSC #450; the apprenticeship contract is predated to begin on 25 May 1668. This apprenticeship was originally made with Jude Meares as the master, but was transferred to Lawrence King on 16 May 1673.

[2] *Civic Enrolments – 1662-1699* (L.5.4), page 659 = CSC #533; *Husting and Mayors Courts – 1672-1677* (M.4.7), folio 79 verso (Mayors).

[3] *Civic Enrolments – 1662-1699* (L.5.4), page 114 = CSC #452. This apprenticeship was originally made with Jude Meares as the master, but was transferred to Lawrence King on 22 August 1670.

[4] *Civic Enrolments – 1662-1699* (L.5.4), page 160 = CSC #485; the apprenticeship contract is backdated to 24 June 1670.

[5] *Civic Enrolments – 1662-1699* (L.5.4), page 626 = CSC #574.

[6] *Civic Enrolments – 1662-1699* (L.5.4), page 195 = CSC #504; the apprenticeship contract is backdated to 25 March 1672.

[7] *Civic Enrolments – 1662-1699* (L.5.4), page 208 = CSC #517; the apprenticeship contract is predated to begin on 1 May 1673. James Leverett is here named as a recipient of 'Mr Bogan's charity'. This was a charity set up in 1659 by the wealthy benefactor named Zacharias Bogan, an MA from Corpus Christi College. Bogan gave £500 to the city to help pay for apprenticeships for children of poor families from the parishes of St Ebbe's, St Peter-in-the-Bailey, St Thomas, St Mary Magdalen, and St Giles.

[8] *Civic Enrolments – 1662-1699* (L.5.4), page 232 = CSC #529. There is some confusion about the spelling of the surname within this record: a correction from 'Mason' to 'Nason' is made, although it seems certain that Joseph Mason/Nason is the son of the glover Thomas Mason with whom Lawrence King had several dealings (see pages 114-5 below).

[9] *Civic Enrolments – 1662-1699* (L.5.4), page 236 = CSC #531.

[10] *Civic Enrolments – 1662-1699* (L.5.4), page 245 = CSC #537; the apprenticeship contract is predated to begin on 24 July 1675.

[11] *Civic Enrolments – 1662-1699* (L.5.4), page 523 = CSC #664.

[12] *Civic Enrolments – 1662-1699* (L.5.4), pages 311 = CSC #591. The contract is backdated to 1 October 1679.

[13] *Civic Enrolments – 1662-1699* (L.5.4), pages 554 = CSC #635.

[14] *Civic Enrolments – 1662-1699* (L.5.4), page 363 = CSC #613.

suppression of Dissenters was at its height, and it is possible that this gives us an indication as to why it was terminated. No reason is given for the transferral of the apprenticeship away from Lawrence King to a second master glover, but it happens to come within a month of his being cited to appear before the ecclesiastical court to answer for non-attendance at the local parish church. It is possible that Nathaniell Lloyd, or his family, did not want to be associated with King at a time when he was under public censure as a 'seditious sectarye'. Alternatively it could be an indication of the inherent inability of Nathaniell to stay the course, given the fact that he transferred to a *third* master glover within the span of eighteen months, and had only been taken on by Lawrence King in the first place when an earlier apprenticeship with the sadler Richard King failed.[1]

3. *Civic Offices and Responsibilities*

Soon after being granted his 'Freedom of the City', King began to take an active role in municipal affairs. He was appointed as 'Constable' for the south-east ward of the city on 30 September 1652,[2] and on 27 September 1653 he was designated as one of twelve Common Council members to benefit from a charity established by a Mrs Brooks.[3] The money was apparently lent to King for five years, after which time it was to be re-paid to the city, which administered the charity. There is record of a re-payment of £10 being made by Lawrence King five years later on 29 September 1658 in connection with this loan.[4] Interestingly King's fellow Baptist Richard Tidmarsh is listed as one of the three people offering securities on the loan, a detail which helps establish a relationship between the two men as early as 1653. King also received a loan of £6, probably sometime in 1657, from a legacy set up by a Mr Bosworth. The loan was re-paid in 1663; once again Richard Tidmarsh is listed as one of the three people offering securities on the loan.[5] King also subsequently offered securities on loans available through the various charities of the city. On four separate occasions he offered securities for loans being granted to others: once on 25 March 1677 for a loan to the fuller Thomas King (a relative?) in connection with Alderman Harris's charity;[6] once on 7 May 1681 for a three-

---

[1] See page 111, note 7 above.
[2] *City Council Proceedings – 1629-1663* (A.5.7), folio 209 verso.
[3] *City Council Proceedings – 1629-1663* (A.5.7), folio 215 verso.
[4] *Civil War, Charities & General Minutes – 1645-1695* (E.4.6), folio 71 verso.
[5] *Civil War, Charities & General Minutes – 1645-1695* (E.4.6), folio 72 recto.
[6] *Civil War, Charities & General Minutes – 1645-1695* (E.4.6), folio 100 recto. It is possible that Thomas King was a distant relative, although the precise family connection is unknown. In this record Lawrence King stands as one of two people offering securities for the loan (*Civil War, Charities & General Minutes – 1645-1695* (E.4.6), folio 100 recto). The other person offering security for the loan is Zacheus Smith, who is listed as a 'dier' (dyer). It appears that the favour of standing securities was returned four years later on 7 May 1681 when Thomas King stood as a guarantor for a three-year loan of £10 which was granted to the glover Francis Carter in

year loan of £10 to Michael Stockford in connection with Mrs. Fulseye's charity;[1] once on 21 December 1684 for a ten-year loan of £12 6*s* 8*d* to Jude Meares in connection with Mrs Lloyd's charity;[2] and once on 29 September 1686 for a five-year loan of £5 to Richard Leverett, again in connection with Mrs Lloyd's charity.[3] The last two cases are particularly interesting in that they are both loans made to glovers, and guaranteed by glovers: the second guarantor on the loan to Jude Meares was the glover John Cantwell, and the second guarantor on the loan to Richard Leverett was the glover Thomas Mason. Interestingly, Thomas Mason was a man whom King had supported in a civil suit some years before in June of 1669, so it was not the first time the

---

connection with Mrs Fulseye's charity (*Civil War, Charities & General Minutes – 1645-1695* (E.4.6), folios 104 recto and 110 recto). Francis Carter had been one of Lawrence King's apprentices from 1664-71, and it looks as if there is an overlap between family and business associations in operation here.

Some details of Thomas King the fuller are extant, including an apprenticeship contract with William White which was agreed on 29 June 1665 (*Civic Enrolments – 1662-1699* (L.5.4), page 58 = CSC #417, the apprenticeship contract is backdated to 29 September 1664). As a fuller Thomas appears to have been moderately successful, and agreed an apprenticeship with William Durling on 3 October 1691 (*Civic Enrolments – 1662-1699* (L.5.4), page 449). However, on 22 February 1692 this was deemed to have been an attempt to defraud the city, and King was reprimanded and the apprenticeship was voided (*City Council Proceedings – 1663-1701* (B.5.1), folio 295 recto). Thomas King the fuller married Elizabeth Floyd on 11 November 1671 (*Parish Register of St Cross, Hollywell – 1654-1812* (Par 199/1/R1/1), folio 169 verso). He and Elizabeth had at least three children: a daughter named Anne who was baptized on 5 April 1673 (*Parish Register of St Peter-in-the-Bailey – 1659-1689* (Par 214/1/R1/2), folio 17 recto), a son named Thomas who was baptized on 22 January 1678 but died and was buried on 9 June 1686 (*Parish Register of St Peter-in-the-Bailey – 1659-1689* (Par 214/1/R1/2), folios 24 verso and 49 recto), and probably another daughter named Mary who died as a young girl and was buried on 21 March 1689 (*Parish Register of St Peter-in-the-Bailey 1659-1689* (Par 214/1/R1/2), folio 45 verso). Elizabeth King herself died and was buried between the death of these two children on 29 January 1686 (*Parish Register of St Peter-in-the-Bailey 1659-1689* (Par 214/1/R1/2), folio 49 verso). Thomas re-married within eight months of his wife's death; his second wife was named Mellesent Bigersap and they were married on 2 August 1686 in the parish church of St Peter-in-the-Bailey (*Parish Register of St Peter-in-the-Bailey – 1659-1689* (Par 214/1/R1/2), folio 44 recto). There are baptismal records relating to four children who were born to the couple: a daughter Sarah baptized on 31 October 1687, a son Thomas baptized on 1 April 1689, a daughter Mellesent baptized on 26 March 1691, and a daughter Elizabeth baptized on 8 March 1697 (*Parish Register of St Peter-in-the-Bailey – 1684-1742* (Par 214/1/R1/3), folios 5 verso, 7 verso, 9 verso and 14 verso. The entry for Thomas explicitly describes him 'the second of the name'). The son Thomas also went on to become a fuller in his own right and was granted his Oxford citizenship on 30 July 1722 (*Civic Enrolments – 1697-1780* (L.5.5), folio 346 recto).

[1] *Civil War, Charities & General Minutes – 1645-1695* (E.4.6), folios 104 recto and 110 recto.

[2] *Civil War, Charities & General Minutes – 1645-1695* (E.4.6), folio 111 verso.

[3] *Civil War, Charities & General Minutes – 1645-1695* (E.4.6), folio 112 recto.

two glovers had co-operated professionally.[1]   Indeed, Mason and King had other points of professional and personal contact, notably the fact that King took on Mason's son Joseph as an apprentice in 1674 (see page 112 above). More importantly the recipients of the loans were both men with whom King had a professional, as well as a personal, connection. Jude Meares was the son of Thomas Meares, King's own original apprenticeship master, and he had a son whose name was Thomas (after his grandfather). As noted above, King took on this Thomas, as an apprentice in 1675, and upon successful completion of the apprenticeship was granted Oxford citizenship in 1695. Also noted above was the fact that King took over two of Jude Meares's apprenticeships, those of Jeffery Hands and James Newton, guiding both to successful careers and Oxford citizenship. In other words, the King-Meares family connection seems to extend across many years and to be responsible for several generations of glovers in Oxford. Similarly, the willingness of King to guarantee a loan to the glover Richard Leverett in 1686 is all the more understandable when we remember that Leverett's son James had probably just completed an eight-year apprenticeship under King in 1681. Then as now, business was conducted on the basis of personal contacts; by their very nature apprenticeship contracts tended to follow family lines. Nowhere is this more evident than in the life of Lawrence King himself, whose son Jonathan succeeded him professionally. King's family glover's business was obviously quite successful and was carried on by his son Jonathan well into the next century. There are details of six apprenticeships contracted with Jonathan King contained within the various City Council documents. Several of these apprenticeships serve as the basis for the citizenship of the person concerned, long after Jonathan King dies. The six apprenticeships are:

Name	Date of Contract	Duration	Citizenship Granted
Richard Meares	11 January 1695[2]	Seven years	29 January 1705[3]
John Sheppard	24 September 1701[4]	Seven years	19 May 1710[5]
William Carter	13 June 1704[6]	Seven years	15 February 1713[1]

---

[1] Mason appeared before the Petty Sessions court on 22 June 1669 having been indicted for illegally trading as a glover without having served an apprenticeship. Lawrence King is recorded as offering a financial guarantee of £10 to have the case heard in the following Hilary sessions (*Oxford Petty Sessions Roll – 1656-1678* (O.5.11), folio 110 verso = CSC #471). The case came before the court again on 13 January 1670, where the court ruled in favour of Mason and he was discharged (*Oxford Petty Sessions Roll – 1656-1678* (O.5.11), folio 114 recto = CSC #481).

[2] *Civic Enrolments – 1662-1699* (L.5.4), page 480 = CSC #661; the apprenticeship contract is backdated to 24 June 1694.

[3] *Civic Enrolments – 1697-1780* (L.5.5), folio 20 recto.

[4] *The Enrolments of Apprentices – 1697-1800* (F.4.9), folio 26 recto = CSC #674.

[5] *Civic Enrolments – 1697-1780* (L.5.5), folio 37 recto.

[6] *The Enrolments of Apprentices – 1697-1800* (F.4.9), folio 44 recto = CSC #679; the apprenticeship contract is backdated to 24 June 1703. William Carter was the son

John Brooker (Brucker)	14 February 1705[2]	Seven years	18 March 1733[3]
John Wells	5 May 1712[4]	Seven years	18 January 1733[5]
Martin Williams		Seven years	18 January 1733[6]

To return to Lawrence King: two further indications of his involvement in civic matters are worth highlighting, both of which illustrate his activity within his local parish in precisely the same way as did his fellow Baptist conventicler Richard Tidmarsh. First, he was appointed an 'Overseer of the Poor' for the parish of All Saints' in the spring of 1668;[7] second, he serves as a tax assessor for the parish in the same year. As noted above (page 9), in 1668 a tax was levied relating to the 'Act for Granting £1,256,347 13s for the War against the Dutch'. Within the city of Oxford each parish appointed two assessors who were responsible for helping to facilitate the tax collection in their parish. Lawrence King is listed three times as an assessor for the parish of All Saints' for the taxes collected on 26 June 1668, 26 September 1668, and 26 December 1668.[8] Interestingly, King's fellow assessor in each instance is the goldsmith Daniel Porter, his neighbour, who also later took on Lawrence's son Lemuel as an apprentice in 1672 (see page 103 above).

Finally, it is worth noting that Lawrence King did hold one other civic office within Oxford, albeit only for a brief period of time and under controversial circumstances. He was one of the political appointees listed in James II's new charter of Oxford issued 15 September 1688, and as such is another of the Dissenters elevated to positions of responsibility by a devious monarch intent on weakening the Anglican power structures of the day (see pages 138-9 below).

C. Public Baptisms, Illegal Conventicles, and the Licensed Baptist Meeting-House (1659-1672)

1. Abingdon Association Records

There is no doubt that Lawrence King was a Baptist leader of some repute. The *Abingdon Association Records Book*, containing accounts of meetings which took place between 1652 and 1660, firmly establish him as a Baptist leader

---

of Francis Carter, a glover who had served his apprenticeship under Lawrence King from 1664-71 (see *Civic Enrolments – 1662-1699* (L.5.4), pages 39 and 684).

[1] *Civic Enrolments – 1697-1780* (L.5.5), folio 48 verso.

[2] *The Enrolments of Apprentices – 1697-1800* (F.4.9), folio 48 verso = CSC #680.

[3] *Civic Enrolments – 1697-1780* (L.5.5), folio 131 recto.

[4] *The Enrolments of Apprentices – 1697-1800* (F.4.9), folio 88 verso = CSC #683; the apprenticeship contract is backdated to 1 May 1712.

[5] *Civic Enrolments – 1697-1780* (L.5.5), folio 122 recto.

[6] *Civic Enrolments – 1697-1780* (L.5.5), folio 122 recto.

[7] *Husting and Mayor's Court 1662; Licenses and Overseers* (N.4.3), folio 57 recto = CSC #451.

[8] *War Taxes – 1667-1668* (P.5.8), folios 125 verso, 126 recto, and 127 verso.

within Oxford. The records show that he once served as a delegate from Oxford, at the meetings held at Tetsworth which began on 14 September 1658, although he apparently arrived a day late at the meetings. This act of tardiness engendered a mild rebuke from the rest of the delegates to the congregation in Oxford, who 'sent a loving epistle to that church, beseeching them to consider their acting in this respect'.[1]

2. *Public Baptisms in an Atmosphere of Mistrust*

Perhaps the most celebrated passage mentioning Lawrence King is one contained within Anthony Wood's manuscript *MS Wood F 31*, and dated December 1659. Here Wood claims to have witnessed a noisy public baptism at High Bridge being performed by an Anabaptist preacher named King who was being heckled by the crowd.[2] The passage comes as a marginal comment on Wood's more general discussion of disruptions taking place within Oxford at the time, disruptions which Wood suggests included public declamations against the University. The political atmosphere throughout the country was highly-charged, with great uncertainty about what the future might hold in the face of the collapse of Richard Cromwell's Protectorate. Was there to be a return to Parliamentary rule, or was a restored monarchy likely? One popular perception was that Anabaptists up and down the country were planning a military coup, and indeed, some of them were doing precisely that, as the Venner uprising in London was soon to make clear. Inevitably this led to clashes between Baptists and the legal authorities in many towns and cities, including Oxford. Thus, Anthony Wood makes passing reference to 'a great meeting of ye Anabaptists at abingdon' on 2 June 1659 which caused a great disturbance to the nation.[3] Wood also tells of a rather humorous incident which took place on 31 July 1659 in which a great wind storm hit the city of Oxford and blew some roofing slates from Carfax Tower. This act of nature was interpreted by some residents worshipping in St Martin's Church next door as heralding the day of judgement, and, as Wood relates, some thought 'y^e Anabap[tists] & quakers were co[m]e to cutt their throats'.[4] Wood similarly comments on the turmoil surrounding the Restoration of Charles II, noting in an entry dated 7 January 1661 that Oxford was 'in a posture of defence because of

---

[1] *AARB*, folio 35 recto = White (1974): 186 = CSC #267.

[2] *MS Wood F 31*, folio 7 verso = CSC #305.

[3] *MS Wood Diaries 3*, folio 17 verso.

[4] *MS Wood Diaries 3*, folio 19 verso = CSC #288; *MS Tanner 102, Part 1*, folio 32 recto = CSC #289. The incident was also reported in several newspapers of the time, including *The Loyall Scout* (Friday, July 29 to Friday, August 5, 1659): page 120); *The Weekly Post* (Tuesday August 2, to Tuesday August 9, 1659): page 116) = CSC #290. A similar panic was reported as taking place in Tiverton in Devon on 25 July 1659 in *The Loyall Scout* (Friday, July 22 to Friday, July 19, 1659): page 108; *The Publick Intelligencer*, No. 187 (Monday, July 25 to Monday, August 1, 1659): page 617.

Anabaptists & phanaticks'.[1] Like other fellow Baptists in the city, King was named as one of the insurrectionists in the so-called 'Presbyterian Sham-plot' of 1661 (see pages 43-4 above). Throughout the turbulent 1660s Dissenters like King were regarded as troublemakers, and King was regularly called to give an account of himself before both civil and ecclesiastical authorities in Oxford.

3. Petty Session Court Records

The very first record of Lawrence King appearing before the Oxford courts demonstrates something of the fear of violent revolution which was thought by many to be a masterplan being orchestrated by fanatical 'Anabaptists' up and down the land. As noted above (page 47 above), the Oxford Petty Sessions court records for 4 October 1660 mention King, alongside Richard Tidmarsh, in connection with an incident involving a man named William Robins who was charged with sedition and hiding illegal arms. Also noted above was King's appearance before the court on 9 January 1662 as one of four members of the Baptist conventicle charged with being 'seditious sectaryes and disloyal persons'.

Other instances of King's indictment before the Petty Sessions court are extant. On 15 January 1663 King, together with John Toms senior, Edward Wyans senior, Richard Quelch junior, and James Jennings, appeared before the Petty Sessions court on the indictment that he had attended an unlawful conventicle. The men were all fined 10s each for their misconduct in this regard, the money being collected 'to ye use of the howse of Common'.[2] At the same Petty Sessions three of the five (King, Quelch, and Jennings) were additionally fined by the court for 'refusing the Oath of Allegience' demanded of them by the officers of the court.[3]

Interestingly, the question of the taking of oaths was one of the issues debated by the various messengers of the fifteen Baptist churches attending the Association meetings held four years earlier on 14-15 September 1658. It is to be recalled that Lawrence King was the sole messenger sent from the church in Oxford to these meetings. The matter of oaths was raised by the church in Kingston:

[From the] church of Kingston.
[Query]. Whether saints in gospell dayes may lawfully take an oath before a magistrate yea or no. And, if it be judged by any that they may, we desire to know in what cases and in what forms, with reasons and grounds from Scripture.
A[nswer]. In some cases we conceive it may be lawfull solemnly to call God to witnesse to the truth of an action or expression and that this may be done before a magistrate, which is accepted as, and usually termed, an oath, Heb[rews] 6.16,

---

[1] *MS Tanner 102, Part 2*, folio 80 recto.
[2] *Oxford Petty Sessions Roll – 1656-1678* (O.5.11), folio 49 verso = CSC #366.
[3] *Oxford Petty Sessions Roll – 1656-1678* (O.5.11), folio 49 verso = CSC #367.

Ro[mans] 9.1, 2 Cor[inthians] 1.23. That of James 5.12 we beleeve to be of the like purpose with that of Matt[hew] 5.34 and considering the time when the Lord gave the direction, we conclude that no part of the Law was then abrogated and particularly that Ex[odus] 22.10,11, Deut[eronomy] 6.13 and ch[apter] 10.20 remained still in force.[1]

In short, the swearing of oaths was considered by the Baptist messengers as something acceptable for Christians to do – *under certain circumstances*. Assuming that Lawrence King agreed with this opinion, it means that he would have no qualms about swearing of oaths as a general rule. However, the Petty Sessions court records of 20 March 1663 suggest that for Lawrence King and his four fellow conventiclers oaths of political allegiance to the king were a different matter altogether. Oaths of this nature fell outside the bounds of what was permitted to be sworn before a magistrate.

The passing of *The Conventicle Act* in July 1664 brought a fresh legal basis upon which Dissenters could be suppressed by the prevailing religious authorities. The Act was specifically brought in as an attempt to offer 'Remedies against the growing and dangerous Practices of Seditious Sectaries, and other disloyal persons, who under pretence of Tender Consciences, do at their Meetings contrive Insurrections' (see Appendix E). The restrictions imposed by the Act were severe (meetings of more than five persons were declared illegal), and the financial penalties heavy (fines ranging from £5 for the first offence to transportation to the colonies for the third). Lawrence King and his fellow Dissenters in Oxford were to fall foul of the stipulations of the Act, as can readily be seen in some of the surviving civil and ecclesiastical court records. However, in many respects *The Conventicle Act* was a rather blunt and double-edged instrument with which to assert the supremacy of the established Church of England. For one thing, it was difficult to prove someone guilty of attendance at an illegal conventicle. As Roger Thomas remarks:

> The Conventicle Act depended for its effectiveness on the use of informers; and, if an informer so much as tripped in some particular in his accusation, he might find himself charged with perjury, and then it would be the informer and not his victim who found himself in gaol. Confronted with such discouragements in attacking Dissenters the pursuers resorted more and more to certain old Elizabethan statutes that imposed penalties, including heavy fines, for non-attendance at church.[2]

Nevertheless, fears about the growing number and size of illegal meetings of Dissenters within Oxford prompted the City Council to take action. The Hilary term Petty Sessions court record for 14 January 1664 warned that 'diverse Quakers Anabaptists & other seditious sectaryes doe frequently on the Lords Day riotously & unlawfully assemble themselves togeather in great numbers

---

[1] *AARB*, folio 35 verso–36 recto = White (1972): 187.
[2] Thomas (1962): 222-3.

in many places w[i]th in this Citie'. Bailiffs were ordered to take whatever means was necessary to disturb these 'unlawful assemblies' and to apprehend any conventiclers that they could.[1]   Occasionally, the paranoia about illegal conventicles resulted in some rather humorous incidents involving innocent members of the public, such as a night-time raid on a warehouse of the bookseller Richard Davies in December of 1663.   It seems that some over-zealous and slightly inebriated students thought they had stumbled upon an illegal conventicle when they heard the couple speaking through a window, and promptly fetched the authorities.   When the door was broken down and the house entered the couple were found sorting out books in preparation for a London sale – apparently the students 'listning under the window, heard Davies say to his wife O the bible! I had almost forgot ye bible, which made them verily suspect there had bin a conventicle.'[2]

King is mentioned in the Petty Sessions court records for 14 April 1664, where he and two of the same Dissenting colleagues (Richard Quelch junior and Edward Wyans senior) were indicted for 'not rep[air]ing to Church for Four Sondayes'.[3]   The quandary about what to do with illegal conventiclers continued to occupy the civic courts for several years, although stamping out Dissent proved difficult. A good example of this is found in an entry within the records of the Oxford Petty Sessions court dated 22 April 1669.[4]   While the entry attempts to encourage the constables of the city to suppress conventicles, it also gives details of penalties they will incur if they fail to pursue their duty with diligence.   This suggests that there was some reluctance on the part of some constables to implement the orders of the court.

Nevertheless, illegal conventiclers continued to be indicted to appear before the Petty Sessions court and answer for their religious activities. Thus a group of eight conventiclers appeared before the court on 7 October 1669, having been indicted during the Easter sessions for attending an illegal conventicle.[5] This group of eight included Ralph Austen (with whom King had been indicted for sedition some years before on 9 January 1662), John Sheene (under whom King had served his apprenticeship as a glover), and Abraham Davies (the husband of a teacher who, as we shall see, later got into trouble for teaching at a conventicle held in King's house).   The eight appeared later in the Petty Sessions court on 7 April 1670 where they threw themselves on the favour of the court and were fined.[6]

Similarly, a group of five Dissenters are mentioned in the records for 13 January 1670, again charged with being at an unlawful conventicle; this group,

---

[1] *Oxford Petty Sessions Roll – 1656-1678* (O.5.11), folio 62 recto = CSC #389a.
[2] *MS Wood Diaries 7*, folio 36.
[3] *Oxford Petty Sessions Roll – 1656-1678* (O.5.11), folio 66 verso = CSC #392.
[4] *Oxford Petty Sessions Roll – 1656-1678* (O.5.11), folio 108 verso = CSC #467.
[5] *Oxford Petty Sessions Roll – 1656-1678* (O.5.11), folio 112 recto.
[6] *Oxford Petty Sessions Roll – 1656-1678* (O.5.11), folio 115 recto = CSC #483. Also included within the eight was Walter Cave Junior, the brother-in-law of Abraham Davies.

which included Richard Tidmarsh, John Toms senior and John Higgins, almost certainly constituted a meeting of the Baptist conventiclers at the house of Lawrence King in the High Street.[1] King was himself indicted to appear before the court on 7 April 1670; this time the charge was his failure to attend his local parish church and he was fined 4*s* for the infraction.[2]

Interestingly, within the surviving documents Peter Mews, the Vice-Chancellor of the University, makes an unusual appearance in connection with the suppression of Dissenters such as King. This is contained within the Petty Sessions court records for 6 October 1670, where it is stated that Mews officially handed over to the court monies levied in fines upon the illegal conventiclers. Mews does so by virtue of his being one of the Justices of the Peace of the city, and as such was presiding over the court sessions. The amount collected is stated to be £7 10*s*, a substantial sum for the time.[3] More importantly, Mews was thereby ingratiating himself to Charles II, for a healthy percentage of money gleaned by such fines went to the crown. No doubt this was political toadyism at some level, for Mews had earlier in the year been the object of praise and encouragement by Charles II and the Privy Council for his eagerness to stamp out such conventicles in Oxford (more on this below).

4. *Ecclesiastical Court Records (1662-1670)*

Records of King's numerous clashes with ecclesiastical courts are extant; frequently he is cited along with 'his wife [blank], of the same parish'. It is significant that King's wife, Anne, has such a prominent role alongside him in these ecclesiastical confrontations, even though she is never cited by name and no record of her formal excommunication from the parish of All Souls exists.

The Act of Uniformity, requiring assent to the *Book of Common Prayer*, was passed on 24 August 1662 and formed the basis of a systematic crack-down on all Dissenters. A number of Baptists within Oxford were targeted in the months prior to its becoming law. Several people attending a Baptist conventicle were cited to appear in the Diocesan court on 28 June 1662; these included Ralph Austen, Edward Wyans senior, Thomas Tisdale, and Lawrence King and his wife.[4] This record sets the scene for the dispute between Lawrence and Anne King and their parish church, a conflict no doubt exacerbated by the fact that the couple lived immediately opposite the church on the other side of the High Street and were thus high-profile Dissenters. The court record states that, although he appeared before the court, King refused to

---

[1] *Oxford Petty Sessions Roll – 1656-1678* (O.5.11), folio 114 recto = CSC #480. Confirmation that this meeting took place on Sunday, 9 January 1670 at the house of Lawrence King comes in SP 29/272, folios 76 recto-75 verso) (see page 129 below).

[2] *Oxford Petty Sessions Roll – 1656-1678* (O.5.11), folio 115 verso = CSC #484.

[3] *Oxford Petty Sessions Roll – 1656-1678* (O.5.11), folio 119 verso = CSC #490.

[4] *ODR: 1 February 1660 – 4 October 1662* (c. 3) folios 29 recto, 29 verso, and 30 recto.

respond to the charges that were laid against him.[1] Subsequent court dates for all of them were made, with King and his wife being cited to appear on three further Saturdays during the following month, namely on 5, 19 and 26 July 1662.[2] Four further records from 1662 are also extant, with King cited to appear on his own on 8 and 15 November and on 6 and 13 December.[3] The record from 8 November is the fullest of these four later entries and gives details of King's response to the charges made by the church wardens against him. It states that 'he [King] doth not goe to Church to heare Divine service, for he sayeth hee doth not conceive hee is bound thereto by the Lawe of God'.[4] King was ordered by the court to attend both morning and evening services on the next day, a Sunday, and to produce a certificate that he had done so. He was told that failure to do so meant that excommunication proceedings might be set in motion against him. King returned a week later (15 November) and was told by the court 'to conferre with some learned divine and to conforme himselfe to the Church Discipline'.[5]

The records for 1662 set up a formal censure of King by the relevant ecclesiastical authorities, instituted through a court-appointed official named Richard Witt.[6] Eventually this resulted in the production of a formal deposition against King by the local parish officials. This three-page document is dated toward the end of 1662, probably after the passing of the *Act of Uniformity*, and represents the culmination of the legal proceedings against him up to this point. It gives a record of the Consistory Court's charges against King and calls upon him to give reasons for his failure to attend his local parish church services during 1661-1662.[7] However, despite the formal deposition King continued his life as active Dissenter, attending illegal conventicles, and refusing to attend the Church of England services.

Not surprisingly, King continued to be mentioned regularly in the records of the Saturday Diocesan court sessions during the years 1664-1669. In the Diocesan court records for 23 and 30 July 1664 his failure to conform to the Church of England was again noted and his case bound over to the next session of the court.[8] King and his wife are mentioned eight times for various offences within the Oxford Diocesan records for the year 1665. The first of these is

---

[1] *ODR: 1 February 1660 – 4 October 1662* (c. 3) folio 29 verso = CSC #345.

[2] *ODR: 1 February 1660 – 4 October 1662* (c. 3) folios 32 recto, 35 verso, and 38 verso.

[3] *ODR: 27 September 1662-15 April 1665* (c. 4), folios 29 recto, 36 recto, 51 verso and 57 verso.

[4] *ODR: 27 September 1662-15 April 1665* (c. 4), folio 29 recto = CSC #354.

[5] *ODR: 27 September 1662-15 April 1665* (c. 4), folio 36 recto = CSC #356.

[6] He is named in the record for 26 July 1662 (*ODR: 1 February 1660 – 4 October 1662* (c. 3) folio 38 verso = CSC #352).

[7] *OAR: Allegations and Depositions – 1621-1672* (c. 175), folios 141 recto & verso and 142 recto = CSC #361.

[8] *ODR: 27 September 1662 – 15 April 1665* (c. 4), folios 214 recto and 222 recto. The entry for 23 July notes that King was cited by the apparitor to appear before the court two days earlier on 21 July 1664.

dated 29 April 1665 where King offered what to his interrogators must have been a frustrating reply to the query about his church attendance. The record noted that King said 'he doth goe to Church, but being Interrogated whither he gooeth to divine Service & Sermons, refused to give any answer thereunto'. [1] King appeared again before the court a week later on 6 May 1665; once again he appeared without his wife Anne alongside him. [2]

The case against Lawrence and Anne King featured in the court records for the sessions held four weeks later on 3 June 1665; here an abbreviated entry was made noting that the case against the couple was held over to the next week's session. [3] The fourth time his name appears in these records is the entry for 10 June 1665, where the entry is headed by the explanatory note 'For not coming to Church'. Once again King appeared on his own, and because she did not appear, Anne was pronounced 'contumacious' by the court with penalty being reserved 'out of grace' until the next session of the court. [4] The court's decision to reserve imposing a penalty may indicate a reluctance to pronounce judgement on wives in this way. The court records for 17 June 1665 have an abbreviated entry for King and his wife in which the dispute between the couple and the church wardens was rehearsed. Interestingly, an entry from 21 June records that Anne appeared before the court in her own right and, when challenged about her failure to attend her local parish, she stated that 'shee us not satisfied in her own Conscience touching the matter'. [5] Anne petitioned that more time be granted her, which the court did, although it made conditions, notably that she consult with 'some Learned & Orthodox Divine of the Church of Engl[an]d' and her attendance at her local church before the next Feast of Saint Michael. The next appearance of Lawrence King within the Diocesan records for 1665 took place two days later in the final days of the court session. Thus, there is a brief mention within the records for Friday, 23 June 1665 in which the basic accusations made against him hitherto were repeated; reference to Anne within this particular entry is dropped. The record concludes with an explanatory note to '*Vide in fine huius Curie* (See at the end of this Court)'. [6] The records of the next day, Saturday, 24 June 1665, offer something of a resolution to his case; once again specific reference to Anne is dropped, suggesting that her case had been dealt with during the session held on 21 June. [7] The same terms and conditions granted to Anne were applied to his case.

On 21 July 1666 Lawrence King and his wife were again cited to appear before the Diocesan court officials to answer charges made against them by the church wardens of All Saints' parish. In this case King appeared on his own

---

[1] *ODR: 15 October 1664 – 30 September 1665* (d. 12), folio 144 recto = CSC #406.

[2] *ODR: 15 October 1664 – 30 September 1665* (d. 12), folio 155 recto = CSC #407.

[3] *ODR: 15 October 1664 – 30 September 1665* (d. 12) folio 169 verso.

[4] *ODR: 15 October 1664 – 30 September 1665* (d. 12) folio 182 recto = CSC #410.

[5] *ODR: 15 October 1664 – 30 September 1665* (d. 12) folio 198 verso = CSC #414.

[6] *ODR: 15 October 1664 – 30 September 1665* (d. 12) folio 205 verso.

[7] *ODR: 15 October 1664–30 September 1665* (d. 12), folio 210 verso = CSC #415.

before Dr Alworth, the Bishop of Oxford's Vicar General.[1] On 26 January 1667 he was again cited by the apparator, John Brees, to appear in court. King failed to appear and, like his wife, was pronounced 'contumacious'.[2] Both King and his wife are named within the court records dated 30 March 1667 as members of a group of fourteen Dissenters in Oxfordshire who were required by the court to certify their attendance at the local parish church at the forthcoming Easter services. Four people from Oxford were listed in this regard: Lawrence King and his wife (Anne), John Toms senior and Richard Tidmarsh.[3] Moreover, King and his wife are twice mentioned in the court proceedings for 1667 (22 June and 6 July).[4] Meanwhile King also appears on his own in records for the Diocesan court sessions held on 18 January 1668; 8 February 1668; 15 February 1668; 29 February 1668, 7 March 1668, and 14 March 1668.[5] There are eight such records relating to Lawrence King for the Archdeaconry court for 1668 (6, 13, 20 and 27 June; 4, 11 and 18 July; 10 October);[6] King was listed, together with three other people from the parish of All Saints', in a further nine records for the Archdeaconry court (17, 24 and 31 October; 7, 14, 21 and 28 November; and 5 and 12 December).[7] Within these last nine records King was listed in a combined entry together with John Toms senior, James Jennings, and Ellinor Seale, the wife of Martin Seale;[8] the unified

---

[1] *ODR: 23 June 1666–22 January 1670* (c. 9), folio 40 verso = CSC #430.

[2] *ODR: 7 October 1665–7 March 1668* (c. 5), folio 176 recto = CSC #436.

[3] *ODR: 7 October 1665–7 March 1668* (c. 5), folio 226 recto.

[4] *OAR: 11 May 1667–21 July 1669* (c. 17), folios 28 verso, 37 recto.

[5] *ODR: 7 October 1665–7 March 1668* (c. 5), folios 263 recto, 265 recto, 272 recto, 278 verso and 284 verso; *OAR: 11 May 1667–21 July 1669* (c. 17), folio vii recto.

[6] *OAR: 11 May 1667–21 July 1669* (c. 17), folios 109 verso, 118 verso, 128 verso, 137 verso, 148 recto, 159 verso, 170 verso, and 180 verso.

[7] *OAR: 11 May 1667–21 July 1669* (c. 17), folios 187 recto, 194 recto, 201 recto, 207 verso, 214 recto, 221 recto, 227 verso, 234 recto and 240 recto.

[8] Ellinor Seale had been a Dissenter for several years; she appeared before the Petty Sessions court on 15 January 1662 where she was fined 4s 'for not going to divine service for fower Sundays past' (*Oxford Petty Sessions Roll – 1656-1678* (O.5.11), folio 49 recto). In addition to the citations alongside King, Toms and Jennings during 1668, Ellinor Seale is also individually named in 95 other ecclesiastical court records for the years 1667-1671. These are dated 22 June; 6, 13, 20 and 27 July; 9, 16, and 23 November; 7 and 14 December 1667; 1 February; 6, 13, 20 and 27 June; 4, 11 and 18 July; and 10 October 1668; 16 and 23 January; 6, 13, and 27 February; 13, 20 and 27 March; 3 April; 8, and 15 May; 12, 19 and 26 June; 3, 17, 24 and 31 July 1669; 16 and 30 October; 6, 13, 20 and 27 November; 4, 11 and 18 December 1669; 15, 22 and 29 January; 5, 19 and 26 February; 5, 19 and 26 March; 23 and 30 April; 7 May; 4, 18 and 25 June; 2, 9, 16, 23 and 30 July; 15, 22 and 29 October; 12, 19 and 26 November; 3, 10 and 17 December 1670; 14, 21 and 28 January; 4, 11 18 and 25 February; 4, 11 and 18 March; 1, 8, and 15 April; 20 and 27 May; 3 June; 15, 22 and 29 July; 14 October 1671 (*OAR: 11 May 1667–21 July 1669* (c. 17), folios 28 verso, 37 recto, 43 recto, 48 recto, 54 recto, 58 verso, 62 verso, 65 verso, 68 verso, 71 verso, 74 verso, 116 verso, 118 verso, 128 verso, 138 recto, 148 verso, 159 verso, 170 verso, 180 verso, 246 recto, 249 verso, 252 verso, 255 verso, 258 verso, 261 verso, 263 verso, 265 verso, 268 recto,

270 verso, 273 recto, 276 recto, 279 verso, 283 recto, 286 verso, 291 recto; *OAR: 24 July 1669-July 1672* (c. 19), folios 4 recto, 9 verso, 17 recto, 21 recto, 24 verso, 28 verso, 31 verso, 35 verso, 38 verso, 41 recto, 43 verso, 46 verso, 48 verso, 50 verso, 52 verso, 54 verso, 56 verso, 58 verso, 61 verso, 63 verso, 66 recto, 67 recto, 68 recto, 69 recto, 70 verso, 73 verso, 76 recto, 79 recto, 82 verso, 86 verso, 90 verso, 96 recto, 98 verso 101 recto, 103 verso, 106 recto, 108 verso, 110 verso, 112 verso, 114 verso, 116 verso, 118 verso, 120 verso, 122 verso, 124 verso, 126 verso, 128 verso, 130 verso, 132 verso, 134 verso, 136 verso, 139 recto, 140 verso, 142 verso, 144 verso, 146 recto, 147 verso, 150 verso, 154 verso, 161 verso). The record for 14 October 1671 shows that the patience of the court was finally exhausted with Ellinor, and it declared her excommunicated ('*Dec[revi]t exco[mmu]n[i]can[dam]*'). She is also listed in an excommunication decree dated 29 January 1679 (*ODR: Excommunications – 1633-1791* (c. 99), folio 226 recto), and in a ecclesiastical court citation dated 9 June 1680 (*ODR: Miscellaneous Citations* (c. 62), folio 39 recto). Like Edward Wyans senior and John Toms senior, her husband Martin Seale was a cordwainer by trade. He was apprenticed to John Bannister on 31 July 1635 (*MS Morrell 23 – List of Cordwainers' Apprentices (1590-1660)*, folio 75 recto; *Civic Enrolments – 1613-1640* (L.5.2), folio 271 verso). Seale was admitted into the Guild of Cordwainers on 16 October 1647 (*MS Morrell 14 – Minutes of Meetings of the Guild of Cordwayners (1614-1711)*, folio 49 verso), and was granted his 'Freedom of the City' on 30 September 1648 (*Civic Enrolments – 1639-1662* (L.5.3), folio 251 verso). There is record of him taking on several apprentices, including Edmond Parsons on 17 October 1648 (*MS Morrell 23 – List of Cordwainers' Apprentices (1590-1660)*, folio 86 recto; *Civic Enrolments – 1639-1662* (L.5.3), folio 78 recto), Thomas Vaughan on 2 February 1653 (*MS Morrell 23 – List of Cordwainers' Apprentices (1590-1660)*, folio 89 verso; *Civic Enrolments – 1639-1662* (L.5.3), folio 117 verso), John Stiles from Cumnor on 4 April 1659 (*MS Morrell 23 – List of Cordwainers' Apprentices (1590-1660)*, folio 93 verso; *Civic Enrolments – 1639-1662* (L.5.3), folio 173 recto), John Evans on 8 June 1664, who went on to become a citizen of the city on 14 July 1671 (*Civic Enrolments – 1662-1699* (L.5.4), pages 36 and 685; *Husting and Mayors Courts – 1666-1672* (M.4.6), folio 170 verso (Mayors), John Greeneway on 12 December 1668, an apprenticeship which was transferred to Henry White on 29 June 1674 (*Civic Enrolments – 1662-1699* (L.5.4), page 131), and John Deverell on 28 August 1671, an apprenticeship which was transferred to Thomas Hanns on 5 June 1674 (*Civic Enrolments – 1662-1699* (L.5.4), page 187). Seale rose steadily through the ranks of the guild, and was granted a warden's place on 5 October 1652 (*MS Morrell 14 – Minutes of Meetings of the Guild of Cordwayners (1614-1711)*, folio 54 verso), and was granted a master's place on 20 October 1667 (*MS Morrell 14 – Minutes of Meetings of the Guild of Cordwayners (1614-1711)*, folio 83 recto; *MS Morrell 12 - Gylde of Cordwayners (1648-1758)*, folio 49 recto). Seale was twice elected one of the four keykeepers of the guild, first on 25 October 1652 and then on 24 October 1670 (*MS Morrell 12 - Gylde of Cordwayners (1648-1758)*, folios 14 recto and 55 recto). He died and was buried on 1 April 1674 (*Parish Register of All Saints' – 1559-1810* (Par 189/1/R1/1), folio 99 recto). Martin and his wife Ellinor had four children: a daughter Sarah who was baptized on 29 August 1651, a daughter Ellinor who was baptized on 13 August 1659, a son Martin who was baptized on 22 February 1662, and a daughter Elizabeth who died and was baptized in April of 1666 (*Parish Register of All Saints' – 1559-1810* (Par 189/1/R1/1), folios 22 recto, 28 recto, 25 verso, and 96 recto). The son Martin agreed an apprenticeship with the cordwainer Thomas Nicholls on 7 June 1678 (*Civic Enrolments*

entry suggests that the four all belong to the same conventicle. Most of these records from 1667-1668 are simply notices of their cases being bound over to the next court session, presumably because the defendants failed to appear. The overall impression is that the courts were in a quandary as to how to deal with the kind of intransigence exhibited by Lawrence and Anne King and their fellow Dissenters. The entry dated 12 December 1668 shows the court patience of the court ran out, as the presiding official pronounced King and his colleagues John Toms senior and James Jennings contumacious and declared that they should be excommunicated.[1]

Matters soon came to a head for King on 7 January 1669 when the formal declaration of his excommunication from the Church of England was issued to him.[2] As noted above (page 36), Richard Tidmarsh was also formally excommunicated from the Church of England on the same day, both orders being written at the same time and in the same hand. As required by law, King's excommunication order was publicly read out in the local parish church, in this case the church of St Mary the Virgin, on 17 April 1670.[3]

All indications are that Lawrence King's brother Thomas also become an active Dissenter while living in the parish of St Peter-in-the-Bailey. There are seven records from 1664 of him being cited to appear before the Diocesan court (dated 10, 18 and 25 June and 2, 16, 23 and 30 July),[4] and three such records from 1665 (dated 17 and 23 June, and 1 July).[5] There is also record of his excommunication from the Church of England on 1 July 1665;[6] this excommunication document is a joint declaration covering King and Thomas Mason, with whom he probably shared a house.[7] This is an intriguing

---

– *1662-1699* (L.5.4), page 258). Ellinor Seale made a will dated 21 October 1680 which was probated on 19 February 1681 (*Ellinor Seale* (OWPR 149/9/19)).

[1] *OAR: 11 May 1667–21 July 1669* (c. 17), folio 240 recto = CSC #459.

[2] *OAR: Excommunications – 1610-1783* (c. 121), folio 294 recto CSC #461.

[3] Ironically, King had been forced to attend Sunday services at this church just three months before on 9 January 1670 (see page 129 below).

[4] *ODR: 27 September 1662-15 April 1665* (c. 4), folios 180 verso, 186 recto, 191 verso, 197 recto, 205 recto, 213 recto, and 221 recto.

[5] *ODR: 15 October 1664 – 30 September 1665* (d. 12) folios 196 recto, 208 verso and 220 verso.

[6] *ODR: Excommunication Schedules – 1662-1667* (c. 100), folio 149 recto = CSC #418. The excommunication is elsewhere said to be 'for not duely rep[air]ing to Church' (*ODR: Excommunications – 1633-1791* (c. 99), folios 243 verso). His name appears in *MS Morrell 6 – Election and Order Book of the Company of Taylors (1572-1711)* in the lists for 1661 (folio 173 verso).

[7] See CSC #544 for the probable location of this property in David Loggan's *Oxonia Illustrata* (1675). There are records of King paying 4*s* on a four-hearth property in the Hearth Tax of Michaelmas 1662 (*Hearth Tax of August-November 1662* (E 179/255/4), Part 2, page 69), and of Mason being relieved of the responsibility of paying for one hearth on the grounds of poverty (*Hearth Tax of August-November 1662* (E 179/255/4), Part 2, page 68). The payments for Michaelmas 1665 and Lady Day 1665 show King as sharing the property in St Peter-in-the-Bailey with Thomas Mason (*Hearth Tax of Michaelmas 1665* (E 179/164/513), membrane 28 verso; *Hearth Tax of*

connection, given that Thomas King's brother Lawrence supported Thomas Mason in a court action in 1669 when Mason was accused of illegally trading as a glover (see page 115, note 1 above). The excommunication order testifies to King's lack of integration into parish church life, although his excommunication also needs to be set against the intriguing record of his appointment as an 'Overseer of the Poor' in the spring of 1666.[1] In any event, it appears that Thomas King briefly left Oxford in the face of his excommunication; there is no record of him in the Poll Tax of 1667, nor in the Subsidy Tax of 1667. He appears himself to have returned to Oxford some time in the 1670s, re-establishing his friendship with Thomas Mason. Thus, King and Mason appear in a document from October 1679 which lists them as two of five Dissenters within the parish of St Peter-in-the-Bailey who were not attending their local parish church.[2] Other occasional glimpses of King appear

---

24 April 1666 (E 179/164/514), membrane 23 verso). It looks as if Mason and his wife Emma then and took over the property on their own, for the Poll Tax of 1667 shows him and his wife paying 2*s* in tax (*Poll Tax of 1667* (P.5.7), folio 43 verso). Apparently the couple lived in the property for a number of years, for Mason is mentioned in a Balliol College lease document dated 27 April 1676 (see Salter (1913): 178, 350-351, for details). Interestingly, the document mentions that the mercer Thomas Tisdale, a fellow Dissenter, rented a plot of ground adjoining. Another Dissenter, Ralph Austen, lived in a property immediately to the west. A Thomas Mason of St Michael's parish is known to have paid 1*s* 6*d* in the Lay Subsidy of 23 June 1647 (*Lay Subsidy of 23 June 1647* (E 179/164/498), membrane 2), and 1*s* in the Lay Subsidy of 17 March 1648 (*Lay Subsidy of 17 March 1648* (E 179/164/499), membrane 3), although this is probably a different person.

[1] *Husting and Mayor's Court 1662; Licenses and Overseers* (N.4.3), folio 39 recto = CSC #425.

[2] *OAR: Returns of Recusants – 1679-1706* (c. 430), folio 41 verso = CSC #589. Mason and his wife Emma also appear in a number of other ecclesiastical court documents from 1662, including those dated 28 June, 5, 19 and 26 July (*ODR: 1 February 1660 – 4 October 1662* (c. 3) folios 29 recto, 31 verso, 35 recto and 38 verso). These indictments culminated in the excommunication of both Thomas and Emma Mason on 26 July 1662; the reason given is 'for absenting from prayers & sermons for ye yeare paste & neglecting Min[inister's] dues & baptism of his childe & for impious speeches by the s[ai]d Tho[mas] touching ye Sacram[en]t' (*ODR: Excommunications – 1633-1791* (c. 99), folios 238 recto).

Despite this censure Thomas Mason continued to be an active Dissenter, and two other excommunication orders were issued against him: the first on 23 July 1664, and the second (as noted above) on 1 July 1665, which covered him and Thomas King (*ODR: Excommunications – 1633-1791* (c. 99), folios 242 recto and 243 verso = CSC #423). Mason also appears in a number of other documents, including those dated 17 and 23 June, 1 July 1665 (*ODR: 15 October 1664–30 September 1665* (d. 12) folios 196 verso, 208 verso, 221 recto), and those dated 18 January, 8, 15, and 29 February, 7 and 14 March 1668 (*ODR: 7 October 1665–7 March 1668* (c. 5), folios 263 recto, 265 recto, 272 recto, 278 verso, 284 verso; *OAR: 11 May 1667–21 July 1669* (c. 17), folio vii recto). He died and was buried on 15 May 1687 (*Parish Register of St Peter-in-the-Bailey – 1659-1689* (Par 214/1/R1/2), folio 48 recto); his widow Emma died and was buried less than two months later on 7 July 1687 (*Parish Register of St Peter-in-the-*

in the surviving sources. He was still in the parish in 1692 and made several payments in the Poll Taxes of 1692-1695.[1] Thomas King died and was buried 28 June 1702; his wife died and was buried a few months earlier on 9 March 1702.[2] Their son Thomas King junior also appears to have been active as a Dissenter while living in the parish of St Thomas; there is a record dated 2 July 1693 of him being excommunicated from the Church of England.[3] This is all the more tantalizing, given the reputation of his uncle, Lawrence King, as a Dissenter and his association with Richard Tidmarsh of the parish of St Thomas; it raises the possibility that Thomas King junior may have helped pick up the Dissenters' cause in the parish once Tidmarsh, who had been active there for so long, had left Oxford. Unfortunately, no other records of his activities as a Dissenter in the parish are extant. Thomas King junior died and was buried in the parish church of St Michael's on 10 May 1711; the parish register entry specifically notes that he was from the parish of St Thomas, suggesting that special arrangements had been made for the burial in an adjoining parish.[4]

5. State Papers of Charles II (1670)

As an important Baptist leader within Oxford, Lawrence King would have naturally come to the attention of those within the city and the University who saw it as their duty to stamp out Dissent and contain the unlawful conventicles. One of the key establishment figures attempting to do just that was Peter Mews, the President of St John's College. It is not surprising to find that King and Mews clashed over the question of religious worship. Mews was certainly no scholar (the only thing of substance that he ever wrote was a short piece on *The Ex-ale-tation of Ale* in 1663), but what he lacked in intellectual abilities was

---

Bailey – 1659-1689 (Par 214/1/R1/2), folio 47 verso).

[1] *Taxes – 1691-1694* (P.5.9), folios 37 verso, 73 verso, 120 recto, 146 verso.

[2] *Parish Register of St Peter-in-the-Bailey 1684-1742* (Par 214/1/R1/3), folios 64 verso and 64 recto.

[3] *ODR: Excommunication Schedules – 1633-1791* (c. 99), folio 117 recto = CSC #655. The excommunication was publically read out by Jonas Proast, one-time chaplain of All Souls, who is best known for his three critiques of John Locke's *A Letter Concerning Toleration* (1689). Anthony Wood relates that he was expelled by Leopold Finch, the warden of All Souls, on 3 April 1688 for failing to support him in his bid to have the Camden History Professorship conferred upon him (*MS Wood Diaries 32*, page 26). He also tells us that Proast was restored to his chaplaincy by the Archbishop of Canterbury in 1693 (*MS Wood Diaries 36*, folio 61 verso). In 1693 Finch published his version of the removal of Proast from the chaplaincy in a pamphlet entitled *The Case of Mr Jonas Proast*. See Clark (1894): 4.263; Goldie (1991): 362-368; Schochet (1992): 153; Vernon (1993): 95-106, for more on Proast

[4] *Parish Register of St Michael-at-the-Northgate – 1683-1736* (Par 211/1/R1/3), page 95. Interestingly, both Lawrence King and Thomas King junior were buried in the parish of St Michael while Jonathan King, Lawrence's son, lived there. Perhaps Jonathan King was responsible for the burial arrangements.

more than compensated for by boundless energy and enthusiasm, especially when it came to strengthening the Anglican church against what he felt to be her detractors.[1] Mews's obsession with Dissenters meeting in secret conclaves bordered on paranoia, particularly after he became Vice-Chancellor of the University in 1669.[2] Indeed, news of his activism in suppressing the conventicles in Oxford reached the court of Charles II, and the Privy Council wrote him a letter on 31 December 1669 encouraging him to keep up the good work.[3] The Privy Council declared that they were 'much satisfied with the vigilancy' with which Mews had acted, exhorting him 'to continue a Watchfull Eye for suppressing the groweth of all Scismaticall meetings of the like nature in that your University'. This Mews undoubtedly endeavoured to do, which brought him into direct contact with a number of illegal conventicles, including one meeting at King's house on 9 January 1670. This was all reported to the Privy Council, who once again wrote a letter on 13 January 1670 praising Mews for his sterling efforts.[4] Apparently Mews had broken up the meeting at King's house and forced him and 'another of the Chiefs', presumably Richard Tidmarsh, to attend Anglican services at the University Church of St Mary the Virgin as a punishment. Unfortunately, there is no record of the Dissenters' reaction to this punishment, and if the pair's continuation in illegal activities is anything to go by, their being brought to religious conformity by this means was a forlorn hope on Mews's part.

The Privy Council letter of 13 January 1670 also contains an interesting note about 'Mrs. Davies y^t teaches younge women, being one in ye former Conventicles'. Almost certainly she was the wife of Captain Abraham Davies, who was specifically identified as a ringleader of Dissent in the Privy Council letter to Mews in 1669.[5] Davies himself had an earlier encounter with the

---

[1] Mews was fiercely royalist in sympathy. He served in the King's Army during the Civil War and was made a prisoner at the battle of Naseby. He was President of St John's 1667-1673; Bishop of Bath and Wells 1672-1684; Bishop of Winchester 1684-1706. Mews was wounded in the battle of Sedgmoor in 1685 defending the cause of James II against the Duke of Monmouth (see Milne-Tyte (1989): 129-130). He was also a key figure in the final days of the reign of James II and served as a member of the Provisional Government of 11-28 December 1688 (see Beddard (1988): 49-50, 63-64).

[2] Anthony Wood in *Athenae Oxonienses* records that in January of 1672 Mews objected to the publication of the book entitled *Animadversions upon Sr Richard Baker's Chronicle* by Thomas Blount simply because the book suggested that the use of the term 'conventicle' was not a recent invention but went back to the days of Wycliffe (see Bliss (1813): 1.lxx, for details).

[3] *Privy Council Register – 1 October 1669–28 April 1671* (PC 2/62), page 92 = CSC #479.

[4] SP 29/272, folios 76 recto-75 verso = CSC #482. The incident is also discussed in *HMC 78 Hastings 2* (1930): 315-316.

[5] Mrs Davies was the daughter of Walter Cave junior (1602-1663), a brewer from St Aldate's who was elected mayor of Oxford in 1650. She and Abraham Davies had at least five children, whose names were Walter, Thomas, Katherine, John, and Cave

ecclesiastical authorities in March of 1663 who cited him for not attending his parish church in St Aldate's.[1] He appeared before the court on 19 March and admitted his non-attendance, saying that 'hee was not setled or resolved in his judgem[en]t of his conformity therein'. The court ordered him 'to frequent his p[ar]ish Church at time of divine service and sermons and to receive the holy Sacram[en]t from the hands of his Minister upon or before Whitsunday next'. It is uncertain if he obeyed the court's order, although he was appointed one of the 'Overseers of the Poor' for the parish in 1664.[2] Davies also appears in a number of court records from 1665 (29 April, 6 May, 3 and 10 June and 14 July).[3] The matter of his non-attendance was specifically addressed on 6 May 1665, where Davies was 'P[rese]nted as a Sectary for not duely rep[air]ing to his p[ar]ish Church to heare Divine service and Sermons'.[4] He denied the charge and the court ordered the churchwardens to produce evidence supporting their accusation. Within these same Hilary court sessions of 1665 Davies was also presented by the churchwardens for failing to have a child baptized. He also denied this charge, saying that the child, a son, had been baptized 'by A Minister Episcopally ordained', but he refused to reveal who the minister was.[5] The court ordered that he have the child re-baptized by the parish minister in front of the Saint Aldate's congregation and in accordance with the laws and rites of the Church of England. Davies failed to appear before the court on 10 June 1665 and was pronounced contumacious as a result.[6] Davies next appeared before the court in person on 14 July 1665 where he produced a certificate of baptism for the son, duly signed by the minister. He also admitted that he did not attend his parish church as required, but requested more time to consider the matter. The court exhorted him to go to his parish church, and required him to produce evidence that he had done so at the next Michaelmas court sessions, suspending all proceedings against him in the meantime.[7]

However, this was not the end of the Dissenting activity of the Davies family, as the letter from the Privy Council in 1669 demonstrates. This letter is the only time that Mrs Davies appears in connection with the Baptist Dissenters, assuming that the reference to her as 'being one in y^e former Conventicles' is in

---

(*PCC – Will of Walter Cave* (PROB 11/311), pages 197 verso-198 recto); the will was probated on 2 June 1663).

[1] *ODR: 27 September 1662-15 April 1665* (c. 4), folios 154 recto = CSC #370, 158 recto = CSC #371, and 161 verso.

[2] *Husting and Mayor's Court 1662; Licenses and Overseers* (N.4.3), folio 23 recto = CSC #391.

[3] *ODR: 15 October 1664-30 September 1665* (d. 12), folios 147 recto, 155 recto and verso, 170 recto, 182 verso, 244 verso and 245 recto.

[4] *ODR: 15 October 1664-30 September 1665* (d. 12), folio 155 verso = CSC #409.

[5] *ODR: 15 October 1664-30 September 1665* (d. 12), folio 155 recto = CSC #408.

[6] *Diocesan Records – 15 October 1664-30 September 1665* (d. 12), folio 182 verso = CSC #411.

[7] *ODR: 15 October 1664-30 September 1665* (d. 12), folios 244 verso and 245 recto = CSC #419.

fact an indication of her attendance at the meeting at King's house. If this
assumption is correct, then Mrs Davies' name can be added to the list of people
known to have been associated with the Baptist church in Oxford. In any
event, it seems clear from this that Mrs. Davies was exercising her gifts as a
teacher, and (apparently) was doing so in such a way as to advance the cause of
sexual equality, for she was teaching young women at a time when it was far
from socially acceptable so to do.[1] More important, at least as far as the
religious establishment was concerned, was the fact that she was teaching
without having been licensed by the religious authorities. The fact that the
Privy Council instructed Vice-Chancellor Mews to 'to pull down her Scoole &
not p[er]mit her to teach till a license from the B[isho]p of Oxon' had been
obtained suggests that her actions as a teacher were deemed just as dangerous
and socially undermining as her unlawful activity in attending the conventicles.
Indeed, her teaching young women may have been a constituent part of the life
of the conventicle she attended.[2]

Less we outrun ourselves and think that Baptists meeting at King's house
were on the cutting edge of the sexual revolution and were advocating equal
rites for men and women, we do well to recall a discussion that took place at
the Abingdon Association in March of 1658. There the question of how far,
and in what circumstances, a woman was allowed to speak or teach in public
were vigorously debated.[3] Not surprisingly, a number of qualifying conditions
were thought necessary before such activities should happen.

Under the auspices of the conventicles, such as those meeting at the Kings'
house, however, Mrs Davies appears to have found her calling, setting up a

---

[1] Fraser (1985): 132-57, discusses the educational opportunities open to women in
the 17th century. She notes that there was one boarding school for women in Oxford;
Thompson (1974): 190, states that there were two such schools. Also see Mendelson
and Crawford (1998): 321-7, and Keeble (2002): 183-205, for more on the role of
women and women teachers in the period. None of these writers specifically mentions
Mrs. Davies, or her school for young women. Teague (2000): 240-69, discusses the
philosophical debate about women's education which took place between such notable
writers as figures as John Milton, Samuel Hartlib and Bathsua Makin in the 17th
century.

[2] There is an intriguing record from 26 February 1664 involving an Anna Pierce
who was cited to appear before the ecclesiastical court to answer a case of dilapidation,
probably involving the parish church property in Eynsham where her late husband
(apparently)was the minister. She was personally cited by Abraham Lawrence, the
court apparitor, on 7 February 1664 'at the house of Abraham Davies in the p[ar]ish of
Saint Aldate' (*ODR: Citations 1662-1664* (c. 39), folio 103 recto and verso). Lawrence
also attempted to cite her at Abraham Davies's house on 24 June 1664 (*ODR: Citations
1664-1667* (c. 40), folio 16 recto and verso). This second citation notes that the home
of Abraham Davies house was 'her place of habitation'. Perhaps Anna Pierce was
attending or assisting with the school of Mrs Davies?

[3] *AARB*, folio 34 verso = White (1974): 184-185 = CSC #257. See Thomas (1958):
42-62, for a discussion on the wider issue of the role of women within the dissenting
traditions during the period. Crawford (1992): 112-128, and Kent (1999): 1-24, provide
interesting background discussions.

school for young women which seems to have been flourishing - at least until such time as she found herself a pawn in the game of religious power-politics being played by Charles II in 1670. In this regard, she may have been a victim of the battle being waged by Peter Mews upon Dissenters like Lawrence King. However, Mews did not always have things his own way. In an interesting letter dated 26 June 1672, and thus immediately after the issuing of *The Declaration of Indulgence*, he wrote to Archbishop Sheldon of the changes in the king's political and religious policies. Ironically, the *Declaration* meant that Mews, as Vice-Chancellor, was now required to defend the rights of Oxford students to attend conventicles, such as the one meeting at the house of King. Mews states: 'The meeting houses here are so odious to the young men, yet 'tis very difficult to restrain them from falling on them. I was forced on Sunday last (weak as I was) to appear in Person to protect those who would have hanged mee had I fallen into their hands.'[1]

6. A Licensed Meeting House for Baptists (1672)

Some relief from legal proceedings against Dissenters under the strictures of the Clarendon Code came in the form of *The Declaration of Indulgence*, issued by Charles II on 15 March 1672 (see Appendix F).[2] This allowed for the licensing of Dissenting preachers and teachers, along with Dissenting meeting houses. In April of 1672, in response to the *Declaration*, Lawrence King and Richard Tidmarsh together made an official application to have Tidmarsh's house in St Thomas's parish within the city licensed with the two of them licensed as the leaders of the congregation (see page 38 for details). The licensing of King and Tidmarsh as Baptist leaders did not mean that persecution was completely lifted, however. One particular way that such oppression continued in the case of King demonstrates an interesting change in tactic on the part of the religious authorities. With the promise of *The Declaration of Indulgence* in the air the grounds for prosecuting King for failing to attend his local parish church were lost - at least temporarily. However, an alternative was quickly found.

In an unusual move, King was cited by the parish church authorities on 14 February 1672 for failure to attend to the spiritual welfare of his children: he

---

[1] *MS ADD* (c. 302), folio 250 = CSC #509. Ironically, it was Mews, as Vice-Chancellor of the University who hosted a visit by William of Orange to Oxford on 19-20 December 1670. Mews and other university officials received the Prince at St Mary the Virgin Church, the very place that Lawrence King and Richard Tidmarsh(?) were forced to listen to sermons earlier in the year. As it turned out, both King and Tidmarsh benefited from William III's policy of religious toleration, as embodied in *The Act of Toleration* (1689), and swore allegiance to him as the rightful king of the realm following the assassination attempt of 1696 (see page 139 below).

[2] Although *The Declaration of Indulgence* is often viewed as an expression of the Earl of Clarendon's own political views, the political debate underlying its composition was very complex and multi-sided. See Abernathy (1960): 55-73, for an oft-cited discussion; also see Thomas (1962): 189-253; Hutton (1985): 196-200.

was accused of not having had them baptized. The case was brought to the Archdeaconry court held on Saturday, 17 February 1672 in the church of St Mary the Virgin.[1] The record presents some unusual details which are difficult to explain. For instance, the description of Lawrence King as being cited at his house in the parish of St Mary the Virgin is out of keeping with the majority of other records which list him as a resident of the parish of All Saints'. This may indicate that King has temporarily moved from one parish to the other. On the other hand the two parishes were geographically adjoining, and the reference to the parish of St Mary the Virgin may simply be a reflection of the flexibility of parish boundaries, or even an error on the part of the court clerk. There is also the possibility that the association of King with the parish of St Mary the Virgin is because the church of All Saint's was temporarily unusable due to problems with its spire. The building was plagued with structural weaknesses, even having to evacuate nearby residents in February of 1662 when, according the Anthony Wood, the 'steeple rocked',[2] and it was feared the buildings would collapse (as they eventually did in 1700). Indeed, problems with the buildings of the parish church of All Saint's may explain why King's excommunication order was publicly read in the church of St Mary the Virgin, even though the excommunication declaration specifically identifies him as a resident of the parish of All Saint's.

In any event there are seventeen subsequent records within the Archdeaconry court documents which show that the case against King was being pursued within the Saturday court sessions through most of 1672.[3] It is difficult to know how representative King's response to the matter of having his children baptized in the local parish church was among Baptists within the city of Oxford. Certainly there is some evidence which suggests that other Baptists in Oxford did, on occasion, permit their children to be baptized in conformity to the laws of the church of England (we noted the case of Richard Tidmarsh above on pages 50-51). However, it appears that King continued to resist the paedo-baptist line over a long period of time. The resolution of this particular court case against Lawrence King is unknown, although it represents the last time that he was cited to appear before the ecclesiastical courts during the turbulent 1670s. The next time that King and his wife appear within court records is in the summer of 1680. However, there is one further record which is worth noting, namely the ecclesiastical survey from 1676 known as *The Compton Census*. This document reported that within the parish of All Saints' in Oxford there were 300 Conformists, 7 Papists and 6 Nonconformists; it is

---

[1] *OAR: 24 July 1669–Michaelmas 1672* (c. 19), folio 195 recto = CSC #501.

[2] *MS Tanner 102, Part 1*, folio 89 verso.

[3] *OAR: 24 July 1669–Michaelmas 1672* (c. 19), folio 197 recto (24 February 1672); folio 199 recto (2 March); folio 201 recto (9 March); folio 202 verso (16 March); folio 203 verso (30 March); folio 205 verso (18 May); folio 207 verso (8 June); folio 209 recto (15 June); folio 210 recto (22 June); folio 211 verso (13 July); folio 213 verso (20 July); folio 215 recto (27 July); and folios 216 verso, 218 recto, 219 verso, 221 recto and 224 verso (unspecified dates in the Michaelmas sessions).

probable with Lawrence and Ann King, were reckoned among these six Dissenters.[1]

D. Controversial Burials, Political Intrigues, and the Registered Baptist Church (1680-1689)

1. The Controversial Burial of Anne King (1681)

The precise juridical relationship between the Diocesan and the Archdeaconry courts within Oxford is a complicated matter. At times the same men served as officials for both courts, a situation which means that at times court cases which were heard on a particular day appear within the records of both courts. This is precisely the situation with Lawrence and Anne King during the summer of 1680. The ecclesiastical court included both Lawrence and his wife Anne in a document issued on 9 June 1680. Along with Richard Tidmarsh from St Thomas parish, and John and Frances Toms, fellow Baptist Dissenters from the parish of All Saint's, they were cited for 'not comeing to Church to hear divine service'.[2] On 23 July Lawrence King appeared before the courts and was questioned by them; Diocesan and Archdeaconry documents dated 24 July 1680 both record the event.[3] The couple appear in the records of both courts for the following week, 31 July 1680.[4] It appears that they were again questioned by the court on that day, but the judge was not impressed by their answers; the Diocesan court entry records '*non Emendatur* (he/she is not improved)'. In any event, Lawrence and Anne continued in their Dissenting ways and and the couple were cited again for not coming to church in a document issued on 1 October 1680. In this instance, the citation lists not only John Toms senior and his wife Frances, but also James Jennings, another of the Baptists from the parish of All Saint's.[5]

King was again cited to appear before the Archdeaconry court on 20 January 1681. The records do not mention the nature of the charge against him, although his name appears in the court records for the sessions held on 22 January, 29 January, and 19 February following.[6] Somewhat anomalously the records describe King as a resident of the parish of St Martin's, rather than the

---

[1] *The Compton Census* (1676), page 361 = Whiteman (1986): 426.

[2] *ODR: Miscellaneous Citations* (c. 62), folio 39 recto = CSC #592.

[3] *OAR: 1 June 1678-30 July 1681 and 4 July 1674-17 October 1674* (c. 22), folio 134 recto; *ODR: 1 June 1678–27 November 1680* (c. 2134), folio 109 verso.

[4] *OAR: 1 June 1678-30 July 1681 and 4 July 1674-17 October 1674* (c. 22), folio 136 recto; *ODR: 1 June 1678–27 November 1680* (c. 2134), folio 111 recto = CSC #595.

[5] *ODR: Miscellaneous Citations* (c. 62), folio 32 recto = CSC #599. John and Frances Toms and James Jennings are also cited in another undated document, which probably comes from February of 1681 (*ODR: Miscellaneous Citations* (c. 62), folio 41 recto = CSC #602).

[6] *OAR: 1 June 1678-30 July 1681 and 4 July 1674-17 October 1674* (c. 22), folios 148 verso, 149 verso and 152 recto.

parish of St Mary the Virgin or the parish of All Saints'.[1] King's wife Anne is not named in these particular records, but there may be a good explanation for it. It is likely that she was in a poor state of health at the time, since records show she died less than four months later.

All appearances are that Anne King was a constant support to her husband as a Dissenter and that she remained unreconciled to her local parish church in All Saint's. However, when she died in June of 1681, she was buried in the graveyard of All Saints'.[2] At one level this makes perfect sense, since the church was located across the street from the house where she appears to have lived most of her adult life.[3] The surviving church records note that she was interred in accordance with the prevailing legislature concerning burial garb as specified in *The Woollen Act* of 1678.[4] However, even in death Anne King was to prove a source of controversy. Her burial in hallowed ground as an excommunicant without the appropriate 'divine service' prompted an indictment against the minister of the parish church, Roger Cooper. A summons was issued against Cooper on 29 June 1681[5] and he appeared before at the Archdeacon's court on 2 July 1681.[6] He offered an explanation, but the case did not end simply. There are records of Cooper appearing before the ecclesiastical court on two subsequent dates (16 and 30 July 1681).[7] In the end, Cooper submitted himself to the judgment of the court and the case was then dismissed.[8]

---

[1] He is described on two other occasions as being from the parish of St Martin's (*ODR: 16 January 1686–13 November 1686* (c. 14), folios 3 recto and 4 verso). Bishop Fell's records from 1682 list three Dissenters within the St Martin's parish in the city (*ODR: Memoranda from Diocesan Books – 1679-1814* (b. 68), folio 6 verso). It is possible that Lawrence King should be reckoned among them.

[2] *Parish Register of All Saints' – 1678-1812* (Par 189/1/R1/2), folio 5 verso = CSC #604.

[3] Houlbrooke (1998): 336, states that 'most Presbyterians, Congregationalists, and Baptists were buried in churchyards until long after 1700, despite being permitted their own places of worship by the Toleration Act of 1689'. He notes that theoretically excommunication included exclusion from burial in churchyards, but that this was not a major concern for ecclesiastical courts.

[4] For more on this *Act*, which was brought in to support a flagging wool industry, see Tate (1969): 67-69, and Tomlinson (1981): 2-10; the *Act* was not officially repealed until 1814. Interestingly, the burial register for All Saints' parish has a copy of *The Woollen Act* (1678) bound in the front of the manuscript (*Parish Register of All Saints' – 1678-1812* (Par 189/1/R1/2)).

[5] *ODR: Citations 1678-1681* (c. 46), folio 149 = CSC #605.

[6] *OAR: 1 June 1678-30 July 1681 and 4 July 1674-17 October 1674* (c. 22), folio 163 recto = CSC #606. A very similar case involving the burial of Ann Durham in the churchyard of St Helen's in Abingdon in February of 1682, is discussed by Preston (1935): 125.

[7] *OAR: 1 June 1678-30 July 1681 and 4 July 1674-17 October 1674* (c. 22), folios 165 recto and 166 verso respectively.

[8] This did not affect Cooper's position in the church, for he served as clerk of the parish church from 5 August 1670 until his death in February of 1697 (*Parish Register*

2. Lawrence King Listed as a Dissenter in the Parish by the Bishop of Oxford (1679)

The next time that Lawrence King appears within the sources is in a manuscript entitled *Returns of Recusants – 1679-1706*; the relevant section of this document was probably compiled circa June 1679. As part of his attempt to ascertain the state of health of the Church of England, Bishop Fell had a list of recusants and Dissenters within the diocese of Oxford compiled. The list is geographically arranged by parishes. Under the heading 'The names of those who are presented for not going to church', the entry for All Saints' parish has five men listed, each of whom is cited with his wife (*'et ux[or]'*). These five are Richard Quelch junior, Thomas Swan, John Toms senior, Laurence King, and James Jennings.[1]

3. The Rye House Plot and its Implications (1683-1686)

The remaining records relating to Lawrence King demonstrate his increasing involvement within the political arena. His place as a leader among the Dissenters of Oxford made him an object of fear and suspicion during the last years of the reign of Charles II. Thus, Anthony Wood records that King's house was searched on the evening of 25 June 1683 by royalist leaders, including Lord Norris,[2] Sir Charles Doyly, and Sir George Pudsey;[3] ostensibly they were looking for arms in the aftermath of the so-called Rye House plot to assassinate Charles II.[4]

The assassination plot created a political backlash against those who were perceived to be anti-royalist in sentiment, and ultimately led to the highly-publicized trial and public execution of Sir William Russell and Sir Algernon

---

of All Saints' – 1678-1812 (Par 189/1/R1/2), folio 119 recto; *Parish Register of All Saints' – 1559-1810* (Par 189/1/R1/1), folio 15 verso.

[1] *OAR: Returns of Recusants – 1679-1706* (c. 430), folio 41 verso = CSC #589. Thomas Swan was later excommunicated on 12 December 1663 'for not coming to Church' (*OAR: Excommunications – 1610-1783* (c. 121), folio 268 recto and verso = CSC #387; *ODR: Excommunications – 1633-1791* (c. 99), folio 241 recto = CSC #423). His excommunication was publicly read out in the parish church of All Saints' on Sunday, 17 January 1664; Richard Quelch junior's excommunication was read out at the same time.

[2] This was Montague Bertie, the eldest son of James Bertie, the Earl of Abingdon.

[3] Sir George Pudsey's star was in the ascendency at this time. Less than three months later, on 17 September 1683, he was given a Bayliffe's place within the Oxford City Council and then was made the Recorder following the death of Sir Richard Crook (*City Council Proceedings - 1663-1701* (B.5.1), page 217 recto).

[4] *MS Wood Diaries 27*, folio 29 verso = CSC #611. Luttrell (1857): 1.263, records that similar house searches were taking place in London on 26 June 1683: 'The same day also the officers of the militia for the city of London went from house to house to search for arms, and 'tis said at some places quantities were seized.'

Sidney.[1] The plot had implications at a much lower level as well. One of the results of the whole incident was an increase in the prosecution of Nonconformists by local parish officials.[2] One tangible means whereby this was accomplished can be seen in the pamphlet issued on 27 July 1683 by the Court at Whitehall. This was entitled *His Majesties Declaration to All His Loving Subjects Concerning the Treasonable Conspiracy Against His Sacred Person and Government Lately Discovered* (1683). The pamphlet gives details of the plot from the king's perspective, noting that his opponents involved themselves 'in Tumults and Riots, and Unlawful and Seditious Conventicles (4)'. The pamphlet concludes with instructions about how its contents were to be disseminated, together with an order declaring Sunday 9 September a national Day of Thanksgiving:

> For which end We do hereby Appoint the Ninth day of *September* next, to be observed as a day of Thanksgiving in all Churches and Chappels within this Our Kingdom of England, Dominion of Wales, the Town of Berwick upon Tweed, in such manner as shall be by Us Directed, in a Form of Prayer with Thanksgiving, which We have Commanded to be prepared by Our Bishops, and Published for that purpose.
> And it is Our Pleasure, That this Declaration be Publickly Read in all the Said Churches and Chappels, as well on Sunday the Second of September next, as upon the Day of Thanksgiving aforesaid (19-20).

The instructions for the Day of Thanksgiving were faithfully carried out in Oxford, with Thomas Heylyn of Christ Church preaching at the church of St Mary the Virgin. Predictably, however, celebrations extended far beyond mere attendance at worship services in church. Anthony Wood suggests that the Day of Thanksgiving was arranged on a Sunday 'to spite the Presbyterians', and records some of the celebrations within the city:

> Many bonefiers at night in ye City & University. The city at penniless bench had an entertainment of wind-musick, a barrel of ale, & a fier. On ye pump below the Star Inn was a tub set & presbyter therein preaching. The smart lads of the city march'd downe ye street with cudgells in their hands, cryinge for ye K[ing] & Duke of York, & all people had York in their mouths, & his health was drank publickly in most Halls at Dinner.[3]

The said Duke of York ascended the throne upon the death of his brother Charles II on 6 February 1685. James II was on the throne for only three years (1685-88), and, as noted above, much of his reign was embroiled in

---

[1] For more on the various political plots to assassinate Charles II, most of which were driven by anti-Catholic sentiment and fear of a collapse of the monarchy and a descent back into the uncertainties of the Civil War, see Kenyon (1974); Scott (1990); Marshall (1999).

[2] See Milne (1951): 91-108, for details.

[3] *MS Wood Diaries 27*, folios 43 recto and verso.

controversy. Within Oxford this came to a head in the form of a clash between rival religious and political groups. Yet despite the coronation of a more overtly Catholic monarch, it was at one level business as usual as far as the suppression of Baptists conventiclers in Oxford was concerned – or at least this was the case initially. Indeed, the last records that we have about Lawrence King appearing before the ecclesiastical courts are from the Diocesan court sessions held on 19 and 26 June 1686.[1] Within these two brief one- or two-line entries we discover that on 16 June 1686 King was personally cited to appear before the Diocesan court; the exact charge is unspecified. Regardless, the records go on to describe King with the words '*decernitur excommunicatus*' ('is declared excommunicated') – a clear sign of his continuing unacceptability within the religious establishment.

4. *A Testimony to Truth, Agreeing with an Essay for Settlement* (1659), *The Charter of Oxford* (1688), *and The Act of Toleration* (1689)

As noted above (pages 73-4) both Richard Tidmarsh and Lawrence King were signatories of the politically-charged broadsheet entitled *A Testimony to Truth, Agreeing with an Essay for Settlement* (1659), issued at a time when it looked as if there was a real possibility of a return to a Commonwealth ruled by the 'rule of the Saints'. This seems to have been the highpoint in political activism within King's life. The nation followed a very different political direction with the Restoration under Charles II and the hopes expressed within *A Testimony to Truth* were quickly dashed. Strangely enough, it was Charles II's brother, James II, who was to bring Lawrence King back into Oxford politics, even if only for a brief period.

Along with their colleague Richard Tidmarsh, Lawrence King and John Toms senior were identified by James II among the Dissenters put forward for civic advancement within *The Charter of Oxford* issued 15 September 1688. Both King and Toms were named within the City Council records as among of the city's 24 Common Councilmen, and both men are mentioned twice within the four sheets of the charter: King appears on line 93 of sheet two and on line 184 of sheet four; Toms appears on line 94 of sheet two and on line 185 of sheet four. Neither man appears to have become nearly as involved in the schemes of James II as did Tidmarsh, and neither is a signatory of the pamphlet *Innocency Vindicated: or, Reproach Wip'd Off* (1689), which effectively served as a public apology for accepting political office from the king. Nevertheless, there is record of Lawrence King swearing his oath of office as one of the 24 Common Councilmen before the Mayor on 28 September 1688.[2] However, none of the three Baptists (Tidmarsh, King and Toms) are recorded as being active in civic government after the revocation of the charter on 22 October

---

[1] *ODR: 16 January 1686–13 November 1686* (c. 14), folios 3 recto and 4 verso. Once again, within both of these particular entries King is said to be from the parish of St Martin's in Oxford.

[2] *City Council Proceedings – 1663-1701* (B.5.1), folio 266 verso = CSC #629.

1688.   Interestingly, all of the appointees mentioned in the charter were
excused from taking the usual oaths of allegiance to the king, as well as being
relieved of the requirement to receive the sacrament according to the rites of the
Church of England.   As noted above in the discussion of some of the
ecclesiastical court records, these were matters of particular importance to the
Baptist conventiclers and had often served as points of conflict between them
and the governing authorities.

King seems to have spent the remaining years of his life in Oxford serving the
Baptist church that met in Richard Tidmarsh's house.   No doubt he was
encouraged in this by the passing of *The Act of Toleration* in May of 1689.
Indeed, it was Lawrence King who took the first steps in testifying to the Petty
Sessions court that the house of Richard Tidmarsh was being used as a
'Congregation or Assembly for religious worship' on 15 April 1689,[1] and it
was he who saw to it that the house was duly registered as such three months
later on 15 July 1689.[2] King William III's policy of religious toleration also
engendered the allegiance of Lawrence King, if his signature on the
Association Oath roll, compiled by the citizens of Oxford, in 1696, is anything
to go by.[3] This document was signed by 1825 citizens of the city and stands as
a gesture of support for William III following the discovery of an assassination
plot (see pages 81-2 for more on this).

Lawrence King died and was buried on 4 January 1710.   The record of his
burial is recorded in the parish register of St Michael's church, the parish in
which his son Jonathan lived with his wife Ann; a small indication of the
respect in which the elder glover and tradesman was held is the fact that the
entry describes him as '*Mr* Larance King'.[4] Interestingly, Jonathan probably
also arranged for his cousin Thomas, the Dissenter from St Thomas and the son
of Lawrence King's brother Thomas, to be buried within the parish a year later.
Thomas King junior died and was buried on 10 May 1711; the entry in the
parish register records that he was from the parish of St Thomas.[5]

However, the old glover Lawrence King provides one final anecdote of 17th-
century history - or to be more precise, the house where he once lived and
traded along the High Street offers such an anecdote.   Archaeological
investigations of 113-119 High Street in 1993-5 revealed an intriguing artefact,
for hidden stashed in one of the chimneys in the house was a Civil War
passport signed by Sir Thomas Fairfax guaranteeing safe conduct out of the city

---

[1] *Oxford Petty Sessions Clerk's Notebook – 1687-1701* (O.2.1), folio 18 verso =
CSC #630.

[2] *Oxford Petty Sessions Roll – 1679-1712* (O.5.12), folio 66 verso = CSC #633.

[3] *Association Oath Roll – Oxford – 1696* (c. 213/208) = CSC #668.

[4] *Parish Register of St Michael-at-the-Northgate – 1683-1736* (Par 211/1/R1/3),
page 92.

[5] *Parish Register of St Michael-at-the-Northgate – 1683-1736* (Par 211/1/R1/3),
page 95.

for its bearer, one Samuell Smith, after the siege of 1645.[1] How the pass came to be stashed there is anybody's guess. Apparently the pass was overlooked by the militia men of Charles II who searched King's house for arms in June of 1683.[2]

E. John Toms senior: Shoemaker and Royal Appointee in James II's *Charter of Oxford* (1688)

I have already noted several times in passing the association between Lawrence King and John Toms senior as Baptist conventiclers, particularly in the turbulent and repressive 1660s and 1670s. Like Lawrence King, John Toms senior was a native Oxonian; the wider Toms family was well established within the city of Oxford, particularly within the parishes of All Saints' and St Peter-in-the-East. There are records of at least six generations living within the parishes in the 1600s, although it is very difficult to sort out the complicated family relationships, particularly since several variations of the spelling of the family name are extant (Toms, Tomms, Tomes, Tombes, Thoms, and Thomes all appear).[3] The situation is made all the more problematic by the frequency of the first name John within the surviving documents. Thus, there is record of a John Toms, the son of Tobias Toms, being baptized on 1 November 1605 in the parish of All Saints',[4] of a John Toms, the son of William and Frances Toms, being baptized on 5 June 1622 in the parish of All Saints',[5] of a John Toms, the son of Anthony Toms, being baptized on 27 July 1624 in the parish church of All Saints',[6] of a John Toms, the son of William Toms, being

---

[1] Munby (2000): 442. The document is now part of the archives of Lincoln College, Oxford. The connection between Samuell Smith and the property is unknown. The Lay Subsidy of 1648 records a Mr Berry as paying 3*s* in tax on the house, but there is no mention of any Smith as a tenant (*Lay Subsidy of 17 March 1648* (E 179 164/499); folio 2).

[2] This is assuming that King and his family lived in the house at the time. As noted above, although most records list King as a resident of All Saints' parish, there are some documents from 1670-1672 and 1692-96 which describe him as being from the parish of St Mary the Virgin, and some from 1681-2 and 1686 which describe him as being from the parish of St Martin's.

[3] The Toms family connections in the parish of St Peter-in-the-East are especially complex and intertwined. The parish registers contain 35 entries for the family in the 1600s and early 1700s, and it is impossible to sort them out with precision.

[4] *Parish Register of All Saints' – 1559-1810* (Par 189/1/R1/1), folio 10 verso.

[5] *Parish Register of All Saints' – 1559-1810* (Par 189/1/R1/1), folio 15 verso.

[6] *Parish Register of All Saints' – 1559-1810* (Par 189/1/R1/1), folio 15 recto. Anthony Toms married Mary Emerson in the parish church of St Peter-in-the-East on 20 September 1621 (*Parish Register of St Peter-in-the-East – 1559-1653* (Par 213/1/R1/1), folio 32 verso). The register entry notes that he was from 'Allhallowes' (All Saints') parish. It is likely that the wedding took place here because the bride was from the parish of St Peter-in-the-East. Anthony Toms died and was buried on 4 April 1635 (*Parish Register of All Saints' – 1559-1810* (Par 189/1/R1/1), folio 88 recto). Several other children were born to Anthony and Mary Toms; these include a son

baptized on 31 December 1629 in the parish of All Saints',[1] of a John Toms, the son of John Toms, being born on 15 January 1660 in the parish of All Saints',[2] of a John Toms, the son of John Toms, being baptized on 26 April 1667 in the parish church of St Peter-in-the-Bailey,[3] of a John Toms, the son of John Toms, being baptized on 11 April 1672 in the parish of St Peter-in-the-East,[4] of a John Toms, the son of John Toms, being baptized on 5 August 1683 in the parish of St Peter-in-the-East,[5] and of a John Toms, the son of John Toms, being baptized on 20 December 1684 in the parish of St Peter-in-the-East.[6] There is also record of a John Tombes being buried in the parish of All Saints' on 7 June 1632,[7] another record of a John Tombes being buried in the parish on 18 March 1636,[8] and a third of a Johannis Tomes being buried in the parish on 7 December 1643.[9] Unfortunately, the precise relationship that any of these men had to the Baptist John Toms is rarely explicitly stated, although a reasonable reconstruction of the family connections can be made (see the accompanying chart on 'The Family Tree of John Toms senior' for details of

---

named Robert who was baptized on 8 September 1622 (*Parish Register of All Saints' – 1559-1810* (Par 189/1/R1/1), folio 14 verso); a son named John who was baptized on 27 July 1624 (*Parish Register of All Saints' – 1559-1810* (Par 189/1/R1/1), folio 15 recto); and a daughter named Ellenor who was born on 29 January 1626 and baptized 8 February 1627 (*Parish Register of All Saints' – 1559-1810* (Par 189/1/R1/1), folio 15 verso). Robert Toms is mentioned within the will of Ann Toms which is dated to 26 August 1650 (*Ann Toms* (OWPR 66/2/64)); he is also described as a 'grandchild' of the said Ann Toms within the inventory list of her goods which is dated 20 November 1651. Ann Toms died on 11 November 1651 and is described in the parish registry entry as 'the wife of John Toms the Elder' (*Parish Register of All Saints' – 1559-1810* (Par 189/1/R1/1), folio 94 recto). In addition to Anthony, there are also records of several other children born to John and Ann Toms: a daughter named Phrysia who was baptized on 19 March 1606 (*Parish Register of All Saints' – 1559-1810* (Par 189/1/R1/1), folio 10 verso), and a daughter named Margareta who was baptized on 29 September 1608 (*Parish Register of All Saints' – 1559-1810* (Par 189/1/R1/1), folio 11 verso). The daughter Margareta died and was buried on 4 October 1610 (*Parish Register of All Saints' – 1559-1810* (Par 189/1/R1/1), folio 85 recto). It is likely that three other sons were also born to the couple: William, John, and Tobias, who was the grandfather of the Baptist John Toms.

[1] *Parish Register of All Saints' – 1559-1810* (Par 189/1/R1/1), folio 17 verso.

[2] *MS Top Oxon* (b. 40), folio 1 verso; *Poll Tax of 1667* (P.5.7), folio 12 recto.

[3] *Parish Register of St Peter-in-the-Bailey – 1659-1689* (Par 214/1/R1/2), folio 8 verso.

[4] *Parish Register of St Peter-in-the-East – 1653-1807* (Par 213/1/R1/3), folio 4 recto.

[5] *Parish Register of St Peter-in-the-East – 1653-1807* (Par 213/1/R1/3), folio 9 verso.

[6] *Parish Register of St Peter-in-the-East – 1653-1807* (Par 213/1/R1/3), folio 10 recto.

[7] *Parish Register of All Saints' – 1559-1810* (Par 189/1/R1/1), folio 87 verso.

[8] *Parish Register of All Saints' – 1559-1810* (Par 189/1/R1/1), folio 88 recto.

[9] *Parish Register of All Saints' – 1559-1810* (Par 189/1/R1/1), folio 91 verso.

some of these family relationships).[1] The Poll Tax of 1667 lists two John Tomses within the city of Oxford: one in the parish of All Saints', and one in the parish of St Peter-in-the-Bailey. The geographical distinctions will serve as a convenient way to distinguish beween the two men within this discussion: the John Toms from the parish of All Saints' is the Baptist conventicler, and the John Toms from the parish of St Peter-in-the-Bailey is his cousin. Records associated with the Baptist conventicler John Toms show that he lived within the parish of All Saints' for the whole of his life, whereas records of his younger cousin show that at some point he moved from the parish of St Peter-in-the-Bailey to the parish of St Peter-in-the-East.

Some details about the life and family history of the Baptist conventicler John Toms can be gleaned from surviving sources. According to the record of his apprenticeship contract, which is dated 17 October 1644, Toms was 'the son of John Tomes senior, late of the Citty of Oxon, Barb^{our} Chirurgeon, deceased'.[2] There is record of the burial of his father, John Toms, on 7 June 1632 in the parish of All Saints'.[3] The probate documents of John Toms from 1633 also describe him as a surgeon in the parish of St Peter-in-the-East;[4] the likelihood is that he was the 'John Toms son of Tobias Toms' who was baptized on 1 November 1605.[5] Tobias Toms, who is also described as a surgeon, died the year after his son John, and was buried in the parish of All Saints' on 29 May 1633.[6] According to a probate record, he was survived by his wife Abigail, a son named William, and a daughter named Jane.[7] The daughter Jane was baptized on 25 November 1607,[8] and later married Thomas Price on 17 October 1634.[9] Tobias's probate record was witnessed by his widow Abigail,[10] and a John Toms, probably his older brother.

---

[1] There is also a record of a John Tombs being paid 6*d* 'for the carriage of iron brought from London from the wharfe to the theatre on 24 December 1668'. This is found in *MS Bodl 898*, page 312, the official financial accounts relating to the construction of the Sheldonian Theatre. This John Tombs was a boatmen and he is known to have held lease on two tenements in Bullocks Lane (see *City Council Proceedings – 1663-1701* (B.5.1), folios 76 verso, 77 recto, 78 recto, and 78 verso).

[2] *Civic Enrolments – 1639-1662* (L.5.3), folio 42 verso = CSC #46.

[3] *Parish Register of All Saints' – 1559-1810* (Par 189/1/R1/1), folio 87 verso.

[4] *John Tombs* (OWPR 87/3/5).

[5] *Parish Register of All Saints' – 1559-1810* (Par 189/1/R1/1), folio 10 verso.

[6] *Parish Register of All Saints' – 1559-1810* (Par 189/1/R1/1), folio 87 verso. Interestingly, the probate document record relating to Tobias was altered from describing him as living in the parish of All Saints' to living in the parish of St Peter-in-the-East (*Tobias Toms* (OWPR 66/1/43)).

[7] There is record of the baptism of another daughter named Editha on 2 January 1613 (*Parish Register of All Saints' – 1559-1810* (Par 189/1/R1/1), folio 12 verso); Editha apparently died before her father, for she is not mentioned in his probate records.

[8] *Parish Register of All Saints' – 1559-1810* (Par 189/1/R1/1), folio 11 recto.

[9] *Parish Register of St Peter-in-the-East – 1559-1653* (Par 213/1/R1/1), folio 34 recto.

[10] There is record of the widow Abigail Toms living with John Lambe and his family in the parish of St Aldates (*Poll Tax of 1667* (P.5.7), folio 34 recto).

No record of the Baptist John Toms's marriage survives, although it appears that he and his wife Frances (whose name is known to us through other sources) had at least four children, including a son named Tobias who was born 11 February 1655,[1] a son named John who was born 15 January 1660,[2] a daughter named Abigale (Abigail) who was baptized on 9 June 1662,[3] and another child whose name and birth date are unknown. He paid 6*s* in the Poll Tax of 1 March 1667 while living in the parish of All Saints'; this covers himself, his wife Frances, and their four children.[4] The same entry records that Richard Mullis and Henry Mills (Miles) paid 2*s* as apprentices living with the Toms family, and that a widow named Elizabeth Wise, possibly Frances Toms's mother, also lived with them and paid 1*s* in the tax. In addition, there are several other records of Toms paying taxes in the years 1667-68 as a resident within the parish of All Saints'. He pays 2*s* in the tax of 24 June 1667; 2*s* 2*d* in the tax of 29 September 1667; 2*s* 9*d* in the tax of 21 December 1667; 2*s* in the tax of 26 March 1668; 2*s* in the tax of 26 June 1668; 1*s* 6*d* in the tax of 26 September 1668; and 2*s* in the tax of 26 December 1668.[5]

As noted, the Baptist John Toms made his living as a cordwainer in the city, having served an eight-year apprenticeship under Richard Phillips, the record of which is dated 17 October 1644;[6] Phillips had also served as the master of Edward Wyans senior, Toms's fellow Baptist conventicler (see page 62 above). After the completion of his apprenticeship Toms was granted his 'Freedom of the City' on 20 June 1652.[7] The professional career of Toms is worth considering briefly, particularly as it helps explain something of why he becomes one of the Oxford tradesmen singled out by James II for advancement

---

[1] *MS Top Oxon* (b. 40), folio 1 recto.

[2] *MS Top Oxon* (b. 40), folio 1 verso. The birth of this son on 15 January 1660 may help explain why Toms did not accompany his Baptist colleagues Roger Hatchman and Ralph Austen to hear the controversial John Belcher preach at St Peter-in-the-Bailey parish church the next day, Monday the 16th of January (see pages 137-138).

[3] *Parish Register of All Saints' – 1559-1810* (Par 189/1/R1/1), folio 25 verso. The fact that this entry records the baptism of the daughter Abigail may illustrate something of the flexibility that Baptists in Oxford had over the matter of infant-baptism. There is evidence which suggests that Richard Tidmarsh, the acknowledged leader of the Baptists in Oxford, also had a daughter baptized within his local parish church (see the discussion on pages 50-1 above for more on this matter).

[4] *Poll Tax of 1667* (P.5.7), folio 12 recto. There are records of other members of the wider Toms family paying the Poll Tax of 1 March 1667, but it is difficult to determine what their relationship was to John Toms of All Saints' parish.

[5] *War Taxes – 1667-1668* (P.5.8), folios 4 recto, 23 verso, 42 recto, 59 verso, 79 verso, 98 recto and 107 recto. See pages 5-6 for more details about these various taxes.

[6] *Civic Enrolments – 1639-1662* (L.5.3), folio 42 verso = CSC#; the apprenticeship contract is backdated to 24 June 1644. Also see *MS Morrell 23 – List of Cordwainers' Apprentices (1590-1660)*, folio 82 verso.

[7] *Civic Enrolments – 1639-1662* (L.5.3), folio 240 recto = CSC #115. A similar entry dated 15 July 1652 is found in *MS Morrell 14 – Minutes of Meetings of the Guild of Cordwayners (1614-1711)*, folio 53 verso = CSC #118.

within the new *Charter of Oxford* granted to the city in 1688 (see pages 138-9 above).

Several documents relating to John Toms's career as a cordwainer are extant, including *MS Morell 14 - Minutes of Meetings of the Guild of Cordwayners (1614-1711)* and *MS Morrell 12 - Gylde of Cordwayners (1648-1758)*, official records of the early years of the guild (see pages 62-6 for discussion of these manuscripts). In *MS Morrell 14*, where a list of members of the guild was compiled annually, his name appears every year, virtually without fail, for over a forty year period.[1] In addition, the first reference to Toms in *MS Morrell 12* is an entry which appears in the account of receipts dated 12 November 1652; it notes, 'Rec'd of John Toms for his admission into ye company - £ 0 3s 4d'.[2] A second entry dated 23 October 1665 records that Toms was elected 'Searcher' for the guild for the year;[3] a third reference dated 20 October 1673 similarly records that he was appointed 'Searcher' for that year as well.[4] He began to advance within the guild's structures, paying £1 10s as a fine for a warden's place in records dated 25 October and 12 November 1669.[5] He was

---

[1] He is named in the minutes for 20 October 1652 (folio 56 recto); 24 October 1653 (folio 57 verso); 23 October 1654 (folio 60 verso); 22 October 1655 (folio 61 verso); 20 October 1656 (folio 62 verso); 29 October 1657 (folio 64 verso); 25 October 1658 (folio 66 verso); 24 October 1659 (folio 68 recto); 22 October 1660 (folio 69 recto); 21 October 1661 (folio 71 verso); 21 October 1662 (folio 74 verso); 19 October 1663 (folio 75 verso); 24 October 1664 (folio 77 recto); 23 October 1665 (folio 79 recto); 22 October 1666 (folio 81 recto); 20 October 1667 (folio 83 recto); 19 October 1668 (folio 85 recto); 25 October 1669 (folio 87 recto); 24 October 1670 (folio 88 verso); 23 October 1671 (folio 90 verso); 20 October 1673 (folio 93 recto); 19 October 1674 (folio 95 verso); 25 October 1675 (folio 97 verso); 23 October 1676 (folio 99 verso); 22 October 1677 (folio 101 recto); 21 October 1678 (folio 103 recto); 20 October 1679 (folio 104 verso); 25 October 1680 (folio 105 verso); 24 October 1681 (folio 107 recto); 24 October 1682 (folio 108 recto); 22 October 1683 (folio 110 verso); 20 October 1684 (folio 113 recto); 19 October 1685 (folio 115 recto); 25 October 1686 (folio 118 recto); 24 October 1687 (folio 120 recto); 21 October 1689 (folio 124 verso); 20 October 1690 (folio 127 recto); 19 October 1691 (folio 129 recto); 24 October 1692 (folio 131 verso); and 23 October 1693 (folio 133 recto) where his death is recorded ('*mort[uus]*'). The only exceptions are in the records for the years 1672 and 1688, where pages are missing from the manuscript.

[2] *MS Morrell 12 - Gylde of Cordwayners (1648-1758)*, folio 14 verso. The entry also records Toms's payment of £1 'in leiue of a Breakfast'.

[3] *MS Morrell 12 - Gylde of Cordwayners (1648-1758)*, folio 45 recto.

[4] *MS Morrell 12 - Gylde of Cordwayners (1648-1758)*, folio 61 verso.

[5] *MS Morrell 14 – Minutes of Meetings of the Guild of Cordwayners (1614-1711)*, folio 86 verso = CSC #477; *MS Morrell 12 - Gylde of Cordwayners (1648-1758)*, folio 53 verso. Toms had made an earlier bid to be elected a warden in 1661 but was defeated by Richard Edwards for the place (*MS Morrell 14 – Minutes of Meetings of the Guild of Cordwayners (1614-1711)*, folio 73 verso. Edwards received 40 votes, Thomas Harris 8 votes and John Toms 5 votes in the election.

admitted to a 'Master's place' within the guild on 25 October 1675,[1] and there is an accounting record dated 12 November 1675 of him paying £2 10*s* as a fine for a master's place.[2] Along with his fellow Baptist Edward Wyans senior, Toms also assisted in the renewal of the guild's orders on 20 April 1666, helping to ensure that they were appropriately presented to the judges at the Oxford assizes.[3] He also signed a minute on 18 January 1688 in which all members of the guild agreed 'that all constitutions, orders and by laws should be kept and observed'.[4] There are also several interesting records of Toms being fined six pence for failing to appear at meetings of the guild, including those held on 14 January 1679,[5] 30 December 1687,[6] and 2 January 1690.[7]

There are also several mentions within *MS Morrell 12* of a John Toms *junior*, who, as can best be determined, was the second-cousin of the Baptist John Toms.[8] For example, in the financial accounts dated to 19 October 1668 John Toms junior is elected 'to have £5 8*s* of Mr Carter's money', obviously a reference to a legacy left by a deceased benefactor.[9] It appears that John Toms junior followed in his cousin's footsteps as a cordwainer, serving an apprenticeship under Richard Meares which commenced 10 July 1657.[10] He

---

[1] *MS Morrell 14 – Minutes of Meetings of the Guild of Cordwayners (1614-1711)*, folio 96 verso = CSC #538.

[2] *MS Morrell 12 - Gylde of Cordwayners (1648-1758)*, folio 66 recto.

[3] *MS Morrell 14 – Minutes of Meetings of the Guild of Cordwayners (1614-1711)*, folio 80 verso = CSC #426.

[4] *MS Morrell 14 – Minutes of Meetings of the Guild of Cordwayners (1614-1711)*, folio 122 recto = CSC #623.

[5] *MS Morrell 14 – Minutes of Meetings of the Guild of Cordwayners (1614-1711)*, folio 104 recto = CSC #585.

[6] *MS Morrell 14 – Minutes of Meetings of the Guild of Cordwayners (1614-1711)*, folio 121 recto = CSC #622.

[7] *MS Morrell 14 – Minutes of Meetings of the Guild of Cordwayners (1614-1711)*, folio 128 recto = CSC #640.

[8] As noted, the Baptist John Toms was the son of John Toms the surgeon, and thus also a *junior*. Indeed, he is described in his apprenticeship record as 'John Tomes junior'. However, it appears that after his father's death the 'junior' was dropped, and was then later applied to his younger cousin John, the son of Thomas, as a way to distinguish between the two cordwainers. Moreover, starting in 1695, following the death of the Baptist John Toms in 1693, the younger cousin begins to be described as 'John Toms *senior*'. At the same time, his son, who was also named John, is designated as 'John Toms *junior*' in records dating from 1689-96 which relate to his membership within the cordwainers' guild.

[9] *MS Morrell 12 - Gylde of Cordwayners (1648-1758)*, folio 51 verso.

[10] *Civic Enrolments – 1639-1662* (L.5.3), folio 157 verso. He is said to be 'sonne of Thomas Tommes, late of the University of Oxon, Cook, dec[eas]ed'. Also see *MS Morrell 23 – List of Cordwainers' Apprentices (1590-1660)*, folio 91 verso. There is also record of a Thomas Tomes (Toms) signing an engagement as a journeyman within the cordwainers' guild in circa 1632 (*MS Morrell 24 – Guylde of Cordwayners*, folio 39 verso); and record of the baptism of a child of a daughter Elizabeth to Thomas

was granted his 'Freedom of the City' on the basis of the successful completion of that apprenticeship on 19 February 1666,[1] and was admitted into the cordwainers' guild upon payment of 3*s* 4*d* on 9 November 1666.[2] John Toms junior appears regularly in the annual lists of members of the guild, starting in 1666 and continuing until his death in 1708.[3] It looks as if this John Toms junior established himself as a shoemaker in the parish of St Peter-in-the-East soon after he finished his apprenticeship. He married Sarah Clarke in 1666,[4] although they probably lived in the parish of St Peter-in-the-Bailey for the first year or so of the marriage.[5] The couple had several children, including a son

---

Toms, a 'cuttler' on 10 December 1643 (*Parish Register of St Mary Magdalen – 1602-1662* (Par 208/1/R1/1), folio 18 verso).

[1] *Civic Enrolments – 1662-1699* (L.5.4), page 718; *Husting and Mayors Court 1665-1666* (M.4.5), folio 102 recto (Husting). .

[2] *MS Morrell 12 - Gylde of Cordwayners (1648-1758)*, folio 47 verso; *MS Morrell 14 – Minutes of Meetings of the Guild of Cordwayners (1614-1711)*, folio 80 recto = CSC #434 (dated 15 November). There is also record of him making a gift of £1 to the guild on 8 November 1667 (*MS Morrell 12 - Gylde of Cordwayners (1648-1758)*, folio 49 verso).

[3] There is record of his burial on 22 December 1708 (*Parish Register of St Peter-in-the-East – 1670-1812* (Par 213/1/R1/5), folio 13 verso). Toms is named within *MS Morrell 14 – Minutes of Meetings of the Guild of Cordwayners (1614-1711)* in the minutes for 22 October 1666 (folio 81 verso; 20 October 1667 (folio 83 verso); 19 October 1668 (folio 85 verso); 25 October 1669 (folio 87 verso); 24 October 1670 (folio 89 recto); 23 October 1671 (folio 91 recto); 20 October 1673 (folio 93 recto); 19 October 1674 (folio 95 verso); 25 October 1675 (folio 97 verso); 23 October 1676 (folio 99 verso); 22 October 1677 (folio 101 recto); 21 October 1678 (folio 103 recto); 19 October 1679 (folio 104 verso); 25 October 1680 (folio 105 verso); 24 October 1681 (folio 107 verso); 23 October 1682 (folio 108 recto); 22 October 1683 (folio 110 verso); 20 October 1684 (folio 113 recto); 19 October 1685 (folio 115 recto); 25 October 1686 (folio 118 recto); 24 October 1687 (folio 120 recto); 21 October 1689 (folio 124 verso); 20 October 1690 (folio 127 recto); 19 October 1690 (folio 130 recto); 24 October 1692 (folio 132 recto); 23 October 1693 (folio 133 recto); 22 October 1694 (folio 134 verso); 21 October 1695 (folio 136 verso); 19 October 1696 (folio 138 recto); 19 October 1697 (folio 140 recto); 24 October 1698 (folio 141 verso); 23 October 1699 (folio 142 recto); 21 October 1700 (folio 144 verso); 20 October 1701 (folio 146 verso); 25 October 1703 (folio 153 recto); 23 October 1704 (folio 155 verso); 22 October 1705 (folio 158 verso); 161 verso 21 October 1706 (folio 161 verso); 20 October 1707 (folio 164 recto); and 22 November 1708 (folio 167 recto) where his death is recorded (*'mort[uus]'*). The only exceptions are in the records for the years 1672, 1688 and 1702, where pages are missing from the manuscript. There is also an interesting records of John Toms junior being fined 6*d* for failing to appear at a meeting of the guild held on 4 January 1695 (*MS Morrell 14 – Minutes of Meetings of the Guild of Cordwayners (1614-1711)*, folio 135 recto = CSC #660).

[4] Toms signed a bond for this marriage on 19 February 1666 (*OAR: Marriage Bonds – 1665* (c. 456), folio 234). His bride was from the parish of St Peter-in-the-East, although the wedding was licensed to take place in Wolvercote.

[5] There is record that a John Toms and his wife paid 2*s* in the Poll Tax of 1667 while living in the parish of St Peter-in-the-Bailey (*Poll Tax of 1667* (P.5.7), folio 46

named John who was baptized on 26 April 1667,[1] a daughter named Elinor who was baptized on 5 October 1668 but died and was buried on 15 November 1687,[2] a daughter named Alice who died and was buried on 20 October 1671,[3] and a son named William who was baptized on 24 October 1678.[4]   Moreover, there is also record of a 'Widow Toms' being buried in the parish church of St Peter-in-the-Bailey on 19 November 1669.[5]   What relationship this 'Widow Toms' had to John Toms junior is unclear; perhaps she was his (unnamed) mother, the wife of Thomas Toms. John Toms junior's younger son William, as the eldest surviving son of an Oxford citizen, was granted his own 'Freedom of the City' on 27 April 1705.[6]   It appears he never served an official apprenticeship or joined the cordwainers' guild in his own right, and is once simply described in the cordwainers' guild minutes for 1708 as an 'Older Worker'.[7]   He does not appear again within the minutes in this capacity, which is not surprising given that he died a little over three years later and was buried on 30 December 1711.[8]   However, it is worth noting that at the time of his death he was serving as the clerk in the parish of St Peter-in-the-East, a position he appears to have taken over from his father.[9]

---

verso = Salter (1923): 279). However, it is possible that this refers to the John Toms who married Judith Crase on 13 July 1665 (*Parish Register of St Peter-in-the-Bailey – 1659-1684* (Par 214/1/R1/2), folio 37 recto). There are also several tax records from 1692-1695 which relate to a John Toms of the parish of St Peter-in-the-Bailey (*Taxes – 1691-1694* (P.5.9), folios 38 recto, 74 recto and 119 verso).

[1] *Parish Register of St Peter-in-the-Bailey – 1659-1684* (Par 214/1/R1/2), folio 8 verso.

[2] *Parish Register of St Peter-in-the-East – 1670-1812* (Par 213/1/R1/2), folio 17 recto; *Parish Register of St Peter-in-the-East – 1670-1812* (Par 213/1/R1/5), folio 5 recto.

[3] *Parish Register of St Peter-in-the-Bailey – 1659-1684* (Par 214/1/R1/2), folio 64 verso.

[4] *Parish Register of St Peter-in-the-East – 1653-1807* (Par 213/1/R1/3), folio 7 verso.

[5] *Parish Register of St Peter-in-the-Bailey 1659-1684* (Par 214/1/R1/2), folio 66 verso.

[6] *Civic Enrolments – 1697-1780* (L.5.5), folio 22 recto = CSC #682.

[7] *MS Morrell 14 – Minutes of Meetings of the Guild of Cordwayners (1614-1711)*, folio 167 verso.

[8] *Parish Register of St Peter-in-the-East – 1670-1812* (Par 213/1/R1/5), folio 15 recto.

[9] The burial notices of both John Toms in 1708 and William Toms in 1711 describe them as 'parish clerk'. Toms's active role in the parish of St Peter-in-the East may also help explain how it is that he signed a number of marriage bonds for couples either from the parish, or wanting to get married in the parish church. Thus, Toms signed a marriage bond for John Gunyon and Susanna Meyricke on 10 February 1666 (*OAR: Marriage Bonds – 1665* (c. 456), folio 91); a marriage bond for Thomas Carter and Mary Hanson on 12 January 1674 (*OAR: Marriage Bonds – 1673* (c. 462), folio 24); a marriage bond for William Roebuck and Anne Slatter on 30 August 1687 (*OAR: Marriage Bonds – 1687* (c. 475), folio 106); and a marriage bond for James Winch and

Several other City Council documents also pertain to the Baptist John Toms's life as a cordwainer within Oxford. For example, he was appointed one of the city's four 'Leather Searchers and Sealers' on 30 September 1659; one of his fellow Baptist conventiclers, Edward Wyans senior, also served in this capacity for the year.[1] In addition, there are a number of apprenticeship records which are dated between the years 1654-1695 which bear the name of John Toms (it is difficult to know if the older man or his younger cousin is meant in the records between 1670 and 1688 since both were active master cordwainers). The apprenticeships concerned are as follows:

Name	Date of Contract	Duration	Citizenship Granted
William Stubbes	1654[2]		8 May 1661[3]
William Goodson	21 July 1657[4]	Seven years	
Richard Mullis	30 March 1664[5]	Seven years	
Henry Mills (Miles)	1 March 1667[6]	Eight years	22 July 1678[7]
John Johnson	10 June 1667[8]	Seven years	4 March 1677[9]
Thomas George	29 August 1670[1]	Seven years	22 July 1678[2]

Elizabeth Francklyn on 4 June 1697 (*ODR: Marriage Records: W 1634-1704* (d. 92/2), folio 206). In each of these Toms is described as either a 'cordwinder' or a 'shoemaker'.

[1] *City Council Proceedings – 1629-1663* (A.5.7), folio 265 recto; *Council Minutes – 1657-1668* (A.4.4), folio 47 verso.

[2] *MS Morrell 23 – List of Cordwainers' Apprentices (1590-1660)*, folio 90 recto. This apprenticeship is not recorded in the official register of *Civic Enrolments – 1639-1662* (L.5.3), suggesting that Toms failed to register it when it was agreed in 1654. This may account for the fact that Stubbes's citizenship was later granted by an act of the City Council, and not on the basis of him having completed an apprenticeship.

[3] *Civic Enrolments – 1639-1662* (L.5.3), folio 215 verso = CSC #325; Stubbes was admitted to the guild of cordwainers on 25 April 1661 (*MS Morrell 14 – Minutes of Meetings of the Guild of Cordwayners (1614-1711)*, folio 72 verso = CSC #323). He is also mentioned in the minutes of the City Council dated 16 April 1661 (*City Council Proceedings – 1629-1663* (A.5.7), folio 288 recto).

[4] *Civic Enrolments – 1639-1662* (L.5.3), folio 158 recto = CSC #252; the apprenticeship contract is backdated to 25 July 1670. Also see *MS Morrell 23 – List of Cordwainers' Apprentices (1590-1660)*, folio 175.

[5] *Civic Enrolments – 1662-1699* (L.5.4), page 31 = CSC #390; the apprenticeship contract is predated to begin on 24 June 1664. Mullis is recorded as living with John Toms senior in the Poll Tax of 1667 (see page 143 above).

[6] *Civic Enrolments – 1662-1699* (L.5.4), page 86 = CSC #439; the apprenticeship contract is backdated to 2 February 1667.

[7] *Civic Enrolments – 1662-1699* (L.5.4), page 636 = CSC #581. Miles (Mills) is recorded as living with John Toms senior in the Poll Tax of 1667 (see page 143 above).

[8] *Civic Enrolments – 1662-1699* (L.5.4), page 96 = CSC #444; the apprenticeship contract is predated to begin on 24 June 1667.

[9] *Civic Enrolments – 1662-1699* (L.5.4), page 636 = CSC #561. Johnson was admitted to the guild of cordwainers on 12 April 1678 (*MS Morrell 14 – Minutes of Meetings of the Guild of Cordwayners (1614-1711)*, folio 72 verso = CSC #576).

Michael Whately	3 April 1676[3]	Seven years	
William Cannon	14 June 1676[4]	Seven years	14 May 1688[5]
Edward Drinkwater	4 March 1681[6]	Seven years	13 April 1694[7]
John Charman	14 May 1688[8]	Seven years	23 September 1695[9]

Taken together these apprenticeships demonstrate the professional competency of both John Toms senior (of the parish of All Saints')[10] and his younger cousin John Toms (of the parish of St Peter-in-the-East).

So much for the professional career of John Toms as an Oxford tradesman; what do we know about his life as a Dissenter? Records of many clashes between the ecclesiastical authorities and John Toms are extant; generally these can confidently be reckoned to concern the John Toms senior who lived in All Saints' parish. Like other Baptists in the city, Toms was named as one of the insurrectionists in the so-called 'Presbyterian Sham-plot' of 1661 (see pages 43-4 above). I also noted in discussion above that he was one of five people indicted for attending a Baptist conventicle on 20 March 1663 (see page 119); that on 30 March 1667 he and three others (Lawrence and Anne King and Richard Tidmarsh) were required by the court to certify their attendance at the local parish church at the forthcoming Easter services (see page 124); and that on 13 January 1670 he and four others (Abraham Ward, Richard Tidmarsh, John Higgins and Lawrence King) appeared before the Petty Sessions court

---

[1] *Civic Enrolments – 1662-1699* (L.5.4), page 162 = CSC #487; the apprenticeship contract is backdated to 25 July 1670.

[2] *Civic Enrolments – 1662-1699* (L.5.4), page 623 = CSC #580.

[3] *Civic Enrolments – 1662-1699* (L.5.4), page 256 = CSC #553; the apprenticeship contract is predated to begin on 1 May 1676.

[4] *Civic Enrolments – 1662-1699* (L.5.4), page 259 = CSC #554; the apprenticeship contract is backdated to 1 May 1676.

[5] *Civic Enrolments – 1662-1699* (L.5.4), pages 566 and 561 = CSC #627.

[6] *Civic Enrolments – 1662-1699* (L.5.4), page 323 = CSC #603.

[7] *Civic Enrolments – 1662-1699* (L.5.4), page 524 = CSC #659. This record specifies John Toms *senior* as the master under whom Drinkwater served his apprenticeship.

[8] *Civic Enrolments – 1662-1699* (L.5.4), page 413 = CSC #626; the apprenticeship contract is backdated to 24 June 1687.

[9] *Civic Enrolments – 1662-1699* (L.5.4), page 523 = CSC #665. Charman was admitted to the guild of cordwainers on 12 July 1696 (*MS Morrell 14 – Minutes of Meetings of the Guild of Cordwayners (1614-1711)*, folio 137 recto = CSC #667).

[10] There is a ballad broadsheet entitled *A True Relation of a Notorious Cheater one Robert Bullock* (1663) which contains an interesting reference to John Tombes (Toms), describing him as one of the people that Robert Bullock swindled. The relevant lines read: 'A good man, a rich Sadler,/for my custom courted me,/Both Pillion-cloth and Bridle,/were at my service free,/With Tombes, for boots & shoos/I quickly did agree,/And for mine offences I did flie.' Anthony Wood annotated a copy of the pamphlet which is now in the Bodleian Library. He annotated the relevant paragraph with the words: 'Tombes ye shomaker over against S. Maries church' (see *Wood 402* (92)).

charged with attending an unlawful conventicle at Lawrence King's house (see page 129). A number of other documents are extant which also need to be considered.

Interestingly, Frances, the wife of the Baptist John Toms, is frequently cited in her own right within several of these additional ecclesiastical court documents. In this regard the cases of John and/or Frances Toms are mentioned regularly in the records of the Saturday court sessions during the years 1665-1671, usually being cited for not attending their local parish church. They are mentioned four times in the records for the ecclesiastical court proceedings for 1665 (on 29 April; 6 May; 3 and 10 June),[1] and twice in the records of the ecclesiastical court proceedings for 1666 (on 14 and 28 July).[2] They also appear nineteen times in the records of the ecclesiastical court proceedings for 1667 (on 9, 16, 23 and 30 March; 27 April; 11 and 18 May; 8, 15 and 22 June; 6, 13, 20 and 27 July).[3] Similarly, there are twenty-three such records for 1668 (18 January; 8, 15 and 29 February; 7 March; 6, 13, 20 and 27 June; 4, 11 and 18 July; 10, 17, 24 and 31 October; 7, 14, 21 and 28 November; and 5 and 12 December);[4] fifteen such records for 1670 (25 June; 2, 9, 16, 23 and 30 July; 15, 22 and 29 October; 12, 19 and 26 November; 3, 10, and 17 December);[5] twenty-one such records for 1671 (14, 21 and 28 January; 4, 11, 18 and 25 February; 4, 11 and 18 March; 1, 8 and 15 April; 20 and 27 May; 3 June; 15, 22 and 29 July; 14 October; 11 November);[6] and eighteen such records for 1672 (17 and 24 February; 2, 9, 16, and 30 March; 18 May; 8, 15 and 22 June; 13, 20 and 27 July; and 5 unspecified dates in the Michaelmas sessions).[7]

---

[1] *ODR: 15 October 1664–30 September 1665* (d. 12), folios 144 verso, 155 recto, 169 verso, and 182 recto.

[2] *ODR: 23 June 1666–22 January 1670* (c. 9), folios 21 recto and 50 verso.

[3] *ODR: 7 October 1665–7 March 1668* (c. 5), folios 204 recto, 210 verso, 218 recto, 223 recto, 226 recto, 227 verso, 232 recto, 232 verso, 236 verso, 238 recto, 239 verso, 241 recto, 242 verso, 244 recto; *OAR: 11 May 1667–21 July 1669* (c. 17), folios 29 recto, 37 verso, 43 recto, 48 recto, and 54 verso. The Diocesan and Archdeaconry court records overlap for several dates during the year.

[4] *ODR: 7 October 1665–7 March 1668* (c. 5), folios 259 verso, 265 recto, 271 verso, 278 verso, 284 verso; *OAR: 11 May 1667–21 July 1669* (c. 17), folios vii recto, 109 verso, 118 verso, 128 verso, 138 recto, 148 recto, 159 verso, 170 verso, 180 verso, 187 recto, 194 recto, 201 recto, 207 verso, 214 recto, 221 recto, 227 verso, 234 recto and 240 recto. The Diocesan and Archdeaconry court records overlap for 7 March 1668.

[5] *OAR: 24 July 1669-July 1672* (c. 19), folios 73 verso, 76 recto, 78 recto, 82 verso, 86 verso, 90 verso, 96 recto, 98 verso, 101 recto, 103 verso, 106 recto, 108 verso, 110 verso, 112 verso and 114 verso.

[6] *OAR: 24 July 1669-July 1672* (c. 19), folios 116 verso, 118 verso, 120 verso, 122 verso, 124 verso, 126 verso, 128 verso, 130 verso, 132 verso, 134 verso, 136 verso, 139 recto, 140 verso, 142 verso, 144 verso, 146 recto, 147 verso, 150 verso 154 verso, 164 verso, and 170 verso.

[7] *OAR: 24 July 1669-July 1672* (c. 19), folios 195 recto, 197 recto, 199 recto, 201 recto, 202 verso, 203 verso, 205 verso, 207 verso, 209 recto, 210 recto, 211 verso, 213

Every indication is that John Toms senior and his wife Frances continued to be active as Dissenters through to the issuing of *The Act of Toleration* in 1689. *The Compton Census* (1676) notes that within the parish of All Saints' in Oxford there were 300 Conformists, 7 Papists and 6 Nonconformists; it is probable that John and Frances Toms, along with Lawrence and Anne King, were reckoned among these Dissenters.[1] There is record of John Toms senior being cited for not attending his local parish church in 1679.[2] In addition, as noted above (on page 136), he was named, along with his wife, as among those from All Saints' parish identified as Dissenters in the list compiled for Bishop Fell in about October of that year. Indeed, some of the last records we have of Toms being described on the basis of his religious convictions date to circa 1679-81, where he is again named as among the Dissenters residing within the parish of All Saints'. One particular record refers explicitly to 'Jo[hn] Toms, shoemaker & his wife'.[3] John and Frances Toms are also named in three ecclesiastical court citations from 1680-1, all of which accuse them of 'not coming to Church to hear divine service'. The first of these is dated 9 June 1680, the second is dated 1 October 1680, and the third is undated but probably comes from February of 1681.[4] There is also an entry relating to John Toms within the court records dated 16 July 1681.[5] It appears that the couple lived the last few years of their lives together in relative obscurity, for they are absent from further ecclesiastical records.

As discussed above, there is a fleeting glimpse of John Toms as one of the Dissenters identified for political advancement within James II's new *Charter of Oxford* (1688). Toms was named as one of the 24 men appointed as members of the Common Council, but the appointment was inconsequential at the end of the day and there is no record of him ever serving in this capacity. There is record of a quarterly payment of 2s for Toms and his wife in the Poll Tax of 27 June 1692, while living in the parish of All Saints'.[6] The last appearances of Toms within surviving documents are in probate records associated with his death which took place on 20 November 1693.[7] An inventory of his goods was made on 27 February 1694 and the related bond

---

verso, 215 recto, 216 verso, 218 recto, 219 verso, 221 recto and 224 verso.

[1] *The Compton Census* (1676), page 361. See Whiteman (1986): 426.

[2] ODR: *Memoranda from Diocesan Books – 1679-1814* (b. 68), folio 4 recto = CSC #590. In this instance Toms is cited together with six other Dissenters, including his fellow Baptist James Jennings.

[3] ODR: *Bishop Fell's Notes on Dissenters – 1679-1685* (d. 708), folio 57 recto.

[4] ODR: *Miscellaneous Citations* (c. 62), folios 32 recto, 39 recto and 41 recto.

[5] OAR: *1 June 1678-30 July 1681 and 4 July 1674-17 October 1674* (c. 22), folio 164 recto.

[6] *Taxes – 1691-1694* (P.5.9), folio 61 recto. A record from 1693 shows he was taxed for rents and stocks (*Taxes – 1691-1694* (P.5.9), folio 68 verso).

[7] He was buried in the All Saints' parish churchyard on 27 November 1693 (*Parish Register of All Saints' – 1678-1812* (Par 189/1/R1/2), folio 14 verso). His widow Frances paid the tax on rents and stocks in 1694 (*Taxes – 1691-1694* (P.5.9), folio 106 verso).

pertaining to the distribution of his property is dated 2 March 1694.[1]   No
mention is made in either the inventory list or the associated property bond of
Frances Toms, although we know that she died the following autumn; there is
an entry in the All Saints' parish register of her burial on 4 September 1694.[2]
Interestingly, the principal executor of his property is John Toms's son-in-law
Benjamin Thornton, who is described as a 'tobacco pipe-maker' from
Abingdon; he probably married Abigail, the daughter of John and Frances,
although when and where the marriage took place is unknown.   The bond also
names the Baptist John Toms's son John, who is described as a 'cordwinder'
from the parish of St Thomas in the city of Oxford.[3]   At some stage John Toms
junior was apparently apprenticed to his father, for on the strength of the
completion of that apprenticeship he was admitted into the cordwainers' guild
on 27 September 1689.[4]   He was a member of the guild until 1696, when he
probably moved to London.[5]   There is record of a marriage bond between him
and Sara Tull which is dated 28 June 1687 (the wedding was to take place in
the parish church of All Saints').[6]   There is also record of Toms making a
number of tax payments in the Poll Taxes of 1692-1695 while living in the
parish of St Thomas.   The first of these from 10 March 1692 is for £1 4s and
covers 'John Toms, teacher & his Wife & two children'.[7]   In the end, the

---

[1] *John Toms* (OWPR 175/2/27) = CSC #657 and CSC #658.

[2] *Parish Register of All Saints' – 1678-1812* (Par 189/1/R1/2), folio 14 verso.

[3] There is record of this son John being granted a 40-year lease on a property in the
South Oseney area of St Thomas parish on 16 July 1689.   Salter (1929): 2.523-524,
gives details of the leases on the property which is designated the 'Eighteenth
Tenement' of the South Oseney leases.   The lease was eventually taken over by the
Morrell family who based their famous Lion brewery there.   The property is depicted in
Loggan's *Oxonia Illustrata* (1675) as having several buildings on it (see CSC #550).

[4] *MS Morrell 14 – Minutes of Meetings of the Guild of Cordwayners (1614-1711)*,
folio 123 verso = CSC #637.

[5] Toms is named in the minutes for 21 October 1689 (folio 125 recto); 20 October
1690 (folio 127 verso); 19 October 1691 (folio 130 recto); 24 October 1692 (folio 132
recto); 23 October 1693 (folio 133 verso); 22 October 1694 (folio 135 recto); 21
October 1695 (folio 136 verso); and 19 October 1696 (folio 138 recto), where an '+' by
his name probably indicates his relocation during the year.   Toms is consistently
identified as 'Junior' in all of these entries except that for 1689.

[6] *OAR: Marriage Bonds – 1687* (c. 475), folio 136 = CSC #619.   Interestingly, the
marriage bond is signed by Roger Cooper, perhaps the same man who appeared before
the Oxford Petty Sessions court in connection with his allowing Lawrence King's wife
Anne to be buried within the parish churchyard while she technically was an
excommunicate (see above 135 above).

[7] *Taxes – 1691-1694* (P.5.9), folio 6 verso.   A second similar payment is dated 27
June 1692 (*Taxes – 1691-1694* (P.5.9), folio 41 recto).   Another three quarterly
payments dated 2 May 1694, 27 August 1694 and 25 February 1695 are for 3s and
cover Toms, his wife and *one* child, suggesting that one of the children had died (*Taxes
– 1691-1694* (P.5.9), folios 141 recto, 162 recto and 185 verso).   A record from 1693
shows he was also taxed for rents and stocks (*Taxes – 1691-1694* (P.5.9), folio 90

couple had four children, and appear to have been active members of the Baptist congregation which met in the house of Richard Tidmarsh. The fact that John and Sarah Toms had none of their four children baptized in the parish church of St Thomas may be an indication of their Baptist commitments.[1] What happened to this John Toms after his relocation to London is unclear, although all indications are that he made his living as a cordwainer and continued his involvement with Baptists. Thus, Thomas Crosby relates a story about a John Toms in his *The History of the English Baptists* (1740). Crosby describes him as 'a worthy gentleman of an unblemished character, and universally respected as an honest and sober man', who, when he still lived in Oxford, used to preach to the Baptist congregation which met at Richard Tidmarsh's house near the castle after he (Tidmarsh) had moved to Tiverton.[2] It is likely that Toms soon became involved with the Baptist church which was led by William Kiffen and met in Devonshire Square Baptist Church, London.[3] Benjamin Stinton mentions Toms as a messenger of the church at Devonshire Square in London, and records that he attended a meeting held on 4 June 1717 designed to establish a Particular Baptists Fund.[4] There are records of Toms serving as both a deacon and minister of the church into the 1720s, and he was instrumental in facilitating the merger with the sister-church at Turner's-Hall in 1727.[5] Perhaps the most interesting example of Toms's activity within the Devonshire Square church concerned a complicated case of church discipline involving William Kiffen's second wife, Sarah. On 2 March 1698 Sarah Kiffen was brought before the church and made to answer a number of charges, including lying, theft and falsely accusing her husband.[6] After lengthy deliberations, she was found guilty and asked to appear before the church again on 24 April 1698. This she refused to do, and as a consequence the church

---

recto), whereas an entry from 1694 records that he was taxed for his house and tenements (*Taxes – 1691-1694* (P.5.9), folio 115 verso).

[1] The parish register simply records the birth, rather than the baptism, of the four children: Sarah on 29 March 1690 (*Parish Register of St Thomas – 1655-1755* (Par 217/1/R1/1), folio 16 recto), John on 29 June 1691 (*Parish Register of St Thomas – 1655-1755* (Par 217/1/R1/1), folio 17 recto), Joseph on 2 January 1694 (*Parish Register of St Thomas – 1655-1755* (Par 217/1/R1/1), folio 18 verso), and Benjamin on 13 November 1695 (*Parish Register of St Thomas – 1655-1755* (Par 217/1/R1/1), folio 19 verso).

[2] Crosby (1740): 4.138-9. See Kreitzer (forthcoming) for more on this.

[3] Ivimey (1823): 3.322, notes that in 1704 he attended the General Assembly which met in Lorimer's Hall as a representative of the church.

[4] *A Journal of the Affairs of ye Antipaedobaptists beginning with ye Reign of King George whose Accession to the Throne was on the first of August 1714* (Reg Angus 3.h.30): page 135.

[5] *Devonshire Square (Particular) Baptist Church* (MS 20 228 1A). Ivimey (1823): 3.327-30, was critical of this merger, suggesting that it was driven by dubious financial considerations.

[6] *Devonshire Square (Particular) Baptist Church* (MS 20 228 1A), folio 13 recto-verso = CSC #670a.

initiated proceedings to withdraw table fellowship from her. On 17 July 1698 communion was withdrawn from her 'until it please God that she do returne to repentance'. She disappears from further church records after this incident, and all indications are that she was estranged from her husband until his death in 1701. Thus John Toms was an active participant in what must have been a very painful incident for the octogenarian Kiffen, one which rose like a dark storm cloud in the last years of his influential life.

3. The Soldier:

Roger Hatchman

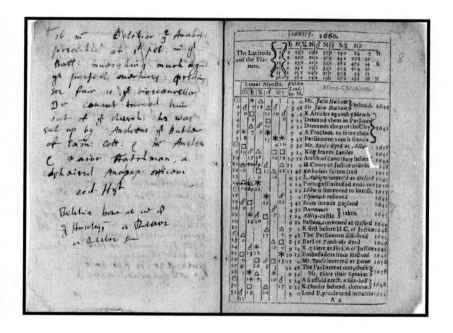

Illustration #6: Page from the almanac diaries of Anthony Wood in which he records that the controversial Fifth Monarchist John Belcher preached at St. Peter-in-the-Bailey church in Oxford on 16 January 1660. Wood notes that "he was set up by Andrews ye Butler of Exon Coll: & Mr Austen & Maior Hatchman, a casheired Anabap officer". The manuscript is part of the collection of the Bodleian Library, Oxford (*MS Wood's Diaries 4*, folios 7 verso – 8 recto).

3. The Soldier:

Roger Hatchman

Within this chapter I shall consider the life and career of Roger Hatchman, a prominent Oxford resident censured by Charles I, who became a professional military man and served in the New Model Army in Scotland under General Monck before falling foul of his commanders because of his radical religious and political beliefs. As noted above in the introduction (pages 17-18), Roger Hatchman, together with Richard Tidmarsh, Lawrence King, and Ralph Austen, appeared before the Oxford Petty Sessions court on 9 January 1662, charged, among other things, with being 'seditious sectaryes & disloyal persons'. As a result, Hatchman, Tidmarsh and King were jailed in the Bocardo prison at the North Gate of the city until such time as they would swear an oath of allegiance to Charles II and satisfy the court as to their behaviour and intentions. Despite the attempts to make him conform, Hatchman continued to be an active Dissenter. He appeared again before the Petty Sessions court a year later on 30 April 1663, where the assessment of him as a 'seditious sectary and a disloyall person' was again asserted.[1] The chapter will conclude with a brief discussion of another important Baptist Disssenter with whom Hatchman had some contact, namely John Higgins, an Oxford weaver and a signatory of *A Testimony to Truth, Agreeing with an Essay for Settlement* (1659).

A. Family Background

1. Family in Dorchester-on-Thames, Oxfordshire

Roger Hatchman was not a native Oxonian, but came from Dorchester-on-Thames in south Oxfordshire.[2] The date of his birth is unknown as the

---

[1] *Oxford Petty Sessions Roll – 1656-1678* (O.5.11), folio 52 recto = CSC #374. The court fined Hatchman 5s, but had to pursue him once again for the Dissenter 'slipt out of Courte without paying the fyne'.

[2] *The Compton Census* (1676), page 360, records that there were 13 Nonconformists in the village. See Whiteman (1986): 426, for details.

surviving records for the parish church in the village do not begin until 1638, and consequently there is no record of his baptism. However, there are a number of wills from members of his immediate family that allow us to reconstruct a fairly detailed family tree extending over six generations (see the accompanying chart of 'The Family Tree of Roger Hatchman'). The wills present some difficulties in sorting out the various Roger Hatchmans that are named within them (Roger appears as a favourite first name within the wider family). There is a son Roger named within the will of John Hatchman, a farmer from Dorchester-on-Thames, which was probated on 15 April 1588.[1] At the same time, there is also reference to a Roger Hatchman within the will of John Hatchman's wife Agnes, dated to 8 November 1610.[2] Somewhat mysteriously however, Agnes's will, in addition to bequeathing gifts to her five children (William, Elizabeth, Alice, Barbara, and Margaret), appoints Roger Hatchman as one of the overseers, describing him as her 'son in lawe'. How he can be so described is problematic; the most likely solution is that he was the son of John Hatchman from an earlier marriage.[3]

More important for this study is the will of William Hatchman, a son of John and Agnes Hatchman, which was probated on 1 August 1642.[4] The will mentions five children (three sons and two daughters),[5] and three 'God children', probably grand-children (one boy and two girls)'. The first of his sons was named John, who appears to have remained in the village of Dorchester-on-Thames and raised a family of his own there, making his living as a stonemason.[6] The second son of William and Elizabeth was named

---

[1] *John Hatchman* (DPWPR 69/1/2).

[2] *Agnes Hatchman* (DPWPR 30/1/17) = CSC #1.

[3] A second son of this earlier marriage is also named Richard Hatchman; his will has also survived (*Richard Hatchman* (DPWPR 69/1/20)), but it does not clarify the family relationships. Both Roger and Richard Hatchman gave evidence in a long and protracted court case in the Star Chamber in 1612-1614 (*Star Chamber Depositions* (STAC 8/114/18). This involved the enclosure of certain fields in Dorchester-on-Thames and the effects upon local farmers grazing their cattle on common ground. The deposition by Roger Hatchman gives his age as 56; that of Richard gives his age as 55.

[4] *William Hatchman* (DPWPR 69/1/24) = CSC #32. The will does not specifically mention William's wife, probably because she had died; most likely she was the Elizabeth Hatchman who was buried on 18 June 1638 (*Dorchester Parish Register – 1638-1726* (Par 87/1/R1/1), folio 31 recto).

[5] There was apparently a sixth child who died between 1610 and 1642; this unnamed child is mentioned in an earlier will (see *Agnes Hatchman* (DPWPR 30/1/17) = CSC #1).

[6] There is record of John Hatchman from Dorchester-on-Thames paying tax for a property containing one hearth in the Hearth Tax of Michaelmas 1662 (*Hearth Tax of August-November 1662* (E 179/255/4), Part 3, page 28). The circumstances of his marriage are unknown, although parish records indicate that he and his wife had at least five daughters (Elizabeth, Mary, Anne, Martha and one unnamed daughter) and two sons (John and Philip). The baptisms of these seven children are recorded in the parish register between the years 1638-57 (*Dorchester Parish Register – 1638-1726* (Par 87/1/R1/1), folios 1 recto, 2 recto, 4 verso, 5 recto, 5 verso and 6 recto). The daughter

Richard, and their third son was named Roger – he is the person described in this study as Roger Hatchman, the Anabaptist soldier of Oxford. Precisely when Roger was born is unknown, although it is clear from the will of Agnes Hatchman that he was alive at the time of her death in 1610. On this basis we can tentatively place his birth at about 1605.

William Hatchman was certainly not a wealthy man when he died, and each of the five children mentioned in his will was bequeathed a mere 12*d*. On 23 July 1642 his goods were valued at a total of £20 5*s* 0*d*, and all but 5*s* of that was in obligations owed him by others. The impression left is that William Hatchman was a poor farmer, whose only real riches were his children and family. He does not appear to have been an educated man, and was probably illiterate as he did not sign the will but simply left his mark (*'signum'*).[1] It looks as if Roger, the third son in the family, left a struggling farm in the country to seek his fame and fortune in Oxford, established himself there as a stonemason and later pursued a military career which took him to Scotland.

2. Family in Oxford

Unfortunately, there are no records giving details of the time and place of Hatchman's marriage to his wife Alice (whose name is known from other records). The couple appear to have been married prior to the move to Oxford, for there is record in the Dorchester-on-Thames parish register of the baptism of a son named John on 17 September 1639.[2] It appears that the couple had at least three other children while living in Dorchester-on-Thames; the children were probably born during the late 1620s or early to mid-1630s. There are no records of the baptism of any of these three other children, whose names were Thomas, Ann and Elizabeth. However, the fact that all three of these children pay the Poll Tax of 1667 in Oxford suggests that they lived independently and were earning their own salaries. by that time Indeed, Thomas was himself starting a family of his own by that time, as there is record of him marrying a

---

Elizabeth married John Thompson in October 1666 (*Dorchester Parish Register – 1638-1726* (Par 87/1/R1/1), folio 25 recto). The son Philip married Anne Fellow on 1 April 1676 (*Dorchester Parish Register – 1638-1726* (Par 87/1/R1/1), folio 25 verso), and the couple went on to have four children of their own: Philip junior, Martha, John and Richard. The baptisms of these four children are recorded in the parish register between the years 1678-85 (*Dorchester Parish Register – 1638-1726* (Par 87/1/R1/1), folios 10 verso, 11 verso, 12 recto and 13 recto).

[1] A grammar school for boys was established in the village in 1652, and a full record of boys enrolled within it has survived. However, there are *no* Hatchman boys included within the register, which covers some 192 names from 1652-1714. See *Dorchester-on-Thames Grammar School* (1976) for further details.

[2] *Dorchester Parish Register – 1638-1726* (Par 87/1/R1/1), folio 1 verso. The fate of this son is inknown. He may have been a victim of the cholera epidemic that swept through Oxford in the summer of 1643.

Margret Higgins of St Giles on 9 November 1657.[1] Margret was probably the daughter of another of the Baptist conventiclers, John Higgins, a signatory of *A Testimony to Truth, Agreeing with an Essay for Settlement* (1659) and one of the five people later arrested for attending a meeting at the house of Lawrence King on 9 January 1670 (for more on Higgins see pages 191-7 below). The couple had a child, who died shortly after birth and was buried in the parish church of St Mary Magdalen on 3 November 1659.[2] Meanwhile, within the Poll Tax of 1667 Ann Hatchman is recorded as living in the parish of St Ebbe's within the city of Oxford. She was a servant to George Price, his wife and three children, and is listed as receiving 30*s* in wages and paying 2*s* in tax.[3] Elizabeth Hatchman is also recorded as living in the parish of St Ebbe's; she is listed as receiving 40*s* in wages and pays 3*s* in tax.[4]

At some point Hatchman and his family settled in the parish of St Thomas in Oxford. He held the lease on a property within the parish for many years, as is evidenced by a variety of records including leases, tax records, and wills and probate documents. The earliest of these is a forty-year lease from Christ Church granted on 20 December 1636.[5] The lease was on a property in an area of South Osney known as the Hammell, just along what is now known as Osney Lane.[6] It is described as 'the Seventh Tenement & the first on the west side of the Ham[m]ell';[7] the lease carried the standard rent of 6*s* 8*d* and one capon (or 18*d* in lieu), and Hatchman's occupation within the lease document is given as 'Freemason'. Subsequent tax records show a 'Mr Hatchman' as living in the parish of St Thomas and paying 9*d* in the Lay Subsidy of 23 June 1647[8] and 1*s* in the Lay Subsidy of 17 March 1648.[9] The Christ Church lease was

---

[1] *Parish Register of St Michael-at-the-Northgate – 1654-1683* (Par 211/1/R1/2), folio 40 verso = CSC #255.

[2] *Parish Register of St Mary Magdalen – 1602-1662* (Par 208/1/R1/1), folio 75 recto. The entry states 'A Chrisom child of Mr Hatchmans was buried'. The description of the unnamed child as a 'chrisom child' suggests that he or she had recently been baptized, and may indicate how flexible some of the early Baptists were in such matters.

[3] *Poll Tax of 1667* (P.5.7), folio 68 recto = Salter (1923: 307).

[4] *Poll Tax of 1667* (P.5.7), folio 65 verso = Salter (1923: 303). Salter mis-transcribed the surname as 'Hatchin'.

[5] *Christ Church Lease – Roger Hatchman* (22 December 1636) = CSC #13.

[6] See CSC #545 for the probable location of this property in David Loggan's *Oxonia Illustrata* (1675). This means that the Hatchman family residence was probably a hundred yards or so away from the house of Richard Tidmarsh, later one of the acknowledged leaders of the Baptist church in Oxford.

[7] *Book of Evidences, Part 1* (Ch Ch MS c.2), page 41.

[8] *Lay Subsidy of 23 June 1647* (E 179 164/498), membrane 3. Hatchman's name does not appear in the records of the earlier collection of this tax (*Lay Subsidy of 23 June 1647* (E 179 164/498a), membrane 4), although it is possible that he also made this payment. The membrane is torn and has a large piece missing, which probably accounts for the absence of his name.

[9] *Lay Subsidy of 17 March 1648* (E 179 164/499), membrane 2.

renewed on 25 April 1654,[1] although, interestingly, within the renewal Hatchman is described not as a 'Freemason', but as a 'Gentleman',[2] and his parish address is now given as 'St Gyles' rather than St Thomas.[3] This may be a simple clerical error, although it is possible that the alterations indicate Hatchman's relocation to that parish. However, there are no other records associating Hatchman with the parish of St Giles, although there are several later records mentioning him as living in the nearby village of Headington, as well as records of him being granted a lease in the parish of St Peter-in-the-Bailey.

There are several intriguing records which associate Hatchman with the parish of St Peter-in-the-Bailey. The most important is a lease dated 16 November 1652 on a New College property containing two houses along the west side of the lane traditionally called 'the Seven Deadly Sins', now known as New Inn Hall Street. Interestingly, this property is within a stone's throw of the property of Ralph Austen, who built a new house along Queen Street and opened a cider-making business on the site in 1659 (Austen is discussed more fully in chapter 4). Thus, Hatchman and Austen, two of the men who facilitated the Fifth Monarchist John Belcher coming to preach at the nearby St Peter-in-the-Bailey on 16 January 1660 (see pages 179-81 below), were neighbours.

Fortunately, the lease for the property in St Peter-in-the-Bailey has survived in fairly good condition and it has a clear signature of Hatchman.[4] It seems likely that he signed the lease prior to his military career and eventual posting to Scotland, which took place probably in the middle of 1654 (Hatchman's career as a soldier is discussed below). Early in that year he and a neighbour named Mr. Gilpin became involved in a dispute over property boundaries as Hatchman prepared to build on the site. City viewers were appointed by the City Council to render an opinion in the matter and made their report on 4 March 1654, siding with Hatchman in the matter.[5] Construction on the property seems to have been overtaken by political events, as Hatchman took up a military commission and was posted to Scotland to help defend the nation against a resurgence of the 'Scots invasion'.

---

[1] *Christ Church Lease – Roger Hatchman* (25 April 1654) = CSC #171. The 1636 lease is in a poor state of preservation, although the 1654 lease is in good condition with the original wax seal, as well as Hatchman's signature, clearly visible. Both leases were copied into the *Christ Church Lease Book 4 – 1635-1658* (Ch.Ch. MS xx.c.4), pages 18-19 and 362-364.

[2] For a discussion of the title of 'Gentleman', the lowest rank in the gentry, and its relation to the higher title of 'Esquire' and the lower title of 'Mister', see Aylmer (1973): 394-395.

[3] See Salter (1929b): 2.530. Hayden (1981-2): 127), wrongly gives the duration of the 1654 lease as twenty years.

[4] *New College Archives: Leases* (Steer #2244) = CSC #121. The lease was also copied into the New College's *Lease Book #10 – 1649-1654* (Steer #9765), pages 219 and 222.

[5] *New College Archives: Valuations* (Steer #1446) = CSC #169.

When he returned from Scotland, Hatchman seems to have settled in the village of Headington. Several records place him in the village no later than the summer of 1661. The earliest of these is a record of him serving as one of the people responsible for collecting the village's contribution to the Subsidy of 29 December 1660. Hatchman and his fellow collector Thomas Hanckes submitted £3 2*s* 7*d* to the Oxfordshire county officers Sir Thomas Clerk and Vincent Barry in a document dated 12 July 1661.[1] There is also record of Hatchman paying tax on a Headington property containing four hearths in the Hearth Tax of Michaelmas 1662.[2] In addition, Roger Hatchman and another man named William Cannon jointly paid 2*s* 8*d* in the Lay Subsidy of 27 July 1663 while living in the village; the tax was collected on 17 October 1663.[3] Interestingly, Hatchman and Cannon, are described as 'non communicants' within this document.[4] There are two entries relating to Hatchman within the Diocesan court records which fill out this picture of Hatchman as an active Dissenter within the village of Headington. The first of these is dated 6 December 1662 and concerns the failure of Hatchman and his wife, whose name is (mistakenly) given as Mary, to attend their local parish church.[5] The

---

[1] *Subsidy of 29 December 1660* (E 179/164/501a), folio 2 recto.

[2] *Hearth Tax for Michaelmas 1662* (E 179/255/3), page 72. This payment is dated 9 November 1662.

[3] *Subsidy of 27 July 1663* (E 179/164/503), folio 4 recto = Weinstock (1940): 249. Weinstock misprints the amount paid by Cannon and Hatchman as £10 2*s* 08*d* (the total collected from the village).

[4] Both were excommunicated, although Cannon appealed against his excommunication, citing bad weather and the great distance he lived from the parish church as reasons for his non-attendance. Humorously, he also attempted to justify his wearing a hat during services as due to his poor health (*ODR: 27 September 1662-15 April 1665* (c. 4), folio 214 verso).

The description of Hatchman as a 'non communicant' needs to be viewed alongside other ecclesiastical records of Dissenters in Headington, including the returns for Headington recorded within *The Compton Census* of 1676. Within these returns the parish of Headington is recorded as having 237 Conformists and one Nonconformist within it (*The Compton Census* (1976) , page 361 = Whiteman (1986: 426). Meanwhile, the Bishop of Oxford John Fell records two Dissenters for the parish of Headington within his accounts of 1682; they are named as John Webb, an Anabaptist, and John Freeman, a Quaker (*ODR: Bishop Fell's Notes on Dissenters* (d. 708), folio 75). Similarly, the list of Dissenters presented to the Archdeacon Timothy Halton at his visitation in 1683 records one unnamed Dissenter for the parish of Headington (*ODR: Memoranda from Diocesan Books 1679-1814* (b. 68), folio 6 verso). It is significant that Hatchman is *not* named in any of these three subsequent documents. This suggests that Hatchman, who was identified by name as one of two Dissenters in the parish of Headington in 1663, had died by the time that the later ecclesiastical records from 1676 and 1682-3 were compiled. However, it appears that William Cannon had further contacts with the Baptists: his son William was apprenticed to John Toms senior, probably the Baptist cordwainer, on 14 June 1676 (*Civic Enrolments – 1662-1699* (L.5.4), page 259) (see page 114 above).

[5] *ODR: 27 September 1662-15 April 1665* (c. 4), folio 51 verso = CSC #359.

record relates that Hatchman 'disputeth the case, and denyeth any p[ar]ochiall church'. The court ordered them to attend their parish church the next Sunday 'and to certifie thereof the next Court day, or otherwise to shewe cause that hee should not be excommunicated'. The second record is dated a week later on 13 December 1662 and has Hatchman admitting that 'he hath not beene at church nor hath he a c[er]tificate', whereupon the court pronounced him contumacious and set in motion the process of excommunication.[1] In this second record Hatchman's wife is not named at all, which suggests that the court clerk may have been confused over her name and realized the error in the previous week's entry.

Another important document associating Hatchman with Headington is the caveat on the estate of a John Hatchman of Shirborne which is dated 8 November 1661.[2] This document mentions a 'John Hatchman of Dorchester', a 'Roger Hatchman of Heddington', and an 'Edward Wyans of the parish of St Martin's, Carfax' as people to be contacted in connection with the settlement of goods and property. It is initially difficult to determine what the relationships are between the various Hatchmans mentioned within this caveat record, for they are never explicitly stated in the document itself. Clearly John Hatchman from Shirborne near Dorchester-on-Thames in Oxfordshire has died, and the post-mortem distribution of his goods and property is being considered. The caveat's legal notice concerns Roger and John Hatchman, presumably the closest surviving relatives of the deceased John Hatchman (probably his cousins[3]). The geographical connections contained in the caveat are confirmed in the probate bond of John Hatchman from 11 November 1661, which the said

---

[1] *ODR: 27 September 1662-15 April 1665* (c. 4), folio 57 verso = CSC #360. It appears that the court clerk made an error as to the name of Hatchman's wife within these records, calling her Mary instead of Alice. At the bottom of the folio there is another entry referring to 'Mariam ux[orem] Georgii Hatchman de Heddington (Mary the wife of George Hatchman from Headington)'. Elsewhere in the court proceedings Mary is the wife of George *Potter* from St Aldate's parish (*ODR: 27 September 1662-15 April 1665* (c. 4), folios 120 verso, 123 recto and 127 recto). Apparently the clerk confused *Alice* Hatchman with *Mary* Potter. The same error is made in a listing of those excommunicated which was composed in circa 1665 (*ODR: Excommunications – 1633-1791* (c. 99), folios 239 recto). Beyond these, there are no other records of a Mary Hatchman; elsewhere Roger Hatchman's wife is always called Alice.

[2] *Oxford Caveats – 1643-1677* (MS Wills 307), folio 47 recto = CSC #332. It is this document which provides the primary geographical clue to Roger Hatchman's family roots in Dorchester-on-Thames.

[3] I take the deceased John Hatchman, who is described as a shepherd from Shirborne, to be the son of Roger Hatchman of Dorchester-on-Thames, the son of John Hatchman. This Roger Hatchman was thus the half-brother of William Hatchman, who was the father of both John and Roger (our Baptist Dissenter). This reconstruction fits well with the description in the probate inventory, dated 4 January 1662; John Hatchman from Shirborne is described as the 'cousin Germane' of John Hatchman of Dorchester-on-Thames (*John Hatchman* (OWPR 80/4/17) = CSC #333). The record mistakenly describes the administrator of the probate accounts as 'John Hatchman of Sherborne', instead of correctly giving his residence as Dorchester-on-Thames.

John Hatchman from Dorchester-on-Thames and Roger Hatchman of Headington sign as witnesses.[1]

Moreover, one other interesting feature of the caveat document from 1661 is also worthy of special comment for it confirms a connection between Hatchman and other Baptists in Oxford. The caveat mentions the cordwainer Edward Wyans, who serves in some capacity as an executor of the John Hatchman's estate (Wyans was discussed above on pages 59-72). It appears that he was a long-standing friend of Hatchman, and that the two men had worked together in 1642 on the construction of the Great Quadrangle in Christ Church (see below).[2] The fact that Wyans's name later appears in connection with documents relating to the death of a Hatchman family member nearly twenty years later in 1661 is another illustration of the close interconnections that existed among the Baptists of the city over a long period.

After being cashiered from the army in late 1659 or early 1660 (see pages 175-9 below) Hatchman returned to Headington, but this apparently was only intended as a temporary arrangement until the construction of a new house on the property in St Peter-in-the-Bailey was complete. Several records confirm the possession of the property along New Inn Hall Street and Hatchman's intent to build on it. There is record of him paying two installments in a tax subsidy dated 11 April 1664 in connection with the property. The entry is given as 'Roger Hatchman in Lands'; the first payment is for 20*s* and the second for 8*s*.[3] There is also a document providing the official measurements of the property, as determined by a carpenter employed by New College officials who witnessed the survey on 20 March 1665.[4] This was almost certainly done in anticipation of building or expanding or remodelling the two tenements on the site. This document is especially interesting in that it gives the location and name of the property – 'Roger Hatchmans house Olive Rosehall by Trillocks In[n]e'.[5] Most significant are the records of another property dispute with a neighbour, a well-established Quaker surgeon named Richard Betteris (or Betterice) who also lived along New Inn Hall Street in the property to the south

---

[1] *John Hatchman* (OWPR 80/4/17) = CSC #333. There is a scribal mistake in the introductory paragraph which confuses Roger Hatchman's surname with his occupation. He is described as 'Rogerum Mason de Heddington in Com[ita]t[u] p[re]dicto, Freemason'. Interestingly, his relative John Hatchman is also described in the document as a 'Mason', which suggests there was a tradition of masonry within the Hatchman family.

[2] Wyans's name appears six times in two of the summary account sheets that mention Hatchman (*Disbursements Book 1641-2* (Ch. Ch. MS xii b 85), folios 11 recto and verso).

[3] *Lay Subsidy of 11 April 1664* (B.1.4f).

[4] *New College Archives: Valuations* (Steer #1442) = CSC #403.

[5] The property was just to the south of New Inn Hall (Trillock's Inn), with the two tenements now known as No. 3 and No. 5 New Inn Hall Street (see Salter (1969): 2.179-180 for details of the leases relating to the property).

of Hatchman's (see page 57 above).[1] Hatchman and Betteris had a legal wrangle over the ownership of a wall between their properties,[2] and viewers were appointed by the City Council on 3 February 1665 to render an opinion.[3] Other records of this dispute survive in the New College archives, including a legal resolution of the dispute, which was signed and sealed by Betteris on 10 April 1665.[4] Interestingly, these documents mention 'the house of Roger Hatchman', but give prominence to Alice Hatchman as the tenant and active agent in the affair. This gives the impression that Alice Hatchman was pursuing the legal dispute on behalf of her husband, a possible indication that he was seriously ill and unable to do so himself. Indeed, he appears to have died within the next year or two, for there is a record of 'Alice Hatchman wife of Rog[er] Hatchman' paying 1s in the Poll Tax of 1 March 1667 while living in the parish of St Michael.[5] This suggests that her husband had died leaving her responsible for payment of the tax; apparently she moved to the parish of St Michael soon after his death.

Hatchman's death sometime in late 1667 or 1668 also seems indicated by records associated with the Christ Church property for which he held a lease in the parish of St Thomas. That Hatchman was still alive at the beginning of 1664 is suggested by the lease of an adjoining property, namely, that pertaining to Tenements 8-11 on the west side of the Hammell. This lease, granted to Henry Whitehead on 20 January 1664, names Roger Hatchman as occupying the property to the south, indicating that he was still the leaseholder of the Christ Church property at the beginning of the year. However, Hatchman's lease for this property came up for renewal on 10 September 1669. Records show that the lease passed on to a freemason named Philip Tomlinson, which suggests that Hatchman had died by this time. Nevertheless, it seems that for a short time after his death the Hatchman family still retained legal rights and responsibilities for the property in the parish of St Thomas, which was probably rented out to tenants. There are records of a 'Mr. Hatchman' of the parish of St Thomas paying a number of War Taxes in 1667-1668,[6] commencing with a quarterly payment of 2s 3d for his 'tenements' on 24 June 1667.[7] Two further such quarterly payments, assessed at the same rate, were made for Hatchman's

---

[1] Betteris lived in what is now known as No. 1 New Inn Hall Street (see Salter (1969: 2. 179)). He paid tax on four hearths on the property in the Hearth Taxes of Michaelmas 1662 (*Hearth Tax of August-November 1662* (E 179/255/4), Part 2, page 69 reverse), Michaelmas 1665 (*Hearth Tax of Michaelmas 1665* (E 179/164/513), membrane 28 verso) and Lady Day 1665 (*Hearth Tax of 24 April 1666* (E 179/164/514), membrane 23 verso).

[2] The wall is clearly visible in David Loggan's *Oxonia Illustrata* (1675). See CSC #547.

[3] *Husting and Mayors Court 1665-1666* (M.4.5), folio 25 verso (Husting) = CSC #402.

[4] *New College Archives: Valuations* (Steer #1442) = CSC #405.

[5] *Poll Tax of 1667* (P.5.7), folio 50 recto.

[6] See pages 5-6 for an explanation of these taxes.

[7] *War Taxes – 1667-1668* (P.5.8), folio 15 verso.

tenements on 29 September 1667[1] and 21 December 1667.[2]   There is also a quarterly tax record dated 26 March 1668 in which 2s 4d in tax was paid for Hatchman's tenements.[3]   Finally, there are also three further quarterly tax records dated 26 June 1668, 26 September 1668, and 26 December 1668; within all three collections 2s 4d was paid for 'Hatchman's tenements'.[4]   It is probable that Hatchman's son Thomas took over responsibility for these tenements after his father's death and paid the taxes concerned until the lease was taken over by Philip Tomlinson.

What about the other property in the parish of St Peter-in-the-Bailey?   It appears that the New College lease to Hatchman's property in this parish was sold after his death.   The property is mentioned within the will of one John Johnson which was signed on 21 April 1677: 'I give and bequeath unto my said loveing wife Mary Johnson thos houses that [I] purch[as]ed of Mr Hatchman lying & being on New Inn Hall Lane in the Citty of Oxford which I hold by lease from New Colleg in the University of Oxford'.[5]

B. The Controversial Stonemason: From Royal Censure to Oxford Citizenship (1642-1654)

1. Work as a Stonemason (1642)

Although Hatchman came from a farming family he does not appear to have been interested in life as a husbandman.   Instead, his occupation is generally described in surviving records as 'stonemason' or, as in the 1636 lease from Christ Church, as 'freemason'.   The city of Oxford, with its many colleges and University buildings, was an ideal place for a skilled stonemason to work, and there is evidence that Hatchman made a good living in the profession, contracting himself out to the colleges of the University.   Within the archives of Christ Church there are account books covering the construction of the Great Quadrangle, work that was done under the supervision of Samuel Fell, the Dean of Christ Church.[6]   Fell was an ardent royalist and later proved himself to be a thorn in the side of the Parliamentary Visitors to the University, the very

---

[1] *War Taxes – 1667-1668* (P.5.8), 37 verso.

[2] *War Taxes – 1667-1668* (P.5.8), 46 verso.

[3] *War Taxes – 1667-1668* (P.5.8), 62 verso.

[4] *War Taxes – 1667-1668* (P.5.8), folios 74 verso, 100 recto, and 115 verso.

[5] *John Johnson* (OWPR 38/1/3).

[6] Hiscock (1946): 201, makes passing reference to the mason Hatchman.   Hayden (1981-82): 132, cites Hiscock (incorrectly giving the page number as 200) and then adds, 'The same mason, or a namesake, worked on the Sheldonian Theatre under Wren in 1664.'   This is a complete misreading of Hiscock and represents a confusion between Roger Hatchman and Thomas Robinson, another mason who worked on the project (see Hiscock [1946]: 202).   In point of fact, the Bodleian Library contains a manuscript (*MS Bodl 898*) which gives a detailed account of the finances expended on the construction of the theatre.   It is a meticulous record of where every penny went, to whom and on what date, and in all its 361 pages there is not a *single* reference to Roger Hatchman.

group which, as we shall see, other documents suggest Hatchman supported. One particular account book includes several pages detailing regular payments made to Hatchman for his work as a stonemason on the project. This account book records Hatchman signing for payments made on 29 October 1641; 6, 19 and 26 November 1641; 3, 10, 17 and 24 December 1641; 7, 14, and 21 January 1642; on 28 January 1642; 4, 11, 18 and 25 February 1642; 4, 11, 18 and 26 March 1642; 1, 8 April 1642; on 15, 22 and 29 April 1642; on 5, 20 and 27 May 1642; on 10, 17 June 1642; on 1, 8, 15, 22 and 30 July 1642; on 5, 13, 19 and 26 August 1642; and 1 September 1642.[1] Roger Hatchman's name also appears in the summary accounts for the four termly periods of the fiscal year: his name is listed seven times for Term 1, 6 times for Term 2, 3 times for Term 3, and 5 times for Term 4.[2]

Relations between the city of Oxford and the University, with its various constituent colleges, were often strained, particularly in matters of employment. The guild of freemasons guarded their profession jealously, which meant that occasionally there were disputes between them and college or University officials over the employment of unqualified masons in the construction of college buildings. For example, according to University records, some freemasons working on the chapel of University College were imprisoned on 25 August 1640 by the Vice-Chancellor of the University, Christopher Potter from Queen's College, for refusing to allow some roughmasons to work with them in the project. The basis for the refusal appears to have been the fact that the roughmasons had not joined the official guild.[3] It is unknown whether Hatchman worked as a freemason on the University College project, but we can reasonably deduce that he was all too aware of the clash between University officials and members of his own trade guild in the matter. This appears to be a classic example of the tension between 'Town' and 'Gown' which characterized so much of life within Oxford. As a 'freemason' Hatchman presumably would have known of the pressures being place upon the professional guild by the prevailing political and economic powers in the University, particularly as they tended to try and dominate the city and its inhabitants. This situation had important political implications, for it is generally recognized that the students and teaching fellows of the colleges of the University were largely royalist in sympathy, while the majority of the support for the Parliamentary cause within the city came from its resident

---

[1] *Disbursements Book 1641-2* (Ch. Ch. MS xii b 85), folios 1 verso, 2 recto, and 2 verso.
[2] *Disbursements Book 1641-2* (Ch. Ch. MS xii b 85), folios 11 recto, 11 verso, 27 recto, 43 recto, and 59 recto
[3] The matter is discussed in *MS Twyne-Langbaine IV*, folio 87 recto and verso = CSC #17. Crossley (1979): 327, discusses this manuscript briefly, but inaccurately cites the reference for it and fails to give the full date of the incident (which is found at the top of folio 87 recto). The incident was also recorded within the official University archives in *Gerard Langbaine's Collections Volume 3* (WP γ 26 1) page 454 = CSC #18.

population. The arrival of Charles I and his entourage in the city on 29 October 1642 seems to have heightened tensions between royalists and Parliamentarians within the city. It was not long before some members of the Parliamentarian camp decided that they could not live in Oxford any longer and left for greener pastures. Hatchman was among these disaffected inhabitants.

2. The Flight to Abingdon and Censure by Charles I (1642-3)

There is evidence to suggest that Hatchman left Oxford in late 1642 for the relative safety of the near-by town of Abingdon. The City Council proceedings dated 14 September 1643 detail what can only be described as Hatchman's anti-royalist stance and his support for the Parliamentary cause.[1] On that date the Mayor of Oxford reported that he had received a letter from Charles I outlining his dissatisfaction with a number of citizens who had abandoned Oxford and 'many moneths since have gone from hence into the Rebellion or have adhered unto them'. An investigation was conducted by the City Council into the matter and Roger Hatchman was specifically identified as one of those citizens who left Oxford because he was so 'ill affected to his Ma[jes]tie'. In accordance with the king's demands, Hatchman and the others, including Thomas Williams who later was to become an active Dissenter, were disenfranchised and, where relevant, had their citizenship revoked.

In short, Hatchman is listed among a group of prominent civic officials and tradesmen within Oxford whose departure from the city was being construed by the king as disloyalty, not to say outright sedition against the crown. Precisely what official role Roger Hatchman had within civic government at this point is unknown. He may simply have been a man who held strong Parliamentarian convictions and found that the presence of the king in Oxford was too much to stomach psychologically; he also may have been in danger of being imprisoned at the king's pleasure. The City Council record does not tell us explicitly where the disaffected Parliamentarians went, but there is good evidence to suggest that many of them went to the market town of Abingdon, a mere six miles to the south.[2]

One contemporary witness, Brian Twyne, an Oxford antiquarian and the first curator of the University archives, records an unusual incident prior to the royal occupation of Oxford which also helps explain the background to Hatchman's censure by the king in September of 1643. This concerns events which took place in August of 1642, during the run-up to the battle of Edgehill, when royalist and Parliamentary forces were both jockeying for position and testing each other's strengths and weaknesses. It seems that three troops of horse under the command of Sir John Byron had a confrontation with Parliamentary militia at Brackley in Northamptonshire on Sunday 28 August 1642. Byron's royalist cavaliers came off much the worse in the engagement – over 60 horses

---

[1] *City Council Proceedings – 1629-1663* (A.5.7), folio 130 verso = CSC #43.

[2] Philip (1937): 152-165, discusses the important river traffic that existed between Oxford and other towns downstream on the Thames during the Civil War.

were captured, and a great deal of money and supplies were commandeered by the men of the county militia. Byron and the remaining troops under his command were forced to flee for their lives across the open fields and headed south, eventually taking refuge in Oxford, where they arrived late at night, hungry and exhausted.[1] Twyne describes the entry of these royalist troops into the city on that Sunday night, an act which caused great consternation amongst the people of the city since they did not know if the soldiers were royalist or Parliamentary forces, or what their intentions were.[2] Anthony Wood, who consulted Twyne's manuscript and wrote marginal notes into it, also describes how anxious the people of Oxford were over rumours of the imminent arrival of soldiers during the summer of 1642. Although Wood shamelessly copied from Twyne without acknowledgement when compiling his own study of Oxford, he adds at this point the interesting detail that some of the 'puritanical Townsmen', including the Alderman John Nixon, were fearful of ill-treatment or imprisonment, and *fled the city for nearby Abingdon.*[3]

There are other indications within contemporary documents which suggest that the disaffected Parliamentarians left Oxford for Abingdon. The six-page pamphlet entitled *A True Relation of the Manner of Taking the Earl of Northampton* (1642), in relating the events surrounding the capture of Spencer Compton, the Second Earl of Northampton, by Parliamentary soldiers under the command of Colonel Hampden and Colonel Goodwin,[4] records a reference to the flight of some townspeople from Oxford to Abingdon. Here it is noted that the entry of the cavaliers into Oxford at night 'much affrighted the townsmen in so much that some of them removed to Abingdon for safety'.[5] The exodus was not restricted to a few frightened and disaffected individuals, for according to one contemporary news-sheet, the number of townspeople who fled to Abingdon was said to have been 'above 100 families'.[6]

There are several news-sheets and pamphlets which help explain the circumstances surrounding this incident involving the arrival of troops into the city and the flight of some of the townspeople to nearby Abingdon. Most of these deal with the period between 24 August 1642, when rumours of the advance of Colonel Hampden's cavalry towards Oxford was received in the city, and 29 October 1642, when the king's troops entered Oxford following the

---

[1] For details of Sir John Byron's outrageous behaviour in the whole incident, see *A Declaration of the Lords and Commons ... Concerning an insolent Letter sent to M. Clarke ... from Sir John Biron, Knight* (1642).

[2] *MS Ballard 68*, page 5 = CSC #33. The manuscript was stolen from the library of the Ashmolean Museum at one point, but it was later deposited within the Bodleian Library.

[3] *MS Wood F 1*, page 900 = Gutch (1796): 2.444-5 = CSC #34.

[4] At the time, John Hampden and Arthur Goodwin were fellow MPs for Buckinghamshire.

[5] *A True Relation of the Manner of Taking the Earl of Northampton* (1642): 6.

[6] *Speciall Passages and certain Informations from severall places* (Number 5: 6-13 September 1642): 33. A census taken on 7 June 1643 gives the adult male population of Oxford as 3,320 (see *Bodleian MS 28189*, folio 17).

battle of Edgehill and set up what was to become a royalist force of occupation. During these crucial six weeks, both royalist and Parliamentary forces made preliminary excursions into Oxford, although neither side appeared to appreciate fully the strategic and political importance of the city at the time. Three documents in particular are worth noting briefly, for they not only help illustrate the fears and anxieties of the inhabitants about soldiers entering the city, but also demonstrate the complexities and tensions between royalist and Parliamentary factions, citizens and University members alike.

The first is the pamphlet entitled *Exceeding Good News from Oxfordshire* which was written following the capture of the Earl of Berkshire by Colonel Hampden and Colonel Goodwin and is dated 24 August 1642. The pamphlet relates how royalists in Oxford, 'those of the University and City that were ill-affected to the King and Parliament', were so disconcerted by rumours that Colonel Hampden was heading towards them with his troops that they 'caused many great pieces of timber to be laid crosse the Bridge to keep out his horse'.[1] Here we see both University members and town citizens working together to fortify Magdalen Bridge against the incursion of Parliamentary forces.   The second is the pamphlet entitled *True News from Oxford* which is dated to 29 August 1642.   This is ostensibly a letter written by an anonymous Oxford scholar to his brother in London and purports to give an account of the ongoing preparations that are being made in anticipation of the arrival of Parliamentary forces in Oxford.[2]   It is clearly written by a supporter of the Parliamentary cause and is highly ironic in tone.   The pamphlet describes the 'scholars' of the University as busily engaged in training exercises, marching up and down the streets of the city.   This was done under the watchful eyes of Lord Lovelace and Lord Wilmot, the representatives of Charles I sent to prepare for his entry into, and eventual occupation of, the city of Oxford.[3]   The pamphlet's anonymous author invokes biblical imagery from 1 Samuel 17 to describe the false bravado of these 'scholars':

> They were ... courageously marching, every one looking like a son of Goliath, [when] there came unexpected news, that there were troopers marching towards them, but now the stout courage of these before brav Cavaleers, for they hearing this news, the major part was in such haste to be gone, they never staied to examine the truth, or whether they were for them or against them, but runne as hard as their heeles could carry them out of the field, leaving field and courage

---

[1] *Exceeding Good News from Oxfordshire* (1642): 3.

[2] In the face of this advance Lord Byron's troops left the city on 10 September. Interestingly, Parliamentary soldiers under the command of William Fiennes, the Viscount Lord Say and Sele, entered Oxford on 10 September 1642 and made a thorough search of the colleges. See *A Perfect Diurnal of the Passages of the Souldiers that are under the Command of The Lord Say in Oxford* (1642) for details of their activities, including the notorious incident in which soldiers shot up the statue of the Virgin Mary at the entrance to St Mary's church and then were chased by an angry, stone-throwing mob down the High Street to the east gate of the city (3).

[3] John Lovelace, second baron Lovelace and Charles, Viscount Wilmot of Athlone.

all at once, the rest being encouraged by the two Lords to stand and see the event, staid, but with such courage that each of them were like to fall down in the places where they stood, which did plainly appear by their pale faces, so that I am confident had the imagined troopers come to fight, they would have showed them their backes, and made known what swift footmen they could (on such an occasion) be.[1]

The third document is a related eight-page pamphlet dated to 10 September 1642 and entitled *University News, or, the Unfortunate Proceedings of the Cavaliers in Oxford.* It too takes the form of a letter written by an Oxford resident to his brother in London, giving details about life within the University city. The unnamed author also relates how, on the evening of Sunday 28 August, approximately 250 Cavalier troopers rode into Oxford, supposedly to 'assist the University against the Parlamenteers'.[2] What is intriguing about this third pamphlet is the way in which it suggests that it is not only the Townspeople but also some students of the University who were becoming disaffected with the royalist troops and were deserting to nearby Abingdon. Much of the pamphlet is given over to relating how the behaviour of the troopers within the city alienated both students and townspeople from any sympathy for the royalist cause. Speaking of the 'merciless mercies' of the Cavaliers, and the way they had conducted themselves in Oxford, the author noted that

> there is a daily declining of the University as well as of the Towne from them …
> insomuch that some of the scholars (as its reported) that trained for them are
> now gone to *Abington*, to combine with those that intend to oppose them, so that
> now the number of the Schollars that train here are scarce 300 which formerly
> was neere 500 or more.[3]

In short, all of this suggests that in the autumn of 1642 there was in Oxford a fairly widespread disaffection with Charles I and the royalist troops housed in the city. Many could read the signs of the times and withdrew from Oxford to the nearby market-town of Abingdon.[4] It seems that Hatchman was among the

---

[1] *True News from Oxford* (1642): 5-6.

[2] *Exceeding True Newes* (1642): A3, reported on 7 September that some Oxford students who supported the royalist cause had carried great stones to the top of Magdalen Tower in order to 'throw them downe upon the heads of those that shall oppose them.' A bloody skirmish between Cavaliers entrenched in the city and a county militia took place on 7 September 1642 (see *A Happy Victory Obtained by the Trained Band of Oxford* (1642)).

[3] *University News, or, the Unfortunate Proceedings of the Cavaliers in Oxford* (1642): A3.

[4] There are numerous tracts and newspaper reports of the Cavaliers' abuses in Oxford. See *A Continuation of certain Speciall and Remarkable passages from both Houses of Parliament*, Number 26 (2-9 September 1646): 3. The behaviour of the royalist troops during an earlier incursion into Abingdon itself, while under the

Oxford townspeople who left the city rather than face living there alongside Charles I and his royal entourage. Indeed, it is probably not coincidental that the last payment Roger Hatchman received for his work as a stonemason is dated 1 September 1642, just three days after the royalist troops led by Sir John Byron entered Oxford. The evidence suggests that Hatchman's work on the Great Quadrangle in Christ Church stopped with the arrival of the soldiers. As far as can be determined, Hatchman went to Abingdon with his family, and only returned to Oxford when Charles I left and the city was in the hands of the Parliamentary army.

3. The Return to Oxford and the Granting of Citizenship (1646)

On 27 April 1646 Charles I fled from the besieged city of Oxford in a rather ignominious fashion: shorn of his beard, he rode out on horseback, under cover of darkness, accompanied by a few loyal friends. A woodcut from the time proclaimed 'The King escapes out of Oxford in a disguised manner'.[1] Once the king was gone Parliamentary forces under Lord Fairfax soon took control, capturing the city in June of 1646. The stage was thus set for the return of the Parliamentarians who had fled for Abingdon three or four years before.

Indeed, the second mention of Hatchman within the Oxford City Council records points in precisely this direction. His name appears in the entry for 29 June 1646, where the earlier matter of royal censure is again taken up and overturned by the City Council. Something of the urgency felt over the matter is seen by the fact that this Council dealt with the matter just five days after the royalist troops commenced their evacuation from Oxford. Hatchman and others, including Thomas Williams, were 'restored to theire freedom and such places as they had before in this Citie by a full Consent of this howse'.[2]

The restoration of rights and privileges for those listed opened the door for their further civic involvement within the life of the city of Oxford. Alderman John Nixon, by all accounts one of the leaders of the anti-royalist faction who were disenfranchised by Charles I, was elected the new Mayor in September of 1646.[3] Clearly the surrender of the city of Oxford to the Parliamentary army under Thomas Fairfax meant that the winds of change were blowing. For Hatchman, the altered political situation provided an opportunity for him to pursue civic advancement and make an application to be granted the 'Freedom of the City'. There is record of him being granted Oxford citizenship within the proceedings of the Oxford City Council for 1 July 1651, having paid a 'Fyne of Fyve poundes, paying the Officers fees, & Five shillinges towards the

---

command of Lord Wilmot in 1642, was far from exemplary. See *Abingdons and Alisburies Present Miseries* (1642): 6-8, for details.

[1] Vicars (1652): 19. Wilson (2000): 352, discusses Charles I's flight from Oxford.

[2] *City Council Proceedings – 1629-1663* (A.5.7), folio 147 recto = CSC #47. The matter is also recorded in *City Council Minutes – 1635-1657* (A.4.3), folio 161 verso = CSC #48.

[3] His coat of arms is presented in *MS Wood F 4*, page 101.

buyinge of a cushion'.[1] Somewhat unusually, his citizenship is also recorded within *two* other Oxford City documents, the *Audit Book – 1592-1682*,[2] and the *Oxford Civic Enrolments – 1639-1662*.[3]

C. Captain Hatchman – Officer in the Parliamentary Army (1655-1659)

Roger Hatchman is the only person of significance in the first generation of Baptists in Oxford known to have been a commissioned military officer with active service. Moreover, he served in the Parliamentary army as a captain in a regiment of foot during the period of the Commonwealth and Protectorate, when the military was a very important player on the stage of national politics. By all accounts, Hatchman was one of the more 'fanatical' officers within the army and sided with Major General Fleetwood and Major General Lambert in the tumults of late 1659, an act which cost him his military career.

1. The Oxford Militia (1651-54)

Records of Hatchman's early career as an officer in the Parliamentary army are sketchy, although it seems clear that the immediate context of his military career is the aftermath of the Anglo-Scottish war of 1650-52. On 31 July 1651 a Scots army of 16,000 men, headed by Charles II, left Stirling in Scotland and headed south across the border into English territory, crossing the border on 6 August. This was a desperate gamble on the part of the king and his ill-matched Scots supporters, and it sent shockwaves throughout England, including Oxfordshire.[4] There is mention within the City Council records of 13 August 1652 of a decision to form a militia in Oxford, so that 'the Citty might

---

[1] *City Council Proceedings – 1629-1663* (A.5.7), folio 199 recto = CSC #92; *City Council Minutes – 1635-1657* (A.4.3), folio 246 verso = CSC #91. Hayden (1981-2): 127, states that Hatchman was 're-admitted to the freedom of the city'. However, the City Council record is not about the *re-admission* of Hatchman to that privilege, but about the initial granting of citizenship to him. Hayden appears to misunderstand the record, probably due to the misleading paraphrasing of it within Hobson and Salter (1933): 183. White (1974): 215 n. 126, appears to suggest on the basis of these three mentions of Roger Hatchman within the City Council records that there were *two* Roger Hatchmans, father and son, both of whom lived in Oxford and were active in the Parliamentarian cause. He states that Hatchman was the 'son of a radical Parliamentarian citizen of Oxford'. Although it is not explicitly stated, White, by this comment, seems to take the references to Roger Hatchman in the City Council records for 1643 and 1646 as referring to the *father*, and the reference to Roger Hatchman in the City Council records for 1651 to refer to the *son*.

[2] *Audit Book – 1592-1682* (P.5.2), folio 280 recto = CSC #95.

[3] *Oxford Civic Enrolments – 1639-1662* (L.5.3), folio 33 recto = CSC #94. This entry is dated 11 July 1651.

[4] See Grainger (1997): 113-127, for details.

be put into a posture of defence'.[1]   The Oxford militia joined the forces commanded by Major General John Lambert as part of the Parliamentary army.[2]   In the end Cromwell and his generals crushed the ill-fated excursion into England by Charles II and his army of Scots in the battle of Worcester between 27 August–3 September 1651.   It is possible that Hatchman was involved with the Oxford militia at this time, and may have even participated in the battle of Worcester, although no record of his military commission in connection with this campaign appears to have survived.   However, cavaliers continued to present a threat to the peace and security of the Commonwealth during the next few years and Cromwell responded by calling for more militia forces to be formed in response.   There is record of Cromwell writing with some urgency to the Oxford City Council on 12 November 1654, calling for the 'raysing of A Troope of voluntier horse for the use of your towne and as many Foote as you can well for y[e] security of that place'.[3] Cromwell also mentions in passing within this letter of his 'having occasion to send the troops from you which lay w[i]th you' to meet the cavaliers who have 'gathered themselves into some bodyes'.   This suggests that the militia forces of the city have been deployed sometime earlier, although when and under what circumstances is not exactly clear.   All indications are that Hatchman was part of this earlier force and that he eventually was sent to Scotland as part of Cromwell's army of occupation.

2. The Governor of Peebles in Scotland (1654)

There are few details about Hatchman's early military career, although it seems that sometime between April and November of 1654[4] he joined the famous Foot Regiment of Lieutenant-General George Monck (the Regiment was reformed after the Restoration in 1661 and is now better known as the 'Coldstream Guards').[5]   Monck had been made Commander-in-Chief of the Army in Scotland on 8 April 1654,[6] and his Foot Regiment was stationed in

---

[1] *City Council Proceedings – 1629-1663* (A.5.7), folio 199 verso = CSC #97. The matter of the raising of the militia was again raised within the City Council a week later. It was agreed on 21 August 1651 that a loan of £150 was to be granted to help offset the burden of such a costly exercise (*City Council Proceedings – 1629-1663* (A.5.7), folio 200 recto).

[2] Atkin (1998): 59, 175.

[3] *Civil War Charities and General Minutes 1645-1695* (E.4.6) folio 15 recto = CSC #195. Along with the letter Cromwell sent some blank commissions to the City Council and asked them 'to put them into y[e] hands of such as you can bee confident of and will bee friends to the peace of the Nation'. News of the Lord Protector's letter was presented to the City Council on 22 March and it was agreed to form a new regiment to replace those already sent to meet the cavalier insurgents (*City Council Proceedings – 1629-1663* (A.5.7), folio 225 verso).

[4] Hatchman signed the renewal of his Christ Church lease on 25 April 1654.

[5] Mackinnon (1833): 70-1, 451; Firth (1940): 534, 540.

[6] *MS Rawlinson A 34*, folio 40.

Edinburgh as part of the English occupational forces. There are occasional glimpses of Hatchman's military career under General Monck, including an interesting reference to 'Captain Hatchman' in Monck's *Order Books* which relates to an incident that took place in 1654 in the town of Peebles, twenty-two miles south of Edinburgh in the Borders region. Hatchman is described within the order book as the 'Governor of Peebles'; Peebles was an important outpost and included Neidpath Castle, a base for Scottish guerrillas which had only been subdued by Major-General Lambert on behalf of the Parliamentary cause in November of 1650.[1] Hatchman's Governorship of Peebles suggests a position of some authority and influence, and we see something of this in the latitude of discretion accorded to him by General Monck in dealing with the matter of a local robbery. The entry in General Monck's *Order Book* for 23 November 1654 affirms the fines that Hatchman imposed in a court martial of the persons concerned.[2]

3. Arrest for Radicalism and Dismissal from the Army (1659)

Roger Hatchman's commission as an officer within Monck's Foot Regiment was re-affirmed by Parliament on Saturday, 30 July 1659. According to the *Journal for the House of Commons*, Hatchman was re-commissioned as one of the seven captains within this unit by an Act of Parliament.[3] However, confidence in Hatchman's abilities evaporated by October 1659, and questions as to his loyalty to the rule of Parliament were soon raised. In Scotland, Baptists began to give more and more cause for concern in the political unrest and uncertainty that dogged the Protectorate of Richard Cromwell.[4] Alarms were ringing up and down the country, with Baptists frequently being identified as potential troublemakers who threatened to take advantage of the political struggle between Cromwell and factions within Parliament and plunge the country into another war. Indeed, in mid-October of 1659 Monck sent a missive to London entitled *The Northern Queries from The Lord Gen: Monck his Quarters; sounding an Allarum to all Loyal Hearts and Freeborn English men*, which was said to be 'Printed in the Year of Englands Confusion' and 'sold at the Sign of Wallingford House'.[5] One of the queries raised by Monck

---

[1] Grainger (1997): 72.

[2] *MS Clark 46* (23 November 1654) = CSC #196. The order is cited in Firth (1899): xxxiv.

[3] See *JHC* 7: 742 = CSC #287, for the complete list of officers commissioned within the unit. According to Mackinnon (1833): 458, Hatchman was an Ensign in July 1650, although I have been unable to confirm this within the primary sources. Anthony Wood's description of him as a 'Major' (see page 137 below) is probably a misunderstanding about military ranks.

[4] There are reports of 'Anabaptist' activity made to the Secretary of State John Thurloe by Captain Timothy Langley, one of his agents in Leith. See Birch (1742): 7. 194; 371-2; 403; 527.

[5] Thomason dates the pamphlet to 7 September 1659, although this is clearly incorrect given that the tract mentions the disruption of Parliament on 13 October 1659.

within the pamphlet concerned the loyalty and trustworthiness of Baptists who supported the attempt of Major-General Charles Fleetwood and Major-General John Lambert to stop the sitting of the Parliament called by Richard Cromwell.[1] Monck put the essential point about Baptist involvement in the crisis in the form of a rhetorical question. He queried,

> Whether ever any Common-wealth will trust the Baptized Churches again, seeing they have dealt thus perfidiously with the Honourable Parliament, (who as the Fathers of the Nation) were pleased to put part of the Militia into their hands, for the security of the Priviledge of Parliament, and Freedoms of all men, against Domestick and Forreign Enemies; yet they have maliciously and shamefully betrayed their Trust, in opposing the Parliament, from whom they had their Commissions; and have sided with those Traytors which interrupted the Parliament in October 13, 59. which will be as a Brand upon the Church-men for ever, except they come in, and now appear with General *Monck*, and the rest of the true *English* men, for the re-establishing of Parliament?[2]

This military intervention in London was part of a very difficult political period involving complicated manoeuvrings by a number of interested parties, including London Baptists led by William Kiffen and Samuel Moyer.[3] The timing is significant, for the year 1659 was, in the words of Christopher Hill, 'a year of political crisis, the last year of hope for the radicals'.[4] Essentially Fleetwood and Lambert sought to promote the military's cause and force the government to address grievances within the political arena by first re-instating, and then staging a coup against, the so-called 'Rump' Parliament. These events were eyed nervously back in Scotland and things finally came to a head in October of 1659 when news of the ousting of the 'Rump' Parliament reached Monck on 17-18 October 1659. The arrest and dismissal of suspect military officers within his army regiments quickly followed. General Monck arrested Captain Hatchman and five other 'Anabaptist' officers who had supported the actions of Fleetwood and Lambert. In short, the arrest of Hatchman and his fellow officers was part of a bold, deliberate strategy adopted by Monck to support the 'Rump' Parliament as the legitimate government of the country. As Thomas Gumble, the royalist biographer of Monck and a cleric who had served as one of his chaplains, notes:

> On the Eighteenth of *October*, 1659 (St *Lukes*-day) he took his own guards with him from *Dalkeith*, and marched to *Edenburgh*, (there his own Regiment of Foot

---

[1] Mackinnon (1833): 74; Firth (1940): 541. Also see Ashley (1954): 211-6; (1977): 166-79.

[2] *The Northern Queries from The Lord Gen: Monck his Quarters; sounding an Allarum to all Loyal Hearts and Freeborn English men* (1659): 6-7.

[3] Brown (1912): 171-205, discusses the role that London Baptists had in the collapse of the Protectorate.

[4] Hill (1975): 233.

quartered, which was not drawn forth) he seized all such Officers as he knew were not well satisfied with such an undertaking, and secured them afterwards.[1]

On 20 October General Monck sent a letter from Edinburgh to William Lenthal, the Speaker of Parliament, in which he acknowledged that he had made the arrests, but asserted that he was acting within the bounds of his Parliamentary commission:

> I have according to your Act of the Eleventh instant, being constituted a Commissioner of the Government of the Army, put out such persons as would not act according to your Commission. I do call God to witness that the Asserting of a Commonwealth is the only intent of my heart.[2]

However, others did not view Monck's actions as motivated by such noble, altruistic ideals. Within a week a letter was sent to General Monck by Colonel Cobbet and the General Council of Officers in London in which concern was expressed about Monck's proceedings. Monck replied to this in a letter dated 27 October; both were published soon afterwards, together with a one-page document entitled 'The Substance of a Letter intended to have been sent from the Militia of London to General Monck and the Officers under his Command in Scotland'. This letter from Colonel Cobbet linked the arrest of the Anabaptist officers and the proposed march of Monck's army into England:

> We understand, That you are preparing to march with an Army into England, having displaced and imprisoned several Officers of the Army of known Integrity to the Commonwealth, and appointed others in their Commands; and that you are making great and warlike Preparations hereunto; ... We think fit to present unto you our earnest desires ... that you would please to set free the said Officers from their Imprisonments, restoring them to their Commands, and desist your further Actings in that kind.[3]

It appears that although the officers concerned were under house-arrest, they were not harshly treated or incarcerated under extreme conditions. Indeed, a letter from Monck's secretary William Clarke (1623?-1666)[4] in Linlithgow, directed to Lord Fleetwood and the army officers in England and dated 12 October 1659, emphasizes the benevolence shown to the officers who had been arrested:

---

[1] *The Life of General Monck, Duke of Albemarle, &tc. With Remarks Upon His Actions* (1671): 133.

[2] *A Declaration of the Commander in Chief of the Forces in Scotland* (1659): 7. The letter is reprinted in *Several Letters from the Lord General Monck* (1660): 1.

[3] *A Letter Sent by Col. Cobbet from the General Council of Officers to Gen. Monk* (1659): 8. A letter dated 28 October 1659 from a royalist to Lord Chancellor Hyde similarly notes: 'Monck has not only declared against our proceedings, but imprisoned several Officers, and is preparing for a new war' (Clarendon (1786): 3.591).

[4] Aylmer (1973): 261-262, summarizes Clarke's career.

And we shall also assure you. That though the present Emergency hath made our Commander in chief, to put some of the Officers from their Commands, whose actings have not been such as might promise they can cordially joyn in this business, yet he hath continued to them their Sallaries out of the Contingencies of the Army, till the Parliaments pleasure be further known.[1]

A similar comment about the payment of the officers' salaries is made by John Price in his *The Mystery and Method of His Majesty's Happy Restauration Laid Open to Publick View* (1680), a work which was issued in praise of Monck's role in the restoration of Charles II. Price notes, however, that Monck's generosity in this regard was not without its limits, and that some of the officers 'opened their Mouths against him, and their Tongues were Exercised to Debauch his soldiers from their Duty'. At this point payment of arrears to some of the cashiered officers was stopped.[2] A similar declaration about the payment of arrears is made in a postscript to a letter sent to Fleetwood and the army officers in London by Monck and his officers in Scotland. The letter, written from Edinburgh, was in reply to an earlier enquiry sent by Fleetwood and his supporters and is dated 7 November 1659. Monck said that the imprisoned officers were still regarded as 'Brethren', that their pay was to be continued, and that the restraints which were put upon them for reasons of security 'we hope will be very short, shorter than either you or we can expect'.[3] Reports of the arrest of the Baptist officers appears in several news-sheets published in the beginning of November, with several of them specifically naming Hatchman as one of the officers concerned.[4]

Ultimately, as a result of the action by Monck, the six company commanders, including Hatchman, were either cashiered, or resigned their commissions.[5] Details of precisely what happened to the officers concerned at this point are sketchy. However, there is a record in General Monck's order book dated 19 November 1659, written by his Secretary William Clarke, which records Hatchman's dismissal from the army.[6] In addition, Hatchman's name appears in a list of 20 soldiers who either deserted Monck or were not allowed to take

---

[1] See *A Letter of the Officers of the Army in Scotland under the Commander in Chief there to the Officers of the Army in England* (1659): 7; reissued in *A Collection of Several Letters and Declarations Sent by General Monck* (1660): 6.

[2] Price (1680): 55-56.

[3] *The Answer of the Officers at Whitehall to the Letter from the Officers of the Parliaments Army in Scotland from Linlithgow, Oct. 22, with a Return of the General and Officers in Scotland thereunto* (1659): 8; reissued in *A Collection of Several Letters and Declarations Sent by General Monck* (1660): 22 = CSC #302.

[4] *The Publick Intelligencer*, No. 201 (31 October – 7 November 1659): 840-842 = CSC #299; *The Loyall Scout* 28 (4-11 November 1659): 223 = CSC #300; *The Weekly Post*, No. 27 (1-8 November 1659): 216 = CSC #301. These reports are based upon the anonymous letter from Edinburgh dated 25 October 1659 (see below).

[5] Firth (1940): 540-1.

[6] *MS Clarke 49* (19 November 1659) = CSC #303.

up their commissions under his command.   This list was published in a broadsheet entitled *A Letter from a Person of Quality in Edenburgh* on 25 October 1659,[1] shortly before Monck made his carefully-timed march into England the following January.[2]   It records that command of Hatchman's company was handed over to Captain John Collins, who had transferred over from the regiment of foot commanded by Colonel George Fenwick and Colonel Timothy Wilkes.[3]

Unfortunately, there are no further records of Hatchman's career as an active military officer.   Precisely when he was released from his imprisonment in Scotland, and how he managed to make his way from Edinburgh to Oxford, are matters unknown.   However, after his return to Oxford in late 1659 or early 1660, Hatchman quickly became involved in the politics of Dissent, and was soon marked out as a Baptist 'sectarye' charged with sedition.   Not surprisingly, he was named as one of the insurrectionists in the so-called 'Presbyterian Sham-plot' of 1661 (see pages 43-4 above).

D. Radical Dissenter and Messenger of the Baptist Church (1660-1667)

1. The 'Casheired Anabaptist Officer' and the Fifth Monarchist John Belcher (1660)

The Oxford antiquarian Anthony Wood tells us that on 16 January 1660 an Anabaptist named John Belcher (whom Wood spells as *Belchior*)[4] preached at St Peter-in-the-Bailey church in the centre of Oxford.   Wood notes that Belcher's anti-Restorationist[5] views were so controversial that the Vice-Chancellor John Conant[6] had him removed from the church.   More importantly, at least from the standpoint of this study, is that Wood also mentions in passing that Belcher, a Fifth Monarchist, was supported by, among others, a 'Major Hatchman', whom he describes as 'a casheired Anabaptist officer'.   Wood's comments on this incident are contained in two documents now in the Bodleian Library.   The first of these is the manuscript for Wood's *The History and*

---

[1] *A Letter from a Person of Quality in Edenburgh to an Officer of the Army, wherein is given a true account of Generall Moncks proceedings* (1659) = *Wood 276a* (331) = CSC #298. See Mackinnon (1833): 81, for a discussion of this rare broadsheet; Also see Firth (1901): 101; Hutton (1985): 68-71.

[2] McDonald (1990): 363-76, discusses the reasons for Monck's well-planned movement.

[3] This is discussed in Firth (1940): 392, 541.

[4] Belcher's surname is variously spelled in the primary sources.

[5] Hopes for the return of the monarchy were widespread at the time. In fact, Charles II arrived at Dover on 25 May 1660, just a few weeks before the Abingdon Association meetings of 19-20 June 1660 where the matter of John Belcher's discipline by the member churches was discussed (see page 181 below).

[6] John Conant was Vice-Chancellor from October 1657 to August 1660, and later archdeacon at Norwich. He died on 12 March 1694 (see Clark (1894): 3.447). Burrows (1881): xlv-lii, offers a brief biography of him.

Antiquities of the University of Oxford,[1] and the second a printed almanac from 1660 to which Wood made annotations.   The almanac is the later of the two, with Wood's annotation for 16 January offering a compressed version of the event:

> 16 m[onday] Belchior ye Anabap[tist]
> preached at st pet[er] in y^e
> Ball[y], inveighing much ag[ain]st
> ye present overtures, pr[o]c[ee]ding
> soe farr as ye vicecancellor
> Dr conant turned him
> out of ye church; he was
> set up by Andrews[2] ye butler
> of Exon coll[ege] & Mr Austen
> & Major Hatchman, a
> casheired Anabap[tist] officer
>   vid[e]   H[i]st[oria]
>   Belcher borne at one of
>   ye Haseleys, a Butcher
>   or Butchers son[3]

Belcher was known as an influential Fifth Monarchist, and continued to be identified with radical dissent even after the failure of the Venner up-rising in 1661. He is named as one of the leaders of the Fifth Monarchists in two letters written by Captain William Pestell to Secretary Edward Nicholas on 26 September 1661[4] and 28 November 1661.   In the latter Pestell stated that Belcher 'is at Limehouse, where Venner's plot was hatched, and goes about to seduce the people as he did then'.[5]   After preaching a politically-charged sermon to his congregation at Bell Lane on 24 June 1671,[6] Belcher was imprisoned in the Tower.   A record relating to his imprisonment describes him as 'John Bellchar, a most notorious knafe came out of Oxfordshire'.[7]   Belcher was certainly a controversial figure among Baptists in Oxfordshire, but this was not the first contact that he had with members of the Oxford church.   There is record of him having represented the Baptist church at Kingston Blount at the meeting of the Abingdon Association which took place at Tetsworth on 11-14

---

[1] *MS Wood F 1*, pp. 1110-1111 = Gutch (1796): 2.697 = CSC #306.

[2] Andrews was later indicted to appear before the ecclesiastical court on 28 June 1662, charged with not attending his parish church (*ODR: 1 February 1660 – 4 October 1662* (c. 3) folio 29 recto).   He responded by asserting that 'hee doth frequent his p[ar]ish church at prayers and sermons'.

[3] *MS Wood Diaries 4*, folio 7 verso = CSC #307.

[4] SP 29/42, folios 68 recto-69 verso = CSC #330.

[5] SP 29/44, folios 258 recto-259 recto = CSC #335.   Greaves (1986): 81, briefly discusses this letter.

[6] The occasion was reported by two informants who were present at the service (SP 29/291, page 148 = CSC #497).

[7] SP 29/291, page 149.

March 1656,[1] the very meeting at which the church at Oxford was welcomed into the Abingdon Association. It is possible that the Oxford messengers Richard Tidmarsh and Thomas Tisdale first came into contact with the fiery Belcher at these meetings, which also had the equally contentious John Pendarves of Abingdon in attendance. It was not to be the last time that Belcher and Tidmarsh were to cross paths; it was noted above (page 72) how Tidmarsh in 1689 was called in to help adjudicate in a dispute between two London churches, Belcher's in Bell Lane, Spitalfields and Francis Bampfield's in Pinners' Hall, Broad Street. Belcher seemed to court controversy wherever he went and later became one of the prime advocates of sabbatarianism, writing a preface to Edward Stennet's influential pamphlet entitled *The Seventh Day is the Sabbath of the Lord* (1664). His name also heads a list contained in a manuscript from 1690 of Sabbatarian Baptists in England; the manuscript is in the possession of Llanwenarth Baptist Church, Monmouthshire. Belcher died in 1695, and Joseph Stennet, the son of Edward Stennet, preached the funeral sermon which was later published as *The Groans of a Saint under the burden of a mortal body* (1695).[2]

2. Messenger to the Abingdon Association Meeting (1660)

The records of the Abingdon Association firmly establish Hatchman as a Baptist leader and note that he was the sole messenger from the church in Oxford at the meetings held at Tetsworth on 19-20 June 1660. There were eleven messengers representing eleven different churches in the Association at the meeting, as well as one messenger from the neighbouring association of Bedfordshire and Hertfordshire.[3] This is the only time within these records that Hatchman is specifically named as a messenger of the church in Oxford. At the meeting Hatchman reported on the life of the congregation, noting among other things that 'two members are lately fallen to the Quakers'.[4] Interestingly, one of the issues raised at this Association meeting concerned the exercise of church discipline upon a member of one of the churches represented, namely John Belcher. It appears that the controversial leader Belcher had been excommunicated some time earlier by the Baptist church in Abingdon. However, he seems to have been openly accepted by some of the other churches in the area and was continuing a contentious ministry among them. Clearly, Belcher's excommunication was still a bone of contention among the

---

[1] *AARB*, folio 13 verso = White (1974): 145. In connection with this church, Belcher is also mentioned in Bishop Walter Blandford's report about conventicles in the Oxford diocese compiled in 1669 (*Lambeth MS. 951/1*), folio 112 recto). See Clapinson (1980): 43, for details.

[2] For more on Belcher as a Fifth Monarchist and as a Sabbatarian Baptist, see Burrage (1910): 745-6; Payne (1951-2): 161-166; Rogers (1966): 124, 131; Capp (1972): 242; Greaves (1982): 52-3; Sanford (1992): 67-8; Ball (1994): 175-7, 211.

[3] *AARB*, folio 44 recto = White (1974): 203 = CSC #311.

[4] *AARB*, folio 44 verso = White (1974): 204 = CSC #312.

Baptist churches in the area and the matter surfaced within the messengers' deliberations on 20 June 1660. A vote was taken concerning a public censure of him, and 'all messengers, save one did approve' of it.[1] Of course it is impossible to know for certain which of the twelve messengers listed as being in attendance at the Association meeting did *not* agree with the censure of John Belcher, but a good case can be made for Hatchman from the church in Oxford being the lone dissenting voice. His support of Belcher's preaching at Hatchman's local Anglican church in the parish of St Peter-in-the-Bailey suggests that the two men were like-minded, particularly when it came to the matter of the restoration of the monarchy. Indeed, there may have been an even closer connection between Belcher and Hatchman's son, Thomas, who was likewise disciplined by his church in Oxford and became the subject of discussion amongst the churches of the Abingdon Association.

3. Hatchman's Son Thomas - The Wayward Butcher

It is worth noting that in Wood's almanac note entry from January of 1660 (cited above) John Belcher is specifically said to be either a butcher, or the son of a butcher. It is possible that a business association served as the initial point of contact between Belcher and the Hatchman family, for Roger Hatchman's son Thomas was known to have been a butcher within Oxford from the mid-1650s and even had the lease on one of the lucrative stalls in the centre of the city. According to the city rental records of 1658 the seventeenth shop in the so-called Butchers' Row was owned by a Thomas Hatchman, the son of Roger Hatchman.[2]

Thomas Hatchman is uniformly described as a 'butcher' within the primary sources which mention him. The earliest of these concerns his being granted the 'Freedom of the City' of Oxford on 16 June 1654 pursuant to his paying a fee of £10, the customary officers' fees, and 5s for a cushion.[3] Hatchman made the payment on 16 August 1654, although the 5 shillings was applied to the

---

[1] *AARB* 45 recto–45 verso = White (1974): 205 = CSC #313. John Belcher was also excommunicated from his local parish in Aston Rowant on 19 July 1662 (*ODR: Excommunication Schedules – 1662-1667* (c. 100), folio 3 recto = CSC #348). He does appear within the village records for the Hearth Tax of Michaelmas 1665, but was 'discharged by poverty' from having to pay on the two hearths in his house (*Hearth Tax of Michaelmas 1665* (E 179/164/513), membrane 9 reverse).

[2] There is also record listing the twenty shops with the Butchers' Row, the rents levied, and the names of the butchers assigned to them (*Civil War Charities and General Minutes – 1645-1695* (E.4.6), folio 15 verso). This document lists Hatchman as the seventeenth butcher concerned, and states that 'they entred in Jan[uar]ii 1656'. This page appears to be the rough draft of the rent roll of 1658.

[3] *City Council Proceedings – 1629-1663* (A.5.7), folio 220 verso = CSC #176. The entry leaves a blank for the first name of Hatchman, which may explain why there is a further entry pertaining to his citizenship in August.

purchase of a leather bucket rather than a cushion.[1] His citizenship was also entered in the *Civic Enrolments – 1639-1662* for the same date, where it is said to be 'according to an Act of Common Councell' as opposed to the more usual means of the completion of an apprenticeship.[2] This may be due to some behind-the-scenes manoeuvrings on the part of his father, who took up a military commission and was posted to Scotland sometime after April of 1654. It looks as if Captain Hatchman was finalizing family arrangements, making sure that his son's place in the civic life was secure before departing from Oxford. It is interesting that Thomas Hatchman's citizenship was granted during the Mayoral year of Thomas Williams, a prominent tradesman within the city who was well-known for his religious piety and his political activism. Mayoral consent would have been all-important in a case such as this; not insignificantly, Williams was one of the fellow anti-royalists who, with Roger Hatchman was censured by Charles I in 1643 (see page 168 above).

As a butcher Thomas Hatchman was a member of a powerful, and controversial, guild of traders. The butchers' trade in Oxford was well-established, and had been operating in the centre of the city for many years. In 1556 butcher's stalls were erected in an area consequently named Butchers' Row, in what is now Queen Street between the parish church of St Peter-in-the-Bailey and Carfax. There were only twenty licensed butchers in Oxford at any given time during the middle part of the 17th century and their trade was strictly regulated by the city.[3] By long-standing tradition the shops were leased to butchers based on the seniority of the butcher concerned; when one of the twenty licensed died or moved away those below him moved up in rank and a new butcher was enrolled at the bottom of the order.[4] Hatchman's placement within this arrangement within the surviving city rental records is evident, even if only for a brief period of time. The rental records for 1658 list Hatchman as holding the license for the seventeenth shop in Butchers' Row and show him as having paid £1 3s 4d in rent for the year.[5] However, the records for the year 1660 show that his name was dropped from the list of the butchers, with those above and below him in the 1658 list advancing accordingly. Clearly something happened to Hatchman's position as a licensed butcher within the city between 1658 and 1660 (unfortunately the rental records for 1659 have not survived to help clarify the situation).

---

[1] *City Council Proceedings – 1629-1663* (A.5.7), folio 221 recto = CSC #188. The purchase of a leather bucket, presumably for use as a water container in the event of a fire, was not unusual and was a standard fee in such matters.

[2] *Civic Enrolments – 1639-1662* (L.5.3), folio 234 verso = CSC #189.

[3] Cooper (1979): 307, notes that there were only twelve shops in Butchers' Row in 1623. Also see Crossley (1979): 320-1.

[4] See Ogle (1890): 30-9, for a convenient collection of City Council documents relating to the butchers' trade in Oxford.

[5] *Rent Roll for 1658* (A.1.1 – CT.1.E.02). Salter (1926): 16, mistakenly gives this as the shop of *Edward* Hatchman. See CSC #551 for its location in the parish of St Peter-in-the-Bailey in David Loggan's *Oxonia Illustrata* (1675).

Where and when butchers were allowed to carry on their business was a matter of considerable debate in the 1640s and 1650s, and there is frequent mention of them within the Oxford City Council records. For example, the record for 10 June 1642 contains a detailed comment about the butchers, including an act by the City Council setting out the laws governing their trade.[1] Unfortunately, much of the western portion of the city, including the butchers' shops in Butchers' Row, was destroyed by the great fire of 1644 and had to be rebuilt at great cost to the city.[2] However, trading practices become a matter of dispute within the newly erected and re-edified Butchers' Row, as can be seen in the records for 16 December 1656. Most significantly, this act of City Council stipulated that butchers were only allowed to trade on Wednesdays and Saturdays, the traditional days for the sale of butcher's meat, and then only at their own shops or stalls. Severe penalties of 20s per day were imposed for anyone offending against these regulations.[3] The matter continued to be a subject of controversy within the city, and again flared up in the following spring. The City Council records for 24 March and 7 April 1657 show that controversy between the butchers, or at least some of them, and the City Council.[4]

Thomas Hatchman is named within several City Council records in connection with his illegal trading activities as a butcher. The town clerk's notebook records that on 4 June 1658 he appeared before city officials and had three acts of the City Council concerning regulation of the butchers' trade in the newly erected Butchers' Row (probably those dated 16 December 1656, 24 March 1657 and 7 April 1657) read to him.[5] Similar action was taken by the city officials against another butcher named Henry Hedges three weeks later on 25 June 1658.[6] Although the precise nature of Hatchman's and Hedges' offences are not here stated, it seems clear that they were in breach of the strict regulations governing the public sale of meat within the city market. Hatchman's public rebuke, presumably by the Mayor of the city of Oxford, Thomas Dennis, was witnessed by Leonard Smith, the High Sheriff of Oxfordshire, who served as a Bailiff for the city, and John Hym, a tailor.[7] The

---

[1] *City Council Proceedings – 1629-1663* (A.5.7), folio 123 recto = CSC #30.

[2] City Council records for 19 August 1656 (*City Council Proceedings – 1629-1663* (A.5.7), folio 232 verso) and 14 November 1656 (*City Council Proceedings – 1629-1663* (A.5.7), folio 236) show the matter of rebuilding being discussed.

[3] *City Council Proceedings – 1629-1663* (A.5.7), folio 237 recto and verso = CSC #244.

[4] *City Council Proceedings – 1629-1663* (A.5.7), folios 239 verso and 240 recto = CSC #248 and CSC #250.

[5] *Civil War Charities and General Minutes – 1645-1695* (E.4.6), folio 21 recto = CSC #260. The document also records that John Pitman, who had the butcher's stall next to Hatchman's, was cited for breaking the regulations on 4, 6 and 7 May.

[6] *Civil War Charities and General Minutes – 1645-1695* (E.4.6), folio 21 verso.

[7] Hobson and Salter (1933): 222, records that the Honourable Colonel Smith had been given citizenship of the city and appointed as a Bailiff on 14 August 1657. A further point to consider in this regard is that Hatchman, in standing before Colonel

same two witnesses signed a citation against Hatchman and two other butchers on 28 June 1658, charging them with keeping 'a shopp, stall or standing with Butchers Meate in places not allowable'.[1]

The butchers' controversy is given two further mentions within the City Council records a week later. Neither of these records mention Hatchman by name, but they do seem to be a continuation of the dispute over regulations governing the time and place that butchers were allowed to sell their wares. Indeed, the matter seems to have spilled over into a row among the butchers themselves, some of whom were content to abide by the prevailing regulations and some of whom were not. The record for 2 July 1658 notes that some butchers made a formal complaint that their licensed stalls in the Butchers' Row were being used by others to sell meat on the days that were not designated butchers' market days (Wednesdays and Saturdays). The City Council imposed a penalty of 2*s* 6*d* per day on anyone so offending.[2] Undeterred, the offending butchers, led by one named William Hedges, the son of Henry Hedges mentioned above, seem to have moved from the stalls in the Butchers' Row to the street itself, which necessitated that the City Council address the matter yet again. In a Council meeting held on 15 July 1658 a fine of 20*s* per day was set for this further abuse.[3]

In short, all of this suggests that Hatchman was breaking the law with regard to the way that he was carrying out his business as a butcher, either attempting to sell his produce from an unlicensed site, or doing so at an unlawful time. Why was this such a controversial act on the part of the butchers? One possible explanation involves viewing it as closely intertwined with the debate over sabbatarianism, a matter which was known to have preoccupied some Baptists at the time.[4] This is made all the more likely when it is remembered that John Belcher, the fiery preacher whom Hatchman's father supported when he returned from the army eighteen months later (see pages 179-80 above), was known to have harboured sabbatarian principles.[5] Indeed, it is worth noting that Belcher, the (son of a) butcher, preached in the Church of St Peter-in-the-

---

Smith, was brought face to face with a representative of the wider authority of Parliament, and not just a local Oxford magistrate.

[1] *Civil War Charities and General Minutes – 1645-1695* (E.4.6), folio 21 verso = CSC #262.

[2] *City Council Proceedings – 1629-1663* (A.5.7), folio 250 recto = CSC #263.

[3] *City Council Proceedings – 1629-1663* (A.5.7), folio 261 recto = CSC #264. William Hedges was also prosecuted for his activities within the Oxford City Petty Sessions court on 10 June 1658 (*Oxford Petty Sessions Roll – 1656-1678* (O.5.11), folio 16 recto). His slaughter house was located in All Saints' parish.

[4] Ball (1994): 164-166, discusses the matter as it concerned Baptists in Oxford. His monograph is now the definitive treatment of sabbatarianism of the period.

[5] See Payne (1951-52): 161-6, for more on this matter. Payne records an important document sent by the Seventh Day Church in Bell Lane, Spiralfields, London to the Seventh-day Baptists in Rhode Island. The document is dated 26 March 1668 and is signed by eleven people, including John Belcher.

Bailey, which was located just twenty yards or so from the Butchers' Row with Hatchman's tenements in the parish just a few yards to the north.

If Belcher's fellow-butcher Thomas Hatchman had taken up sabbatarian ideas, he may have found the fact that Saturdays were specifically designated as one of the two days upon which butchers were allowed to sell meat objectionable. Perhaps what we are seeing in the City Council records is a reflection of this sabbatarian debate, with Hatchman (and other like-minded butchers) trying to force the issue about the sanctity of Saturday and attempting to sell meat from their stalls on other days of the week. Operating on an alternative day may also have involved using the empty stalls in the Butchers' Row (which would have stood unused on days other than Wednesday or Saturday), or using alternative (illegal) sites for laying out their wares – matters which seem to have been focal points for the debate with the City Council. Presumably, Hatchman felt that by acting in this way the Old Testament command of 'keeping the sabbath holy' could be obeyed, even if it meant that opening the unlawful stalls on other days of the week was breaking the law as far as the city of Oxford was concerned. Everything points to Hatchman coming into conflict, not only with the butchers' guild (who appear to have lodged the complaint against him and others which is recorded in the minutes for 2 July 1658), but also the city authorities.[1]

Thomas Hatchman's relationship with the city officials was not the only area of his life embroiled in controversy. He also brought the Baptist church in Oxford into disrepute in the following spring, for he is specifically mentioned as an errant church member in the Abingdon Association records for the meetings held on 5-7 April 1659. The sole Oxford delegate to those meetings, Richard Tidmarsh, reported about the church members:

> Two among them doe ob-
> serve the Seventh-day Sabbath yet forsake not y[e] church.
> Two have bene lately cast out, viz., Thomas Hatchman,
> a butcher who brake and ran away and hath wronged many,
> and much blurred the gospell; the other is a sister who
> is cast out for backbiting, and other wills.
> One member is very low in spirit, and in a very sad
> condition. Another also is low, but not in so great extremity.[2]

Precisely what it was that Hatchman had done to 'much blurr the Gospell' is now very difficult to determine, although the fact that other members of the congregation were under the influence of sabbatarian ideas does offer a

---

[1] Interestingly, in 1435 nineteen of the master butchers of Oxford agreed among themselves that they would restrict the hours of their trade. They agreed not to trade on Sundays after 8:00 p.m. (see Salter (1924): 315-7).

[2] *AARB*, folio 38 recto = White (1974): 191 = CSC #279. There is a slight error in White's transcription of the manuscript at this point; he has omitted the words 'Another also is low'. The text refers to two different church members, rather than the one that White's transcription implies.

suggestive clue. So too does the fact that at an earlier meeting of the Abingdon Association, commencing on 27 May 1656, the matter of sabbatarianism was raised by the Oxford messengers as a topic for open discussion and debate.[1] They asked 'whether the seven-day Sabbath, as it was given in Ex. 20.10, be in force to be observed by the saints'. In addition, the Oxford messengers raised a question about the interpretation of the book of Revelation, 'what the Beast is which is spoken of in the Revelation of John, and what is his Image, and what it is to worship him and to receive his mark upon theire foreheads or in their right hand'.

What is so interesting about this particular portion of the Abingdon Association records is that it sets the concern about sabbatarianism within a wider question about apocalyptic expectations of the day, expectations which were based on the book of Revelation. Some Baptist historians have argued that there was an easy passage for Baptists from holding sabbatarian convictions to involvement with more radical political movements such as the Fifth Monarchists.[2] William T Whitley, for example, goes so far as to suggest that sabbatarianism was introduced to Baptists by Fifth Monarchists. He suggested that the '"Fifth Monarchy" movement flamed up like a phoenix and out of its ashes arose the Seventh-Day Baptist Movement.'[3]

The biblical imagery which lends itself to the idea of the *Fifth* Monarchy comes from the book of Daniel wherein four visions of successive empires are said to rule. It is impossible to overestimate how important the apocalyptic timetables of Daniel and Revelation were for the Fifth Monarchy movement, and we certainly see the influence of the biblical books at work here.[4] This becomes all the more understandable when it is remembered that Jews began to return to England under Cromwell's Protectorate, and their return was closely bound up in popular thinking with the belief that the conversion of the Jews

---

[1] *AARB*, folio 20 verso = White (1974): 158 = CSC #237. Unfortunately, the names of the Oxford messengers to this Association meeting are not given in the record.

[2] Perhaps a little less than half of the 150 signatories of the so-called 'Fifth-Monarchy Manifesto of 1654', the pamphlet entitled *A Declaration of Several of the Churches of Christ and Godly People in and about the Citie of London* (1654), were Baptists. See Thirtle (1912-13): 129-153, for details.

[3] Whitley *Men of the Seventh Day* (no date). Also see Whitley (1946-48): 252-4. Whitley contends that the rise of sabbatarianism amongst Baptists only took place *after* 1656. This is probably an inaccurate judgement, given the fact that Jacob Trask (c. 1585-1636) did much to promote interest in Judaism and sabbatarian principles beginning in 1617-20 and in later life may have influenced the thinking of Henry Jessey, the pastor of the Baptist church Trask attended, along these lines (see White (1968): 223-233; Tolmie (1977): 34-5; Katz (1982): 18-31; Ball (1994): 7, 154-155).

[4] Farrer (1910-11): 166-180, and Rogers (1966): 1-13, 134-49, give some examples of how these apocalyptic books were interpreted by the Fifth Monarchists. Also see Hill (1962b): 323-8; Capp (1984): 165-176; Smith (1989): 85-109. Watts (1978): 134-142, has an interesting discussion of the conflict between John Owen, the Vice-Chancellor of Oxford University, and the Fifth Monarchists, much of it involving matters of biblical interpretation.

was a necessary precursor to the second coming of Jesus Christ.[1]   Many Baptists were committed to such beliefs, and sometimes were in positions of power and influence which allowed them to turn their theological convictions into political policy. The most important illustration of this is Henry Jessey (1603-1663) who in November-December 1655 served on a committee of twenty-eight delegates appointed by Oliver Cromwell's Council of State to consider the question of allowing Jews to be readmitted to England. Jessey published a pamphlet in 1656 detailing the proceedings of the committee entitled *A Narrative Of the late Proceeds at White-Hall, Concerning the Jews.*[2] Little wonder, then, that some Baptist sabbatarians, including Henry Jessey and Francis Bampfield (c. 1615-1683), were ridiculed by their opponents as being 'Jews'.[3] This idea leads to a consideration of one further point arising from the reference to the Book of Revelation contained in the Abingdon Association record cited above.

It is significant that the evocative imagery of Revelation 13, with its symbolic description of the Roman empire as the beast rising from the sea, is being alluded to here. Not only does the phrase 'the image of the beast' derive from this chapter, but, more importantly, the idea of 'receiving the mark on the forehead or hand' comes straight from 13:16-17. In theses verses the power of the beast is demonstrated:

> It causes all, both small and great, both rich and poor, both free and slave, to be marked on the right hand or on the forehead, so that no one can buy or sell unless he has the mark, that is, the name of the beast or the number of its name.

What is striking about these verses is the way that the right to buy or sell, to function as a merchant or tradesman, is tied to acceptance of the authority of the state.[4] It is precisely these same issues that Hatchman seems to be facing in his own day, with the Oxford city authorities imposing restrictions upon where and when he could carry on his trade as a butcher. When these restrictions are linked to the violation of sabbatarian principles (as appears to be the case for Hatchman) , then the question raised by the Oxford delegates at the Abingdon Association about the nature of the 'beast' (a cipher for the state) suddenly makes sense.

---

[1] See Hill (1962b): 141-2; Rogers (1966): 150-1; Katz (1982); Capp (1989): 300-1; Coulton (2001): 21-38; Coward (2002): 60-2.

[2] For more on Jessey's involvement with Jewish matters, see Katz (1989): 117-138; Van der Wall (1990): 161-184.

[3] See White (1968): 228; Capp (1979): 153; Van der Wall (1990): 164. This recalls the case of Jacob Trask, who in 1626 was sentenced by the Star Chamber 'to bee burnt in the forehead w[i]th the l[ett]re 'J', in token that hee broached Jewish opynions' (*Addit. MSS c. 303,* folio 45 recto).

[4] The idea of 'marking the forehead or hand' as a sign of ownership is a frequent theme in Revelation (see 7:3; 9:4; 14:1, 9; 17:5; 20:4; 22:4). However, only in 13:16-17 is it specifically linked to buying or selling.

In any event, it seems clear that the 'Hatchman affair' was the cause for considerable debate, for the minutes of the meeting of the Abingdon Association held on 5-7 April 1659, the meeting at which Richard Tidmarsh reported the wayward conduct of Hatchman, also records a question put forward by the church at Oxford for public discussion. The query was raised, 'How, and how farre a church is to deale with a member that holds communion with one lawfully cast out by another true church?'[1] It looks as if Hatchman was thrown out of the Oxford church, and found fellowship within another Baptist church nearby. The church in Oxford felt that this undermined the discipline they had invoked on one of their members and were asking for a clarification of policy on such cases by the Association. Unfortunately, a veil is cast over the incident and no further reference to it is made within the Abingdon Association records. In fact, Thomas Hatchman disappears from further Oxford records altogether after this incident (as noted, his last appearance in City Council records was in connection with his illegal trading as a butcher in July of 1658). His disappearance is so rapid and his absence from surviving documents so complete that it raises questions about whether he left the city of Oxford and moved for a place more suitable to his beliefs and interests. A relocation to London is perhaps the most likely possibility, particularly given that the country was undergoing something of a political upheaval in 1659-1660, dealing not only with the collapse of the Protectorate of Richard Cromwell, but also with the Restoration of Charles II. Unfortunately, what happened to Thomas Hatchmen after his expulsion from the Baptist church is unknown.

However, there is one further tantalising possibility involving Thomas Hatchman that is worth pursuing further. If correct it means that he was directly involved in the Parliamentary cause during the Civil War, just as his father was. The issue revolves around the fact that one of the spies of Sir Samuel Luke, the Scout Master General of the Earl of Essex during the Civil War, was named Thomas *Hitchman*. Given the vagaries of spelling during the 17th century, this may well be Thomas Hatchman, especially since this spy clearly knows Oxford well and could travel in and out of the city with relative ease. Thus, the manuscript journal of Sir Samuel Luke, which since 1905 has been part of the collection of the Bodleian Library,[2] records that Thomas Hitchman is sent on reconnaissance missions to Oxford on several occasions in the early part of 1643.[3] For example, he went to Oxford on 14 February 1643 and returned to Luke's camp eight days later on 22 February.[4] The report he

---

[1] *AARB*, folio 41 recto = White (1974: 196) = CSC #281.

[2] *MS Eng. hist. c. 53*. It has been edited and published in three parts by Philip (1950a, 1950b, 1953).

[3] His employment as a scout for Sir Samuel Luke's army is summarized towards the end of the manuscript; see *MS Eng. hist. c. 53*, folio 133 verso = CSC #38.

[4] *MS Eng. hist. c. 53*, folios 8 verso and 12 recto = Philip (1950a: 6, 13). Hitchman also makes a report of a reconnaissance visit to Oxford on 8 March 1643 (*MS Eng. hist. c. 53*, folio 16 verso = Philip [1950a]: 24).

tendered about this spying mission demonstrates not only how difficult it was for soldiers to separate those townspeople supporting the royalist cause from those supporting the Parliamentarians, but also the relative ease with which Hitchman could get himself released from prison once he was arrested as a spy. At one point while he was in custody in Oxford, Hitchman was even able to get close enough to Charles I to see the king's fury as news reached him about an offer from Parliament concerning the cessation of hostilities.[1]

Hitchman was frequently dispatched to London, probably as a message courier for Sir Samuel Luke: specific mention is made of him going there on 23 February, on 9 March, on 1 May, on 18 May, on 1 August, on 26 September, on 25 October, on 1 November 1643, on 12 January 1644, on 16 March 1644;[2] and of him returning from there on 30 April and on 17 May 1643, on 11 January, and on 5 February 1644.[3] He was also dispatched to Maidenhead on 16 April 1643,[4] is said to have carried letters to a Colonel Harvey on 28 August 1643,[5] and to have returned from Newport on 16 March 1644.[6]

Given the nature of the sources concerned, it is impossible to prove that the identification of Thomas Hatchman, the Oxford butcher, with Thomas Hitchman, the Parliamentary spy, is correct. However, there is one final incident recorded within the journal which may be relevant. One of Sir Samuel Luke's scouts reported about a reconnaissance mission in Oxford that was made on 22 August 1643, saying 'that hee saw a Butchers man hangd by Pr[ince] Ru[perts] command for refusing to say God blesse the King'.[7] One cannot help but wonder if there is a connection between this event and the career of Thomas Hitchman/ himself. Perhaps the butcher who was hanged was a friend, or fellow butcher, and his execution indicates that the Oxford butchers were a hot-bed of anti-royalist sentiment.[8] Interestingly, Thomas *Hitchman's* last recorded reconnaissance visit to Oxford was in March of 1643. Perhaps the public execution of a butcher by the royalist camp in August of 1643 meant that it was just too dangerous for him to enter the city again, particularly if he was in any way associated with the trade in the city. On this point, circumstantial evidence points to Thomas *Hitchman* and Thomas *Hatchman* as possibly one and the same person, although such an identification cannot be proven.

---

[1] *MS Eng. hist. c. 53*, folio 12 recto and verso = Philip (1950a): 13-14 = CSC #39.

[2] *MS Eng. hist. c. 53*, folios 12 verso, 16 verso, 35 recto, 39 verso, 60 recto, 75 recto, 85 verso, 88 recto, 111 recto, and 125 recto = Philip (1950a): 15, 24, 68, 78; (1950b): 127, 156, 175; (1953): 187, 237, 265.

[3] *MS Eng. hist. c. 53*, folios 35 recto, 39 recto, 111 recto, and 115 verso = Philip (1950a): 67, 77; 1953: 234, 246).

[4] *MS Eng. hist. c. 53*, folio 31 verso = Philip (1950a): 61.

[5] *MS Eng. hist. c. 53*, folios 69 recto = Philip (1950b): 143.

[6] *MS Eng. hist. c. 53*, folio 125 recto = Philip (1953): 265.

[7] *MS Eng. hist. c. 53*, folio 67 recto = Philip (1950b): 140.

[8] See MacCulloch (1986): 306, for a related observation about the radical nature of butchers' trade.

Roger Hatchman and his son Thomas were among the first generation of Baptists in Oxford, and each in his own way had a distinctive contribution to make to the life of the church that met there. Both men appear in the earliest records of the Abingdon Association, the former as a messenger to the meetings held in Tetsworth on 19-20 June 1660, and the latter as a subject of censure in the meetings held 5-7 April 1659. A careful examination of the available 17th-century documents also reveals that both men had lively and controversial careers within the municipal affairs of Oxford, beginning in the tumultuous days of the Civil War and extending well into the years of the Protectorates of both Oliver and Richard Cromwell. Their chosen career paths also offer an important angle on such matters, with Roger Hatchman pursuing a career as a Parliamentary military officer and Thomas Hatchman working as a member of a guild which was itself a source of anti-royalist sentiment and a breeding ground for political dissent.

E. John Higgins: Weaver and Signatory of
A Testimony to Truth, Agreeing with an Essay for Settlement (1659)

As noted above (page 159) Thomas Hatchman was married to Margret Higgins, who was probably the daughter of John Higgins, one of the signatories of the Baptist broadsheet *A Testimony to Truth, Agreeing with an Essay for Settlement* (1659). Higgins's signature to this controversial tract is the primary evidence of his involvement with Baptists; he does not appear in other Baptist publications of the period, nor is he mentioned in the *Abingdon Association Records Book*. Most of his activity as a Dissenter has to be gleaned from the records of the civil and ecclesiastical courts, and his association with other known Baptists mentioned within such documents.

Precise identification of members of the Higgins family is made difficult by the fact that a number of variations of the spelling of the surname are found in the sources, including Higgens, Higgons, Huggins, and Huginges. In addition, several members of this wider family had the first name of John which complicates matters considerably, particularly when attempting to identify individuals in the second half of the 1600s. A number of these John Higginses went on to successful careers in their chosen fields.[1] The Dissenter John Higgins was a weaver or clothier by trade, although he apparently was not a native Oxonian, but a foreigner ('farriner'), that is to say, someone who lived

---

[1] John Higgins the son of Anthony Higgins was apprenticed as a farrier to John Holdship on 1 June 1685 (*Civic Enrolments – 1662-1699* (L.5.4), page 376), and upon completion of that apprenticeship was granted his citizenship on 26 August 1692 (*Civic Enrolments – 1662-1699* (L.5.4), page 539. There is record of him agreeing an apprenticeship contract with Ferdinando Smith on 27 August 1695 (*Civic Enrolments – 1662-1699* (L.5.4), page 488).

outside the bounds of the city.[1] Parish records suggest that many of the Higgins family were located in the northern part of the suburbs, mainly in the parishes of St Mary Magdalen and St Giles (see the accompanying chart on 'The Family Tree of John Higgins' for details of his larger family connections). The immediate family circumstances of Higgins himself are unclear, although it it likely that his father was a tailor from the parish of St Mary Magdalen.[2] Higgins was conditionally granted his 'Freedom of the City' by an act of Common Council on 2 December 1651,[3] and, after paying the normal fees and giving a bond of £200, was enrolled as such on 2 April 1652.[4] Having established himself as a master weaver Higgins began to take on apprentices, starting with his own son John who succeeded him as a master weaver and continued the family tradition as a craftsman, at least for a while. Records of four apprenticeships for John Higgins senior and one apprenticeship for John Higgins junior are extant. The names and dates for these apprenticeship contracts, and the dates when the apprentices were granted their 'Freedom of the City', are as follows:

Name	Date of Contract	Duration	Citizenship Granted
John Higgins	2 April 1652[5]	Seven years	11 April 1659[6]
Adam Turner	1 October 1659[7]	Seven years	
Thomas Davies	21 November 1663[8]	Seven years	5 February 1672[9]
William Milday	31 March 1671[1]	Seven years	

---

[1] He may have lived in Headington. There is a record of a John Higgins of Headington paying 1s 5½d in tax in the summer of 1647 (*Lay Subsidy of 23 June 1647* (E 179/164/497), membrane 3).

[2] There is record of a Thomas Higgins who was buried on 13 November 1616 (*Parish Register of St Mary Magdalen – 1602-1662* (Par 208/1/R1/1), folio 51 recto), and of an Edward Higgins who was buried on 19 July 1620 (*Parish Register of St Mary Magdalen – 1602-1662* (Par 208/1/R1/1), folio 52 verso). Both men are described as 'taylor' within their respective register entries.

[3] *City Council Proceedings – 1629-1663* (A.5.7), folio 203 verso = CSC #100.

[4] *Civic Enrolments – 1639-1662* (L.5.3), folio 241 verso = CSC #109. The accounting record for this is dated 9 December 1652 (*Audit Book – 1592-1682* (P.5.2), folio 284 recto).

[5] *Civic Enrolments – 1639-1662* (L.5.3), folio 109 recto = CSC #1·10.

[6] *Civic Enrolments – 1639-1662* (L.5.3), folios 221 verso and 222 recto = CSC #282 and CSC #283.

[7] *Civic Enrolments – 1639-1662* (L.5.3), folio 178 verso = CSC #295; the apprenticeship contract is backdated to 21 December 1658.

[8] *Civic Enrolments – 1662-1699* (L.5.4), page 23 = CSC #386. This apprenticeship was originally made with James Ward as the master, but was transferred to John Higgins on 2 April 1666.

[9] *Civic Enrolments – 1662-1699* (L.5.4), page 679 = CSC #500; *Husting and Mayors Courts – 1666-1672* (M.4.6), folio 199 recto (Hustings).

| Edward Dubber | 7 January 1668[2] | Seven years | 7 December 1674[3] |

There is record of a John Higgins, probably the father, applying for 'a lease for some voyd ground in Broken Hayes' on 14 November 1659.[4] It appears that a substantial property was built upon this site which became the family home, as well as the place from which the family's weaving business was conducted. Several tax records are associated with the Higgins's residence in this property which was located outside the north gate of the city. There are two records of John Higgins making a voluntary contribution to the Subsidy of 8 July 1661; a John Higgins senior(?) made a contribution of 5s, and a John Higgins junior 'in St Giles' made a contribution of 4s.[5] In addition, there are two records of a John Higgins serving as one of the officers of the parish of St Giles responsible for overseeing the collection of the Hearth Tax of Michaelmas 1662,[6] and of a John Higgins who was appointed one of the 'Overseers of the Poor' for the parish in 1663.[7] More importantly, there is also record of a John Higgins of the parish of St Mary Magdalen paying for six hearths in the Hearth Tax of Michaelmas 1665.[8] Apparently by 1667 both father and son and their families lived near to one another, or perhaps shared the property noted above; the record of the Poll Tax of 1667 pertaining to them is a joint entry.[9] It records that John Higgins senior paid 3s in tax, covering himself, his wife, (whose name we know from other sources was Elizabeth), and one child; John Higgins junior paid 5s in tax to cover himself, his wife, and three children. The entry also lists an apprentice, Thomas Davies, who paid 1s in tax, and a Joanne Lay, probably a family servant, who paid 2s in tax on her wages of £1.[10] As a resident of the parish of St Mary Magdalen, Higgins is listed as paying 5s 6d for the War Tax collections dated 24 June, 29 September

---

[1] *Civic Enrolments – 1662-1699* (L.5.4), page 175 = CSC #493a. This apprenticeship was originally made with John Higgins as the master, but was transferred to William Hamblen on 26 July 1672.

[2] *Civic Enrolments – 1662-1699* (L.5.4), page 108 = CSC #445a; the apprenticeship contract is backdated to 1 November 1667.

[3] *Civic Enrolments – 1662-1699* (L.5.4), page 660 = CSC #532; *Husting and Mayors Courts – 1672-1677* (M.4.7), folio 58 verso (Mayors). John Higgins junior is listed as one of two people who offered sureties for Edward Dubber when he was awarded £5 from Mr Wilson's charity on 29 September 1676 (*Civil War Charities and General Minutes 1645-1695* (E.4.6) folio 108 verso).

[4] *City Council Proceedings – 1629-1663* (A.5.7), folio 267 verso.

[5] *Free and Voluntary Present of 8 July 1661* (E 179/255/5/4), membrane 4.

[6] *Hearth Tax of August-November 1662* (E 179/255/4), Part 2, pages 66 and 110. He signed declarations excusing those who were unable to pay the tax due to their poverty.

[7] *Husting and Mayor's Court 1662; Licenses and Overseers* (N.4.3), folio 15 recto = CSC #372.

[8] *Hearth Tax of Michaelmas 1665* (E 179/164/513), membrane 34.

[9] *Poll Tax of 1667* (P.5.7), folio 39 recto.

[10] *Poll Tax of 1667* (P.5.7), folio 39 recto.

and 29 December 1667, 26 March, 26 June, 26 September and 26 December 1668.[1] He also signed a marriage bond on 5 November 1673 for the marriage of John Faulkner and Rebecca Atley while living in the parish.[2]

There are not many records of John Higgins's activity following the collapse of the Protectorate. There is record of a John Higgins who gave assistance to the Oxford militia in the summer of 1661, probably in anticipation of celebrations surrounding the restoration of Charles II. This probably is Higgins the Baptist Dissenter – he is listed as one of three people who provides supplies for John Colton, who was likely a young soldier.[3]   After the Restoration, however, Higgins was active as a Dissenter in the city over a number of years. There are many records in which he is cited to appear before the ecclesiastical courts. The earliest of these are three records from the spring of 1662, dated 8, 15 and 22 March, 19 and 26 April.[4] They record Higgins's failure to appear before the court, despite being called three times, and note that his name was being entered into the schedule of excommunications. The excommunication document itself does not appear to have survived, although there is an intriguing record of Higgins making an appeal against his excommunication on 30 December 1662.[5]   The document notes the 'heavy censure' of the excommunication, and relates that Higgins

is informed his Ma[jes]ties
Writt *de Exco[mmu]n[i]cato Capiendo* is issued out against him.
But at p[re]sent hee is made sensible of this excesse and
is sory for the same, and humbly prayeth that hee may bee
obsolved from the exco[mmu]n[i]cat[i]on and restored to the Communion
of Christian people upon p[ro]mise that hereafter hee wilbee
obedient to the Kings Eccl[es]i[as]t[i]cal Lawes and the commands
of the ordinary.

However, Higgins's conformity was not permanent, for he and his wife Elizabeth were again cited to appear before the ecclesiastical courts on 2, 23 and 30 May, and 6 June 1668.[6] The record of the court appearance on 6 June is the most interesting of these, with Higgins admitting their failure to attend their parish church and confessing that 'Neither hee nor his wife did receive y^e Sacram[en]t at Easter last'.[7] Higgins appeared also before the court on his own

---

[1] *War Taxes – 1667-1668* (P.5.8), folios 13 recto, 25 verso, 56 verso, 69 recto, 83 recto, 99 verso, 114 verso.

[2] *OAR: Marriage Bonds – 1673* (c. 462), folio 43 = CSC #522.

[3] *Civil War Charities and General Minutes 1645-1695* (E.4.6) folios 35 recto and 35 verso.

[4] *ODR: 1 February 1660-4 October 1662* (c. 3), folios 11 recto, 13 recto, 15 recto, 17 recto, and 18 recto.

[5] *ODR: 27 September 1662-15 April 1665* (c. 4), folio 60 verso = CSC #360.

[6] *OAR: 11 May 1667 – 21 July 1669* (c. 17), folios 86 verso, 89 verso, 98 verso and 108 verso.

[7] *OAR: 11 May 1667 – 21 July 1669* (c. 17), folio 108 verso = CSC #455.

a year later on 21 July 1669, again answering accusations that he had failed to attend his parish church.[1] He was ordered to certify his church attendance and his participation in the Lord's Supper by the following Feast of St Michael (29 September).

Higgins continued as an active Dissenter despite the ecclesiastical court's attempts to make him conform. As noted above (page 160), Higgins was one of the five people indicted to appear before the Petty Sessions court and charged with attending a meeting at the house of Lawrence King on 9 January 1670.[2] Higgins also made another court appearance before the Petty Sessions court on 3 October 1672, and was discharged after an (unnamed) brother spoke up for him.[3] By this stage of his life Higgins was a widower; his wife Elizabeth died and was buried sometime in November of 1671.[4] In addition, there are records from 6, 13 December 1673; 17, 24, 31 January, 7, 14, and 21 February 1674 which signal that Higgins was involved in yet another round of conflict with ecclesiastical authorities.[5] Interestingly, John Higgins junior is also cited to appear at each of these eight court dates; he is described as being from the parish of St Mary Magdalen, his name generally appearing alongside that of Richard Tidmarsh in the court entries.[6] Matters reached a critical point for John Higgins senior when he appeared before the court on the morning of 28 February 1674 and responded to the charge that he did not attend his local parish by saying that he had in fact 'hath bin there lately at a Funerall'. The court officials, Nicholas Vilett and John Baylie, warned him 'to goe to his p[ar]ish Church to heare divine service & to frequent it betweene this & Easter' and to certify that he had done so at the next court.[7]

John Higgins is cited fifteen times ecclesiastical court records for 1680 while living in the parish of St Giles. These records are dated 31 January, 7, 14, 21 and 28 February, 6 and 13 March, 9, 10, 12, 17, 19, 26 June, 3, and 17 July

---

[1] *OAR: 11 May 1667 – 21 July 1669* (c. 17), folio 296 verso = CSC #473.

[2] *Oxford Petty Sessions Roll – 1656-1678* (O.5.11), folio 114 recto = CSC #480.

[3] *Oxford Petty Sessions Roll – 1656-1678* (O.5.11), folio 134 verso = CSC #513. This brother may have been Thomas Higgins, a farrier, who signed a bond for a marriage between Henry Cockson and Mary Belcher on 24 November 1668 (*OAR: Marriage Bonds – 1668* (c. 458), folio 12). Mary Belcher is here described as coming from Westcott Barton in Oxfordshire and may have been related to the controversial Fifth Monarchist preacher John Belcher.

[4] *Parish Register of St Giles – 1576-1680* (MS DD Par Oxford – St Giles b.1), page 134. The exact day of her burial is not recorded in the parish register.

[5] *OAR: 29 November 1673-20 February 1675* (c. 21), folios 6 verso, 9 verso, 13 verso, 17 verso, 22 verso, 27 verso, 32 recto, and 37 verso.

[6] *OAR: 29 November 1673-20 February 1675* (c. 21), folios 5 verso, 9 recto, 13 recto, 17 recto, 22 recto, 27 recto, 32 recto, and 37 verso.

[7] *OAR: 29 November 1673-20 February 1675* (c. 21), folio 40 recto = CSC #524. Ironically, Higgins had appeared before these same two officials three months earlier when signing the marriage bond for John Faulkner and Rebecca Atley.

1680.[1] He was also listed in an excommunication order dated 30 August 1680, where he is named as one of three people from the parish of St Giles so excommunicated.[2] It is likely that Higgins was among the unnamed Dissenters who are mentioned in the list presented to the Archdeacon Timothy Halton at his visitation in 1683; the list notes seven Dissenters from the parish of St Mary Magdalen and ten from the parish of St Giles.[3] This is the last record of Higgins as a Dissenter, for he died and was buried in the parish church of St Giles on 13 February 1685.[4]

Surviving records relating to his son John Higgins junior are more difficult to sort out, but it appears that he died and was buried eight years later on 20 February 1693.[5] His will describes him as a farmer or husbandman from the parish of St Giles, which suggests that he had moved away from the profession of a weaver; this may help explain why there is only one apprenticeship contract (dated to 1668) which lists him as a master weaver (see pages 192-3 above). His wife Mary died and was buried on 8 November 1696.[6]

A number of tax records confirm the residence of John and Mary in the parish of St Giles throughout the whole of their married life. There is record of John Higgins paying the Poll Tax of 10 March 1692 covering himself, his wife, one son, two daughters and a man-servant while living in the parish.[7] Another quarterly payment of 2s in the Poll Tax dated 27 June 1692 covers just Higgins and his wife Mary, whereas a payment from 1693, made after John Higgins had died, shows 'Widow Higgins' paid the tax on her own.[8] Early in 1694 she paid for herself and one other person (presumably one of her children), whereas in the collections of 2 May, 27 August and 17 December 1694, and 25 February 1695 she paid for herself and two of her children.[9]

---

[1] *OAR: 1 June 1678-30 July 1681 and 4 July 1674-17 October 1674* (c. 22), folios 91 verso, 94 recto, 94 verso, 99 verso, 102 verso, 105 verso, 109 recto, 119 recto, 122 recto, 124 verso, 126 verso, 129 verso; *ODR: 1 June 1678–27 November 1680* (c. 2134), folios 63 recto, 64 verso, 67 verso, 72 verso, 76 recto, 79 verso, 83 verso, 96 verso, 98 verso, 102 verso and 106 verso; *ODR: Miscellaneous Citations* (c. 62), folios 32 recto.

[2] *ODR: Excommunications – 1633-1791* (c. 99), folio 60 recto and verso = CSC #598.

[3] *ODR: Memoranda from Diocesan Books – 1679-1814* (b. 68), folio 6 verso.

[4] *Parish Register of St Giles – 1679-1768* (MS DD Par Oxford – St Giles c. 1), page 184.

[5] *Parish Register of St Giles – 1679-1768* (MS DD Par Oxford – St Giles c. 1), page 187; *John Higgins* (OWPR 132/4/21).

[6] *Parish Register of St Giles – 1679-1768* (MS DD Par Oxford – St Giles c. 1), page 188; *Mary Higgins* (OWPR 34/5/4).

[7] *Taxes – 1691-1694* (P.5.9), folio 17 recto.

[8] *Taxes – 1691-1694* (P.5.9), folios 42 recto and 79 recto. The second entry from 1693 also records her paying £16 in tax on a house and lands; a similar payment was made in 1694 (*Taxes – 1691-1694* (P.5.9), folio 108 recto).

[9] *Taxes – 1691-1694* (P.5.9), folios 108 recto, 144 verso, 158 recto, 167 recto and 187 recto.

In all, the couple had at least ten children, five of whom survived the death of their parents, including a daughter Mary who had married the bookbinder John Browman from the parish of St Mary the Virgin in 1684,[1] and a son named John who was apprenticed to the upholsterer Adrian Roberts on 2 July 1683.[2] Upon successful completion of his apprenticeship this John Higgins, the grandson of the Baptist Dissenter, was granted his 'Freedom of the City' on 27 September 1690.[3] There is record of him paying 1s in the Poll Tax of 2 May, 27 August and 17 December 1694 and 25 February 1695, while living in the parish of St Giles,[4] although he eventually established himself in the parish of St Martin as an upholsterer. He married Anne Godfrey from the parish of St Mary the Virgin in September of 1696,[5] and the couple had a daughter named Sarah who was baptized on 22 June 1697,[6] and a son named Godfry who died and was buried on 2 June 1698.[7] This John Higgins paid 2s in the Window Tax of 1696 for a house with seven windows in the parish of St Martin's,[8] and £2 16s in the Poll Tax of 1696.[9]

---

[1] *OAR: Marriage Bonds – 1684* (c. 472), folio 10. There may have been some tension within the marriage as Mary Higgins specifically notes that the legacy left to her namesake daughter 'shalbe paid and given to her & not to her husband' (*Mary Higgins* (OWPR 34/5/4)). Browman is not named in her will, as he was in that of his father-in-law John Higgins junior (*John Higgins* (OWPR 132/4/21).

[2] *Civic Enrolments – 1662-1699* (L.5.4), page 353.

[3] *Civic Enrolments – 1662-1699* (L.5.4), page 548.

[4] *Taxes – 1691-1694* (P.5.9), folios 144 verso, 158 verso, 167 verso and 187 verso.

[5] *OAR: Marriage Bonds – 1696* (c. 482), folio 71.

[6] *Parish Register of St Martin's – 1678-1789* (Par 207/1/R1/4), folio 20 recto.

[7] *Parish Register of St. Giles – 1679-1768* (MS DD Par Oxford – c. 1), page 189.

[8] *Taxes – 1694-1746* (P.5.10), folio 48 recto.

[9] *Taxes – 1694-1746* (P.5.10), folio 41 verso.

4. The Gardener:

Ralph Austen

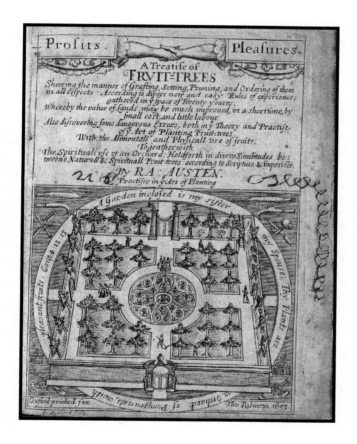

Illustration #7: Title page from the first edition of Ralph Austen's *A Treatise of Fruit-Trees* (1653). The central image of an enclosed garden is taken from Song of Songs 4:12-13: 'A Garden inclosed is my sister, my Spouse; Thy Plants are an Orchard of Pomegranats, with pleasant fruits.' The first edition was limited to 500 copies.

4. The Gardener:

Ralph Austen

I have already noted above (pages 17-18) in the discussion of Major Roger Hatchman, the 'casheired military officer', that on 9 January 1662 Ralph Austen was indicted for being a 'seditious sectarye' and a 'disloyall person' and for attending an unlawful conventicle in Oxford. Along with Roger Hatchman, Richard Tidmarsh and Lawrence King, Austen was brought before the Petty Sessions court and made to answer for his involvement with these openly Baptist leaders. I also noted in this regard Anthony Wood's assertions of Austen's public support for John Belcher, the fiery Baptist leader and Fifth Monarchist, who caused such controversy when preaching at St Peter-in-the-Bailey in January of 1660 (see pages 179-80 above). In many respects Ralph Austen is the most significant of the four 'seditious sectaryes' who appeared before the Petty Sessions court on that Thursday in January of 1662. Of the four men only Ralph Austen has an entry within the newly revised *Dictionary of National Biography*, albeit one that has significant gaps in it.[1]

I shall now examine Austen's life in more detail, noting not only his involvement as a Dissenter, but also his association with Baptists in Oxford. Special attention will also be given to Austen's role as the Regstrar[2] of the Visitors of Parliament to Oxford, and his activities as a gardener, horticulturalist and cider-maker. The chapter will conclude with a brief discussion of two other controversial Baptist Disssenter with whom Austen appears to have been in contact, namely Richard Quelch junior, a watchmaker who served as an agent for the Fifth Monarchists in Oxford, and James Jennings, a button-maker and the under-butler of New College.

---

[1] Turner (2004) makes significant improvements on the earlier article by Henderson (1908): 702-3, notably suggesting that a distinction be made between Austen the Dissenter and another man of the same name who served as a proctor of the University of Oxford.

[2] The title is frequently spelled 'Register' within many of the original documents.

A. An Active Dissenter in Oxford with Baptist Associations

Austen's involvement with the Dissenters in Oxford was not just a passing whim, but extended over a long period of time. This can be readily demonstrated through a number of primary source documents, notably the pamphlet entitled *The Complaining Testimony of Some ... of Sion's Children* (1656). This little pamphlet is one of the most interesting of the period, not only for its contribution to the study of Baptist involvement in religious and political movements such as the Fifth Monarchy movement, but also for the insight if offers to into Baptist life in the city of Oxford.

1. The Complaining Testimony of Some ... of Sion's Children (1656)

Although Austen's name is not among those listed at the end of the pamphlet as officially representing the church in Oxford, the pamphlet does contain a short paragraph detailing the involvement of the various people who had gathered in Abingdon for the funeral of John Pendarves and were involved in a confrontation with the authorities. In this regard, passing mention is made to 'our Brother Austen, a member of the Church at Oxford, who was late a member of the Army exercising.'[1]

The military connection ('late a member of the Army exercising') is important, and may be an additional point of contact for Ralph Austen, Richard Tidmarsh and Roger Hatchman and help explain how they ended up appearing together before the Petty Sessions court in January of 1662. As noted above (page 32), there is evidence that Austen and Tidmarsh both received commissions within the Oxfordshire militia in August of 1659.[2] In fact, Austen was commissioned an ensign in the sixth of seven companies of a regiment of foot under the command of Colonel Scroope, although he probably did not serve in this capacity in any substantial way, or at least not for very long. Political circumstances were changing rapidly and on 23 February 1660 Parliament issued a declaration revoking all orders pertaining to county militias.[3] More significantly, the commanding officer of the regiment, Colonel Adrian Scroope, was executed as a regicide on 17 October 1660.[4] However, Austen's military connections probably extended even earlier, and gave rise to the provocative phrase in the pamphlet from 1656.

---

[1] There is record of a George Astin being member of the Baptist church in Oxford, and it is possible that this is who is meant here (see page 10). However, the difference in the spelling of the surname needs to be taken into account and suggests that Ralph Austen is the person indicated in *The Complaining Testimony of Some ... of Sion's Children* (1656).

[2] *JHC* 7: 752-3 = CSC #291.

[3] *Resolved upon the question by the Parliament, that all the militias in the respective counties, and the powers given to them, be and are hereby revoked* (1660).

[4] Payne (1951): 150-5, summarizes his life.

Austen counted other Army officers as his friends, as several of his surviving letters indicate. Fortunately, a wealth of information can be extracted from the correspondence that he shared with others. Austen's reputation as a gardener and horticulturalist brought him into contact with a number of important intellectual figures, particularly within the burgeoning scientific community. One of the most important of these contacts was Samuel Hartlib (c. 1600-1662), the influential polymath who, together with his circle of friends and contacts, helped form the Royal Society in 1660.[1] A lively correspondence between Austen and Hartlib took place between 1652 and 1661, most of Austen's side of which has survived. A total of seventy-one letters written by Austen to Hartlib are extant, as well as a number of copies of Austen's letters to other friends of Hartlib, notably the horticulturalist and fellow cider enthusiast John Beale (1603-1683).[2] Together these documents provide remarkable insight into the horticultural and religious concerns which dominated Austen's life. They also give incidental details into the circle of Austen's military contacts.[3]

For example, a letter dated 8 February 1654 was delivered to Hartlib in London by a Captain John Hunt, whom Austen describes as 'my very loving & worthie freind & neighbour'.[4] Similarly, he makes mention of a Colonel Kelsey in a letter dated 29 April 1655, suggesting that 'worthie' Kelsey might be very instrumental in getting his ideas about gardening and horticulture reviewed by the Lord Protector Cromwell.[5] Thomas Kelsey was an influential Parliamentary officer during the Civil War, having helped to draw up the

---

[1] The Hartlib papers are now part of the library of the University of Sheffield. References to Austen's letters to Hartlib are taken from *The Hartlib Papers Project* (1995). See Crawford (1995) for details.

[2] There are copies of two letters from Austen to Beale, one dated 30 July 1658 (*Hartlib 45/2/3A-4B* = CSC #265), and the other 7 September 1658 (*Hartlib 52/169A-171A* = CSC #266). In addition, copies of two letters of reply from John Beale to Austen, one dated 23 August 1658 (*41/1/123A-124B*) and one dated 16 September 1658 (*Hartlib 52/169A-171B-172B*) also survive within the Hartlib collection.

[3] They also reveal that a financial dispute between Austen and Hartlib's son Sam. It appears that Sam Hartlib was paid £100 by Austen to search through land records and locate crown properties that were being sold off or awarded by Parliament for services rendered (Austen intended to petition for a suitable plot of land). However, although he accepted the money, Sam Hartlib did not do what he had promised he would. Austen mentions the son's unreliability in a number of letters, attempting to persuade the father to influence his son to attend to his promises (see *Hartlib 41/1/74A* = CSC #194; *41/1/76A* = CSC #197; *41/1/78A* = CSC #201; *41/1/83B* = CSC #207; *41/1/86A* = CSC #212; *41/1/98A* = CSC #225; *41/1/110A* = CSC #238; *45/2/5A* = CSC #268; and *45/2/7A* = CSC #271). Turnbull (1947): 8-9, gives details of difficulties that Hartlib had with his son Sam.

[4] *Hartlib 41/1/64B* = CSC #165. Austen lists Captain John Hunt as one of the ten people willing to offer a testimonial on his behalf in a letter dated 20 August 1655 (*Hartlib 41/1/94A-95B* = CSC #220).

[5] *Hartlib 41/1/82A-83B* = CSC #207.

articles of surrender for Langford House on 17 October 1645;[1] he was also appointed Deputy Governor of Oxford following the surrender of the city in June 1646. Kelsey was given a Bailiff's place on the City Council on 10 March 1648;[2] he also served in 1649, 1650 and 1652 as one of the Parliamentary Commissioners for assessing the city's contribution towards the finances needed to maintain the military forces of the nation.[3] Kelsey was known to have been an active supporter of the Parliamentary Visitors to the University and in that capacity would have been in frequent contact with Ralph Austen as Registrar of the Visitors.[4] Indeed, Kelsey was one of the four Parliamentary Visitors who appointed Austen as Register.[5] Within the letter from 29 April 1655, Austen says that Kelsey, 'hath frequent accesse to him [Cromwell] & hath a great interest in his Highnesse: I have received many favours from him [Kelsey] in Oxon: hee well knowes my way.'[6]

Austen also had some contact with the regicide Colonel John Barkstead, and attempted to elicit his support for the proposal he made to Parliament concerning the planting of trees (more on Austen's horticultural vision below). Barkstead was a London goldsmith and silversmith who joined the Parliamentary cause at the start of the Civil War, notably participating in the siege of Basing House in the summer of 1644,[7] and serving with Sir Thomas Fairfax at the siege of Colchester in July of 1648. Barkstead worked closely with Cromwell's spymaster John Thurloe in intelligence work during the 1650s, uncovering various plots against the government. He was appointed military governor of Middlesex during the Rule of the Major Generals and was knighted by Cromwell for his services during the Protectorate. At the Restoration Barkstead fled to Germany where he was welcomed and given the freedom of the Lutheran city of Hanau. However, Barkstead, who had been tried *in absentia* for his participation in the execution of Charles I, made the fatal error of crossing into Holland to meet his wife, and was arrested by Dutch authorities who handed him over to the English Resident George Downing.[8]

---

[1] See *Lieutenant General Cromwells Letter to the Honourable William Lenthall Esq; Speaker of the House of Commons* (1645): 4-5.

[2] *City Council Proceedings – 1629-1663* (A.5.7), folio 165 recto.

[3] Firth and Rait (1911): 2.306, 475 and 672.

[4] *Wood 514* (29), contains an order dated 31 March 1648 from Sir Thomas Fairfax to Kelsey to use the troops in Oxford to support the Parliamentary Visitors as needed (see CSC #56a). There is a similar letter of Kelsey's contained in *MS Wood F 35*, folio 243, which is dated 5 July 1648. Kelsey was made an MA on 14 April 1648 (*Athenae Oxonienses, Volume 2* (1692): 745).

[5] Greaves (1983): 154-5, summarizes Kelsey's life.

[6] *Hartlib 41/1/82A* = CSC #207.

[7] *A Description of the Seige of Basing Castle Kept by the Lord Marquisse of Winchester for the Service of His Majesty: Against, the Forces of the Rebells, under Command of Colonell Norton* (Oxford, 1644) gives details of the long struggle over this house.

[8] Walker (1948): 113-114, discusses Downing's unscrupulous manoeuvrings in the matter of the extradition of the regicides.

Despite the protests of the Dutch Anabaptist churches on his behalf,[1] Barkstead was returned to England and executed on 19 April 1662.

To return to Barkstead's role in the Commonwealth period, he had been appointed the Lieutenant of the Tower in 1652 and it is in this capacity that Austen approached him through the agency of Samuel Hartlib. There are four letters to Hartlib in which Austen mentions Colonel Barkstead, all of written when Barkstead was at the height of his influence and power.[2] With the last of these four letters, dated 9 February 1657, Austen sends four copies of his latest book to Hartlib and asks that they be given away as gifts, specifically asking that one go to Colonel Barkstead. He describes Barkstead and the other intended recipients in hopeful terms:

> These men are the fittest, & likliest to doe something of any that I know; Coll[onel] Barksted hath beene a meanes to promote [a] thing of the same nature heretofore; & perhaps he may do something now.

As a final illustration of Austen's familiarity with military personnel, we note that he also makes brief mention to a Captain Smith in a letter dated 24 April 1656, remarking that he has heard the Captain had recently been in London and had spoken to Lord Fleetwood on his behalf, presumably meeting Fleetwood at his home in Wallingford House.[3]

In short, it seems that Austen moved comfortably among military leaders, counting several of them as personal friends and acquaintances, and numbering others as potential colleagues in the promotion of his aims. All of this helps to confirm Austen's involvement in the events surrounding John Pendarves's funeral in Abingdon in 1656 and the passing mention of him in *The Complaining Testimony of Some ... of Sions Children* (1656). In short, there is good evidence to suggest that Austen was a member of a Dissenting conventicle in Oxford and that he counted some of the prominent Baptists within the city as among his fellow conventiclers. Is there any additional

---

[1] *A Memoriall Intended to be delivered to the Lords States, Monday 10 March, Stilo Novo, to the High and Mighty Lords, the States of Holland, by the Forraign Anabaptist Churches, upon the apprehending and giving up Colonel Barkestead, Colonel Okey and Mr. Miles Corbet to the English Resident* (1662). The three men wrote a letter to some churches in London who had supported them, published as *A Letter from Collonell John Barkstead, Collonell Okey and Miles Corbet to the Congregations at London* (1662). The fullest account of their capture, trial and execution was published as *The Speeches, Discourses, and Prayers of Col. John Barkstead, Col. John Okey, and Miles Corbet; upon the 19th of April, being the Day of their Suffering at Tyburn* (1662). Interestingly, Barkstead describes himself as a follower of 'the Congregationalist way' in his final speech before his execution (page 58).

[2] Letters dated 26 December 1654 (*Hartlib 41/1/76A-77B* = CSC #197); 12 June 1655 (*Hartlib 41/1/88A-89B* = CSC #213); 10 December 1655 (*Hartlib 41/1/104A-105B* = CSC #231); and 9 February 1657 (*Hartlib 41/1/121A-122B* = CSC #247).

[3] *Hartlib 41/1/108A-109B* = CSC #236.

evidence which links Ralph Austen to Oxford Baptists? Fortunately, there are other records from the Oxford City archives which shed further light.

Austen's brush with the legal authorities in January of 1662 (noted above) was by no means an isolated instance. Like his fellow Baptists, he was named as one of the insurrectionists in the so-called 'Presbyterian Sham-plot' of 1661 (see pages 43-4 above). In addition, Austen appeared before the ecclesiastical and civic courts on a number of other occasions. These court records are worth considering in some detail for they provide additional circumstantial evidence of Austin's association with Baptists and other Dissenters in the city of Oxford.

2. Diocesan Court Records

Austen's name appears several times in the Diocesan Court records for the 1660s, usually in connection with some offence involving his religious activities. Thus, we find Austen, together with his (unnamed) wife, residents of the parish of St Peter-in-the-Bailey, cited in court records for 28 June 1662. The couple were summoned by the court apparitor the day before, but they failed to appear and were provisionally fined 20 shillings.[1] This court citation was followed by another a week later on 5 July. Once again Austen and his wife, though summoned, did not appear before the court and the fine was levied.[2] There is also a record dated 18 January 1668 which specifically mentions allegations that Austin's failed to attend services at his local parish church in St Peter-in-the-Bailey. In this instance Ralph Austen alone is cited; his wife does not appear in further records of the period.[3]

Austen's name appears in records for five subsequent sessions of the Diocesan Court, namely those held on 8, 15 and 29 February,[4] and those on 7 and 14 March 1668.[5] The record for 8 February notes that Austen had been judicially warned to be present at the proceedings and give answer to the charges against him; however, it does not make clear if he was actually present.[6] The records for 15 and 29 February and 7 March simply note that Austen's case was to be addressed in the next meeting of the court sessions. The record dated 14 March is slightly more expansive, however, and indicates Austen's physical appearance before the court.[7] His case was dismissed until such time as he was summoned again to the next court sessions. Interestingly,

---

[1] *ODR: 1 February 1660–4 October 1662* (c. 3), folio 29 recto = CSC #343.

[2] *ODR: 1 February 1660–4 October 1662* (c. 3), folio 31 verso = CSC #346.

[3] *ODR: 7 October 1665–7 March 1668* (c. 5), folios 263 recto and verso = CSC #446.

[4] *ODR: 7 October 1665–7 March 1668* (c. 5), folios 265 verso, 272 recto, and 279 recto.

[5] The relevant pages are contained in *OAR: 11 May 1667-21 July 1669* (c. 17), folios i recto and vii verso. However, folios i-xi of this manuscript are mis-bound and actually belong to *ODR: 7 October 1665–7 March 1668* (c. 5).

[6] *ODR: 7 October 1665–7 March 1668* (c. 5), folio 265 verso = CSC #447.

[7] *OAR: 11 May 1667-21 July 1669* (c. 17), folio vii verso = CSC #449.

the records for these particular court sessions also list Richard Tidmarsh, Lawrence King, John Toms senior, James Jennings, and Thomas Mason, all of whom were fellow Baptist conventiclers in the city.[1]

3. The Petty Sessions Court Records

On 21 May 1668 Austen was indicted to appear before the Petty Sessions court, although the exact nature of his offence is not clear (records for the previous court session in April are incomplete). In any event, Austen submitted himself to the court, which discharged him after payment of court fees.[2] Interestingly, one of the judges presiding over the Petty Sessions was John Fell, the Vice-Chancellor of the University and one of the students who was dismissed from his college place at Christ Church by Austen and the Parliamentary Visitors twenty years before in May of 1648 (more on this below). On 7 October 1669 Austen was again indicted, along with seven others, to appear before the Petty Sessions court in the Town Hall in Oxford. The charge was 'for goeing unto meetings', and 'being p^{re}sent at A unlawfull meeteing or conventicle under p^{re}tence of excerciseing religion'. In all eight men who were indicted, and they all offered financial sureties for one another before the court.[3] One interesting feature about this particular episode is that one of Austen's fellow sectaryes was the glover John Sheene, who I noted above was the master glover under whom Lawrence King served his apprenticeship (see page 108 above). The case of Austen and the others was brought before the following Easter Quarter Sessions court on 7 April 1670, whereupon the eight men withdrew their pleas of not guilty, threw themselves upon the mercy of the court, and paid fines.[4]

There are two important dimensions to Ralph Austen's life which help shed light on his involvement with the dissenting conventicle in Oxford. The first of these concerns his service within as an official with a Parliamentary commission, and the second concerns his role as an ordinary citizen in Oxford seeking to integrate his passion for gardening with his religious commitments and beliefs.

---

[1] *ODR: 7 October 1665–7 March 1668* (c. 5), folios 259 verso (John Toms senior and James Jennings); folio 263 recto (Lawrence King); folio 265 recto (John Toms senior, James Jennings and Lawrence King); folio 271 verso (John Toms senior and James Jennings); folio 272 recto (Lawrence King); folio 278 verso (John Toms senior, James Jennings and Lawrence King); folio 280 verso (Richard Tidmarsh). Folio 284 verso (pertaining to court sessions held on 7 March 1688) also is relevant (John Toms senior, James Jennings, Lawrence King and Thomas Mason).

[2] *Oxford Petty Sessions Roll – 1656-1678* (O.5.11), folio 104 recto = CSC #454.

[3] *Oxford Petty Sessions Roll – 1656-1678* (O.5.11), folio 112 recto.

[4] *Oxford Petty Sessions Roll – 1656-1678* (O.5.11), folio 115 recto = CSC #483.

B. Registrar of the Visitors of Parliament to Oxford

Anthony Wood's *Fasti Oxonienses* has a full and engaging note about Ralph
Austen and his activities, commencing with his application to have access to
the University Library while serving as Deputy Registrar to the Parliamentary
Visitors in 1652. I shall discuss various aspects of Wood's comments below,
but for now give the record in its entirety:

> In the latter end of *July* this year, *Ralph Austen* Deputy Regi-
> trary to the Visitor, for *Will[iam] Woodhouse*, and Registry afterwards
> in his own right, was entred a Student into the publick Library, to
> the end that he might find materials for the composition of a book
> which he was then meditating. The book afterward he finish'd
> and entit[led] it *A treatise of Fruit-trees, shewing the manner of graft-
> ing, planting, pruning, and ordering of them in all respects, according
> to new and easie rules of experience*, &c. Oxon. 1657, sec[ond] edit[ion] qu[arto].
> Ded[icated] to *Sam[uel] Hartlib* Esq[uire]; This book was much commended for a
> good and rational piece by the honourable Mr. *Rob[ert] Boyle*, who, if I
> mistake not, did make use of it in a book or books which he after-
> wards published: And it is very probable that the said book might
> have been printed more than twice had not he, the author, added
> to, and bound with it, another treatise as big as the former entit[led]
> *The spiritual use of an Orchard, or garden of Fruit-trees*, &c. Which
> being all divinity and nothing therein of the practice part of Gar-
> dening, many therefore did refuse to buy it. He hath also written
> *A dialogue, or familiar discourse and conference between the Husband-
> man and Fruit-Trees, in his nurseries, orchards and gardens: wherein
> are discovered many useful and profitable observations and experiments
> in nature in the ordering of Fruit-Trees for temporal profit*, &c. prin-
> ted 1676, 79 in oct[avo] much of the former book, is, I presume, in-
> volv'd in this. This Mr. *Austen*, who was either a Presbyterian or
> an Independent I know not whether, was a very useful man in his
> generation, and spent all his time in *Oxon* to his death, in planting
> gardens there and near it, in grafting, in oculating, raising Fruit-
> trees, &c. He was born in *Staffordshire*, and dying in his house
> in the Parish of S[aint] *Peter in the Baylie* in *Oxon*, was buried in the
> Church belonging thereunto, in the Isle joyning on the S[outh] side of
> the Chancel, on the 26. of *Octob[er]* 1676, after he had been a prac-
> tiser in gardening 50 years.[1]

It is difficult to determine precisely when it was that Austen set up his tree-
planting business in Oxford; his own claims get more and more exaggerated as
the years go by. Samuel Hartlib has a note from 1652 which states 'Austen had
made some years agoe a Nursery of 15. thousand plants for Fruit-trees, which
have been much destroyed by the souldjery'.[2] This suggests that his tree-

---

[1] *Athenae Oxonienses, Volume 2* (1692): 780 = Bliss (1820): 2.174 = CSC #654.
[2] *Hartlib 28/2/37A.*

planting nursery may have had its origins in Oxford during the Civil War period and that the troops of Charles I inflicted damage upon it.

Wood's comment mentions only in passing Austen's role as an official of the Parliamentary Visitors, summarizing within the opening sentence what was a very influential position of power and responsibility held for several years. It seems reasonable to assume that Austen was active within the Parliamentary cause throughout the period of the Civil War, for he was appointed as the Deputy Registrar for the Parliamentary Visitors soon after their arrival in Oxford in 1648, and it hardly seems likely that they would appoint someone to this position whose abilities and loyalties were not well-known to them.[1] Like many others, Austen had high hopes for the political changes that the new Parliament might bring about within the nation. In a letter to Samuel Hartlib dated 18 March 1653 he wrote, 'Wee heare there is like to be a new Representative ere long, which (as is expected) will goe through with affaires for the good of Church & State, with life & zeale: Wee trust the time is neere when God will visite his people with greater light, & glory, & happinesse then former ages have seene.'[2]

The aims and intentions of the Parliamentary Visitors, particularly those associated with the Barebones Parliament of 1653,[3] have undergone something of a reassessment in recent years. In the past the Parliamentary Visitors to Oxford have often been seen as driven by an anti-intellectual zeal which sought only to destroy, rather than reform, the University. However, this rather negative interpretation of their intentions is now generally recognized as one-sided and inaccurate.[4] The Parliamentary Visitors are best viewed as attempting to carry out what they saw as the necessary task of the reformation of the University of Oxford, and Ralph Austen served as one of the chief administrative agents of this work.

1. The Register of the Visitors

The official *Register of the Visitors* is contained within the Bodleian Library in Oxford; it is a 568-page manuscript designated *Ms e Musaeo 77*. It covers the work of the three Boards of Visitors during the period 30 September 1647

---

[1] There is record of another Ralph Austen who matriculated at Magdalen College in 1617 and went on to serve as a proctor in the University in 1630. The *DNB* article by Henderson (1908): 732, incorrectly equates the two men, as does Burrows (1881): viii. The revised *DNB* article by Turner (2004) corrects this error.

[2] *Hartlib 41/1/19A* = CSC #131. A similar remark is found in a letter dated 25 April 1653: 'many of the people of god are carried on with a beleife & perswaded that peaceable, & more happy times are approching: notwithstanding any troubles at present' (*Hartlib 41/1/24A-25B* = CSC #134).

[3] For more on the Barebones Parliament, see Firth (1893): 526-534 ; Watts (1978): 142-151; Woolrych (1965): 492-513; (1982).

[4] Hill (1972); Aylmer (1973): 333. Aylmer notes Kearney (1970): 119-120, as a proponent of the earlier negative viewpoint.

through 8 April 1658 and is the most important single document for our reconstruction of this tumultuous period of the University's history. The manuscript contains ten specific mentions of Ralph Austen within its pages: one document Austen signed as Deputy Registrar; two documents which give details of his appointment as Registrar by the first and second Boards of Visitors; four documents in which Austen copied orders received from Parliament and verified their authenticity; one document in which he signed receipt of testimony in the case of a Fellow of Merton College; one document in which he gave evidence in the trial of a man accused of royalist sympathies; and one document in which he acknowledged receipt of a letter from the Lord Protector Oliver Cromwell.

It seems likely that the *Register* was in the possession of Ralph Austen when the work of the Parliamentary Visitors was completed in April of 1658; the inside flyleaf of the manuscript volume bears his name and title, *'Ralph Austen Reg[iste]r.'* It is uncertain how this manuscript came to be placed in the Bodleian Library, but it is possible that it was donated by the executors of Ralph Austen's estate after he died in 1676.[1] As best as can be determined, Austen served as Deputy Registrar to Mr Newhouse from Merton College, who had been appointed Registrar in 1647. Austen's first order as Deputy Registrar was issued on 12 May 1648, when Newhouse was away in London at the time. Austen stepped in to issue an order concerning the collection of rents from tenants in Magdalen College.[2] Soon thereafter Austen was made *Registrarius Commissionariorum* in his own right, with offices in Christ Church.[3] An entry

---

[1] So Burrows (1881): viii suggests. He goes on to comment: 'It is needless to inquire why this valuable document was not formally received amongst the University archives, instead of being placed in the Bodleian Library. The very proposal would certainly at the time have been considered a deadly insult, its acceptance a foul desecration: the book would have been burnt. Ralph Austen, or his representatives, knew what they were about. Entombed in the venerable library it would at least be safe. If not worthy to be reckoned part of the archives of the University, to which indeed it had no absolute claim, it might yet reappear as general history. The Visitation, too detestable in the reign of Charles the Second to be mentioned without a curse, might perhaps in some future age receive at least fair play.' Austen's will specifically mentions his library, with his books being valued at the not insignificant sum of £4.10.0, but no specific mention is made of the *Register of the Visitors* itself. Moreover, there is some evidence to suggest that the manuscript was deposited in the Bodleian Library *prior* to Austen's death in 1676. This comes in the form of a short notation on the manuscript of the *Register of the Visitors* made by Anthony Wood, who offers a description of the manuscript: 'It begins 30 Sept. 1647 and ends 8 April 1658; written by William Newhouse and Ralf Austen ... registers successively to the said Visitors. It contains not only the acts of the Visitors appointed 1647, but of those (though slenderly) anno 1651 and anno 1654. It is kept in Dr. Say's hands.' (*MS Wood E 4*, folio 218 recto). This suggests that the *Register* was deposited in the Bodleian Library by 1674. See Clark (1891): 1.142, for details.

[2] *Ms e Musaeo 77, (Register of the Visitors)*, page 82 = CSC #59.

[3] *Ms e Musaeo 77, (Register of the Visitors)*, page 334 = CSC #88. A letter to Hartlib dated 14 June 1653 has Austen make passing reference to 'my offise at Christ

in the *Register* dated 14 January 1651 gives details of the circumstances of Austen's appointment; the relevant order of his appointment was signed by five of the Visitors, including Lieutenant Colonel Kelsey. The entry also explained how he was paid for his work as Register to the Visitors, with every college bursar being told to 'allow 2*s* 6*d* to the Register for everie Order that is brought to the Colledges'. A similar letter of appointment is contained in another entry dated 20 June 1653, with Austen's position as the official Register re-affirmed by the new set of Visitors to the University.[1]

What is particularly interesting about this entry is the list of seven people who confirm the re-appointment. They were all men of power and influence during the period of the Commonwealth and the Cromwellian Protectorate and several were later reckoned by Austen as personal friends and colleagues.[2] Confirmation of this comes in the form of a letter that Austen wrote to Samuel Hartlib on 20 August 1655. Within the letter Austen lists ten people in Oxford whom he wishes to nominate as Commissioners for any proposed land-grant that he might receive. Both John Owen and Thankfull Owen are included among his proposed referees.[3] Meanwhile, several other letters indicate that Austen had been in regular contact with Thomas Goodwin, initially to serve as a delivery agent for materials sent to him by Samuel Hartlib. There are references to Austen visiting the house of Goodwin at Magdalen College five

---

Church' (*Hartlib 41/1/34A* = CSC #140). Unfortunately, there are few records of Christ Church from the Commonwealth period, and no mention of Austen's office have survived to help us determine where it was located.

[1] *Ms e Musaeo 77, (Register of the Visitors)*, page 393 = CSC #141.

[2] The seven named people were all important figures within the various constituent colleges of the University of Oxford: John Owen was Dean of Christ Church and Vice-Chancellor from September 1652 to October 1657; Edmund Staunton was President of Corpus Christi College; Thomas Goodwin was President of Magdalen College; Jonathan Goddard was Warden of Merton College; John Conant was Rector of Exeter College and Vice-Chancellor from October 1657 to August 1660; Thankfull Owen was President of St John's College; and Francis Howell was a Fellow of Exeter College, becoming the Principal of Jesus College on 1657 on Cromwell's orders. Thomas Goodwin and Thankfull Owen remained friends throughout their lives, and were even united in death; the two share a tomb vault in Bunhill Fields in London. The marble top on their tomb is broken, having been struck by lightning.

[3] The other eight referees were: John Nixon, Thomas Weekes, Henry Cornish, Tobias Garbrand, Thomas Berry, Captain John Hunt, Matthew Martin, and Elisha Coles. Apparently John Owen was a friend of several years standing. Passing mention is made to him by Austen in a letter he wrote to Benjamin Martin dated 26 February 1652 (*Hartlib 41/1/2B* = CSC #106), and in letters to Samuel Hartlib dated 10 February 1654 (*Hartlib 41/1/66A-67B* = CSC #166) and 20 February 1654 (*Hartlib 41/1/68A-69B* = CSC #167). According to Anthony Wood, Elisha Coles was the steward of Magdalen College and stepped in as Registrar to the Visitors when Austen was away (see Clark (1891): 1.142).

times in May-July 1655.[1]　Thomas Goodwin (1600-1680) is known to have been a friend of the Particular Baptist leader William Kiffen when he lived in London, and may have served as a link between the Independents and the Baptists in Oxford.[2]

Within the *Register of the Visitors* Austen verifies copies of several orders issued on behalf of Parliament and bearing the name of Francis Rous (1579-1659) on them.　Rous was a key figure of the day and was later to become the Speaker of the Parliament for the so-called Barebones Parliament of July-December 1653; he also served on Cromwell's Council of State following the establishment of the Protectorate on 16 December 1653.　More importantly for our interests here, Rous served as the Chairman for the London Parliamentary Committee for the Universities, a job which brought him in direct contact with life in the University of Oxford.[3]　In this regard Austen's name appears on four orders from Rous's Parliamentary Committee contained within the *Register*, each of them dealing with matters of finance and discipline within the colleges. The first of these is dated 22 May 1648 and concerns the collection of college fees by bursars,[4] and the second example is dated 30 May 1648 and concerns the suspending of two fellows and a servant from Magdalen College for financial misconduct.[5]　Another topic frequently addressed within the *Register* is the expulsion of staff and students for not submitting to the Parliamentary rules and requirements or refusing to accept the authority of Parliament over them.　Austen's name appears in connection with the verification of two such orders issued by Francis Rous on behalf of the Parliamentary Committee.　For example, an order dated 14 June 1648 concerns the expelling of a total of 21 staff and students from Magdalen College, St John's College, Queen's College, Corpus Christi College, All Souls College, University College, and Trinity College.[6]　The most comprehensive list of expulsions from the University is dated 15 May 1648 and takes up six full pages in the manuscript.[7]　It details the expulsion of a host of staff and students from Oxford.　Fifteen of the eighteen constituent colleges of the University (All Souls; Brasenose; Christ Church;

---

[1] On 8 May (*Hartlib 41/1/84A* = CSC #208), 5 June (*Hartlib 41/1/86A* = CSC #212), 12 June (*Hartlib 41/1/88A* = CSC #213), 19 June (*Hartlib 41/1/90A* = CSC #214), and 5 July (*Hartlib 41/1/92A* = CSC #216).

[2] Kiffen published *A Glimpse of Sions Glory* (1641) based on a sermon Goodwin preached while in exile in the Netherlands; Kiffen wrote 'The Preface to the Reader' for the book.　The book was an extremely important step in the formulation of a theology for the Independents, as well as in the development of full-blown millenarian beliefs such as were espoused by the Fifth Monarchists a few years later. Goodwin had also served as one of the 'Dissenting Brethren of the Assembly of Divines' in 1643. See Liu (1973): 1-9.

[3] Burrows (1881): lxii-lxiii, gives details. Rous died on 7 January 1659.

[4] *Ms e Musaeo 77, (Register of the Visitors)*, page 144 = CSC #62. See E 2771 for a copy of the original.

[5] *Ms e Musaeo 77, (Register of the Visitors)*, page 144 = CSC #66.

[6] *Ms e Musaeo 77, (Register of the Visitors)*, page 148 = CSC #70.

[7] *Ms e Musaeo 77, (Register of the Visitors)*, page 127 = CSC #60.

Corpus Christi; Exeter; Lincoln; Magdalen; Merton; New; Oriel; Pembroke; Queen's; St John's; Trinity; Wadham) are included in a list that stretches to 324 names (many names appear more than once).[1] Austen's name appears in the concluding paragraphs of this particular order, where once again he verifies the Parliamentary declaration issued by Francis Rous to the Visitors requiring them 'to cause this Order to be put in Execution, & to desire the souldiery in Oxford to assist them therein if there shalbe occation.'

Complaints about misconduct during the Civil War and the royal occupation of Oxford are also registered by Austen within two records which date to 6 June 1648 and 13 April 1652. The first of these is part of an extended entry within the Register which concerns John Greaves, a Fellow of Merton College, who fell foul of the Visitor's and had the testimony of Edward Copley, also a Fellow of Merton College, lodged against him.[2] The second entry is dated 13 April 1652 in the aftermath of the battle of Worcester (27 August - 3 September 1651).[3] Here Ralph Austen gives evidence in a report to the Parliamentary Visitors about the case of Mr Holloway, an Oxford royalist who supported the (losing) cause of Charles II in the battle. Austen's contribution to the judicial proceedings is to state that no official submission to the Parliamentary Visitors by Mr Holloway was on file. Interestingly, one of Austen's fellow witnesses at Holloway's trial was Thomas Williams, who was to become the Mayor of the city of Oxford for the next year of 1653-4. Williams was an active Dissenter and had been persecuted, along with several others including Roger Hatchman, in the 1640s (see page 168 above). A second fellow witness was Richard Phillips, who served as the master for the apprenticeships of both Edward Wyans senior and John Toms senior (see pages 62-3 and 143 above).

At times Austen, as Registrar, was in direct correspondence with the ruling powers of the Commonwealth. Perhaps the best example of this is dated 5 September 1653, the final occurrence of Austen's name within the manuscript, in which he acknowledges receipt of a letter from Oliver Cromwell.[4]

2. Anthony Wood's Manuscripts: MS Wood F 1 and MS Wood F 35

It seems likely that Anthony Wood knew of Austen's *Register of the Visitors*, and almost certainly consulted it in the Bodleian Library following Austen's death in 1676 (frequent references are made to specific page numbers of the *Register* within Wood's manuscripts). Occasionally there are other glimpses of Ralph Austen, the *Registrarius Commissionariorum*, within Anthony Wood's own manuscripts and diaries. For example, Wood has a handwritten copy of an order dated 22 January 1651 in which Austen issues an order concerning

---

[1] Only University, Jesus and Balliol are not listed as colleges here. The University also included seven Halls (St Mary, Hart, New Inn, Magdalen, Gloucester, St Alban and St Edmund) none of which appear in this particular list.

[2] *Ms e Musaeo 77, (Register of the Visitors)*, page 302 = CSC #68.

[3] *Ms e Musaeo 77, (Register of the Visitors)*, page 378 = CSC #112.

[4] *Ms e Musaeo 77, (Register of the Visitors)*, page 398 = CSC #148.

Edward Wood, a fellow of Merton College and the brother of Anthony. Edward Wood is here cited for various moral and political offences. As Registrar of the Commissioners, Austen orders Edward Wood's activities as a college tutor at Merton be suspended forthwith.[1]

There are several bound volumes of manuscripts in the Bodleian which contain additional documents illustrating Austen's role as the Registrar of the Parliamentary Visitors. One of the most important of these is *Wood F 35*, a volume containing 386 leaves of miscellaneous papers relating to the period of the Visitations to the University of Oxford. The manuscript is important because it includes autograph letters and papers from some of the principal figures involved, including John Fell, Dean of Christ Church and Vice-Chancellor of the University (folios 1, 123); Gilbert Sheldon, who later became the Archbishop of Canterbury (folio 152); Christopher Rogers (folio 16), and Thomas Barlow (folio 144). There are also copies of many other documents, some of which are in Anthony Wood's own hand. There are 19 pages within the volume which bear Ralph Austen's name, many of which appear to be original documents written by Austen himself.[2] Once again, some of these original documents are certifications of orders issued by Parliamentary leaders, such as Francis Rous. A good example of a document issued on 30 May 1648 by Rous, and certified by Austen, dealing with the disposition of Dr. Gilbert Sheldon. Sheldon was incarcerated in prison in Oxford, but his continuing presence in the city was viewed as so politically dangerous that it was ordered he be moved to Wallingford castle.[3] Another example is dated 18 October 1649 and deals with matters of public subscription to Parliamentary directives.[4]

Three documents from April-May 1648 bears Austen's title of Deputy Registrar to the Visitors. They all are issued following the publication of an order by the House of Commons on 21 April 1648 enabling the Visitors of Oxford 'to displace such Fellows, and other Officers and Members of Colledges, as shall contemn the Authority of Parliament'.[5] The first of these is

---

[1] The order is pasted into one of Wood's manuscripts (*MS Wood F 1*, page 1062) = CSC #89). A copy of the order is contained in the *MS Musaeo e 77*, (Register *of the Visitors*), page 345), but there it does not bear Austen's name. Clarke (1891): 1.166, suggests that this order in *MS Wood F 1* may even be the original document issued by Ralph Austen which Anthony Wood somehow came to possess, possibly because it related to his eldest brother and was passed on to him directly. This seems correct, as it matches several others in *MS Wood F 35* in terms of both handwriting and paper size and texture. See Burrows (1881): 322, for more on the incident involving Edward Wood. Edward Wood was elected Junior Proctor of the University in 1655 and died after serving a month in that office on 22 May 1655 at the age of 28.

[2] *MS Wood F 35*, folios 226, 227, 231, 232, 233, 234, 235, 236, 239, 240, 241, 244, 245, 246, 297, 349, 353, 355 and 363.

[3] *MS Wood F 35*, folio 235 recto = CSC #67.

[4] *MS Wood F 35*, folio 353 recto = CSC #83.

[5] *Die Veneris, 21 April 1648 – An Order of the Commons assembled in Parliament enabling the Visitors of Oxford to displace such Fellows, and other Officers and Members of Colledges, as shall contemn the Authority of Parliament* (1648).

dated to 27 April 1648 and directed the treasurers and bursars of several colleges to turn over documents relating to their office.[1] The second is dated 9 May 1648 and required fellows and members of Brasenose College to appear before the Visitors and answer questions put to them.[2] The third of these concerns a summons issued to the students and staff of Lincoln College on 20 May 1648.[3] Three other notes are all dated 26 May 1648, after Austen had taken over as Registrar. The first is an order requiring the professors and lecturers of the University to repair to Oxford within eight days and attend to their duties,[4] the second is an order prohibiting any member of the University from leaving Oxford without permission,[5] and the third is an order requiring all members of the University to state whether they submit to the authority of Parliament.[6] A further note dated 6 June 1648 was issued pertaining to all that laid claim 'to any University fellowship, scholarship, place of power, trust, or advantage in ye University of Oxford, or any Colledge or hall'. Such persons were required to return to Oxford within fifteen days and assume their responsibilities.[7] Four further notices from June-July of 1648 deal with matters pertaining to Exeter College. The first is dated 27 June 1648 and ordered Mr Henry Tozer to hand over all records and keys of the college within his possession,[8] the second is dated 29 June 1648 and ordered that Tozer and five others from Exeter College be expelled from the University,[9] the third is dated 5 July 1648 and ordered the replacement leaders of the college,[10] and the fourth, also dated 5 July 1648, ordered the suspension of a Mr Proctor from his fellowship, 'for his contempt of Parliam[en]t, in not appearing before the Visitors'.[11]

Another order from 18 October 1648 concerns an allegation of stealing horses which was levelled against Dr. Gilbert Sheldon, the expelled Warden of All Souls; it appears that the order was countermanded two months later after further evidence was gathered.[12]

The most detailed list of expulsions within *MS Wood F 35* which bears Ralph Austen's name occurs in two notes dated 29 June and 7 July 1648. The first of

---

[1] *MS Wood F 35*, folio 226 recto = CSC #57.

[2] *MS Wood F 35*, folio 227 recto = CSC #58. Anthony Wood adds an explanatory comment on the back of the notice: 'This pap[er] was put uppon y^e wall on y^e left/ hand going up y^e staires to y^e Chappell about/ 7 of y^e clock in y^e morning May y^e 10th 1648.'

[3] *MS Wood F 35*, folio 231 recto = CSC #61.

[4] *MS Wood F 35*, folio 232 recto = CSC #63.

[5] *MS Wood F 35*, folio 233 recto = CSC #64.

[6] *MS Wood F 35*, folio 234 recto = CSC #65.

[7] *MS Wood F 35*, folio 236 recto = CSC #69. Anthony Wood adds an explanatory comment on the folio: 'This order not ~~published~~ set up till y^e 8th of June in y^e morning.'

[8] *MS Wood F 35*, folio 239 recto = CSC #71.

[9] *MS Wood F 35*, folio 240 recto = CSC #72.

[10] *MS Wood F 35*, folio 244 recto = CSC #74.

[11] *MS Wood F 35*, folio 245 recto = CSC #75.

[12] *MS Wood F 35*, folio 297 recto = CSC #77. The order is also contained on page 218 of the *Register of the Visitors* (see Burrows (1881): 207)

these contains the names of 64 persons from sixteen colleges,[1] and the second of these contains the names of 73 persons from ten colleges within the University.[2]   One order from 8 August 1649 gives details about general regulations imposed upon all of the colleges and halls of the University, while being specifically directed to the Provost of Queen's College.[3]   Another example of a general order issued to all of the colleges and halls of the University is dated 9 November 1649.[4]   The order gives details of an engagement to be sworn: 'I doe declare & promise that I will bee true & faithful to the Commonwealth of England, as the same is now established, without a king or house of Lords'.   The final document bearing Ralph Austen's name within the manuscript is dated 25 November 1650 and concerns the appointment of George Hitchcock to a fellowship in Lincoln College, a matter apparently bitterly contested by college officials.[5]

3. Christ Church Deanery Papers

One document written to Christ Church by Austen as Registrar has survived within the Deanery papers of the college.   This is an order dated 21 January 1656 and concerns the monitoring of the religious conduct of students by college authorities.   Earlier, on 27 June 1653 the Visitors issued an order that all students be required every Sunday to report 'to some person or persons of knowne ability & piety' and give account of the sermons they had heard and the other religious activities they had been involved with on that day.   In the order from 1656 the Visitors required the 'Heads, Governors & Officers of the severall societies' to report personally to them and verify that 'the said Order hath beene constantly observed'.[6]

4. The Vice-Chancellor's Account Books

Brief glimpses of Austen's role as the Registrar to the Parliamentary Visitors can been seen within the official financial records of the University.   For example, within the Vice-Chancellor's account books there are also several receipts for payments made to Ralph Austen in this regard.   Thus, the *Liber Computus Vicecancellarii Oxon 1547-1666* records as an entry pertaining to the academic year 1652-3, when John Owen was Vice-Chancellor, noting a payment of £5 4s made to Austen as Registrar and John Langley as Mandatory and for twelve weeks and two days of service.[7]   A similar entry for the

---

[1] *MS Wood F 35*, folio 241 recto and 241 verso = CSC #73.
[2] *MS Wood F 35*, folio 246 recto = CSC #76.
[3] *MS Wood F 35*, folio 349 recto = CSC #81.
[4] *MS Wood F 35*, folio 355 recto = CSC #84.
[5] *MS Wood F 35*, folio 363 recto = CSC #87.
[6] *Christ Church Deanery Papers* (DP ii.c.1), folio 52 = CSC #232.
[7] *Liber Computus Vicecancellarii Oxon 1547-1666* (WPB/21/4), folio 147 verso. The account book also contains a supplementary note for this expenditure dated 27

academic year 1653-4 records a payment of £23 12*s* which was made to the two men.[1]

This fits perfectly well with the instructions that were issued by the Lord Protector and Parliament within the Ordnance for Appointing Visitors for the Universities. The instructions issued on 2 September 1654 state:

> And it is further Ordained by the Authority aforesaid, That the said Visitors, or any seven or more of them for each University respectively, Are hereby impowered to finde out and setle some equal and just way of Competent Allowances to their Register and Mandatory for their attendance and pains during the time of their Visitation.[2]

C. Oxford Citizen: Gardener, Horticulturalist, and Cider-Maker

For the last seventeen or so years of his life Ralph Austen lived in the parish of St Peter-in-the-Bailey with his wife Sarah.[3] The couple were childless, and apparently had little by way of immediate family within the city of Oxford. Few details of Austen's extended family are certain, although an indenture from 30 June 1675 relating to his house and property shows that he had a brother named Thomas and a nephew (the son of Thomas) named Joseph who hailed from Leeke in Staffordshire.[4] There is also mention within this indenture to a sister named Mary Lownes, a sister named Helen Brindley, and a niece named Mary Leigh, although their places of residence, presumably in Staffordshire, are not given.[5] In letters to Samuel Hartlib, Austen does mention in passing that his mother and aunt lived in Staffordshire, and that through them he was related to Henry Ireton, Oliver Cromwell's son-in-law (more on this below). The only additional detail about family matters contained in Austen's

---

January 1654: 'Agreed that the allowance made to Mr Zimran and that to Mr. Austen & Mr. Langley be reported to the Convocation for their assent.' It is probable that this is John Langley, the School-Master of St Paul's School in London, who was a member of the Assembly of Divines and preached the Fast sermon before the House of Commons on 25 December 1644 (see his *Gemitus Columbae: The Mournfull Note of the Dove* (1644) for the text). He died in September 1657 (see Edward Reynolds *A Sermon Touching the Use of Humane Learning* (1658), for the text of the sermon preached at his funeral). His will was probated on 20 September 1657 (*PCC – Will of John Langley* (PROB 11/267), folios 256 recto and verso). Austen also mentions Langley in letters dated 18 November 1652(?) = CSC #123, 6 December 1653 = CSC #159, 12 December 1653 = CSC #160, 6 February 1654 = CSC #163, and 2 October 1656 = CSC #241.

[1] *Liber Computus Vicecancellarii Oxon 1547-1666* (WPB/21/4), folio 149 recto.

[2] Firth and Rait (1911): 2.1028.

[3] See CSC #548 for the location of their property in David Loggan's *Oxonia Illustrata* (1675).

[4] It can be deduced, as Turner (1978): 39 does, that Ralph Austen was from the same village as his brother. Unfortunately, the parish records for the village of Leeke only begin in 1634, so there is no record of who Ralph Austen's parents were, or when he was baptized.

[5] *MS Ch Oxon c. 50* (#4501) = CSC #536.

letters is a passing reference to his brother-in-law named Job Hancock, probably the brother of Austen's wife Sarah (see the accompanying chart on 'The Family Tree of Ralph Austen' for details of the larger family connections, including the link to Ireton). It does not appear, however, that any of his family were residents of, or ever visited him in, the city of Oxford. Nevertheless, by all accounts Austen led a full and active life in Oxford, continuing many of the avenues of life which his position as Registrar of the Visitors had opened. For example, the surviving documents of the Oxford City Council record Austen's name as a 'suitor' (the Latin term used is 'sectator') at the so-called Husting's Court, generally held in the Guildhall.[1] Austen's name first appears in this regard in the Mayoral year of Henry Southam in 1658-59, where Austen takes over the suitor's place of one John Fletcher.[2] Following this initial appearance as a suitor in the Hustings court, Austen's name appears regularly in the court records for the next twenty years.[3] The records for the year 1676-7 contain a note of Austen's death; the word 'mort[uus]' is written as a marginal note alongside his name. Only his death in October of 1676 led to eventual removal of Austen's name from the Hustings court records, and even then it continued to appear in the annual lists for the years 1676-7 and 1677-8.[4] Austen's attendance at these court sessions appears to have been entirely regular, faithful and consistent. Indeed, it is only in the records for the years 1677-8 and 1678-9, *after his death*, that there is any hint that Austen was ever fined for missing a meeting of the Hustings court. The record for 1677-8 shows one fine of 3s 4d alongside marks denoting three attendances for the year; the fine was presumably paid on Austen's behalf out of his estate. Similarly, the record of 1678-9 lists three fines of 3s 4d, alongside a second declaration of Austen's death two years earlier (the word 'mort[uus]' is again in the margin).[5]

While living in St Peter-in-the-Bailey Austen continued his interest in gardening and horticulture and built up a moderately successful cider-making business to supplement his selling of fruit-tree saplings to interested customers. There is record of Austen living in the parish of St Thomas as late as 1652, but he appears to have moved his main residence to the parish of St Peter in the

---

[1] This identifies Austen as an Oxford freeholder who is not a citizen of the city. See Salter (1928): xiii, for details. As noted above (page 65), Edward Wyans senior was also a 'sectator' of the Hustings Court.

[2] *Civic Enrolments – 1639-1662* (L.5.3), folio 222 verso.

[3] See *Civic Enrolments – 1639-1662* (L.5.3), folio 220 verso (1659-60); folio 218 recto (1660-1); folio 214 verso (1661-2); folio 212 recto (1662-3); *Civic Enrolments – 1662-1699* (L.5.4), page 741 (1662-3); page 730 (1663-4); page 724 (1664-5); page 719 (1665-6); page 714 (1666-7); page 708 (1667-8); page 702 (1668-9); page 695 (1669-70); page 687 (1670-1); page 681 (1671-2); page 675 (1672-3); page 669 (1673-4); page 662 (1674-5); page 655 (1675-6); page 650 (1676-7).

[4] *Civic Enrolments – 1662-1699* (L.5.4), page 641 (1677-8) and page 633 (1678-9). The place where Austen's name was entered in the sequence of suitors is maintained with a blank for the nine years 1679-80 through to 1687-8 (pages 617, 611, 605, 600, 595, 588, 582, 574, 567).

[5] The standard fine for non-attendance was 3s 4d.

Bailey shortly thereafter.[1] It looks as if Austen pursued the cider-making business from his home in St Peter-in-the-Bailey, although he also maintained gardens and tenements in St Thomas. Probably the bulk of his fruit-trees were kept there in orchards near the river. City Council tax records show that Austen pays tax on both properties for the War Taxes of 1667-1668.[2] Thus, the property in St Thomas is taxed at 1*s* 1*d* for the seven consecutive quarterly periods between June 1667 and December 1668.[3] Similarly, the property in St Peter-in-the-Bailey is taxed at 2*s* 2*d* for the same period.[4] It is also worth noting that Austen served as one of the tax assessors of the parish of St Peter-in-the-Bailey during this taxation period.[5] His fellow assessor for most of these quarterly periods was Thomas Francklin, although Timothy Box joined as a third assessor for the return of 26 March 1668.[6] Interestingly, Austen was also appointed an 'Overseer of the Poor' for the parish in the spring of 1665.[7]

Despite Austen's movement to and greater involvement within the parish of St Peter-in-the-Bailey, he also maintained an interest in local affairs in the parish of St Thomas where his orchards were located. There is one interesting record which illustrates Austen's involvement in a contentious local affair, namely the repair and maintenence of the so-called Quaking Bridge near the Castle Mills. I noted Richard Tidmarsh's involvement in this matter above (see page 36 above), but in a minute of the agreement dated 15 February 1658 Austen is named as one of six inhabitants of the parish of St Thomas who represented the parish interests and signed on their behalf.[8] This brief insight into a local parish matter is also significant in that it demonstrates another point of contact between Ralph Austen and the Baptist leader Richard Tidmarsh.

---

[1] In a letter to Samuel Hartlib dated 8 April 1652, Austin mentions that his house was in St Thomas's parish (*Hartlib 41/1/4A-5B* = CSC #111).

[2] See pages 9-10 for an explanation of these taxes.

[3] See *War Taxes – 1667-1668* (P.5.8), folio 15 verso (24 June 1677); 37 verso (29 September 1667); 46 recto (21 December 1667); folio 62 verso (26 March 1668); 74 recto (26 June 1668); folio 100 recto (26 September 1668); and 115 verso (26 December 1668).

[4] See *War Taxes – 1667-1668* (P.5.8), folio 7 verso (24 June 1677); 27 verso (29 September 1667); 51 recto (21 December 1667); folio 72 verso (26 March 1668); 76 recto (26 June 1668); folio 94 verso (26 September 1668); and 112 recto (26 December 1668).

[5] See *War Taxes – 1667-1668* (P.5.8), folio 8 verso (24 June 1677); 29 recto (29 September 1667); 52 recto (21 December 1667); folio 73 verso (26 March 1668); 77 recto (26 June 1668); folio 95 verso (26 September 1668); and 113 verso (26 December 1668). Austen is also named as an assessor of taxes for the parish of St Peter-in-the-Bailey on folios 132 verso, 128 verso, 127 verso, 126 recto, and 125 verso.

[6] Timothy Box was later to serve as one of the two witnesses to Ralph Austen's will (see pages 241-3 below). Box was sworn onto the City Council on 30 September 1653 (see *City Council Proceedings – 1629-1663* (A.5.7), folio 217 recto).

[7] *Husting and Mayor's Court 1662; Licenses and Overseers* (N.4.3), folio 31 recto = CSC #404.

[8] *Civil War Charities and General Minutes – 1645-1695* (E.4.6), folio 23 verso.

According to a Oxford City Council record dated 20 September 1655, Austen's renewed the lease on the property in the parish of St Peter-in-the-Bailey and began to make plans to build a new house there.[1] Viewers were appointed to survey Austen's building proposals along Shoe Lane at a further City Council meeting held on 16 December 1656.[2] Work on the house progressed over the course of the next few years and it became the subject of a subsequent City Council record dated 15 July 1659. Apparently the house exceeded the allowed dimensions and encroached into the street some 21 inches. Austen petitioned the City Council that this be allowed, which was agreed on the condition that he pay a yearly fee for it.[3]

There are several tax records relating to Austen's residence in this property, now designated No. 30 Queen Street.[4] It is known that Austen made a contribution of 10s in the Free and Voluntary Present granted by Parliament on 8 July 1661, probably while living at the house.[5] There are also records of Austen paying 4s for the Michaelmas Hearth Tax of 1662,[6] as well as 4s for the Michaelmas and Lady Day collections of the Hearth Tax of 1665.[7] All three of these hearth tax payments are connected with the house in the parish of St Peter-in-the-Bailey, and they give us some indication of the size of the house (the tax was levied at 2 shillings per year per each hearth or chimney within a property). Austen and his wife paid 2s in the the Poll Tax of of 1667 while living at this property in St Peter-in-the-Bailey.[8] Austen appears to have leased the land upon whch his house was built from All Souls college. Unfortunately, the initial lease document agreed between Austen and All Souls does not appear to have survived, although Austen's name is found on rental rolls and associated documents from the college.[9] Thus, he is listed in the All Souls rental rolls for the years 1661-1677, where he pays £1 00s 00d per annum on the property.[10] Austen's widow Sarah stayed in the property following her

---

[1] City Council Proceedings – 1629-1663 (A.5.7), folio 228 recto.

[2] City Council Proceedings – 1629-1663 (A.5.7), folio 237 recto.

[3] City Council Proceedings – 1629-1663 (A.5.7), folio 260 verso = CSC #286; also see Council Minutes – 1657-1668 (A.4.4), folio 38 recto. There is a record from 20 August 1669 which shows that this arrangement was re-negotiated for an annual fee of 3s (Languables – 1668-1737 (P.5.3), page 20 = CSC #474).

[4] See Salter (1969): 2.138-139, for details of the leases relating to the property.

[5] Free and Voluntary Present of 8 July 1661 (E 179/255/5/4), membrane 3. Austen made his contribution on 8 November 1661.

[6] Hearth Tax of August-November 1662 (E 179/255/4), Part 2, page 69 reverse.

[7] Hearth Tax of Michaelmas 1665 (E 179/164/513), membrane 28 verso, and Hearth Tax of 24 April 1666 (E 179/164/514), membrane 23 verso.

[8] Poll Tax of 1667 (P.5.7), folio 43 verso. The entry also lists a Michael Roberts as paying 1s on wages of 40s; this was probably a servant of the Austen household.

[9] Austen's occupation of the Shoe Lane property is mentioned in a record of the adjoining property dated to 10 March 1676 (Oxford City Ledgers – 1675-1696 (D.5.7), folios 9 verso–10 verso.

[10] MSS DD All Souls College – Rent Rolls 1657-1665 (c. 338); MSS DD All Souls College – Rent Rolls 1666-1672: (c. 339); MSS DD All Souls College – Rent Rolls 1673-

husband's death in October of 1676, although the rental records continued to be in his name for the year 1677. However, commencing in 1678 the rental lease on the property was taken over by another man named Christopher Mathews, who continued to pay the rate of £1 per annum on it.[1] In any event, it appears that Austen began to put into motion changes to the legal ownership of the house on the property as early as the summer of 1675, probably in recognition of his age and failing health. On 30 June 1675 he signed an indenture on the freehold which handed it over to two gentlemen from his native Staffordshire, namely Thomas Bagnall and William Thornburie, who, apparently, acted as agents for Austen's brother Thomas and his nephew Joseph (the son of Thomas).[2] At the same time the indenture guaranteed that he and Sarah could continue to reside in their house until the end of their natural lives. Ralph Austen died the next year, and the right of his widow Sarah to continue to reside in the house in the parish of St Peter-in-the-Bailey is explicitly stated in a subsequent indenture signed by the nephew Joseph Austen dated 27 June 1678.[3] The indenture grants Sarah a ninety-nine year lease at the token yearly rent of 'one Pepper Corne, if the same be lawfully demanded'.[4] Interestingly, one of the two witnesses to this indenture was Austen's friend Richard Tidmarsh, who also served as a witness to his last will and testament (see pages 241-3 below).[5] These two documents not only illustrate the close connection that existed between Ralph Austen and Richard Tidmarsh, but also serve as part

---

1679 (c. 340). Also see the documents contained in *MSS DD All Souls College – Rentals 21-40* (b. 20) for the years 1661 (*Rental 21*); 1662 (*Rental 22*); 1665 (*Rental 23*); 1666 (*Rental 24*); 1667 (*Rental 25*); 1669 (*Rental 26*); 1670 (*Rental 27*); 1672 (*Rental 28*); 1673 (*Rental 29*); 1674 (*Rental 30*); 1675 (*Rental 31*); 1676 (*Rental 32*). The rent rolls record three payments made by a Mr Austen to All Souls College, all under the heading of 'Recepta Alias'. Thus, the rent roll for 1671 has the entry 'Received of Mr Astyn for ye Coll[ege] expenses in a Letter of Attorney &c. ag^t Mr Prettima[n] - £10 02s 02d'; the rent roll for 1672 has an entry: 'Received of Mr Austin his Fine being VI ^{li} - £4 0s 0d'; and the rent roll for 1673 has an entry: 'Of Mr Austin for a Writt & Warrant ag[ains]^t Madge of Crendon - £00 09s 11d'.

[1] *MSS DD All Souls College – Rent Rolls 1673-1679* (c. 340). Also see the documents contained in *MSS DD All Souls College – Rentals 21-40* (b. 20) for the years 1678 (*Rental 33*); 1679 (*Rental 34*); 1680 (*Rental 35*); 1681 (*Rental 36*); 1683 (*Rental 37*); 1684 (*Rental 38*); 1685 (*Rental 39*); 1686 (*Rental 40*).

[2] *MS Ch Oxon c. 50* (#4501) = CSC #536.

[3] *MS Ch Oxon c. 50* (#4502) = CSC #579.

[4] Sarah Austen is also mentioned in an indenture dated 10 December 1690 in which the property is sold on to a John Greeneway (*MS Ch Oxon c. 50* (#4503a) = CSC #645). There was a query raised about the legal ownership of the property in 1691 (*MS Ch Oxon c. 50* (#4503b) = CSC #648).

[5] The other signatory was Arthur Madle, who was one of those indicted with Austen on 22 June 1669 for attending an unlawful conventicle (*Oxford Petty Sessions Roll – 1656-1678* (O.5.11), folio 112 recto = CSC #472). Madle was also one of the Dissenters singled out for advancement by James II in his new charter for Oxford issued in 1688; Madle was given one of the twelve Bailiffs' places (see Appendix H, lines 89 and 182).

of the flimsy 'paper trail' of surviving documents which actually bear Tidmarsh's signature.

One final point concerning Austen's property in St Peter-in-the-Bailey is worth noting. The Oxford antiquarian Anthony Wood mentions visiting here in his diary entry for 2 June 1669, saying that he spent 10*d* at 'Austens ye gardner for Cider'. The cider must have been to his liking for he returns there on 15 June with two friends and spends 6*d*, and goes a third time on 23 June with a different friend and again spends 6*d*.[1] Clearly the making of cider was something very close to Ralph Austen's heart; he built much of his life around it, and it is a matter that he turned to frequently in his books and surviving correspondence.[2] However, it is as an author on books on horticulture, in which his religious convictions and his expertise as a gardener converged, that Austen made his most enduring contribution.

1. Austen's Books on Gardening: A Treatise of Fruit-trees (1653) and its Successors

Ralph Austen authored several books in which he set out his imaginary vision of applying horticultural principles to society so as to create the kingdom of God on earth. In this regard Austen builds upon the Biblical image of the Garden of Eden, and sees human beings as following the god-given task of tilling the soil and raising crops as Adam did. In fact, Austen goes so far as to cite Genesis 2:15 and suggest that Adam was assigned the care of fruit-trees in the Garden of Eden, 'the meetest place upon all the Earth for Adam to dwell in'.[3] I shall summarize Austen's publications before moving on to discuss the wider circle of friends that he made through his wide-ranging horticultural interests.

Austen first contacted the influential educationalist and philanthropist Samuel Hartlib in London in February of 1652 through Benjamin Martin, a mutual friend. He asked Martin to deliver to Hartlib a manuscript copy of his proposed book, *A Treatise of Fruit-trees*, so that Hartlib might comment upon it and

---

[1] *MS Wood Diaries 13*, folio 18 recto.

[2] Austen discusses cider in his letter to Hartlib dated 10 October 1656 (*Hartlib 41/1/119A-120B* = CSC #243); in his letter to John Beale dated 30 July 1658 (*Hartlib 45/2/3A-4B* = CSC #265). Webster (1975): 480, describes Austen and his friend and colleague John Beale, a fellow cider enthusiast, as 'the two prima donnas of arboriculture'.

[3] Austen (1653): 12. Also see his letter to Samuel Hartlib dated 11 May 1659 (*Hartlib 41/1/129A-130B* = CSC #285). Webster (1975): 465-6, discusses this, pointing out that Milton portrayed Adam as a gardener in *Paradise Lost* (1668): iv: 436-9. There is considerable debate about the influence of Milton's vision upon the horticulturalists such as Austen, Hartlib, Evelyn, and Beale. See Hunter (1989): 84-87; Poole (2004): 77-88.

suggest any improvements.[1] This Hartlib gladly did; the two men shared a vision of the importance of fruit trees as a scientific and economic facet of the nation's life. Hartlib had published his *Designe for Plentie by a Universall Planting of Fruit Trees* the previous year in 1652, and effectively used its publication as a springboard for promoting Austen's forthcoming work on the subject. In his introductory note 'To the Reader' Hartlib mentions his 'experienced friend' Austen, and the book which 'he was putting to the Presse'.[2]

As mentioned above, Austen showed his appreciation for Hartlib's support by dedicating the proposed book to him.[3] Most of the early letters exchanged between Austen and Hartlib concerned details surrounding the publication of Austen's book.[4] He consulted Hartlib about who might publish the book, the number of copies to be produced and at what commission, and even bemoaned the fact that a Mr. Goddard, the person hired by the publisher Thomas Robinson to produce the engraving used as a frontis-piece, was a deceitful and unreliable drunkard.[5]

Thus, Austen's first publication on gardening was a book entitled *A Treatise of Fruit-trees Shewing the manner of Grafting, Setting, Pruning and Ordering of them ... With the Alimentall and Physical Use of Fruits* (1653).[6] This was published together with another study of Austen's entitled *The Spiritual Use of an Orchard, or Garden of Fruit Trees.*[7] The two works were complementary in

---

[1] *Hartlib 41/1/2A-3B* = CSC #106. It is possible that Martin also delivered a letter written by Austen to Hartlib; there is an undated letter which appears to be a letter of introduction (*Hartlib 41/1/144A-145B* = CSC #107).

[2] *Designe for Plentie by a Universall Planting of Fruit Trees* (1652) = CSC #128. Austen's negotiations with the publisher Thomas Robinson are also mentioned in several letters to Samuel Hartlib, including those dated 12 July 1652 (*Hartlib 41/1/8A-9B* = CSC #117), and 1 November 1652 (*Hartlib 41/1/12A-13B* = CSC #120).

[3] The dedication is discussed in letters from Austen to Hartlib dated 7 and 17 January 1653 (*Hartlib 41/1/14A-15B* = CSC #129; *Hartlib 41/1/16A-17B* = CSC #130).

[4] See the letters dated 8 April 1652 (*Hartlib 41/1/4A-5B* = CSC #111); 23 April 1652 (*Hartlib 41/1/6A-7B* = CSC #113); 12 July 1652 (*Hartlib 41/1/8A-9B* = CSC #117); 26 July 1652 (*Hartlib 41/1/10A-11B* = CSC #119); 1 November 1652 (*Hartlib 41/1/12A-13B* = CSC #120); 18 November 1652? (*Hartlib 41/1/142A-143B* = CSC #123); 7 January 1653 (*Hartlib 41/1/14A-15B* = CSC #128); 17 January 1653 (*Hartlib 41/1/16A-17B* = CSC #129); 18 March 1653 (*Hartlib 41/1/18A-19B* = CSC #132); 1 April 1653 (*Hartlib 41/1/20A-21B* = CSC #132); 12 April 1653 (*Hartlib 41/1/22A-23B* = CSC #134); 25 April 1653 (*Hartlib 41/1/24A-25B* = CSC #135); 6 May 1653 (*Hartlib 41/1/26A-27B* = CSC #136); and 6 June 1653 (*Hartlib 41/1/32A-33B* = CSC #139).

[5] Goddard (1631-1663) was an engraver based in Gutter Lane in London. He is specifically mentioned in Austin's letters dated 6 May 1653 (*Hartlib 41/126A-27B* = CSC #135) and 16 May 1653 (*Hartlib 41/1/28A-29B* = CSC #137). See Worms (2004) for more on him.

[6] It is worth noting that the *Oxford English Dictionary* (1994, second edition) contains 112 quotations from Austen's *A Treatise of Fruit-Trees* (1653). This stands as one small measure of the importance of the work.

[7] Bennett and Mandelbrote (1998): 49-51, offer a brief discussion.

subject matter and were popular enough to see subsequent editions, both expanded and reissued together, and in the case of *The Spiritual Use of an Orchard*, as an independent work reissued nearly 200 years later. The first edition of *A Treatise of Fruit-Trees* contains a number of introductory pages, while the body of the book runs to 97 pages. Included within the introductory pages is a 2-page note 'To the Reverend Dr. Langley, Master of Pembrook Coll[edge] in Oxon'. He offered an autobiographical note in the midst of this dedication to Langley, saying that he wrote it:

> As a testimony of my thankfulnessse for all your labours in the Lord, and care for mee, from time to time, especially in my great afflictions, which befell me about six years agoe in this place, when I was even strip naked both of inward, and outward comforts, walking in darknesse, seeing neither Sunne, not Starres, for many Months together, out of which the Lord (I will speake it to his praise) hath delivered me with great advantages.

The first edition also contained a 5-page 'Preface to the Reader' and a list of twenty 'Propositions Shadowed out unto us by Observations in Nature, and Cleared by Scripture and Experience'; a second 5-page dedicatory epistle 'To the Worshipfull Samuel Hartlib, Esquire, My much Honoured Friend'; a second 4-page epistle 'To the Reader'; a 9-page description of 'The Analysis' in which a chart of divine and human arguments and their strengths and shortcomings are detailed; and a 4-page index described as 'A Table shewing the Principall things Contained in the Naturall part of the Ensuing Worke'. The second part of the book, *The Spiritual Use of a Garden of Fruit-Trees* contains the twenty propositions in 41 pages. The initial print run for the book was 500 copies and it appears to have retailed at 18d per copy.[1]

Hartlib and Austen shared a number of other specialized horticultural interests, including experimentation with the cultivation of mulberry trees for use in raising silk-worms. In fact Hartlib published one of the earliest records of this in English in 1655 under the title *The Reformed Virginian Silk-Worm, or, a Rare and New Discovery of a speedy way, and easie means, found out by a young Lady in England she having made full proof thereof in May, Anno 1652*. Within the book Hartlib cited Austen at one point, mentioning the experiments that his friend in Oxford had been conducting on silk worms and gave the text of a letter written to him by Austen on 18 February 1654.[2]

---

[1] In a letter to Hartlib dated 23 April 1652 Austen tried to persuade him to help secure funding for the publication of the book. He intended to distribute copies to all the members of Parliament (*Hartlib 41/1/6A-7B* = CSC #113). According to a letter dated 30 May 1653, after the book appeared in 1653, Austen sent copies to Hartlib so that they may be distributed as he saw fit (*Hartlib 41/1/30A-31B* = CSC #138). There is some suggestion that Austen also attempted to have the book advertized in the newspaper *Mercurius Politicus* (see *Hartlib 41/1/36A-37B* = CSC #142).

[2] See *Hartlib 41/1/80A-81B* = CSC #203 and CSC 203a. There are slight discrepancies between the actual letter and Hartlib's relation of it in his book.

A second edition of *A Treatise of Fruit-Trees* appeared in 1657.[1] Although this is a slightly smaller book in size, it is in fact an expanded edition and contains many new experiments and observations, which means that the work swells from 97 to 140 pages.[2] This second edition was published with an expanded version of *The Spiritual Use of an Orchard* which also considerably expanded the propositions drawn from nature from 20 to 100. Interestingly, the second edition also includes a extra 2-page supporting declaration dated to 24 December 1656 which reads 'To my dear Friend & brother in the Lord' and is signed 'Your very loving Friend J.F., A Minister in the Gospell'. The volume also contains a 3-page declaration addressed 'To the Reader' which is written by Stephen Ford, who describes himself as 'Pastor in Chippin-Norton'. Ford writes:

> Reject not the work because it is not done by a publique minister of the gospel, for many private experienced Christians have been (in this way) very profitable to the church of God; these are the last *times*, wherein God fulfils his great gospel promise, in powring out his Spirit upon all flesh; and those whom God intends for any speciall service, he prepares them for it by some special preparations (p xxii).

Ford's comments are important for they not only describe Austen as a Christian layman but also establish further links between him and the wider group of Dissenters in Oxford and Oxfordshire. Stephen Ford is known to have been an active Independent (Congregational) minister in Chipping Norton and records of his making an application for registering the village Town Hall as a place of worship in April of 1672 are extant, as are records of his involvement in a church in Miles Lane (between Eastcheap and Thames Street, parallel to St Martin's Lane) in London during the same period.[3] In 1657, while pastor of the congregation in Chipping Norton, he published a church manual of rules for use within the congregation which gives great insight into how it functioned under his leadership. Within this pamphlet, entitled *An Epistle to the Church of Christ in Chippin-Norton* (1657), Ford mentions in passing that he tarried in the University of Oxford until his call to the church became clear to him. It seems that he was subsequently ejected from Chipping Norton and made his way to London where he took up his preaching ministry again.[4] Precisely how Stephen Ford came to know Ralph Austen is unknown, although it probably was when he was in Oxford and may have been through the agency of Thankfull Owen, one of the Parliamentary Visitors to Oxford with whom

---

[1] Austen sent a hand-written copy of the title-page of the book to Hartlib on 3 October 1656 (*Hartlib 41/1/116A-118B* = CSC #242).

[2] Austen discusses some of the additions in a letter dated 2 October 1656 (*Hartlib 41/1/114A-115B* = CSC #241).

[3] SP 44/38A, page 6. See Turner (1911): 1.211; 2.828, 982, 984.

[4] See Turner (1914): 3.387-390; Matthews (1934): 206; Clapinson (1980): xxiii.

Austen would have been in regular contact.[1]   According to the so-called Episcopal Returns of 1669, Ford was at one time a servant to Thankfull Owen, who himself was an Independent minister.[2] Ford is also mentioned in one of Austen's letters to Samuel Hartlib, hand-delivering a letter of introduction to Hartlib at his home in Charing Cross in London.[3]

In 1658 Austen published *Observations upon some part of Sr Francis Bacons Naturall History as it concernes, Fruit Trees, Fruits, and Flowers: especially the Fifth, Sixth, and Seaventh Centuries, Improving the Experiments mentioned to the best Advantage.*   The book contains a two-page dedication 'To the honourable Robert Boyle, Esq. Sonne to the Lord Boyle Earl of Corke'.   It also has two two-epistles directed 'To the Reader', the first of which is from Austen himself, and the second is by R Sharrock. The body of the book runs to 48 pages, including a table summarizing the various observations that Austen makes.   It appears that Austen had some contact with his fellow Oxonian Robert Boyle in Oxford. For example, there is mention of Boyle in a letter to Hartlib dated 3 May 1658; here Austen notes in passing that Boyle had conveyed to news that some of his (Austen's) letters written to Hartlib had gone missing in the post. A fuller period of contact with Boyle takes place later in that year, apparently after Boyle had travelled to London in connection with business with the establishment of the Royal Society. Thus, in a letter to Hartlib dated 7 October 1658, written in the aftermath of Oliver Cromwell's death, Austen informed Hartlib of his desire to get Boyle to make contact with Lord Fleetwood.[4] In another letter dated 8 December 1658 it is made clear that Boyle did as Austen requested, although Lord Fleetwood does not appear to have actively pursued the matter in Parliament, despite his expressed intentions to do so.[5] The situation dragged on for over a year, and in a letter to Hartlib dated 16 December 1659, Austen noted that he had met with Boyle in Oxford and discussed the matter further.[6] The final reference to Boyle which appears in Austen's letters occurs in a letter dated 11 March 1661.[7] Here Austen

---

[1] Owen was appointed to the body of Visitors to the University of Oxford by Oliver Cromwell on 2 September 1654.

[2] Turner (1911): 1.143.

[3] The letter is dated 26 October 1654 (*Hartlib 41/1/74A-75B* = CSC #194). Ford signed his last will and testament on 9 April 1693 (*PCC – Will of Stephen Ford* (PROB 11/431), folios 185 verso – 186 verso. The will was probated on 14 May 1696.

[4] *Hartlib 45/2/5A* = CSC #268.

[5] *Hartlib 45/2/7A-8B* = CSC #271.

[6] *Hartlib 41/1/131A* = CSC #304. According to Austen, Boyle even offered to deliver some copies of his second edition of his *Treatise of Fruit-Trees* to Hartlib when he next travelled to London. The intention was that the books be distributed to members of what came to be the Royal Society, which Austen describes in later letters (dated 5 June 1660, 22 July 1660, and 11 March 1661) as a 'secret society, rich & wealthy' (*Hartlib 41/1/133A* = CSC #310); 'a 'secret society of worthy, & welthy persons, who as they are able to doe good, are (it seems) willing' (*Hartlib 41/1/135A* = CSC #314); and 'a secret society that intend some good to the Nation' (*Hartlib 41/1/137A* = CSC #321).

[7] *Hartlib 41/1/137A-138A* = CSC #321.

described Boyle as 'my very good freind' and 'my noble friend', and again mentioned Boyle's kind offer to speak on his behalf and help distribute his books among members of the Royal Society. Despite Boyle's support, enthusiasm for Austen's proposals for planting of fruit-trees was not forthcoming within the Royal Society, and Austen admits despair over the situation:

> I have beene at so much expences in sending, & receiving Letters for above this 7 yeares, & in giving, & distributing of Books both in the Citty & Country, about this business that I am aweary of it, & discouraged; & indeed disabled, reaping no fruit after so much seede sown.

Boyle did send a copy of Austen's proposals to the secretary of the Royal Society in London; this was read to the Society on 14 December 1664 and then referred to the Committee for Agriculture for further consideration.[1]

A third expanded edition of *A Treatise of Fruit-Trees* appeared in 1665. It was entitled *A Treatise of Fruit-Trees, Shewing the manner of Planting, Grafting, Pruning, and ordering of them in all respects according to Rules of Experience Gathered in the space of Thirty-seven Years, whereunto is Annexed Observations Upon Sr. Fran. Bacons Natural History as it concerns Fruit-trees, Fruits, and Flowers, Also, Directions for Planting of Wood for Building, Fuel, and other uses, whereby the Value of Lands may be much improved in a short time, with small Cost and little Labour.* The third edition bears the Imprimatur of the Vice-Chancellor of the University of Oxford, Robert Say, dated 9 June 1665.[2] The dedications to Henry Langley and Samuel Hartlib are here replaced with a 10-page dedication 'To the Honourable Robert Boyle, Esq; The Worthy Patron and Example of all Vertue'; the 'Epistle to the Reader' is also substantially reworked.[3] There is also an eight page 'Epistle to the Reader', a thirteen-page Analysis chart, and a thirteen-page table showing the principal things covered in the work. The body of the book is 260 pages and covers numerous experiments and observations on trees and plants performed by Austen and offered by him to the interested reader. This book has a slightly more scientific feel about it, and it is significant that the third edition drops the companion treatise on *The Spiritual Use of an Orchard* and replaces it with *The Observations Upon some part of Sr. Francis Bacon's Natural History.*[4] This work consists of a further 82 pages introduced by a supporting four-page declaration 'To the Reader' by R Sharrock of New College, and a three-page

---

[1] The original proposal is within the Royal Society archives (*CL.P. X (iii) 7*). Also see Birch (1756): 1.504.

[2] Austen says in a letter to Samuel Hartlib dated 8 July 1653 that the Vice-Chancellor of the University, John Owen, had authorized publication of the first edition of the book, 'giving me great encouragements in it' (*Hartlib 41/1/38A* = CSC #143).

[3] Hartlib had died in 1662 and Langley was a political outcast following the Restoration of the monarchy in 1660.

[4] Webster (1975): 470-1, discusses the attempt by Austen and others to place husbandry on a sound scientific and philosophical basis.

'Epistle to the Reader' by Austen himself. It is possible that Robert Boyle was influential in the repackaging of the third edition into a more scientific volume. Indeed, it has even been suggested that Boyle made it a condition of his patronage to Austen that the religious annotations be removed.[1] There is an interesting letter written from Boyle to his friend Henry Oldenburg on 17 September 1665 which points in this direction. Within the letter Boyle says that he 'easily perswaded him [Austen] ... to leave out many things w[hi]ch for ought I know good on themselves were of a Theological not a rurall nature'.[2]

Given such a remark, it is understandable why it has often been thought that Austen acquiesced to Boyle's opinion in the matter. However, there is a letter (hitherto unpublished) that Austen wrote to Boyle which suggests otherwise. The letter was written from Oxford nine months earlier, on 14 January 1665, and was sent to Boyle at the house of his sister Lady Ranelagh in Pall Mall in London.[3] What is significant about the letter is that Austen states that he has himself come to the opinion that the third edition of his *A Treatise of Fruit-Trees* should not include the 'spiritual part' dealing with the similitudes between natural and spiritual fruit-trees. He notes that the book thus 'will be more profitable to my selfe, and more acceptable to others'.

In any event. Austen certainly did not abandon the spiritual dimension of his publications on gardening. In fact Austen's last major publication in the field of gardening was published in 1676 (the year of his death) and was entitled *A Dialogue, or Familiar Discourse, and conference between the Husbandman, and Fruit-trees in his Nurseries, Orchards, and Gardens,.* The body of the book is divided into 25 sections covering 87 pages. The text is filled with scriptural quotations and examples from history, as well as offering Latin citations of historians of antiquity and early church fathers, notably St Augustine.

One striking note within the work is the way in which Austen formulated what traditionally has been described as 'general versus particular revelation' from God; he comes firmly down on the side of general revelation as being operative in the world. Thus, the opening words of the 'Epistle to the Reader' state:

> God hath given to man two greate Books to read and study; viz: His workes, and his word; whereby we may come to know God, and learn our duty to him. The Creatures of God do all of them speake out the Praises of God; and are not only Examples to us of Obedience, but also do call aloude unto Man, and instruct, and teach him, what he ought to do.

---

[1] Jacob (1977): 156.

[2] *Royal Society MS B 1*, no. 90 = Hall and Hall (1966): 509 = CSC #421. A handwritten copy of this letter is to be found in the *Royal Society Letter-Book – Supplement, Volume 2, B-C (1663-1693)*, pages 31-33.

[3] *Royal Society Library (BL.1.16)* = CSC #401.

His religious zeal comes through in the concluding paragraph of the 'Epistle to the Reader':

> Every *created being*, instructs us concerning our Creature, *of his wisdom, and goodnesse*, and of our *duty, and thankfulnesse* we owe unto him; so that as many Creatures as are in the world, so many *Teachers* there are in the world: Therefore none shall be excused at the last day, for their *ignorance of God*; seeing we have not only *the word of God*, but *all the Creatures of God* to instruct us; concerning God and our duty to him. So then; with these breife instructions concerning *discourse with Fruit-trees*, I commit the Ensuing *Dialogue* to thy use, for thy profit. Who am thy Friend to serve thee in love.
>
> RA: AUSTEN

One of the most interesting examples of the dialogue between the Husbandman and the fruit trees occurs on pages 60-1 in Section 16 of the book and concerns the reason why there has been much planting of fruit trees in recent days. Here, once again, Austen's passion for cider came to the fore:

> FRUIT TREES: The Reason is evident; Because men of late time have inquired, and made search into the Nature of our Fruits: And have found out the particular *Profitts, and advantages that come by us*, in many respects; not only as to the *sale of the Fruits* to those that buy them; but also as to *pleasant, and wholesome Foode*, all the yeare long in the family; And particularly for *Cider*, which is of late time concluded generally, to be the *most wholesome liquor in the world*; being found so to be *by* Experience: Not only preventing diseases, which other drinks do breed in the Body; but also cures many already contracted: And therefore no marvell Fruit-trees are in esteeme now, more than formerly.

> Cider; the most wholesome drink: especially of the best fruits.

> HUSB: It is undoubtedly true; That *Cider* in generall, is the *most wholesome drink*, in reference both to *health, and Long life*; though made of ordinary, and common Fruits. But there are certaine peculiar Fruits (now of late time,) found out, and known, which makes *Cider* far beyond, (and better, then) the *common Cider*: As the *Redstrake, the double Red-redstrake; Gennet Moyles*; and some other kinds that might be named: And so long as *health and long life* is in esteeme with men, so long will *Cider* be in esteeme also; as the cheif meanes to attaine *these Ends*.

2. *Austen's Book on Quakers and Quakerism:* The Strong Man Armed not Cast out (1676)

The fourth, and last, book which Ralph Austen wrote was one entitled *The Strong Man Armed not Cast out, But Removed to a stronger Hold: Viz. From Profaneness to Hypocrisie* (1676). This is a moderately sized work; the body of the text is 118 pages, which is introduced by a two page 'Epistle to the Reader' and a four-page description of the contents. Effectively it is a reply to the pamphlet by the Quaker James Jackson of Nottingham which was entitled

The Strong Man armed Cast Out, and his goods spoiled: or, The poor man sitting at Jesus' feet clothed, and in his right mind (1674), and is in effect is a critique of what Austen perceived to be the excesses of Quakerism.   In particular, he criticized Jackson for claiming that the 'Strong Man' of the title (i.e. Satan), had been cast out of his life, and that the life he now lead was Christ-centred. Austen rebuked him sharply for this, describing him and those who followed this line of thought as 'the Seducers among the Quakers' (page 32). Much effort was spent on challenging the Quaker belief that Christ was present in all men and women. The work is filled with scriptural allusions and citations, from both the Old and New Testaments. Occasionally there are indications of Austen's own life and commitments within the discussion.

For example, on pages 6-7 we get an indication of Austen's own denominational allegiances, as he picked up Jackson's claims about his spiritual journey away from the Dissenters into Quakerism. Austen wrote:

> First, That Spirit in thee Declares to all People, That thou art now *Converted, and turned from Darkness to* Light, and from the power of Satan unto God; that thou art changed from a wicked Profane course of Life, unto a Holy Life, walking with a Holy People, and that thou hast left off to be *a Parish Priest*; yea, and after that hast left off from being *a Teacher among the Independents*, and hast disowned, and forsaken the Congregations and Assemblies of the Independents; and art now come and joined with the People called *Quakers*. And thou tellest us, That these are the *onely Holy People of God upon Earth*; and that all other *Churches, Assemblies, and Congregations* (Naming the *Presbyterians, Independents, Baptists*, and others) are out of the way; and that though they differ in *Forms or Perswasions*, yet they agree in the *same Faith, Foundation, and Root*.
>
> *Answ.* For Answer hereunto briefly; I shall not speak to Reproach thee, or rail upon thee, or any of thy way, as thou hast done against many of the Precious Saints in the Churches of Christ, saying of the *Independents* (whose Assemblies thou has forsaken) That there was sufficient ground for thee to separate from the Tents of the ungodly Men, their Teachers, who are no better than *Filthy Dreamers, Blind Guids, and Belly-gods*, which belch out nothing but *Lies, Slanders, Blasphemies, and evil speeches* against Christ, his Ways, Truths, and People; and this (thou sayest) thou seest and declarest against them in the Light. I say, I will not bring against thee Railing Accusations, as thou dost against others; but *the Lord Rebuke thee*, and the *Lying Spirit* in thee, and Convince *thy Spirit* of the Truth.

What is clear from this is that Austen was well acquainted with a range of Dissenting traditions; he noted that Presbyterians, Independents and Baptists all helped to form what he described as the 'precious saints of the Church of Christ'. It is also significant that Austen did not include mention of the Church of England here, or at any point within the book; he has clearly nailed his colours to the mast of Nonconformity and feels himself to be part of the Dissenting congregations.

It is partly because this book is so overtly religious in tone that it has been attributed to another Ralph Austen, a different person than the author of the various publications on gardening discussed above. This is the opinion of T.F. Henderson, whose entry in the *Dictionary of National Biography*, one of the very few places where Austen's life is discussed, boldly asserts:

> A work by a Ralph Austen appeared in London in 1676 entitled 'The Strong Man Armed:)' but the fact that it was published at London, not Oxford, and that it is entirely controversial, and contains no reference to gardening, militates against the supposition that its author was identical with the subject of the present notice.[1]

This is a bizarre judgment, to say the least. In point of fact, there *are* references to gardening contained within the book, and they match what Austen wrote elsewhere in terms of both style and substance. Even his long-standing interest in his beloved *'Fruit-trees'* appears here, as can be seen in a passage where Austen drew lessons from the world of gardening in a manner that is wholly consistent with what he wrote about earlier in his *Spiritual Use of an Orchard* (1653) . Within this passage he was attacking the Quaker suggestion that Christ can be found in all people, whether they are upright or wicked:

> Christ is not in wicked Men and Women. This Truth may be illustrated, and shadowed out unto us by a plain *Similitude* between *Natural and Mystical Fruit-trees*: *Similitudes* of things with which we daily Converse, obvious to our *Natural Senses*, are very helpful unto us *to shadow out, and Illustrate Spiritual things* which are *Dark, Abstruce, and Difficult*, as they lye in intricate Spiritual notions; which without some plain Similitude would be discerned but dimly, as in this particular. As Windows are to a House, so are Similitudes to a Discourse: They both let in Light. We know the *Root, Body, Boughs, Branches, and Twiggs of a Fruit-tree are all joined together, and do make but one Body or Substance*: And that the *Root* gives no *Sap, Life or Nourishment* but only to those parts of the Tree that are *United to it*; all those *Boughs and Branches* are Nourished from the *Root*; they Receive *Sap, Spirit and Life, the Innate, Intrisical Form and Virtue of the Tree is in all the parts*: But the *Virtue and Influence of the Root* is not *in any other Branches or Boughs*, which do not grow upon the *Root*, though they are never so near this Tree, though they are contiguous, and mixed among, or hand among the Living Branches, yet they have *no Life in them, no Sap, no Virtue from the Root*, because they are no parts of it.
>   Even so it is here, in this *Mystical Fruit-tree, Christ and his* Members; his People who are *Members of his Body*; they Receive *Life, Nourishment and Virtue from him*; he is *in them* by his Effectual Operations (pages 53-54).

Or again, where the words of Jesus recorded in Matthew 7:17-18 and Luke 6:43-44 were creatively reworked into a stinging rebuke of Jackson:

> As for Thee, *James Jackson (Author of the strong Man Armed cast out)* it is plain and manifest to a Spiritual Eye, that thou art yet *in the Gall of bitterness,*

---

[1] Henderson (1908): 733.

and in the Bond of Iniquity; for certainly, *The Tree is known by its fruits; a good Tree cannot bring forth bad Fruits*: By the Fruits of Trees we know of what Kind or Nature the Tree is that brings them forth; dost thou doubt of this? Thou needest not, if thou dost but remember who it was that said it; and all Agree, and know it is a Truth. So then, Thy *Fruits* Discover thee to be *a very Corrupt Tree, bringing forth sower, bitter, poysonous, deadly Fruits; Thy Grapes are Grapes of Gall, the Clusters are bitter* (pages 65-66).

As to Henderson's comment about the book being published in London, rather than in Oxford (where Austen's other works appeared), one has to wonder if this argument has much weight. One answer as to why Austen's *The Strong Man Armed not Cast out* was published in London is contained within the text itself. This appears on page 101 where Austen mentioned a book by the Particular Baptist minister Thomas Hicks entitled *Three Dialogues between a Christian and a Quaker* (1674).[1] Indeed, the last page of Austen's book is an advertisement for the 'Three Dialogues, Sold by Peter Parker at the *Leg and Star* in Cornhill, against the Royal Exchange'. In short, the anti-Quaker nature of Austen's book, and the fact that the London-based publisher had an interest in such anti-Quaker literature, is probably the reason why it was published in London rather than Oxford. In any event, the exchange between Jackson and Austen continued yet one further stage. In 1676 Jackson published a small 10-page pamphlet in reply to Austen's *The Strong Man armed not Cast out* in which he responded to the stern challenges put forward by this book. Jackson's pamphlet was published in 1676, probably in London, and picked up on Austen's reputation as a gardener and horticulturalist. The title is a clever allusion to Jesus' parable about the wicked husbandmen (Matthew 21:33-46/Mark 12:1-12/Luke 20:9-19); the pamphlet was entitled *The Malice of the Rebellious Husband-men against The True Heir, Plainly discovered in this Brief Reply to the Blasphemies, Lies, and Slanders, of Ra. Austen*. Jackson's reply is filled with accusation and bitterness at what he felt was the un-Christian way in which he has been treated by Austen in the earlier book from 1674. As Jackson puts it, his opponent Austen 'dreads not to shoot so many envenomed Arrows' (page 1). Much of Jackson's pamphlet was given over to discussion of Biblical texts, many of them revolving around the Quaker conviction of 'the inner light'. Jackson cited numerous examples of Austen's exegetical inconsistencies as far as Biblical passages were concerned, and turned the tables on him by using the parable of the wicked husbandmen against the gardener who had built his reputation as an expert gardener and husbandman: 'Woe unto thee Austen, for thou art one with those husbandmen, who despise the Heir, and therefore conspire against him to keep him out of his Inheritance' (page 3). Perhaps the most interesting additional insight that the pamphlet gives about Austen himself comes in two passing comments about his hypocrisy. Jackson noted that Austen had several dealings with Quakers and

---

[1] Horle (1975-6): 344-62, discusses the often-hostile relationship between Baptists and Quakers. Also see Underwood (1977).

appeared to be open and accepting of them, only to turn around later and write such negative things about them. The two passages give some details of Austen's travels and associations with Quakers in London:

> But pray thee *Ra. Austen*, how ill do's this become thee thus to scandalize and reproach the leading Quakers, as thou calls them, I say, how ill do's this become thee to call those spreaders of false Doctrines, Errors, Heresies &c. with thy Pen, whom thou hast justified and commended with thy Tongue, and at the same *juncto*, thou went to most meetings of Friends in *London*, and heard several Friends declare; nay, after thou hadst heard *Alexander Parker*, thou went to him, and discours'd with him, and came and told *B. Clarke*, Stationer in *George Yard Lumbard-street*, how sound thou found this *Parker*, and how well thou liked such and such, and could willingly joyn with them. Ah thou self-condemning *Pharisee*, what kind of dissimulation is this; who speaks Lies in Hypocrisie like unto thee? [5]

> But this is nothing with thee who heard Friends declare, bought Friends Books, and justified their Doctrines and Principles to *Ben. Clarke*, and yet hast forged those Lies in thy Book against us and our principles. [9]

The circumstances and date of Austen's visit to London are unknown. There is no record of Austen's reply to Jackson's pamphlet, nor any proof that he was even aware of its publication. No doubt Austen's death in October of 1676 precluded any further exchange between the two men.

Further occasional glimpses of the religious convictions of Austen can also be gleaned from his letters to Samuel Hartlib. A good example of this is contained within a letter dated 1 April 1653 in which he brought up the subject of the annual May Day celebration in Oxford, describing it as 'a sinfull superstitious Custome' which promoted 'many vaine, & sinfull things ... to the dishonour of God'.[1] May Day celebrations, including the erection of 'phallic' May-poles, were frequently condemned by the pious Puritans of the time, particularly among the leading Presbyterians and Independents.[2] Such festivals frequently were at times thinly veiled religious and political declarations against what was perceived to be an excessively repressive policy concerning holy days and Sabbath observances. They also came to be visible symbols of a those who desired the restoration of the monarchy.[3] In fact, Anthony Wood records that in Oxford in 1660 a May pole was erected outside the Mitre Hotel in the High Street as part of the May Day celebrations, and when John Conant, the Vice-

---

[1] *Hartlib* 41/1/20A = CSC #133. Within the letter Austen alludes to the traditon that the May-pole ceremony commemorated the death of a Roman harlot named Flora. Hill (1964): 186, noted that in 1661 Adam Martindale made a similar remark when a May-pole was erected in his parish in Cheshire: 'many learned men were of opinion that a maypole was a relic of the shameful worship of the strumpet Flora in Rome.'

[2] See *True and New Newes with an example from Warwick Castle, and also other parts, especially upon the anti-round-heads* (1642) for a typical example of a pious reaction against May-poles.

[3] See Keeble (2002): 40-46.

Chancellor, and his beadles attempted to cut it down they were prevented from doing so by a mob.[1] It was set up, Wood notes, 'to vex the Presbyterians and the Independents'. Later that month after the return of Charles II, on Holy Thursday (31 May), Wood records that 'the people of Oxon were soe violent for Maypoles in opposition to the Puritans that there was numbered 12 Maypoles besides 3 or 4 morrises, etc.'[2] The association between the Church of England and the monarchy in this matter is clear. As Christopher Hill puts it, 'After 1660 the phallic maypole became almost a symbol of the restored church and (more appropriately) of Charles II.'[3]

3. Austen the Horticultural Visionary: The Petitions to Cromwell and Parliament

Shortly after his book *A Treatise of Fruit-trees* (1653). was published, Austen shared with Samuel Hartlib his plan to have copies of his book distributed to members of Parliament.[4] The hope was that this might further induce them to adopt his bold scheme for planting fruit trees as a nation-wide strategy for economic and spiritual regeneration of the country.[5] Thus, in a letter dated 25 July 1653 he wrote to Hartlib that he has received news of the setting up of a Parliamentary Commission for Trade whose task it was to 'receive proposals for the profit & welfare of the Common wealth, also to advance & encourage Learning, honest designs &c'.[6] Austen put pressure on his friend to have the Parliamentary Commission consider his proposals for the planting of fruit-trees, as set out in both his book and Hartlib's own *A Designe for Plentie* (1652). In a letter dated 30 August 1653 he even suggested to Hartlib that the Parliamentary Committee might like to consider granting him a piece of land so that he might carry on his tree-planting business, given that he is restricted in terms of space and finance in Oxford.[7] Austen pursued this idea with Hartlib again in a letter dated 12 December 1653. Here he had a particular piece of land in mind, namely the area around Shotover hill on the outskirts of Oxford:

---

[1] Clark (1891): 1.314. Clark gives *MS Tanner 102, Part 2* as his source for this, but I have been unable to locate it within the manuscript.

[2] *MS Wood Diaries 3*, folio 16 verso. See Davies (1955): 270, and Underdown (1985): 274-275, for more on this.

[3] Hill (1969): 196.

[4] In a letter dated 2 July 1656 Austen admitted that the scheme 'has beene to so little purpose' and stated, 'I judg it no way necessary, or convenient, to give Coppies to any Parlim[en]t men, but only to two or 3 of those that wee know are spirited for the worke (*Hartlib 41/1/112A-113B* = CSC #239).

[5] Like many prominent figures who supported the ideals of the Commonwealth, Austen was a supporter of the policy of land enclosure as a means to introducing farming and agricultural innovations. He mentions land enclosure in a number of letters (see *Hartlib 41/1/56A-57B* = CSC #159).

[6] *Hartlib 41/1/40A-41B* = CSC #144.

[7] *Hartlib 41/1/44A-45B* = CSC #146.

There is a Forrest (Shattofer) neere Oxon; a mile off: I humbly desire your advice whether it be worth the while for me to Peticion the Committye, (who sell these Lands) for a few Acres 10 or a dozen &c: to bestow them on me in recompence of my many yeares labours for the Common wealth: seeing also the same would have an influence (through my improvement) further upon a great part of the Nation: At least that they would please to allot me (by their surveyours), some part vpon easier Rates then some others: & if not in Shattofor Forest, then somewhere els: I am very much Straitened in my Nurssery here at present.[1]

Later, after the government was re-organized and Cromwell was appointed Lord Protector, Austen continued to press for being given a piece of land around Shotover Hill, even suggesting that the matter be put before Cromwell himself.[2] Eventually Austen had to abandon this idea, for the number of people who needed to be compensated in the Shotover area in order make it happen proved too great. A letter to Hartlib dated 30 August 1655 Austen explained:

Upon serious consideration, & good advice, I find it best, & necessary, to desist in the presentation of my Petition to his Highnesse for a parcel of Land in the Forrest of Shat-over: in regard I find it so difficult, (if not altogether impossible) to satisfy a multitude: There being divers more Townes, & Villages who have Common there, then I heard, or thought of before: & divers of the persons will not be satisfied by any meanes.[3]

Austen also prepared a proposal for the consideration of the Parliamentary Trade Commission, taking heart in the fact that on 3 September 1653 Parliament had turned down a scheme put forward for expanding tobacco plantations in Gloucestershire;[4] it would be much better, he suggested in a letter to Hartlib dated 31 August 1653, to make a law governing the planting of fruit-trees.[5] A copy of the proposal which he prepared for the Barebones Parliament survives amongst Hartlib's papers.[6] The proposal itself is undated but most likely is to be associated with Austen's letter to Hartlib dated 26 September 1653.[7] Similarly, Austen enclosed within a letter sent to Hartlib on 6 February

---

[1] *Hartlib 41/1/58B* = CSC #160.

[2] *Hartlib 41/1/60A-61B* = CSC #162.

[3] *Hartlib 41/1/96A-97B* = CSC #223. In a letter to Hartlib dated 3 May 1659 Austen mentioned a proposal made by a Dr Tonge to provide him with some barren wasteland on which to plant fruit-trees (see *Hartlib 41/1/125A-126B* = CSC #284).

[4] Parliament issued an Act prohibiting the planting of tobacco in England on 1 April 1652.

[5] *Hartlib 41/1/46A-47B* = CSC #147. Austen also mentioned the Committee for Trade in a letter dated 5 September 1653 (*Hartlib 41/1/48A-49B* = CSC #149).

[6] *Hartlib 41/1/146A-47B* = CSC #151.

[7] *Hartlib 41/1/52A-53B* = CSC #150. Also see the letter dated 21 October 1653 in which Austen expressed the prayer that 'The Lord give them wisdome & discerning Judgments to receive and those with things of reall & spetiall advantage to his people' (*Hartlib 41/1/54A-55B* = CSC #155).

1654[1] a copy of a proposal addressed Oliver Cromwell, who had assumed the title of Lord Protector in December of 1653.[2] The proposal is extremely interesting for its breadth of vision and demonstrates something of Austen's passion for his subject. The copy which survives among Hartlib's papers was corrected and annotated by Hartlib, but Austen's original version can be readily reconstructed.[3]

Two points are worth highlighting about Austen's proposal to Cromwell concerning the planting of fruit trees. First, Austen his political savvy here by identifying, as the first advantage to be gained by the adoption of his proposal, a matter which clearly was of great interest to Cromwell himself. By suggesting that 'Hereby would bee a supply of all sort of Timber, fit for building ships, which hath beene of late yeares exceedingly wasted & destroyed', he was saying something that Cromwell wished to hear. It is well-known that in 1649 Cromwell and the Rump Parliament set out on an ambitious ship-building programme, despite the fact that the country had a severe timber shortage.[4] The programme was so successful that the Commonwealth had 180 ships by 1653, more than any of her rivals in Europe. This helped to transform England's role in foreign politics and meant that she became a major player on the international scene.[5] Austen was pushing all the right buttons here, linking together his ambitious plans for tree-planting and the building up of the Commonwealth's navy, a matter which would have fallen on receptive ears in the immediate aftermath of the naval war with the Dutch in 1652-4. In fact, he continued in just this regard in several subsequent letters to Hartlib. Thus, in a letter to Hartlib dated 1 December 1655 he made the point about planting trees in order to ensure that materials would be available for the building of ships, noting that future generations will need wood 'for ships for safty of the Nation: wise men ought to forsee evils afar off, & labour to prevent them: Our forefathers Planted and wee in this generation destroy, without making any considerable supplys for time to come'.[6]

Second, it is possible that there is also a more private concern being expressed within the petition when Austen identified the advantages for tanners as his second major point. He states that 'there would bee a supply not only of Timber for building, but also of Barke for Tanners'. At first glance, it is a bit odd to have something so seemingly inconsequential and insignificant feature in this way. However, when it is remembered that Richard Tidmarsh, Austen's

---

[1] *Hartlib 41/1/62A-63B* = CSC #163.

[2] For a recent assessment of Cromwell's Protectorate, see Coward (2002).

[3] *Hartlib 66/22A-B* = CSC #164.

[4] Wilson (1965): 80-1, discusses this.

[5] See Capp (1989): 4-6; Coward (2002): 123, on this point.

[6] *Hartlib 41/102A-103B* = CSC #230. A letter to Hartlib dated 6 March 1656 similarly lamented: 'What shall our successours doe for Timber to build ships for defence of the Nation, if there be noe planting, wee all know & acknowledg how it hath beene destroyed of late, but what preparation is there for a future supply:' (*Hartlib 41/1/106A* = CSC #234).

friend and the leader of the Baptist conventicle in Oxford, was a prominent tanner within the city, then it is easier to understand why tanners figured so high on Austen's agenda.

Austen also approached several figures of power and prominence close to Cromwell in these matters. Perhaps the best example of this is Major-General Charles Fleetwood, one of the foremost military leaders of the Protectorate and Cromwell's chosen instrument in Ireland, where he was appointed Lord Deputy in early 1654. Austen and Fleetwood shared a perspective on religious matters; Fleetwood was an intensely religious man and was renowned as a supporter of the rights of Independents and Baptists within the army. As Ronald Hutton remarks:

> Charles Fleetwood was a man of profound personal piety. He may, in fact, have the distinction of having mentioned the name of God more frequently in his correspondence than any other English soldier.[1]

However, the real reason for Austen's approach seems more to lie in the fact that Fleetwood was Cromwell's son-in-law, he having married Cromwell's daughter Bridget on 8 June 1652.[2] More significantly, Bridget Fleetwood was also the widow of Henry Ireton (1611-1651) who had previously served as Cromwell's Deputy in Ireland.[3] The reason for Austen's boldness in this regard becomes clear in his correspondence with Samuel Hartlib.

In approaching Bridget Fleetwood, Austen sought to exploit the fact that he was distantly related to her first husband Henry Ireton, commonly regarded as Cromwell's most accomplished, and trusted, military officer. Ireton had commanded the left wing of Cromwell's army at the battle of Naseby on 14 June 1645, and married Cromwell's daughter Bridget the following year on 15 June 1646, just ten days before the surrender of Oxford to the Parliamentary forces.[4] He served as a moderating influence in Parliament's difficult dealings with the Levellers, drafting the important document known as *The Heads of the Proposals* (1947).[5] He was also responsible for *A Remonstrance of His Excellency Thomas Lord Fairfax, Lord Generall of the Parliaments Forces, and of the Generall Councell of Officers Held at St Albans the 16 of November, 1648,* an influential document which provided an ideological justification not

---

[1] Hutton (1985): 17.

[2] Bridget was the third of Cromwell's nine children and was born in Huntingdon in 1624.

[3] The marriage took place on 15 June 1646 (*Parish Register of Holton – 1633-1794* (Par 135/1/R1/1), folio 13 verso = CSC #46a). See Fox (2004): 23-29, for more on their marriage. Hutchinson (2000): 227, 251, also mentions Ireton's marriage to Bridget, as well as her subsequent marriage to Fleetwood.

[4] Wedgwood (1939): 62; Ramsey (1949): 43; Kaplan (1983): 131.

[5] This was published with *A Declaration from His Excellencie Sr Thomas Fairfax and His Councell of War concerning their proceeding in the Proposalls prepared and agreed on by the Councell of the Armie* (1947). It is discussed in Woodhouse (1938): 422-426.

only for the army's moves against Parliament, but also for the trial and execution of the king based on his crimes against the nation.[1] Other indications of Ireton's importance in the military and political arenas include the fact that he was also one of the fifty-nine signatories of Charles I's death-warrant on 27 January 1648, and the fact that he served as Cromwell's military commander against rebellious royalists and Catholics in Ireland during most of 1650-1. Unfortunately, Ireton caught fever during the siege of Limerick and died on 28 November 1651 at the age of 40; he was given a state funeral and interred at Westminster Abbey on 6 February 1652, with John Owen, the Dean of Christ Church preaching the funeral sermon.[2] His death meant that he was thus not available to serve as a direct channel of influence for Austen, who nevertheless invokes the memory of Cromwell's right-hand man in several letters written to Samuel Hartlib during 1654-6. For example, in a letter dated 2 June 1654 Austen explains the family connection: 'my Mother and Aunt yet living [told me] that their father, & his father were Brothers, so he & they first Cosins'.[3] On the basis of this Austen then wrote: 'I was further credibly informed that his hignesse hath expressed his redinesse and resolution to shew favour to any of the Iretons, or any related to them for his late sonne in Law's sake'.[4] Similarly, Austen wrote to Hartlib on 29 April 1655 and again invoked his family connection to Ireton as a potential means of leverage in getting Cromwell's attention on the matter of being granted a small plot of land: 'And Sir if my neere Relation to the late Col[onel] Ireton may be any inducement (& surely humble Christians will take notice of such bonds), then (if you please) it may be mentioned.'[5]

The family connection was brought up again in a letter to Hartlib dated 5 July 1655. Here Austen described himself as 'a poore kinsman of his (Cromwell's) sonnes', while specifically asking for a small piece of land (20 or 30 acres):

> I doubt not Sir but if you please to observe an opportunity to move his Highnesse in my behalfe, for my help, & encouragement, it would easily be granted, if not also as it concernes the Publique: It were noe more for his Highnesse to assigne me 20: or 30 acres of ground, somewhere, for an Orchard, and Nursery, then it is for me to give a Penny to one that has neede, which I hope I shall neuer be unwilling to: The truth is I am much straitned for ground

---

[1] See Woodhouse (1938): 456-465; Underdown (1971): 107-123.

[2] Ramsey (1949): 200.

[3] *Hartlib 41/1/70A-71B* = CSC #175. Austen's mother and aunt lived in Staffordshire; several of Austen's letters record his visits to the county (notably *Hartlib 45/2/1A-2B* = CSC #259).

[4] *Hartlib 41/1/70A-71B* = CSC #175. Also see the letter dated 25 June 1654 in which Austen described a letter written to Lady Fleetwood (*Hartlib 41/1/72A-73B* = CSC #181).

[5] *Hartlib 41/1/82A* = CSC #207.

where I am, & want abilities to enlarg; Now if his Highnesse please to graunt this small request to a poor kinsman of his sonnes;[1]

A letter dated 10 December 1655 continued in the same vein, with Austen pleading with Hartlib to bring up the family relationship to Colonel Ireton when he next met with the Lord Protector Cromwell[2] In several surviving letters Austen asked his friend Samuel Hartlib to bring up the matter of his family connection with Lord Fleetwood,[3] and in a bold letter even wrote to Lord Fleetwood himself. Unfortunately the petition to Fleetwood himself is undated, but it probably was written sometime in 1658 when Fleetwood was still serving as Cromwell's Deputy in Ireland. What is interesting about this letter (a copy of which survives in Hartlib's correspondence) is the way in which Austen appealed to the biblical story of Jonathan and David (2 Samuel 9:1-13) as a suitable basis upon which Cromwell might act on his (Austen's) behalf. Austen wrote:

> And unto these considerations I desire your Lordship would please to ioyne that of King David whose loue was so great towards Ionathan that he enquired if there were any of the house of Saul that he might shew kindnesse to him for Jonathans sake: I know the very remembrance of that worthy person deceased, the late Lord Ireton, is so pretious, that his neere Relations shall fare the better, & haue kindnesse shewed vnto them for his sake[4]

It is unknown if Ralph Austen ever encountered his relative Henry Ireton face-to-face, although it is possible that the two did meet in Oxford when they were young men (the two were roughly the same age). Ireton entered Trinity College, Oxford in 1626 at the age of fifteen;[5] Austen claimed in the Preface to his 1676 book that he had been working as a gardener in Oxford for some fifty years, which put him in the city at roughly the same time. However, any proposed meeting of the two cousins must remain speculative.

Austen mentioned Ireton's widow Bridget, now Lady Fleetwood, a number of times in his letters to Samuel Hartlib. However, these appeals to Lord and Lady Fleetwood were, in the end, unproductive and he never did result in any material advantage for Austen. Cromwell died in September of 1658, and Lady Fleetwood died in 1662, and with their passing the basis for Austen's attempt to exploit his family connection to Henry Ireton was lost.

---

[1] *Hartlib 41/1/92B* = CSC #216. Passing mention was also made by Austen to his 'relation to the late Lord Ireton' in a letter dated 1 December 1655 (*Hartlib 41/1/102A* = CSC #230).

[2] *Hartlib 41/1/104A* = CSC #231.

[3] Including the letter dated 28 November 1655 (*Hartlib 41/1/100A-101B* = CSC #229).

[4] *Hartlib 45/2/9A* = CSC #273.

[5] Ramsey (1949): 3.

4. Austen the Oxford Citizen: Horticulturalist and Cider-Maker

Occasionally we do find hints that Austen's work did enjoy some success among his fellow Oxonians, particularly as a cider-maker and a horticulturalist specializing in fruit trees. One of the best examples of this in Oxford itself is Brome Whorwood, an influential civic leader in the Oxford City Council, who was mentioned in the letter from John Beale to Henry Oldenburg dated 6 August 1671 (see below). Austen had helped Whorwood to plant an orchard, probably at his manor in Halton, and at some stage had approached him about his proposal to Parliament, as can be seen in a letter to Hartlib dated 3 May 1661.[1]

One of the last glimpses that we find of Ralph Austen within the primary sources occurs in the *Petty Sessions Records* for the city of Oxford. The records for 30 March 1676 state that he was one of two people nominated to be 'Overseer of the Poor' within the parish of St Peter-in-the-Bailey,[2] a position that Austen had held some years before in 1665. This is an interesting appointment in that it does not require an active involvement with the local parish church. However, 'Overseers of the Poor' had to be property owners and maintain a substantial household within the parish they served,[3] and Austen's house and orchard in Queen Street certainly would have qualified him for this post.

5. Austen as Horticultural Visionary: The Petition to the Royal Society in London

After the Restoration the normal channels through which Austen sought to gain a hearing for his horticultural vision were very much restricted. He had been too long associated with the Parliamentary cause for much interest to be generated among the royalists who now held the levers of power. Still, Austen was not lacking in resourcefulness and he turned his attention to another possible ally – the developing scientific community which came to be known as the Royal Society. A good example of Austen's contacts in London in this regard is Henry Oldenburg, who went on to become the Secretary of the Royal Society and was an influential member in the scientific and philosophical circles of the day. On 6 August 1671 John Beale wrote to Henry Oldenburg and, in passing, mentioned Austen's gardening business in Oxford, noting some of the influential people Austen was supplying.[4]

Similarly, Isaac Newton wrote to his friend Henry Oldenburg from Trinity College, Cambridge and asked that he might effect an introduction to Austen.

---

[1] *Hartlib 41/1/139A-140B* = CSC #324. Brome Whorwood was also MP for Oxford from 1679-84.

[2] *Oxford Petty Sessions Roll – 1656-1678* (O.5.11), folio 158 recto. His fellow Overseer was Robert White.

[3] See Tate (1969): 30-32, for more on the role of 'Overseer of the Poor'.--

[4] *BL ADD MS 4294*, folio 17 recto = Hall and Hall (1966): 188-9 = CSC #498.

This letter is dated 14 November 1676 and mentions Austen, 'ye Oxonian planter', from whom Newton wished to obtain some grafts of cider fruit trees.[1] Unfortunately, Oldenburg's reply to Newton on this occasion has not survived, although Newton probably received it around 25 November 1676. He alludes to Oldenburg's reply in a postscript to another letter written to his friend in London on 28 November 1676, once again mentioning the desired introduction to Austen: 'Yours about Planting I received, & am obliged to you & your Friends for making our way to Mr Austin'.[2] Further exchanges between Newton and Oldenburg took place in the next couple of months, although not all of these letters have survived. However, Oldenburg wrote to Newton again on 2 January 1677 and informed him of Austen's death.[3] This subsequent letter from Oldenburg to Newton is also significant in that it gives independent confirmation of the fact that Ralph and Sarah Austen had no children, a matter which may be deduced by the lack of mention of any children within his will, which is dated 24 September 1673.

6. Austen's Last Will and Testament

Sarah Austen remains very much a figure living in the shadows of her husband's life; very few details are known about her. Apparently, no record of their marriage exists, nor indeed, very much solid information about Sarah's family background. In a letter to Samuel Hartlib dated 7 October 1658 Ralph Austen makes mention of a brother-in-law named Job Hancock (he serves as the person carrying the letter to Hartlib);[4] it is possible that this is Sarah's brother, and an indication that her maiden name was Hancock.[5] The only other mention of her in the Hartlib letters is in a letter dated 22 July 1660; here Sarah is the bearer of the letter, having travelled to Hartlib's house in Axe Yard, King's Street, Westminster in London on her husband's behalf.[6]

Ralph Austen died and was buried on 26 October 1676 in his local parish church, the parish register recording his name as 'Mr Ralph Aughstion'.[7]

---

[1] *BL ADD MS 4294*, folio 12a-d = CSC #556.

[2] *Cambridge University Library MS Add 3976*, folio 16a = Turnbull (1960): 185.

[3] *Cambridge University Library MS Add 3976*, folio 17a = Turnbull (1960): 187 = CSC #559.

[4] *Hartlib 45/2/5B* = CSC #268.

[5] There is record that a Job Hancock married Catherine James at St Bartholomew the Less, in London on 4 June 1661. A London ironmonger named Job Hancock made a will on 5 October 1680 which was probated on 8 December 1680, naming his wife Catherine, and two sons, James and George, as beneficiaries (*PCC – Will of Job Hancock* (PROB 11/364), folios 327 recto-327 verso). It is possible that the London ironmonger is Sarah Austen's brother, although the will makes no mention of her as a beneficiary.

[6] *Hartlib 41/1/135A* = CSC #314.

[7] *Parish Register of St Peter-in-the-Bailey – 1663-1689* (Par 214/1/R1/2), folio 59 verso. His death is also recorded in Anthony Wood's *Fasti Oxonienses* 2.780 = CSC #654. Elsewhere Wood wrongly recorded Austen's death as occurring in 1677. Thus,

Because he had the status of a 'Privileged Person' within the University of Oxford, his will was proven in the Vice-Chancellor's court on 11 December 1676. The will, and the accompanying inventory list, gives details of the house contents, including items stored in his cider-house.[1] Although they followed the conventions of the day, there is no reason to believe that the pietistic opening paragraphs of the will are anything but genuine expression of Austen's own religious convictions.[2]   All indications are that Austen remained a devoutly religious man until his death, even though he does appear to waiver in how he expressed his beliefs, alternating between outright Nonconformity and allegiance to his local Anglican church in the parish of St Peter-in-the-Bailey. According to Anthony Wood, Austen was buried in the local parish church, the church of St Peter-in-the-Bailey, 'in the Isle joyning on the S[outh] side of the Chancel'.[3]   Thus, he was buried within a few dozen meters of the site of his home and cider-making shop, and in the very church at which he, together with the 'cashiered Anabaptist officer' Roger Hatchman, had so controversially supported the preaching of the Fifth Monarchist John Belcher in January of 1660.

Perhaps it is not too surprising to discover that Richard Tidmarsh, one of the main leaders of the Baptists in Oxford, was one of the two signatories to witness Austen's will on 24 September 1673. Although Austen was not to die until three years later in 1676, the making of a will suggests that he had begun to have a sense of his own mortality. Perhaps the circumstances of Richard Tidmarsh himself had something to do with this, for Tidmarsh had buried his own wife Jean less than three weeks before on 6 September 1673. What is certain is that Tidmarsh agreed to serve as a legal witness to Austen's last will and testament. Given the known associations between the two men over the years it was a fitting tribute to offer to a fellow 'seditious sectarye'. Tidmarsh's involvement with Austen extended beyond the death of his friend, for in 1678, as noted above, Tidmarsh also served as one of the witnesses to the property indenture which secured Sarah Austen's right to live within the house in St Peter-in-the-Bailey until the end of her life. However, she does not appear to have done so, since there is record of her paying the Poll Tax of 10 March 1692 while living in the parish of St Michael-ar-the-Northgate.[4]   This is the last record of her; where and when she died remain unknown, although she it is

---

MS Wood Diaries 21, folio 2 recto: 'Ralph Austen ye Gardiner died in Apr[il] or May 1677, in st. pet[er] par[ish] of y^e bayly – q[uare]' (the entry is marked through as an error); *MS Wood Diaries 21*, folio 15 recto: 'Raph Austen died in Ap[ril]. or May, v[ide] sup[ra] in 2d last leaf'. On this see Clark (1892): 2.374.

[1] *Bodleian Wills – Austen, Ralph* = CSC #519 and CSC #557. Also see Griffiths (1862): 3.

[2] See Marsh (1990): 215-249; Spufford (1995): 15-18; Aylmer (2002): 148-149, for more on the religious sentiments contained in 17th-century wills. Houlbrooke (1998): 110-146, offers a more generalized discussion.

[3] *Athenae Oxonienses, Volume 2* (1692): 780 = CSC #654.

[4] *Taxes – 1691-1694* (P.5.9), folio 13 recto.

possible she died in the spring of that year, for her name does not appear in the records for the quarterly tax collected on 24 June 1692.

I turn now to consider one other member of the Baptist church in Oxford with whom Austen was in contact – Richard Quelch junior, arguably the most politically radical of the first generation of Baptists within Oxford.

D. Richard Quelch junior: Watchmaker and Fifth Monarchist Agent in Oxford

I noted above (page 42) that Richard Quelch junior and Richard Tidmarsh attended the funeral of John Pendarves in Abingdon on 30 September 1656 and that both men were signatories of the short pamphlet *The Complaining Testimony of Some ... of Sions Children* (1656) which was issued following the clash with government soldiers there. The evidence suggests that Ralph Austen also was in attendance at Pendarves's funeral, making it one of the few public occasions where he and Richard Quelch junior are described in surviving documents as being in the same place at the same time. However, this was almost certainly not the first time that the two men were in contact one with another.

There are some indications that Austen had earlier encountered the Quelch family in connection with his role as an official of the Parliamentary Visitors to the University of Oxford. For example, in *Ms e Musaeo 77*, the Register of the Visitors, there is an entry dated 10 April 1649 which names both a Richard Quelch (senior) and a James Jennings as among those inhabitants of Oxford to be placed in college positions by the Visitors of the University of Oxford.[1] Both Quelch and Jennings are named in a subsequent entry within the manuscript; the relevant page is headed 'The Names of Such as are chosen unto Colledges'.[2] The page lists a number of appointees and the dates of their appointments within the colleges concerned, starting on 18 July 1648 and running through 22 April 1650. The entry mentioning Quelch and Jennings pertains to appointments made to New College on 22 June 1649. Quelch is here described as a 'Porter', and Jennings is listed as an 'Under-butler'. Quelch's appointment as a college porter appears to have been a temporary or part-time position, probably made to Quelch as he was coming towards retirement and beginning to hand over his business responsibilities to his son, who was also named Richard and was coming toward the end of an apprenticeship with his father. There are some indications that the elder Richard Quelch was active in civic affairs and favoured the cause of the Parliamentarians. Perhaps the best illustration of this is a petition made to Parliament by a group of citizens in Oxford, including Quelch, who protested

---

[1] *Ms e Musaeo 77, (Register of the Visitors)*, page 244 = CSC #79. The order was signed by Francis Rous on behalf of the Parliamentary Committee for the Reformation of the University.

[2] *Ms e Musaeo 77, (Register of the Visitors)*, page 184.

the city elections held in September of 1647.[1] This petition was signed by 28 citizens and was submitted to Parliament in London; it protested against the annual elections for the Mayor and Bailiffs which took place on 20 September. The signatories effectively submitted a vote of no confidence in the vintner Humphrey Boddicott,[2] who had been elected Mayor, and the two Bailiffs, whose names were Henry Hodges (Hedges?) and Francis Greenway (Greeneway?). The petitioners asked that the results of the elections be overturned and other people be put in their place who were capable of doing the job. What is so intriguing about this document is that a number of the signatories, or their sons, were later to become prominent Dissenters, several of them with connections to the Baptist conventicles meeting within the city. Thus, we find that Richard Quelch and James Jennings were signatories, together with Matthew Langley (Richard Tidmarsh's apprenticeship master), John Sheene (Lawrence King's apprenticeship master), Richard Phillips (the apprenticeship master of Edward Wyans senior and John Toms senior), and, most significantly, Thomas Williams, the milliner, who was later elected Mayor in 1653 (see chapter 5 below).

The Baptist Dissenter Richard Quelch junior came from a family of watchmakers who were well-established in the city of Oxford. Richard Quelch senior came from Wallingford in Berkshire and married Anne Fisher at St Martin's parish church on 11 September 1625;[3] the couple had at least eight children, although three of them did not survive childhood (see the chart on the 'Family Tree of Richard Quelch junior' for details of the wider family). One of the daughters, Mary, married the influential sabbatarian Edward Stennet in 1654.[4] As best can be determined, Richard Quelch senior, his wife Ann, and their children lived in the parish of St Michael's in the north of the city.[5]

Richard Quelch senior served a seven-year appenticeship with Triumphe de St Paule which commenced on 11 August 1608,[6] and upon completion of it was granted his 'Freedom of the City' on 9 September 1616.[7] Three of his sons (Richard, John and Martin) became watchmakers in the city. In many respects John was the most successful of these three watch-making Quelch brothers. He not only had a successful career as a master watchmaker, with four known

---

[1] *MS Wood F 35*, folios 13 recto and verso = CSC #53.

[2] Boddicott issued trade tokens advertising his business (see Leeds (1923): 385-589, and Dickinson (1986): 179, #124, for details).

[3] *Parish Register of St. Martin's – 1569-1705* (Par 207/1/R1/2), folio 68 recto.

[4] The record of their marriage on 19 July 1654 has survived (*Parish Register of St Michael-at-the-Northgate – 1653-1683* (Par 211/1/R1/2), folio 28 verso) = CSC #186. Stennet died in 1705.

[5] A record of a property dispute between Quelch and a neighbour survives; it is dated 7 December 1639 and concerns the responsibility of repairing a lead gutter separating the two properties (*Husting and Mayors Court 1639-1641* (M.4.3), folio 7 recto (Mayors).

[6] *Civic Enrolments – 1590-1614* (L.5.1), folio 174 verso.

[7] *Civic Enrolments – 1613-1640* (L.5.2), folio 411 recto.

apprenticeship contracts on record,[1] but also took up civic responsibilities later in life. On 30 September 1686 he was elected one of the city Bailiffs, as the Mayor's 'child';[2] he continued to serve as a Bailiff until 1691.[3] Most records relating to John Quelch show him as living in the parish of All Saints'. He is listed as paying 1s in the Poll Tax of 1667 while living in the parish of All Saints', perhaps taking over the house on which his brother Richard paid the Hearth Taxes in 1665.[4] The Poll Tax entry is for John Quelch alone, probably because he married soon after it was collected. There is record of a marriage bond with Elizabeth Hutt of All Saints' parish which is dated 12 August 1667,[5] and there are records of the baptism of four of their children within the parish records: Richard (on 2 November 1668), Katherine (on 23 January 1671), Mary (on 9 August 1674), and John (on 24 March 1678).[6] In addition, there are several other records of a 'Mr Quelch', presumably John, paying the War Taxes of 1667-1668 as a resident within the parish of All Saints'. He pays 1s 9d in the tax of 24 June 1667; 1s 10d in the tax of 29 September 1667; 1s 9d in the tax of 21 December 1667; 1s 9d in the tax of 26 March 1668; 1s 9d in the tax of 26 June 1668; 1s 9d in the tax of 26 September 1668; and 1s 9d in the tax of 26 December 1668.[7] There is also record of him signing a marriage bond on 30 March 1665.[8]

---

[1] Thomas Langley on 4 April 1673 (*Civic Enrolments – 1662-1699* (L.5.4), page 207), with citizenship to follow on 2 December 1687 (*Civic Enrolments – 1662-1699* (L.5.4), page 565); Henry Godfrey on 24 June 1676 (*Civic Enrolments – 1662-1699* (L.5.4), page 260; Edward Pope on 24 July 1684 (*Civic Enrolments – 1662-1699* (L.5.4), page 365), and Joseph Rustin on 30 July 1686 (*Civic Enrolments – 1662-1699* (L.5.4), page 392).

[2] *City Council Proceedings – 1663-1701* (B.5.1), folio 245 verso.

[3] He is listed as holding a Bailiff's place in the City Council lists from 1686–1694 (*City Council Proceedings – 1663-1701* (B.5.1), folios 246 verso, 257 verso, 268 recto, 276 verso, 286 recto, 292 verso, 302 recto, 309 verso, 319 recto).

[4] *Poll Tax of 1667* (P.5.7), folio 12 verso.

[5] *ODR: Marriage Bonds* (d. 76), folio 3. The marriage was licensed to take place in the parish church of St Peter-in-the-East.

[6] *Parish Register of All Saints' – 1559-1810* (Par 189/1/R1/1), folios 27 recto, 28 recto, 30 recto, and 31 verso. The son John Quelch appears to have moved to the village of Wolvercote on the outskirts of Oxford where he established himself as a papermaker. There is record of his son, also named John, entering into an apprenticeship under the papermaker John Beckford of Wolvercote on 29 June 1711 (*The Enrolments of Apprentices - 1697-1800* (F.4.9), folio 84 verso), and being granted his citizenship upon successful completion of that apprenticeship on 8 June 1724 (*Civic Enrolments – 1697-1780* (L.5.5), folio 339 verso). It is likely that the papermaker John Beckford was related to the John Beckford who registered the Wolvercote church as a Baptist meeting house on 5 September 1672 (SP/44 38A, page 249. See Turner (1911): 2.830.

[7] *War Taxes – 1667-1668* (P.5.8), folios 4 recto, 23 verso, 42 recto, 59 verso, 79 verso, 98 recto and 107 verso. See pages 9-10 for more details about these various taxes.

[8] *OAR: Marriage Bonds – 1665* (c. 456), folio 110. The marriage was between Richard Herne and Alice Newe and was licensed to take place in Merton College chapel.

As noted, Richard Quelch junior served an apprenticeship with his father, and upon the successful completion of it was given his citizenship on 26 November 1652.[1] He took on several apprentices, starting with that of his younger brother John, the contract for which was agreed just three days after Richard's citizenship was granted. He also took over the apprenticeship of his brother Martin after their father died in early 1653. In total there are records of five apprenticeships involving Richard Quelch junior, the details of which are as follows:

Name of Apprentice	Date of Contract	Duration	Citizenship Granted
Martin Quelch	16 February 1650[2]	Seven years	
John Quelch	29 November 1652[3]	Nine years	7 September 1663[4]
Thomas Creed	3 September 1657[5]	Eight years	
James Browne	18 May 1663[6]	Eight years	
William Fowler	25 June 1677[7]	Eight years	

Quelch joined a small but select group of watchmakers and clockmakers who practised their trade in Oxford during the 17th century. Several of these artisans, notably the Knibb brothers (John and Joseph), produced a number of watches and clocks, many of which have survived and are now in museums or private collections. Unfortunately, this is not the case with Richard Quelch junior. Indeed, it appears that only one watch bearing his name has survived; this is a small silver-gilt octagonal watch dating to circa 1650, now within the collection of the Ashmolean Museum.[8] It is uncertain whether this watch was actually made by Richard Quelch senior, or his son Richard Quelch junior – the engraved inscription on the inside of the watch simply reads 'Richard Quelch fecit Oxon'.[9]

For a time Richard Quelch junior lived in the parish of All Saints', and there is record of him paying for a property containing two hearths there in the Hearth Taxes of Michaelmas 1665,[10] and Lady Day of 1665.[11] He married

---

[1] *Civic Enrolments – 1639-1662* (L.5.3), folio 238 verso = CSC #124.
[2] *Civic Enrolments – 1639-1662* (L.5.3), folio 90 verso = CSC #85. The apprenticeship was backdated to 29 September 1649. Richard Quelch junior took over the apprenticeship contract on 18 February 1653.
[3] *Civic Enrolments – 1639-1662* (L.5.3), folio 116 recto = CSC #125. The apprenticeship was backdated to 24 June 1652.
[4] *Civic Enrolments – 1662-1699* (L.5.4), page 733 = CSC #383; *Husting and Mayors Court 1660-1664* (M.4.4), folio 128 recto (Husting).
[5] *Civic Enrolments – 1639-1662* (L.5.3), folio 159 verso = CSC #253.
[6] *Civic Enrolments – 1662-1699* (L.5.4), page 13 = CSC #376.
[7] *Civic Enrolments – 1662-1699* (L.5.4), page 274 = CSC #564.
[8] Ashmolean Museum Department of Antiquities #1910-317.
[9] Beeson (1989): 135, assigns the watch to Richard Quelch senior, but it could just as easily be the handiwork of his son.
[10] *Hearth Tax of Michaelmas 1665* (E 179/164/513), membrane 31 verso.
[11] *Hearth Tax of 24 April 1666* (E 179/164/514), membrane 25 verso.

Amy Wright from Chastleton in Oxfordshire on 4 February 1656, the entry in the register describing Quelch as from 'the parrish of All-Hallowes'.[1] There are records of the couple having three sons, one of whom died as a young boy in 1671.[2] It is also possible that they had a daughter named Margaret, who married William Stukeley, a waterman from Abingdon, on 30 December 1693.[3]

The Baptist credentials of Richard Quelch junior are clear and unambiguous, and his activities as a Dissenter in Oxford well documented. There are records of Quelch making several court appearances before the civic and ecclesiastical authorities where he was asked to give account for his actions. Together with eight others he was indicted to appear before the Petty Sessions court on 30 June 1661 for failure to obey a legal summons and serve on a grand inquest; each man was fined 3s 4d for this disobedience.[4] Like his fellow Baptists, he was named as one of the insurrectionists in the so-called 'Presbyterian Sham-plot' of 1661 (see pages 43-4 above). Quelch is also named within the Diocesan court records for 24 and 31 October 1663, entries which note that he was a resident of the parish of All Saints' and describe him as being an excommunicant ('*exc[ommunicari]*').[5] There is record of Quelch's excommunication on 31 October 1663 'for not goeing to church',[6] and his name appears within a list of excommunicated persons which was composed circa 1665.[7] Quelch was also indicted to appear before the Petty Sessions court on 15 January 1663 along with Lawrence King, John Toms senior, Edward Wyans senior, and James Jennings for attending an illegal conventicle, and along with Lawrence King and James Jennings was also indicted on the same day for refusing to swear an oath of allegiance to the king.[8] Finally, on 14 April 1664 Quelch, King and Wyans were again indicted for not attending their local parish church.[9]

---

[1] *Parish Register of St Michael-at-the-Northgate – 1653-1683* (Par 211/1/R1/2), folio 34 verso = CSC #233.

[2] A son named John was born on 4 February 1658 (*MS Top Oxon* (b. 40), folio 1 verso), and a son named Nicholas was baptized on 26 January 1671 (*Parish Register of St Martin's – 1569-1705* (Par 207/1/R1/2), folio 33 recto). A third son named Richard was buried just a week before on 18 January 1671 (*Parish Register of All Saints' – 1559-1810* (Par 189/1/R1/1), folio 97 verso).

[3] *OAR: Marriage Bonds – 1693* (c. 479), folio 84. The marriage bond states that Margaret was from the parish of St Michael-at-the-Northgate within the city.

[4] *Oxford Petty Sessions Roll – 1656-1678* (O.5.11), folio 41 verso = CSC #326.

[5] *ODR: 4 April 1663-12 December 1663* (c. 6), folios 35 verso and 38 verso.

[6] *OAR: Excommunications – 1610-1783* (c. 121), folio 265 recto and verso = CSC #385. His excommunication was publicly read out in the parish church of All Saints' on Sunday, 17 January 1664; Thomas Swan's excommunication was read out at the same time.

[7] *ODR: Excommunications – 1633-1791* (c. 99), folio 240 recto.

[8] *Oxford Petty Sessions Roll – 1656-1678* (O.5.11), folio 49 verso = CSC #366 and CSC #367.

[9] *Oxford Petty Sessions Roll – 1656-1678* (O.5.11), folio 66 verso = CSC #392.

As noted, Quelch was one of the two messengers from Oxford who attended the funeral of John Pendarves on 30 September 1656, and he was a signatory of *The Complaining Testimony* (1656) which was issued in light of the confrontation between mourners and government troops at the funeral (see Appendix A). Quelch also signed the pamphlet *A Testimony to Truth* (1659), one of the eight signatories from the Baptist church in Oxford so to do (see Appendix B). The timing of the funeral is of crucial importance for understanding the significance of the event, for the last months of 1656 were a period of great fear and uncertainty for Cromwell and his government. Radical political forces in opposition to Cromwell's Protectorate were at their height, with much of it focusing on the Fifth Monarchists who threatened outright rebellion. Indeed, there was a plot to kill Oliver Cromwell life by a group of would-be assassins led by the disgruntled Leveller Miles Sindercombe. Initially Sindercombe planned to shoot Cromwell on the morning of 17 September 1656 as the Lord Protector traveled from Westminster Hall to Hampton Court; Cromwell was in the habit of spending the weekend there away from the noise and commotion of Westminster.[1]   News of the assassination plot hit the headlines with the publication of two pamphlets in early 1657: *The Whole Business of Sindercombe from first to last, it being a Perfect Narrative of his Carriage during the time of his imprisonment in the Tower of London* which appeared in February, and the provocative pamphlet by Edward Sexby and Silius Titus (published under the pseudonym William Allen) entitled *Killing; No Murder* which appeared in May.[2]   The plot, of course, failed, but the incident serves to illustrate the tense atmosphere of the time and helps provide a backdrop for the actions of government troops in harassing Baptist mourners at Pendarves's funeral.

Quelch's involvement with the Fifth Monarchy movement is frequently asserted, and there is some indication that in 1657 he was an agent in Oxford for them. Fifth Monarchists were known to have been active in Oxford at several points in the late-1650s, often with the support of Baptists. Anthony Wood tells us that one of the Fifth Monarchist leaders, the fiery Welshman Vavasor Powell, preached in All Saints' Church in the High Street on 15 July 1657. He notes Powell as an example of preachers who ranted against the Universities and sought 'to reforme ye Universitie after their owne way', viewing them as 'nurseries of wickedness' and, alluding to the description of fallen Babylon in Revelation 18:2, 'cages of uncleane birds'.[3]

---

[1] See Marshall (2003): 20-25.

[2] Firth (1902): 308-311, discusses the authorship of the controversial pamphlet, suggesting that it was a joint effort by Sexby and Titus. Hardacre (1961-2): 292-308, offers a study of the controversial Allen.

[3] *MS Wood F 1*, page 1099 = CSC #251. Wood also provides another comment about the Anabaptist antipathy against the University of Oxford, this time in connection with the uprising which was thought to have taken place on 8 May 1658 (see *MS Wood F 1*, page 1101 = CSC #261).

More to the point, at least one contemporary source mentions 'a brother from Oxford' as being involved in the Fifth Monarchy movement led by Thomas Venner in London in 1657.[1] Some historians have argued that this is a reference to Richard Quelch junior,[2] although he is not specifically identified in the document by name and much of the evidence on this point is circumstantial in nature. John Thurloe, the Secretary to the Council of State for Oliver Cromwell, discussed the rise of the Fifth Monarchists in a report submitted in report April of 1657, and although Thurloe specifically notes that Fifth Monarchy men had converged on Abingdon following the funeral of the Baptist pastor John Pendarves in September of 1656, he does not name Quelch as one of them.[3] However, one later document *does* appear to assert that Quelch was indeed a member of the Fifth Monarchy movement. This comes in the form of a document captured from some Fifth Monarchists, namely a list of some of their contacts around the country. It is in this regard that a cryptic, possibly coded, reference is made to Richard Quelch junior. The relevant line from the captured document reads:

| 10 | 6 | Warwick Lane at Oxford Armes | 2 & 5 day Agent | Oxford the White swann in Oxford[4] | Mr Quelch | Watchmaker o^{ur} |

It is difficult to know exactly what the reference to 'the White Swan' means. It is probably a reference to the Swann Inn in the parish of St Thomas where Quelch lived, and very near to the house of Richard Tidmarsh.[5] The important point for our consideration is the fact that, whatever its worth, the note clearly describes Quelch as the Fifth Monarchists' 'agent in Oxford'.

It is unknown how long and in what capacity Quelch continued to be active within the Fifth Monarchy movement, although it is likely that his involvement waned following the failure of Venner's revolt in 1660. As noted, Quelch does show up in a number of records of the ecclesiastical courts alongside other Baptist Dissenters; it looks as if his activities were confined to the Baptist conventicles of the city of Oxford. His name does appear alongside those of

---

[1] See *BL ADD MS 4459*, folio 111 verso = CSC #246.   For more on Venner's uprising, see Hutton (1985): 150-2.

[2] So Payne (1951): 47, argues.

[3] *MS Rawlinson A 64*, folio 141 = Birch (1742): 6.184-186.

[4] *MS Rawlinson A 54*, folio 225 = Birch (1742): 6.186-187.

[5] There was a Swan Inn located at the corner of what is now King Edward Street and High Street. This is mentioned by Anthony Wood in a diary entry dated 11 February 1663 which records that Wood was a witness to a rental agreement between his cousin and Abraham Davies (*MS Wood Diaries 7*, folio 2 recto). Samuel Brayne, the spy for the Earl of Essex's scout-master Sir Samuel Luke, mentions in his report of 13 February 1642 that he spent two nights 'at the White Swann at Oxford' on one of his reconnaissance missions (see Philip (1950): 1.4). It is possible that Brayne means the Swan Inn in the High Street, but it may also be that he means the Swan Inn in the parish of St Thomas. If so, the St Thomas property may have been known as the *White* Swan to distinguish it from the Swan Inn along the High Street.

Lawrence King, Thomas Swan, John Toms senior and James Jennings in Bishop Fell's list of Dissenters for the parish of All Saints' compiled in circa 1679.[1]

E. James Jennings: Buttonmaker and Under-Butler of New College

James Jennings was not a signatory to any of the documents issued by Oxford Baptists in the latter part of the 17th century, nor does his name appear within the *Abingdon Association Records Book*. However, his involvement with the Baptist conventicles meeting in Oxford at the homes of Lawrence King and Richard Tidmarsh is certainly indicated by the surviving ecclesiastical and civil court records. Like Lawrence King, Jennings was a resident of All Saints' parish in the city and there are several tax records which confirm this, including the Poll Tax of 1667 which show him paying 7*s* for himself, his wife and five children.[2] There is record of Jennings paying a property in All Saints' parish containing three hearths in the Hearth Tax of Michaelmas 1662,[3] in the Hearth Tax of Michaelmas 1665,[4] and in the Hearth Tax of Lady Day 1665.[5] There is also record of Jennings making a voluntary contribution of 5*s* to the the Free and Voluntary Present of 8 July 1661, probably while living in the parish.[6] He probably lived at the same property until his death in 1679, for Jennings signed an agreement on 23 August 1670 to pay an annual fee of 1*s* for an encroachment his house made onto the city street.[7]

Jennings was born into a prominant family of tradesman who had been established in Oxford for several generations, many of them making their living as tailors in the parishes of All Saints' and St Michael's (see the chart on the 'Family Tree of James Jennings' for details of the wider family). Jennings's father Humphrey was himself a haberdasher and there is record of James Jennings agreeing a seven-year apprenticeship with his father on 19 October 1632.[8] Upon successful completion of this apprenticeship Jennings was

---

[1] *OAR: Returns of Recusants – 1679-1706* (c. 430), folio 41 recto = CSC #588 (see the discussion above on page 14). There is a record of a Richard Quelch and two others (James Maynard junior and Robert Ayres) being appointed as deacons in the Baptist church in Reading in January of 1679 (see Davis (1891): 15; White (1967-68): 253). It is possible that this is the Oxford Dissenter.

[2] *Poll Tax of 1667* (P.5.7), folio 13 recto. None of the names of the children are given. It is possible that one of them was a daughter named Sarah; there is record of a marriage bond being agreed for her and James Pound on 8 January 1684, the marriage to take place in St Mary's parish church (*OAR: Marriage Bonds – 1683* (c. 471), folio 127).

[3] *Hearth Tax of August-November 1662* (E 179/255/4), Part 2, page 8.

[4] *Hearth Tax of Michaelmas 1665* (E 179/164/513), membrane 31 recto.

[5] *Hearth Tax of 24 April 1666* (E 179/164/514), membrane 25 recto.

[6] *Free and Voluntary Present of 8 July 1661* (E 179/255/5/4), membrane 2.

[7] *Languables – 1668-1737* (P.5.3), page 30 = CSC #486.

[8] *Civic Enrolments – 1613-1640* (L.5.2), folio 229 verso) = CSC #9; the apprenticeship contract is backdated to 1 May 1632.

granted his 'Freedom of the City' on 11 September 1640.[1] Jennings's older brother Edward followed the more accepted family tradition and became a tailor. Edward agreed an eight-year apprenticeship with Richard Astell (alias Myles) on 19 October 1632 (the same day as his brother James),[2] and was granted his 'Freedom of the City' on 4 September 1640, a week before his younger brother.[3] He joined the Company of Journeyman Taylors soon thereafter; there are records of him regularly paying his quarteridge dues of 2*d* to the company for the years 1640-1642, although his name is *not* included in the accounts for 1643.[4] The records are patchy after this, and only regularize again in the Restoration, but Jennings is not mentioned again in the Company accounts. Edward Jennings eventually became a member of the Company of Taylors, which vigorously regulated the trade and sought to stamp out unlicensed tailors from working within the city.[5] He was admitted to the Company on 14 August 1662[6] and remained a member until his death in 1673;[7] his name also appears regularly in the Company's annual list of members.[8]

---

[1] *Civic Enrolments – 1639-1662* (L.5.3), folio 277 verso = CSC #19; *Husting and Mayors Courts – 1639-1641* (M.4.3), folio 257 recto (Mayors).

[2] *Civic Enrolments – 1613-1640* (L.5.2), folio 229 verso. The apprenticeship was also entered in *MS Morrell 22 – The Company of Taylors: Enrolling Book (1604-1807)*, folio 34 recto.

[3] *Civic Enrolments – 1639-1662* (L.5.3), folio 277 verso; *Husting and Mayors Courts – 1639-1641* (M.4.3), folio 255 recto (Mayors).

[4] *Journeyman Tailors' Company Accounts – 1613-1697* (F.4.2), folios 63 verso, 64 verso, and 65 verso.

[5] There is record of Thomas Kelsey, the Governor of Oxford, issuing an order on 3 January 1649 for the suppressing of soliders who were illegally working as tailors (*MS Morrell 6 - Election and Order Book of the Company of Taylors (1572-1711)*, folio 142 recto = CSC #78). No doubt this order was issued at the instigation of the guild of tailors who wanted to protect their own interests. It suggested that illegal tailors in Oxford 'wilbe the utter undoeing and impov[er]isheing of a greate number of the said Company being very poore'.

[6] *MS Morrell 21 - Company of Taylors Minute Book (1658-1689)*, folio 84 recto = CSC #352. Interestingly, Jennings had to clear an outstanding fine of 20*s* before his admission was allowed, although the relevant entry recorded 'this Companye was Contented to take of him 2*s* 6*d*' (*MS Morrell 21 - Company of Taylors Minute Book (1658-1689)*, folio 84 verso). It is probable that the fine was for illegally trading as a tailor without being a member of the guild.

[7] He was buried on 25 July 1673 (*Parish Register of St Michael-at-the-Northgate – 1653-1683* (Par 211/1/R1/2), folio 25 verso). His widow Edith lived much longer; she died and was buried on 26 March 1702 (*Parish Register of St Michael-at-the-Northgate – 1683-1736* (Par 211/1/R1/3), page 77).

[8] His name appears in *MS Morrell 6 - Election and Order Book of the Company of Taylors (1572-1711)* in the lists for 1661 (folio 173 verso), 1662 (folio 178 recto), 1663 (folio 180 recto), 1664 (folio 182 recto), 1665 (folio 184 verso), 1666 (folio 186 verso), 1667 (folio 190 verso), 1668 (folio 193 verso), 1669 (folio 196 verso), 1670 (folio 198 verso), 1671 (folio 202 verso), 1672 (folio 203 verso), 1673 (folio 205 verso), and 1674 where the annotation '*d[efunctus]*' is given (folio 207 recto). In the entries for 1661,

Similarly, Edward's son Humphrey was admitted to the Company of Taylors on 16 February 1669, after having been enrolled as the son of a freeman of the company in 1662-3;[1] he had been granted his 'Freedom of the City' as the eldest son of a citizen on 1 April 1660.[2] He remained a member of the Company of Taylors until his death in 1685,[3] and his name also appears regularly in the annual lists of members.[4] Both Humphrey and Edward had difficulties establishing themselves within the restrictions imposed by the guild, although both signed an agreement promising to abide by the regulations governing the employment of apprentices and journeymen and the commissioning of work, thereby preserving 'the Craft and mistery of Taylors'.[5] There are records from 17 January and 2 February 1671 of Humphrey being fined 20s by the Company for 'Begings of Worke contrary to the good order of the Company'.[6] There is also record of a meeting held on 14 February 1671 at

---

1662 and 1665 Jennings's first name is corrected from Richard to Edward, suggesting a confusion with another branch of the larger Jennings family.

[1] *MS Morrell 6 - Election and Order Book of the Company of Taylors (1572-1711)*, folio 194 recto = CSC #464; *MS Morrell 22 – The Company of Taylors: Enrolling Book (1604-1807)*, folio 54 recto.

[2] *Civic Enrolments – 1639-1662* (L.5.3), folio 217 verso = CSC #309a; *Husting and Mayors Court 1660-1664* (M.4.4), folio 35 recto (Husting).

[3] He died and was buried on 9 August 1685 (*Parish Register of St Michael-at-the-Northgate – 1683-1736* (Par 211/1/R1/3), page 33). He died without leaving a will, although there is a probate bond signed by the 'Overseers of ye poor of ye p[ar]ish of St Michaell' who dealt with his estate (*Humphrey Jennings* (OWPR 82/2/6)).

[4] His name appears in *MS Morrell 6 - Election and Order Book of the Company of Taylors (1572-1711)* in the lists for 1669 (folio 196 verso), 1670 (folio 198 verso), 1671 (folio 202 verso), 1672 (folio 203 verso), 1673 (folio 205 verso), 1674 (folio 207 recto), 1675 (folio 209 verso), 1676 (folio 211 recto), 1677 (folio 214 verso), 1678 (folio 217 recto), 1679 (folio 219 recto), 1680 (folio 221 verso), 1681 (folio 223 verso), 1682 (folio 226 recto), 1683 (folio 228 verso), 1684 (folio 230 verso), and 1685 where the annotation '*mort[uus] est*' is given (folio 233 recto).

[5] *MS Morrell 6 - Election and Order Book of the Company of Taylors (1572-1711)*, folio 174 verso = CSC #338. This agreement, which contains about 200 names, is undated but probably comes from 1661. Apparently, neither Edward nor Humphrey was able to write, for both make a 'marke' on the document as opposed to a signature: Edward makes a '+' and Humphrey makes a large 'H'. A similar agreement was signed by tailors of the Company in 1670 (*MS Morrell 6 - Election and Order Book of the Company of Taylors (1572-1711)*, folio 200 recto).

[6] *MS Morrell 21 - Company of Taylors Minute Book (1658-1689)*, folio 57 verso and recto; *MS Morrell 6 - Election and Order Book of the Company of Taylors (1572-1711)*, folios 200 verso and 201 recto. On 14 February 1671 4d of the fine was remitted, and on 26 June 1671 Jennings was given 10s of his fine back because he was poor (*MS Morrell 21 - Company of Taylors Minute Book (1658-1689)*, folio 57 recto and 55 recto; *MS Morrell 6 - Election and Order Book of the Company of Taylors (1572-1711)*, folios 201 and 202 recto).

which Edward was given 5*s* in relief 'being a poore member of the Company'.[1] Both Edward and Humphrey are named in a couple of other records: on 8 September 1668 Edward was fined 5*s* 'for contempt' for failing to attend a meeting of the Company when he was ordered to do so, although the fine was eventually countermanded;[2] similarly, both Edward and Humphrey were among a group of fifteen tailors fined 4*s* apiece for failing to attend a meeting of the Company held at the Guildhall on 31 October 1670.[3] Despite these difficulties, Humphrey took on at least two apprentices, namely Samuel Denny on 10 March 1669,[4] and his younger brother Joseph (see below).[5] Humphrey and his wife Anne[6] had a son of their own named James who was enrolled in Alderman Nixon's School for Boys on 27 September 1683,[7] agreed an apprenticeship with Thomas Day on 16 July 1686,[8] and upon completion of that apprenticeship was granted his 'Freedom of the City' on 16 July 1694.[9] He was later admitted to the Company of Taylors on 7 November 1701,[10] and remained a member until his death in 1756.[11] In addition, Humphrey had three other sons, named

---

[1] *MS Morrell 21 – Company of Taylors Minute Book (1658-1689)*, folio 57 recto; *MS Morrell 6 - Election and Order Book of the Company of Taylors (1572-1711)*, folios 201 recto.

[2] *MS Morrell 21 – Company of Taylors Minute Book (1658-1689)*, folio 66 recto = CSC #456.

[3] *MS Morrell 21 – Company of Taylors Minute Book (1658-1689)*, folio 58 verso = CSC #492. Edward's name is crossed out in the entry, which suggests that his fine was remitted.

[4] *MS Morrell 22 – The Company of Taylors: Enrolling Book (1604-1807)*, folio 57 recto; *Civic Enrolments – 1662-1699* (L.5.4), page 133 = CSC #465. The seven-year apprenticeship was backdated to commence 17 February 1668; it was not successful and was cancelled on 21 November 1673 by mutual consent of master and apprentice.

[5] The apprenticeship was originally made with George Blackwell on 14 October 1668, but was shifted to his brother Joseph on 10 January 1669 (*MS Morrell 22 – The Company of Taylors: Enrolling Book (1604-1807)*, folios 57 recto and verso); *Civic Enrolments – 1662-1699* (L.5.4), page 126 = CSC #458.

[6] There is a marriage bond dated 5 February 1669 between Humphrey and Anne Denham of the parish of St Mary the Virgin in Oxford (*ODR: Marriage Bonds* (d. 58), folio 6 = CSC #463.

[7] *Alderman Nixon's Free School –1658* (Q.5.1), page 165. As noted above (page $$) Thomas Tisdale was one of the trustees of the Nixon School. It is possible that he helped facilitate the enrolment of the young James Jennings into it.

[8] *Civic Enrolments – 1662-1699* (L.5.4), page 392 = CSC #616. The young James did not have an easy ride through his apprenticeship. His contract was transferred first to Robert Books on 7 November 1691, and then to John Shelfox on 8 May 1692. The apprenticeship is also recorded in *MS Morrell 22 – The Company of Taylors: Enrolling Book (1604-1807)*, folio 66 recto.

[9] *Civic Enrolments – 1662-1699* (L.5.4), page 529.

[10] *MS Morrell 6 - Election and Order Book of the Company of Taylors (1572-1711)*, folio 280 verso.

[11] His name appears in *MS Morrell 6 - Election and Order Book of the Company of Taylors (1572-1711)* in the lists for 1702 (folio 281 verso), 1703 (folio 284 verso), 1704 (folio 287 recto), 1705 (folio 289 recto), 1706 (folio 291 verso), 1707 (folio 293 recto),

Samuel, Joseph and Thomas. Samuel and Joseph were apparently adopted by their uncle Joseph, after their father died in 1684 and left them orphans (the boys were aged seven and one at his death). The fate of the younger son Thomas is unknown, and the only record of him pertains to his entry into Alderman Nixon's School for Boys on 2 July 1694.[1] Both Samuel and Joseph were apprenticed to their uncle Joseph[2] although Samuel died in 1695 at the age of nineteen when he was half way through the apprenticeship.[3]

As noted, Humphrey's apprenticeship with Joseph was successful, and upon completion of it he was granted his 'Freedom of the City' on 16 July 1677,[4] and was admitted to the Company of Taylors two weeks later on 30 July 1677.[5] In many respects Joseph was the most successful tailor of the Jennings family. He was a member of the Company until his death in 1713[6] and his name also appears regularly in their annual list of members.[7] More significantly, he

---

1708 (folio 295 recto), 1709 (folio 297 recto); *MS Morrell 7 - Election and Order Book of the Company of Taylors (1710-1833)*, 1710 (folio 4 recto); 1711 (folio 7 verso); 1712 (folio 10 verso); 1713 (folio 12 verso); 1714 (folio 15 verso); 1715 (folio 17 verso); 1716 (folio 20 verso); 1717 (folio 22 verso); 1718 (folio 24 verso); 1719 (folio 26 verso); 1720 (folio 29 verso); 1721 (folio 31 verso); 1722 (folio 33 verso); 1723 (folio 36 recto); 1724 (folio 38 verso); 1725 (folio 40 verso); 1726 (folio 42 verso); 1727 (folio 44 verso); 1728 (folio 46 verso); 1729 (folio 48 verso); 1730 (folio 50 verso); 1731 (folio 52 recto); 1732 (folio 54 verso); 1733 (folio 56 verso); 1734 (folio 58 verso); 1735 (folio 59 verso); 1736 (folio 61 verso); 1737 (folio 63 recto); 1738 (folio 64 verso); 1739 (folio 66 recto); 1740 (folio 68 recto); 1741 (folio 69 verso); 1742 (folio 71 recto); 1743 (folio 73 recto); 1744 (folio 74 verso); 1745 (folio 76 recto); 1746 (folio 77 verso); 1747 (folio 79 recto); 1748 (folio 81 recto); 1749 (folio 82 verso); 1750 (folio 83 verso); 1751 (folio 84 verso); 1752 (folio 85 verso); 1753 (folio 86 verso); 1754 (folio 88 recto); 1755 (folio 88 verso); 1756 (folio 89 verso).

[1] *Alderman Nixon's Free School - 1658* (Q.5.1), page 171. Again, Thomas Tisdale may have helped facilitate the enrolment of the young Thomas Jennings into the Nixon School (see footnote $$ above).

[2] Samuel's apprenticeship is dated 13 May 1691 (*Civic Enrolments – 1662-1699* (L.5.4), page 444). Also see *MS Morrell 22 – The Company of Taylors: Enrolling Book (1604-1807)*, folios 67 verso.

[3] *Parish Register of St Michael-at-the-Northgate – 1683-1736* (Par 211/1/R1/3), page 58.

[4] *Civic Enrolments – 1662-1699* (L.5.4), page 646; *City Council Proceedings – 1663-1701* (B.5.1), folio 156 recto. The second entry is dated 17 July 1677.

[5] *MS Morrell 6 - Election and Order Book of the Company of Taylors (1572-1711)*, folio 215 recto; *MS Morrell 21 - Company of Taylors Minute Book (1658-1689)*, folio 37 recto.

[6] He died and was buried on 23 July 1713 (*Parish Register of St Michael-at-the-Northgate – 1683-1736* (Par 211/1/R1/3), page 98). His will was signed on 19 June 1712 and was probated on 1 August 1713 (*Joseph Jennings* (OWPR 137/1/23)).

[7] His name appears in *MS Morrell 6 - Election and Order Book of the Company of Taylors (1572-1711)* in the lists for 1678 (folio 217 recto), 1679 (folio 219 recto), 1680 (folio 221 verso), 1681 (folio 223 verso), 1682 (folio 226 recto), 1683 (folio 228 verso), 1684 (folio 230 verso), 1685 (folio 233 recto), 1686 (folio 235 recto), 1687 (folio 236 verso), 1688 (folio 239 recto), 1689 (folio 241 verso), 1690 (folio 244 verso), 1691

progressed through the Company's administrative ranks, being elected to a Warden's place on 26 June 1693,[1] and was elected the Master, the highest position within the guild, on 26 June 1699.[2] There are records of the birth of two daughters to Joseph and his wife Mary: a daughter named Mary who was born on 17 December 1691,[3] and a daughter named Hannah who was born on 2 January 1693 but died and was buried eighteen months later on 2 September 1694.[4] There is record of Jennings paying 4*s* in the Poll Taxes of 1692-1695 to cover himself, his wife, one daughter and a servant while living in the parish of St. Michael.[5] Similarly, entries for 27 August, 17 December 1694 and 25 February 1695 show him paying 3*s* to cover just himself, his wife, and one daughter.[6]

There is also one intriguing court record of a dispute between Joseph and Mary Jennings and another couple, Edward and Frances Higgins, distant relatives of the Baptist John Higgins.[7] It seems that Frances Higgins made accusations against Mary Jennings, publically calling her a whore. A suit was brought against the said Frances Higgins and she was cited to answer charges in the matter on 7 June 1689,[8] and appeared before the ecclesiastical court the next day.[9] The court ordered that Frances Higgins 'make a publick acknowlegm[en]t of her s[ai]d crime in ye p[ar]ish Ch[urch] of St Mich[ael]

(folio 247 verso), 1692 (folio 260 verso), 1693 (folio 262 recto), 1694 (folio 264 recto), 1695 (folio 266 recto), 1696 (folio 268 recto), 1697 (folio 270 verso), 1698 (folio 273 recto), 1699 (folio 275 verso), 1700 (folio 277 verso), 1701 (folio 279 verso), 1702 (folio 281 verso), 1703 (folio 284 verso), 1704 (folio 287 recto), 1705 (folio 289 recto), 1706 (folio 291 verso), 1707 (folio 293 recto), 1708 (folio 295 recto), 1709 (folio 297 recto); *MS Morrell 7 - Election and Order Book of the Company of Taylors (1710-1833)*, 1710 (folio 4 recto); 1711 (folio 7 recto); 1712 (folio 10 recto); 1713 (folio 12 recto).

[1] *MS Morrell 6 - Election and Order Book of the Company of Taylors (1572-1711)*, folio 261 verso.

[2] *MS Morrell 6 - Election and Order Book of the Company of Taylors (1572-1711)*, folio 275 recto.

[3] *Parish Register of St Michael-at-the-Northgate – 1683-1736* (Par 211/1/R1/3), page 358.

[4] *Parish Register of St Michael-at-the-Northgate – 1683-1736* (Par 211/1/R1/3), pages 350 and 53.

[5] *Taxes – 1691-1694* (P.5.9), folios 14 recto, 59 recto, 78 recto, 117 recto, and 133 verso. His nephew Samuel is specifically named in the entry for 2 May 1694.

[6] *Taxes – 1691-1694* (P.5.9), folios 152 recto, 178 recto and 186 verso.

[7] Edward Higgins was apprenticed to the painter Richard Goode on 12 July 1670 (*Civic Enrolments – 1662-1699* (L.5.4), page 61). There is record of a marriage bond between him and Francis Denny which is dated 11 October 1676 (*OAR: Marriage Bonds – 1676* (c. 464), folio 61). It is likely that Frances Higgins was related to the Samuel Denny whom Humphrey Jennings took on as an apprentice (see page 253 above). Perhaps the bad blood between the two families stemmed from this failed apprenticeship.

[8] *ODR: Citations 1688-1691* (c. 49), folio 38 = CSC #631.

[9] *OAR: 15 October 1681-16 December 1693* (c. 23), folio 120 recto = CSC #632.

Oxon on y^e 16 instant'. This was apparently done and ended the matter; the court record for 22 June simply notes that in the matter of Jennings contra Higgins an agreement had been reached (*'concordatt'*). [1] It is impossible to tell given the sparseness of detail what caused this dispute. There appears to have been no further animosity between the two women, though they lived in close proximity to one another for a number of years. [2]

To return to James Jennings: there are several documents which suggest that he was active in the Parliamentarian cause during the civil war. One of the earliest records indicating his political allegiance is dated 20 September 1647. On this date Jennings signed a petition against the election of anti-Parliamentarians to civic offices, setting his name alongside others, notably Richard Quelch senior and Thomas Williams, who later became an active Dissenter and attended Baptist conventicles. [3] As noted above (page 243) James Jennings is twice mentioned in *Ms e Musaeo 77* as among those citizens from Oxford who are given college positions by the Visitors of the University of Oxford. [4] In particular, Jennings was listed as an 'Under butler' at New College in an entry dated 22 June 1649. Jennings's appointment to this post is also noted in an annotated copy of the ballad broadsheet entitled *A True Relation of a Notorious Cheater one Robert Bullock* (1663). [5] The broadsheet contains an interesting reference to Jennings, describing him as one of the people that Bullock swindled. The relevant lines read in the broadsheet read:

> I was a general marchant,
> for Buttons I did trade,
> I cheated brother Jennings,
> and a pure virgin maid.

In connection with these lines, Anthony Wood's copy of the ballad broadsheet in the Bodleian Library has the marginal annotation: 'Jennings a Buttonmaker, lately und[er]-butler of New Coll[ege], and his sister'. [6] Another copy of the broadsheet is similarly annotated by Wood and describes Jennings as the 'crop-ear'd under-butler of New College'. [7] It is likely that the virgin maid/sister referred to in the ballad was Martha Jennings, who was baptized on 26 June 1623 [8] and apparently never married. Like his fellow Baptists, Jennings, together with his brother Edward, was named as one of the

---

[1] *OAR: 15 October 1681-16 December 1693* (c. 23), folio 121 recto.

[2] Mary Jennings died in 1698 (*Parish Register of St Michael-at-the-Northgate – 1683-1736* (Par 211/1/R1/3), page 68); Frances Higgins died in 1723 (*Frances Higgins* (OWPR 134/1/20).

[3] *MS Wood F 35*, folios 13 recto and verso.

[4] *Ms e Musaeo 77, (Register of the Visitors)*, pages 184 and 244 = CSC #79.

[5] Anthony Wood recorded in his diary for 1663 'Rob[ert] Bullock, a great cheat this year. v[ide] Ballad' (*MS Wood Diaries 7*, folio 1 verso).

[6] *Wood 402* (92).

[7] *Wood 401* (198).

[8] *Parish Register of All Saints' – 1559-1810* (Par 189/1/R1/1), folio 15 recto.

insurrectionists in the so-called 'Presbyterian Sham-plot' of 1661 (see pages 43-4 above).

James Jennings appeared before the ecclesiastical court on 8 and 15 November 1662, the same sessions at which his fellow conventicler Lawrence King appeared and answered charges about his failure to attend his local parish church. However, Jennings was presented for a different offence - failing to pay his parish tithes.[1] He replied to the accusation of the court, saying that it was 'against his conscience to paye his taxe to the Church.' The threat of excommunication was also levelled against him by the court, and was in fact set in motion soon thereafter. There are two documents detailing the excommunication of James Jennings within the ecclesiastical records: one dated 15 November 1662,[2] and the other dated 15 June 1665.[3] The first excommunication order was publicly read out in the parish church of All Saints' on 20 April 1663 by the local vicar; the second order was similarly read out on 7 January 1666. Clearly the second excommunication order put severe pressure upon Jennings, for on 13 August 1666 he made a petition to the ecclesiastical court that the 'heavy Censure' of the writ *De Excommunicato Capiendo* against him 'may bee superseded, and a Competent time assigned him better to informe himselfe of those things w[hi]ch hee at p[re]sent scruples at & cannott conforme to.'[4] On this occasion Jennings did not appear before the court himself, but had his case presented by Timothy Box, who, apparently, was well disposed to Dissenters (as noted on page 219 above, Box was one of the witnesses to Ralph Austen's will). The court responded to Jennings's petition, temporarily suspending the excommunication order, and gave him no later than the next Easter to better inform himself.

Other instances of Jennings's appearance before the Petty Sessions court are extant for 1663. On 15 January 1663 Jennings, appeared, together with Lawrence King, John Toms senior, Edward Wyans and Richard Quelch junior, before the Petty Sessions court charged with attending an unlawful conventicle. The men were all fined 10s each for their misconduct in this regard, the money being collected 'to ye use of the howse of Common'.[5] At the same Petty Sessions three of the five (King, Quelch, and Jennings) were additionally fined by the court for 'refusing the Oath of Allegience demanded of them by the officers of the court.[6]

---

[1] *ODR: 27 September 1662-15 April 1665* (c. 4), folios 29 recto and 36 recto = CSC #354 and CSC #356.

[2] *ODR: Excommunication Schedules – 1662-1667* (c. 100), folio 20 recto = CSC #357.

[3] *ODR: Excommunication Schedules – 1662-1667* (c. 100), folio 137 recto = CSC #413. Also see *ODR: Excommunications – 1633-1791* (c. 99), folios 238 verso and 243 verso, where the two excommunication orders are recorded.

[4] *ODR: 23 June 1666-22 January 1670* (c. 9), folio 57 verso = CSC #433.

[5] *Oxford Petty Sessions Roll – 1656-1678* (O.5.11), folio 49 verso = CSC #366.

[6] *Oxford Petty Sessions Roll – 1656-1678* (O.5.11), folio 49 verso = CSC #367.

Throughout the late 1660s and early 1670s Jennings continued to be an active Dissenter and his name appears regularly in the ecclesiastical court records, often alongside his fellow Baptists John Toms senior and Lawrence King. He is cited together with his wife Hannah in two records from 1667 (22 June and 6 July);[1] unfortunately her first name is not given and has to be derived from other sources. There are eighteen records from 1668 (14 March; 6, 13, 20 and 27 June; 4, 11, 18 July; 10, 17, 24 and 31 October; 7, 14, 21, and 28 November; 5 and 12 December);[2] fifteen records from 1670 (25 June; 2, 9, 16, 23 and 30 July; 15, 22 and 29 October; 12, 19, and 26 November; 3, 10 and 17 December);[3] twenty-one records from 1671 (14, 21 and 28 January; 4, 11, 18 and 25 February; 4, 11 and 18 March; 1, 8 and 15 April; 20 and 27 May; 3 June; 15, 22 and 29 July; 14 October; 11 November);[4] nineteen records from 1672 (10, 17 and 24 February; 2, 9, 16 and 30 March; 18 May; 8, 15 and 22 June; 13, 20 and 27 July; and five undated entries from the Michaelmas Sessions).[5]

One of the last documents which mentions James Jennings is Bishop John Fell's list of recusants and Dissenters from 1679. Under the heading 'The names of those who are presented for not going to church', the entry for All Saints' parish has five men listed, each of whom is cited with his wife ('*et ux[or]*'). These five are Richard Quelch junior, Thomas Swan, John Toms senior, Laurence King, and James Jennings.[6] Jennings and his fellow Baptist conventicler John Toms senior are also explicitly named in two other documents from 1679 which are associated with this visitation: the first is a note that the churchwardens of the parish of All Saints' presented them 'for not comeing to Church to hear divine service';[7] and the second is a note by Fell which includes them in his parish-by-parish listing of Dissenters.[8] In one sense Fell's fears about Jennings as a dangerous Dissenter were unfounded, for Jennings died and was buried in the parish church of All Saints' on 6 June

---

[1] *OAR: 11 May 1667–21 July 1669* (c. 17), folios 28 verso and 37 recto.

[2] *OAR: 11 May 1667–21 July 1669* (c. 17), folios vii recto, 109 verso, 118 verso, 128 verso, 138 recto, 148 recto, 159 verso, 170 verso, 180 verso, 187 recto, 194 recto, 201 recto, 207 verso, 214 recto, 221 recto, 227 verso, 234 recto and 240 recto.

[3] *OAR: 24 July 1669-July 1672* (c. 19), folios 73 verso, 76 recto, 78 recto, 82 verso, 86 verso, 90 verso, 96 recto, 98 verso, 101 recto, 103 verso, 106 recto, 108 verso, 110 verso, 112 verso and 114 verso.

[4] *OAR: 24 July 1669-July 1672* (c. 19), folios 116 verso, 118 verso, 120 verso, 122 verso, 124 verso, 126 verso, 128 verso, 130 verso, 132 verso, 134 verso, 136 verso, 139 recto, 140 verso, 142 verso, 144 verso, 146 recto, 147 verso, 150 verso 154 verso, 164 verso, and 170 verso.

[5] *OAR: 24 July 1669–Michaelmas 1672* (c. 19), folios 197 recto, 199 recto, 201 recto, 202 verso, 203 verso, 205 verso, 207 verso, 208 verso, 210 recto, 211 verso, 213 verso, 215 recto, 216 verso, 218 recto, 219 verso, 221 recto and 224 verso.

[6] *OAR: Returns of Recusants – 1679-1706* (c. 430), folio 41 recto = CSC #588.

[7] *ODR: Memorandum from Diocesan Books: 1679-1814* (b. 68), folio 4 recto = CSC #590.

[8] *ODR: Bishop Fell's Notes on Dissenters – 1679-1685* (d. 708), folio 57 recto.

1679. Bishop Fell held the first session of his visitation in the St Mary the Virgin Church, less than a hundred metres away, six days later on 12 June; he probably was unaware of the passing of the Baptist button-maker.[1]

There are clear indications that other members of James Jennings's family also became active Dissenters. His brother Edward apparently shared his Baptist convictions, and a handful of ecclesiastical records illustrate that he and his wife Edith were indicted to appear before the courts on a number of occasions, including 15 and 22 March, 26 April, 3 and 10 May, 7 and 28 June, 5, 12, 19 and 26 July 1662.[2] There is also record of Edward and Edith both being officially excommunicated on 26 July 1662 'for absenting from divine service'.[3] Edward and his wife are also included in Bishop Fell's list from 1679 of recusants and Dissenters from the parish of St Michael's.[4] However, the most interesting records relating to Edward Jennings are from 1663 and concern the issue of infant baptism. On 21 February 1663 he appeared before the court and was admonished to have his five-year old son baptized, and to certify that he had done so through his parish minister at the next court session.[5] The matter was pursued in the courts over the next three months, with Edward being indicted to appear on 7, 14, 21, 28 March, 4 April, and 2, 9, 16, 23 and 30 May.[6] The most revealing of these records is the one dated 2 May 1663, which states that Edward appeared before the court with documents certifying that he had attended his parish church. The court entry also records that Edward 'offered him selfe willing to have his child baptized'.[7] He was ordered by the court to have the child baptized by 30 May and to certify that he had done so at the next court sessions. Apparently Edward did *not* have his son baptized as

---

[1] Jennings name also appears in two ecclesiastical court citations from 1680-1, charged with 'not comeing to Church to hear divine service' (*ODR: Miscellaneous Citations* (c. 62), folios 32 recto and 41 recto). He is also named in one court record dated 11 December 1680 (*OAR: 1 June 1678-30 July 1681 and 4 July 1674-17 October 1674* (c. 22), folio 146 verso), and in four records dated 15, 22, and 29 January and 19 February 1681 (*OAR: 1 June 1678-30 July 1681 and 4 July 1674-17 October 1674* (c. 22), folios 147 verso, 148 recto, 149 recto, 151 verso). There is nothing of substance within these latter entries – just his name and parish are recorded. It looks as if the court records had not yet registered that Jennings had died months before.

[2] *ODR: 1 February 1660 – 4 October 1662* (c. 3) folios 13 verso = CSC #340, 15 recto, 16 recto, 18 verso, 19 verso, 22 recto, 24 verso, 30 verso, 32 verso, 33 verso, 34 verso, 36 recto, 36 verso, 39 recto and 39 verso. Some of the records are for Edith on her own, some for Edward on his own, and others are joint entries.

[3] *ODR: Excommunications – 1633-1791* (c. 99), folio 238 recto.

[4] *OAR: Returns of Recusants – 1679-1705* (c. 430), folio 41 verso = CSC #589. Edith's name is here wrongly given as *Hannah*, probably because she was being confused with her sister-in-law, the wife of James Jennings.

[5] *ODR: 27 September 1662-15 April 1665* (c. 4), folio 85 verso = CSC #369.

[6] *ODR: 27 September 1662-15 April 1665* (c. 4), folios 88 recto, 91 recto, 94 recto, 100 recto, 103 recto, 111 recto, 112 verso, 113 verso, 114 verso and 116 verso.

[7] *ODR: 27 September 1662-15 April 1665* (c. 4), folio 111 recto = CSC #375. The record mistakenly describes Jennings as being from the parish of All Saints', probably as a result of the clerk confusing him with his brother James.

stipulated, for the record for 30 May simply notes that he was 'to certify the baptism of his son in these [sessions]' (*Ad certificand[um] de baptiz[i]o[n]e filii sui in hos [sessiones]*)'. The entry also has the marginal annotation of the court's pronouncement of judgment '*Exc[ommunicandum]* (To be excommunicated)'. Unfortunately, the name of the son is never given in these records, although the most likely candidate is Joseph, who, as noted above, served an apprenticeship under his uncle Humphrey and became a prominent tailor in his own right. If this is correct, then it suggests that Joseph was born to Edward and Edith Jennings in about 1658, that is to say, somewhat later than the births of their other children. This fits well with the Poll Tax entry for 1667 which lists Edward Jennings paying 3*s* to cover himself, his wife and one child while living in the parish of St Michael.[1]

In any event, despite his apparent willingness to conform to the Church of England rules, Edward Jennings continued in his Dissenting ways. On 22 February 1667 he petitioned the court that the excommunication order against him be lifted.[2]   When Jennings again promised to be obedient to the ecclesiastical laws of the Church of England, the court granted him absolution and warned him to frequent his parish church at divine services.

Another example of James Jennings's extended family being active as a Dissenter is Anne Jennings, the wife of his brother Humphrey. Anne was cited to appear before the courts in her own right two times in 1674 (3 and 10 December),[3] and two times in 1675 (12 and 19 February).[4] Unfortunately, the records do not tell us the reason for her being called before the court. However, the record from 12 February does have a marginal annotation of the court's judgment that she 'is declared excommunicated' (*dec[ernitu]r exc[ommunicari]*). She died and was buried on 20 June 1684;[5] her husband Humphrey died and was buried a little more than a year later on 9 August 1685.[6]

[1] *Poll Tax of 1667* (P.5.7), folio 51 recto.

[2] *ODR: 23 June 1666-22 January 1670* (c. 9), folio 140 verso = CSC #437.

[3] *ODR: 28 August 1675-7 July 1677* (c. 13), folios 26 recto and 27 verso.

[4] *ODR: 28 August 1675-7 July 1677* (c. 13), folios 31 recto and 34 recto.

[5] *Parish Register of St Michael-at-the-Northgate – 1683-1736* (Par 211/1/R1/3), page 31.

[6] *Parish Register of St Michael-at-the-Northgate – 1683-1736* (Par 211/1/R1/3), page 33.

5. The Milliner:

Thomas Willliams

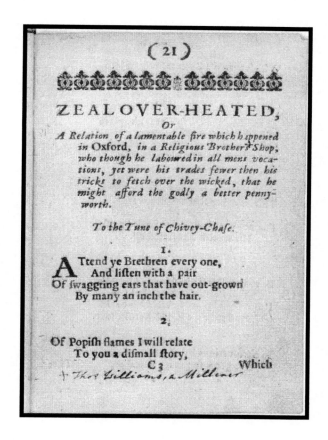

Illustration #8: Title page of a poem entitled 'Zeal Overheated', published in 1654 by Thomas Weaver in his book entitled *Songs and Poems of Love and Drollery* (1654). The Bodleian Library copy of the book has a contemporary footnote identifying the religiously-minded Thomas Williams, who was Mayor of Oxford in 1653-4, as the subject of the satirical verse (*Malone 402*).

5. The Milliner:

Thomas Williams

Within this chapter I shall consider the life and career of Thomas Williams, a milliner by trade, who became a prominent civic leader within Oxford and rose to the office of Mayor in 1653-4. Williams had a number of contacts with some of the acknowledged Baptists, and he has already figured at several points within the discussion. As noted above in the chapter on Roger Hatchman, Williams was among those City Councilmen who was accused of disloyalty and removed from his civic office by Charles I in September of 1643 (see page 168 above). In the chapter on Ralph Austen, it was noted that both he and Williams served as witnesses in the trial of a Mr Holloway, who was accused in April 1652 of taking up arms in support of Charles II in the battle for Worcester and charged with being generally 'disaffected to the Parli[a]m[en]t' (see page 213 above). Similarly, in the discussion of Richard Quelch senior and James Jennings, it was noted that they and Williams were among the 28 signatories of a petition sent to Parliament in September of 1647 protesting against the election of anti-Parliamentarians to civic offices in Oxford (see page 244 above).

This chapter will discuss Thomas Williams's life, beginning with his family background and his being granted the 'Freedom of the City'. I will then proceed to consider his professional life as a tradesman and civic leader within Oxford, and then move on to examine his role as a religious leader among the Dissenters who met in the city.

A. Family Background and Residence in All Saints' Parish

Thomas Williams is one of the earliest Dissenters from Oxford about whom we have a moderate amount of information, particularly as it relates to an active civic life which culminated in his being elected Mayor of the city in September of 1653.[1] However, study of him is at some points complicated by the fact that there were several men with the name Thomas Williams who lived and worked in Oxford during the 17th century. The Poll Tax of 1667 lists *four*

---

[1] *City Council Proceedings – 1629-1663* (A.5.7), folio 215 verso.

such men: one an attorney from Saint Martin's parish,[1] the second a 'gentleman' from Hollywell whose father was an apothecary,[2] the third from the parish of Saint Peter-in-the-East, who possibly made his living as a fuller, [3] and the fourth, our Dissenter from All Saints' parish.[4]

This Poll Tax of 1667 lists the Dissenter Williams and his unnamed wife, together with one son and a household maid named Mary Nash.[5] No record of a lease appears to have survived, although records of adjoining properties show that the Williams family lived in what is now 120 High Street.[6] At the time of

---

[1] *Poll Tax of 1667* (P.5.7), folio 7 recto. He paid 15*s* in tax to cover himself, his practice, his wife Mary, and their children John, Mary and Roger. This Thomas Williams also paid 20*s* and 8*s* in the two collections of tax taken up in 1664 (*Lay Subsidy of 11 April 1664* (B.1.4f). There is record of his apprenticeship to George Banger on 17 April 1650 (*Civic Enrolments – 1639-1662* (L.5.3), folio 92 recto), and of his citizenship upon the successful completion of that apprenticeship on 20 June 1656 (*Civic Enrolments – 1639-1662* (L.5.3), folio 230 verso). Williams later became active in the debate with the University over the rights and privileges of Oxford citizens. There is record of a University court leet which took place in the Guildhall on 25 October 1658 at which a Mr Rowney put forward the city's views on key matters. Interestingly, the minutes of this meeting are verified as being a true copy of the proceedings by two lawyers, Thomas Williams and Joseph Harding (*Civil War Charities and General Minutes 1645-1695* (E.4.6), folios 9 recto and verso).

[2] *Poll Tax of 1667* (P.5.7), folio 25 verso. This Thomas Williams was enrolled in an apprenticeship contract with John Nixon on 22 August 1629 (*Civic Enrolments 1613-1640* (L.5.2), folio 184 verso = CSC #5. His father John was an established apothecary in the city and a member of the University (*Bodleian Wills – Williams, John – 4 June 1641*). It appears that in October of 1657, and again in March of 1658, this Thomas Williams was appointed a farmer of excise taxes by Richard Cromwell (SP 25/78, pages 213-214 and 516). In November 1660 he signed a petition which was presented to Charles II claiming extenuating circumstances for failure to deliver the amounts prescribed (SP 25/78, page 276).

[3] *Poll Tax of 1667* (P.5.7), folio 57 recto. There is an apprenticeship record from 29 March 1644 for a fuller named Thomas Williams which suggests this identification (*Civic Enrolments – 1639-1662* (L.5.3), folio 266 recto).

[4] *Poll Tax of 1667* (P.5.7), folio 10 recto.

[5] The maid paid 3*s* in tax on her wages of 40*s*.

[6] There are records for Williams being a tenant to the west of the property designated 117-119 High Street in the All Saints' district of the city, that is to say, in 120 High Street. He is so described in leases dated to 10 May 1637, 30 April 1652 and 6 June 1665 (*Oxford City Ledgers, 1636-1675* (D.5.6), folios 12 verso–13 verso, 140 recto–141 recto, 363 verso–164 verso, and 533 recto–534 recto; *Old Leases and Counterparts: All Saints' Parish* (S 1.1c). A lease for 3 June 1674 granted to the goldsmith Daniel Porter gives the name of '[blank] Williams, wid[ow] ' as the person occupying the property to the west, confirming Thomas Williams's death in the spring of 1674 (*Old Leases and Counterparts: All Saints' Parish* (S 1.1d); *Oxford City Ledgers, 1636-1675* (D.5.6), folios 533 recto – 534 recto). A lease document from New College dated 2 March 1672 also records Williams as occupying part of what is now 120 High Street (*Estate Administration* (Steer #1422). For more on the rental arrangements of the property, see Cole (1972): 205-207; Salter (1926): 127; (1960):

the Poll Tax in 1667 Williams's spouse was named Alice, but she was not his first wife (see the accompanying chart on 'The Family Tree of Thomas Williams' for details of his larger family connections). There is also record of the marriage of a Thomas Williams to the 'wydow Sibell[a] Rose' on 10 November 1628.[1] It is possible, though unlikely, that this was Williams's first marriage. However, there is record of a Thomas Williams from All Saints' parish who married Elizabeth Hulcock of St Mary Magdalen parish on 2 February 1629; she is in all probability the Dissenter's first wife.[2] As best can be determined Thomas and Elizabeth had at least eight children: a son William who was baptized on 30 July 1630 but died and was buried on 14 November 1631,[3] a daughter named Katherine who was baptized on 12 June 1636,[4] a son named Thomas who was baptized on 5 December 1637,[5] a son named Benjamin who was baptized on 26 January 1640,[6] a daughter named Sarah who was baptized on 14 July 1642,[7] a son named John who was baptized on 24 September 1646 and later died and was buried on 23 June 1673,[8] a daughter named Mary who died and was buried on 3 February 1651,[9] and another son named Thomas who was baptized on 24 April 1653 and later died and was

---

1.179. See CSC #540 for its location in the parish of All Saints' in David Loggan's *Oxonia Illustrata* (1675).

[1] *Parish Register of St Martin's – 1569-1705* (Par 207/1/R1/2), folio 69 recto. Sibell's maiden name was Mawditt and she married William Rose on 28 April 1617 (*Parish Register of St Martin's – 1569-1705* (Par 207/1/R1/2), folio 67 verso).

[2] *Parish Register of St Giles – 1576-1680* (MS DD Par St Giles b.1), page 92.

[3] *Parish Register of All Saints' – 1559-1810* (Par 189/1/R1/1), folios 16 recto and 88 recto.

[4] *Parish Register of All Saints' – 1559-1810* (Par 189/1/R1/1), folio 17 recto. There is record of the burial of a Katherine Williams on 11 December 1636 (*Parish Register of All Saints' – 1559-1810* (Par 189/1/R1/1), folio 88 recto). However, it is uncertain if this refers to the daughter of Thomas and Sibell, since she is not identified as such in the entry.

[5] *Parish Register of All Saints' – 1559-1810* (Par 189/1/R1/1), folio 17 verso. It appears that this son died and was buried on 15 July 1646 in the adjoining parish of St Mary the Virgin (*Parish Register of St Mary the Virgin – 1599-1694* (Par 209/1/R1/1), page 43). The fact that the burial is recorded in the register of an adjoining parish may be tied up with William's removal from civic office from 1643-6. It is possible that the family relocated to Abingdon during this period, and only returned to Oxford in June of 1646 (see page 168 above).

[6] *Parish Register of All Saints' – 1559-1810* (Par 189/1/R1/1), folio 17 verso. There are records of the baptism of two of his daughters: Catherine on 24 November 1685, and Elizabeth on 10 April 1687 (*Parish Register of All Saints' – 1559-1810* (Par 189/1/R1/1), folios 34 recto and 35 recto).

[7] *Parish Register of All Saints' – 1559-1810* (Par 189/1/R1/1), folio 18 recto.

[8] *Parish Register of All Saints' – 1559-1810* (Par 189/1/R1/1), folios 20 verso and 98 verso.

[9] *Parish Register of All Saints' – 1559-1810* (Par 189/1/R1/1), folio 93 verso.

buried on 12 June 1653.[1] Records of two or three grandchildren, two born to his son Benjamin and one perhaps born to his daughter Sarah, are also extant. Elizabeth Thomas (or Izabell, as she was apparently known) died and was buried on 18 December 1662.[2] Thomas Williams then married Alice Hitch, who was from a village near Dorchester, on 18 August 1664;[3] it is she who is described as the wife of Williams in the Poll Tax of 1667.

The Williams family lived a number of years within the parish of All Saints', in the southeast ward of the city, and there are records of Williams paying taxes on goods in connection with his business there. These payments include subsidies granted Charles I by Parliament to help pay for his army in 1640 and 1641, and subsidies granted by Parliament in 1647 and 1648 to maintain the armies under Sir Thomas Fairfax's command.[4] Records show that Williams paid £3 16*s* in the two collections of the Lay Subsidy of 10-23 December 1640;[5] 20*s* 8*s* in the Lay Subsidy of 6 December 1641;[6] 3*s* in two assessments of the Lay Subsidy of 23 June 1647;[7] and 3*s* 6*d* in the Lay Subsidy of 17 March 1648.[8]

A number of other tax records from the 1660s are extant which relate to the Williams' residence along the High Street. There is record of Williams making a voluntary contribution of £5 to the Free and Voluntary Present of 8 July 1661, probably while living there.[9] There is record of Williams paying for five hearths in the Hearth Tax of Michaelmas 1662 as part of the returns for All Saints' parish in the south-east ward of the City.[10] There is also record of him paying for five hearths in the Hearth Tax of Michaelmas 1665 and the Hearth Tax of Lady Day 1665.[11] In addition, he paid 20*s* and 8*s* in the two

---

[1] *Parish Register of All Saints' – 1559-1810* (Par 189/1/R1/1), folios 23 recto and 94 verso.

[2] *Parish Register of All Saints' – 1559-1810* (Par 189/1/R1/1), folio 94 verso. The entry describes her as 'Izabell the wife of Mr Tho[mas] Williams'.

[3] *ODR: Marriage Records: W 1634-1704* (c. 92/2), folio 4 = CSC #396. The record gives the village as 'Baldwyn neere Dorchester'. This probably means Baldon where there are parish records relating to other members of the Hitch family. There is record of a nuncupative will of John Hitch, a stapler from Baldon, which was dated 13 June 1658 and probated on 16 December 1658. The probate record names Alice Hitch and the couple's unnamed son as benefactors (*PCC – Will of John Hitch* (PROB 11/285), folio 158 verso = CSC #260a).

[4] See Jurkowski, Smith and Crook (1998): 190-2, 237 and 240 for details of these subsidies.

[5] *Lay Subsidy of 10-23 December 1640* (E 179/164/477) – the Oxford record of this is found in *Lay Subsidy of 20 March 1641* (B.1.4c), and *Lay Subsidy of 10-23 December 1640* (E 179/164/495).

[6] *Lay Subsidy of 6 December 1641* (B.1.4d).

[7] *Lay Subsidy of 23 June 1647* (E 179/164/498a), membrane 3; *Lay Subsidy of 23 June 1647* (E 179/164/498), membrane 1.

[8] *Lay Subsidy of 17 March 1648* (E 179/164/499), membrane 5.

[9] *Free and Voluntary Present of 8 July 1661* (E 179/255/5/4), membrane 1.

[10] *Hearth Tax of August-November 1662* (E 179/255/4), Part 2, page 8.

[11] *Hearth Tax of Michaelmas 1665* (E 179/164/513), membrane 30 recto; *Hearth*

collections of the Lay Subsidy of 11 April 1664,[1] and is listed as paying a number of the War Taxes of 1667-1668,[2] commencing with a quarterly contribution of 4s 6d for the collection dated 24 June 1667.[3] Two further such quarterly payments, assessed at the same rate, were made by Williams on 29 September 1667[4] and 21 December 1667.[5] There is also a quarterly tax record for dated 26 March 1668 in which Williams paid 4s 6d in tax.[6] Finally, there are also three further quarterly tax records dated 26 June 1668, 26 September 1668, and 26 December 1668; within the first two collections Williams was assessed at 4s 6d for his contribution to the taxes, and within the third his contribution rose to 4s 8d.[7]

B. Master Milliner and Oxford Citizen

1. 'Freedom of the City'

Much information about Williams as a tradesman and citizen of Oxford can be gleaned by a careful combing through of the surviving municipal records. He appears on the scene rather unexpectedly, with no records of an apprenticeship entered in the city's books of *Civic Enrolments*. The most likely explanation of this is that Williams was not a native of Oxford, but moved to the city as a young man to make his fame and fortune (the earliest record of him is his marriage to Elizabeth Hulcock in 1629). Nevertheless, he was granted his 'Freedom of the City' on 21 February 1632, having paid £5 2s 6d in fees; he is described as a 'haberdasher of small wares' within the relevant records.[8] He became a well established trader in Oxford, and his name appears regularly within surviving records of the Guild of Mercers, Grovers and Linendrapers, commencing in 1648 where he is listed as one of eighteen members holding an ordinary place in the 'Cominalty'.[9] Williams was elected to a master's place the next year, leapfrogging over the position of warden in the process. More importantly, he was elected the ruling master of the guild for the year 1653-4, overlapping some of the time with his term of office as Mayor of the city (see

---

Tax of 24 April 1666 (E 179/164/514), membrane 25 recto.

[1] *Lay Subdsidy of 11 April 1664* (B.1.4f).

[2] See pages 9-10 for an explanation of these taxes.

[3] *War Taxes – 1667-1668* (P.5.8), folio 3 verso.

[4] *War Taxes – 1667-1668* (P.5.8), 23 recto.

[5] *War Taxes – 1667-1668* (P.5.8), 41 verso.

[6] *War Taxes – 1667-1668* (P.5.8), 59 recto.

[7] *War Taxes – 1667-1668* (P.5.8), folios 79 verso, 97 verso and 107 recto.

[8] *Civic Enrolments – 1613-1640* (L.5.2), folio 359 verso = CSC #7; *City Council Proceedings – 1629-1663* (A.5.7), folio 31 verso = CSC #8.

[9] *Mercers, Grocers & Linendrapers Guild Book – 1572-1855* (G.5.4), folio 18 recto. It is unknown when Williams first joined the guild; unfortunately the records between the years 1576-1647 are missing.

pages 271-9 below).[1]   Williams continued to hold a master's place within the guild until his death in March of 1674; the entry for the year 1673-4 has the annotation '*mort[uus] est*' next to his name.[2]

2. Apprenticeship Contracts

Generally within the surviving records Williams is described as a 'milliner'. He took on three apprentices within that trade, including his own son John, and Thomas Eustace, who went on to become a successful tradesman in his own right, even rising to the office of Mayor in 1678-9. The names and dates for these apprenticeship contracts, and the dates when the apprentices were granted their 'Freedom of the City', are as follows:

Name	Date of Contract	Duration	Citizenship Granted
William Davis	22 May 1637[3]	Eight years	2 November 1646[4]
Thomas Eustace	15 December 1652[5]	Eight years	20 December 1660[6]
John Williams	20 December 1660[7]	Eight years	

The fifteen-year gap between his first and second apprentice is somewhat unusual and requires some explanation, although milliners do not appear normally to have taken on more than one apprentice at a time. Moreover, it needs to be kept in mind that Williams was removed from his civic office by order of Charles I in 1643, and was only reinstated in 1646 (see pages 168 and 172 above).   Inevitably this caused some disruption to Williams taking on apprentices, and this, together with the fact that he seems to have poured his energy into civic office, offers some answer as to why he had so few apprentices.

---

[1] *Mercers, Grocers & Linendrapers Guild Book – 1572-1855* (G.5.4), folio 22 verso.
[2] *Mercers, Grocers & Linendrapers Guild Book – 1572-1855* (G.5.4), folio 42 recto.
[3] *Civic Enrolments – 1613-1640* (L.5.2), folio 296 recto = CSC #14; the apprenticeship contract is backdated to begin on 25 March 1637.
[4] *Civic Enrolments – 1639-1662* (L.5.3), folio 257 verso. His citizenship was granted by an Act of Council, probably a reflection of the disruption in his apprenticeship caused by Williams's censure by Charles I.
[5] *Civic Enrolments – 1639-1662* (L.5.3), folio 117 recto = CSC #127; the apprenticeship contract is dated to begin on 21 December 1652.
[6] *Civic Enrolments – 1639-1662* (L.5.3), folio 216 verso; *City Council Proceedings – 1629-1663* (A.5.7), folio 284 recto = CSC #318. He became a city bailiff in 1671.
[7] *Civic Enrolments – 1639-1662* (L.5.3), folio 188 verso = CSC #319; the apprenticeship contract is dated to begin on 21 December 1660.

3. Civic Offices and Responsibilities

All indications are that the milliner Thomas Williams was an energetic citizen of the city of Oxford, having established himself as a leading tradesman with active interests in civic government. He was appointed a 'Constable' for the south-east ward of the city on 2 October 1633.[1] The next year he was nominated by the then-Mayor John Sare as a 'fitt man to have a chamberlaines place in lieue of his sonne', a motion which met the full approval of the house on 2 October 1634.[2] On 10 October Sare appointed him to be one of the 'Auditors'.[3] On 31 August 1635 Williams agreed to join a scheme whereby boys in the 'house of correction' were sponsored by the citizens of the city who agreed to clothe them.[4] He was elected to the City Council on 16 October 1639 and was named by the then-Mayor John Smith as an 'Auditor' on 17 October 1639.[5] He then progressed to a bailiff's place on 30 September 1640,[6] was appointed one of the 'Money Masters' of the year on 3 November 1640,[7] and continued as an active council member until, as already noted, he was removed from his office by order of Charles I on 14 September 1643.[8] After the surrender of the city to the Parliamentarian forces in 1646 Williams quickly again became an important figure within civic government and rose through the various civic offices. He was reinstated to his bailiff's position within the City Council on 29 June 1646,[9] was appointed one of the five 'Key-keepers' of the city on 4 October 1647,[10] and was elected one of the two 'Senior Bailiffs' on 14 September 1648,[11] one of the 'Money Masters' for the year on 12 October 1648,[12] and an 'Assistant' on 2 December 1651.[13]

---

[1] *City Council Proceedings – 1629-1663* (A.5.7), folio 45 verso.

[2] *City Council Proceedings – 1629-1663* (A.5.7), folio 54 verso.

[3] *City Council Proceedings – 1629-1663* (A.5.7), folio 56 recto. He was also appointed one of the auditors in 1636 and 1639 (*City Council Proceedings – 1629-1663* (A.5.7), folios 72 recto, 102 recto).

[4] *City Council Proceedings – 1629-1663* (A.5.7), folio 58 verso = CSC #11.

[5] *City Council Proceedings = 1629-1663* (A.5.7), folio 102 recto.

[6] *City Council Proceedings – 1629-1663* (A.5.7), folio 107 verso = CSC #20.

[7] *City Council Proceedings – 1629-1663* (A.5.7), folio 110 recto.

[8] *City Council Proceedings – 1629-1663* (A.5.7), folio 130 verso = CSC #43.

[9] *City Council Minutes – 1635-1657* (A.4.3), folio 161 verso = CSC #47; *City Council Proceedings – 1629-1633* (A.5.7), folio 147 recto = CSC #48.

[10] *City Council Proceedings – 1629-1663* (A.5.7), folio 162 recto = CSC #55. He was also one of the keykeepers elected in 1649 (*City Council Proceedings – 1629-1663* (A.5.7), folio 180 recto).

[11] *City Council Proceedings – 1629-1663* (A.5.7), folio 168 recto. He swore his oath and paid the entrance fee of £5 on 29 September (*City Council Proceedings – 1629-1663* (A.5.7), folio 170 recto). Williams continued to serve as a bailiff from 1649-51.

[12] *City Council Proceedings – 1629-1663* (A.5.7), folio 172 verso.

[13] *City Council Proceedings – 1629-1663* (A.5.7), folio 204 recto = CSC #101.

Numerous documents illustrate Williams's activities during this period. A number of records in the account books for the key-keepers bear his signature, including his acknowledgment of receipt of £129 6s 5d in the common chest at the commencement of his year of office.[1] In addition, Williams was one of the signatories to a letter aimed to prevent Humphrey Boddicott from becoming Mayor following the disputed elections of 1647, a document which alleged that Boddicott held anti-Parliamentarian views (see page 244 above).[2] On 8 November 1647 he was also one of the council members chosen to meet together and try and heal the differences which were dividing the house.[3] On 19 May 1648 he was appointed one of the city viewers given responsibility of viewing a piece of waste ground near Merton College.[4] On 21 June 1649 he was, in his capacity as one of the two senior bailiffs, part of a delegation that went to London to meet with the Parliamentary Committee for the Regulation of the University. The aim of this delegation was to air the grievances that the city had against the University.[5] Williams handed over his responsibilities as a senior bailiff to his successor on 17 September 1649.[6] There is a copy of a receipt for re-imbursement made to Richard Butler which is dated 16 May 1650 and witnessed by Williams,[7] and there is record of him signing an order issued by the City Council on 17 November 1652 pertaining to the abuses of the market clerks in collecting toll corn from the population.[8] There is also an interesting record of him giving unto the city the gift of 'a Paule or buryeing cloth of Velvett', no doubt part of his inventory as a milliner who specialized in cloth and fine goods.[9]

Williams was one of the twelve members of the Mayor's council in 1652, 1654-61. As such he also served as one of the justices of the peace of the city, and there are several documents which illustrate this, including a testimonial letter for Thomas Denver of St Michael's parish which Williams signed on 24 February 1655.[10] He also signed an order dated 1 February 1655 to lend £50

---

[1] *Audit Book- Accounts of the Common Chest 1644-1685* (P.4.2), folios 13 recto. The annual accounts show that Williams signed 6 other receipts during the year (*Audit Book – Accounts of the Common Chest 1644-1685* (P.4.2), folios 14 verso, 15 recto, 16 recto).

[2] *MS Wood F 35*, folios 13 recto and verso = CSC #53. Boddicott was later removed from the City Council by an act of Parliament on 12 September 1648 (*City Council Proceedings – 1629-1663* (A.5.7), folio 167 verso).

[3] *City Council Proceedings – 1629-1663* (A.5.7), folio 164 recto = CSC #56.

[4] *City Council Proceedings – 1629-1663* (A.5.7), folio 166 recto.

[5] *City Council Proceedings – 1629-1663* (A.5.7), folio 177 verso = CSC #80.

[6] *City Council Proceedings – 1629-1663* (A.5.7), folio 180 recto = CSC #82.

[7] *City Council Minutes – 1635-1715* (E.4.5), folio 310 verso = CSC #86.

[8] *City Council Minutes – 1635-1715* (E.4.5), folio 291 verso = CSC #122.

[9] *Benefactions – 1630-1824* (E.4.2), page 7. The benefaction is undated, but it probably was made circa 1651 since Williams is described as a 'sometimes Alderman' and no mention is made of him ever having yet served as Mayor.

[10] *MS Rawlinson A 29*, page 633 = CSC #204.

for the relief of soldiers sequestered in the city.[1] In 1652 he was one of the people who offered sureties for loans made from a charity established in the name of Sir Thomas White: one for £25 made to Edward Lloyd,[2] and the other for £25 made to Lawrence Williard (Willier).[3] In both cases the money was to be repaid in 1658. However, the capstone of his municipal career was his election as Mayor of the city on 19 September 1653.[4]

Williams's activities as Mayor are wide and varied. As the chief justice of 'the Court of his Highnesse the Lord Protector', he presided over the transferral of the apprenticeship of John Bushnill to the fellmonger William Bushnill on 27 January 1654,[5] of John Clark to the glazier William Cole on 10 February 1654,[6] of Barnard Teasler to the butcher Stephen Clarke on 24 April 1654,[7] of William Tippet to the cordwainer George Staynoe on 22 May 1654,[8] and the discharge of Richard Flexon from any further service to the glover Simon Eusters on 3 July 1654.[9] He similarly served as a witness to an agreement dated 20 October 1653 that Robert Veisy, an apprentice to the tailor Thomas Danson, should serve an eighth year of his apprenticeship at an agreed rate of pay of forty shillings.[10] Williams also presided over a meeting of the Guild of Taylors on 5 July 1654 in which three members were sued for breaking the rules concerning the enrolment of apprentices.[11] As the 'Keeper of the greater parte of the Seal', there are also records of him sealing the enrolment of five merchants in the city between February and August of 1654.[1]

---

[1] *Civil War Charities and General Minutes – 1645-1695* (E.4.6) folio 13 recto = CSC #202.

[2] *Civil War, Charities & General Minutes – 1645-1695* (E.4.6), folios 60 verso and 72 verso. The other two guarantors were John Ryland and William Bayly (Baylie).

[3] *Civil War, Charities & General Minutes – 1645-1695* (E.4.6), folios 61 recto and 72 verso. The other two guarantors were John Wildgoose and John Holder.

[4] *City Council Proceedings – 1629-1663* (A.5.7), folio 215 verso = CSC #152. It was expected for the Mayor to have held all the lesser civic offices, as indeed Williams had.

[5] *Civic Enrolments – 1639-1662* (L.5.3), folio 75 recto. As one of the senior bailiffs, he similarly participated in the decision to transfer the apprenticeship of William Swift to the butcher William Attwell (alias Stevens) on 19 March 1649, the apprenticeship of Robert Sanders to the tailor John Allen on 9 June 1649, the apprenticeship of Robert Taylor to the locksmith William Birmingham on 9 July 1649, and the apprenticeship of Stephen Cawdry to the cordwainer Martin Seale on 23 July 1649 (*Civic Enrolments – 1639-1662* (L.5.3), folios 43 recto, 77 verso, 69 verso and 47 verso).

[6] *Civic Enrolments – 1639-1662* (L.5.3), folio 66 recto.

[7] *Civic Enrolments – 1639-1662* (L.5.3), folio 79 recto.

[8] *Civic Enrolments – 1639-1662* (L.5.3), folio 98 verso.

[9] *Civic Enrolments – 1639-1662* (L.5.3), folio 108 verso.

[10] *Civic Enrolments – 1639-1662* (L.5.3), folio 123 verso.

[11] *MS Morrell 6 – Election and Order Book of the Company of Taylors (1572-1711)*, folio 154 recto = CSC #185.

1654.[1] There is also record of Williams paying £5 to the John Nixon, one of the key-keepers of the city for the year 1653-4, 'for not makinge the Com[m]ons a dynner in the tyme of his mayoralty'.[2]

Something of the significance of Williams' religious and political convictions can also be seen through the kinds of activities he undertook as Mayor of the city. For example, new laws passed by Parliament on 24 August 1654 allowed justices of the peace to perform marriages.[3] There are records of Williams performing sixteen marriages as one of the justices of the peace of the city of Oxford, including nine which were solemnized during his Mayoral year. Details of these marriages, including the parish church or public place where the banns were published, are as follows:

Name of Couple	Date of Marriage	Banns Published
William Hanmore & Elizabeth Beale	26 November 1653	St. Peter-in-the-East[4]
Robert Jones & Elizabeth Green	27 February 1654	St. Peter-in-the-East[5]
Baldwin Hodges & Marie Clinch	23 March 1654	St. Peter-in-the-East[6]
William Horne & Anne Adams	29 May 1654	Common Market Place[7]
Stephen Gilkes & Margaret Basely	17 June 1654	Common Market Place[8]
John Bishop & Mary Caudry	19 June 1654	St Mary the Virgin[9]
Thomas Smith & Elizabeth Barksdale	22 June 1654	Common Market Place[1]

---

[1] *Enrolment Book of Statute Merchants – 1637-1675* (F.4.1), folios 97 verso, 98 recto, 98 verso, and 99 recto.

[2] *Audit Book – Accounts of the Common Chest 1644-1685* (P.4.2), folio 49 recto.

[3] *An Act Touching Marriages and the Registring thereof; and also touching Births and Burials* (1653. There is also record of him functioning as one of the justices of the peace of the city and swearing in Matthew Jellyman as registrar to five parish churches on 10 October 1653 (*MS Rawlinson B 402a*), folio 1 recto = CSC #154). A similar entry is extant about Jeremy Digbie as registrar to four parish churches (*Parish Register of St Mary Magdalen – 1602-1660* (Par 208/1/R1/1), folio 33 verso = CSC #145). Digbie went on to serve alongside Ralph Austen in Colonel Scroope's regiment of foot in the Oxfordshire militia in August of 1659 (see pages 32 and 202 above). The competence of some parish registrars was called into question during the Restoration. On 8 January 1663 Matthew Jellyman was presented by his parish churchwardens for not baptizing his own children, a charge he vigorously denied (*ODR: 27 September 1662-15 April 1665* (c. 4), folio 61 verso = CSC #363).

[4] *Parish Register of St Michael-at-the-Northgate – 1653-1683* (Par 211/1/R1/2), folio 26 recto = CSC #158.

[5] *Parish Register of St Michael-at-the-Northgate – 1653-1683* (Par 211/1/R1/2), folio 27 recto = CSC #168.

[6] *Parish Register of St Michael-at-the-Northgate – 1653-1683* (Par 211/1/R1/2), folio 27 recto = CSC #170.

[7] *Parish Register of St Michael-at-the-Northgate – 1653-1683* (Par 211/1/R1/2), folio 32 recto = CSC #174.

[8] *Parish Register of St Michael-at-the-Northgate – 1653-1683* (Par 211/1/R1/2), folio 27 verso = CSC #177.

[9] *Parish Register of St Michael-at-the-Northgate – 1653-1683* (Par 211/1/R1/2), folio 27 verso = CSC #178.

John Godbyheare & Ann Silverside	24 June 1654	Common Market Place[2]
Christopher Brook & Margaret Outridd	4 September 1654	St Mary the Virgin[3]
Thomas Browne & Elizabeth Dely	25 April 1655	Common Market Place[4]
John Bresier & Mary Nash	9 May 1655	Common Market Place[5]
Thomas Potter & Anne Sky	10 May 1655	Common Market Place[6]
Richard Cadbury & Anne Archer	14 May 1655	Common Market Place[7]
William Pule & Anne Alsappe	? June 1655	Common Market Place[8]
Christopher Prudix & Joane Blackwell	6 August 1655	St Mary the Virgin[9]
Henry Johnson & Elinor Kookoe	25 August 1655	Common Market Place[10]

Another indication of Williams's religious and political convictions was the way he dealt with Quakers within the city. It is probably no accident that the arrival of Quakers in Oxford is specifically dated by Anthony Wood to the autumn of 1654;[11] this would have been towards the end of Thomas Williams' term of office as Mayor of the city of Oxford (Mayoral elections were held annually in September and tied to the Feast Day of Saint Michael the Archangel). By all accounts Williams was welcoming to the Quakers, who were despised and ridiculed by many people everywhere they went, including Oxford. A number of stories involving contact between Williams and the early Quaker witnesses have survived, and together they provide a fairly consistent picture of benevolence and charity on his part.

For example, Williams is reported to have intervened on behalf of two Quakers who were being abused by Oxford residents early in 1654. The two are named in one contemporary source as Thomas Castle and Elizabeth Williams, who were 'Evilly Intreated by yᵉ Rude schollars & townsmen'. When he was informed, Thomas Williams, as Mayor, stepped in and 'Sent his

---

[1] *Parish Register of St Michael-at-the-Northgate – 1653-1683* (Par 211/1/R1/2), folio 27 verso = CSC #179.

[2] *Parish Register of St Michael-at-the-Northgate – 1653-1683* (Par 211/1/R1/2), folio 28 recto = CSC #180.

[3] *Parish Register of St Michael-at-the-Northgate – 1653-1683* (Par 211/1/R1/2), folio 29 recto = CSC #190.

[4] *Parish Register of St Michael-at-the-Northgate – 1653-1683* (Par 211/1/R1/2), folio 31 recto = CSC #206.

[5] *Parish Register of St Michael-at-the-Northgate – 1653-1683* (Par 211/1/R1/2), folio 32 verso = CSC #209.

[6] *Parish Register of St Michael-at-the-Northgate – 1653-1683* (Par 211/1/R1/2), folio 31 verso = CSC #210.

[7] *Parish Register of St Michael-at-the-Northgate – 1653-1683* (Par 211/1/R1/2), folio 31 verso = CSC #211.

[8] *Parish Register of St Michael-at-the-Northgate – 1653-1683* (Par 211/1/R1/2), folio 28 recto = CSC #215.

[9] *Parish Register of St Michael-at-the-Northgate – 1653-1683* (Par 211/1/R1/2), folio 31 verso = CSC #218.

[10] *Parish Register of St Michael-at-the-Northgate – 1653-1683* (Par 211/1/R1/2), folio 33 recto = CSC #221.

[11] *MS Wood F 1*, folio 1082 recto.

Sergeants & rescued them from yt wicked company & conveyed ym to y^e Mayors house'.[1]

Another very interesting incident involving Williams, has survived in this regard and was published by the Quaker Joseph Besse in 1753. Thomas Williams is not mentioned by name within the story, but appears masked under the title of his Mayoral office. The incident is dated to June 1654 and concerns two women, named Elizabeth Heavens and Elizabeth Fletcher, who were abused by Oxford students.[2] The students forced the women under a water-pump at St John's College, 'where they pump'd Water upon their Necks, and into their Mouths, till they were almost dead', and then severely injured Elizabeth Fletcher by throwing her 'over a Grave-stone into a Grave, whereby she received a Contusion on her Side, from which she never recovered'.[3] A few days later the women attended a church service where they were confronted by two justices of the peace who ordered that they be sent to the Bocardo prison. The next day Williams, as the Mayor of the city, was approached about the matter as the women were brought before the magistrates and Vice-Chancellor of the University, Dr John Owen. Attempts were made to force Williams to agree to having the women whipped out of the city, but this he refused to do 'because he could not in Conscience consent to a Sentence he thought undeserved'. Nevertheless, despite his intervention on their behalf, the women were severely whipped and driven from the city. The incidents in Oxford left Elizabeth Fletcher badly injured, and although she was to go on to continue as a Quaker prophetess for a few years more in Ireland,

---

[1] *Manuscripts – First Publishers of Truth: Portfolio 7*, folio 64 recto = CSC #199. This story is cited in Penney (1907): 209.

[2] In addition, there are several recorded instances of trouble between the townspeople of Oxford and the students of the University in the years immediately prior to Williams' election as Mayor. In December of 1651 some of the citizens of Oxford signed a petition to government complaining about the disruption to Dissenters' worship services caused by unruly scholars. The Council of State wrote stiff letters of rebuke to the Mayor of Oxford and to the Vice-Chancellor of the University, requiring them to deal with the matter (see SP 25/66, pages 117-118 = CSC #102, and SP 25/97, pages 51-52 = CSC #103). In response to this rebuke by the Council of State, Daniel Greenwood, the Vice-Chancellor of the University, and the University Heads of Houses issued several declarations, including one dated 9 January 1652 which warned the students about involvement in such riots and disturbances, and strictly enjoined them to observe the University statutes against carrying arms or weapons (Greenwood (1652a) = CSC #103a). Similarly, he issued a declaration on 22 March 1652 which decried the 'rude carriage of severall Schollars' within the city, noting that 'severall tumultuous disorders have been lately committed, to the disturbance of the publique Peace, and great scandall of the University' (Greenwood (1652b)). Another declaration was issued by the Vice-Chancellor on 5 July 1652 noting the 'Disturbances, Disorderly carryages, and Incivilities, of many younger Scholars of this University in Publike meetings' (Greenwood (1652c) = CSC #116).

[3] Besse (1753): 1.562-563 = CSC #184. Also see Penney (1907): 209-211, 258-259.

the physical abuses she suffered took their toll and she died before she was twenty years old.[1]

The account of this incident as presented by Besse is an amalgamation of two earlier works published in 1654, namely a pamphlet written by eight Quakers which is entitled *Here followeth a true Relation of Some of the Sufferings inflicted upon the servrnts [sic] of the Lord who are called Quakers,*[2] and Richard Hubberthorne's *A true Testimony of the zeal of Oxford-professors and University-men.*[3] On the surface it appears that the Vice-Chancellor involved in this incident was John Owen, the Dean of Christ Church, a preacher and scholar of great renown. He was an appointee of Oliver Cromwell, and served as Vice-Chancellor of the University from 1652-7. However, Owen was generally known to be a man of charity and tolerance, and on at least one occasion demonstrated he could be personally well-disposed to a Quaker, a man named Thomas Taylor. Taylor had been imprisoned at Owen's orders for preaching at the University Church of St Mary the Virgin. A delegation of Quakers attempted to visit Taylor in prison and were prevented from doing so by the gaoler. One of the Quaker women, Jane Betteris, the wife of the surgeon Richard Betteris, approached Owen and intervened on Taylor's behalf. In the end, Owen relented, paid Taylor's gaoler's fees and had him released from the Oxford Castle prison. The record suggests that the fact that Taylor had once been a student at Oxford was a factor in the matter.[4] In this sense the story about Elizabeth Heavens and Elizabeth Fletcher seems somewhat out of character for Owen. Moreover, it needs to be viewed against what is known about the stern attitude that Vice-Chancellor Owen took in challenging the

---

[1] She wrote one pamphlet entitled *A Few Words in Season to all the Inhabitants of the Earth* (1660). Within it she describes herself as 'a Servant of the Lord, who hath known his terror for sin', and declares herself to be 'a Stranger to the World, and longeth for the Redemption thereof' [8]. She was also a signatory to a pamphlet entitled *The Standard of the Lord Lifted Up Against the Kingdom of Satan* (1653). The tract was written by Quakers who were imprisoned in Kendal in September of 1653 and was directed against the justices and magistrates of England.

[2] *Here followeth a true Relation of Some of the Sufferings inflicted upon the servrnts [sic]of the Lord who are called Quakers* (1654): 1-2 = CSC #183. The eight Quakers were Jeremiah Haward, Abraham Allin, Thomas Ryland, Henry Traine, Lawrence Willyer, Thomas Swan, Alexander Green, and Abraham Badger. Anthony Wood wrote a note on the inside page of his copy: 'This simple pamphlet, containing a relation of the sufferings of certaine Quakers done by Oxford scholars, then under the government of Presbyterians and Independents, was published 1654 in the raigne of Oliver. Some, but not all, things in this pamphlet are true.' (*Wood 515* (14)). Another version is contained in *Manuscripts – First Publishers of Truth: Portfolio 7*, folio 64 recto-64 verso = CSC #199.

[3] Hubberthorne (1654): 1-4 = CSC #182. Elizabeth Fletcher is also mentioned in passing in Burrough's *Declaration of the present Sufferings of above 140 Persons of the people of God ... called Quakers* (1659): 20.

[4] A version of this incident is contained in *Manuscripts – First Publishers of Truth: Portfolio 7*, folio 64a verso-65 recto = CSC #199. See Braithwaite (1970): 395; Penney (1907): 214; Gill (2005): 60-62, for more discussion of it.

immoral and frivolous behaviour of some of the students of Oxford.   For example, in July of 1654, a month after the incident involving the two Quaker women, Owen delivered an oration at the *Comitia*, a ceremony marking the end of the academic year. Within his speech he denounced students who had forsaken the ideals of academic study and thought the occasion merely a time for debauchery and excess, with the promise of their University degree guaranteed by rank of family privilege:

> Do not expect wine merchants, pantomime-girls, and buffoons laid-low, beer-swillers, night prowlers, debauchers and other human riff-raff brought suppliant on to the stage, the bounds of the community of the gown expanded in all directions, the trappings of hoods and gowns restored, made famous by honourable names. This is the renown and this the glory of those who under the influence of multifarious and lasting leisure have been pleased to undertake these multifarious and important tasks.[1]

Owen is known to have sat in Parliament in London for some of 1654, and made frequent visits to the city on business matters relating to the University, so perhaps it was a deputy who initiated this shameful incident with the two Quaker women. On the other hand, the Quaker writer Samuel Fisher, in his *The Rustics Alarm to the Rabbires* (1660), clashed frequently and violently with Owen over Quakerism, so there may be some grounds for viewing the incident between Owen and Elizabeth Heavens and Elizabeth Fletcher as a genuine incident involving Owen as Vice-Chancellor of the University. [2]

In any event, the story of the persecution of the two Quaker women from Kendal in the Lake District by the University of Oxford appears to have grown in the telling. In point of fact the original pamphlet *Here followeth a true Relation of Some of the Sufferings inflicted upon the servrnts [sic] of the Lord who are called Quakers* (1654) does not mention the Vice-Chancellor at all within the story, although it does go on to say that an unnamed *Proctor* of the University mistreated other Quakers who were worshipping at the house of the Quaker leader Richard Betteris (Betterice).   It is only within Richard Hubberthorne's subsequent account that the (unnamed) Vice-Chancellor made an appearance within the story involving the two women Elizabeth Heavens[3] and Elizabeth Fletcher. The Vice-Chancellor was described as the 'chief actor in this persecution', and he was likened by Hubberthorne to the chief priest who was instrumental in the condemnation of Jesus Christ by the Jewish

---

[1] Toon (1971): 10.

[2] Certainly some biographers of Owen think that the incident involving Elizabeth Heavens and Elizabeth Fletcher was a genuine example of Owen's antipathy against Quakerism. See Toon (1971): 47.

[3] There is some confusion over this name; Croese   (1696): 1.108, gives it as Elizabeth *Havens*; the Quaker matriarch Margaret Fell gives it as Elizabeth *Levens* (*Swarthmore MS, Volume 352/208*). Many later Quaker historians give her name as Elizabeth *Leavens*, and note that she married another Quaker named Thomas Holmes in the autumn of 1654 (see Brailsford (1915): 148-156; Braithwaite (1970): 93, 207).

Sanhedrin. Thus, the Vice-Chancellor, together with the accusing justices, are castigated by Hubberthorne for their shameful actions in this matter. Interestingly, this is in stark contrast to Hubberthorne's opinion about the Mayor of the city of Oxford, Thomas Williams. About Williams, Hubberthorne writes: 'the Maior had no hand in any of this cruel usage and persecution.'[1]

A similar story describing Thomas Williams's intervention in the maltreatment of Elizabeth Fletcher was also told by early Quaker chroniclers. This involved an incident in which Elizabeth Fletcher, at the time a young sixteen year-old woman, stripped naked and paraded through the streets of the city, inspired by the scriptural warrant contained in Micah 1:8. The Quaker writer Thomas Camm described Elizabeth Fletcher and her shocking display in Oxford:

> And although they s[ai]d Elizebeth Fletcher was a very modest, grave, yong woman, yet Contrary to her owne will or Inclination, in obedience to ye Lord, went naked through ye Streets of that Citty, as a signe against the Hippocreticall profession they then made there, being then Presbetereans & Independents, w[hi]ch profession she told them the Lord would strip them of, so that theire Nakedness should Appear, w[hi]ch shortly after, at ye returne of King Charles ye 2[d], was fulfilled upon them, they being turned out or made Hippocritically to Conforme.[2]

As a final illustration of Thomas Williams' favourable attitude toward Quakers, it is worth noting that the Quaker Richard Hubberthorne visited Oxford in the summer of 1654 and began to preach openly. After one incident at the University Church of St Mary the Virgin, Hubberthorne was driven by an angry crowd from the church into the street. He sought refuge at the nearby house of Thomas Williams, who took him in and later allowed him to hold a Quaker meeting in his home. As a result of this incident Thomas Williams's son was brought to religious commitment. As one Quaker record of the incident notes:

> (Further, its to be noted) that y[e] afores[ai]d Tho[mas] Williams, Mayor of y[e] City, after y[e] Meeting kept att his House, had a son conuinced of y[e] Truth.[3]

Following the establishment of the Protectorate in December of 1653, it was decided on 1 May 1654 that the city of Oxford should send a delegation to see Oliver Cromwell.[4] This Williams did as Mayor, taking a letter of

---

[1] Hubberthorne (1654): 4.

[2] Cited in Penney (1907): 259. Carroll (1978): 69-87, and Bauman (1983): 84-94, discuss the phenomenon of 'going naked' as a prophetic protest.

[3] *Manuscripts – First Publishers of Truth: Portfolio 7*, folio 64a recto = CSC #199. See Penney (1903): 212; Allott (1952): 3; and Colvin (1979): 415.

[4] *City Council Proceedings – 1629-1663* (A.5.7), folio 220 recto = CSC #172.

congratulations from the city to the Lord Protector.[1] No doubt the incident would have been generated by Williams's desire to greet a fellow religious reformer, although we do see another intriguing aspect of Williams's character coming through as well, for he was careful to submit a bill for £20.00 to cover travel expenses and another for 11s for a new piece of luggage in the process.[2]

During Williams's Mayoral year in office several Baptists were brought in or promoted to positions of civic responsibility. For example, Richard Tidmarsh was appointed to the city's common council on 30 September 1653,[3] and on 16 August 1654 Thomas Hatchman was admitted as a freeman of the city.[4] Ironically, while in office as Mayor Williams oversaw improvements being made to the Bocardo prison at the north gate of the city, the very prison that some of these Baptist leaders were to be incarcerated a decade or so later when the monarchy was restored and the religious and political climate had changed so dramatically for the worse against Dissenters.[5] All indications are that Williams was clearly deeply committed to the ideals of the Commonwealth and an avid supporter of the more radical elements within Parliament. One intriguing illustration of how he was regarded by the prevailing political powers was his appointment by Parliament on 24 November 1653 as one of Oxford's thirteen tax commissioners. The commissioners served from 25 December 1653–24 June 1654, which happened to come in the middle of Williams's Mayoral year.[6] The commissioners were responsible for helping to raise money to cover the costs of maintaining the Commonwealth's army and navy, with Oxfordshire contributing £1933 6s 8d per month in the effort.

Finally, it is worth noting that the City Council agreed on 4 September 1654 to provide the parish church of St Martin's with a pulpit cloth and two new cushions, 'one to bee for Mr Mayor and thother for the preachers'. This took place just two weeks before the city Mayoral elections were held, and thus

---

[1] An incomplete draft of what appears to be this declaration survives (*Civil War Charities and General Minutes 1645-1695* (E.4.6) folios 12 recto and verso = CSC #173). Unfortunately it is not dated, although Hobson and Salter (1933): 459-461, suggest that the reference to the 'foreign war lately buried' contained within it refers to the war with Holland that was concluded by a peace treaty in April 1654.

[2] *Audit Book – 1592-1682* (P.5.2), folio 290 verso. Williams is also shown to have been reimbursed for an earlier matter which he dealt with in 1651 when he was involved in a legal wrangle in Wycroft Lane leading to Portmeadow, possibly to do with some locks on the entrance way there. He was reimbursed £1 10s 0d by the city chamberlains (*Audit Book – 1592-1682* (P.5.2), folios 281 verso and 286 verso.

[3] *City Council Proceedings – 1629-1663* (A.5.7), folio 217 verso = CSC #152.

[4] *City Council Proceedings – 1629-1663* (A.5.7), folio 221 recto = CSC #188.

[5] *City Council Proceedings – 1629-1663* (A.5.7), folio 218 verso = CSC #156. A similar note about the upkeep of the Bocardo prison is contained in the council records for 14 November 1659 (see *City Council Proceedings – 1629-1663* (A.5.7), folio 267 verso.

[6] *An Act for An Assessment at the Rate of One hundred and twenty thousand Pounds by the Moneth, for Six Moneths; From the Twenty fifth day of December 1653, to the Twenty fourth day of June then next ensuing* (1653): 292 = CSC #157.

perhaps serves as a parting gesture of Williams's commitment to the religious reformation taking place within Oxford, including the public preaching by such worthies as Henry Cornish in St Martin's parish church in the centre of the city.[1] Williams completed his Mayoral term of office on 29 September 1654 and dutifully handed over 'the Keyes of the Five Gates togeather w[i]th the Citty treasure (vizt.) 19 li[bras]' to the Bailiffs.[2]

Following his year as Mayor of Oxford Williams continued to be an active agent for the Parliamentarian party in the city. He was again appointed one of Oxford's seventeen tax commissioners to serve from 25 March to 24 June 1657.[3] These commissioners were responsible for helping to raise money to cover the costs of the war against Spain, with Oxfordshire contributing £966 13s 4d per month in the effort. Williams was also appointed one of the city's fifteen tax commissioners in a tax published on 26 January 1660.[4] They were responsible for helping to raise money to defend the Commonwealth against royalists seeking to restore the monarchy, with Oxfordshire contributing £1,127 15s 6d per month.

Following the Restoration Williams continued to serve on the City Council, and there are several records which show him performing standard duties expected of a man in his position as 'Assistant'. In one record dated 22 April 1661 he even presided over the City Council meeting as 'Deputy Mayor'.[5] In a council meeting held 16 April 1661 he was appointed one of the scrutineers of the city elections which sent two citizens from Oxford to serve in the new Parliament.[6] Williams is also included in a list of 58 citizens, probably drawn up in June 1661, who committed themselves to 'walke the rounds to Oversee

---

[1] *City Council Proceedings – 1629-1663* (A.5.7), folio 221 verso = CSC #191. Cornish was paid £20 for his service as a lecturer during the year (*Audit Book – 1592-1682* (P.5.2), folios 289 verso). Members of the City Council were required to contribute quarterly to the cost of the lecturers according to a strict schedule: the Thirteen paid 2s 6d each, Bailiffs paid 1s 4d, Chamberlains 1s, and Members of the Common Council 10d each (*City Council Proceedings – 1629-1663* (A.5.7), folio 167 verso).

[2] *City Council Proceedings – 1629-1663* (A.5.7), folio 222 verso = CSC #192. Williams was paid £40 for his services as Mayor during the year (*Audit Book – 1592-1682* (P.5.2), folio 289 verso).

[3] *An Act for An Assessment upon England, at the Rate of Sixty thousand Pounds by the Moneth, for Three Moneths; From the Twenty fifth day of March 1657, to the Twenty fourth day of June then next ensuing* (1657): 35 = CSC #249 = Firth and Rait (1911): 2.1077. The copy of this publication in the Thomason collection is dated 9 June 1657. See Jurkowski, Smith and Crook (1998): 250, for details of the tax.

[4] *JHC* 7: 844 = CSC #308. A published version of this is *An Act for An Assessment of One Hundred Thousand Pounds by the Moneth, upon England, Scotland, and Ireland, for six Moneths* (1659), although Thomas Williams is *not* named as a commissioner within it. See Jurkowski, Smith and Crook (1998): 253, for details of the tax.

[5] *City Council Proceedings – 1629-1663* (A.5.7), folios 288 verso.

[6] *City Council Proceedings – 1629-1663* (A.5.7), folio 288 recto = CSC #322. Richard Croke and Brome Whorwood were the successful candidates.

the watch'.[1] This was in response to a long-standing dispute between the city and the University over who was responsible for maintaining a night patrol. On 5 July 1661 he was appointed one of the viewers of a property under the Guildhall for which a lease renewal had been proposal, and again on 30 July 1661 he was appointed a viewer to help determine the boundaries of a city property adjoining the Bocardo prison.[2] He was present at a meeting on 13 October 1661 in which the musicians who were to receive city fines (probably those levied in connection with the coronation celebrations) were decided.[3]

As a person with long-standing Parliamentarian commitments, Williams's response to the Restoration is a matter of special interest, especially given the fact that he had been openly 'rebellious' and the object of censure by Charles I in 1643. Apparently, however, Williams was more accommodating to his son, Charles II. Indeed, as one of the Assistants on the City Council, Williams is among those who, in a record dated 24 May 1660, was described as 'being desirious by some publique Act to expresse theire Loyalty to his Ma[jes]tie'. Williams voluntarily took the Oath of Supremacy to Charles II a week later on 1 June 1660, something which his fellow councilman Richard Tidmarsh refused to do (see page 33 above).[4] Oxford was much in a state of frenzy as preparations were made for the king's coronation on 23 April 1661; most of the City Council members were engaged in elaborate preparations months before and after the coronation itself. A letter of congratulation was sent to the king by the City Council, and it was decided that a new ceremonial mace was to be made which reflected the change in political circumstances.[5] Charles II visited Oxford in August of 1661 as part of the post-coronation celebrations, and much time and effort went into establishing the proper pecking order of the Oxford entourage as they went to greet him in parade. There is an intriguing minute dated 8 August 1661, signed by the Mayor Sampson White and various members of the Mayor's council, including Williams, in which they all agree to meet regularly, no doubt in order to prepare for the king's arrival and to ensure that the return to monarchial rule went smoothly.[6] The council records for 16 August 1661 show Thomas Williams listed as the twelfth man after the Mayor within the parade, a placement suitable to his position as a member of the Mayor's council. He was to ride a horse and wear a scarlet robe within the

---

[1] *Civil War Charities and General Minutes – 1645-1695* (E.4.6), folio 36 recto.

[2] *City Council Proceedings – 1629-1663* (A.5.7), folios 289 verso and 290 recto. The viewers reported about the Bocardo to a council meeting held on 27 September 1661 (*City Council Proceedings – 1629-1663* (A.5.7), folio 292 verso).

[3] *Civil War Charities and General Minutes – 1645-1695* (E.4.6) folio 28 verso = CSC #331.

[4] *City Council Proceedings – 1629-1663* (A.5.7), folio 273 verso.

[5] *City Council Proceedings – 1629-1663* (A.5.7), folio 273 recto and verso. *MS Tanner 466*, folio 64 recto–65 recto contains some satirical verses by Henry Thomas of University College on the new mace.

[6] *Civil War Charities and General Minutes – 1645-1695* (E.4.6) folio 26 recto = CSC #327.

procession, paying for them out of his own pocket.[1] Apparently, not all of the City Council members were eager to participate in this parade, and a fine of 40*s* was 'levied by distresse to the use of the Citty' on those who did not attend. Interestingly, Williams was included as a sponsor in 'A Lyst of the trained Soldiers & Supplies for the Citie of Oxon, & whose armes they beare'.[2] The document is undated, but probably comes from the early summer of 1661 and is best seen as a further instance of the city militia making preparations for the royal visit.

However, neither his attention to pomp and circumstance, nor his having been an important figure in the corridors of power within Oxford for the best part of two decades was enough to save Thomas Williams from the purge that was to come. Like his fellow Dissenting citizens, he was named as one of the insurrectionists in the so-called 'Presbyterian Sham-plot' of 1661 (see pages 43-4 above). More importantly, Charles II wiped the civic slate clean, sacking city officials who had (to his mind) unsavoury political and religious connections and replacing them with his own men. Thus, the record for the City Council meeting held on 31 May 1662 tells how two of the Presbyterian preachers appointed by the Parliamentary visitors in 1648, namely Dr Henry Wilkinson and Henry Cornish, were removed from their places as Lecturers at Carfax and replaced with more acceptable appointees.[3] This must have been quite a blow to Williams, for as we have already noted, there appears to have been a close association between himself and Henry Cornish. However, this was just the beginning of the troubles as far as Williams himself was concerned, for just a week later on 6 June 1662 he, along with three others, was relieved of his place as an 'Assistant' on the City Council by order of the Commission for Regulation of the Corporations and replaced by Francis Heywood.[4] As a political appointee, he had lived by the sword, and now he perished by that same sword. This former Mayor thus drops from the lists of City Council members altogether, and he never figures in another entry within the council records.[5]

---

[1] *City Council Proceedings – 1629-1663* (A.5.7), folio 291 recto = CSC #328.

[2] *Civil War Charities and General Minutes – 1645-1695* (E.4.6) folios 35 recto and verso = CSC #329. There are 36 soldiers named within the list and Williams is the sole sponsor of a soldier named Silvester Webster. Webster was a tailor and was later elected to be a member of the common council on 30 September 1662; he swore his oath on 10 October 1662 (*City Council Proceedings – 1629-1663* (A.5.7), folios 303 recto and 304 verso).

[3] *City Council Proceedings – 1629-1663* (A.5.7), folio 299 recto.

[4] *City Council Proceedings – 1629-1663* (A.5.7), folio 299 recto = CSC #342.

[5] There are a number of City Council records relating to a Thomas Williams during the years 1662-71. However, these almost certainly refer to the lawyer who resided in St Martin's parish. He was elected as one of the 24 members of the Common Council on 30 September 1662 (*City Council Proceedings – 1629-1663* (A.5.7), folio 303 recto), and swore his oath of office on 10 October 1662 (*City Council Proceedings – 1629-1663* (A.5.7), folio 304 verso). He took the oath of subscription on 14 March 1663 (*City Council Proceedings – 1629-1663* (A.5.7), folio 309 verso), and is listed as a

C. Religious Dissenter and Political Agitator

Occasionally it has been boldly asserted that Williams the Dissenter was a Baptist, although the evidence for this is circumstantial.[1] He is never listed as one of the named delegates to any of the twenty-two Abingdon Association meetings from 1652-60 for which we have records, nor is there a *direct* reference to his being a Baptist in any publications issued by, or about, them. However, his name does appear in an intriguing entry within Oxford Diocesan records for 7 July 1666 and it is primarily on this basis that he has been identified as a person involved with the Baptist conventicle in Oxford. This entry needs to be more examined carefully for what it might reveal about Williams's credentials as a Baptist Dissenter.

1. Ecclesiastical court records

The Diocesan court entry for 7 July 1666 records that church wardens of All Saints' parish presented Williams and his wife Alice for not receiving the sacrament during the past Easter; they also accused him of being an Anabaptist.[2] The record goes on to state that Williams responded to these charges, admitting that it was true that he did not receive the sacrament at Easter last, but noted that he 'Denyeth that hee is an Anabaptist'. It is possible that the carefully couched reply that Williams gave to his ecclesiastical accusers was a subtle, but all important, indication of his true religious beliefs. He explicitly denies that he is an *Ana*baptist, but is not (apparently) questioned further if he is a *Baptist* or not. It is known that many Baptists were at this point in time keen to distinguish themselves from association with popular perceptions of the more radical Dissenters on the continent and insisted on

---

member of the Common Council from 1662-7 (*City Council Proceedings – 1663-1701* (B.5.1), folios 2 recto, 16 verso, 33 verso, 43 recto, and 57 verso). Most of his activity as a City Councillor during this period involves the viewing of property for lease renewals and boundary assessments, or offering assistance with regard to legal wrangles (*City Council Proceedings – 1629-1663* (A.5.7), folios 306 verso, 321 recto; *City Council Proceedings – 1663-1701* (B.5.1), folios 4 verso, 5 verso, 6 recto, 10 verso, 11 recto, 21 verso, 25 verso, 26 recto, 29 recto). Occasionally other glimpses of him are available. For example, he was fined for leaving the council meeting of 16 September 1664 early (*City Council Proceedings – 1663-1701* (B.5.1), folio 13 recto), and fined for not attending the meeting of 30 June 1665 at all (*City Council Proceedings – 1663-1701* (B.5.1), folio 28 verso). In 1668 he is given a chamberlain's place again and held that from 1668-1670 (*City Council Proceedings – 1663-1701* (B.5.1), folios 69 recto, 82 recto, and 92 recto). He died and was buried on 6 January 1671 (*Parish Register of St Martin's – 1569-1705* (Par 207/1/R1/2), folio 60 verso). He died intestate (*Thomas Williams* (OWPR 88/2/34)).

[1] This is explicit stated by Colvin (1979): 415, Hibbert and Hibbert (1988): 122, and Tyacke (1997): 596; (2001): 288.

[2] *ODR: 23 June 1666-22 January 1670* (c. 9), folio 13 recto = CSC #428.

describing themselves as *Baptists* rather than *Anabaptists*. Williams's reply was more than a simple matter of theological hair-splitting; it embodied a theological conviction about the nature of baptism which was at the heart of Baptist theology. William's wife Alice was clearly an active Dissenter in her own right and cited twice more in the Diocesan court sessions for the year (14 and 21 July).[1] She also was the subject of an excommunication order issued on the latter of these two dates (21 July).[2]

Several other subsequent examples of both Thomas and Alice Williams appearing before the ecclesiastical courts are also extant. Alongside other Dissenters from the parish of All Saints' (namely Lawrence King, John Toms senior, and James Jennings), Thomas was cited three times in records from the year 1668 (6, 13, and 20 June),[3] and together with his wife Alice was cited ten times in records from the year 1671 (27 May; 3 June; 15, 22, and 29 July; 14 October; 4, 11, 18, and 25 November; 2 and 9 December).[4] The first of these joint entries noted that the summons to appear before the court was issued by John Brees, the apparitor, at the Williams's home on 20 May.[5] What is intriguing about these records is that all of the entries relating to Thomas Williams being cited to appear before the ecclesiastical courts come *after* his marriage to Alice on 18 August 1664. It appears that Alice Williams's Dissenting activity served as a catalyst for that of her husband, or at least raised his public involvement as a 'seditious sectarye' to a new level. Thomas Williams was, as has been seen, a man whose political and religious convictions were brought to bear within his public life as a civic official. But prior to his marriage to Alice this activism was channelled in more conventional ways, and Williams seemed content to work within the prevailing religious and political structures of the time. The Restoration brought changes that inevitably meant someone with Williams's convictions became more and more isolated and driven to the margins of civic society. The ecclesiastical court records from 1666-71 are a reflection of this situation.

2. Petty Sessions Court Records

Williams is also mentioned within a Petty Sessions court record dated 6 June 1667 where he and a number of other city merchants were indicted for 'useing the trade of a Salesman of Clothes'.[6] In the end, the indictment was quashed

---

[1] *ODR: 23 June 1666-22 January 1670* (c. 9), folios 21 recto and 38 recto.

[2] *ODR: Excommunication Schedules – 1662-1667* (c. 100), folio 157 recto = CSC #431.

[3] *OAR: 11 May 1667-21 July 1669* (c. 17), folios 116 verso, 118 verso, 128 verso.

[4] *ODR: 19 November 1670-27 June 1672* (c. 11), folios 139 recto, 145 recto, 151 recto, 159 recto, 165 verso, 173 recto, 177 recto, 181 recto, 187 recto, 192 recto, 196 recto, 200 recto and 205 recto.

[5] *ODR: 19 November 1670-27 June 1672* (c. 11), folio 139 recto = CSC #496.

[6] The suit was probably brought against them by the Company of Taylors. There is a later record from 30 July 1677 of them deciding 'to undertake the presenting of y^e

and the case dismissed.[1] However, the trading dispute continued to be a matter of contention within the City Council, for the matter came up again in the Petty Sessions court two years later on 22 April 1669, with writs being produced by the accused which were to be sent to King Charles himself.[2]

In addition, in September of 1670 Williams and seven others were involved in a public disturbance over the election of the new Mayor, Francis Greeneway. The City Council took strong action against the protest and made moves to discover the ringleaders involved.[3] They were all indicted to appear before the Petty Sessions court on 6 October 1670 and charged with 'disturbing the peace' and 'hissing at the Mayor'. In the end, Williams apologized for this offence and was fined 2s 6d.[4]

D. A Satire of Thomas Williams:
Thomas Weaver's *Songs and Poems of Love and Drollery* (1654)

Ironically, one of the most important sources for reconstructing the religious convictions of Thomas Williams comes from the pen of a rather unusual source. The Bodleian Library in Oxford has within its collection an intriguing 17th-century document, designated *Malone 402*, which offers an important insight into the life of the Dissenter Williams. This small book of 124 pages is a leather-bound volume, the spine of which has gilded lettering reading *Love Poems*. The title page of the book reads '*Songs and Poems of Love and Drollery* by T.W. Printed in the Year 1654'; other contemporary sources enable the author to be identified as Thomas Weaver. Most importantly, there is within the book a song entitled 'Zeal Overheated', which contains a marginal note at the bottom of page 21 (the opening page of the piece). This note is linked to a + in the opening lines of the text identifying the 'Religious Brother' about whom the work is written as 'Thos. Williams, a Milliner' (see page 261 above).[5] This marginal note gives us a vital clue as to the association

---

Milliners att the next Sessions for selling Sale Cloathes' (*MS Morrell 21 – Company of Taylors Minute Book (1658-1689)*, folio 38 recto). A similar action was taken against glovers who were making 'Breeches and other Leather App[ar]rell to the manifest Injury of the Members of this Company' on 2 January 1688 (*MS Morrell 21 – Company of Taylors Minute Book (1658-1689)*, folio 11 verso).

[1] *Oxford Petty Sessions Roll – 1656-1678* (O.5.11), folio 97 verso = CSC #443.

[2] *Oxford Petty Sessions Roll – 1656-1678* (O.5.11), folio 108 recto = CSC #466. The writs were returned to the Crown Office on 10 June 1669 (*Oxford Petty Sessions Roll – 1656-1678* (O.5.11), folio 110 recto = CSC #469). Interestingly, a Thomas Williams also initiated proceedings against John Rutter for illegal trading practices at the same court sessions (*Oxford Petty Sessions Roll – 1656-1678* (O.5.11), folio 110 verso = CSC #470). It is probable that this is the lawyer Thomas Williams from the parish of St Martin's.

[3] *City Council Proceedings – 1663-1701* (B.5.1), folio 91 recto = CSC #489.

[4] *Oxford Petty Sessions Roll – 1656-1678* (O.5.11), folio 119 verso = CSC #491.

[5] This marginal note suggests that the book was handled by someone sometime after its publication in 1654 and that this person was aware of the identity of Thomas

of the song with the Oxford tradesman Williams. In short, the song 'Zeal Overheated' gives us an unusual insight into the life of the Dissenter Thomas Williams, who rose to the height of civic power in Oxford in 1653, precisely the time when Anabaptists were, arguably, in the ascendancy. The song helps not only to fill out some of the details of Williams's own religious commitments, but how those convictions were perceived by others. It also helps to provide a backdrop against which to understand Williams's more direct confrontations with the civic and ecclesiastical authorities in the 1660s and 1670s noted above.

However, at this stage another curious factor needs to be taken into consideration. This concerns the fact that an earlier version of the song 'Zeal Overheated' was published in 1642 as an appendix to an obscure tract, entitled *A Three-fold Discourse Betweene Three Neighbours, Algate, Bishopsgate, and John Heyden the late Cobler of Hounsditch, a Professed Brownist.* The title page of this 8-page tract also declares, *Whereunto is added a true Relation (by way of Dittie) of a lamentable fire which happened at Oxford two nights before Christ-tide last, in a religious brothers shop, known by the name of John of All-trades.*[1] The song (or 'dittie') 'Zeale Over-heated' is found on the last two pages of the tract (pages 7-8), and consists of 12 eight-verse stanzas, together with a final three-line concluding paragraph. The full text of the song reads:

> *Zeale over-heated:*
> A Relation of a lamentable fire which happened
> at *Oxford* two nights before *Christ-tide*, in a relig-
> ious brothers shop, who though hee laboured in all mens
> trades, yet his were trades fewer than his tricks, to
> fetch over the wicked, that he might
> afford the godly a better
> Penny-worth.

To the Tune of *Chivey-Chase*

Attend you brethren, everie one,
  And listen with a paire
Of swaggering ears, which have outgrowne
  By many an inch the haire:
Of Popish flames I will relate
  To you a dolefull storie,
Which turn'd a zealous shop of late

By slight of tongue he could fetch ore
  all Sparks that came unto him,
Except those which two nights before
  Christ-tide had like to undoe him.
When he to sleep himselfe had set,
  and dream'd of no more fire,
Than those his zeale and little Pet[2]

Williams. A second marginal note also appears on the second page of the song in connection with the reference to 'holy Cornish' in stanza 3 of the song. The marginal note here reads: 'Henry Cornish, Canon of Christ Church, 1648'.

[1] It is sometimes attributed to John Taylor (1580-1653), the so-called 'Water Poet', who visited Oxford in July and August of 1641 and then lived in the city from April 1643 until July of 1646. See Capp (1994): 150-153, for details of Taylor's time in Oxford.

[2] 'Pet' here means 'peat'.

Into a Purgatorie.

kindled in his desire.

There dwels in Oxon neere the place
    Where holy Cornish teacheth,
One that in all trades hath such grace,
    The wicked he overreaches
This brother first a Stoick was
    Peripateticall;
For 'bout the world as he did passe,
    His wealth he carried all.

He heard some cry, Fire, fire, amaine,[1]
    and said that were he slack,
Great John of All trades[2] would againe
    be brought to his first pack:
Then hasting downe to see what burn'd,
    the smoke did almost stop
His breath: the new Exchange was turn'd
    to a Tobacco shop.

But when his sin had made his pack
    Too heavie for his shoulder,
I' th' foresaid place he eas'd his back,
    And turn'd a staid house-holder.
In all occasions by and by
    He grew so great a Medler,
That if th' Exchange his shop stood nigh,
    You'd take him for no Pedler.

His wife came downe at that report,
    her cloaths hung in such pickle,
As she were new come from the sport
    after a Conventicle:
And first in these flames she espide
    a pure Geneva Bible,
With gilded leaves, and strings beside,
    that were not contemptible.

The second Part, to the same Tune

But with lesse griefe he could have seen't,
    as he then said to some one,
Had but the Apocrypha beene in't
    and Prayers that we call Common:
The Practice there of Pietie,
    and good St Katherine Stubs
Were martyr'd, which oft quoted hee
    had heard in severall Tubs.[5]

Of Canes[3] there smoaking lay great store
    his eyes had soone espied them,
They never were fired ones before,
    though he had oft bely'd them:
Mirrors and Prespectives[4] then might
    be burning glasses call'd;
The fever grew so hot that night,
    the periwigs grew bald.

---

    [1] 'Amain' here means 'loudly' or 'forcefully'.

    [2] 'John of all trades' is probably a nick-name for Williams, building on the traditional image of a merchant as a 'Jack of all trades'. Interestingly, this phrase is used in an obscure newsletter entitled *A Preter-Pluperfect, Spick and Span New Nocturnall*, probably issued by John Taylor in Oxford on Friday, 11 August 1643. The relevant paragraph refers to events that took place on the night of Wednesday, the 9th of August and notes 'some worthy Citizens of *Oxford* ... namely, *T. Gol. Jacke* of all Trades, W.G. a diligent zealous brother in warning and meeting at holy Conventicles, with many others meritorious brethren and sisters, who have forsaken *Oxford*, and their King, Religion, and Allegeance' (see CSC #42). The *T. Gol.* is likely a reference to Williams's surname ('Gulielmus' in Latin), and the reference to his having 'forsaken Oxford' probably alludes to his move to Abingdon when Charles I entered Oxford with his royal entourage.

    [3] 'Canes' here probably means long, thin sticks of tobacco.

    [4] 'Perspectives' here means 'spectacles' or 'eyeglasses', perhaps an allusion to the name of Williams's shop (see page 289 below).

    [5] 'Tub' was a term used contemptuously of a pulpit, usually by members of established churches about nonconformist pulpits. Tolmie (1977): 205, suggests that

Then being of his Dods bereft,
 and Cleavers all and some,
You may presume that there was left
 of Comforts never a Crum.
A chest of Cambricks[1] and Holland[2]
 was turn'd to a box of tinder,
His virgins tapers out were brand,
 the' Extinguishers could not hinder.

They that his Taffities[3] did seee,
 and various Ribbonds straight
Concluded that in burnt silks hee,
 was richly worth his weight:
His Hobby horses[5] erst so tame,
 some babes of grace might run,
A race upon them, now become
 Hot as the Steeds o' the' Sun.

The Mouse-traps, Fly-traps, and whole shelves
 of whips, with other some
Such dreadfull instruments themselves
 suffer'd a martyrdome:
But to conclude, the flame being done,
 some that were there did sweare,
Though Christ-tide were not yet begun,
 yet was Ashwednesday there.

Deare brethren, be not thou too hot,
 for if unto your harme
Your zeale like this take fire, I wot,[4]
 you'll wish 'twere but luke-warme.
God blesse the King the Queene and Issue,
 Nobles and Parliament,
And may all such affrightments misse you
 of the furious element.

And keep all from disasters,
And such as now good servants are,
May never prove bad masters.

FINIS

   The song is filled with numerous references to the varieties of things that would have been sold by a milliner/haberdasher, and alerts us to the success that Williams no doubt enjoyed as a merchant. More importantly, it helps us gain a better picture of Williams himself, who clearly had a reputation not only as a wealthy tradesman, but also as something of a religious zealot.

   Several rather obscure references to religious themes and ideas, which presumably were part and parcel of the Dissenter's world, are also contained in the song. A good example is the reference in stanza 3 to the 'pack' of sin which Thomas Williams was said to have carried on his back. The image of a 'burden on one's back' was well known in Puritan circles and was most famously taken up within John Bunyan's devotional classic *The Pilgrim's Progress* (1678), a book which was later so beloved by Baptists and other Dissenting groups of the day who were undergoing persecution. In *Pilgrim's*

---

the origin of the phrase goes back to January of 1639 when a lay-preacher named Samuel How preached in the Nag's Head Tavern in Coleman Street in London.

   [1] 'Cambrick' was a fine white linen imported from Cambray in Flanders.

   [2] 'Holland' is a linen fabric that comes from the province of Holland in what is now known as The Netherlands.

   [3] 'Taffities' refers to fine fabrics, generally made out of silk, or a wool and silk blend.

   [4] 'Wot' here means 'know'.

   [5] 'Hobby horses' refers to child's toys made out of a stick with a horse's head attached.

Progress this image refers to an incident early on in the story where the pilgrim Christian is weighed down by the burden of sin on his back. He must travel through life thus burdened until such time as he finds that he is released by the saving work of Christ and his burden falls from his back, tumbles down the hill of Calvary and is swallowed up by an open tomb.

Significantly, a number of published books are alluded to in stanzas 7 and 8. In effect, the overall impression gained here is of the library of a religiously-minded reader, one who is given over to collecting books of a devotional and pietistic nature. For example, in stanza 7 there is mention made to 'the Practice ... of Pietie'. This is probably a reference to a book entitled *The Practise of Pietie* by Lewis Bayly (1575-1631). Bayly was the Bishop of Bangor and first published this popular devotional volume early in his career.[1] Similarly, the stanza mentions 'St. Katherine Stubs' (or Stubbs). This is a reference to the wife of a man named Philip Stubbs, a young woman who died at the age of twenty-one and was memorialised by a tract first published by her husband in 1591 (the exact date of her death is unknown).[2] The tract was entitled *Christial Glas for Christian Women: contayning a most excellent Discourse of the Godly Life and Christian Death of Mrs. Katherine Stubbs*, and the copyright went through several different publishers up to 1689. The little quarto volume served as popular devotional reading in some quarters, although it was satirized by William Cartwright in 1635.[3] The author of the song 'Zeale over-heated' appears to have another dig at the religious beliefs of the Anabaptists and other Dissenters when he describes her as *Saint* Katherine Stubbs Presumably he would have been fully aware that they would have objected most vehemently against the very notion of the worship of the saints, since that was a matter associated with both the Roman Catholic church and the Church of England.

Stanza 8 similarly contains other allusions to writers of devotional literature, including mention of Williams being 'bereft' of his 'Dods' and 'Cleavers'. This is a veiled reference to the work of two Puritan writers from Oxfordshire, John Dod (1550-1645) and Robert Cleaver (1562-1625) who jointly authored a number of popular theological books. Perhaps the most important was *A Godly Form of Household Government for the Ordering of Private Families, According to the Direction of God's Word* (first published in 1598 but frequently reprinted in the first half of the 17th century). Both Dod and Cleaver were known as preachers renowned for their nonconformity. Finally, the reference in stanza 8 to 'of Comforts never a Crum' is also worth noting. It probably refers to the popular devotional book by the London bookseller Michael Spark (c. 1586-1653) entitled *The Crums of Comfort with Godly Prayers* (1628). This was a hugely successful book, and effectively functioned

---

[1] The date of the first edition is unknown, but the second edition is dated 1612.

[2] See Bliss (1813): 1.646.

[3] Green (2000): 415-6, notes that this popular tract went through thirty editions between the 1590s and the 1690s. He suggests that the shortness of the tract (only twenty quarto pages) contributed to its popularity. Also see Watt (1991): 267, 282-3.

as a Dissenter's alternative to the official daily prayer books sanctioned by the Church of England.

Similar anti-establishment beliefs are projected onto Williams and the Dissenters by the reference to the incineration of a Geneva Bible in stanzas 6 and 7. The Geneva Bible was a favourite translation among Dissenters,[1] and the two stanzas seem to infer that Williams could have better have accepted the loss of the Bible in the fire that destroyed his shop if it had been a copy which had been bound with a copy of the Apocrypha (used by Catholics and Anglicans), or a copy of *The Book of Common Prayer*.[2] Meanwhile, the satirical reference to 'Ashwednesday' in stanza 11 may also be directed against Dissenters who would have frowned on such celebrations within the liturgical calendar. Here we are presented with the amusing image of a Dissenting shopkeeper being forced by the wholesale destruction of his shop to recognize, amidst the ashes, the very high-church religious traditions he rejected. A similar comment can be made about the mention of 'Purgatory' in stanza 1, and perhaps the mention of 'Virgin Tapers' in stanza 8. The 'Virgin Tapers' is probably a reference to candles which were bought by customers and then lit and offered to the Virgin Mary in an act of religious worship. This would have smacked of idolatry to many of the Dissenters and perhaps there is a none-too-subtle jibe at Williams' hypocrisy in selling the candles in the first place. In any event, the stanza suggests that the candles were completely consumed and that not even the metal 'Extinguishers', the candle snifters usually employed to put them out, were of any use in fighting the fire.

Unfortunately, the exact date of the fire that destroyed Williams's shop is unknown. It appears from the mention of 'Christide' in stanza 4 and 'Christmas' in stanza 10 that it happened sometime in December, probably in 1641, just prior to the publication of the pamphlet in 1642. Little is known for certain about the shop that Williams owned, or what it was called. From the references in stanzas 6 and 11 it could be inferred that it was called *The Exchange*, although a more likely possibility is that it was called *The Spectacles*. Perhaps the best piece of evidence supporting this idea is the fact that the trade token issued by Williams in the 1650s has as its obverse an image of a pair of spectacles. The inscriptions on the front and back of these tokens together read 'Tho[mas] Williams At Y^e Spectacles in Oxon'.[3]

---

[1] When, in 1643, Edmund Calamy compiled biblical verses in order to publish the *Souldier's Pocket Bible* for the use of troops within the Commonwealth army, it was the Geneva Bible translation that he used.

[2] It was not uncommon for book owners to have all three volumes bound together.

[3] For more on the token, see Thompson and Dickinson (1993): Plate 32, #3757 and #3758; Leeds (1923): 450-451; Dickinson (1986): 180, #185. Whittet (1986): 111, attributes the token to Thomas Williams, the apothecary who died in 1668, but this is unlikely.

Illustration #9: Thomas Williams Trade Token

This leads us to consider again the version of the song 'Zeale over-heated' which was published by Thomas Weaver in his *Songs and Poems of Love and Drollery* (1654). [1] In the main, Weaver's version corresponds fairly closely to the 1642 version, although there are a number of stylistic alterations of spelling and changes in the meter and phrasing of some of the lines. In terms of presentation, the version from 1654 sets out the song in 24 four-verse stanzas instead of 12 eight-verse stanzas; it also numbers the stanzas. [2] More importantly, there are one or two significant changes to the song, which reflect the fact that it was being re-published twelve years after the original, and the political landscape had changed dramatically since 1642. The clearest example of this is found in the stanza with which the song ends. The final four lines are altogether different from those in the 1642 version; the concluding stanza reads:

> God blesse this Land, and keep it Aye
>   Against all that oppose:
> And let the Supream head bear sway
>   In stead o' th' Supream nose.

This means that the reference to the monarchy ('God bless the King, the Queen and Issue') in the 1642 version is replaced by a negative allusion to Oliver Cromwell (the 'Supream nose'). No doubt this is a cheap shot at Cromwell's physiognomy and the fact that he had a large, bulbous nose. [3] The

---

[1] The song is found on pages 21-27 of the book. However, there is a pagination error that occurs throughout the seven pages of the song itself, with the page numbers given at the top of the pages running in the order 21, 18, 19, 24, 25, 22, 23. This is probably just an error in the process of printing and folding the pages of the original, for the order of the numbered stanzas of the song is correct and the pagination picks up again on page 28 and continues without error for the rest of the book.

[2] The full text of this is given in CSC #200a.

[3] See Underdown (1996): 101. It may also be a reference to the large nose of Henry Langley, one of the Presbyterian preachers sent to Oxford, by the Parliamentary party to ensure sound religious teaching was taking place within the University. In a sarcastic tract published in 1648 entitled *An Owl at Athens: Or, A True Relation of the Enterance*

alteration makes sense given the fact that the song was being reworked in 1654
to address the changed political circumstances of this later time.

Interestingly, a notebook in the Bodleian Library in Oxford has survived
which also is of relevance at this point. It contains a version of the song which
was copied out in longhand. The notebook was once owned by Thomas
Weaver, and contains some personal notes about the birth of members of
Weaver's family between 1650-62.[1] However, the final lines of the song in the
notebook are different from the printed version of 1654. The final lines in the
notebook version, which correspond to stanza 24 cited above, read:

> From Rome, from Amsterdam & Spain
>   God blesse our King & Nation
> And may he still this Church maintaine
>   'Gainst Clubbes of Reformation.

In terms of political sentiment both of these re-workings of the original 1642
ending of the song are clearly expressive of an avowedly royalist stance. They
lament the recent triumph of the Parliamentary forces and wait for the
restoration of the monarchy and the return of the Church of England to its
place of ecclesiastical privilege. As the 1654 version puts it, the loyal royalists
long for a time when 'the Supream head', the exiled king Charles II, will once
again 'bear sway'.

As to the question why the song was re-published eleven years after it had
first appeared, the answer sees quite obvious: it is because the subject of the
song, Williams the milliner, had been elected Mayor of the city of Oxford.[2]
Then as now, there is no better way to deflate a politician's career, and burst
the bubble of his ego, than to drag up some unflattering incident from the past
and make it the object of public scrutiny. In any event, the re-publication of
the song 'Zeal Overheated' in 1654 caused something of a stir within the
religiously-minded authorities in Oxford city. Not only did Thomas Weaver's
Songs and Poems of Love and Drollery contain several songs and poems which
bordered on being pornographic,[3] but also several that were considered

---

of the Earle of Pembroke into Oxford, April xi. 1648, Langley is lampooned as taking
part in a public parade. He is introduced into the ceremonies with these lines:
>   Th' next thing was *Langley's Nose* that came in sight,
>   (Pox tak't I lost halfe th'e Show; that stood ith' light)

[1] *MS Rawlinson poet 211*, folios 78 recto–80 verso. A note on the opening page of
the notebook suggests that it was the property of one Charles Williams in 1646; this
probably indicates that Williams owned the book and had it bound in calf-skin. How it
became to be owned by Thomas Weaver is unknown.

[2] It may also have something to do with the fact that John Taylor, the supposed
author of the original tract to which the song was appended, died in 1653. Perhaps
Thomas Weaver felt free to reprint the piece once the original author had passed away.

[3] There are several bawdy songs, such as 'To Jean of Chippen-Norton' which
describes attempts to get a maiden to surrender her virginity, and 'A Dialogue Betwixt a
Cavalier and a Lady, Upon Occasion of a sudden Alarm in the Night' which describes a

downright seditious.   Eventually the anonymous author of the work was identified as Thomas Weaver and he was prosecuted by the city authorities because the work was considered ungodly and libellous.   According to Anthony Wood, the judge of the trial, upon reading some of the verses within the book, declared Weaver to be a scholar and a wit, and the jury eventually brought in a verdict of 'Not Guilty'.[1] Incidentally, it is to Anthony Wood's entry on Thomas Weaver in his *Athenae Oxonienses* that we owe confirmatory identification of Thomas Williams as the subject of the song. Wood notes in this entry that 'The said religious brother was Tho[mas] Williams a milliner living sometime against Allsaints church where holy Cornish teached'.[2]

A measure of the song's popularity is to be seen by the fact that William Hicks re-published it in his *Oxford Drollery, Being New Poems and Songs* (1671).[3] The substance of the twenty-four stanzas of the song is the same as the 1654 version published by Thomas Weaver; only small alterations in spelling and punctuation are made. However, the title 'Zeal Overheated' is not given in this version, nor is the opening paragraph describing its contents and the notice that it is to be sung to the tune of 'Chevy-Chase'.[4] In other respects, Hicks' version is taken straight from that published by Weaver seventeen years before.

It looks as the memory of the fire in Christmas of 1641 remained with Williams for years to come. There is no direct mention of the fire which destroyed Williams's shop within the City Council records, although there is an intriguing reference to a decision made on 3 January 1642 to repair the city's fire fighting equipment 'in the tyme of anie suddden fier'.[5] This focused upon the repairing of hooks used to pull down burning houses and the provision of two ladders emergency ladders to be kept in a public place. It looks as if the fire, which proved so disastrous to Williams and his business, here galvanized the City Council into action. In addition, the city records for 7 August 1654 record that Williams, then Mayor, again raised the matter of 'ye buyeing of An Engine for ye Quenching of Fire' in the City and suburbs', to the City Council.[6] Another indication of how concerned the city was about the

---

woman's attempts to use sexual favours to prevent a soldier from leaving to fight for the King in the royalist cause.

[1] *Athenae Oxonienses, Volume 2* (1692): 212-213 = CSC #651. Weaver died on 3 January 1662.

[2] The reference is important because it helps establish that Thomas Williams ran his milliner's business from his home. Cornish is also discussed briefly in *Athenae Oxonienses, Volume 2* (1692): 771 = CSC #653. Interestingly, Kennett (1699): 13, mentions the reference to Cornish contained within the song 'Zeal Overheated' in his published eulogy for the preacher.

[3] It appears in 'Part III: Old Songs made in Oxford, many years since', pages 132-136.

[4] Fox (1998): 1-5, discusses the history of this extremely popular tune.

[5] *City Council Proceedings – 1629-1663* (A.5.7), folio 121 recto = CSC #29. This is the first council meeting held after the fire in the preceding December.

[6] *City Council Proceedings – 1629-1663* (A.5.7), folio 221 recto = CSC #187.

threat of fire is found in the town clerk's records for a meeting in the Guildhall of Oxford, held on 23 March 1655. This mentions a proposal put forward by John Nixon, who succeeded Williams as Mayor, for the purchase of a fire-engine which was to be paid for by a special city-wide tax.[1] It looks as if Williams, as a City Councilman, helped guide this particular item through the agenda of the finance committee of the City Council; one could hardly argue with a man who had once watched his own shop go up in flames.[2]

Unfortunately, as noted above, the last few years of Williams's life are all but shrouded in mystery, and he disappears from the scene rather dramatically after his appearance before the ecclesiastical court in December of 1671. Indeed, he dies less than three years later, and the only record of these final years is his last will and testament which is dated 12 January 1674.[3] According to All Saints' parish records Thomas Williams was buried on 5 March 1674;[4] sadly, it appears his son John, who had apprenticed with his father and was apparently being groomed to take over the milliner's business in the High Street, died the year before him and was buried on 23 June 1673.[5] Interestingly, another son, Benjamin, was specifically named within Thomas Williams's will; it appears that he was the only child who survived his father. Benjamin, was bequeathed £100 provided that (as his father put it) 'the Goods and Wares of my shopp doe amount to the sum[m]e of Fyve hundred Pownds'. Thomas Williams's widow Alice was named as the executrix and main benefactor within the will, although what happened to her immediately after the death of her husband is unknown. She appears to have moved to the village of Cutteslowe outside Oxford, perhaps living with family members or friends there until her death in November of 1699.[6] Somewhat curiously, in his will Williams leaves £5 to the Oxford surgeon Theophilus Poynter, describing him as 'my sonn in law'. This suggests that Poynter had married a daughter of Thomas Williams, probably his daughter Sarah who was born in 1642. No record of their marriage appears to have survived, and she probably

---

[1] *Civil War Charities and General Minutes – 1645-1695* (E.4.6), folio 11 recto. No doubt the great fire on 1644, which burned a good portion of the western part of the city, also helped contribute to the concern here. Porter (1984): 289-300, provides an overview. Martin Lluelyn's poem 'A Curse to Vulcan', first published in 1646 within his *Men-Miracles, with Other Poems*, offers some important details.

[2] By 1661 there were *three* fire engines in the city with special consideration taken for their placement and storage (*City Council Proceedings – 1629-1663* (A.5.7), folio 291 verso). Porter (1985): 251-255, discusses the fire regulations put into efffect in Oxford in 1671.

[3] *PCC – Will of Thomas Williams* (PROB 11/345), folios 318 verso-319 recto) = CSC #523a. The will was probated on 8 July 1674.

[4] *Parish Register of All Saints' – 1559-1810* (Par 189/1/R1/1), folio 98 verso.

[5] He was buried on 23 June 1673 (*Parish Register of All Saints' – 1559-1810* (Par 189/1/R1/1), folio 98 verso.

[6] She was buried on 5 November 1699 (*Parish Register of St Mary the Virgin – 1678-1812* (Par 209/1/R1/4), page 23.

died soon after the marriage, for the widower Theophilus Poynter married again in the summer of 1664. His second wife was Mary Crips and the couple had at least five or six children.[1] Poynter's will, which is dated 21 August 1706 and was probated on 13 March 1709, named his second wife Mary as his executor.[2] One other intriguing incident involving Theophilus Poynter is worth noting here. Poynter is recorded as having surrendered his 'Freedom of the city' of Oxford to the City Council on 28 September 1666; the circumstances of this unusual action are unclear, although it may have something to do with a clash with the prevailing Anglican establishment over religious matters.[3] Poynter certainly came from a strongly pietistic family, if the sentiments expressed in the will of his father John Poynter are anything to go by. He signed and sealed his will on 26 September 1683, describing himself as 'John Poynter the elder of the University of Oxford, Minister of God's word'. At the end of the will, Poynter issued an exhortation to his sons:

> And I doe beseech all my said upon my knees by all the endearing mercies of God and merits of Jesus Christ to feare and obey God and keep his Sabbaths and goe to heare his word preached and Sacraments administered constantly and read the Sacred Scriptures and pray in their families Morning and evening and likewise by themselves morning and evening and labour to bee rooted and built up in Jesus Christ and to live in Charity and to Councell poore Timothy my loveing and afflicted sonne to helpe him.[4]

It looks as if Thomas Williams maintained his contacts with the Baptists of Oxford until the very end of his life. Within his will he named the glover Lawrence King, for many years his neighbour along the High Street in All Saints' parish, as one of the two overseers of the document, describing him as 'my loving freind'.[5]

---

[1] The Poll Tax entry for 1667 shows Theophilus Poynter paying £1 5s in taxes for himself, his wife, one unnamed child, and a servant girl named Elizabeth Fox while living in the parish of St Michael-at-the-Northgate (*Poll Tax of 1667* (P.5.7), folio 54 verso). It is possible that the unnamed child was from his first wife Sarah. Interestingly, the parish register entry for his second daughter, also named Sarah, records her birth rather than her baptism (*Parish Register of St Michael-at-the-Northgate – 1653-1683* (Par 211/1/R1/2), folio 3 verso). Perhaps this is an indication of Poynter's own Nonconformity.

[2] *PCC – Will of Theophilus Poynter* (PROB 11/514), folios 225 verso-229 recto. Poynter and members of his family were buried in the parish church of Saint Mary the Virgin (see CSC #682a for details).

[3] *City Council Proceedings – 1663-1701* (B.5.1), folio 41 recto.

[4] *PCC – Will of John Poynter* (PROB 11/375), folio 254 verso; the will was probated on 17 March 1684.

[5] The other overseer was the maltster John Hitch, who was probably Williams's step-son, the son of his second wife Alice. John Hitch's will, which is dated 23 January 1688, names 'Alice Williams of Cutslow in the County of Oxon, Widow' as one of the beneficiaries of his properties in St Aldate's parish (*John Hitch* (OWPR 34/3/26)).

6. Tom Pun's House and the Antiquated Dancing School:

The Search for Early Baptist Meeting Houses

Illustration # 10: Record of the Oxford City lease granted to Thomas Ayres on 11 July 1642 for a piece of land in a derelict area in the west of the city known as Broken Hayes. Here Ayres built a house that was used as a meeting place by Baptists and other Dissenters. The document is part of the Oxford City archives (*Oxford City Ledgers – 1636-1675* (D.5.6) folio 48 verso).

6. Tom Pun's House and the Antiquated Dancing School:

The Search for Early Baptist Meeting Houses

Anthony Wood, the 17th-century antiquarian and diarist, whose works are so important for a study of Oxford during this period, mentions Baptists (whom he generally describes as 'Anabaptists') at a number of points. Wood was an ardent Anglican royalist and his opinions of (Ana)Baptists are coloured accordingly. Thus, he lumps them together with Quakers and describes them as a 'fanatick party', an 'unstable people', and 'notorious sectaries'.[1] Most of Wood's references to Baptists have been combed over by historians over the years, but two intriguing suggestions made by Wood have not yet received the attention they deserve. The first concerns a house associated with a man named Tom Ayres (or Aires), otherwise known as Tom Pun; the second concerns an upper-story room in a property just outside the north gate which was at one time used as a dancing-school.

I will discuss both of these properties in turn, as they were places where Wood suggests Baptists and other Dissenters in Oxford met to hold their religious services together. These two properties are best seen as complementary to the private homes of Richard Tidmarsh and Lawrence King, where Baptist conventiclers met beginning in the 1650s. In the course of the discussion a number of supportive manuscripts and publications will be used to help fill out the overall picture. This allows a fuller understanding not only of where and when these places were established as Dissenting meeting houses, but how the Dissenters who worshipped in them were perceived by others.

A. Tom Pun's House in Thamestreet along Broken Hayes

Although Tom (Pun) Ayres remains an elusive figure, some details about him can be gleaned from surviving sources. He was baptized on 24 May 1607 in the parish church of Radley in Berkshire; his father's name was also Thomas.

---

[1] *MS Wood F 1*, page 1123 ('fanatic party'); *MS Wood F 31*, folio 7 verso ('Anabaptists, Quakers & such like unstable people'); *MS Tanner 102, Part 2*, folio 80 recto ('Anabaptists & phanaticks'); *MS Wood F 31*, folio 14 recto ('Anabaptists and other notorious sectaries').

There is record of his seven-year apprenticeship to the baker William Baylie which dates to 1622.[1]   Little is known of Ayres's family circumstances, although there is record of his marriage to his wife Elizabeth on 29 January 1629.[2]   The couple apparently had several children, including an unnamed daughter, a son whose name was Thomas,[3] and another son whose name was John.   Sadly, the couple were not destined to share a long life together. Anthony Wood mentions in passing that Tom (Pun) Ayres was buried in the churchyard of Saint Mary the Virgin on 8 September 1643, and his burial is duly recorded in the parish register for that date.[4]   Elizabeth died and was buried in the parish church of Saint Mary's on 14 April 1645.[5]   It is unknown how Tom Ayres died; perhaps he was a victim of one of the many plagues to which Oxford was prone during the early 1640s.[6]   One record of Ayres taking on an apprentice has survived.   This involved a William Baselye who was enrolled in a standard seven-year contract on 4 October 1642; within this contract Tom Ayres is described as a 'yeoman'.[7]   However, it is the property associated with Tom (Pun) Ayres that is of most concern for this investigation into Oxford's Dissenters.

Anthony Wood has an intriguing remark within which his comments about the publication of *The Act of Toleration* on 15 March 1672.   He records in his diary entry for that day that the 'fanaticks (were) brisk about it', and then goes on to note meetings of the 'presbyter[ians] & Anabap[tists] in Tom Puns h[ou]se in brokenhayes'.[8]   Interestingly, Wood also mentions Tom (Pun) Ayres

---

[1] *Civic Enrolments – 1613-1640* (L.5.2), folio 101 recto.

[2] *Parish Register of St Martin's – 1569-1705* (Par 207/1/R1/2), folio 69 recto; the entry does not give the bride's surname.

[3] *MS Wood F 29a*, folio 79 recto. Thomas Ayres junior is listed in the parish of St Peter-in-the-Bailey and paid 5d in the tax of 24 June 1667 (*War Taxes – 1667-1668* (P.5.8), folio 8 recto).

[4] *MS Wood F 29a*, folio 79 recto; *Parish Register of St Mary the Virgin – 1599-1694* (Par 209/1/R1/1), page 39.

[5] *Parish Register of St Mary the Virgin – 1599-1694* (Par 209/1/R1/1), page 42. Margaret Rose, a servant of Tom Ayres, died and was buried on 24 September 1641 (*Parish Register of St Mary the Virgin – 1599-1694* (Par 209/1/R1/1), page 37).

[6] The so-called '*morbus campestris*', probably a cholera epidemic, took many lives during August-September of 1643, including Sir William Pennyman, one of Charles I's military leaders and the Governor of Oxford at the time of his death on 22 August 1643 (see Varley (1937): 145).   For a detailed record of the impact of the plague upon one parish church within the city, see Fletcher (1896): 45-9, 137-9. He records that in the Church of St, Martin's (Carfax) ninety burials were recorded between 26 March 1643 and 17 March 1644, many of them soldiers; the average number of funerals per year in that parish church prior to 1643 was about 15.

[7] *Civic Enrolments – 1639-1662* (L.5.3), folio 28 verso = CSC #37; the apprenticeship contract is dated to commence on 5 October 1642.

[8] *MS Wood Diaries 16*, folio 14 recto = CSC #503.   A similar comment is made by Wood about the subsequent *Act of Toleration* granted to Dissenters in July of 1689: 'In the beg[inning] of this month/a discourse of a toleration/ to be given to Dissenters/ the Anabaptists are glad to receive it' (*MS Wood Diaries 30*, folio 42 recto).

at an earlier point in his history of the city of Oxford. He discusses the attempt to extend George Lane (the present George Street) in the direction of High Bridge by clearing the ground around a derelict area outside the city walls known as Broken Hayes (the Gloucester Green area presently occupied by the Apollo Theatre, the Odeon Cinema and the Old Fire Station). In this connection Wood says that Ayres was among those who built 'fair free stone houses' on the cleared ground in 1641.[1] The point here is that in 1672 Baptists and other Dissenters were meeting in the house of one Tom (Pun) Ayres in Broken Hayes, a building which, apparently, had been in existence for thirty years or so. Fortunately, several records relating to Ayres's involvement with this property in Broken Hayes and his erection of a dwelling on it are extant. The matter is first mentioned in a City Council minute dated 30 July 1641 where it is agreed that Ayres be granted a forty-year lease on 'a peece of ground' for the yearly rent of twelve pence;[2] the lease was then sealed with the city seal on 6 September 1641.[3] Ayres built a house on this site and a lease was duly entered into the city ledger books on 30 July 1642.[4] The City Council minutes record that a year later, on 19 September 1642, Ayres again petitioned for an additional piece of ground adjoining his newly erected house.[5] On 3 October 1642 the City Council agreed to allow him some additional land on the east side of his house in exchange for some of his property to the north.[6] Apparently Ayres erected another building on this site, for in some of the subsequent records there is mention of him having 'two tenements'.[7] It appears that there was some move to pull down these houses in 1643, or at least Ayres's tenements are mentioned as among those properties marked for demolition in an obscure note contained in a 17th-century

---

[1] *MS Wood F 29a*, folio 79 recto = CSC #28. There is record dated to 24 September 1641 to the Oxford City Council agreeing to pay £20 out of its treasury for making the highway through Broken Hayes and George Lane (*City Council Proceedings – 1629-1663* (A.5.7), folio 118 recto.

[2] *City Council Proceedings – 1629-1663* (A.5.7), folio 115 verso = CSC #26.

[3] *City Council Proceedings – 1629-1663* (A.5.7), folio 117 recto = CSC #27. There are several records of Ayres paying taxes, probably in connection with this property in Broken Hayes as part of the north-east ward of the city. Two subsidies granted by Parliament to Charles I in order to help pay for his army specifically mention Ayres in this regard. The entries are for 'Thomas Ayres in lands' and records payments of £1 8*s* which were collected on 20 March 1641 (*Lay Subsidy of 10-23 December 1640* (E 179/164/477)), 30 April 1641 (*Lay Subsidy of 10-23 December 1640* (E 179/164/495)), and 6 December 1641 (*Lay Subsidy of 6 December 1641* (B.1.4d)). See Jurkowski, Smith and Crook (1998): 190-2, for details of these subsidies.

[4] *Oxford City Ledgers – 1636-1675* (D.5.6), folios 48 verso–50 recto = CSC #31.

[5] *City Council Proceedings – 1629-1663* (A.5.7), folios 123 verso–124 recto = CSC #35.

[6] *City Council Proceedings – 1629-1663* (A.5.7), folio 125 recto = CSC #36.

[7] See CSC #546 for their probable location in the area of Broken Hayes in David Loggan's *Oxonia Illustrata* (1675).

manuscript within the Bodleian entitled *The Siege of Oxford*.[1] However, this demolition was not carried out, and the stone houses Ayres built in 1642 were sturdy enough to have survived the great fire of 1644 which consumed much of the surrounding area.[2]

There are several minutes from the City Council records from 1655 which refer to Ayres's houses and property in Broken Hayes, all of which passed on to his son John. Viewers were appointed to examine the property on 22 March 1655 in order that appropriate levels of fines could be set.[3] On 20 July 1655 it was agreed that John Ayres be granted a new lease, which not only brought several pieces of land under a single leasing arrangement, but also required that new buildings be erected within seven years.[4] John Ayres, who is described in the lease documents as a 'Gentleman' from London, signed the indenture on 30 August 1655, and on 4 September 1655 the City Council agreed that the leases for these arrangements were to be sealed.[5] According to Anthony Wood, the Ayres's' houses in Broken Hayes stood until 1691 when the stone fronts, which were among 'the forefront of Oxford' at the time they were built, were removed and wooden ('paper') buildings erected in their place.[6] This much seems clear enough; however, matters are slightly complicated by the fact that Tom (Pun) Ayres is also associated with another property in an adjoining parish.

It seems that Ayres made his living as a victualler and that he rented a property in the parish of St Mary Magdalen which was leased by the city to John Treadwell, a lease which commenced on 23 December 1640.[7] This rented house was located outside the city walls to the north in the area now occupied by the Clarendon Building, just east of the Sheldonian Theatre. City records show that the rental for this victualler's property was renewed in a lease granted to John Ovey on 16 June 1649, but also state that it was hitherto occupied by the victualler Edward Wise, suggesting that the previous victualler Thomas Ayres had died.[8] The property appears to have changed hands several more times in rapid succession after that. The city of Oxford granted a forty-year lease to Thomas Wood, a surgeon, on 19 December 1664; he passed on the lease to Anthony Hall, a vintner, on 13 September 1667; Hall promptly conveyed it to the University on 23 December 1667.[9] Once it was in the

---

[1] *MS ADD d. 114*, folio 12 recto = CSC #40.

[2] See Porter (1984): 289-300, for more on this fire, which swept through a substantial part of the western part of the city.

[3] *City Council Proceedings – 1629-1663* (A.5.7), folio 225 verso = CSC #205.

[4] *City Council Proceedings – 1629-1663* (A.5.7), folio 226 recto = CSC #217.

[5] *Oxford City Ledgers – 1636-1675* (D.5.6), pages 172-174 = CSC #222; *City Council Proceedings – 1629-1663* (A.5.7), folio 227 recto.

[6] *MS Wood F 29a*, folio 78 verso.

[7] *Oxford City Ledgers – 1636-1675* (D.5.6), folios 45 verso–46 verso.

[8] *Oxford City Ledgers – 1636-1675* (D.5.6), folios 103 recto–104 recto.

[9] Salter (1926): 296. Also see Madan (1931): xxxiv-xxxv. Anthony Hall issued trade tokens as a means of promoting his vintner's business (see Leeds (1923): 405-7; Dickinson (1986): 179, #137).

University's hands again, the fate of the property was sealed in a sense, for it was demolished in order to make way for the erection of the Clarendon Building in 1712. What is interesting about all of this is the fact that Anthony Wood specifically mentions the property, calling it 'Tom Pun's house', in his diary entry for 22 October 1669.[1] He does this while discussing the construction of the Sheldonian Theatre, a major building project which was going on at the time. The key point is that geographically this is quite a distance from the Broken Hayes area to the west. How are these details about Thomas Ayres's property arrangements to be reconciled?

The simplest way is to assume that in 1641 Thomas (Pun) Ayres began to construct a second house in Broken Hayes which was a couple of hundred yards west of where he ran his victualler's business (the Clarendon Building site).[2] If this is correct, then this *second* house was the one being used by Presbyterians and Anabaptists a generation later in 1672, and the building was still so identified with its builder that it was known simply as 'Tom Pun's house' even though Ayres himself had died some 29 years before. Apparently, the son, John Ayres, chose *not* to continue in the family business after his father died in 1643, but was content to allow it to be taken over by the victualler Edward Wise (as the leasing arrangements noted above state). Why such a decision was made, no doubt, has something to do with the fact that Edward Wise had married Elizabeth, the widow of Tom Ayres, although (as noted) she was not to live more than a year or two after the marriage.[3] Nevertheless, we are still left with the curious fact that the house in which the religious meetings were going on is described by Anthony Wood as 'Tom Pun's house' many years later. It is the persistence of the association of the house with the name of Thomas (Pun) Ayres which is remarkable, especially when it is remembered that Anthony Wood himself was editing his diaries even later, probably in the 1690s. We will probably never know for certain at what point the Ayres's house in Broken Hayes began to be used for religious meetings, or to what extent John Ayres, the lease-holder, supported the

---

[1] *MS Wood Diaries 13*, folio 26 recto. Elsewhere Wood describes this house of Tom Pun as 'Hall's house, behind and northward of the schoole' (*Tanner MS 102, Part 1*, folio 121 verso).

[2] Salter (1926): 294, apparently confuses this victualler's property with Thomas Ayres' house in Broken Hayes, suggesting, 'In Anthony Wood's time it was commonly known as Tom Pun's house.' Having arrived at the conclusion that there were two properties associated with the name of Tom Pun in 17th-century Oxford, I was pleasantly surprised to discover that Colvin (1979): 416, came to the same conclusion some years ago. She does not pursue the implication of this as far as the establishment of a conventicle in the early 1640s, however.

[3] *City Council Proceedings – 1629-1663* (A.5.7), folio 147 verso. Mention of the marriage is made in connection with the City Council's decision on 11 August 1646 to grant citizenship to Edward Wise; no date is given for the marriage itself. Wise paid the relevant fees and swore his oath on 28 August 1646 (*City Council Proceedings – 1629-1663* (A.5.7), folio 148 verso).

Dissenters' cause by allowing such use.[1] However, there are some intriguing suggestions that it may have been very early, perhaps in the early 1640s, soon after the house was built.

One other intriguing story can be added at this point to support the suggestion that Tom (Pun) Ayres' house may have been a gathering point for Dissenters as early as 1641-2. This is a story contained in a pamphlet entitled *True and New Newes with an example from Warwick Castle, and also other parts, especially upon the anti-round-heads*, first published in August of 1642. The story was then slightly re-worked and printed in John Vicars's *A Looking-glass for Malignants, or God's hand against God-haters* (1643), and copied out from there in full by Anthony Wood and pasted into one of his manuscripts. The story, as found in Wood's copy, is as follows:

> Also in ye parish of Holywell neare Oxon, one
> of the inhabitants of the same parish, being a
> most licentious and p[ro]phane fellow, set up a May-pole
> in the sum[m]er-time, 1641; & yt it might trans
> cend the vanities and impieties of other May-poles,
> he set upon this the picture of a man, in a
> tub, thereby (as he said) to describe a Roundhead.
> w[hi]ch picture, as it was credibly reported, he made
> in derision of a godly gentleman, a manciple
> of one of the Colleges in Oxon: and the reason why
> it must represent this gentleman, was, because
> he was truely religious and used repetition of ser
> mons, singing of psalmes, and other holy duties
> in his house. This picture being thus set up on ye
> May-pole, the said p[ro]phane fellow, the author of it,
> with his loose and licentious companions, making themselves
> mad-merry about it, at last must needs go shoot at
> the Roundhead upon it; and having for this ~~pup~~ purpose
> brought muskets with them & other pieces, one of them,
> being the servant of the chief master of this May-game,
> shot, & did hit the picture. At w[hi]ch the said Master
> did fall a laughing extreamly, & on a sudden
> sunke downe, falling into a sharp and terrible ~~coun~~
> convulsion fit, & so continued a long time after
> very sick & in great paine and misery: but whether
> he be since alive or dead, I am uncertaine. This
> relation I had confirmed to me by an honest yong gentle
> man, a scholar of Oxon, then resident in Oxon,
> & an eyewitness of most of it.[1]

---

[1] There are probate records dated 18 December 1663 relating to a John Eyeres the widower of Dorothy, also known as Dorothy Higgs, probably meaning an earlier marriage into the Higgs family (*Dorothy Eyers* (OWPR 164/5/1)). It is possible that Dorothy Higgs was related to Margaret Higgs, the mother of Lawrence King (see page 159 above).

Of course the story does not mention Tom (Pun) Ayres by name, or give any explicit details that would confirm beyond doubt that he was the person whose picture was drawn 'to describe a Roundhead'. On the other hand the date (the summer of 1641) and thr location (the parish of Hollywell) fit remarkably well, and the description of the ridiculed man as 'a manciple' for one of the Colleges in Oxford is exactly what we might expect of a victualler such as Tom (Pun) Ayres. In short, the story describes a man who had a reputation not only as a sympathizer of the Parliamentarian cause, but also as a devout and religious person who opened his house to religious meeting in which sermons were preached and psalms were sung. On this basis it is probable that this is a story about Tom (Pun) Ayres, a devoutly religious man with Parliamentarian leanings, whose newly-erected house in Broken Hayes continued in this pattern and eventually became a meeting-place for Dissenters.

Mention too should be made of another interesting tale from late 1642 or early 1643, this time involving a man named Francis Deane. This appears in a pamphlet entitled *The Arraignment, Tryall, Conviction, and Confession of Francis Deane ... and of John Faulkner ... for the Murther of ... Mr. Daniel*, published in London by Richard Harper in 1643.[2] Deane was involved in a tragic domestic dispute with the said Mr Daniel over the latter's treatment of his (Deane's) wife's sister. Daniel's intentions were less than honourable and the two men, who had been drinking heavily, got into a fight and Deane struck Daniel a fatal blow to the head. He was helped in disposing of the body by John Faulkner (who was thus an accomplice to the crime). The two men were eventually caught and tried in the Old Bailey in London on 13 April 1643; they were executed at the Tyburne four days later. Unfortunately, the pamphlet does not tell us exactly when the murder itself took place, but it does tell us that Deane went on the run after committing the deed. Given the date of the trial, we can infer that Deane was captured in early April and that the murder was committed in either late 1642 or early 1643. What is interesting for our consideration here is the fact that Deane ran away to Oxford in an attempt to escape justice. The pamphlet reports Deane's last words as he confessed his crime just before he is executed. He said in this regard:

> I went after committing this fact to Oxford, where there being some which had formerly known mee, accused me to authority that I was an Anabaptist, for which I was forced to forsake that place, for feare of being discovered for my murder, or being questioned for my Religion. I confess I was baptized (a new) a month before this fact was acted, and after and for which I was grieved in minde and much troubled about it.

---

[1] *Wood MS F 1*, page 888. This is taken over virtually verbatim from Vicars (1643): 13. The earlier version of the story from *True and New Newes* (1642): 4-5, provides some additional details, as well as a drawing of the May-pole, with the picture of the Roundhead attached to it, on its title-page.

[2] Friedman (1993): 90-91, discusses the pamphlet.

The story raises some interesting questions, not the least of which is how Deane's acquaintances in Oxford came to *know* that he was an Anabaptist and make an accusation to that effect to the authorities.   Given the political circumstances of the time, it seems unlikely that Deane would have openly admitted to those who knew him in Oxford that he was an Anabaptist. Perhaps it was an inadvertent slip of the tongue on Deane's part. Or, as seems more likely, it was a deduction on the part of his former acquaintances based on the people that he met and associated with in Oxford once he had arrived there. Of course it is impossible to know for certain what transpired, but the very least we can glean from the story is that there was a common perception about, and a hostile reaction to, the 'Anabaptist' movement within Oxford when Deane was there in late 1642 or early 1643. Anabaptists were known to be active in the city, and were readily identified as such by others. Perhaps Deane sought some assistance for his plight by going to Tom Pun's house and some of his fellow Dissenters there, people already well-known in Oxford for their sectarian views and having to be watchful about how they conducted themselves. In the end, as Deane relates, he needed to flee from Oxford lest his true status as a murderer on the run be discovered.

All of which suggests it is *possible* (and it can never be more than a mere possibility) that Tom (Pun) Ayres' house along Thames Street in Broken Hayes was the first place in which Baptists began to meet in Oxford, or, more precisely, it was one conventicle where Baptists, Presbyterians, Independents and other Dissenters first began to gather together, perhaps as early as the beginning of the 1640s. As noted above, the house in Broken Hayes became a central meeting-point by early 1672, in the immediate aftermath of the issuing of *The Declaration of Indulgence*. Anthony Wood noted some of the key figures involved in this endeavour in a diary entry for 15 March 1672, notably Dr. Henry Langley, Henry Cornish, John Troughton, and Thomas Gilbert, whom he described as 'constant preachers in brokenhayes'.[1]

Three passages in Anthony Wood's *Athenae Oxonienses* (1692) are also relevant here, for they also provide details of the continuing co-operation between these Dissenting leaders in the 1670s. The entry for John Troughton, who was commonly regarded to be the best of the four preachers, specifically noted: 'the place where they held their meetings was in Thamestreet without the north gate, in an house which had been built a little before the civil war began, by Thomas Pun, alias Thomas Ayres.'[2] A related remark is found in connection with the entry on Thomas Gilbert within the *Athenae Oxonienses*, although it is noted that Gilbert, an Independent, was 'the worse preacher of

---

[1] *MS Wood Diaries 16*, folio 14 recto.
[2] *Athenae Oxonienses, Volume 2* (1692), page 511 = CSC #652. According to Anthony Wood (*MS Diaries 25*, folio 39 verso) Troughton died at the home of John Sheene in All Saints' parish on 20 August 1681. This establishes an interesting connection between Lawrence King and John Troughton as Dissenters; as noted above (page 108) King had served his apprenticeship under Sheene.

the four' divines who preached to the conventicle which met in Tom Pun's house in Thames-street.[1] An entry on Henry Cornish pertaining to the year 1649 is also important, for it confirmed his role as a Dissenting leader and preacher even earlier in the decade.[2] Wood noted that Cornish, an MA of New Inn Hall, left Oxford in 1642 when Charles I had entered the city, and joined the Parliamentary cause. Cornish returned to the city when it was occupied by Parliamentary forces and was an appointee of Oliver Cromwell and the Parliamentary Visitors. He was made a Bachelor of Divinity and a Canon of Christ Church in 1648, and attempts were later made to confer upon him the degree of Doctor of Divinity, but Cornish refused the conferral. Cornish died on Sunday, 22 December 1698 and the sermon at his funeral was given by John Ollyffe, rector of Denton, Buckinghamshire. This was later published by Bishop White Kennett as *Some Remarks on the Life, Death, and Burial of Mr. Henry Cornish, B.D.* (1699). Kennett (who was at one time Vice-Principal of St Edmund Hall) describes Cornish's attempts to hold together the divided Protestant church within the city:

> He never, in my hearing, railed at, or run down the Constitution of the Church; but pleaded calmly for Moderation, and Liberty of Conscience and bearing with One Another. He would often chuse to make, as it were, some Apology for keeping up a separate Meeting in Opposition to the Church. He would say, he was brought thither by the Invitation and Importunity of such, as He thought, good people. That it was not his Intention to keep them altogether from the Church; but should sometimes set them the Example of going thither himself. And He did at first resolve to begin and end his Public Exercises at such hours as should not interfere with the Solemn Service of the Church; but dismiss them from one place, to attend at the other.[3]

---

[1] Bliss (1820): 4.407 = CSC #688. Gilbert applied for a license to preach as a Congregationalist in 1672 (SP/29 320, page 190; on this, see Turner (1911): 2.829). He is said to have died at his home in St Ebbs at the age of 80 on 15 July 1694 (Bliss (1820): 4.408-9). Interestingly, Wood (1751): 26, records a joke that circulated in Oxford at the time of the Parliamentary visitation: 'In the year 1646, a little after the City of Oxford was surrendered to the Parliament Forces, were sent six Presbyterian Preachers from the Parliament to settle their Doctrine there; their names were: *Cornish* and *Langley*, two Fools; *Reynolds* and *Harris*, two Knaves, *Cheynell* and *Rabbi Wilkinson*, two Madmen.' A rude comment about Cheynell was printed in a pamphlet entitled *Midsummer-Moon, Or Lunacy-Rampant, Being a Character of Master Cheynell, the Arch Visitor of Oxford, and Mungrell-President of Saint John Baptists Colledge* (1648). Here the anonymous writer says (page 6): 'You may compare Cheynell to the Chymists *aqua Stygia* and him to their *terra damnata*. Hee'l shortly be a Baptist without a voice, and wheases already as if he fed on nothing but Locusts and Grasshoppers.'

[2] *Athenae Oxonienses, Volume 2* (1692), page 771 = CSC #653.

[3] Kennett (1699): 11. However, Bishop Kennett's negative remarks about some aspects of Cornish's stance on Nonconformity were deemed antagonistic enough to prompt John Ollyffe to publish a refutation in *A Sermon Preach'd at the Funeral of the Revd Mr. Henry Cornish, B.D.* (1699).

The Presbyterian Henry Cornish also figures as one of the preachers associated with the second property under discussion, the so-called 'antiquated dancing school'.

B. The 'Antiquated Dancing-School' outside North Gate

Over the years Baptist apologists and historians have often asserted that the Baptists in Oxford met in an 'antiquated dancing-school' which was located outside the north gate of the city.[1] Indeed, there are property records of just such a place dating to the 17th century, but these need to be considered carefully, for the tendency has been to confuse 'the antiquated dancing-school' with Wood's other references to Tom (Pun) Ayres' house in Thamestreet. Moreover, the implication of these ideas about an 'antiquated-dancing school', which ultimately derives from a couple of passages from Anthony Wood, is *not* what it is often made out to be. The relevant section of the first passage from Wood which mentions the 'dancing school' occurs in his discussion of the life of the Presbyterian preacher Henry Cornish. Cornish, at the time when Wood was working on his *Athenae Oxonienses* in 1691, had retired to Stanton Harcourt in Oxfordshire and was conducting an itinerant preaching ministry there. In Stanton Harcourt Cornish found a safe haven and a patron in the form of Sir Philip Harcourt, an influential man who supported the Dissenters' cause, aided no doubt by the fact that his first wife was the daughter of one of the Parliamentary generals of the Civil War, Sir William Waller. In fact, Cornish had a general license as a Presbyterian minister issued to him under the provision of Charles II's *The Declaration of Indulence* on 29 June 1672,[2] with a subsequent confirmation of the license dated 10 August 1672.[3] In any event, this was not the first time that Cornish had retreated to Stanton Harcourt; he went there years before in 1665 when the stipulations of *The Five Mile Act* necessitated his leaving Oxford (Stanton Harcourt lies nine miles west of Oxford, so it satisfied the geographical demands made within the *Act*). More importantly, Wood noted that, after William III came to the throne, Cornish began to 'preach in an antiquated dancing-school just without the

---

[1] Alden (1904): 8; Paintin (1913): 1. One suspects that this is a biased reading of the situation which is motivated in part by a desire to associate the site where Baptists first began to meet with the Alden & Co. Booksellers, a business concern with strong Baptist connections which occupied 35, Cornmarket Street (on the site of the former Bocardo prison) from 1884-1909. Stevens (1948): 8, similarly says that this old dancing school was on the site of 33-35, Cornmarket Street; however, he more correctly associates it with the Presbyterians in Oxford who were being led by Henry Cornish.

[2] SP 44/38A, page 191. The license was granted to Cornish as a 'preacher & general teacher'.

[3] SP 44/38A, page 228. There was also a license granted to Robert Rogers to be a Congregational teacher at his own house in Oxford on 10 August 1672.

north gate of Oxon, to which place many did usually resort.'[1] Wood went on to record that the meeting house was moved to Saint Ebbe's in 1691,[2] and there are tax records from the Window Tax of 1696 which show that the meeting-house was still in operation at that time.[3]

The second passage comes from an entry in Wood's *Diaries* dated February 1689. Again the historical context of the passage is the so-called 'Glorious Revolution' of 1688 in which William of Orange came to the throne. Wood commented:

> The prisbiterians upon this revolu
> tion grow high – preach
> in public – set up their preaching
> places. Mr. James his old dancing
> school without north gate they
> have made a preaching place.
> Mr [Henry] Cornish holds out.
>
> One [Richard] Stratton somtimes an
> Oxonian, afterwards a Nonconfor-
> mist min[iste]r, was sent for & added
> an assistant in June 1690.[4]

---

[1] *Athenae Oxonienses, Volume 2* (1692): 771 = CSC #653. See CSC #552 for its location in David Loggan's *Oxonia Illustrata* (1675).

[2] On the basis of this Stevens (1948): 8, says: 'In 1691 they moved to Anthony Hall's house in St. Ebbe's (probably next door to 20 Pembroke Street), which they converted into a meeting-house at some expense. Their minister until 1695 was Joshua Oldfield.' Although Stevens does not cite his sources for such a suggestion, it seems to be based on Wood's *Athenae Oxonienses*, together with the fact that Anthony Hall's home was licensed as a Presbyterian meeting-house on 9 December 1672 with Robert Pawlyn (Pawling) as a teacher based there (see SP/44 38A, page 278 = Turner (1911): 828) = CSC #514), and the record of the official certificate of damage done to the property of Protestant Dissenters by the riots in May of 1715 (this document is found within the *Special Commission of Inquiry – Exchequer* (E 178/6906); it is usefully summarized by Hoad (1994): 105-7). Three other points seem clear. First, that Joshua Oldfield was the minister of this predominantly Presbyterian congregation in St Ebbe's from 1691-4; second, that Baptists appear to have been meeting at *another* place, probably Richard Tidmarsh's house in the parish of St Thomas, by then in the possession of a John Francklyn (so Crosby (1740): 4.137-8, suggests, noting that the house was 'near the castle'); third, that Anthony Hall's son did not permit the renewal of the lease on his property after the riots of 1715 destroyed the meeting places of both the Baptists and the Presbyterians, a fact which directly led to the purchase of a suitable joint site for Dissenters to worship (i.e. the present location of New Road Baptist Church in Bonn Square).

[3] *Taxes – 1694-1746* (P.5.10), folios 52 verso and 59 verso. The latter is dated 22 April 1696 and records that 'The meeting house in St. Ebbs taken off ~~from~~ upon y[e] Window act being no dwelling house ___ 2s'.

[4] *MS Wood Diaries 33*, folio 11 recto. Wood later added a clarifying note about the time of Cornish's appointment: 'This was not till Nov[ember] 1690'. He also refers to

Three important points need to be made in connection with these two passages, which serve as the ultimate textual basis for traditions about the 'antiquated dancing school' which are so beloved by some Baptist historians. First of all, the comments by Wood are not about a *Baptist* meeting hall as such, but about a meeting hall of Dissenters in general. In other words, the public worship taking place within the 'antiquated dancing-school' refers to a wider body of religious believers than Baptists would sometimes like to admit. In short, it needs to be stressed that whatever was going on in the antiquated dancing-school, it was not exclusively a *Baptist* meeting as such (the terms 'Anabaptist' or 'Baptist' do not even appear in either of the passages from Wood's diaries cited). In addition, the implication of the passages is that the meetings were open and public, no doubt a reflection of the change of fortune which the coming of William III represented for Dissenters. Before 1688 Dissenters had been forced to meet in the safety of favourably disposed colleges,[1] or in private houses, such as the homes of Richard Tidmarsh, Lawrence King, and possibly Thomas Williams, or even Tom (Pun) Ayres. Once they met as illegal conventicles; now they were licensed gatherings. Everything was so out in the open that even a public place such as an 'antiquated dancing school' could be called into service as a place of worship for Dissenters.

Second, the satirical sub-text of the comments by Anthony Wood is generally unappreciated, if not lost altogether. Wood is not just making a comment about the purpose to which the building was originally put, but about the nature of the religious worship that was going on within it. In other words, he may be poking fun at the frenzied physical activity which took place in the (so-called) worship services. Wood describes it as 'an antiquated *dancing* school' because for him this is not true religious worship at all, but is to be equated with something as secular and frivolous as dancing, or as unspiritual and profane as carousing in a tavern. As noted in chapter 5 (page 286), this is precisely the kind of assessment which was made of Dissenters' worship within an intriguing poem entitled 'Zeal Overheated', written and published anonymously first in 1642, and then reworked in 1654 by an Oxford graduate named Thomas Weaver in 1654. The poem satirizes the life of Thomas Williams, the prominent Dissenting businessman whose milliner's shop in the High Street caught fire, probably late in the year 1641. Weaver describes how

---

this entry in a later diary entry for November of 1689: 'Preaching & setting up of conventicles at Oxford – V[ide] Feb[ruary] preced[ing]' (*MS Wood Diaries 33*, folio 44 verso.

[1] On 30 September 1663 the Edward Hyde, the Chancellor of the University, gave Christopher Rogers (principal of New Inn Hall), John Conant (rector of Exeter College), Henry Cornish, and Thomas Gilbert notice that they were to leave the city within thirty days, because 'he had heard very foule things of them in keeping conventicles & meetings in their houses' (*MS Wood D 19* (3), folios 13 recto and verso = CSC #384).

Williams came downstairs in the middle of the night to find the shop ablaze. His wife, also hearing the commotion downstairs, arrives, making an appearance in something of a state of undress:

> His wife came too at the report,
>   Her cloaths hung in such pickle,
> As she had new come from the sport,
>   After a Conventickle.

The poem here is making jest at her appearance, suggesting that she looked as if she had been hoofing it down at a dancing-parlour again.

Third, there is an additional sharp edge to Wood's remark about setting the Dissenter's worship in an old dancing-school, and in order to appreciate it fully we need to take note of its exact geographical location just outside the North Gate. Fortunately the lease records relating to the 'dancing-school' itself are detailed enough to trace its history with a fair degree of certainty. It seems clear that the old dancing-school was part of a large complex of buildings in and around the Bocardo prison at the north end of Cornmarket Street. Helpful illustrations of these buildings can be seen in the pair of etchings from 1789 by E Howorth (based on famous drawings from 1771 by J B Malchair). The first of these etchings affords a view of the Bocardo prison itself as viewed from Cornmarket Street. The second of these affords a view of the North Gate from St Giles, and includes the antiquated dancing-school as the second building on the right side of the scene (see Illustration #11). The dancing school extended across the second floor of two of these buildings on the west side of the street, which later came to be designated 33-35 Cornmarket Street. This property was leased by the city of Oxford on 11 May 1610 to the mercer John Harrington, with the exception of the dancing-school room on the second floor, which had its own staircase and overlooked Harrington's other holdings and was occupied by a musician by the name of John Bosseley.[1] Bosseley was granted a 31-year lease for the dancing-school itself in indentures dated 11 May 1610 and 5 June 1612.[2] The conditions of the lease on the dancing-school itself were quite specific, and stipulated that the Bosseley was not to allow his

> Schollar or Schollars, or any other p[er]son or p[er]sons whatsoever,
> to daunce in and uppon the said Demised Roome, Sellar, or Chamber,
> or any p[ar]te or p[ar]cell thereof, betweene the houres of twoe of the clocke
> in the afternoone and five of the clock in the forenoon.

---

[1] By an ironic twist of fate, this dancing-school, which doubled as a gymnasium, was attended by Charles II when he was a young boy (see Salter (1923): 119-20). By all accounts, the size of the dancing-school room was considerable (approximately 42' by 20' with a 12' high ceiling).

[2] *Oxford City Ledgers – 1578-1636* (D.5.5), folios 180 recto–181 recto, and 189 recto = CSC #2 and CSC #3.

The lease on the larger property changed hands twice, once in 1624 when the lease was taken over by a butcher named William Hodges (or Hedges),[1] and once in 1658 when it was leased to another butcher named John Pitman. Meanwhile, it appears that John Bossley died in 1621 and passed on the lease on the dancing-school itself to his brother-in-law William Stokes. Stokes, together with his nephew, John Bosseley, junior, are listed on the 21-year lease dated 26 September 1636.[2] The lease specifically prohibits students 'to dance in and uppon the said demised roome, Cellar, or Chamber, or any p[ar]te or p[ar]cell thereof, betweene the houres of tenne of the Clocke in the night and five of the Clocke in the morninge'.

However, Stokes died and was buried on 24 August 1643, probably a victim of the same cholera epidemic that seems to have killed Tom (Pun) Ayres mentioned above.[3] A lease for the dancing school property was issued to Maline Hedges, widow of William Hedges, on 6 September 1655, effectively adjoining it to the tenement properties she already leased in the building complex (namely those now designated 33-35 and 36 Cornmarket).[4] Indeed, the rental records for 25 March 1658 show that Widow Hodges pays £4 for rent on the dancing-school and the tenement to the south (36 Cornmarket), although by this time the old dancing-school had seen its better days.[5] Later in the year she decided to sell the property as a whole to John Pitman and John Twicross, and the City Council appointed viewers of the property on 17 December 1658.[6] On 10 January 1659 the City Council agreed to issue a 40-year lease to Twicross for the tenement at 36 Cornmarket and a lease was signed two days later;[7] similarly, Pitman signed a 40-year lease for the property at 33-35 Cornmarket on 12 January 1659.[8] Both men renewed their leases in due course: Pitman's lease on 33-35 Cornmarket was renewed on 12 February

---

[1] The lease was renewed on 19 March 1652 (*Oxford City Ledgers – 1636-1675* (D.5.6), folios 135 verso–136 verso = CSC #108.

[2] *Oxford City Ledgers – 1636-1675* (D.5.6), folio 6 verso = CSC #12. The matter was discussed and agreed by the City Council on 23 September 1636 (*City Council Proceedings – 1629-1663* (A.5.7), folio 68 verso).

[3] *Parish Register of St Mary Magdalen – 1602-1662* (Par 208/1/R1/1), folio 64 verso.

[4] *Oxford City Ledgers – 1636-1675* (D.5.6), pages 177-180 = CSC #224. On 17 September 1655, Widow Hedges, together with her son, offered a security bond of £50 to repair the tenement and dancing school (*City Council Proceedings – 1629-1663* (A.5.7), folio 227 recto = CSC #226). The lease was sealed with the city seal on 20 September (*City Council Proceedings – 1629-1663* (A.5.7), folio 227 recto = CSC #227).

[5] *Rent Roll for 1658* (A.1.1 – CT.1.E.02).

[6] *City Council Proceedings – 1629-1663* (A.5.7), folio 256 recto = CSC #272.

[7] *City Council Proceedings – 1629-1663* (A.5.7), folio 256 verso = CSC #274; *Oxford City Ledgers – 1636-1675* (D.5.6), folios 265 recto and verso = CSC #276. Twicross pays £4 in rent on 'the Daunceing Schoole' in the *Rent Roll for 1660* (A.1.1 – CT.1.E.03) and in the *Rent Roll for 1663* (A.1.1 – CT.1.E.04).

[8] *Oxford City Ledgers – 1636-1675* (D.5.6), folios 264 recto and verso = CSC #275.

1673,[1] and again on 12 October 1674, with the 'antiquated dancing school', which had hitherto been included in John Twicross's lease arrangements, being added to it.[2] Twicross's lease on 36 Cornmarket (minus the 'dancing schoole') was renewed on 6 March 1674 for a period of 20 years. This lease renewal allowed some enlargements of the premisses so as to improve the facilities of the Bocardo prison complex nearby,[3] and Twicross was made gaoler for life.[4]

So where does all this discussion about the leasing arrangements of the 'antiquated dancing-school' leave us? The point of this is to suggest that Anthony Wood's comment from circa 1691 about Dissenters meeting in an 'antiquated dancing-school' is intimately linked to the fact that the building had been part of the Bocardo prison complex, and indeed, from 1658-74, had been leased to John Twicross, the man who was appointed the city gaoler for life in 1674. In other words, after 1688 the Dissenters met in a building which had long been associated with the Bocardo prison. By stating that they worshipped in the 'antiquated dancing-school' Wood, who was no friend of Dissenters, may have been suggesting that their kind of religious worship was best located in a prison, and that was where such Dissenters really belonged. Most importantly, at least as far as our suggestion concerning the Dissenters' conventicle which met at Thomas (Pun) Ayres' house is concerned, there is nothing to suggest that the 'antiquated dancing-school' was ever used as a place of worship prior to 1688. In fact, the 'antiquated dancing-school' only ever appears to come into use as a meeting place in the wake of the arrival of William of Orange on the English throne. Even then it was in use for only a brief period, probably no more than two or three years (1688-91).

However, the question then remains: where did the Dissenters meet *before* they began to use the 'antiquated dancing house' property in the Bocardo complex? The answer, quite simply, is that they met in private houses, such as those belonging to Lawrence King and Richard Tidmarsh, who are known to have had Baptists meeting in their homes from the 1650s right through to the 1690s.[5] But what about meetings *prior* to the 1650s? Is there any indication that Baptist conventiclers were meeting in other places as well? All of which, of course, takes us back to my suggestion about the importance of Tom (Pun) Ayres' house in Thamestreet along Broken Hays. The time has come for due

---

[1] *Oxford City Ledgers – 1636-1675* (D.5.6), folios 503 recto–504 recto = CSC #516.

[2] *Oxford City Ledgers – 1636-1675* (D.5.6), folios 540 verso–541 verso = CSC #530. Pitman also renewed the combined lease on 2 May 1691 (*Oxford City Ledgers – 1675-1696* (D.5.7), folios 268 verso-269 recto = CSC #647.

[3] Salter (1923): 72, provides a helpful map of the area as it stood in 1771.

[4] *Oxford City Ledgers – 1636-1675* (D.5.6), folios 522 verso–524 recto = CSC #525.

[5] It looks as if Richard Tidmarsh's home in the parish of St Thomas was used as a Baptist meeting-house until his acceptance of the pastorate of the Baptist church in Tiverton, Devon in 1691. Moreover, it appears that the Tidmarsh house continued to be used for Dissenters even after Tidmarsh's departure from Oxford. Anthony Wood has a note dated 6 July 1692 to this effect (*MS Wood Diaries 36*, folio 38 recto = CSC #650).

recognition to be given to the importance of Tom (Pun) Ayres' house in Thamestreet along Broken Hayes within the early days of Dissenters in Oxford. Although we do not have a 17th-century source which *explicitly* states that Baptists and other Dissenters were meeting in Tom (Pun) Ayres' house as early as 1641 or 1642, a good case can be made on circumstantial evidence that this was indeed the case. Dissenters must have been meeting *somewhere* in Oxford during the early 1640s, and Tom (Pun) Ayres' house, along with other private residences such as that of Thomas Williams in the High Street, are two of the most likely places.[1] It seems reasonable to suggest that Tom (Pun) Ayres' house on Thamestreet in Broken Hays was one of the meeting places where political and religious friendships were initially made and allegiances were forged.

---

[1] The houses of Lawrence King and Richard Tidmarsh do not really figure at this time; King was probably only fourteen or fifteen in 1641, and Tidmarsh probably did not arrive in Oxford until 1644.

Concluding Observations

Illustration #11: A view of the North Gate from St Giles, including the so-called 'antiquated dancing-school' on the second floor of the second building on the right side of the scene. The etching is one of a pair produced by E Howorth in 1789 and based on famous drawings from 1771 by J B Malchair.

Concluding Observations

This study is the first, full-scale attempt to trace the beginnings of Baptists in Oxford during the seventeenth century. It has concentrated on identifying both the people concerned and the places where they met to worship together as Dissenters. The intention was to provide as full a picture as possible of the first fifty years or so of Baptists in the traditionally royalist stronghold of Oxford. Of course many questions remain unanswered, but considering that virtually nothing has been published before about the central characters of Baptist life in Oxford, the five biographical chapters here presented, which use Richard Tidmarsh, Lawrence King, Roger Hatchman, Ralph Austen and Thomas Williams as focal points, represent a considerable advancement in what has hitherto been uncharted territory. The concluding chapter on early meeting-houses similarly strikes out in a new direction, attempting to sort out some early traditions about Dissenters and offering fresh insight as to when and where Baptists conventiclers in Oxford met together for worship.

The investigation began by suggesting that it is difficult to make hard and fast distinctions between the various religious denominations and bodies active in Oxford during the seventeenth century. The study has shown that this was as true for Baptists as it was for other Dissenting groups, although the Baptist conventiclers of the city had begun to develop a sense of self-identity during the early 1640s, and certainly by the mid-1650s had formed themselves into a cohesive congregation that was recognized as such by others in Oxford. Indeed, by the time that Oxford Baptists joined the so-called Abingdon Association in 1656, the congregation was firmly rooted and well established, with regular patterns of worship and recognized places of meeting. No doubt one of the reasons for this stability was the fact that they were fortunate to have had an active and capable leadership, including such men as Richard Tidmarsh and Lawrence King who were willing to hold worship services in their homes. This they did even though it represented a considerable risk, particularly during the early 1660s when fines and imprisonment were the order of the day for such 'illegal' behaviour.

Regretably, very few records of these initial years of the Baptist congregation in Oxford have survived. Although the names of some of the leaders are known, we do not know what they looked like for there are no surviving portraits, etchings, or drawings of any of them. There are no church minute books, no extant diaries from members of the congregation, and precious little by way of published sermons or tracts from people directly associated with the church. This is not to suggest that source material is altogether lacking for a study of Oxford Baptists, however. In fact the opposite is true, although many of the available primary source documents consulted in the course of this investigation have hitherto remained largely untouched by Baptist historiographers. Thankfully a number of personal letters of Ralph Austen from 1652-61 have survived within the papers of Samuel Hartlib, and these help considerably in the reconstruction of his life, including his political interests and theological convictions. So too do Austen's published books on both horticultural matters and on Quakerism, commencing with *A Treatise of Fruit-trees* (1653), and concluding with *The Strong Man Armed not Cast Out* (1676). Yet revealing as this material is, it does not tell us very much about the Baptist congregation itself, who the members were or how they lived and worshipped together. The closest thing we have to primary source material of that kind are the occasional paragraphs in the *Abingdon Association Records Book* covering the years 1652-60, and the handful of published pamphlets and tracts written for and signed by leaders of the Baptists in Oxford. Included among these published materials are *The Complaining Testimony of Some ... of Sions Children* (1656); *A Testimony to Truth, Agreeing with an Essay for Settlement* (1659); *Innocency Vindicated: or, Reproach Wip'd Off* (1689), and *A Narrative of the Proceedings of the General Assembly* (1689). Taken together all of these documents can be described as primary source materials which are *internal* to the Baptists of Oxford, insofar as the members of the congregation named within them were willing signatories to the documents concerned. In terms of historical methodology these internal materials are very important for they serve as the initial means of identifying eleven individuals who openly aligned themselves with the Baptist cause in Oxford. A further twenty-three people were identified as Baptist conventiclers through a careful consideration of other available *external* sources, meaning documents which were either written about Dissenters, or refer to them, by others who were not so inclined. Generally these external sources consisted of ecclesiastical records of the Church of England which were openly hostile to the cause of Dissenters, labelling them in the tumultuous days following the Restoration as 'seditious sectaryes'.

In addition to the many parish registers, so critical for establishing basic biographical information about baptisms, marriages and burials, a variety of entries from Oxford's Petty Sessions courts and from the Diocesan and Archdeaconry records featured in the course of the discussion. These materials have proved invaluable in helping to trace the struggles that Baptists had within the civil and ecclesiastical courts, and have amply illustrated how undervalued and overlooked they have been as sources for the study of Dissenters during the period. Also essential in terms of reconstructing the lives of the Baptist leaders in Oxford were the numerous manuscripts of the Oxford City Council, supplemented by the Bodleian Library manuscripts from the library of the celebrated antiquarian Anthony Wood (1632-95), and records of trade guilds and specialized craftsmen such as tailors and cordwainers. A careful examination of apprenticeship contracts, citizenship records, City Council minutes, property leases, rental agreements, taxation records, have enabled an astonishingly full picture to emerge of many of the key figures of this study.

In conclusion, I would like to call attention to four specific ways in which this study challenges traditional understandings about the role that Dissenters in general, and Baptists in particular, had within Oxford in the mid-to-late seventeenth century. Methodologically the four areas are all interconnected, and clearly there is much more work to be done in each of them.

First, the study highlighted some intriguing insights into the way that the Baptist conventiclers related to their local parish churches. It seems clear that most of the conventiclers here presented sought to balance their social responsibilites as Oxford citizens with their religious and theological convictions as Baptist Dissenters. Predictably, one of the focal points in this regard was the issue of infant baptism, and I noted several examples where Baptists were cited to appear before the ecclesiastical courts and explain why their children had not been baptized in accordance with the laws of the Church of England. Some of the Baptists acquiesced in this regard, including the minister Richard Tidmarsh, who in 1669 agreed to have one of his young daughters baptized in an apparent attempt to forestall his excommunication from the local parish church. Tidmarsh was by no means alone in this attempt to achieve a compromise on the controversial issue of infant baptism. In 1663 Edward Jennings similarly entered into negotiation with Diocesan officials over the baptism of one of his sons, although he apparently never did have the child baptized and, in the end, was excommunicated from the Church of England. The stance on believers' baptism was one of the key 'identity markers' for Baptists up and down the country during the period. It us clear that Oxford's Baptists were practicising public baptisms in the river near High Bridge during the 1650s. Indeed, Anthony Wood's account of having witnessed Lawrence King performing baptisms near High Bridge in circa 1659 is important independent confirmation of the practice within the city. Interestingly, the study highlighted that several parish registers recorded the birth, as opposed to the baptism, of a number of the children of Baptist Dissenters, including those of Edward Wyans junior and Thomas Wyans.

Oxford Baptists were frequently cited for other offences, including failure to attend worship services at local parish churches, failure to receive the sacrament at Easter, non-payment of church tithes, and failure to swear oaths of allegiance to the king. The frequency and regularity of charges such as these against Baptists, and the excommunications which resulted, might lead one to conclude that the Dissenters were wholly uninterested in their parish churches and that they had adopted a policy of total withdrawal from all things Anglican. However, this would be an incorrect conclusion, for the study also highlighted a number of ways that the Baptists continued to be active participants in the life of their local parishes. It was noted that they were often appointed as 'overseers of the poor', that they served as both tax accessors and collectors, and that they spoke up for local parishioners in matters of public services and amenities. A good example is Richard Tidmarsh's involvement in the parish of St Thomas over the matter of a public foot-bridge over the Thames (Isis) river which had fallen into a state of disrepair. As noted in the course of the study, several of the Baptists were even buried in local parish churches, including Ralph Austen, who was interred in the parish church of St Peter-in-the-Bailey, Lawrence King, who was buried in the graveyard of the parish church of St Michael's, and Elizabeth King, whose burial in the graveyard of the parish church of All Saints' became a matter of some ecclesiastical contention since she was an excommunicant.

Second, the study has challenged the oft-repeated assertion that Baptists were closely associated with the army and came to Oxford with the Parliamentary forces following the surrender of the city in 1646. In fact, only one of the Baptists investigated within this study was a serving military officer for any length of time, namely Captain Roger Hatchman who served under General Monck in Scotland. Even though his military career is fascinating in its own right, the study showed that Hatchman returned to Oxford after being cashiered from the military and resumed his life as a active citizen of the city, albeit one who continued to be a thorn in the side of the ecclesiastical authorities. It is true that several of the Baptist leaders were commissioned by Parliament as officers in the Oxfordshire militia following the collapse of the Protectorate of Richard Cromwell. Richard Tidmarsh, Ralph Austen and Thomas Tisdale were all so commissioned in August of 1659. However, apart from one brief confrontation with Lord Falkland in the aftermath of Booth's uprising, there is no evidence of their military involvement in any substantial way. In any event, the military careers of the republican-minded Oxfordshire militiamen were shortlived and were overtaken by the return of the monarchy less than a year later.

Third, the study has illustrated the fact that most of the Baptist men investigated were merchants, tradesmen and artisans, often with considerable professional skills and abilities. Oxford Baptists included members from a wide tange of guilds and professions. Included were tanners, glovers, cordwainers (shoemakers), mercers, milliners, weavers, tailors, stonemasons, watchmakers, and buttonmakers. Many of them were native Oxonians, and most spent the whole of their adult lives in Oxford and its environs. The Oxford City Council records are such that a fairly detailed account of their professional careers can be reconstructed. The study has detailed how integrated the Baptists were within the structures of Oxford's civic society. As noted, a number of them were active in training apprentices within their respective trade, including the glover Lawrence King for whom there are records of an amazing *seventeen* apprenticeship contracts. Many progressed through the various ranks and offices of their respective trade guilds; some even rising to the top administrative position (including the mercers Thomas Williams and Thomas Tisdale, and the cordwainer Edward Wyans senior). Several enlarged this professionalism by pursuing a career within the municipal government. Undoubtedly the most successful in this regard was Thomas Williams, who rose to the position of Mayor in 1653-4, overlapping part of his mayoral year of office with the sitting of the Barebones Parliament when

Baptist political influence was at a high point nationally. At one level, Thomas Williams may have been exceptional case, for none of the other Baptists explored within this study matched his achievements, although municipal offices and positions of civic authority were the order of the day for many of them. They served as constables, key-keepers, searchers, bayliffes, aldermen and assistants to the mayor. During the reign of James II a number of Dissenters were promoted to high civic office as part of the king's attempt to gain overall political advantage over his opponents. Three Baptists, Richard Tidmarsh, Lawrence King, and John Toms senior, were identified as among those singled out for such advancement in the *The Charter of Oxford* (1688). However, the scheme was short-lived and James II fled the country, leaving Baptist Dissenters to issue what is in effect an apology for their involvement in the form of a sheet entitled *Innocency Vindicated: or, Reproach Wip'd Off* (1689).

Fourth, the study has demonstrated some of the inter-family connections that helped form the warp and woof of life for Oxford's Baptists. Involvement in the Baptist congregation quite often followed along family lines, with parents bringing up children to follow in their footsteps as Dissenters. There are also several examples of marriage between Baptist families, with the marriage between James Tidmarsh (the son of Richard Tidmarsh) and Alice Wyans (the daughter of Edward Wyans senior), and the marriage between Thomas Hatchman (the son of Roger Hatchman) and Margret Higgins (a relative of John Higgins), being cases in point. Such family inter-connections should not come as a complete surprise and are, at one level, perfectly understandable. Occasionally they are evidenced in legal documents, such a marriage bonds, wills and probate records. For example, on 7 March 1667 Richard Tidmarsh served as one of the witnesses to the will of Edward Wyans senior, and also as one of the assessors responsible for compiling an inventory of Wyans's goods on 28 February 1672. Equally interesting are the extended family connections which shows up in apprenticeship records, not only as fathers took on their own sons, nephews and other relatives as apprentices, but also when they took on the sons and relatives of their fellow Baptist Dissenters as apprentices. All of which illustrates how important family ties were as in the social network of the Baptists, as indeed they were for commercial society at large.

Finally, and most importantly, I hope that the study has demonstrated the value of working with primary source materials, even though at first glance they appear to be irrelevant for a study of Baptist history. True, tracking the sources down was often a difficult and rather hit-and-miss process, and forcing musty old documents to yield up their secrets remained a painstakingly slow process throughout. Yet the challenge for such historical investigation remains, and the thrill of the hunt is as addictive as ever. Hopefully this study will encourage others to take on future investigations into the fascinating world of the 'Seditious Sectaryes'.

Appendices

Appendix A: *The Complaining Testimony of some ... of Sions Children* **(1656)**

Appendix B: *A Testimony to Truth* **(1659)**

Appendix C: *Innocency Vindicated* **(1689)**

Appendix D: *A Narrative of the Proceedings of the General Assembly* **(1689)**

Appendix E: *The Conventicle Act* **(1664)**

Appendix F: *The Declaration of Indulgence* **(1672)**

Appendix G: *The Act of Toleration* **(1689)**

Appendix H: *The Charter of Oxford* **(1688)**

Appendix I: *Family Trees of Oxford Dissenters*

Appendix A: *The Complaining Testimony of some ... of Sions Children* (1656)

The Complaining Testimony of some (though weak, and of the least) of *Sions* Children in this Day of their sore Calamity; occasioned at their Meeting to seek the Lord at their *Abingdon* in *Barkshire*, the second day of the eighth Month, 1656.

Being a short Narrative of the inhumane dealings of some Officers and Souldiers, who said, *They had Order from their Lord for so doing.*

Mal. 3.1 5,16. *And now we call the proud happy; yea they that work wickedness are set up; yea, they that tempt God are delivered. Then they that feared the Lord spake often one to another: and the Lord hearkened, And heard, and a book of remembrance was written for them that feared the Lord, and thought upon his Name.*
Act. 7.34. *I have seen, I have seen the afflictions of my people; I have heard their groanings, and am come own to deliver them.*

London:
Printed for *Livewel Chapman*, at the Crown in
Popes-head-Alley, 1656

To the faithful Remnant of the Womans seed, who keep the Commandments of God, and the Testimony of Jesus: together with every Impartial Reader.

When the Lord did first engage our hearts to wait upon him according to the ensuing Relation, it was much upon some of our spirits, that we should see the glory of God, though we could not apprehend the manner of his appearance; much less could we in the least suppose his answer would be as after was manifest. But the onely-wise God, who knoweth how to order all things for his glory, can make the wrath of man praise him, and the remainder thereof restrain: *upon which account, the ensuing Relation being thought necessary to be published, is presented to your perusal; hoping, that as experience of his goodness hath been some refreshment unto us, (who have subscribed the same, being all of us personally present, some at the one part, others at the other part of the transactions therein mentioned, and sufferers in some degree or other in the same) it will administer some refreshment unto you also; that we may be thereby united with one heart in one common Cause, though contemned, despised, and reproached, by those who did formerly walk with us hand in hand therein, from which they have so openly Apostatized, and also, what you and we must expel from them, unless the Lord should leave us to betray him with a kiss, as they have done: But we trust, that relying upon his grace, he will keep us by his mighty power through faith unto the day of salvation, where we shall with rejoicing say,* Lo, this is our God, we have waited for him: we will be glad and rejoice in his salvation.

Your poor unworthy brethren, desirous to be found faithful in this day of Zions tribulations:

Of the Ch. at Abi.	Of the Ch. At Oxf.	Ioseph Neat,	Iohn Woodly,	David Parry,	Iohn Iones.
John Tomkins	Rich. Tidmarsh,	Tho. Buttivan	Fran. Young,	Iohn Clements.	Iohn Waters.
Iohn Combes,	Rich. Quelch.	Ric. Parnham,	Hen. Forty of Tatnes,		
Simon Mayo,	Of Hull.	Iohn Rye,	Rich. Steed of Dartmouth	Churches.	
Edw. Stennet,	Thom. Cann,	Rich. Denton,	George Allom of Exeter,		
Philip Lockton,	Pet. Tindal.	Tho. Wheeler,	Hen. Simmons		
William White,	Of London.	Iohn Tufnel,	Thomas Ruddock,	Of Northwalsham.	
Rich. Green	Iohn Pugh,	Iohn Portmans,	Tho. Hide, Tho. Helsden.		
Rich. Terrell,	Iohn Green,	Iohn Clark,	William Wainford, of Norwich		
Simon Peck.	Fran. Walton,	Iohn Armiger,	Fran: Langden of Cornwal.	Hen. Preston.	

A2

A Word to such of the Army, especially those of the County-
Troops as are in any measure sensible of the Iniquity of
this Day, and mourning for the same.

It was, and is said upon our hearts, that the Lots, or righteous souls grieved for the great transgressions of the Sodomitish generations among whom they live, might be delivered, before the judgements of the Lord break for the: for, if his wrath be kindled (yea) but a little, blessed are all they that trust in him: *and therefore for your sakes was this short Epistle penned, to the end, that if the Lord so please, you might be no longer deceived with vain words, by those from whom you do suppose that the great things you first engaged for on the behalf of Christ and his people might be attained, and that they might return from whence they are fallen, and do their first works; though the bottom upon which they now stand, seems to us to give little ground of hopes or any such thing:* for men do not gather grapes or thorns, or figs or thistles. *Besides, they persecute that Spirit appearing in any of those who are but* enquiring the way to Zion, with their faces thitherward: *witness the many prisoners now suffering for the Cause of our Lord Jesus, besides the cruel usage of others mentioned in this ensuing Relation. This therefore we desire to leave with you, in the fear of the Lord, That you would flee our from the midst of them, and deliver every man his soul, that you may escape the judgements of God, and be free from the blood of your brethren; which you will unavoidably be involved in, so far as we can discern, if you continue in your present station, as some have been already in these last transactions: and if so, as you partake of their sins, you will partake of their plagues. Thus leaving you to the perusal of this Relation, hoping that it may be of some use, either to convince, or else to leave this further Testimony, That if you perish, your blood will be upon your own heads: though it be otherwise longed for, and prayed for, by*

Your unworthy brethren, mourning with you,
And praying for your return:

Of Northwalsham.	Of Cornwal.	Fran: Walton	John Portmans.
Hen. Simons.	Fran: Langden	Jos. Neat.	John Clarke
Thomas Ruddock.	Of Hull	Tho. Buttivant.	John Armiger
Robert Hide,	Tho. Cann,	Rich: Parnham.	John Woodly.
Tho, Helsden.	Peter Tindal.	John Rye.	David Parry.
Of Norwich.	Of London,	Rich: Denton.	Fran: Young.
William Wainford	John Pugh	Tho: Wheeler	John Clark.
	John Green	John Tufnel	

(1)

The complaining Testimony of some of Sions children, though most unworthy;
or, A short Narrative of the inhumane dealings of some Officers and Souldiers at
Abingdon, *the second day of the eighth Month, 1656.*

It having pleased the Lord to take unto himself a choice and eminent Servant of his, to wit, *Ioh. Pendarves*, Minister of the Gospel, and Pastor of that Congregation at *Abingdon*: whose interring we did meet to solemnize the 30th of the 7th Month, that being one end of our coming together: judging it our duty to perform the last office of love to so faithful a Servant as he was, indeed a Prince in *Israel*, who did in his life-time naturally care for *Sions* welfare, wholly giving himself up unto the Lord's work: and hereby a price and opportunity was put into our hands to bring many of the Lord's people together, from several parts of the Nation, in this dark and gloomy day, to seek his face for the understanding of his minde and will, what his Remnant (remaining faithful this great day of Apostacy) ought to do. To which end, there were several heads agreed upon; according to which they might seek his face with understanding, as by these particulars here mentioned, will more plainly appear:

1. That we humble ourselves before the Lord for all our sins and iniquities wherein we have justly provoked the eyes of his holiness, through our lukewarmness, indifferency of Spirit, rashness, and want of love in this great day of open Apostacy and backsliding; wherein, it is to be feared, we have much added to the measure of the iniquity of this day.

2. That notwithstanding all the complaints of the Lord's people, there hath not been that diligent heart-searching into the minde and will of the Lord, what his people ought to do.

3. To remember before the Lord with mourning, that there is not that natural care for *Sion*, as there ought to be, especially, when he hath chastene us by taking away such choice Instruments as he hath done of late: but most men now, seeking their own, and building their own ceiled houses, saying *The time is not yet*: the time that the Lord's house should be built.

4. To entreat earnestly of the Lord, that he would be pleased so to own the present Meeting, that the light which he hath given in amongst the body of his people inquiring after his minde and will in this day, might be so gathered into one as that we might be able to read his minde and will, together with our duty, in this dark and gloomy day: And, that he would pour forth a plentiful portion of his Spirit upon the Remnant of his faithful ones, whereby they may be enabled to prosecute his minde and will so made known unto them.

5. To remember the afflictions of *Joseph* in all the parts and quarters of the world, and particularly in this Nation, wherein the Saints are imprisoned, especially by those that are under so great a profession of Light.

6. That God would be pleased to deliver them that are insnared with the Apostacy of the times, and remove them that stand in the way of his work.

(2)

Nevertheless, leaving the Spirit of the Lord to breath in his people as he should please to minister unto them.

And accordingly upon the day above mentioned, we met together at *Abingdon*, in the house of the late deceased Servant of the Lord: and we may with a holy boldness declare, That we did in some measure behold the light of his countenance that day breathing through such of his servants, whose hearts were stirred up to speak unto and from the Lord. The next day, being the first instance, we were again met together and spent the whole day in waiting upon him: where we desire to acknowledge with humility and thankfulness, That (though we were unworthy to receive any thing from our Father, yet) some of us and many others did behold such tokens of his presence, by his smiling countenance through our Lord Jesus Christ, such quickenings of his Spirit, such melting & brokenness of heart, such tastes of his peace and joy, such renewings of first-love, such endearing of Saints to each other, such longings after the glory of God, and groanings for the prosperity of *Sion*; as some ancient Professors affirmed, they seldom experienced the like: divers of the Souldiers and others (though adversaries to this Meeting) were forced to acknowledge God was amongst us of a truth; and in particular, when the party came on with violence upon our friends, one of the Souldiers had this word, *Psal.* 105, 15. set upon his spirit with much power, (as he profest) *Touch not mine anointed, and do my Prophets no harm*: he was a Brother, and promised to break his sword when he came home.

For which we desire to bless and praise the Name of the most High our Father, because he hath not forsaken them that seek him, njor is it a vain thing to wait at his posts.

The next morning being the second instant, we intended to have met again, the former refreshings having thereunto sweetly engaged us: but being prevented, we shall give a plain account thereof, and bless Jehovah for the worst men have or can do to us, seeing our God will turn that also to his praise, and the same doth and will work together for the exceeding good of them that sincerely love him.

About seven in the morning, several of us lodging at the sign of the Lamb in *Abingdon*, were in the Inn-yard, some looking to their horses, others getting themselves ready, the better to be prepared for the meeting intended, had the Lord pleased to have afforded it unto us: about which time three Troopers came into the Inn; and after they had put up their horses, went up stairs to another of their company who had continued in the Inn (most p-arte of the time that we were there) as a spy, to take notice, and give information of what he could hear and see done amongst us. Presently after, they went into several of our chambers, and took away a Hawking-bag belonging to one *George Allom* of *Exceter*, being a Messenger of the Church there; and took out of it all his writings, being as we understand of private concernment only: whereupon it was asked by what authority they did it: to which they replied, That they had order: but the question being again put, Where their order was, they put their hands upon their swords,

(3)

and said, There was their order: to which some of us said, That if they could produce no other order, a High-way-man, demanding our purses, could produce as good a commission for his action as they did. Upon this, another came in, being, as we afterwards understood, Commander of the party then in the Town, Lieutenant *Barker* by name: some of our Friends asked him also by what authority this search was made; to which he replied, That it was sufficient he said he had order for what he did, and that he was not bound to shew his order, if he had any, to every one that asked him. But our Friends still pressing for a sight of his order, with words spoken to the same purpose aforementioned, by which the said Lieutenant was much inraged, riding furiously about the Inn-yard, striking several of our Friends violently with his cane, endeavouring to ride over them with his horse, using many uncivil words towards us, commanded us to group, we must go, without any further inquiry.

Soon after this, some of us went out of the Inn to the meeting place, intending to have gone in, but two Troopers keeping centinel at the door, refused to give liberty to any man presenting Pistols to their brests to hinder them from going into the place, and in particular our Brother Mayo, who lived there, was so far hindered from coming in, that they cocked their Pistols, and presented them to his brest, so that he was forced suddenly to step back, fearing lest they should fire upon him. From thence, our Friends being disappointed of their meeting, went into the Market-place: one of our Brethren began in prayer, another seconded him in speaking, after him our Brother *Jones* of *Longworth* in *Barkshire*, and ancient grace Christian, who was formerly persecuted by the Bishops proceeded with a word of exhortation: then our Brother *Austen*, a member of the Church at Oxford, who was late a member of the Army exercising. The Souldiers drew round about us, and after a short time made an attempt upon us, hoping to have scattered us, which the Lord prevented, though no opposition was made on our parts: then the Trumpet sounding they drew off, and came on again in a body with much violence: the Commander of the party came in, and broke through violently with his sword drawn (having first broken his Cane) he cut divers, one of out hats being slashed in three or four places; and most of the Souldiers, some with drawn swords, others with swords in their scabbards, violently smiting, and driving us one from another, whereby we were forced to desist from our duty unto God the Lord of hosts, before whose throne we were in prayer, and continued, till pulled down by force: one was forced to tumble over stones to shift their stickes to his hurt, by another *Officer endeavouring to ride over [them] spurring and beating his horse to that purpose; but the Lord suffered it not to be so. Some had their Garments rent and torn on their backs: some offering to go and see their friends (seized upon in the tumult) were threatened to have their swords thrust through their bowels, several being haled about the Market-place so long, that one of their own

*Note, that the Officers carried themselves more uncivily then the common Troopers.

(4)

company cried out, For shame drag not a man thus. Moreover, one speaking to a soldier that he must answer this one day before the Lord: he replied, He would answer our God well enough. At this time also, the ancient Brother before mentioned had many blows made at him; but through the goodness of the Lord received no hurt, though divers others, men and women, were shamefully beaten at this time: and after this, riding about where they saw any together, fell in amongst them to disperse them, taking several as prisoners, and afterwards letting several loose in a private manner, laying nothing to their charge, somwhat like that in *Act*. 16.37. After this, that party of horse, which had been so insolent and inhuman, drew out of the Town, and within a short time after came in with them about seven or eight Troops more, who suddenly divided themselves into several Inns where we lay, shutting up the gates, and securing such as they could finde. Soon after this, one whom they call Major Gen. *Bridges*, with several others, came into the Town, and at the new Inn proceeded to examinations of such whom they had taken and such also whom they had detained in the several Inns as prisoners, but in the end, they were all dismissed except five, who were carried away to *Windsor*-Castle; of whose particular charge, we can give little account, only thus much we are credibly inform'd, that one of them was charg'd only for making an appeal to God in prayer between us & them; there being little against any as spoke or done at the meeting.

That which was chiefly the ground of their commitment, was drawn forth by insnaring questions asked about them when they were examined against themselves, in matters of their judgement and conscience: which we leave to every unbiased person to judge of.

And this we desire further to mention, That one of the subscribers, *Joh. Tomkins*, an Elder of the Church at *Abingdon* being well known for his grace, cautious and very sparing in his expressions at all times, had this laid to his charge when he was examined, That he challenged one of the Souldiers to fight with him upon *Salisbury plain*; also, that he should say we had thirty thousand men more to come to us: and the souldier that spake these words, proffered to bring three more men to swear to the truth of it, although it is well known there were no such words spoken by him directly or indirectly: by which the Reader may observe what sons of Belial they have amongst them, who dare adventure to swear anything: likewise to advise the Reader not to give much credit to reports contrary hereunto.

This Relation is presented to publick view, to prevent any false Information that may come from andy particular person, or from our enemies, who may endeavour to possess men, that there was a design or rising at this meeting, which we do hereby declare against, as wel as testify to the truth of this Relation.

Of the Ch. at Abi.	*Of the Ch. at* Oxf.	*Ioseph Neat,*	*Iohn Woodly,*	*David Parry,*	*Iohn Iones.*
John Tomkins	*Rich. Tidmarsh,*	*Tho. Buttivan*	*Fran. Young,*	*Iohn Clements.*	*Iohn Waters.*
Iohn Combes,	*Rich. Quelch.*	*Ric. Parnham,*	*Hen. Forty of* Tatnes,		
Simon Mayo,	*Of* Hull.	*Iohn Rye,*	*Rich. Steed of* Dartmouth		*Churches.*
Edw. Stennet,	*Thom. Cann,*	*Rich. Denton,*	*George Allom of* Exeter,		
Philip Lockton,	*Pet. Tindal.*	*Tho. Wheeler,*	*Hen. Simmons*		
William White,	*Of* London.	*Iohn Tufnel,*	*Thomas Ruddock,*		*Of* Northwalsham.
Rich. Green	*Iohn Pugh,*	*Iohn Portmans,*	*Tho. Hide, Tho. Helsden.*		
Rich. Terrell,	*Iohn Green,*	*Iohn Clark,*	*William Wainford, of* Norwich		
Simon Peck.	*Fran. Walton,*	*Iohn Armiger,*	*Fran: Langden of* Cornwal.		*Hen. Preston.*

Had there been an opportunity to get friends together, there would have been many more Subscribers. FINIS.

Appendix B: *A Testimony to Truth* (1659)

A Testimony to truth,
agreeing with an ESSAY for Settlement upon a sure Foundation.

To all the upright in heart in Parliament, Army, and the three Nations that do adhear to, and for the prosecution of the late Declaration put forth by the Parliament, bearing date the 9th of May 1659 which Declaration (that all may understand what we mean) we have hear inserted, viz. The Parliament doth declare that all such as shall be in any place of trust or power within this Commonwealth be able for the discharge of such truth, and that they be persons fearing God, and that have given testimony of their love to all the people of God, and of their faithfulnesse to the Cause of this Commonwealth, &c.

Whereas the Lord hath by his late powerful appearance made us sensible of his love towards us in bringing down our enemies, who were to much inraged against his people, in such a day when their distractions were so many, and their friends so few, having their preservation onely from him, and being it some good measure affected therewith, we judge it our duty to endeavour after an improvement of so great a mercy fearing lest this (as well as many others) may be onely made use of a particular advantage: We therefore to acquit ourselves have agreed to be calling for those things that are Gods peoples due, and have been declared for, and meeting with this Essay for settlement, wherein our hearts do fully agree, our minds being therein fully exprest, we do therefore declare our content thereto, defining that all the upright in heart will pursue after the things therein contained, which until it be effected, we cannot judge we have the price of that blood that hath been spilt, nor of those tears and prayers that hath been powered forth unto the Lord for what he hath promised: we do therefore in pursuance of those things assert the Essay subscribed by *John Owen, Hen. Jessey, Vav. Powell, J. Vernon, H. Courtney, Will. Allen, Phil. Pinchons, John Poortman, Clement Ireton, Rob. Rumsey, P. Goodrick, R. Price, James Hill, Jo. Wigan, H. Danvers, Rich. Goodgroome, Hen. Parsons, Ro. Overton, Rich. Saltonstall, Wentw. Day*. Is as followeth.

Though we cannot but see cause bitterly to bewail our great iniquities and failings under the profession of Christ, both as King of Saints and Nations, and the abominations of an haughty and abusive spirit, found in the late single person (in a professed pursute of reformation) not distinguishing the precious from the vile; in the force he exercised upon the long Parliament, (after the Lord had so honoured in his work and preserved in the very fire a faithful seed amongst them) which, with the like insulting and contempt that afterwards triumphed over a faithful people in the little assembly that followeth; hath returned in just reproach and shame upon their heads, who so insulted and could not therefore in that spirit make any blessed use of the best of men, who cleaved to them, the most hopeful means bringing little forth but meer confusion: yet we cannot but acknowledge to the glory of God on high that such rebuke was justly powred out upon the prevailing party of the said Parliament, and none but the upright and truly penitent amongst them in sense both of neglect of duty and great corruptions, ought of right, or acceptably in our esteem to be sharers in the trust of rule over the so hardly ransomed people of this Nation.

First then we do in humility and fear witnesse against the setting up or introducing any person whatsoever, as King or chief Magistrate, or a House of Lords or any other thing of like import, under what name or title soever, or any power arising from the Nation, as a Nation upon the old corrupt and almost ruinated constitution, apprehending that the great work of taking the Kingdome from man and giving it to Christ hath its beginning in the revolutions we have been under.

Secondly, We do humbly witness against the foundation of future Violence, of bringing into, or continuing in Authority any who joined with the late single Person, otherwise then by first manifesting fruit meet for repentance, for such misdemeanors, by which our Rights, both as Christians and as Men have been so much betrayed, and the name of our heavenly Father, after all his works of wonder with us, so much thereby prophaned, to our greatest grief even throughout and beyond the bounds of these three Nations.

Thirdly, we do hereby humbly witnesse against the imploying in the Armies, or Navy, any Commanders who have been active in the Resignation of the Government to the deceased single Person, or in the abusing any Christians met to mourn over their backslidings and abominations, or that informed against or supplanted their dissenting Brethren, or were principal in contriving or presenting any of the blasphemous or flattering addresses, or were Jaolers or Keepers of their Brethren in Holds or Prisons, or that received extraordinary rewards or titles of honour from the late single Person or his successor, or any deriving power from them, or that acted by either of their Arbitrary Commands, to the banishment of any (without legal Trial) out of the Nation, or that contrived or acted in the unrighteous and shameful proceeding against such of the late Enemy as lived peaceably, and had no hand in the insurrection, by decimating of them contrary to Articles and publique faith of the Nation, unless some good proof of repentance in truth be manifested for these or such of these abominations as they shall be guilty of.

And positively, we doe now desire to witnesse for, and humbly assert, that the right of making and giving laws unto men, is originally in God, who hath given this power, as well as the execution thereof, unto Christ, as he is the Son of man, and therein made universal Lord and Sovereign over the whole World, and under Christ as his Ministers, a certain number of men qualified and limited according to his Word, ought to be set apart to the Office of chief rule and Government over these Nations, as part of Christs universal Kingdom. And we do claim, that only men of courage, fearing God, and hating Covetousness, might be imployed in the trust of Rule, and in all places of publique Judicature; yea, if it be possible in every place of publique Trust in these three Nations. And that all the laws respecting the right of men, might be so truly ordered by the Scriptures to the exaltation of Christ, our Lord, King, and Lawgiver, as that in point of right no difference might be made betwixt good and bad, nor this or that profession in Religion, but by one right Rule the offender may be punished, and the injured effectually relieved without expedition: The said laws being first so plainly declared, as the poorest in the Land may understand their case, and that it be dispenced so nigh their dwellings, as that Judgement might not be turned into Wormwood, as hitherto it hath been through partiality and intricacy, vexatious delaies and distances: That as an intolerable burthen and oppression, inconsistent with the Rights aforesaid or true liberty of conscience unto all: the Rulers over men forbear for ever to impose any National Parochial Ministry, so as to inforce any form of worship suited to their interest or compel men of one perswasion, to maintain any man of another, in the Ministry.

That thus doing Justice, loving Mercy, and walking humbly with our God, which is the good he hath shewed to us, as onely tending to true Setlement, the whole Nation may be blest, and all iniquity may stop her mouth, is the Publique good Old Cause. We desire may be so revived in truth as that all the upright in heart throughout the Land may follow it against every private factious or carnal (though national) spirit and opposition whatsoever, which under the shadow of the Lord our God Almighty, we set forth as out Testimony.

Subscribed in the Name and by the Appointment of the Baptized Churches in and about Abingdon in the County of Berks.

Abingdon	*Wantadge*	*Oxford*	*Longworth*	*Farringdon*	*Wallingford*
William Dyer	Robert Keate	Rich. Tidmarsh	John Jones	Fran. Briton	Consolation Fox
Robert Payne	John Beale	Thomas Tesdall	Francis Wase	Joh. Addams	Tho. Gale
William White	Barth. Tull	John Higgins	Tho. Tuckwell	Joh. Peck	Ralph Clack
Arthur Hearne	Rich. Brooks	Laurance King	Tho. Jones	Christo. Elloway	Rich. Cox
John Tomkins	Robert Burchall	George Astin	Tho. James	Joh. Comes	Will. Roberts
Phillip Lockton	Tho. Peck	Rich. Quelch	Tho. Wate	Rich. Steed	
John Wise		John Edwards	Hen. Wyatt	Joh. Turner	
Richard Tesdall		Humphrey Gilet	etc.	Richard Day	
				etc.	

Judges 19.30, Consider of it, take advice, & speak your minds

Appendix C: *Innocency Vindicated* (1689)

Innocency Vindicated; or,
Reproach Wip'd Off.

The Assembly of Elders, Messengers, and Ministring Brethren sent by, and concerned for, more than one hundred Baptized Congregations of the same Faith with them-selves, from many parts of England and Wales, met together bin London, (from Sept. 3 to 12, 1689) to consider of several things relating to the well-being of the same Churches. And having that Opportunity, judged it their Duty to clear themselves from those Reproaches cast upon them, occasioned by the Weakness of some few of their Perswasion, who in the late King's Reign, were imployed as Regulators of Corporation, &c for the Support of his Dispensing Power.

There having been many Reflections cast upon us, under the Name of *Anabaptists*, as such, as having in the late times, for our Liberties-sake, complied with the Popish Party, to the hazard of the Protestant Religion, and the Civil Liberties of the Nation: We being met together, some from most parts of this Kingdom, judg it our Duty to clear our selves from the said Reflections cast upon us. And we do first declare, That to the utmost of our Knowledg, there was not one Congregation that had a Hand, or gave Consent, to any thing of that Nature, nor did ever countenance any of their Members to own an Absolute Power in the late King, to dispense with the Penal Laws and Tests; being well satisfied, that the doing thereof by his sole Prerogative, would lay the Foundation of Destruction of the Protestant Religion, and Slavery to this Kingdom.

But yet we must confess, that some few Persons (from their own Sentiment) which were of our Societies, used their Endeavours for

(2)

the taking off the Penal Laws and Tests; and were imployed by the late King *James* to go into divers Counties, and to several Corporations, to improve their Interest therein; but met with little or no Encouragement by any of our Members: though, considering the Temptations some were under [their Lives being in their Enemies Hands; the great Sufferings by Imprisonments, Excommunications, &c.that did attend from the Ecclesiastical Courts, as also by the frequent Molestations of Informers against our Meetings, by means whereof many Families were ruined in their Estates, as also deprived of all our Liberties, and denied the common Justice of the Nation, by the Oaths and Perjury of the vilest of Mankind] might be some Abatement to the severe Censures that have attended us, though if some amongst us, in hopes of a Deliverance from the heavy Bondage they then lay under, might miscarry, by falling in with the late King's Design. It being also well known that some Congregations have not Only reproved those among then that were so employed, but in a Regular way have further proceeded against them. From whence it seems unreasonable, that for the Miscarriage of a few

Persons, the whole Party should be laid under Reproach and Infamy. It being our professed Judgment, and we on all Occasions shall manifest the same, to venture our *All* for the Protestant Religion, and Liberties of our Native Country.

And we do with great Thankfulness to God acknowledg his special Goodness to these Nations, in raising up our present King *William*, to be a blessed Instrument, in his Hand, to deliver us from Popery and Arbitrary Power; and shall always (as in Duty bound) pray that the Lord may continue Him and his Royal Consort long to be a Blessing to these Kingdoms; and shall always be ready to the utmost of our Ability, in our Places, to joyn our Hearts and Minds with the rest of our Protestant Brethren, for the Preservation of the Protestant Religion, And the Liberties of the Nation.

William Kiffin,	*Robert Keate,*
Hanserd Knowllys,	*Richard Tidmarsh,*
Andrew Gifford,	*James Webb,*
Robert Steed,	*John Harris,*
Thomas Vauxe,	*Thomas Winnel,*
John Tomkins,	*James Hitt,*
Toby Wells,	*Edward Price,*
George Barret,	*William Phips,*
Benjamin Keach,	*William Facey,*
Samuel Buttall,	*John Ball,*
Isaac Lamb,	*William Hankins,*
Christopher Price,	*Paul Fruin.*

London,   Printed by *J. Darby,*   MDCLXXXIX.

Appendix D: *A Narrative of the Proceedings of the General Assembly* (1689)

A Narrative of the Proceedings of the General Assembly)

Of divers Pastors, Messengers and Ministring-
Brethren of the *Baptized Churches*, met together
in *London*, from *Septemb*. 3. to 12. 1689, from
divers parts of *England* and *Wales*; Owning the
Doctrine of Personal Election, and Final Perserverance.

Sent from, and concerned for, more than one hundred
Congregations of the same Faith with themselves.

Acts 15.6 *And the Apostles and Elders came together for
to consider of the matter.*
2 Cor. 8.23. — *Or our Brethren be enquired of, they are
the Messengers of the Churches, and the Glory of Christ.*

London, Printed in the Year, 1689

(3)

The Elders, Messengers, and Ministring-
Brethren of the Churches met together in their General Assembly in the
City of *London, Septemb*. from the
3*d* to the 11*th*, 1689.

To all the Churches of *Baptized Believers*, owning
the Doctrine of Personal Election, and final
Perserverance, in *England* and *Wales*.

Beloved in our Lord Jesus Christ,

It doth not a little affect our Souls to see how readily you were to comply with that
Christian and Pious Invitation you had, to send one or two worthy Brethren, as your
Messengers, to meet with the rest of us in this great Assembly; for which we return you
our hearty Thanks: hoping, that not only we, and the Churches of the Saints to whom we

are related, at this present time will have cause to bless, praise and magnify the Father of Mercies, and the God of all Comfort and Consolation upon this account; bu that the Ages to come will have some Grounds to rejoice amd praise his holy Name, hoping through the riches of his Grace, and Divine Blessing upon our holy Endeavours, such great and gracious Effects will attend the result of our Consultations in this Assembly; which were chiefly to consider of the present state and condition of all the Congregations respectively under our Care and Charge; and what might be the causes of that Spiritual Decay , and loss of Strength, Beauty and Glory in our Churches; and to see (if we might be helped by the Lord herein) and might be done to attain to a better and more prosperous State and Condition.

(4)

And now, Brethren, in the first place, with no little Joy we declare unto you how good and graciou the Lord hath been to us, in uniting our Hearts together in the Spirit of Love, and sweet Concord, in our Debates, Consultations, and Resolves, which are sent unto you, there being scarcely one Brother who dissente from the Assembly in the Sentiments of his Mind, in any one thing we have proposed to your serious Considerations, either in respect of the cause of our Witherings, nor what we have fixt on as a means of Recovery to a better state, if the Lord will.

And therefore, in the second place, be it known unto you that we all see great cause to rejoice and bless God, that after so dismal an Hour of Sorrow and Persecution, in which the Enemy doubtless designed to break our Churches to pieces, not only us, but to make the whole *Sion* of God desolate, even so as she might become a plowed Field, the Lord was pleased to give such Strength and Power in the time of need to bear up your Souls in your Testimony for Jesus Christ, that your Spirits did not faint under your Burdens in the time of your Adversity; so that we hope we may say in the Words of the Church of old, *Though all this is come upon us, yet we have not forgotten thee, neither have we dealt falsly in thy Covenant. Our Heart is not turned back, neither have our Steps declined from thy way. Though thou hast sore broken us un the place of Dragons, and covered us with the shadow of Death,* Psal. 44.17, 18, 19. Yet nevertheless we fear Christ may say, *I have somewhat against you, because you have left your first Love,* as he once charged the Church of *Ephesus,* and may possibly most Churches in *England,* it is therefore good *to consider from whence we are fallen, and repent, and do our first works,* Rev. 2.5.

We are persuaded one chief cause of our decay is for want of holy Zeal for God, and the House of our God; few amongst us living up (we fear) to what they profess of God, not answering the terms of that sacred Covenant they have made with him; the Power of Godliness being greatly decayed, and but little more than the Form thereof remaining amongst us. The Thoughts of which are enough to melt our Spirits, and break our Hearts to pieces, considering those most amazing Providences of the ever blessed God under which we have been, and more especially now are exercised, and the many signal and most endearing Obligations he is pleased to lay us under. The Spirit of this World we clearly discern is got too much into the

(5)

Hearts of most Chrisatians and Members of our Churches, all seeking their own, and none, or very few, the things of Jesus Christ; if therefore in this there be no Reformation, the whole Interest of the blessed Lord Jesus will still sink in our Hands, and our Churches left to languish, whilst the Hands of poor Ministers become as weak as Water, and Sorrow and Grief seize upon their Spirits.

Thirdly, We cannot but bewail that great Evil, and neglect of Duty in many Churches concerning the Ministry.

1. In that some though they have Brethren competently qualified for the Office of Pastors and Deacons, yet omit that sacred Ordinance of Ordination, whereby they are rendred uncapable of preaching and administring the Ordinances of the Gospel, so regularly, and with that Authority which otherwise they might do. Those who have failed herein, we desire would in the fear of God lay it to Heart, and reform.

2. In neglecting to 'make that Gospel-Provision for their Maintenance, according to their Abilities, by which means many of them are so incumbred with Worldly Affairs, that they are not able to perform the Duties of their holy Calling, in preaching the Gospel, and watching over their respective Flocks.

Fourthly, We find cause to mourn that the Lord's Day is no more religiously and carefully observed, both in a constant attendance on the Word of God in that Church to whom Members do belong, and when the publick Worship is over, by a waiting on the Lord in Family Duties, and private Devotion.

But because we have sent unto you the whole Result of this great Assembly particularly, we shall forbear to enlarge further upon these Causes of our Withering and Decays.

One Thing you will find we have ha before us, and come to a Resolve about, which we are perswaded will prove an exceeding great Blessing adn Avantage to the INterest of Jesus Christ in our Hands; and if the Lord enlarge all our Hearts, give a revival to the sinking Spirits of the Mourners in *Sion*, and to languishing Churches too, which is, that of a general or Publick Stock, or Fund of Mony to be raised forthwith. First, By a Free-will Offering to the Lord: And, secondly, by a Subscription, every one declaring what he is willing to give, Weekly, Monthly, or Quarterly, to it.

And now, brethren, we must say, the Lord is about to try

(6)

you in another way than ever you have been tried to this Day, because, till now, no such Thing was settled amongst us, and so not propounded to you. It will be known now, whether you do love Jesus Christ, and his Blessed Interest, Gospel, and Church, or no; i.e. Whether you love him more than these, or more than Son or Daughter. O that you would at this time shew your Zeal for God, and let all Men see the World is not so in your Hearts, but that Jesus Christ hath much room there: 'Tis to be given towards God's Holy Temple, to build up his Spiritual House which hath a long time lain as waste. Remember how willingly the Lord's People offered upon this Account formerly; 'tis some great as well as good Thing the Lord, and we his poor and unworthy Servants and Ministers, do expect from you. God has wrought a great Work for us, O let us make some suitable return of Duty to him, and act like a People called, loved, and saved by him. Shall so much be spent needlessly on your own ceiled Houses, on costly Attire and Dresses, and delicious Diet, when God's House lies almost waste! We are therefore become hunble Supplicants for our dear Master, nd could entreat you on our bended Knees, with Tears in our Eyes, to pity *Sion*, if it might but move your Hearts to Christian Bounty and Zeal for Her and the Lord of Hosts. We fear God did let in the Enemy upon us to consume us and waste our Substance, because to this Day we have with hel it from him, when his Cause, Gospel, and Churches called for more than ever yet you parted with, and that a Blast has been upon our Trades an Estates for our remissness in this Matter. May we not say, *Ye looked for much, and lo it came to little; and when ye brought it home, the Lord did blow upon it?* Why, *because*, saith God, *mine House that is waste, and ye run every one to his own House*, Hag. 1.9. But if now we reform our Doings, and shew our Zeal for Christ and his Gospel, and love to him, and act as ecomes a willing People professing his Name, you will see you will be no losers by it: *For I will*, saith the Lord, *open the Windows of Heaven, and pour out a Blessing that there shall not be room enough to receive it*, Mal. 3.10. If the Worth of Souls, the Honour of God, the Good of the Church, the glorious Promulgation of the Gospel in the Nation, the Credit of your Profession, your own Peace, and that weight of Eternal Glory be upon your Spirits, we doubt not

(7)

but you will give evidence of it at this Time; and so shall you *build the old waste Places, and raise up the Foundations of many Generations; and be the Repairers of the Branches, and Restorers of Paths to dwell in*, Isa. 58.12.

We to these great and good Ends, have thought upon and appointed a Solemn Day to Fast and Mourn before the Lord, and to humble our selves, and seek his Face, that a Blessing may attend all that we have done, and you with us may yet further do for his Holy Name sake.

A General Fast appointed in all the Congregations on the 10th of October next, 1689, with the Causes and Reasons thereof.

The main and principal Evils to be bewailed and mourn'd over before the Lord on that Day, are as followeth.

First, Those many grievous Backslidings, Sins, and Provocations, not only of the whole Nation, but also of the Lord's own People, as considered in our publick and private Stations; particularly that great decay of first Love, Faith, and Zeal for the Ways and Worship of God; which hath been apparent, not only in our Churches, but also in private Families.

Secondly, That this Declension and Vacksliding hath been, we fear, for a long series of time, and many sore Judgments God has brought upon the Nation; and a strange Death of late come upon the Lord's faithful Witnesses, besides divers painful Labourers in Christ's Vineyard called Home, and but few raised up in their stead; little success in the Ministry; storms of Persecution having been raised upon us, a new War commenc'd by the Beast, (through the Divine Permission of God, and Hand of his Justice) to a total overcoming to appearance the Witnesses of Christ in these Isles, besides his more immediate Strokes by Plague and Fire, etc. God blasting all Essays used for deliverance, so that we were almost without hope, therefore our Sins that provoked the Righteous and Just God to bring allthese Evils upon us, we ought to bewail adn mourn for before him. But withal not to forget his Infinite Goodness, who when he saw our Power was gone, and that there was none shut up or left, that he shold thus appear for our Help and Deliverance, in a way unexpected and unthought of by us.

Thirdly, The Things we should therefore in the next place pray and cry to the Lord for, ot, that he would give us true, brokens, and penitent Hearts for all our Iniquities, and the Sins of his People, and wash and cleanse away those great Pollutions with which we have been defiled; and also pour forth more of his Spirit upon us, and open the Mysteries of his Word

(8)

that we may understand whereabouts we are, in respect of the latter Time, and what he is a doing, and we know our Work, and that a Blessing may attend all the Churches of his Saints in these Nations, and that greater Light may break forth, and the Glory of the Lord rise upon us, and that the Word may not any more be as a miscarrying Womb and dry Breasts, but that in every place Multitudes may be turned out to the Lord, and that Love and sweet Concord may be found among all the Lord's People in these Nations, that the great Work began therein so unexpectantly, may go on and be perfected, to the praise of his own Glory.

Likewise to put up earnest Cries and Supplications to the Lord for the lineal Seed of *Abraham*, the poor Jews, that they may be called, and both Jews and Gentiles made one Sheepfold, under that one Shepherd Jesus Christ.

These are some of those Things we have thought good to lay before you, and which we hope we shall be helped with you to spread before the Lord on that Day, with whatsoever else you or we may be help'd to consider or: hoping you will not forget your Pastors and Ministers in your Prayers, and what we have been enabled to come to a Resolve about, so that all may be succeeded with a glorious Blessing from the Almihty, that the present Churches, and those Saints who shall come after us, may have cause to praise hiw Holy Name. Which is the unfeigned Prayer adn Desire of us, who subscribe our selves your Servants for Jesus sake.

Hanserd Knollys	*Samuel Battall*	*Leonard Harrison*
William Kiffin	*Isaac Lamb*	*Edward Price*
Andrew Gifford	*Christopher Price*	*William Phips*
Robert Steed	*Robert Keate*	*William Facey*
Thomas Vauxe	*Richard Tidmarsh*	*John Ball*
William Collins	*James Webb*	*William Hankins*
John Tomkins	*John Harris*	*Samuel Ewer*
Toby Willes	*Thomas Winnell*	*Paul Frase*
George Barfitts	*James Hitt*	
Benjamin Keach	*Hercules Collins*	In the Name and behalf
Daniel Finch	*Richard Sutton*	of the whole Assembly.
John Carter	*Robert Knight*	

[*Memorand.* 'Tis agreed to by us, that the next General Assembly be held in London, on that Day which is called *Whitsun-Monday*, 1690.]

(9)

The NARRATIVE *of the Proceedings of the Elders and Messengers of the Baptized Congregations, in their* General Assembly, *met in* London *on* Septemb. 3, *to* 12, 1689.

Whereas we the Pastors and Elders of the several Churches, in and about *London*, did meet together, and seriously take into our consideration the particular States of the *Baptized Churches* among our selves, and after a long Presecution, finding the Churches generally under great Decays in the Power of Godliness, and Defects of Gifts for the Ministry; Also, fearing that the same Decays and Defects might be among the Churches of teh same Faith and Profession throughout *England* and *Wales*, many of their

Ministers being deceased, many having ended their Days in Prison, many scattered by Persecution to other Parts, far distant from the Churches to which they did belong. From a due sense of these Things did by their Letter, dated *July* 28, 1689, write to all the aforesaid Churches throughout *England* and *Wales*, to send their Messengers to a General Meeting at *London*, the 3*d* of the 7*th* Month, 1689. And being met together, the first Day was spent in humbling our selves before the Lord, and to seek of him a right way to direct the best Means and Method to repair our Breaches, and to recover our selves into our former Order, Beauty, and Glory. In prosecution thereof, upon the 4*th* day of the same Month, We, the Elders, ministring Brethren and Messengers of teh Churches in and about *London*, and Elders, Ministring Brethren & Messengers of the several Churches from several parts of *England* and *Wales* hereafter mentioned, being aain come together, after first solemn seeking the Lord by Prayer, did conclude upon these following Preliminaries, and lay them down as the Foundation of this our Assembly, and Rules for our Proceedings; Wherein all the Messengers of the Churches aforesaid, in City and Country (as well for the Satisfaction of every particular Church, as also to prevent all Mistakes, Misapprehensions and Inconveniencies that might arise in time to come concerning this General Assembly) do solemnly, unanimously, profess and declare:

(10)

1. That we disclaim all manner of *Superiority*, *Superintendency* over the Churches; and that we have no *Authoriuty* or *Power*, to prescribe or impose any thing upon the Faith or Practice of any of the Churches of Christ. Our whole Intendment, is to be helpers together of one anothre, by way of Counsel and Advice, in the right understanding of that perfect Rule which our Lord Jesus, the only Bishop of our Souls, hath already prescribed, and given to his Churches in his Word, and therefore do severally and jointly agree.

2. That in those things wherein one Church differs from another Church in their Principles or Practices, in point of Communion, that we cannot, shall not, impose upon any particular Church therein, but leave every Church to their own liberty, to walk together as they have received from the Lord.

3. That if any particular Offence doth arise betwixt one Church and another, or betwixt one particular Person and another, no Offence shall be admitted to be debated among us, till the Rule Christ hath given (in that Manner) be first Answered, and the Consent of both Parties had, or sufficiently endeavoured.

4. That whatever is determined by us in any Case, shall not be binding to any one Church, till the Consent of that Church be first had, and they conclude the same among themselves.

5. That all things we offer by way of Counsel and Advice, be proved out of the Word of God, and the Scriptures annexed.

6. That the Breviats of this Meeting be transcribed, and sent to every particular Church with a Letter.

7. That the Messengers that come to this Meeting, be recommended by a Letter from the Church, and that none be admitted to speak in the Assembly, unless by general Consent.

The Letters from several Churches being read, the Meeting was dismissed till next day, and concluded in Prayer.

Septemb. 5, 1689.

After solemn seeking the Lord, all the Elders, Ministring Brethren, and Messengers aforesaid, considered, debated and concluded, That a publick Fund, or STock was necessary: And came to a Resolve in these three Questions; 1. How to Raise it. 2. To what Uses it should be disposed. 3. How to Secure it.

(11)

Quest. 1. *How or by what Means this Publick Fund, or Stock, should be raised?* Resolved,

1. That it should be raised by a *Free-Will Offering*. That every Person should communicate (for the Uses hereafter mentioned) according to his Ability, and as the Lord shall make him willing, and enlarge his Heart; and that the Churches severally among themselves do order the Collection of it with all convenient speed, that the Ends proposed may be put into present practice.

2. That for the constant carrying it on, there be an annual Collection made in the several Churches, of a Half-penny, Penny, 2*d*, 3*d*, 4*d*, 6*d*, *per* Week, more or less, as every Person shall be made willing, and that every Coingregation do agree among themselves to collect it, either Weekly, Monthly, or Quarterly, according to their own convenience, and that Ministers be desired to shew a good Example herein. *Exod.* 35.4, 5. *1 Chron.* 29.14. *Mal.* 3.10. *Hag.* 1.9. *2 Cor.* 8. 11,12.

3. That every particular Church do appoint their Deacons, or any other faithful Brothers to collect, and to acquaint the Church with the Sum collected, and remit it Quarterly into the Hands of such Person as are hereafter nominate and appointed to receive it at *London*; the first quarterly Paiment to be made the 5th of *December* next.

4. That the Persons appointed to receive all the aforesaid Collections, be our Honoured and well-beloved Brethren, whose Names we have sent you in a printed Paper by it self, all living in and about *London*; and when any of these aforesaid Brethren die, then the major part of the Survivors of them, shall nominate and appoint another Brother in his stead, to be confirme, or refused, at the next General Meeting of this Assembly. And that the said nine Brethren shall disburse it, from time to time, for the uses hereafter mentioned, according to the satisfaction they, or the major part of them, shall have from the Information and Testimony of any two Churches in this Assembly, or from the Testimony of any particular Association of Churches in the Country, or from the Satisfaction they shall have by any other means whatsoever.

Quest. 2. *To what Uses this Fund, or Pulick Stock, shall be disposed?* Resolved,

(12)

1. To communicate thereof to those Churches that are not able to maintain their own Ministry; and that their Ministers may be encouraged wholly to devote themselves to the great Work of Preaching the Gospel.

2. To send Ministers that are ordained (or at least solemnly called) to preach, bot in City and Country, where the Gospel hath, or hath not yet been preached, and to visit the Churches; and these to be chosen out of the Churches in *London*, or in the Country, which Ministers are to be approved of, and sent forth by two Churches at the least, but more if it may be.

3. To assist those Members that shall be found in any of the aforesaid Churches, that are disposed for Study, have an inviting Gift, and are found in Fundamentals, in attaining to the knowledge and understanding of the Languages, Latin, Greek, and

Hebrew. These Members to be represented to the Nine Brethren in *London*, by any two of the Churches that belong to this Assembly.

Resolved, The Mony collected, be returned, as is expressed in a printed Paper aforesaid, of all the Receipts and Disbursements belonging to this aforesaid Fund, or Stock: With an Account signed by them, or the major part of them, shall be sent and transmitted to one Church in every County and from that Church to be communicated to all the rest of the Churches aforesaid within the same County, with all convenient speed. The first Account to be mae and sent the 5th of *January* next.

Resolved, That what Charges soever the said Nine Brethren are at in the Service of this Assembly, shall be discharged out of the aforesaid Stock.

(13)

The Questions Proposed from the several Churches, Debated and Resolved.

Quest. Whether it be not expedient for Churches that live near together, and consist of small numbers, and are not able to maintain their own Ministry, nto join together for the better and more confortable support of their Ministry, and better Edifications one or another?
Answ. Concluded in the Affirmative.

Q. Whether it is not the Duty of every Church of Christ to maintain such Ministers as are set apart by them, by allowing them a confortable Maintenance according to their Ability?
A. Concluded in the Affirmative. *1 Cor.* 9.9, 10, 11, 12, 13, 14. *Gal.* 6.6.

Q. Whether every Church ought not to endeavour not only to provide themselves of an able Ministry for the preaching of the Word, but also to set apart to Office, and in a solemn manner ordain sch as are duly qualified for the same?
A. Concluded in the Affirmative. *Act.* 14.23. *Tit.* 1.5.

Q. Whether it is not the liberty of Baptized Believers to bear any sober and pious Men of the Independent and Presbyterian Persuasion, when they have no opportunity to attend the preaching of the Word in their own Assembly, to have no other to preach unto them?
A. Concluded in the Affirmative. *Act.* 18.24, 25, 26.

Q. Whether the continuing of Gifted Brethren many Years upon trial for Eldership, or any Person for the Office of a Deacon, without ordaining them, altho qualified for the same, be not omission of an Ordinance of God?
A. Concluded in the Affirmative.

Q. What is the Duty of Church-Members when they are disposed to marry, with respect to their Choice?
A. To observe the Apostle's Rule, to marry only in the Lord, *1 Cor.* 7.39.

Q. Whether, when the Church have agreed upon the keeping of one day weekly, or monthly, (besides the first day of the Week) to worship Go, and perform the necessary Services of the Church, they may not charge such Persons with evil that neglect such Meetings, and lay them under

(14)

Reproof, unless such Members can shew good cause for such their Absence?
A. Concluded in the Affirmative, *Heb.* 10.25.

Q. What is to be done with those Persons that will not communicate to the necessary Expences of the Church whereof they are Members, according to their Ability?

A. Resolved, That upon clear Proof, the Persons so offending, as aforesaid, be duly admonished; and if no Reformation, the Church to withdraw from them, *Eph.* 5.3. *Mat.* 25.42. *1 Joh.* 3.17.

Q. What is to be done with those Persons that withdraw themselves from the Fellowship of that particular Church whereof they are Members, and join themselves to the Communion of the National Church?

A. To use all due means to reclaim them buy Instruction and Admonition; and if not thereby reclaimed, to reject them. *Mat.* 18.17. *Luk.* 9.63. *Heb.* 10.38. *Jude* 19.

Resolved. That the like method be taken with those that wholly forsake the Fellowship of that Congregation to which they have solemnly given up themselves.

Q. Whether Believers were not actually reconciled to God, actually justified and adopted when Christ died?

A. That the Reconciliation, Justification, and Adoption of Believers are infallibly secured by the gracious purpose of God, and merit of Jesus Christ. Yet none can be said to be actually reconciled, justified, or adopted, until they are really implanted into Jesus Christ by Faith; and so by virtue of this their Union with him, have these Fundamental Benefits actually conveyed unto them. And this we conceive is fully evidenced, because the Scripture attributes all these Benefits to Faith, as the instrumental cause of them. *Rom.* 3. 25. *Chap.* 5.11. *Chap.* 5.1. *Gal.* 3.26. And gives such Representation of the state of the Elect before Faith as is altogether inconsistent with an actual Right in them, *Eph.* 2.1, 2, 3, - 12.

Q. Whether it be not necessary for the Elders, Ministring-Brethren, and Messengers of teh Churches, to take into their serious consideration those Excesses that are found among their Members, Men and Women, with respect to their Apparel?

A. In the Afirmative. That it is a shame for Men to wear long Hair, or long Perewigs, and especially Ministers, *1 Cor.* 11.14.

(15)

or, strange Apparel, *Zeph.* 1.8. That the Lord reproves the Daughters of *Sion*, for the Bravery, Haughtiness, and Pride of their Attire, walking with stretched-out Necks, wanton Eyes, mincing as they go, *Isa.* 3.16. As if they affected Tallness, as one observes upon their stretched-out Necks, tho some in these Times seem, by their high Dresses, to out do them in that respect. The Apostle *Paul* exhorts, in *1 Tim.* 2. 9, 10. *Women adorn themselves in modest Apparel, with Shamefac'dness and Sobriety: not with Broidered Hair or Gold, or Pearls, or costly Array; but with good Works as becomes Women professing Godliness.* And *1 Pet.* 3. 4, 5. *Whose adorning let it not be the outward adorning, of plaiting the Hair, of wearing of Gold, or of putting on of Apparel: but the Ornament, of a meek and quiet Spirit, which is in the sight of God of great price. For after this* (fashion) *manner, the holy Women who trusted in God adorned themselves.* And therefore we cannot but bewail it, with much Sorrow and Grief of Spirit, That those Brethren and Sisters who have solemnly professed to deny themselves, *Mat.* 16. 24. And who are by Profession obliged in Duty not to conform to this World, Rom. 12.2. should so much comform to the Fashions of this World, and not reform themselves in those Inclinations that their Natures addicted them to in days of Ignorance, *1 Pet.* 1.14. From these Considerations we earnestly desire, That Men and Women, whose Souls are committed to our Charge, may be watched over in this matter, and that care be taken, and that such who are guilty of this crying Sin of Pride, that abounds in the Churches as well as in the Nation, may be reproved; especially considering what Time and Treasure is foolishly wasted in adorning the Body, which would be better spent in a careful endeavour to adorn the Soul; and the charge laid out upon those Superfluities, to relieve the necessities of the poor Saints, and to promote the Interest of Jesus Christ. And though we deny not but in some cases Ornaments may be allowed, yet whatever Ornaments in Men and Women which are inconsistent with Modesty, Gravity, Sobriety, and a Scandal to Religioun, opening the Mouths of the Ungodly, ought to be cast off, being truly no Ornaments to Believers, but rather a Defilement; and that those Ministers and Churches who do not endeavour after a Reformation herein, are justly to be blamed.

(16)

Q. Whether it is not the Duty of all Christians, and Churches of Christ, religiously to observe the Lord's Day, or first Day of the Week, in the Worship and Service of God both in publick and private?

A. It is concluded in the Affirmative. Because we find that Day was set apart for the solemn Worship of God by our Lord Jesus, and his Holy Apostles, through the infallible Inspiration of the Holy Spirit.

1st. Because it appears that the Son of God, who was manifested in the Flesh, had Authority to make a change of the Solemn Day of Worship, being Lord of the Sabbath. *Mat.* 12.8 *Mark* 2.28. *Luke* 6.5.

2dly. It is maniest that our Blessed Lord and Saviour arose on that Day, as having compleated and confirmed the work of our Redemption. *Mat.* 28.1. *Mark* 16.2. *Luke* 2.4. *Joh.* 20.1. whereby he laid the Foundation of the Observation of that Day.

3dly. Our Lord Jesus did then on that Day most plainly and solemnly appear to his Disciples, teaching and instructing them, blessing them, and giving them their Commission, breeathing on them the Holy Ghost. *Luke* 24.13, 31, 36. *Joh.* 20.19, 20, 21, 22.

Moreover, on the next first day of the Week, he appeared to them again, giving them a further infallible proof of his glorious Resurrection. And then convinced the Apostle *Thomas*, who being absent the first Day before, was now with them, *Joh.* 20. 26. Whereby it appears he sanctified and confirmed the religious Observations of that Day, by his own Example.

4thly. Our Lord and Saviour remained with his Disciples forty Days after his Resurrection, and spoke to them of the things pertaining to the Kingdom of God, *Act.* 1.3. And we question not but he then gave command about the Observation of this Day.

5thly. Which appears, in that for a further confirmation thereof, after his Ascension, when his Disciples or Apostles were assembled together, solemnly with one accor, on the Say of *Pentecost*, which (by all computation) was the first Day of the Week; recorded, *Act.* 2.1, 2. He then poured out his Holy Spirit in a marvellous and an abundant Measure upon them.

(17)

6thly. Accordingly, afterwards, we find this Day was solemnly observed by the Churches, as appears, *Acts* 20.7. where we have the Churches assembling on that day plainly asserted, with the solemn Duties then performed, which were Preaching, and breaking of Bread; and all this recorded as their usual Custom, which could be from no other cause but Divine and Apostolical Institution. And it is most remarkable and worthy the serious Observation of all the Lord's People, that although the Holy Apostles, and others that were Preachers of the Gospel, took their opportunities to preach the Word on the Jewish Sabbathpday, and on other days of the Week as they had convenient Seasons afforded; yet we have no Example of the Churches then assembling together to celebrate all the Ordinances of our Lord Jesus peculiar to them, but on the first Day of the Week. Which manifest practice of theirs is evidently as plain a Demonstration of its being a Day set apart for religious Worship, by the Will and Command of our Lord Jesus, as if it had been exprest in the plainest Wors. Forasmuch as they did nothing in those purest Primitive Times in the sacred Worship of God, either as to time or form, but by a Divine Warrant from the Holy Apostles, who were instructed by our Lord Jesus, and were guided in all those Affairs by his faithful and infallible Holy Spirit.

7thly. In like manner the solemn Ordinances of Collection for the necessities of the poor Saints, was commanded by the Lord to be performed on that Day, *1 Cor.* 16. 1, 2. by an Apostolical Ordination; which without question, by reason of their observing that Day for their holy assembling and worship, was then required.

8thly, and *lastly.* It is asserted by all the considerate and able Expositors of the Holy Scriptures, that the denomination or Title of the Lord's Day, mentioned *Rev.* 1.10. was attributed to the First Day of the Week, as the usual distinguishing Name given to that solemn Day by the Christians, or Churches, in the Primitive Times, as being a Day to be spent wholly in the Service and Worship of the Lord, and not in our own worldly and secular Affairs, which are lawful to be attended unto on other Days of the Week.

From all which, laid toether and considered, we are convinced, that it is our Duty religiously to observe that Holy Day in the Celebration of the Worship of God.

(18)

Q. Whether the Graces and Gifts of the Holy Spirit be not sufficient to the making and continuing of an Honourable Ministry in the Churches?

A. Resolved in the Affirmative, *Eph.* 4.8, 9. *1 Cor.* 12.7.

Q. Whether it be not avantageous to our Brethren now in the Ministry, or that may be in the Ministry, to attain to a competent knowledge of the Hebrew, Greek, and Latin Tongues, that they may be the better capable to defend the Truth against Opposers?

A. Resolved in the Affirmative.

Q. Whether an Elder of one Church may administer the Ordinance in other Churches of the same Faith?

A. That an Elder of one Church, may administer the Ordinance of the Lord's Supper to another of the same Faith, being called so to do by the said Church; tho not as Pastor, but as a Minister, necessity being only cnsidered in this Case.

We the Ministers and Messengers of, and concerned for, upwards of one hundred Baptized Congregations in *England,* and *Wales* (denying *Arminianism*) being met together in *London* from the 3*d* of the 7*th* Month to the 11*th* of the same, 1689 to consider of some things that might be for the glory of God, and the good of these Congregations; have thought meet (for the satisfaction of all other Christians that differ from us in the point of Baptism) to recommend to their perusal the Confession of our Faith, Printed for, and sold by, Mr. *John Harris* at the *Harrow* in the *Poultery*: Which Confession we own, as containing the Doctrine of our Faith and Practice; an do desire that the Members of our Churches rewspectively do furnish themselves therewith.

Moreover, this Assembly do declare their Approbation of a certain little book, lately recommended by divers Elders dwelling in and about the City of *London*, Intituled, *The Ministers Maintenance Vindicated.* And it is their Reqiest that the said Treatise ve dispersed amongst all our respective Congregations; and it is desired that some Brethren of each Church take care to dispose of the same accordingly.

(19)

An Account of the several Baptized Churches in England and Wales (owning the Doctrine of Personal Election and Final Perserverance) that sent either their Ministers, or Messengers, or otherwise communicated their State in our General Assembly at London, on the 3d, 4th, and so on to the 11th Day of the 7th Month, called September, 1689.

The Names of the Churches and Messengers

Barkshire.

1	Reading	*William Facy*, Pastor.
		Reynaire Griffin, Messenger.
2	Faringdon	*Richard Steed*, Minister.
		William Mills, Minister.
		Henry Forty, Pastor.
3	Abbingdon	*John Tomkins*.
		Philip Hockton.
4	Newberry	
5	Wantage	*Robert Keate*, Minister.
6	Longworth	*John Man*, Preacher.
		Peter Stephens.

Bedfordshire.

7	Steventon	*Stephen Howtherne*, Pastor
		John Carver.
8	Evershall	*Edward White*, Pastor.

Bristol.

9	Broad-Mead	*Thomas Vans*, Pastor.
		Robert Bodinam.
10	Fryers	*Andrew Gifford*, Pastor.

Buckinghamshire.

11	Haddington	*Paul Tyler*.
12	Stukley	*Robert Knight*, Pastor.

(20)

Cambridg.

13	Cambridg	*Thomas Cowlinge*.
14	Wisbich	*William Ricks*, Preacher.

Cornwall.

15 Looe _____ *Thomas Cowling.*

Devonshire.

16 Holy-Tracy _____ *Clement Jackson*, Minister.
17 Dartmouth _____ *Philip Cary*, Minister.
18 Ladswell _____ *Samuel Hart*, Minister.
19 Luppit _____ *Thomas Halwell*, Minister.
20 Plimouth _____   *Holdenby*, Pastor.
     Samuell Buttall, Minister.
21 South-Molton ' _____ *Thomas Stoneman*, Messenger
22 Tiverton _____ *John Ball.*
     Tristram Trurin, Minister.

Dorsetshire.

23 Dorchester _____ *Thomas Cox*, Minister.
24 Dalwood _____ *James Hitt*, Preacher.
     Thomas Payne, Preacher.
25 Lime _____ *Simon Orchard*, Minister.

Durham.

26 Muggleswick _____ *John Ward.*
     Henry Blackhead.
27 Newcastle on Tine _____ *Richard Pitts*, Pastor.
     John Turner.

Essex.

28 Hadfield-Braddock _____ *William Collins*, Pastor.
29 Harlow _____ *William Woodward*, Pastor.
     James Newton.

Exon County.

30 Exon _____ *William Phipps*, Pastor.
     Richard Adams.

(21)

Gloucestershire.

31 Burton on the Hill and _____ *John Goring*, Pastor.
    Morton Hinmast   *Anthony Freeman.*
32 Cirincester _____ *Giles Watkins*, Minister.
33 Dimmock _____ *William Hankins*, Pastor.
34 Marring-Hampton _____
35 Nimpsfield _____ *Robert Williams.*
36 Sudbury _____
37 Tewksbury _____ *Eleazar Herringe*, Pastor.
     Edward Canter.

Glamorganshire.

38 Swanzey _____ *Lewis Thomas*, Pastor.

Francis Giles.

Hartfordshire.

39	Hempstead	*Samuel Ewer*, Pastor.
		William Aldwin.
40	Kingsworth	*James Hardinge*, Minister.
		Daniel Finch, Minister.
41	Perton	
42	Theobalds	*Joseph Masters*, Pastor.
		Joseph Seward.
43	Tringe	*Richard Sutton*, Pastor.
		John Bishop.

Hampshire.

44	Christ-Church	*Joseph Brown.*
		John Lillington.
45	Ringwood	
46	South-Hampton	*Richard Ring*, Pastor.
		John Greenwood.
47	White-Church	*Richard Kent,* *Stephen Kent.* } Messengers.

Herefordshire.

48	Hereford City	*Edward Price*, Pastor.
49	Weston and Pinnard	*Richard Perkins*, Preacher.

(22)

Kent.

50	Sandwich	*Thomas Fecknam*, Pastor.
		Edward Taylor.

Lancashire.

51	Warrington	*Loe*, Pastor.

Leicestershire.

52	Kilbey	*Henry Coleman*, Pastor.
		Benjamin Winkles.

London.

53	Broken-Wharf	*Hanserd Knowllys,* *Robert Steed.* } Pastors.
		John Skinner.
		Thomas Lampet.
54	Devonshire-Square	*William Kiffin*, Pastor.
		Morris King.
		William Clark.
55	Joyners-Hall	*John Harris*, Pastor.

		Samuel Boneal.
		William Dicks.
56	Hounsditch	*John Merriot.*
		Edward Man, Pastor.
		John Burkes.
57	*Petty-France*	*Richard Hollowell.*
		William Collins, Pastor.
		John Collet.
		Thomas Harrison.

Middlesex.

58	Lime-House	*Leonard Harrison*, Pastor.
		Samuel Booth.
59	Mile-end Green	*John Hunt.*
		George Barret, Pastor.
		Isaac Marloe.
		John Putipher.
60	Culman-Green	*Daniel Hawes.*

(23)

61	Pennington-Street	*Isaac Lambe*, Pastor.
		Humphrey Burroughs.
62	Wapping	*John Gillet.*
		Hercules Collins, Pastor.
		Humphrey Hutchings.
		John Overinge.

Monmouthshire.

63	Abergaviny	*Christopher Price*, Minister.
64	Blainegumt	*William Prichard*, Pastor.
65	Galoen	
66	Lanwamouth	
67	Glanmenock	

Norfolk.

68	Pulham-Market	*Henry Bradshaw.*
69	Norwich	*Austin*, Pastor.
		Thomas Flatman, Minister.

Oxfordshire.

70	Finstock	*John Carpenter*, Minister.
		Joshua Brooks.
71	Hook-Norton	*Charles Archer*, Pastor.
72	Oxford City	*Richard Tidmarsh*, Minister.

Pembrookshire.

73	Neare	*Griffith Howel.*
		William Jones, Pastor.

Somersetshire.

74 Bath-Haycomb _____   *Richard Gay*, Minister.
75 Bridgwater _____   *Tobias Wells*, Pastor.
                                          William Coleman.
76 Chard _____   *William Wilkins*, Minister.
77 Charton _____   *William Woodman.*
78 Dunster and Stockgomer _____
79 Froome _____   *William Randalfe.*
80 Hallitraw _____   *John Andrews.*

(24)

81 Hatch _____   *Jeremiah Day.*
82 Kilmington _____   *Robert Cox*, Minister.
83 Taunton _____   *Thomas Winnell*, Pastor.
84 Wedmore _____   *George Stant*, Minister.
85 Wells _____   *Timothy Brook*, Minister.
86 Yeovel and Perriot _____   *Thomas Miller*, Minister.

Suffolk

87 Framington _____   *Thomas Mills*, Minister.

Surry

Southwark _____
88 Horse-lie-down _____   *Benjamin Keach*, Minister.
                                          John Leader.
                                          Thomas Dawson.
                                          Edward Sandford.

89 Mayes Pond _____
90 Shad-Thames _____   *Richard Adams*, Minister.
                                          Nathaniel Crabb.
                                          John Bernard.
91 Gilford _____   *John Ward.*
92 Richmond _____   *Hezekiah Brent*, Minister.
                                          John Scot, Minister.

Warwickshire

93 Alestree _____   *John Wills.* .
                                          John Higgins.
94 Warwick _____   *Paul Fruine*, Minister.
                                          Robert Paule.

Wiltshire

95 Bradford _____   *John Flouret.*
96 Calne _____
97 Cley-Chase _____
98 Devises _____   *James Webb.*

99 Ecclestocke _____ *William Aldridge.*
Edward Froud.

(25)

100 Knolles _____ *John Williams*, Pastor.
101 Malmsbury _____ *Arch*, Pastor.
102 Milsham _____
103 Porton _____ *Walter Pen.*
John Andrews.
104 Southweeke _____ *Joseph Holton.*
John Layes.
105 Warminster _____ *John Werell*, Pastor.
106 Westbury _____ *Roger Cator.*

Warwickshire

107 Bromsrove _____ *John Eccles*, Pastor.

[Hearty Thanks are returned to you for your great Love
and Charity towards our poor Brother *Richard Dorwood*,
upon the account of his Loss by Fire.]

---

(26)

The Assembly of the Elders, Messengers, and Ministring-Brethren, sent by, and concerned for, more than one hundred Baptized Congregations of the same Faith with themselves, from many parts of *England* and *Wales* (met together in *London Sept. 3* to *12, 1689*, to consider of several things relating to the well-being of the same Churches). And having that opportunity, judged it their Duty to clear themselves from those Reproaches cast on them, occasioned by the weakness of some few of their Perswation, who in the late King's Reign, were imployed as Regulators for the Support of his Dispensing Power.

There having been many Reflections cast upon us, under the Name of *Anabaptists*, as such, as having in the late Times, for out of Liberties-sake, compiled with the Popish Party, to the hazard of the Protestant Religion, and the Civil Liberties of the Nation: We being met together, some from most parts of this Kingdom, judg it our Duty to clear our selves from the said Reflections cast upon us. And we do first declare, that to the utmost of our Knowledg, there was not one Congregation that had a hand, or gave consent to any thing of that Nature, nor did ever countenance any of their Members to own as Absolute Powder in the late King, to dispense with the Penal Laws and Tests; being well satisfied, that the doing thereof by his sole Prerogative, would lay the Foundation of Destruction of the Protestant Religion, and Slavery to this Kingdom.

But yet we must confess, that some few Persons (from their own Sentiment, which were of our Societies, used their endeavours for the taking off the Penal Laws and Tests; and were employed by the late King *James* to to into divers Counties, and to several Corporations, to improve their Interest therein but met with little, or no Encouragement by any of our Members; though considering the Temptations some were under (their Lives being in their Enemies Hands) the great Sufferings, by Imprisonments, Excommunications, etc. that did attend from the Ecclesiastical Courts, as also by the frequent Molestations of informers against our Meetings, by means

(27)

whereof many Families were ruined in their Estates, as also deprived of all our Liberties, and denied the common Justice of the Nation, by the Oaths and Perjury of the vilest of Manking, might be some abatement to the severe Censures that have attended us, tho if some amongst us, in the hopes of a Deliverance from the heavy Bondage thy then lay under, might miscarry, by falling in with the late King's Design. It being also well known that some Congregations have not only reproved those amon them that were so employed, but in a regular way have further proceeded against them. From whence it seems unreasonable, that for the miscarriage of a few Persons, the whole Party should be laid under Reproach and Infamy.

It being our professed Judgment, and we on all Occasions shall manifest the same, to venture our All for the Protestant Religion, and Liberties of our Native Countrey.

And we do with great Thankfulness to God acknowledg his special Goodness to these Nations, in raising up our present King *William*, to be a blessed Instrument, in his Hand, to deliver us from Popery and Arbitrary Power, and shall always (as in duty bound) pray that the Lord may continue Him and His Royal Consort long to be a Blessing to these Kingdoms, and shall always be ready to the utmost of our ability, in our Places, to join our Hearts and Hands with the rest of our Protestant Brethren, for the Preservation of the Protestant Religion and the Liberties of the Nation.

William Kiffin,	*Benjamin Keach,*	*Thomas Winnel,*
Hanserd Knowllys,	*Samuel Buttall,*	*James Hitt,*
Andrew Gifford,	*Isaac Lamb,*	*Edward Price,*
Robert Steed,	*Christopher Price,*	*William Phips,*
Thomas Vauxe,	*Robert Keate,*	*William Facey,*
John Tomkins,	*Richard Tidmarsh,*	*John Ball,*
Toby Wells,	*James Webb,*	*William Hankins,*
George Barret,	*John Harris,*	*Paul Fruin.*

FINIS

Appendix E: *The Conventicle Act* (1664)[1]

An Act to suppress and prevent Seditious Conventicles

Whereas an Act made in the five and thirtieth year of the Reign of our late Sovereign Lady Queen Elizabeth, Entitled, An Act to retain the Queens Majesties Subjects in their due Obedience, hath not been put in due Execution, by reason of some doubt of late made, whether the said Act be still in force; although it be very clear and evident, and it is hereby Declared, that the said Act is still in force, and ought to be put in due execution.

For providing therefore of further and more speedy Remedies against the growing and dangerous Practices of Seditious Sectaries, and other disloyal persons, who under pretence of Tender Consciences, do at their Meetings contrive Insurrections, as late experience hath shewed: Be it by the Kings most Excellent Majesty, by, and with the Advice and Consent of the Lords Spiritual and Temporal, and Commons in this present Parliament Assembled, and by the Authority of the same, That if any person of the age of Sixteen years or upwards, being a Subject of this Realm, at any time after the first of July, which shall be in the year of our Lord, One thousand six hundred sixty and four, shall be present at any Assembly, Conventicle, or Meeting, under colour or pretence of Exercise of Religion, in other manner then is allowed by the Liturgy, or practice of the Church of England, in any place within the Kingdom of England, Dominion of Wales, or Town of Berwick upon Tweed, At which Conventicle, Meeting, or Assembly, there shall be five persons or more assembled together, over and above those of the same household; Then it shall and may be lawful to, and for the Cheif Magistrate of the place where such offence aforesaid shall be committed (if it be within a Corporation where there are not two Justices of the Peace) And they are hereby requited and enjoyned upon proof to them or him respectively made of such offence, either by confession of the party, or Oath of Witness, or notorious Evidence of the fact: (Which Oath the said Justices of the Peace, and Cheif Magistrate respectively, are hereby impowred and required to administer) to make a Record of every such offence and offences under their Hands and Seals respectively; which Record so made as aforesaid, shall to all intents and purposes, be in Law taken and adjudged to be a full and perfect Conviction of every such Offender for such offence: and thereupon the said Justices and Cheif Magistrate respectively, shall commit every such Offender so convicted aforesaid, to the Goal or House of Correction, there to remain without Bail or Mainprize, for any time not exceeding the space of three Months, unless such offender shall pay down to the said Justices or Cheif Magistrate, such Sum of Money not exceeding five pounds, as the said Justices, or Cheif Magistrate (who are hereby thereunto authorized and requited) shall Fine the said offender at, for his or her said offence; which Money shall be paid to the Church Wardens for the relief of the Poor of the Parish where such offender did last inhabit.

And be it further Enacted by the Authority aforesaid, that if such Offender, so convicted as aforesaid, shall at any time again commit the like offence contrary to the

---

[1] The Act lapsed on 1 March 1669.

Act, and be thereof in manner aforesaid, Then such Offender so convict of such second offence, shall incur the penalty of Imprisonment in the Goal, or House of Correction, for any time not exceeding six Months, without Bail or Mainprize, unless such offender shall pay down to the said Justices or Cheif Magistrate (who are thereunto authorized and requited as aforesaid) shall fine the said offender at, for his or her second offence, the said fine to be disposed in manner aforesaid.

And be it further Enacted by the Authority aforesaid, That if any such Offender so convict of a second offence, contrary to this Act in manner aforesaid, shall at any time again commit the like offence contrary to this Act, Then two Justices of the Peace, and Chief Magistrate as aforesaid respectively, shall commit every such Offender to the Goal, or House of Correction, there to remain without Bail of Mainprize, until the next General Quarter Sessions, Assizes, Goal-delivery, great Sessions, or sitting of any Commission of Oyer and Terminer in the respective County, Limit, Division or Liberty which shall first happen; when, and where every such Offender shall be proceeded against by Indictment for such offence, and shall forthwith be arraigned upon such Indictment, and shall then plead the General Issue of Not guilty. And if such Offender proceeded against, shall be lawfully convict of such Offence, either by Confession or Verdict, of if such Offender shall refuse to plead the General Issue, or to confesse the Indictment, then the respective Justices of the Peace at their General Quarter Sessions, Judges of Assize and Goal-delivery at the Assizes and Goal-delivery, Justices of the great Sessions at the great Sessions, and Commissioners of Oyer and Terminer, at their sitting, are hereby enabled and required to cause Judgement to be entred against such Offender. That such Offender shall be Transporter beyond the Seas to any of his Majesties Foreign Plantations (Virginia and New England onely excepted) there to remain for Seven years; And shall forthwith under their Hands and Seals make out Warrants to the Sheriff or Sheriffs of the same County where such Conviction or Refusal to Plead or to Confesse as aforesaid, shall be, safely to convey such Offender to some Port or Haven nearest or most commodious to be appointed by them respectively; And from thence to Embargue such Offender to be safely Transported to any of his Majesties Plantations beyond the Seas, as shall be also by them respectively appointed (Virginia and New England only excepted:) Whereupon the said Sheriff shall safely Convey and Embargue, or cause to be Conveyed or Embargued such offender, to be Transported as aforesaid, under pain of forfeiting for default of so Transporting every such Offender, the sum of Forty pounds of lawful money, the moyety thereof to the King, and the other moyety to him or them that shall Sue for the same in any of the Kings Courts of Record, by Bill, Plaint, Action of Debt, or Information; in any of which, no Wager of Law Essoign or Protection shall be admitted. And the said respective Court shall then also make out Warrants to the several Constables, Head-boroughs, or Tythingmen of the respective places where the Estate real or personal of such Offender so to be Transported shall happen to be, commanding them thereby to Sequester into their hands the profits of the Lands, and to distrain and sell the Goods of the Offender so to be Transported, for the reimbursing of the said Sheriff all such reasonable charges as he shall be at, and shall be allowed him by the said respective Court such Conveying and Embarguing of such Offender so to be Transported, rendring to the party , of his or her Assigns, the overplus of the same, if any be; unless such Offender, or some other on the behalf of such Offender so to be Transported, shall give the Sheriff such Security As he shall approve of for the paying all the said Charges unto him.

And be it further Enacted by the Authority aforesaid, That in default of defraying such Charges by the parties so to be Transported, or some other on their behalf, or in default of Security given to the Sheriff as aforesaid, It shall and may be lawful, for every such Sheriff to Contract with any Master of a Ship, Merchant, or other person, for the

Transporting of such Offender at the best rate he can. And that in every such Case it shall and man be lawful for such persons so Contracting with any Sheriff for Transporting such Offender as aforesaid, to detain and employ every such Offender so by them Transported, as a Labourer to them or their Assigns for the space of Five years, to all intents and purposes, as if he or she were bound by Indentures to such person for that purpose: And that the respective Sheriffs shall be allowed or paid from the King, and upon their respective Attempts in the Exchequer, all such charges by them expended, for Conveying, Embarguing and Transporting of such persons, which shall be allowed by the said respective Courts from whence they received their respective Warrants, and which shall not have been by any of the ways aforementioned paid, secured, or reimbursed unto them as aforesaid.

Appendix F: *The Declaration of Indulgence* (1672)
(David Neal *The History of the Puritans or Protestant Non-Conformists, Volume 4*
(London: 1738): 443-445)

Charles Rex

Our Care and Endeavours for the Preservation of the Rights and Interests of the Church, have been sufficiently manifested to the World, by the whole Course of our Government since our happy Restoration, and by the many and frequent Ways of *Coercion* that we have used for reducing all erring or dissenting Persons, and for composing the unhappy Differences in Matters of Religion, which we have found among our Subjects upon our Return: but it being evident by the sad Experience of twelve Years, that there is very little Fruit of all these forcible Courses, *We think ourselves obliged to make use of that supreme Power in Ecclesiastical Matters, which is not only inherent in us, but hath been declared and recognized to be so, by several Statutes and Acts of Parliament*; and therefore we do no accordingly issue this our Declaration, as well for the quieting of our good Subjects in these Points, as for inviting Strangers in this Conjecture to come and live under us; and for the better Encouragement of all to a chearful following of their Trades and Callings, from whence we hope, by the Blessing of God, to have many good and happy Advantages to our Government; as also for preventing for the Future the Dangers that might otherwise arise from private Meetings and seditious Conventicles.

And in the first Place, we declare our express Resolution, Meaning and Intention to be, that the Church of *England* be preserved, and remain entire in its Doctrine, Discipline and Government, as now it stands established by Law; and that this be taken to be, as it is, the Basis, Rule, and Standard of the general and publick Worship of God, and that the Orthodox conformable Clergy do receive and enjoy the Revenues belonging thereunto, and that no Person, tho' of a different Opinion and Persuasion, shall be exempt from paying his Tithes, or Dues whatsoever. And farther we declare, that no Person shall be capable of holding any Benefice, Living, or Ecclesiastical Dignity or Preferment of any kind, in this our Kingdom of *England*, who is not exactly conformable.

We do in the next Place declare our Will and Pleasure to be, that *the Execution of all, and all manner of Penal Laws in matters Ecclesiastical, against whatsoever Sort of Non-Conformists or Recusants, be immediately suspended, and they are hereby suspended*; and all Judges, Judges of Assize and Gaol Delivery, Sheriffs, Justices of Peace, Mayors, Bailiffs, and other Officers whatsoever, whether Ecclesiastical or Civil, are to take Notice of it, and pay due Obedience thereunto.

And that there may be no Pretence for any of our Subjects to continue their illegal Meetings and Conventicles, we do declare, that we shall from Time to Time allow a sufficient Number of Places, as they shall be desired, in all Parts of this our Kingdom, for the Use of such as do not conform to the Church of *England*, to meet and assemble in order to their publick Worship and Devotion, which Places shall be open and free to all Persons.

But to prevent such Disorders and Inconveniencies as may happen by this our Indulgence, if not duly regulated; and that they may be th better protected by the Civil Magistrate, *our express Will and Pleasure is, that none of our Subjects do presume to meet in any Place, until such Places be allowed, and the Teachers of that Congregation be approved by us.*

And lest any should apprehend that this Restriction should make our said Allowance and Approbation difficult to be obtained, we do further declare, that this our Indulgence, as to the Allowance of the publick Places of Worship, and Approbation of the Preachers, shall extend to all Sorts *of Non-Conformists and Recusants, except the Recusants of the Roman Catholic religion*, to whom we shall in no wise allow publick Places of Worship, but only indulge their Share in the common Exemption from the Penal Laws, and the Exercise of their Worship in their private Houses only.

And if after this our Clemency and Indulgence any of our Subjects shall pretend to abuse this Liberty, and shall preach seditiously, or to the Derogation of the Doctrine, Discipline or Government of the Established Church, or shall meet in Places not allowed by us, we do hereby give them Warning and declare, we will proceed against them with all imaginable Severity. And we will let them see, we can be as severe to punish such Offenders when so justly provoked, as we are inulgent to truly tender Consciences.

Given at our Court at Whitehall this 15ᵗʰ Day of March, in the four and twentieth Year of our Reign.

Appendix G: *The Act of Toleration* (1689)

An Act for Exempting Their Majesties Protestant Subjects, Dissenting from the Church of England from the Penalties of certain Laws

Inasmuch as Ease to Scrupulous Consciences in the Exercise of Religion may be an effectual means to Unite Their Majesties Protestant Subjects in Interest and Affection.

Be it Enacted by the King and Queens most Excellent Majesties by and with the Advice and Consent of the lords Spiritual and Temporal and the Commons in this present Parliament Assembled, and by the Authority of the same, That neither the Statutes made in the Three and Twentieth Year of the Reign of the late Queen Elizabeth, Instituted, *An Act to Retain the Queens Majesties Subjects in their Due Obedience*; Nor the Statue made in the Twenty ninth Year of the said Queen, Intitled, *An Act for the more Speedy and Due Execution of certain Branches of the Statute made in the Three and twentieth Year of the Queens Majesties Reign, Viz.* The aforesaid Act, nor that Branch or Clause of a Statute made in the First Year of the Reign of the said Queen, Instituted, *An Act for the Uniformity of Common Prayer and Service in the Church and Administration of the Sacraments*; Whereby all Persons having no Lawful or Reasonable Excuse to be Absent, are required to Resort to their Parish Church or Chappel, or some usual Place where the Common Prayer shall be used upon pain of Punishment by the Censures of the Church, and also upon pain that every Person so Offending shall forfeit for every such Offence Twelve pence: Nor the Statute made in the Third Year of the Reign of the late King James the First, Intitled, *An Act for the better Discovering and Repressing Popish Recusants*; Nor that other Statute made in the same Year, Entitled, *An Act to Prevent and Avoid Dangers which may grow by Popish Recusants; Nor any other Law, or Statute of this Realm made against Papists or Popish Recusants*, Nor any other Law, or Statue of this Realm made against Papists or Popish Recusants, Except the Statute made in the five and twentieth Year of King Charles the Second, Intitled, An Act for Preventing Dangers which may happen from Popish Recusants; And Except also the Statute made in the Thi8rtieth Year of the said King Charles the Second, Intituled, *An Act for the more Effectual Preserving the Kings Person and Government, by Disabling Papists from Sitting in either House of Parliament*; Shall be Construed to Extend to any Person or Persons Dissenting from the Church of England, that shall takje the Oaths mentioned in a Statute mad this present Parliament, Intituled, *An Act for Removing and Preventing all Questions and Disputes Concerning the Assembling and Sitting of this present Parliament*; And shall Make and Subscribe the Declaration mentioned in a Statute made in the Thirtieth Year of the Reign of King Charles the Second, Intituled, An Act to Prevent Papists from Sitting in either House of Parliament; With the Oaths and Declaration, the Justices of Peace at the General Sessions of the Peace to be held for the County or Place where such Person shall live, are hereby Required to Tender and Administer to such Persons as shall offer themselves to Take, Make, and Subscribe the same, and thereof to keep a Register: And likewise none of the Persons aforesaid, shalt give or pay as any fee, or Reward to any Officer, or Officers belonging to the Court aforesaid, above the Sum of Six pence, nor thaqt more then once for his or their entry of his taking the said Oaths, and Making and Subscribing the said Declaration; Nor above the further Sum of Six pence for any Certificate of the same to be made out, and Signed by the Officer, or Officers of the said Court.

And be it further Enacted by the Authority aforesaid, That all and every Person and Persons already Convicted or Prosecuted in order to Conviction of Recusancy by Indictment, Information, Action of Debt, or otherwise grounded upon the aforesaid Statutes, or any of them, that shall take the said Oaths mentioned in the said Statute made this present parliament, and Make and Subscribe the Declaration aforesaid, in the Court of Exchequer, or Assizes or General, or Quarter Sessions to be held for the County where such Person lives, and to the thence respectively Certified into the Exchequer, shall be thenceforth Exempted and Discharged from all the Penalties, Seizures, Forfeitures, Judgments and Executions, Incurred by Force of any the aforesaid Statutes, Without any Composition, Fee, or further Charge whatsoever.

And be it further Enacted by the Authority aforesaid, That all and every person and persons that shall aforesaid take the said Oaths, and Make and Subscribe the Declaration aforesaid, shall not be liable to any Pains, Penalties, or Forfeitures, mentioned in an Act made in the Five and thirtieth Year of the Reign of the Late Queen Elizabeth Intituled, *An Act to Retain the Queen's Majesties Subjects in their due Obedience*; Nor in an Act made in the Two and twentieth Year of the Reign of the late King Charles the Second, Intituled, *An Act to Prevent and Suppress Seditious Conventicles*; Nor shall any of the said Persons by Prosecuted in in any Ecclesiastical Court, for or by reason of their Nonconforming to the Church of England.

Provided always, and be it Enacted by the Authority aforesaid, That if any Assembly of persons Dissenting from the Church of England shall be had in any place for Religious Worship with the Doors Locked, Barred or Bolted during any time of such Meeting together, all and every person or persons that shall come to and be at such Meeting, shall not receive any benefit from the Law, but be liable to all the Pains and Penalties of all the aforesaid Laws recited in this Act for such their Meeting, notwithstanding his taking the Oaths, and his Waking and Subscribing the Declaration aforesaid.

Provided always, That nothing herein contained shall be Construed to Exempt any of the persons aforesaid from the paying of Tythes or other Parochial Duties, or any other Duties to the Church or Minister, nor from any Prosecution in any Ecclesiastical Court or elsewhere for the same.

And be it further Enacted by the Authority aforesaid, That if any person Dissenting from the Church of England, as aforesaid, shall hereafter be Chosen or otherwise Appointed to bear the Office of High Constable or Petty Constable, Church Warden, Overseer of the Poor, or any other Parochial or Ward Office, and such person shall Scruple to take upon him any of the said Offices in regard of the Oaths, or any other Matter or Thing required by the Law to be taken or done in respect of such Office, Every such person shall and may execute such Office or Employment by a sufficient Deputy, by him to be provided, that shall Comply with the Laws on this behalf.

Provided always the said Deputy be Allowed and Approved by such person or persons, in such manner as such Officer or Officers respectively should by Law have been Allowed and Approved.

And be it further Enacted by the Authority aforesaid, That no person Dissenting from the Church of England in Holy Orders, or pretended Holy Orders, or pretending Holy Orders, nor any Preacher or Teacher of any Congregation of Dissenting Protestants, that shall Make and Subscribe the Declaration aforesaid, and take the said Oaths at the General or Quarter Sessions of the Peace to be held for the County, Town, Parts or Division where such person lives, which Court is hereby impowered to Administer the same, and shall also Declare the Approbation of, and Subscribe the Articles of Religion mentioned in the Statute made in the Thirteenth Year of the Reign of the late Queen Elizabeth. Except the Thirty fourth, Thirty fifth, and Thirty sixth, and these words of the Twentieth Article, Viz. *[The Church hath power to Decree Rights or Ceremonies, and Authority in Controversies of Faith, and yet]* shall be liable to any of the Pains or Penalties mentioned in an Act made in the Seventeenth Year of the Reign of King Charles the Second, Intituled, *An Act for Restraining Non-Conformists from Inhabiting in Corporations*; Nor the Penalties mentioned in the aforesaid Actmade in the Two and Twentieth Year of the said late Majesties Reign, for or by reason of suchy persons Preaching at any Meeting for the Exercise of Religion; Nor to the Penalty of One hundred pounds mentioned in an Act made in the Thirteenth and Fourteenth of King Charles the Second, Intituled, *An Act for the Uniformity of Publick Prayers, and Administration of Sacraments, and other Rites and Ceremonies: And for Establishing the Form of Making, Ordaining and Consecrating of Bishops, Priests and Deacons in the Church of England*, for Officiating in any Congregation for the Exercise of Religion permitted and allowed by this Act.

Provided always, that the Making and Subscribing the said Declaration and the Taking the said Oaths, and Making the Declaration of Approbation and Subscription to the said Articles, in manner as aforesaid, by every respective person or persons herein before mentioned, at such General or Quarter Sessions of the Peace as aforesaid, shall be then and there Entred of Record in the said Court, for which Six pence shall be paid to the Clerk of the Peace and no more.

Provided that such Person shall not at any time Preach in any place, but with the Doors not Locked, Barred, or Bolted, as aforesaid.

And Whereas some Dissenting Protestants Scruple the Baptizing of Infants, Be it Enacted by the Authority aforesaid, That every Person in pretended Holy Orders, or Pretending to Holy Orders, or Preacher, or Teacher, that shall Subscribe the aforesaid Articles of Religion, Except before Excepted, and also Except part of the Seven and twentieth Article touching *Infant Baptism*, and shall take the said Oaths, and Make & Subscribe the Declaration aforesaid, in nammer aforesaid, every such Person shall enjoy all the Priviledges, Benefits and Advantages which any other Dissenting Minister as aforesaid might have, or enjoy by vertue of this Act.

And be it further Enacted by the Authority aforesaid, That every Teacher or Preacher in Holy Orders, or pretended Holy Orders, that is a Minister, Preacher, or Teacher of a Congregation, that shall take the Oaths herein Required, and Make and Subscribe the Declaration aforesaid, And also Subscribe such of the aforesaid Articles of the Church of England, as are Required by this Act in manner aforesaid, shall be thenceforth Exempted from serving upon any Jury, or from being Chosen or Appointed to bear the Office of Church Warden, Overseer of the Poor, or any other Parochial or Ward Office, or other Office in any hundred of any Shire, City, Town, Parish, Division, or Wapentake.

And be it further Enacted by the Authority aforesaid, That every Justice of the Peace, may at any time hereafter Require any Person that goes to any Meeting for Exercise of Religion, to Make and Suscribe the Declaration aforesaid, and also to take the said Oaths or Declaration of Fidelity herein after mentioned, in Case such Person scruples the taking of an Oath, and upon refusal thereof, such Justice of the Peace is hereby Required to Commit such Person to Prison Without Bail or Mainprize, and to Certifie the Nanme of such Person to the next General or Quarter Sessions of the Peace to be held for that County, City, Town, Part or Division where such Person then Resides, and if such Person so Committed, shall upon a second tender at the General or Quarter Sessions refuse to Make and Subscribe the Declaration aforesaid, such Persons refusing shall be then and there Recorded, and he shall be taken thenceforth to all Intents and Purposes, for a Popish Recusant Convict, and suffer accordingly, and incur all the Penalties and Forfeitures of the aforesaid Laws.

And whereas there are certain other persons, Dissenters from the Church of England, who Scruple the taking of any Oath, Be it Enacted by the Authority aforesaid, That every such person shall Make and Subscribe the aforesaid Declaration, and also this Declaration of Fidelity following, Viz.

I, A.B. Do sincerely Promise and Solemnly Declare before God and the World, that I will be True and Faithful to King William and Queen Mary; And I do Solemnly Profess and Declare, that I do from my Heart Abhor, Detest and Renounce as Impious and Heretical, that damnable Doctrine and Position, That Princes Excommunicated or Deprived by the Pope, or any Authority of the See of Rome, may be Deposed or Murthered by Their Subjects, or any other whatsoever. And I do Declare, that no Foreign Prince, Person, Prelate, State or Potentate hath, or ought to have any Power, Jurisdiction, Superiority, Preeminence or Authority Ecclesiastical or Spiritual within this Realm.

And shall Subscribe a Profession of their Christian Belief in these Words,

I, A.B. Profess faith in God the Father, And in Jesus Christ his Eternal Son, the true God, And in the Holy Spirit, one God blessed for evermore; And do acknowledge the Holy Scriptures of the Old and New Testament to be given by Divine Inspiration.

Which Declaration and Subscription shall be made and Entred of Record at the General Quarter Sessions of the Peace for the County, City or Place where every such Person shall then Reside. And every such Person that shall Make and Subscribe the Two Declarations and Profession aforesaid, being thereunto Required, shall be Exempted from all the Pains and Penalties of all and every the aforementioned Statutes made against Popish Recusants, or Protestant Nonconformists, and also from the Penalties of an Act made in the fifth Year of the Reign of the late Queen Elizabeth, Intituled, *An Act for the Assurance of the Queen's Royal Power over all Estates, and Subjects within Her Dominion*; for or by reason of such Persons not making or refusing to take the Oath mentioned in the said ACT; And also from the Penalties of an Act made in the Thirteenth and Fourteenth Years of the Reign of King Charles the Second, Intituled, *An Act for Preventing Mischiefs that may arise by certain Persons called Quakers, refusing to take Lawful Oaths*; And enjoy all other the Benefits, Priviledges and Advantages under the, like Limitations, Provisors, and Conditions which any other Dissenters shall, or ought to enjoy by Virtue of this Act.

Provided always, And be it Enacted by the Authority aforesaid, That in case any person shall refuse to take the said Oaths, when tendred to them, which every Justice of the Peace is hereby Impowered to do, such person shall not be admitted to Make and Subscribe the Two Declarations aforesaid, though required thereunto either before any Justice of the Peace, or at the General or Quarter Sessions before or after any Conviction of Popish Recusancy, as aforesaid, unless such person can within Thirty one days after such tender of the Declarations to him, produce Two sufficient Protestant Witnesses, to Testifie upon Oath that they believe him to be a Protestant Dissenter, or a Certificant under the hands of four Protestants who are Conformable to the Church of England, or have taken the Oaths and Subscribed the Declaration above mentioned, and shall also produce a Certificate under the Hands and Seals of Six or more sufficient Men of the Congregation to which he belongs, owning him for one of them.

Provided also, and be it Enacted by the Authority aforesaid, That until such Certificate under the hands of Six of his Congregation, as aforesaid, be produced, and Two Protestant Witnesses come to attest his being a Protestant Dissenter, or a Certificate under the hands of Four Protestants, as aforesaid, be produced, the Justice of the Peace shall, and hereby is Required to take a Reconizance with Two Sureties in the Penal Sum of Fifty pounds, to be Levyed of his Goods and Chattels, Lands and Tenements to the Use of the King and Queens Majesties, Their Heirs and Successors, for his producing the same; And if he cannot give such Security, to Commit him to Prison, there to remain until he has produced such Certificates, or Two Witnesses, as aforesaid.

Provided always, and it is the true Intent and Meaning of this Act, That all the Laws made and provided for the frequenting of Divine Service on the Lord's Day, commonly called Sunday, shall be still in force, and Execution against all persons that offend against the said Laws. Except such persons come to some Congregations or Assembly of Religious Worship, allowed or permitted by this Act.

Provided always, and be it further Enacted by the Authority aforesaid, That neither this Act nor any Clause, Article, or Thing herein Contained shall Extend or be Construed to Extend to give any Ease, Benefit, or Advantage to any Papist, or Popish Recusant whatsoever, or any person that shall deny in his Preaching or Writing the Doctrine of the Blessed Trinity, as it is Declared in the aforesaid Articles of Religion.

Provided always, and be it Enacted by the Authority aforesaid, That if any person or persons at any time or times after the Tenth day of June, do and shall willingly and of purpose, Maliciously or Contemptuously come into any Cathedral or Parish Church, Chappel, or other Congregation pemitted by this Act, and Disquiet or Disturb the same, or Misuse any Preacher or Teacher, such person or persons upon proof thereof before any Justice of Peace, by Two or more sufficient Witnesses, shall find Two Sureties to be bound by Reconizance in the Penal Sum of Fifty Pounds, and in default of suchy Sureties shall be Committed to Prison, there to remain till the next General or Quarter Sessions; And upon Conviction of the said Offence at the said General or Quarter Sessions, shall suffer the Pain and Penalty of Twenty pounds to the Use of the King and Queens Majesties Their Heirs and Successors.

Provided always, That no Congregation or Assembly for Religious Worship, shall be permitted or allowed by this Act, until the place of such Meeting shall be Certified to the Bishop of the Diocess, or to the Arch-Deacon of that Arch-Deaconry, or to the Justices of the Peace at the General or Quarter Sessions of the Peace for the County, City, or Place in which such Meeting shall be held, and Registred in the said Bishops, or Arch-Deacons Court respectively, or Recorded at the said General or Quarter Sessions; The Register or Clerk of the Peace, whereof respectively is hereby Required to Register the same, and to give Certificate thereof to such Person as shall Demand the same, for which there shall be none greater Fee or Reward taken then the Sum of Six pence.

FINIS

Appendix H: *The Charter of Oxford* (1688) [1]

(Transcription and translation by Larry J. Kreitzer and Deborah W. Rooke)

Text:

[Sheet 1]

[1]   Jacobus Secundus Dei gratia

Anglie Scocie Francie et Hibernie Rex fidei Defensor etc OMNIBUS ad quos p[re]sentes L[itte]re n[ost]re p[er]venerint salutem CUM Civitas n[ost]ra Oxon[ia] in

Com[itatu] n[ost]ro Oxon[iensi] sit Civitas antiqua et valde populosa et divers[is] temporibus antehac divers[is] no[min]ibus Incorporat[a] fuit et In[ha]bitantes eiusdem per divers[a]

no[m]i[n]a Incorporacionis divers[a] lib[er]tat[es] Franches[ia]s Imunitat[es] et Preheminenc[ias] ha[bu]erunt usi et gavisi fuerunt tam r[aci]one divers[orum] Prescripc[i]on[um] us[uum] et Consuetud[inum] in

[5]   eadem Civitat[e] a tempore in cuius contrar[ium] memor[ia] hom[inum] non existit usitat[orum] quam per divers[as] Chart[as] et L[itte]ras Paten[tes] Progenitor[um] n[ost]ror[um] Regium et Reginar[um] Angli[e] eis

p[re]antea fact[as] concess[as] et confirmat[as] CUMQ[UE] seperal[es] Charte et L[itte]re paten[te]s p[re]d[icte] r[aci]one quo[ru]nd[am] abus[uum] defect[uum] seu negligenc[ie] In[ha]bitan[cium] Civitat[is] p[re]d[icte] iam determinat[e] et vacue

existunt unde Incorporacio vel Corpus Corporat[um] eiusd[em] Civitat[is] iam totaliter dissolut[a] existit d[i]ctiq[ue] In[ha]bitan[tes] Civitat[is] illius nos humillime supplicaverint quatenus eisdem

gratiam et munificentiam n[ost]ram Regiam in Concessione ip[s]is tal[ia] lib[er]tat[es] et privileg[ia] qual[ia] nob[is] melius expedire videbitur exhibere et extendere dignaremur SCIATIS

igitur q[uo]d nos meliorac[i]on[em] Civitat[is] n[ost]re de Oxon[ia] gratiose affectant[es] volentes q[uo]d de cetero imp[er]p[etuu]m in Civitat[e] de Oxon[ia] p[re]d[icta] continue h[ab]eatur unus certus et indubitat[us]

[10] modus de et pro Custod[ia] pacis n[ost]re ac p[ro] bono Regimine et gubernac[i]one eiusd[em] Civitat[is] et populi n[ost]ri ib[ide]m de tempore in tempus In[ha]bitanci[u]m et alior[um] illuc de tempore in

tempus confluen[cium] Et q[uo]d Civitas p[re]dicta de cetero imp[er]p[etuu]m sit et p[er]maneat Civitas pacis et quiet[is] ad formidinem et terror[em] malor[um] delinquen[cium] et in p[re]mium bonor[um]

Acetiam ut pax n[ost]ra ceteraq[ue] facta Justicie ib[ide]m melius custodiri possint

---

[1] The Latin text of the Charter was first published by Ogle (1892): 294-314. However there are many inaccuracies within the transcription, notably an error of haplography in lines 76-79 focusing on the word *amovebitur* which results in the omission of 89 words. Ogle's transcription gave no indication of the lacuna within the Latin, a matter which we have attempted to correct here. As far as we are aware, an English translation of this document has never been published before.

et valeant de gra[tia] n[ost]ra sp[ec]iali ac ex certa scientia et mero motu
n[ost]ris voluim[us] ordinavimus
constituimus concessim[us] et declaravim[us] ac p[er] p[re]sentes p[ro] nob[is]
hered[ibus] et Successor[ibus] n[ost]ris volum[us] ordinam[us]
constituim[us] concedim[us] et declaram[us] q[uo]d d[i]cta Civitas Oxon[ia]
in Com[itatu] Oxon[iensi] sit et erit et p[er]maneat de cetero imp[er]p[etuu]m
lib[er]a Civitas de se Et q[uo]d Cives Civitat[is] p[re]dict[e] de cetero
imp[er]p[etuu]m sint et erunt u[nu]m Corpus Corporat[um] et politic[um] in
[15]   re f[ac]to et no[m]i[n]e p[er] no[m]en Maior[is] Ballivor[um] et Co[mmun]itat[is]
Civitat[is] Oxon[ie] in Com[itatu] Oxon[iensi] ac eos p[er] idem no[m]en
Maior[is] Ballivor[um] et Co[mmun]i[tati]s Oxon[ie] in Comitatu
Oxon[iensi] in u[nu]m Corpus
Corporat[um] et politic[um] in re f[ac]to et no[m]i[n]e realiter et ad plen[um] p[ro]
nob[is] hered[ibus] et Successor[ibus] n[ost]ris erigim[us] facim[us]
ordinam[us] constituim[us] cream[us] et declaram[us] p[er] p[re]sentes Et
q[uo]d p[er]
idem no[m]en h[ab]eant Successionem p[er]petuam Et q[uo]d ip[s]i et
Successor[es] sui p[er] nomen Maior[is] Ballivor[um] et Co[mmun]itat[is]
Civitat[is] Oxon[ie] in Com[itatu] Oxon[iensi] sint et erunt modo et
exnunc p[er]petuis futur[is] temporibus p[er]sone h[ab]iles et in lege capaces ac
Corpus Corporat[um] et politic[um] in Lege capac[es] ad h[ab]end[a]
p[er]qui rend[a] recipiend[a] possidend[a] gaudend[a] et retinend[a] Terr[as]
Tenemen[ta] Lib[er]tat[es] Privileg[ia]
Jurisdicc[i]on[es] Franches[ias] et Hereditamen[ta] quecunq[ue] cuiuscunq[ue]
generis no[min]is natur[e] qualitat[is] vel speciei sint vel fuerint sibi et
Successor[ibus] suis in Feodo et p[er]petuitat[e] vel p[ro] termino annor[um]
vel aliter quocunq[ue]
[20]   modo acetiam bon[a] et catall[a] et quascunq[ue] a[lia]s res cuiuscunq[ue] generis
no[min]is nature qualitat[is] vel speciei sint vel fuerint necnon ad dand[a]
concedend[a] dimittend[a] alienand[a] assignand[a] et disponend[a] terr[as]
Ten[emen]t[a] et Hereditament[a] bona et catall[a] et omn[ia] et singula al[ia]
fact[a] et revs faciend[a] et exequend[a] per nomen p[re]dict[um] Et q[uo]d
p[er] idem no[m]en Maior[is] Ballivor[um] et Co[mmun]itat[is] Civitat[is]
Oxon[ie] in Com[itatu] Oxon[iensi] pl[ac]itare et impl[ac]itari
respondere et responderi defendere et defendi valeant et possint in quibuscunq[ue]
Curiis placeis et locis ac coram quibuscunq[ue] Judicib[u]s et Justiciar[iis]
ac al[iis] p[er]son[is] et Officiar[iis] n[ost]ris heredum et Successor[um]
n[ost]ro[ru]m in
o[mn]ib[u]s et sing[u]lis acc[i]o[n]ib[u]s pl[ac]itis querel[i]s secti[s] caus[is]
mater[iis] et demand[is] quibuscunq[ue] cuiuscunq[ue] sint aut erint generis
nominis nature qualitat[is] sive speciei eisdem modo et forma prout aliqui
al[ii] Ligei
n[ost]ri huius Regni Anglie persone h[ab]iles et in lege capaces existent[es] sive
aliquod aliud Corpus Corporat[um] et politic[um] infra hoc Regnum
n[ost]rum Angli[e] h[ab]ere p[er]quirere recipere possidere gaudere retinere
[25]   dare concedere dimittere alienare assignare et disponere pl[ac]itare et impl[ac]itari
respondere et responderi defendere et defendi facere permittere sive exequi
possint aut valeant Et quod Maior
Balli[vi] et Com[mun]itas Civitat[is] p[re]d[icte] et Successor[es] sui h[ab]eant
posthac imp[er]p[etuu]m Co[mmun]e Sigillum p[ro] Causis et negotiis suis
et Successo[ru]m suo[ru]m quibuscunq[ue] agend[is] deservitur[um] Et

q[uo]d bene liceat et licebit eisdem
Maior[i] Balliv[i]s et Co[mmun]itat[i] Civitat[is] Oxon[ie] p[re]d[icte] et
   Successor[ibus] suis de tempore in tempus frangere mutare et de novo facere
   sigillu[m] illud ad libitu[m] su[u]m prout eis melius fieri videbitur ET
ULTERIUS volum[us] ac p[er] p[re]sent[es] p[ro] nob[is] hered[ibus] et
   Successor[ibus] n[ost]ris concedim[us] et ordinam[us] q[uo]d de cetero
   imp[er]p[etuu]m sit et erit infra Civitat[em] p[re]dict[am] unus de
   Pr[i]orib[us] et Discretior[ibus] Civib[us] Civitat[is] p[re]d[icte] in forma
inferius menc[i]onat[a] eligend[us] et constituend[us] qui erit et no[m]i[n]abitur
   Maior Civitat[is] p[re]dicte ac p[ro] melior[i] execuc[i]on[e] voluntat[is]
   n[ost]re in hac parte ASSIGNAVIM[US] no[m]i[n]avim[us] constituim[us]
   et fecim[us] ac p[er] p[re]sent[es] p[ro]

[30]   nobis hered[ibus] et Successor[ibus] n[ost]ris assignam[us] no[m]i[n]am[us]
   constituim[us] et facim[us] dilectum nobis Ric[ard]um Carter arm[igerum]
   fore et esse primu[m] et modern[um] Maiorem Civitat[is] p[re]dict[e]
   volentes q[uo]d idem Ric[ard]us Carter in
Offic[io] Maior[is] Civitat[is] p[re]d[icte] continuabit a data p[re]sentiu[m] sq[ue]
   ad diem Lune p[ro]x[imum] ante Fest[um] Sancti Mathei Apostoli qui erit
   anno D[omi]ni Mill[es]imo Sexcentesimo Octogesimo nono et exinde
   quousq[ue] un[us] al[ius] ad Offici[um] illud
deb[it]o modo elect[us] p[re]fect[us] et jurat[us] fuerit juxta Ordinac[i]on[em] et
   Constituc[i]on[em] inferius in p[re]sentib[us] declarat[as] si idem Ric[ard]us
   Carter tamdiu vixerit nisi interim p[ro] Causa rac[i]onabil[i] vel modo et
   forma inferius menc[i]onat[is]
ab Offic[io] ill[o] amovebitur ET ULTERIUS volum[us] ac p[er] p[re]sentes
   p[ro] nobis hered[ibus] et Successor[ibus] n[ost]ris concedim[us] Maior[i]
   Balliv[is] et Co[mmun]itat[i] Civitat[is] p[re]d[icte] et Successor[ibus] suis
   q[uo]d quilib[e]t Maior Civitat[is] p[re]d[icte] de cetero eligend[us]
no[m]i[n]and[us] sive constituend[us] de tempore in tempus et ad o[mn]ia
   tempora imposter[um] elect[us] no[m]i[n]at[us] et jurat[us] fuerit p[er] tales
   p[er]son[as] ad hui[usm]o[d]i dies et tempora et in tali[bus] modo et forma
   qual[ibus] Maior dict[e] Civitat[is] antehac
[35]   eligebatur no[m]i[n]abatur constituebat[ur] et jurabat[ur] Et q[uo]d quilib[e]t
   Maior dict[e] Civitat[is] p[ro] tempore existen[s] de cetero imp[er]p[etuu]m
   in eodem Offic[io] continuabit duran[te] tal[i] tempore et h[ab]eat teneat
   gaudeat et exerceat et
h[ab]ere tenere gaudere exercere valeat et possit tal[es] Cur[ias] de Record[o] ac
   tot tant[a] tali[a] eadem huiu[sm]o[d]i et consimili[a] al[ia] Potestat[es]
   Privileg[ia] Authoritat[es] Feod[a] jur[a] jurisdicc[i]on[es] perquisita et
   p[ro]fic[ua] ad o[mn]es intenc[i]o[n]es et p[ro]posit[a]
quecunq[ue] quot quant[a] qual[ia] et que Maior d[i]ct[e] Civitat[is] antehac
   quocunq[ue] modo continuavit h[ab]uit tenuit gavis[us] fuit vel exercuit aut
   continuare h[ab]ere tenere gaudere vel exercere potuit aut debuit
AC ETIAM volum[us] ac p[er] p[re]sentes p[ro] nob[is] hered[ibus] et
   Successor[ibus] n[ost]ris concedim[us] et ordinam[us] q[uo]d de cetero sint
   et erint infra eand[em] Civitat[em] duo probi et discreti viri Cives Civitat[is]
   p[re]d[icte] in forma in his L[itt]e[ri]s Patent[ibus]
inferius menc[i]onat[a] eligend[i] qui erunt et no[m]i[n]abunt[ur] Balliv[i]
   Civitat[is] p[re]d[icte] Et p[ro] melior[i] execuci[on]e voluntat[is] n[ost]re in
   hac p[ar]te ASSIGNAVIM[US] no[m]i[n]avim[us] constituim[us] et
   fecim[us] ac p[er] p[re]sentes assignam[us] no[m]i[n]am[us]

[40] constituim[us] et facim[us] dilectos nob[is] Joh[ann]em Weller et Joh[ann]em
Philipps Corne Chandler Cives Civitat[is] p[re]d[icte] fore et esse duos
primos et modernos Ballivos Civitat[is] p[re]d[icte] continuand[os] in eodem
Offic[io]

usq[ue] ad p[re]d[ictum] diem Lune p[ro]x[ime] ante dict[um] Fest[um] Sancti
Mathei Apostoli qui erit Anno D[omi]ni Mill[es]imo Sexcentessimo
Octogesimo nono et de eod[em] die quousq[ue] duo al[i]i de Civib[us]
Civitat[is] p[re]d[icte] ad Offici[u]m illud p[re]fect[i] et jurati

fuerint juxta Ordinacion[em] et Provision[em] in his presentib[us] inf[er]ius
express[as] et declarat[as] si iidem Joh[ann]es Weller et Joh[ann]es Philipps
tam diu vixerint nisi interim ip[s]i vel eor[um] alter ab Offic[io] p[re]d[icto]
p[ro] Causa rac[i]onab[ili] vel modo et

forma inf[er]ius menc[i]onat[is] amoti sint vel amotus sit ET ULTERIUS
volum[us] ac p[er] p[re]sentes p[ro] nob[is] nob[is] *(sic)* hered[ibus] et
Successor[ibus] n[ost]ris concedim[us] Maior[i] Balliv[is] et
Co[mmun]itat[i] Civitat[is] p[re]d[icte] et Successor[ibus] suis q[uo]d
Balliv[i] Civitat[is]

p[re]d[icte] de cetero eligend[i] sive constituend[i] de tempore in tempus et ad
o[mn]ia tempor[a] imposter[um] elect[i] nominat[i] et jurat[i] fuerint Et
eor[um] alter elect[us] nominat[us] et jurat[us] fuerit per tal[es] p[er]sonas
ad hui[us]mo[d]i dies et tempora et

[45] in tali[bus] modo et forma qual[ibus] Ballivi dict[e] Civitat[is] antehac
eligebant[ur] no[m]i[n]abant[ur] constituebant[ur] et jurabant[ur] Et q[uo]d
Ballivi dict[e] Civitat[is] et eor[um] alter p[ro] tempore existen[tes] de
cetero imp[er]p[etuu]m continuabint duran[te]

tal[i] tempore et h[ab]eant teneant gaudeant et exerceant et h[ab]ere tenere
gaudere et exercere valeant et possint tot tant[a] tal[ia] eadem hui[us]m[o]di
et consimil[ia] Potestat[es] Privileg[ia] Authoritat[es] Feoda jur[a]
jurisdicc[i]on[es]

perquisit[a] et p[ro]fic[ua] ad o[mn]es intenc[i]ones et p[ro]posit[a] quecunq[ue]
quot quant[a] qual[ia] et que Ballivi dict[e] Civitat[is] antehac quocunq[ue]
modo continuaver[unt] h[ab]uerunt tenuer[unt] gavis[i] fuer[unt] vel
exercuer[unt] aut continuare

h[ab]ere tenere gaudere vel exercere potuerunt aut debuer[unt] vel eor[um] alter
antehac quocunq[ue] modo continuavit h[ab]uit tenuit gavis[us] fuit vel
exercuit aut continuare h[ab]ere tenere gaudere vel exercere

potuit aut debuit ET ULTERIUS volumus ac per p[re]sentes p[ro] nob[is]
hered[ibus] et Successor[ibus] no[str]is de grac[ia] n[ost]ra speciali ac ex
certa scientia et mero motu n[ost]ris concedim[us] prefat[is] Maior[i]
Balliv[is] Civitat[is]

[50] Oxon[ie] p[re]d[icte] et Successor[ibus] suis q[uo]d de cetero imp[er]p[etuu]m
sint et erunt in Civitat[e] p[re]dict[a] de tempore in tempus Octo probi et
discreti viri In[ha]bitan[tes] et Commoran[tes] infra eand[em] Civitat[em] in
forma in his presentib[us]

inferius menc[i]onat[a] eligend[i] qui erunt et vocabuntur Ald[erman]ni Civitat[is]
pred[icte] ac p[ro] melior[i] Execuc[i]on[e] Voluntat[is] n[ost]re in hac parte
ASSIGNAVIMUS nominavim[us] constituim[us] et fecim[us] ac p[er]
present[es]

p[ro] nob[is] hered[ibus] et Successor[ibus] n[ost]ris assignamus no[m]i[n]am[us]
constituim[us] et facim[us] dilect[os] nob[is] Will[elm]um Wright
sen[iorem] Arm[igerum] Edw[ard]um Walker mili[tem] Thomam Eustace

Ric[ard]um Carter Tobiam Browne Edw[ardu]m Combes
Ric[ard]um Hawkins et Alexand[r]um Wright fore et esse primos et modernos
Aldermannos Civitat[is] predict[e] continuand[os] in eisdem Officiis et
Locis durant[ibus] vitis suis naturalibus
nisi interim pro aliqua Causa rac[i]onab[ili] vel modo et forma inferius
menc[i]onat[is] amovebuntur vel eorum aliquis amovebitur

[Sheet 2]

[55] VOLUMUS insup[er] ac p[er] p[re]sentes p[ro] nob[is] hered[ibus] et
Successor[ibus] n[ost]ris Concedim[us] p[re]fat[is] Maior[i] Ball[ivis] et
Co[mmun]itat[i] Civitat[is] Oxon[ie] p[re]d[icte] quod de cetero
imp[er]p[etuu]m sint et erint infra eandem Civitat[em] de tempore in tempus
quatuor al[ii] probi et discreti
viri Inh[ab]itan[tes] Com[m]oran[tes] infra eandem Civitat[em] in forma inferius
in his L[itte]ris Paten[tibus] menc[i]onat[a] eligen[di] qui erunt Assisten[tes]
Civitat[is] p[re]d[icte] et de tempore in tempus erunt Assisten[tes] et
Auxilian[tes] Maior[is] Balliv[orum] et Co[mmun]itat[is] eiusd[em]
Civitat[is] pro tempor[e] existen[cium] in o[mn]ibus causis et materiis Civitat[em]
p[re]d[ictam] tangen[tibus] seu concernen[tibus] ac pro melior[i]
execuc[i]on[e] voluntat[is] n[ost]re in hac parte ASSIGNAVIMUS
nominavim[us] constituim[us] et fecim[us] ac per
presentes pro nob[i]s hered[ibus] et Successor[ibus] n[ost]ris assignam[us]
nominam[us] constituim[us] et facim[us] dilect[os] nobis Jacobum Pinnell
Ric[ard]um Tidmarsh Will[elm]um Greene et Joh[ann]em Tomkins Cives
Civitat[is] p[re]d[icte] fore et esse
primos et modern[os] quatuor Assisten[tes] Civitat[is] p[re]dict[e] continuan[dos]
in Offic[io] ill[o] duran[tibus] vitis suis na[tu]r[a]l[ibus] nisi interim p[ro]
aliqua causa rac[i]onab[ili] vel modo et forma inferius menc[i]onat[is]
amovebuntur vel aliquis eor[um] amovebitur
[60] ET ULTERIUS volumus ac p[er] p[re]sentes p[ro] nob[is] hered[ibus] et
Successor[ibus] n[ost]ris Concedim[us] p[re]fat[is] Maior[i] Balliv[is] et
Co[mmun]itat[i] Civitat[is] p[re]dict[e] et Successor[ibus] suis quod de
cetero imp[er]p[etuu]m sint et erunt infra Civitat[em] p[re]d[ictam]
duodecim
de Civibus Civitat[is] illius in forma inferius in his p[re]sentibus menc[i]onat[a]
eligend[i] qui erunt et vocabuntur loco Ballivor[um] Ang[li]ce in Bayliffes
places ET ULTERIUS volumus ac p[er] p[re]sentes pro nobis
hered[ibus] et Successor[ibus] n[ost]ris Concedim[us] p[re]fat[is] Maior[i]
Balliv[is] et Co[mmun]itat[i] Civitat[is] p[re]d[icte] et Successor[ibus] suis
q[uo]d de cetero imp[er]p[etuu]m sint et erunt infra eand[em] Civitat[em]
viginti quatuor de Civibus Civitat[is] illius in forma
inferius in his present[ibus] menc[i]onata eligend[i] qui erunt et vocabunt[ur]
Co[mmun]es Consiliar[ii] sive de Co[mmun]i Consilio Civitat[is] illius ET
INSUPER volum[us] ac p[er] p[re]sentes p[ro] nobis hered[ibus] et
Successor[ibus] n[ost]ris Concedim[us]
p[re]fat[is] Maiori Balliv[is] et Co[mmun]itat[i] Civitat[is] p[re]d[icte] et
Successor[ibus] suis q[uo]d ip[s]i et Successor[es] sui de cetero
imp[er]p[etuu]m h[ab]eant et h[ab]ebunt in Civitat[e] p[re]d[icte]
unu[m] viru[m] p[re]claru[m] et discretu[m] in forma in his p[re]sentib[us]
inferius menc[i]onat[a] eligend[um]
[65] et no[m]i[n]and[um] qui erit et no[m]i[n]abit[ur] Capital[is] Sen[esc]all[us]

Civitat[is] p[re]d[icte] Et
Assignavim[us] no[m]i[n]avim[us] constituim[us] et fecim[us] ac p[er]
p[re]sentes assignam[us] no[m]i[n]am[us] constituim[us] et facim[us]
p[er]quam fideli[ter] et sincere dilectu[m] Edw[ard]um
Henricum Co[m]item Litchfield fore et esse primu[m] et modernu[m] Capital[em]
Sen[esc]allum Civitat[is] p[re]d[icte] in eodem Officio continuand[um]
duran[te] vita sua n[atu]rali nisi interim p[ro] causa r[aci]onabili vel modo et
forma inferius menc[i]onat[is]
ab Offic[io] ill[o] amovebitur ET ULTERIUS volum[us] ac p[ro] nob[is]
hered[ibus] et Successor[ibus] n[ost]ris concedim[us] p[re]fat[is] Maior[i]
Balliv[is] et Co[mmun]itat[i] Civitat[is] p[re]d[icte] et Successor[ibus] suis
q[uo]d de cetero imp[er]p[etuu]m sit et erit infra eand[em] Civitat[em]
de tempore in tempus vn[us] p[ro]bus et discretus vir in Legib[us] Angli[e]
erudit[us] qui erit et no[m]i[n]abitur Recordatur eiusd[em] Civitat[is] ac ea
o[mn]ia et singula faciet et exequetur p[er] se vel sufficien[tem]
Deputat[um] suu[m] que ad
Offic[ium] Recordator[is] infra eand[em] Civitat[em] p[er]tinent et p[er]tinere
debent Necnon vnus al[ius] p[ro]bus et discretus homo informa *(sic)* inferius
express[a] eligend[us] qui erit et vocabitur Co[mmun]is Cl[er]icus Civitat[is]
p[re]d[icte] et Cl[er]icus
[70] o[mn]ium Societat[um] Incorporat[arum] et Corpor[um] Politicor[um] Artiu[m]
Misterior[um] sive Manual[ium] Occupac[i]on[um] infra Civitat[em]
p[re]d[ictam] ac ea o[mn]ia et singula faciet et exequetur p[er] se vel
sufficientem Deputat[um] suu[m] p[er] ipsu[m]
imposter[um] no[m]i[n]and[um] et appunctuand[um] que ad Offic[ium]
p[re]d[ictum] infra eand[em] Civitat[em] p[er]tinent et p[er]tinere debent
Necnon vnus al[ius] p[ro]bus et discretus homo in forma inferius express[a]
eligend[us] qui erit et vocabitur Sollicitator
eiusd[em] Civitat[is] ad ea o[mn]ia et singula que ad Offic[ium] illud p[er]tinent
fideliter faciend[a] Ac etiam duo al[ii] probi et discreti ho[m]i[n]es qui erunt
et vocabuntur Coronatores Civitat[is] p[re]d[icte] Et vnus alius probus homo
qui erit
et vocabitur primus Serviens ad Clavam Maior[is] Civitat[is] p[re]d[icte] ac p[ro]
melior[i] execuc[i]on[e] voluntat[is] n[ost]re in hac parte
ASSIGNAVIM[US] no[m]i[na]vim[us] constituim[us] et fecim[us] ac p[er]
p[re]sentes assignam[us] nominamus
constituim[us] et facim[us] delectum nob[is] Henricum Trinder ar[miger]um
Servien[tem] ad Legem fore et esse primu[m] et modern[um]
Recordator[em] Civitat[is] p[re]d[icte] Et dilectu[m] nob[is] Will[hel]um
Wright jun[iorem] Ar[miger]um fore et esse Deputat[um]
[75] Recordator[is] Civitat[is] [1] ad o[mn]ia que ad Offic[ium] p[re]d[ictum]
Recordator[is] p[er]tinent exequend[a] et in eisdem Offic[iis] continuand[os]
durant[ibus] vit[is] suis na[tu]r[a]l[ibus] respectiv[is] nisi interim p[ro]
Causa r[aci]onabil[i] vel modo et forma inferius
menc[i]onat[is] ab Offic[iis] illi[s] amovebunt[ur] aut eor[um] aliquis amovebitur
ASSIGNAVIM[US] etiam no[m]i[n]avim[us] constituim[us] et fecim[us] ac
p[er] p[re]sentes p[ro] nob[is] hered[ibus] et Successor[ibus] n[ost]ris

---

[1] Luttrell (1857): 471, notes in a diary entry dated 24 October 1688: 'Mr. Wright, the aldermans son of the citty of Oxford, is made recorder of the same.'

assignam[us] no[m]i[n]am[u]s constituimus

et facim[us] dilectu[m] nob[is] Thomam Baker gener[osum] fore et esse primu[m] et modernu[m] Co[mmun]em Cl[er]icum Civitat[is] p[re]d[icte] et Cl[er]icum o[mn]ium Societat[um] Incorporat[arum] et Corpor[um] Politicor[um] Misterior[um] Arti[um] sive Manuali[um] Occupac[i]on[um]

infra Civitat[em] p[re]d[ictam] habend[um] et exercend[um] Offic[ium] p[re]d[ictum] p[er] se vel p[er] sufficien[tem] Deputat[um] suu[m] p[er] ip[su]m no[m]i[n]and[um] et appunctuand[um] et in Offic[io] ill[o] continuand[um] duran[te] vita sua n[atu]ral[i] nisi interim p[ro] causa r[aci]onabil[i] vel modo

et forma inferius menc[i]onat[is] amovebitur AC ETIAM assignavim[us] no[m]i[n]avim[us] constituim[us] et fecim[us] et p[er] p[re]sentes p[ro] nob[is] hered[ibus] et Successor[ibus] n[ost]ris assignam[us] no[m]i[n]am[us] constituim[us] et facim[us] dilect[um] nobis

[80] Ric[ard]um Dodwell gener[osum] fore et esse primu[m] et modernu[m] Sollicitator[em] Civitat[is] illius Et dilectos nob[is] Timotheu[m] Box et Ric[ard]um Dodwell gen[erosos] fore et esse primos et modernos Coronatores et dilect[um] nobis

Abrahamu[m] White gen[erosum] fore et esse modern[um] prim[um] Servien[tem] ad Clavam Maior[is] Civitat[is] p[re]d[icte] continuand[os] in respectiv[is] Officiis suis duran[tibus] vit[is] suis n[atu]ral[ibus] respectiv[is] nisi interim ab Offic[iis] il[li]s p[ro] causa r[aci]onabil[i] vel

modo et forma inferius menc[i]onat[is] ip[s]i amovebuntur vel eor[um] aliquis amovebitur VOLUMUS etiam ac p[er] p[re]sentes p[ro] nob[is] hered[ibus] et Successor[ibus] n[ost]ris ordinam[us] et firmit[er] iniungend[o] p[re]cipim[us] q[uo]d p[re]d[ictus] Ric[ard]us

Carter superius in p[re]sentib[us] no[m]i[n]at[us] fore et esse primu[s] et modernu[s] Maior Civitat[is] p[re]d[icte] antequam ad Execuc[i]on[em] Offic[ii] Maior[is] eiusd[em] Civitat[is] admittatur seu aliqualiter se intromittat Sacrament[um]

Corporal[e] super Sacro-Sanct[is] dei Evangeli[is] ad Officium illud in o[mn]ib[us] et per o[mn]ia illud Offic[ium] tangen[cia] bene et fidelit[er] exequend[um] coram dilect[is] nob[is] p[re]fat[is] Will[elm]o Wright sen[iore] Thoma Eustace Will[elm]o

[85] Wright jun[iore] et Thoma Baker aut aliquib[us] duob[us] eor[um] p[re]stabit quibus quidem Will[elm]o Wright sen[iore] Thoma Eustace Will[elm]o Wright jun[iore] et Thoma Baker vel aliquib[us] duobus eor[um] tale Sacrament[um]

p[re]fat[o] Ric[ard]o Carter dand[i] et administrand[i] plen[am] potestat[em] et authoritat[em] dam[us] et concedim[us] p[er] p[re]sentes absq[ue] aliquo ali[o] Warranto sive Com[m]isione a nob[is] hered[ibus] et Successor[ibus] n[ost]ris in ea p[ar]te p[ro]curand[is]

aut obtinend[is] necnon p[re]stabit o[mn]ia tal[ia] Sacra[menta] solita et consuet[a] in tali modo et forma et ad tal[ia] loc[a] et tempora et coram tal[ibus] p[er]son[is] quali[bus] Maior[es] Civitat[is] ill[ius] antehac usi fuer[unt] et consuever[unt] ET

ASSIGNAVIM[US] no[m]i[n]avim[us] constituim[us] et fecim[us] ac p[er] p[re]sentes p[ro] nob[is] hered[ibus] et Successor[ibus] n[ost]ris assignam[us] no[m]i[n]am[us] constituim[us] et facim[us] dilectos Subditos n[ost]ros Wil[lelm]um Ayleworth Wil[lelm]um Badger

Thomam Neale Ric[ard]um Houghton Ric[ard]um Keates Timotheu[m] Perry

Joh[ann]em Knibb Will[elm]um Walker Peruque maker Arthuru[m] Malde
Joh[ann]em Weller Joh[ann]em Philipps et Thomam Kimber generosos
[90] fore et esse primos et modern[os] duodecim loco Ballivor[um] Ang[li]ce in
Bayliffes places Civitat[is] p[re]d[icte] continuand[os] in Offic[iis]
p[re]d[ictis] duran[tibus] vitis suis n[atu]ral[i] respectivis nisi interim
p[ro] causa r[aci]onabil[i] vel modo et
forma inf[er]ius menc[i]onat[is] ab Offic[iis] illi[s] amovebuntur aut eor[um]
aliquis amovebitur AC ASSIGNAVIMUS no[m]i[n]avim[us] constituim[us]
et fecim[us] et p[er] p[re]sentes p[ro] nob[is] hered[ibus] et Successor[ibus]
n[ost]ris assignam[us] no[m]i[n]am[us] constituim[us] et
facim[us] dilect[os] et fidel[es] Subdit[os] n[ost]ros Jacobum Finch Ric[ard]um
Crouch Thomam Blissem Will[elm]um Ryley Michael[em] Ackland
Edw[ard]um Salter Chilton Tubb Will[elm]um Appleby Theodoru[m]
Spencer Anthoniu[m] Mathews
Rob[er]tum Hensly Will[elm]um Stibbs Ric[ard]um Carter Currier Laurentiu[m]
King Will[elm]um Nicholls Henricum Wildgoose Daniel[em] Monday
Rob[er]tum Kenricke Henricu[m] Richardson Josephu[m] Mayo
Will[elm]um Playter
Jacobu[m] Burrowes Joh[ann]em Burrowes jun[iorem] et Joh[ann]em Toms fore
et esse primos et modern[os] viginti quatuor Co[mmun]es Conciliar[ios] vel
de Co[mmun]i Consilio Civitat[is] p[re]d[icte] continuand[os] in eisd[em]
Offic[iis] duran[tibus] vitis suis natural[ibus]
[95] respectiv[is] nisi interim p[ro] causa r[aci]onabil[i] vel modo et forma inferius
menc[i]onat[is] ip[s]i ab Offic[iis] ill[is] amovebunt[ur] aut eor[um] aliquis
amovebitur ET ULTERIUS volum[us] ac p[er] p[re]sentes ordinam[us]
q[uo]d Ballivi Alder[mann]i
Assisten[tes] Capital[is] Sen[esc]all[us] Recordator Deputat[us] Recordator[is]
Co[mmun]is Cleric[us] Sollicitator prim[us] Serviens ad Clavam Maior[is]
p[re]d[icti] Coronator[e]s duodecim loco Ballivor[um] Ang[li]ce in Bayliffes
places et viginti quatuor Co[mmun]es Consiliar[i]i vel de
Co[mmun]i Consilio Civitat[is] p[re]d[icte] et quilibet eor[um] in his
p[re]sentib[us] sup[er]ius no[m]i[n]at[i] et constitut[i] respective
Sacram[entum] Corporal[e] ad Offic[ia] sua p[re]d[icta] in o[mn]ib[us] et
p[er] o[mn]ia officia sua respective tangen[cia] bene et fidelit[er]
exequend[a] coram p[re]fat[o] Ric[ard]o
Carter p[re]stabunt et eor[um] quilibet p[re]stabit Cui quidem Ric[ard]o Carter
tale Sacra[mentum] hui[us]mo[d]i Officiari[is] in his p[re]sent[ibus]
constitut[is] et no[m]i[n]at[is] dandi et administrand[i] plen[am]
pot[estat]em et authoritat[em] dam[us] et concedim[us] p[er] p[re]sent[es]
absq[ue]
aliquo al[io] Warrant[o] sive Com[m]issione a nob[is] hered[ibus] vel
Successor[ibus] n[ost]ris in ea parte p[ro]curand[is] seu obtinend[is] ET
ULTERIUS volumus ac p[er] presentes pro nob[is] hered[ibus] et
Successor[ibus] n[ost]ris dam[us] et concedim[us] p[re]fat[is]
[100] Maior[i] Balliv[is] et Co[mmun]itat[i] Civitat[is] p[re]d[icte] et Successor[ibus]
suis q[uo]d quoties et quandocunq[ue] acciderit aliquem vel aliquos
Ald[e]r[mann]or[um] Assistant[ium] Ballivor[um] aut p[re]d[ictarum]
p[er]sonar[um] in locis Ballivor[um] p[re]d[ictorum] vigint[i] quattuor
Consiliar[iorum] sive de
Co[mmun]i Consilio vel aliquem Capital[em] Sen[esc]all[um] Recordator[em]
Com[munem] Cl[er]icum Solicitator[em] Coronator[em] vel prim[um]

Servien[tem] ad Clavam Maior[is] Civitat[is] p[re]d[icte] p[ro] tempore
existen[tes] obire seu ab Officio suo vel ab Officiis suis

decedere vel amoveri quos et quem p[ro] r[aci]onabil[i] causa amobiles esse et
amoveri volumus q[uo]d tunc et in quolibet tal[i] casu al[ia] idonea
p[er]sona vel al[ie] idonee p[er]sone de tempore in tempus ad et in
Offic[ium] ill[um] respective

deb[it]o modo eligetur et juretur eligent[ur] et jurent[ur] eisd[em] modo et forma
p[er] tal[es] p[er]son[as] et ad hui[us]mo[d]i loc[a] dies et tempora p[ro]ut in
dict[a] Civitat[e] p[er] spatiu[m] septem Annor[um] jam ult[ra]
p[re]terit[orum] usitat[um] et consuet[um] fuit vel fieri

debuit Et Offic[ium] sive Officia loc[um] sive loca ad q[uo]d vel que sic elect[us]
et jurat[us] fuerit vel fuerint exercebit et exercebunt p[ro] tal[i] tempore et
temporib[us] et abinde amot[us] erit vel erunt in tal[i] modo quali in

[105] hu[ius]mo[di] casib[us] infra Civitat[em] p[re]d[ictam] infra tempus p[re]d[ictum]
consuet[um] fuit VOLUMUS etiam ac p[er] p[re]sentes p[ro] nob[is]
hered[ibus] et Successor[ibus] n[ost]ris Concedim[us] Maior[i] Ball[ivis] et
Co[mmun]itat[i] Civitat[is] p[re]d[icte] et Successor[ibus] suis q[uo]d si
contigerit p[re]d[ictum]

Ric[ard]um Carter sup[er]ius p[er] p[re]sentes no[m]i[n]at[um] fore Maior[em]
Civitat[is] p[re]d[icte] vel aliquem al[ium] Maior[em] Civitat[is] p[re]d[icte]
p[ro] tempore existen[tem] obire vel ab Officio suo amoveri duran[te]
tempore Maioralitat[is] sue vel si contiger[it]

aliquam elecc[i]on[em] Maior[is] Civitat[is] p[re]d[icte] imposter[um] frustrari
p[er] incapacitat[em] vel renunciac[i]on[em] illius qui ad Offici[um]
Maior[is] Civitat[is] p[re]d[icte] elect[us] fuerit vel p[ro] aliqua alia Causa
quacunque q[uo]d tunc et toties quoties

casus sic acciderit liceat et licebit senior[i] Ald[e]r[mann]o Civitat[is] p[re]d[icte]
tunc ibid[em] residen[ti] et p[ro]inde capaci p[ro]tinus vocare Ball[ivos] et
Co[mmun]itat[em] Civitat[is] p[re]d[icte] et p[ro]cedere ad elecc[i]on[em] et
jurac[i]on[em] alterius p[er]sone in Offic[ium]

Maior[is] Civitat[is] p[re]d[icte] ut p[re]fertur ET ULTERIUS volum[us] ac p[er]
p[re]sentes p[ro] nob[is] hered[ibus] et Successor[ibus] n[ost]ris
concedim[us] p[re]fat[is] Maior[i] Ball[ivis] et Co[mmun]itat[i] Civitat[is]
p[re]d[icte] et Successor[ibus] suis q[uo]d liceat et licebit Maior[i]
Civitat[is]

[110] p[re]d[icte] p[ro] tempore existen[ti] ad libitu[m] suu[m] facere et constituere de
tempore in tempus un[um] de Ald[ermann]is sive Assisten[tibus] Civitat[is]
p[re]d[icte] qui sint et erunt Justiciar[ium] ad pacem n[ost]ram et hered[um]
et Successor[um] no[st]ror[um] infra Civitat[em] ill[am]

conservand[am] l[eg]ittime constitut[us] fore et esse Deputat[us] ip[s]ius
Maior[is] p[ro] tempore existen[tis] ad ea o[mn]ia et singula que ad
Offic[ium] Maior[is] p[er]tinent et p[er]tinere debent faciend[a] et
exequend[a] duran[te] benep[la]cit[o] Maior[is]

Civitat[is] p[re]d[icte] pro tempore existen[tis] adeo plene libere et integre p[ro]ut
Maior Civitat[is] p[re]d[icte] p[ro] tempore existen[s] si p[re]sens esset
facere et exequi valeat et possit PROVISO semper et volum[us] q[uo]d
`dict[us] Deputat[us] Maior[is] Civitat[is]

p[re]d[icte] Sacram[entum] Corporal[e] coram Maior[e] Civitat[is] p[re]d[icte]
p[ro] tempore existen[te] ad Officiu[m] p[re]d[ictum] bene et fidelit[er]
exequend[um] p[re]stabit antequam se intromittat in Offic[ium] Deputat[i]
Maior[is] Civitat[is] p[re]d[icte] et sic toties quoties casus

sic acciderit cuiquid[em] Maior[i] Civitat[is] p[re]d[icte] p[ro] tempore existen[ti]
  tal[e] Sacramen[tum] administrand[i] potestat[em] et authoritat[em] dam[us]
  et concedim[us] p[er] p[re]sentes ET ULTERIUS volum[us] p[ro] melior[i]
  gub[er]nac[i]on[e] Civitat[is] p[re]d[icte]
[115] p[erp]etuis futur[is] temporibus ac p[er] p[re]sentes p[ro] nob[is] hered[ibus] et
  Successor[ibus] n[ost]ris Concedim[us] p[re]fat[is] Maior[i] Balli[vis] et
  Co[mmun]itat[i] Civitat[is] p[re]d[icte] et Successor[ibus] suis q[uo]d de
  cetero imp[er]p[etuu]m Maior vel Deputat[us] Maior[is] Capital[is]

[Sheet 3]

Senescall[us] Ald[e]r[mann]i Assisten[tes] Ballivi Recordator vel eius Deputat[us]
  Co[mmun]is Cl[er]icus vel eius Deputat[us] Sollicitator Coronator primus
  Serviens ad Clavam Maior[is] duodecim p[er]son[e] in loco Ballivor[um] et
  viginti quatuor Co[mmun]es
Consiliari[i] Civitat[is] p[re]d[icte] p[ro] tempore existen[tes] vel maior pars
  eor[un]d[em] quor[um] Maior[em] Civitat[is] illius p[ro] tempore
  existen[tem] vel eius Deputat[um] unum esse volum[us] in Guihalda vel alio
  loco convenienti Civitat[is] illius assemblati h[ab]eant
et ha[be]bunt o[mn]ia tanta tal[ia] hui[usm]o[d]i et consimil[ia] Franch[esi]as
  lib[er]tat[es] jurisd[i]ccion[es] potestat[em] et authoritat[em] qualia
  Co[mmun]e Consili[um] Civitat[is] illius antehac unquam quocunq[ue]
  modo ha[bu]erunt gavis[i] fuerunt seu exercuerunt aut h[ab]ere
gaudere seu exercere potuerunt vel debuerunt tam ad condend[um] et
  constituend[um] ordinand[um] faciend[um] et stabiliend[um] Leges Statuta
  Constituc[i]on[es] Decret[a] et Ordinac[i]on[es] q[ua]m aliter seu ali[o]
  modo quocunq[ue] PROVISO
[120] semper ac plen[am] potest[atem] et authoritat[em] nob[is] hered[ibus] et
  Successor[ibus] n[ost]ris p[er] p[re]sentes Reservamus de tempore in tempus
  et ad o[mn]ia tempora imposter[um] ad Maior[em] Capital[em]
  Senescall[um] Recordator[em] Deputat[um]
Recordator[is] Co[mmun]em Cl[er]icum et Sollicitator[em] et aliquem vel aliquos
  de Ald[e]r[mann]is Assisten[tibus] Balliv[is] duodecim loco Ballivor[um]
  Angl[ice] Bayliffes places Coronator[em] Prim[um] Servien[tem] ad Clavam
  Maior[is] p[re]d[icti] vel de p[re]d[ictis]
vigint[i] quatuor Consiliar[iis] vel de Co[mmun]i Consilio Civitat[is] illius necnon
  de ali[is] Servien[tibus] ad Clavas eiusd[em] Civitat[is] p[ro] tempore
  existen[tibus] ad libit[um] et Benepl[ac]itum n[ost]rum hered[um] et
  Successor[um] n[ost]ror[um] p[er] aliquem Ordinem
n[ost]rum hered[um] vel Successor[um] n[ost]ror[um] in Privato Consilio
  fact[um] et sub Sigillo Privati Consilii p[re]d[icti] eisdem respective
  significat[um] amovend[os] et amotu[m] et amotos esse declarand[i] Et
  quoties nos hered[es] et Successor[es]
n[ost]ri p[er] tale[m] Ordinem in Privato Consilio fact[um] declarabim[us] vel
  declarabunt hui[us]mo[d]i Maior[em] Capital[em] Sen[esc]allum
  Recordator[em] Deputat[um] Recordator[is] Co[mmun]em Cl[er]icum
  Sollicitator[em] vel aliquem vel
[125] aliquos de Ald[e]r[mann]is Assisten[tibus] Balliv[is] duodecim loco Ballivor[um]
  Ang[li]ce Bayliffes places Coronator[em] prim[um] Servien[tem] ad Clavam
  Maior[is] p[re]d[icti] vel de p[re]d[ictis] viginti quatuor Consiliar[iis] vel de
  Co[mmun]i Consilio
Civitat[is] ill[ius] necnon de Servien[tibus] ad Clavas eiusd[em] Civitat[is] p[ro]

tempore existen[tibus] vel eor[um] aliquem fore et esse amot[um] vel
amotos a respectivis Officiis et locis suis q[uo]d tunc et extunc Maior
Capital[is] Sen[esc]all[us]

Recordator Deputat[us] Recordator[is] Co[mmun]is Cl[er]icus Sollicitator et
aliquis vel aliqui de Ald[e]r[mann]is Assisten[tibus] Ballivis duodecim loco
Ballivor[um] Ang[li]ce Bayliffes places Coronator prim[us] Servien[s] ad
Clavam Maior[is] p[re]d[icti]

vel de p[re]d[ictis] viginti quatuor Consiliar[iis] vel de Co[mmun]i Consilio
Civitat[is] illius necnon de Servien[tibus] ad Clavas Civitat[is] illius p[ro]
tempore existen[tibus] sic amoti vel amotus esse declarat[i] sive declarand[i]
a respectiv[is] Offic[iis] et

locis suis ip[s]o f[ac]to et sine aliquo ulterior[i] processu realiter et ad o[mn]es
intenc[i]ones et p[ro]posita quecunq[ue] amoti sint et erint ac hoc quoties
casus sic acciderit aliquo in contrar[ium] inde non obstante Ac tunc et

[130] in tali casu de tempore in tempus quoties casus sic acciderit infra convenien[s]
tempus post hui[us]mo[d]i amoc[i]on[em] vel amoc[i]o[n]es al[ia] idonea
p[er]sona vel al[ie] idonee p[er]sone in locu[m] et Offici[um] vel in
respectiva loca et

Officia hui[us]m[od]i p[er]sone vel p[er]sonar[um] sic amot[e] vel amotar[um]
eligetur et constituetur eligentur et constituentur et eligi et constitui possit et
possint s[e]c[un]d[um] tenor[em] et appunctuac[i]on[em] har[um]
L[itte]rar[um] Patentiu[m] Acetiam

PROVISO q[uo]d si aliquando imposter[um] infra viginti dies post hu[ius]mo[d]i
amoc[i]o[n]em sive amoc[i]o[n]es alicuius sive aliquor[um] Maior[is]
Ald[e]r[mann]or[um] Assisten[tium] Balli[v]or[um] Capital[is] Seneschall[i]
Recordator[is] Deput[ati]

Recordator[is] Com[m]un[is] Cleric[i] Sollicitator[is] duodecim loco
Ball[iv]or[um] Ang[li]ce Baliffes places Coronator[is] prim[i] Servien[tis]
ad Clavam Maior[is] p[re]d[icti] et p[re]d[ictorum] vigint[i] quatuor
Consilior[um] sive de Co[mmun]i Consilio aut a[lio]r[um]

Officiarior[um] Civitat[is] p[re]d[icte] ab Officiis suis respectivis p[re]d[ictis] aut
post mortem sive decess[um] eor[un]d[em] aut aliquor[um] eor[um] reliqu[i]
de Com[m]un[i] Consilio Civitat[is] p[re]d[icte] p[ro] tempore existen[te]
precept[i] sive mandat[i] fuerint p[er] L[itte]ras Mandator[um]

[135] n[ost]ri seu hered[um] vel Successor[um] n[ost]ror[um] sub Sigillo et Signeto
manual[i] n[ost]ri hered[um] vel Successor[um] n[ost]ror[um] iisd[em]
direct[as] sive dirigend[as] eligere admittere et jurare aliquam aliam
p[er]sonam vel aliquas al[ias] p[er]sonas

no[m]i[n]ac[i]onis n[ost]ri hered[um] vel Successor[um] n[ost]ror[um] ad et in
Sep[ar]al[ia] et respectiva loca et Officia sive Locum aut Officium alicuius
vel aliquar[um] p[er]sonar[um] sic inde amot[arum] mort[e] vel decess[u] ut
p[re]fertur quod tunc

et toties liceat et licebit iisdem Co[mmun]i Consilio Civitat[is] p[re]d[icte] p[ro]
tempore existen[ti] quam pauci in numero iidem esse acciderint aut maior[i]
part[i] eor[un]d[em] qui super publicam noticiam sive sumonic[i]onem

adtunc interesse voluerint eligere et admittere ac iidem p[er] p[re]sentes
requirunt[ur] eligere et admittere quamlib[e]t tal[em] respectiv[am]
p[er]son[am] sive p[er]son[as] respectiv[as] ad et in locum aut Officiu[m]
sive loca aut

Officia p[re]d[icta] p[er]sonar[um] sive p[er]sone respective sic inde amot[arum]
morte sive decess[u] prout in eo casu de tempore in tempus posthac p[er]

hu[ius]mo[d]i L[itte]ras Mandator[um] respectiv[e] nominat[i] sive
appunctuat[i] sint vel
[140] erint Et q[uo]d in tal[i] casu quelibet al[ia] elecc[i]o sive admissio h[ab]ita sive
h[ab]end[a] contra tenor[em] har[um] p[re]sentiu[m] aut contra exigentiam
p[re]d[ictarum] L[itte]rar[um] Mandator[um] ad o[m]nia Intenc[i]on[es] et
p[ro]posita quecunq[ue] vacua et
nullius vigoris erit Etiam p[er] p[re]sentes p[ro] nob[is] hered[ibus] et
Successor[ibus] n[ost]ris dam[us] et concedim[us] Co[mmun]i Consilio
Civitat[is] p[re]d[icte] p[ro] tempore existen[ti] aut tal[ibus] eor[um] per
quos talis elecc[i]o aut admissio s[e]c[un]d[u]m veram
intenc[i]onem har[um] p[re]senciu[m] habit[a] et fact[a] sit et erit plen[am]
pot[estat]em et authoritatem administrand[i] Sacrament[um] Officii sive
Offic[i]or[um] cuilibet Maior[i] Alderman[nis] Assisten[tibus] Balliv[is]
Capital[i] Senescall[o]
Recordator[i] Com[m]uni Cleric[o] Sollicitator[i] duodecim loco Ballivor[um]
Ang[li]ce Bayliffes places Coronator[i] prim[o] Servien[ti] ad Clavam
Maior[is] p[re]d[icti] et p[re]d[ictis] viginti quatuor Com[m]un[ibus]
Consiliar[iis] sive de
Com[m]un[i] Consil[io] aut al[io] Officiar[io] Civitat[is] p[re]d[icte] sic ut
p[re]fertur electi[s] aut admiss[is] sive eligend[is] aut admittend[is] infra
eand[em] Civitat[em] necnon q[uo]d quilibet Maior Ald[e]r[mann]i
Assisten[tes] Balli[v]i Capital[is] Sen[esc]all[us] Recordat[or]
[145] Com[m]un[is] Cl[er]icus Sollicitator Coronator duodecim loco Balli[v]or[um]
Ang[li]ce Bayliffes places prim[us] Servien[s] ad Clavam Maior[is]
p[re]d[icti] et viginti quatuor Consiliar[ii] sive de Com[m]un[i] Consi[li]o
aut al[ius] Officiar[ius] Civitat[is] p[re]d[icte] sic
ut p[re]fertur elect[i] admiss[i] et jurati sive imposter[um] eligend[i] admittend[i]
aut jurand[i] seperal[ia] sua respectiva Officia p[re]d[icta] seu Officiu[m]
p[re]d[ictum] infra Civitat[em] p[re]d[ictam] h[ab]ere gaudere et exercere
possit et valeat sive
possint aut valeant adeo plene et integre ac in tam amplis modo et forma ad
o[mn]ia intenc[i]o[ne]s et p[ro]posita quecunq[ue] sicut aliquis al[ius] Maior
Ald[e]r[mann]i Assisten[tes] Ballivi Capital[is] Senescall[us] Recordator
Co[mmun]is Cl[er]icus Sollicitator duodecim loco Balli[v]or[um] Ang[li]ce
Bayliffes places Coronator prim[us] Servien[s] ad Clavam Maioris
p[re]d[icti] et p[re]d[icti] viginti quatuor Com[m]un[es] Consil[iarii] sive de
Com[m]un[i] Consil[io] aut al[ius] Officiar[ius]
infra eand[em] Civitat[em] in ullo alio modo elect[us] admiss[us] et jurat[us] sive
in futur[o] eligend[us] admittend[us] aut jurand[us] possit aut valeat aliquo
alio modo aut forma elecc[i]o[n]is admiss[ionis] vel Juendment[i] in
presentib[us] sup[er]ius script[o]
[150] vel infra Civitat[em] p[re]d[ictam] antehac usitat[o] in contrar[ium] huius in
aliquo non obstante ET ULTERIUS volum[us] ac p[er] p[re]sentes p[ro]
nob[is] hered[ibus] et Successor[ibus] n[ost]ris concedim[us] p[re]fat[is]
Maior[i] Balliv[is] et Co[mmun]itat[i] Civit[atis] p[re]d[icte] et
Successor[ibus] suis
q[uo]d Maior Balliv[i] et Co[mmun]itas Civitat[is] ill[ius] p[ro] tempore
existen[tes] vel eor[um] maior pars quor[um] Maior[em] Civitat[is] ill[ius]
p[ro] tempore existen[tem] un[um] esse volum[us] eligere no[m]i[n]are et
appunctuare possint de tempore in tempus p[er]petuis
futur[is] temporib[us] ad libit[um] et voluntat[em] suam tot et tant[os]

Camerar[ios] Servien[tes] ad Clava[m] Constabular[ios] et al[ios]
Officiar[ios] et Ministr[os] Inferior[es] infra Civitat[em] p[re]d[ictam] quot
et quant[i] antehac in eadem Civit[ate] elect[i]   no[m]i[n]at[i]
et appunctuat[i] fuer[unt] aut eligi no[m]i[n]ar[i] et appunctuari consuever[unt]
q[uo]dq[ue] Camerar[ii] Servien[tes] ad Clavas Constabular[ii] et al[ii]
Officiar[ii] et Minist[ri] sic imposter[um] eligend[i] et no[m]i[n]and[i]
elect[i] no[m]i[n]at[i] et jurat[i] fuerint
p[er] tali[s] p[er]son[as] ad hui[us]mo[d]i dies et tempora et in tal[ibus] modo et
forma qual[ibus] Camerar[ii] Servien[tes] ad Clavas Constabular[ii] et al[ii]
Officiar[ii] et Ministr[i] Civit[atis] p[re]d[icte] antehac eligebantur
nominabant[ur] constituebantur et
[155] jura[ba]nt[ur] ET ULTERIUS de ampliori gra[tia] n[ost]ra sp[ec]iali ac ex certa
scientia et mero motu n[ost]ris concessim[us] ac p[er] p[re]sentes p[ro]
nob[is] hered[ibus] et Successor[ibus] n[ost]ris concedim[us] p[re]fat[is]
Maior[i] Bal[livis] et Co[mmun]itat[i] Civit[atis] p[re]d[icte] et
Successor[ibus] suis o[mn]ia et omnimod[a] tot tant[a] tal[ia] ead[em]
hui[us]mo[d]i et consi[mi]l[ia] Coronat[ores] Escaetor[es] Cur[ias] de
Recordo Cognic[i]o[n]es pl[ac]itor[um] bona et Catal[la] Felon[um]
Fugitivor[um] et in exigend[o] possit[orum] *(sic)* deodand[a] waviat[a]
extrahur[as]
Mercat[a] Fer[ias] Nundi[n]a[s] Tolnet[a] Theolon[ia] Tol[l]ag[ia] Taxat[iones]
Fin[es] Redempc[i]on[es] Exit[us] Amerciament[a] Forisfact[uras]
p[er]quisit[a] Cur[ie] Gaol[arum] lib[er]tat[es] Concession[es] Franches[ias]
Immunitat[es] Privileg[ia] exempc[iones] quietanc[ias] jurisdicc[i]on[es]
Custum[as] liber[tates] Consuetud[ines] Messuag[ia] Molendin[a] aquas
P[is]car[ias] P[is]cac[i]o[n]es terr[a] tenemen[ta] et hereditament[a]
quecunq[ue] quot quant[a] qual[ia] et que Maior Ball[ivi] et Co[mmun]itas
Civit[atis] p[re]d[icte] modo h[ab]ent tenent gaudent
utuntur aut h[ab]ere tenere uti et gaudere consueverunt debuerunt aut debent aut
eor[um] aliquis vel aliqui vel Predecessor[es] sui p[er] quecunq[ue]
no[m]i[n]a sive p[er] q[uo]dcunq[ue] no[m]en vel p[er] quamcunque
Incorporac[i]on[em] vel p[re]textu
[160] cuiuscunque Incorporac[i]onis antehac h[ab]uer[unt] usi vel gavisi fuer[unt] aut
h[ab]ere tenere uti et gaudere debuer[unt] h[ab]uit tenuit usus vel gavis[us]
fuit debuit aut debuer[unt] eis et Successor[ibus] suis imp[er]p[etuu]m de
statu hereditar[io]
rac[i]on[e] aliquar[um] C[ha]rtaru[m] Concess[ionum] aut L[itte]rar[um]
Patenci[um] p[er] nos vel p[er] aliquem Progenitor[um] vel Antecessor[um]
vel Predecessor[um] n[ost]ror[um] quoquomodo antehac fact[arum] et
confirmat[arum] vel concess[arum] seu quocunq[ue] al[io] legali
p[re]script[i]on[e] us[u] seu consuetud[ine] aut aliquo al[io] legal[i] modo jure seu
titulo antehac habit[is] seu usitat[is] licet ead[em] aut eor[um] aliquod vel
aliqua antehac usa non fuer[int] aut fuit abusa vel male usa vel
discontinuat[a]
seu sursum reddit[a] fuerint aut fuit ac licet ead[em] aut eor[um] aliq[uo]d vel
aliqua forisfact[a] aut dep[er]dit[a] sunt vel fuer[unt] HABEND[A]
tenend[a] et gaudend[a] p[re]fat[is] Maior[i] Ball[ivis] et Co[mmun]itat[i]
Civit[atis] Oxon[ie] p[re]d[icte] et Successor[ibus]
suis imp[er]p[etuu]m Ac Reddend[a] et solvend[a] inde annuatim nob[is]
hered[ibus] et Successor[ibus] n[ost]ris tot tant[a] tal[ia] ead[em]
hu[ius]mo[d]i et consi[mi]l[ia] firm[as] Feoda Redd[itus] servic[ia]

denar[ios] Sum[mas] et demand[a] quecunq[ue] quot quant[a] qual[ia] et
[165] que nob[is] antehac p[ro] eisd[em] reddi seu solvi consuever[unt] seu reddi aut
solvi debuer[unt] et in consi[mi]li[bus] modo et forma p[ro]ut eadem
antehac nob[is] vel Progenitor[ibus] n[ost]ris reddi consuever[unt]
VOLUMUS etiam et p[er]

p[re]sentes p[ro] nob[is] hered[ibus] et Successor[ibus] n[ost]ris conced[imus]
p[re]fat[is] Maior[i] Ball[ivis] et Co[mmun]itat[i] Civit[atis] p[re]d[icte] et
Successor[ibus] suis q[uo]d h[ab]eant teneant utant[ur] et gaudeant ac plene
h[ab]ere tenere uti et gaudere possint

valeant imp[er]p[etuu]m om[n]ia libertat[es] lib[er]as consuetud[ines] privileg[ia]
quietanci[as] Jurisdicc[i]o[n]es et Hereditamen[ta] s[e]c[un]d[um] tenor[em]
et effe[c]tum har[um] L[ittera]rum n[ost]rar[um] p[ate]nci[um] sine
occas[i]o[n]e vel Impedimen[to] n[ost]ri hered[um] vel Successor[u]m
n[ost]ror[um]

quorumcunq[ue] NOLENTES q[uo]d iid[em] Maior Ball[ivi] et Co[mmun]itas
Civitat[is] p[re]d[icte] et Successor[es] sui r[aci]one p[re]missor[um] vel
eor[um] alicuius p[er] nos vel hered[es] n[ost]ros Justic[iarios] vicecom[ites]
Escaetor[es] aut al[ios] Balli[v]os vel Ministr[os] n[ost]ros

hered[um] seu Successor[um] n[ost]ror[um] quor[um]cunq[ue] inde
occ[asi]one[n]tur molestentur vexent[ur] seu graventur molestetur vexetur
gravetur seu in aliquo p[er]turbetur VOLUMUS insuper ac p[er] p[re]sentes
p[ro] nob[is] hered[ibus] et Successor[ibus]

[170] n[ost]ris providem[us] et firmiter iniungend[o] Precipim[us] et mandam[us]
q[uo]d Dissoluci[o] Corporis Corporat[i] Civitat[is] p[re]d[icte] sic ut
p[re]fertur habit[a] nullo modo extendat vel extendere construatur fore in

aliq[uo]d dampn[um] p[re]iudiciu[m] aut enervac[i]onem lib[er]tat[um]
Franches[i]ar[um] Immunitat[um] Privileg[iorum] aut aliquor[um]
hereditament[orum] p[er] p[re]sentes dat[orum] et restitut[orum] p[re]fat[is]
Maior[i] Ball[ivis] et Co[mmun]itat[i] Civitat[is] Oxon[ie] p[re]d[icte] et

Successor[ibus] suis nec ad dand[um] Cancellar[io] Mag[ist]ris et Scholar[ibus]
Uniuer[sit]atis n[ost]re Oxoniens[is] aliqu[a] Preheminentias Privilegi[a] vel
Advantagi[a] quecunq[ue] que ip[s]i vel Predecessor[es] sui non h[ab]uerunt
vel de iure

usi vel gavisi fuerunt ante p[re]d[ictam] Dissoluc[i]o[n]em Corporac[i]o[n]is
Civitatis p[re]d[icte] sed q[uo]d omnes et singuli Lib[er]tat[es] Franchesi[e]
Immunitat[es] Privilegi[a] et Hereditamen[ta] p[re]fat[orum] Maior[is]
Balli[vorum] et Co[mmun]itat[is] Civitat[is] p[re]d[icte]

et Successor[um] suor[um] valid[a] firm[a] et illes[a] et in suo pleno robore
p[er]petuis futur[is] temporibus erunt et reman[ebu]nt aliqua re causa vel
materia quacunq[ue] in Contrar[ium] inde ullo modo non obstante

[175] PROVISO semper ac Regiam voluntat[em] n[ost]ram p[er] p[re]sentes declaramus
q[uo]d nullus Capital[is] Senescall[us] Recordator vel Co[mmun]is
Cl[er]icus dict[e Civitat[is] imposter[um] eligend[us] vel p[ro]ficiend[us] ad
Execuc[i]on[em]

Officii sui respective admittatur nisi approbat[i]o n[ost]ra hered[um] vel
Successor[um] n[ost]ror[um] sub Sigillo vel Signeto Manual[i] n[ost]ri
hered[um] vel Successor[um] n[ost]ror[um] in ea parte prius significabitur
aliquo in p[re]sentibus

superius menc[i]onat[o] aut aliqua al[ia] re Causa vel materia quacunq[ue] in
contrar[ium] inde non obstante ET ULTERIUS pro diversis Causis et
Considerac[i]onibus nos ad hoc specialiter moven[tibus]

[Sheet 4]
gr[aci]a nostra speciali ac ex certa sciencia et mero motu nostris et virtute
  Prerogative n[ost]re Regie DISPENSAVIMUS Pardonavimus Remisimus et
  Exoneravimus ac per
presentes pro nobis Hered[ibus] et Successor[ibus] n[ost]ris Dispensamus
  Pardonamus Remittimus et Exoneramus p[re]d[ictos] Edw[ard]um
  Henricum Comitem Litchfield Ric[ard]um Carter Will[elm]um
[180] Wright sen[iorem] Edw[ard]um Walker Thomam Eustace Ric[ard]um Carter
  Tobiam Browne Edw[ard]um Combes Ric[ard]um Hawkins Alex[and]rum
  Wright Jacobum Pinnell Ric[ard]um Tidmarsh Will[elm]um
Greene Joh[ann]em Tomkins Henricum Trinder Will[elm]um Wright jun[iorem]
  Joh[ann]em Weller Joh[ann]em Philipps Thomam Baker Abrahamum White
  Timothe[u]m Box Ric[ard]um Dodwell Will[elm]um
Ayleworth Will[elm]um Badger Thomam Neale Ric[ard]um Houghton
  Ric[ard]um Keats Timotheum   Perry Joh[ann]em Knibb Will[elm]um
  Walker Arth[ur]um Madle Joh[ann]em Weller Joh[ann]em Phillips
Thomam Kimber Jacobum Finch Ric[ard]um Crouch Thomam Blisse
  Will[elm]um Ryley Michael[em] Ackland Edw[ard]um Salter Chilton Tubb
  Will[elm]um Appleby Theodor[um] Spencer Antonium
Mathews Rob[er]tum Hensley Will[elm]um Stibbs Ric[ard]um Carter
  Laurentiu[m] King Will[elm]um Nicholls Henricum Wildgoose Danielem
  Monday Rob[er]tum Kenrick Henricum Richardson
[185] Josephum Maior Will[elm]um Playter Jacobum Burrows Joh[ann]em Burrows et
  Joh[ann]em Toms existen[tes] Maior[em] p[re]d[ictum] Capital[em]
  Senescall[um] p[re]d[ictum] Recordator[em] Deputat[um] Recordator[is]
  Alderman[nos]
Assisten[tes] Ballivos Coronator[em] Commun[em] Cleric[um] Sollicitator[em]
  duodecim loco Ballivos Ang[li]ce Bayliffes places prim[um] Servien[tem]
  ad Clavam Maior[is] et vigint[i] quatuor Consiliar[ios]
vel de Communi Consilio Civitat[is] predict[e] in presentib[us] nominat[os] et
  quemlibet eorum et quemlibet alium sive alios hui[us]mo[d]i Officiar[ios] ac
  omnes al[ios] Officiar[ios] sive Ministr[os] respective
infra eandem Civitat[em] in futur[um] nominand[os] eligend[os] vel
  admittend[os] de et ab omn[ibus] Prestac[i]one et Recepc[i]one Juramenti
  Primatie Ang[li]ce the Oath of Supremacy menc[i]onat[i]
in quodam Act[o] Parliament[i] fact[o] in Parliament[o] Domine Elizabethe nuper
  Anglie Regine Anno Regni sui primo seu in aliquo alio Statuto sive Act[u]
  Parliament[i]
[190] Acetiam de et ab Prestac[i]one et Recepc[i]one Jurament[i] Ligeantie Ang[li]ce
  the Oath of Allegiance or Obedience menc[i]onat[i] seu express[i] in
  quodam Act[u] Parliament[i]
fact[o] in Parliament[o] Domini Jacobi primi Avi nostri nuper Regis Anglie Anno
  Regni sui tercio tento seu in aliquo al[io] Statut[o] sive Act[u] Parliament[i]
  Acetiam
de et ab Prestac[i]one et Recepc[i]one Jurament[i] menc[i]onat[i] et content[i] in
  quodam Statut[o] fact[o] in Parliament[o] D[omi]ni Caroli Secundi nuper
  Regis Anglie Anno R[eg]ni
sui Decimo tercio tent[o] Entitulat[o] an Act for the well governing and
  Regulateing of Corporac[i]ons Acetiam de et ab omn[i] Recepc[i]one
  Sacrament[i] Cene D[omi]nice

Ang[li]ce the Sacrament of the Lords Supper secund[um] rit[us] seu usus Ecclesie
Anglicane seu secund[um] direcc[i]on[em] aliquorum Canon[um] seu
Statutor[um] vel alicuius Canon[is] vel
[195] Statut[i] huius Regni nostri Anglie acetiam de et ab Prestac[i]on[e] et
Subscripc[i]on[e] Declarac[i]on[is] menc[i]onat[e] seu content[e] in
p[re]d[icto] Statut[o] Anno Decimo Tercio Caroli Secundi
acetiam de et ab prestac[i]one et Subscripc[i]one Declarac[i]on[is] menc[i]onate et
express[e] in quodam al[io] Statut[o] fact[o] in Parliament[o] dicti D[omi]ni
Regis Caroli Secundi Anno R[eg]ni
sui Vicesimo Quinto Entitulat[o] an Act for preventing Dangers which may
happen from Popish Recusants Acetiam de et ab Prestac[i]one et
Recepc[i]one aliquor[um]
Juramentor[um] et Recepc[i]one Sacrament[i] Cene Dominice et Subscripc[i]one
aliquar[um] Declarac[i]onum sive alicuius Declarac[i]on[is]
menc[i]onat[arum] seu express[arum] in Statut[is] pred[ictis]
sive Act[ibus] Parliament[i] superius menc[i]onat[is] aut eor[um] aliquo seu
aliquo al[io] Statut[o] menc[i]onat[arum] sive content[arum] de et
concernen[te] p[re]miss[a] et de et ab omnib[us] Criminib[us]
Convicc[i]on[ibus]
[200] Pen[is] Penalitat[ibus] forisfactur[is] dampn[is] Incapacitat[ibus] et
Disabilitat[ibus] per eosdem vel aliquem eorum incurs[is] vel incursur[is]
seu eisdem aut alicui eorum imputand[is] aut obiiciend[is]
vel cum quibus aliquis vel aliqui eorum modo sint vel sit seu posthac possint vel
possit esse onerabiles vel onerabilis pro eo quod non p[re]stiterunt seu
reciperunt vel
aliquis eorum non prestitit aut recepit aut posthac non p[re]starint seu reciperint
vel aliquis illor[um] non p[re]starit seu reciperit p[re]fat[a] Jurament[a] et
Sacrament[a] Cene D[omi]nice
aut non subscripserint seu fecerint aut posthac non subscripserint vel fecerint aut
eor[um] aliquis non subscripsit aut subscripserit fecit vel fecerit p[re]dict[as]
Declarac[i]on[es]
superius menc[i]onat[as] aut eorum aliquam vel aliquam al[iam] quamcunq[ue]
iniunctas vel p[re]script[as] per Statut[u]m predict[um] seu eorum alter[um]
sive per aliquem (sic) al[ium] Statut[um] preantea
[205] fact[um] seu edit[um] requiren[tem] prestac[i]on[em] Jurament[orum]
predict[orum] vel cuiuslibet eorum vel recepc[i]one[m] Sacrament[i] Cene
D[omi]nice secund[um] rit[us] et us[us] Ecclesie Anglicane vel
prolac[i]on[em]
et subscripc[i]one[m] Declarac[i]on[um] p[re]dict[arum] vel alicuius eor[um] Ac
de et ab omnib[us] et omnimod[is] Informac[i]on[ibus] Presentac[i]on[ibus]
Indictament[is] Prosecuc[i]on[ibus] molestac[i]on[ibus] Clameis et
demand[is] quibuscunq[ue] tam in nomine nostri hered[um] aut Successor[um]
n[ost]ror[um] quam in nomine vel in nominib[us] alicuius al[ie] persone vel
aliquarum al[iarum] personarum p[re]antea
habit[is] prolat[is] et modo dependen[tibus] vel imposterum h[ab]end[is]
proferend[is] seu fore dependen[tibus] in aliqua Cur[ia] n[ost]ra hered[um]
et Successor[um] n[ost]ror[um] sive in aliqu[ibus] al[iis] Cur[iis] seu Locis
quibuscunq[ue] de pro sive
concernen[tibus] aliquod defect[um] neglect[um] omission[em] sive
recusat[i]on[em] capiend[i] prestand[i] recipiend[i] seu subscribend[i]
p[re]d[icta] Jurament[a] Sacrament[um] Cene D[omi]nice aut

Declarac[i]on[es] in Act[ibus] Parliament[i] superius

[210] menc[i]onat[is] aut per eosdem aut per eor[um] aliquem direct[a] seu p[re]script[a]
aut propter aliquod al[iud] defect[um] in p[er]formac[i]one p[re]missor[um]
aut eor[um] alicuius ET ULTERIUS ex abundantiori gra[cia] n[ost]ra et ex

certa scientia et mero motu n[ost]ris volumus et declaramus et per presentes pro
nobis Hered[ibus] et Successor[ibus] n[ost]ris Concedimus iisdem
p[re]dict[is] Maior[i] Capital[i] Seneschall[o] predict[o]

Recordator[i] Deputat[o] Recordator[is] Aldermann[is] Assisten[tibus] Ballivis
Coronator[i] Com[m]uni Cleric[o] Sollicitator[i] duodecim loco Balliv[is]
ang[li]ce Bayliffes places prim[o] Servien[ti] ad

Clavam Maior[is] et Vigint[i] quatuor Consiliar[ios] vel de Com[m]uni Consilio
et omnib[us] al[iis] Officiar[iis] sive Ministr[is] Civitat[is] predict[e] modo
et p[ro] tempore existen[tibus] et cuilibet eorum

plenam et sufficien[tem] abilitat[em] capacitat[em] potestat[em] et authoritat[em]
h[ab]end[i] gaudend[i] et exercend[i] Officia sua respectiva predict[a]
respective et omnia et singula adinde respective spectan[tia]

[215] ac pertinen[tia] sine et absq[ue] prestac[i]one Jurament[orum] predict[orum] vel
eorum alicuius aut recepc[i]one Sacrament[i] Cene D[omi]nice
s[e]c[un]d[u]m rit[us] et us[us] Ecclesie Anglicane vel Prolac[i]one et

Subscripc[i]one Declarac[i]on[um] predict[arum] vel eorum alicuius seu
performand[i] alicuius Iniunct[i]on[is] vel Requisic[i]on[is] quarumcunq[ue]
per aliquod Statut[um] predict[um] direct[arum] fore

Performand[arum] sive incurrend[arum] aut Subject fore aliquibus Criminibus
Offens[is] Inabilitat[ibus] Incapacitat[ibus] Correcc[i]on[ibus]
Prosecuc[i]on[ibus] Pen[is] Penalitat[ibus] Forisfactur[is]
Impetrac[i]on[ibus] seu

dampnis quibuscunq[ue] Et adeo plene et libere ac si iidem Maior Capital[is]
Seneschall[us] Recordator Deputat[us] Recordator[is] Ald[e]r[mann]i
Assisten[tes] Ballivi Coronator Co[mmun]is Cl[er]icus

Sollicitator duodecim loco Ballivor[um] Ang[li]ce Bayliffes places prim[us]
Serviens ad Clavam Maior[is] et viginti quatuor Consiliar[ii] vel de
Com[m]uni Consilio et omnes al[ii] Officiar[ii]

[220] sive Ministri Civitat[is] p[re]d[icte] modo et pro tempore existen[tes] prestitissent
recepissent fecissent et subscripsissent predict[a] Jurament[a]
Sacrament[um] Cene Dominice et Declarac[i]on[es]

secund[um] formam et effectum Statut[orum] predict[orum] et Act[uum]
Parliament[i] superius menc[i]onat[orum] Actibus et Statut[is] predict[is] vel
aliquib[us] eorum aut aliquo in eisdem seu eorum

aliquo content[o] aut aliquo al[io] Statut[o] Act[u] Parliament[i] Lege vel
Provisione in contrar[ium] inde in aliquo nonobstante IN CUJUS rei
Testimoniu[m] has L[itte]ras n[ost]ras fieri

fecimus Patentes TESTE meip[s]o apud Westmonaster[ium] Decimo quinto Die
Septembr[is] Anno Regni nostri quarto.   per ip[su]m Regem

PIGOTT

Translation:

[1] James the Second, by the grace of God [2] King of England, Scotland, France and
Ireland, Defender of the faith, etc. TO ALL [those] whom our present Letter will reach,
greetings. SINCE our City of Oxford in [3] our County of Oxfordshire is an ancient
City, extremely populous, and at differing times prior to this was Incorporated by

differing names, and the Inhabitants of the same [city] under the differing [4] names of Incorporation possessed, used and enjoyed differing rights, Franchises, Immunities and Privileges, both by reason of the differing Prescriptions, usages and Customs habitual in [5] the same City from a time in contradiction of which there is no human memory, and also through the differing Charters and Letters Patent of our Forebears the Kings and Queens of England [6] [that were] previously made, granted and confirmed for them; AND SINCE the individual aforesaid Charters and letters patent, by reason of certain abuses [and] defects or of the negligence of the Inhabitants of the aforesaid City have now come to an end and are null and void, [7] wherefore the Incorporation or Body Corporate of the same City is now completely dissolved, and the said Inhabitants of that City most humbly begged us that [8] we should see fit to display and extend to them our Royal grace and munificence in a Grant to them [of] such liberties and privileges as seem to us to be most expedient, YOU SHOULD KNOW [9] therefore that we, freely aspiring to the improvement of our City of Oxford, desiring that henceforward in perpetuity in the aforesaid City of Oxford there should continually be in force one sure and certain [10] means concerning and for the Protection of our peace and for the good Rule and government of the same City and of [those of] our people who from time to time Live in that same place and of others *[10-11]* who from time to time gather there, [11] And that the aforesaid City henceforward in perpetuity should be and remain a City of peace and calm to the fear and terror of evil men and offenders and for the benefit of good men; [12] And also that our peace and other deeds of Justice in the same place can better be protected and may have authority; as an act of our special grace and from our secure knowledge and our own free will we have desired, ordained, [13] established, granted and declared and through the present documents on behalf of ourselves [and] our heirs and Successors we desire, ordain, establish, grant and declare that the said City of Oxford [14] in the County of Oxfordshire should be now and in the future and should remain henceforward in perpetuity a free City by its very nature; And that the Citizens of the aforesaid City henceforward in perpetuity should be now and in the future one Incorporated and political Body [15] in actual fact and in name, by the name of [the] Mayor, Bailiffs and Commonalty of the City of Oxford in the County of Oxfordshire, *[15-16]* and by the same name of [the] Mayor, Bailiffs and Commonalty of Oxford in the County of Oxfordshire, through the present documents on behalf of ourselves [and] our heirs and Successors we elevate, make, ordain, establish, create and declare them to be one Incorporated and political Body in actual fact and in name actually and fully; [16] Also that under [17] the same name they should have a perpetual Succession; Also that they themselves and their Successors, under the name of Mayor, Bailiffs and Commonalty of the City of Oxford in the County of Oxfordshire should be now and in the future, presently and [18] hereafter for all future times persons who are fit, and legally capable, and an Incorporated and political Body legally capable of having, restoring, receiving, possessing, enjoying and retaining [any] Lands, Tenements, Freedoms, Privileges, [19] Jurisdictions, Franchises and Hereditaments whatsoever of whatever sort, name, nature, kind or species they may be now or in the future, for themselves and their Successors in Fee and perpetuity whether to the end of the years or otherwise in whatever [20] manner; and also goods and chattels and whatsoever other items of whatever sort, name, nature, kind or species they may be now or in the future; also [legally capable] of giving, granting, handing over, transferring, assigning and bequeathing lands, [21] Tenements and Hereditaments, goods and chattels, and doing and carrying out and all and every other deed and matter under the aforesaid name; Also that by the same name of Mayor, Bailiffs and Commonalty of the City of Oxford in the County of Oxfordshire they should be authorised and able to sue and be sued, [22] to answer and be answered, to defend and be defended, in whatsoever Lawcourts, places and locations of judgment and before whatsoever Judges and Judicial personnel and other persons and Officials of ours [and of] our heirs and Successors in [23] all and every single court sitting, assembly, lawsuit, petition, case, matter and claim whatsoever, of whatsoever sort, name, nature, kind or species they may be now or in the future, in the same manner and form just as any other Subjects [24] of ours of this Kingdom of England [who are] fit and legally capable people, or any other Incorporated and political Body within this our Kingdom of England *[25]* are able and authorised *[24]* to hold, restore, receive, possess, enjoy, retain, [25] give, grant, hand over, transfer, assign and bequeath, sue and be sued, answer and be answered, defend and be defended, do, neglect, or carry out; Also that the Mayor, [26] Bailiffs and Commonalty of the aforesaid City of Oxford and their Successors should have hereafter in perpetuity a Communal Seal to be used for the purpose of transacting the legal Affairs and business of themselves and of their Successors, whatever it is; Also that it should be freely permitted now and in the future to the same [27] Mayor, Bailiffs and Commonalty of the aforesaid City of Oxford and to their Successors from time to time to break, to change and to make afresh that seal as they desire, just as it shall seem to them best to be done; AND [28] FURTHERMORE it is our will and through the present documents on behalf of ourselves [and] our heirs and Successors we grant and ordain that henceforward in perpetuity there should be now and in the future within the aforesaid City one from among the more prominent and Discreet Citizens of the aforesaid City, *[28-9]* to be elected and appointed in the form mentioned below, [29] who will be and will be named Mayor of the aforesaid City; and for the better execution of our will in this area WE HAVE ASSIGNED, nominated, appointed and made, and through the present documents on behalf of [30] ourselves [and] our heirs and Successors we assign, nominate, appoint and make our beloved Richard Carter [the] squire to become and be the first modern Mayor of the aforesaid City, desiring that the same Richard Carter *[30-31]* shall continue in the Office of Mayor of the aforesaid City [31] from the date of the present documents up to the Monday next before the Feast of St Matthew the Apostle which will come in the year of the Lord 1689, and thereafter until such time as one other man *[31-2]* has been elected, appointed and sworn in to that Office in the required manner [32] according to the Ordinance and Constitution specified below in the present documents, provided the same Richard Carter lives that long, unless in the meantime because of reasonable Cause or in the manner and form mentioned below [33] he is removed from that Office; AND FURTHERMORE it is our will and through the present documents on behalf of ourselves [and] our heirs and Successors we grant to the Mayor, Bailiffs and Commonalty of the aforesaid City and to their Successors that any Mayor of the aforesaid City who henceforward [34] is to be elected, nominated or appointed from time to time and for all time in the future shall be elected, nominated and sworn in by such persons on the kind of days and times and in such a manner and form as those in which the Mayor of the aforesaid City prior to this [35] used to be elected, nominated, appointed and sworn in; Also that any Mayor of the aforesaid City in office at any given time henceforward in perpetuity shall continue in the same Office for the duration of such a period of time, and should have, hold, enjoy and exercise and [36] should be authorised and able to have, hold, enjoy and exercise such Courts of Record and as many, as great and such of this kind and other similar Powers, Privileges, Authorities, Offices, rights, jurisdictions, acquisitions and profits for all intents and purposes [37] whatsoever, however many, however great and whatever kind and which a Mayor of the said City prior to this in whatever manner continued, had, held, enjoyed or exercised, or was able or ought to continue, have, hold, enjoy or exercise; [38] AND ALSO it is our will, and through the present documents on behalf of ourselves [and] our heirs and Successors we grant and ordain that henceforward there should be now and in the future within the same City two trustworthy and prudent men, Citizens of the aforesaid City, [38-9] to be elected in the form mentioned below in these letters Patent, [39] who shall be and shall be named Bailiffs of the aforesaid City; And for the better execution of our will in this area WE HAVE ASSIGNED, nominated, appointed and made and through the present documents we assign, nominate, [40] appoint and make our beloved John Weller and John Philipps [the] Corn Chandler, Citizens of the aforesaid City, to become and be the first two modern Bailiffs of the aforesaid City, to continue in the same Office [41] up to the aforesaid Monday next before the said Feast of St Matthew the Apostle which will be in the year of the Lord 1689 and from the same day until two other men from among the Citizens of the aforesaid City [41-2] are appointed and sworn in to that Office [42] according to the Ordinance and Provision set out and declared below in these present documents, provided the same John Weller and John Philipps live so long, unless in the meantime [42-3] they are removed or one or other of them is removed from the aforesaid Office because of reasonable Cause or in the manner and form mentioned below; [43] AND FURTHERMORE it is our will and through the present documents on behalf of ourselves [and] our heirs and Successors we grant to the Mayor, Bailiffs and Commonalty of the aforesaid City and to their Successors that the Bailiffs of [44] the aforesaid City who are henceforward to be elected or appointed from time to time and for all time in the future shall be elected, nominated and sworn in, And either one of them shall be elected, nominated and sworn in, by such persons on the kind of days and times and [45] in such a manner and form as those in which the Bailiffs of the said City prior to this used to be elected, nominated, appointed and sworn in; Also that the Bailiffs of the said City and either one of them [who are] in office at any given time henceforward in perpetuity shall continue for the duration [46] of such a period of time, and should have, hold, enjoy and exercise and should be authorised and able to have, hold, enjoy and exercise as many, as great and such of this kind and similar Powers, Privileges, Authorities, Offices, rights, jurisdictions, [47] acquisitions and profits for all intents and purposes whatsoever, however many, however great and whatever kind and which Bailiffs of the said City prior to this in whatever way continued, had, held, enjoyed or exercised, or [47-8] were able or ought to continue, have, hold, enjoy or exercise, [48] or either one of them prior to this in whatever way continued, had, held, enjoyed or exercised, or [48-9] was able or ought to continue, have, hold, enjoy or exercise; [49] AND FURTHERMORE it is our will and through the present documents on behalf of ourselves [and] our heirs and Successors out of our special grace and from certain knowledge and of our own free will we grant to the aforementioned Mayor [and] Bailiffs of the aforesaid City [50] of Oxford and to their Successors that henceforward in perpetuity there should be now and in the future in the aforesaid City from time to time eight trustworthy and prudent men, Inhabitants and Residents within the same City, [50-51] to be elected in the form mentioned below in these present documents, [51] who will be and will be called Aldermen of the aforesaid City; and for the better Execution of our Will in this area WE HAVE ASSIGNED, nominated, appointed and made, and through the present documents [52] on behalf of ourselves [and] our heirs and Successors we assign, nominate, appoint and make our beloved William Wright senior [the] squire, Edward Walker [the] soldier, Thomas Eustace, Richard Carter, Tobias Browne, Edward Combes, [53] Richard Hawkins, and Alexander Wright, to become and to be the first modern Aldermen of the aforesaid City, to continue in the same Offices and Places for the duration of their natural lives [54] unless in the meantime because of some reasonable Cause or in the manner and form mentioned below they are removed or any one of them is removed; [55] IT IS OUR WILL in addition, and through the present documents on behalf of ourselves [and] our heirs and Successors We Grant to the aforementioned Mayor, Bailiffs and Commonalty of the aforesaid City of Oxford that henceforward in perpetuity there should be now and in the future within the same City from time to time four other trustworthy and prudent [56] men, Inhabitants and Residents within the same City, to be elected in the form mentioned below in these Letters Patent, who will be Assistants of the aforesaid City and from time to time will be Assistants and Helpers of the Mayor, Bailiffs and Commonalty of the same [57] City who are in existence at the time, in all the cases and matters affecting or concerning the aforesaid City; and for the better execution of our will in this area WE HAVE ASSIGNED, nominated, appointed and made, and through [58] the present documents on behalf of ourselves [and] our heirs and Successors we assign, nominate, appoint and make our beloved James Pinnell, Richard Tidmarsh, William Greene and John Tomkins, Citizens of the aforesaid City, to become and to be [59] the first four modern Assistants of the aforesaid City, to continue in that Office for the duration of their natural lives unless in the meantime because of some reasonable cause or in the manner and form mentioned below they are removed or any one of them is removed; [60] AND FURTHERMORE it is our will and through the present documents on behalf of ourselves [and] our heirs and Successors We Grant to the aforementioned Mayor, Bailiffs and Commonalty of the aforesaid City and to their Successors that henceforward in perpetuity there should be now and in the future within the aforesaid City twelve [61] from among the Citizens of that City, to be elected in the form mentioned below in these present documents, who will be and will be called *loco Ballivorum*, in English, 'in Bayliffes places'; AND FURTHERMORE it is our will, and through the present documents on behalf of ourselves [62] [and] our heirs and Successors We Grant to the aforementioned Mayor, Bailiffs and Commonalty of the aforesaid City and to their Successors that henceforward in perpetuity there should be now and in future within the same City twenty-four from among the Citizens of that City, *[62-3]* to be elected in the form mentioned below in these present documents, [63] who will be and will be called Common Councillors or [men] of the Common Council of that City; AND IN ADDITION it is our will, and through the present documents on behalf of ourselves [and] our heirs and Successors We Grant [64] to the aforementioned Mayor, Bailiffs and Commonalty of the aforesaid City and to their Successors that they themselves and their Successors henceforward in perpetuity should have now and in the future in the aforesaid City one eminent and prudent man, *[64-5]* to be elected and nominated in the form mentioned below in these present documents, [65] who will be and will be named Head Steward of the aforesaid City; And We Have Assigned, nominated, appointed and made and through the present documents we assign, nominate, appoint and make the very faithfully and sincerely beloved Edward [66] Henry [the] Earl of Litchfield, to become and to be the first modern Head Steward of the aforesaid City, to continue in the same Office for the duration of his natural life unless in the meantime because of reasonable cause or in the manner and form mentioned below [67] he is removed from that Office; AND FUTHERMORE it is our will, and on behalf of ourselves [and] our heirs and Successors, we grant to the aforementioned Mayor, Bailiffs and Commonalty of the aforesaid City and to their Successors that henceforward in perpetuity there should be now and in the future within the same City [68] from time to time one trustworthy and prudent man, learned in the Laws of England, who shall be and shall be named Recorder of the same City; and [either] himself or through his capable Deputy he shall do and carry out all and every single thing that [69] relates and ought to relate to the Office of Recorder within the same City; Also one other trustworthy and prudent man, to be elected in the form set out below, who will be and will be called Common Clerk of the aforesaid City and Clerk [70] of all the Incorporated Societies and Bodies Political, Artistic, Mysterious or of Manual Occupations within the aforesaid City, and *[70-71]* [either] himself or through his capable Deputy whom he himself shall in future nominate and appoint, he shall carry out all and every single thing [71] that relates and ought to relate to the aforesaid Office within the same City; Also one other trustworthy and prudent man, to be elected in the form set out below, who shall be and shall be called Solicitor [72] of the same City, to do faithfully all and every single thing that relates to that Office; And also two other trustworthy and prudent men who shall be and shall be called Coroners of the aforesaid City; And one other trustworthy man who shall be [73] and shall be called chief Mace-bearer of the Mayor of the aforesaid City; and for the better execution of our will in this area WE HAVE ASSIGNED, nominated, appointed and made, and through the present documents we assign, nominate, [74] appoint and make our beloved Henry Trinder [the] squire [and] Sergeant-at-Law to become and to be the first modern Recorder of the aforesaid City; And our beloved William Wright junior [the] Squire to become and to be the Deputy [75] Recorder of the City to carry out everything that relates to the aforesaid Office of Recorder; and they are to continue in the same Offices for the duration of their respective natural lives unless in the meantime because of reasonable Cause or in the manner and form [76] mentioned below they are removed from those Offices, or either one of them is removed; WE HAVE ASSIGNED, also, nominated, appointed and made, and through the present documents on behalf of ourselves [and] our heirs and Successors we assign, nominate, appoint [77] and make our beloved Thomas Baker [the] gentleman to become and to be the first modern Common Clerk of the aforesaid City and Clerk of all the Incorporated Societies and Bodies Political, Mystical, Artistic or of Manual Occupations [78] within the aforesaid City, to hold and exercise the aforesaid Office [either] by himself or through his capable Deputy whom he himself shall nominate and appoint, and to continue in that Office for the duration of his natural life unless in the meantime because of reasonable cause or in the manner [79] and form mentioned below he shall be removed; AND ALSO we have assigned, nominated, appointed and made and through the present documents on behalf of ourselves [and] our heirs and Successors we assign, nominate, appoint and make our beloved [80] Richard Dodwell [the] gentleman to become and to be the first modern Solicitor of that City; And our beloved Timothy Box and Richard Dodwell [the] gentlemen to become and to be the first modern Coroners, and our beloved [81] Abraham White [the] gentleman to become and to be the modern chief Mace-bearer of the Mayor of the aforesaid City, [all of them] to continue in their respective Offices for the duration of their respective natural lives unless in the meantime *[81-2]* because of reasonable cause or in the manner and form mentioned below they are removed, or any one of them is removed, from those Offices; [82] IT IS OUR WILL in addition, and through the present documents on behalf of ourselves [and] our heirs and Successors we ordain and by strong injunctions we order that the aforesaid Richard [83] Carter, named above in the present documents to become and to be the first modern Mayor of the aforesaid City, before he is admitted to the Exercise of the Office of Mayor of the same City or somehow installs himself, *[85]* shall take [84] a Corporal Oath on the most holy Gospels of God, [swearing] to carry out that Office well and faithfully in and through Everything that relates to that Office, in front of our aforementioned beloved William Wright or Thomas Eustace, William [85] Wright junior and Thomas Baker, or any two of them; to which men, indeed, William Wright or Thomas Eustace, William Wright junior and Thomas Baker or to any two of them *[85-6]* we give and grant through the present documents full power and authority to give and administer such an Oath to the aforementioned Richard Carter, [86] apart from any other Warrant or Commission *[86-7]* that must be procured or obtained from us [or from] our heirs and Successors in that area; [87] in addition, he shall take all such Oaths as are usual and customary in such a manner and form and at such places and times and in front of such persons as the Mayors of that City prior to this were used and accustomed [to take]; ALSO [88] WE HAVE ASSIGNED, nominated, appointed and made and through the present documents on behalf of ourselves [and] our heirs and Successors we assign, nominate, appoint and make our beloved Subjects William Ayleworth, William Badger, [89] Thomas Neale, Richard Houghton, Richard Keates, Timothy Perry, John Knibb, William Walker [the] Wig maker, Arthur Malde, John Weller, John Philipps and Thomas Kimber [the] gentlemen, [90] to become and to be the first modern twelve *loco Ballivorum*, in English 'in Bayliffes places', of the aforesaid City, to continue in the aforesaid Offices for the duration of their respective natural lives, unless in the meantime because of reasonable cause or in the manner and [91] form mentioned below they are removed from those Offices, or any one of them is removed; AND WE HAVE ASSIGNED, nominated, appointed and made and through the present documents on behalf of ourselves [and] our heirs and Successors we assign, nominate, appoint and [92] make our beloved and faithful Subjects James Finch, Richard Crouch, Thomas Bliss, William Ryley, Michael Ackland, Edward Salter, Chilton Tubb, William Appleby, Theodore Spencer, Anthony Mathews, [93] Robert Hensly, William Stibbs, Richard Carter [the] Leatherworker, Laurence King, William Nicholls, Henry Wildgoose, Daniel Monday, Robert Kenrick, Henry Richardson, Joseph Mayo, William Plater, [94] James Burrowes, John Burrowes junior, and John Toms, to become and to be the first modern twenty-four Common Councillors or [men] of the Common Council of the aforesaid City, to continue in the same Offices for the duration of their respective natural lives [95] unless in the meantime because of reasonable cause or in the manner and form mentioned below they are removed from those Offices or any one of them is removed; AND FURTHERMORE it is our will, and through the present documents we ordain that the Bailiffs, the Aldermen, [96] the Assistants, the Head Steward, the Recorder, the Deputy Recorder, the common Clerk, the Solicitor, the chief Mace-bearer of the aforesaid Mayor, the Coroners, the twelve [men] *loco Ballivorum*, in English, 'in Bayliffes places', and the twenty-four Common Councillors or [men] of [97] the Common Council of the aforesaid City and any one of those [who are] nominated and appointed respectively above in these present documents *[97-8]*shall each and every one take a Corporal Oath to carry out their aforesaid Offices well and faithfully in and through everything that relates to their respective offices, in front of the aforesaid Richard Carter; [98] to which Richard Carter indeed we give and grant through the present documents full power and authority to give and administer such an Oath of this kind to the Officers appointed and nominated in these present documents, apart from [99] any other Warrant or Commission that must be procured or obtained from us [or from] our heirs and Successors in that area; AND FURTHERMORE it is our will and through the present documents on behalf of ourselves [and] our heirs and Successors we give and grant to the aforementioned [100] Mayor, Bailiffs and Commonalty of the aforesaid City and to their Successors that however often and whenever it should happen that one or more of the Aldermen, Assistant, Bailiffs, or aforesaid persons in the aforesaid Bailiffs' places, [or] twenty-four Councillors or [men] of [101] the Common Council, or any Head Steward, Recorder, Common Clerk, Solicitor, Coroner or chief Mace-bearer of the Mayor of the aforesaid City who is in office at any given time should die or *[101-2]* step down from his Office or from their Offices, [102] or that those whom we want to be removable and to be removed because of reasonable cause are removed; that then and in any [other] such case another suitable person or other suitable persons from time to time *[102-3]* should be elected and sworn in in the required manner, for and into that respective Office, [103] in the same manner and form, through such persons and at the kind of places and days and times as *[103-4]* was or ought to have been the usage and custom in the said City during the period of seven years now past, [104] And he or they shall exercise the Office or Offices and position or positions to which he is or they are elected and sworn in for such a period or periods, and from thence he or they shall be removed in such a manner, as *[104-5]* was the custom in cases of this kind within the aforesaid City within the aforesaid period; [105] IT IS OUR WILL also, and through the present documents on behalf of ourselves [and] our heirs and Successors We Grant to the Mayor, Bailiffs and Commonalty of the aforesaid City and to their Successors, that if it should chance that the aforesaid [106] Richard Carter, nominated above through the present documents to become Mayor of the aforesaid City, or any other Mayor of the aforesaid City in office at any given time should die or be removed from his Office during the period of his Mayoralty; or if it should chance that [107] any election of a Mayor of the aforesaid City in future should be rendered void through the incapacity or resignation of the man who was elected to the Office of Mayor of the aforesaid City, or because of any other Cause whatsoever; that then and as many times as [108] such a case occurs it should be permitted now and in the future for the senior Alderman of the aforesaid City who is at the time resident in the same place and therefore capable, immediately to call the Bailiffs and Commonalty of the aforesaid City and proceed to the election and swearing in of another person to the Office [109] of Mayor of the aforesaid City as previously said; AND FURTHERMORE it is our will and through the present documents on behalf of ourselves [and] our heirs and Successors we grant to the aforementioned Mayor, Bailiffs and Commonalty of the aforesaid City and to their Successors that now and in the future it should be permitted for the Mayor of the aforesaid City [110] who is in office at any given time to make and appoint from time to time at his own pleasure one of the Aldermen or Assistants of the aforesaid City who should be now and in future a Judge, *[110-11]* legally empowered to preserve our peace and [that] of our heirs and Successors within that City, [111] to become and to be the Deputy of the Mayor himself who is in office at any given time for the purpose of doing and carrying out all and every single thing that relates and ought to relate to the Office of Mayor, for as long as the Mayor of the aforesaid City who is in office at the time should desire it, as fully, freely and completely as the Mayor [112] of the aforesaid City who is in office at the time would be authorised and able to do and carry out if he were present; PROVIDED always, and it is our will, that the said Deputy of the Mayor [113] of the aforesaid City shall, in front of the Mayor of the aforesaid City who is in office at the time, take a Corporal Oath to carry out the aforesaid Office well and faithfully, before he installs himself in the Office of Deputy of the Mayor of the aforesaid City; and thus as many times as a case [114] like this occurs, to whoever is Mayor of the aforesaid City at the time we give and grant through the present documents the power and authority to adminster such an Oath; AND FURTHERMORE it is our will for the better government of the aforesaid City for all [115] future times, and through the present documents on behalf of ourselves [and] our heirs and Successors We Grant to the aforementioned Mayor, Bailiffs and Commonalty of the aforesaid City and to their Successors, that henceforward in perpetuity the Mayor or Deputy Mayor, Head [116] Steward, Aldermen, Assistants, Bailiffs, the Recorder or his Deputy, the Common Clerk or his Deputy, the Solicitor, the Coroner, the chief Mace-bearer of the Mayor, the twelve persons in Bailiffs' places and the twenty-four Common [117] Councillors of the aforesaid City who are in office at any given time, or the greater part of the same men, of whom it is our will that the Mayor of that City who is in office at the time or his Deputy should be one, when they are assembled in that City's Guildhall or other appropriate place should have now [118] and in the future all, so great and such of this kind and similar Franchises, liberties, jurisdictions, power and authority such as the Common Council of that City prior to this at any time in whatever manner had, enjoyed or exercised, or [119] were able or ought to have, enjoy or exercise, both to found, appoint, ordain, make and establish Laws, Statutes, Constitutions, Decrees and

Ordinances, and otherwise or in any other way, PROVIDED [120] always that through the present documents We Reserve full power and authority for ourselves and our heirs and Successors from time to time and for all time in the future *[123]* to remove and to declare removed *[120]* the Mayor, Head Steward, Recorder, Deputy [121] Recorder, Common Clerk and Solicitor and any one or more of the Aldermen, Assistants, Bailiffs, twelve [men] *loco Ballivorum*, in English, '[in] Bayliffes places', Coroner, chief Mace-bearer of the aforesaid Mayor, or [one or more] of the aforesaid [122] twenty-four Councillors or [men] of the Common Council of that City, and also of the other Mace-bearers of the same City who are in office at any given time, at the will and Good Pleasure of ourselves and our heirs and Successors through an arrangement [123] of ours [or] of our heirs or Successors made in the Privy Council and under the Seal of the aforesaid Privy Council notified to those same [people] respectively; And however often we [and] our heirs and Successors [124] through such an arrangement made in the Privy Council declare such a Mayor, Head Steward, Recorder, Deputy Recorder, Common Clerk, Solicitor or one or [125] more of the Aldermen, Assistants, Bailiffs, twelve [men] *loco Ballivorum*, in English, '[in] Bayliffes places', Coroner, chief Mace-bearer of the aforesaid Mayor or [any] of the aforesaid twenty-four Councillors or [men] of the Common Council [126] of that City, and also [any] of the Mace-bearers of the same City who are in office at any given time, or any one of them to become and to be removed from their respective Offices and positions, that then and from that point onwards the Mayor, Head Steward, [127] Recorder, Deputy Recorder, Common Clerk, Solicitor and any one or more of the Aldermen, Assistants, Bailiffs, twelve [men] *loco Ballivorum*, in English, 'in Bayliffes places', Coroner, chief Mace-bearer of the aforesaid Mayor [128] or [any] of the twenty-four Councillors or [men] of the Common Council of that City and also [any] of the Mace-bearers of that City who are in office at any given time thus declared or to be declared removed from their respective Offices and [129] positions, thereby and without any further process in actuality and for all intents and purposes whatever should [indeed] be removed, both now and in future; and this however often a case like this occurs, anything to the contrary in respect thereof notwithstanding; And at that time and [130] in such a case from time to time however often a case like this occurs, within an appropriate time period after a removal or removals of this kind another suitable person or other suitable persons *[131]* shall be elected and appointed and can be elected and appointed *[130]* into the position and Office or into the respective positions and [131] Offices of the kind of person or persons thus removed, according to the stipulation and settlement of these Letters Patent; And also [132] PROVIDED that if at any time in the future within twenty days after this kind of removal or removals of one or more of the Mayor, Aldermen, Assistants, Bailiffs, Head Steward, Recorder, Deputy [133] Recorder, Common Clerk, Solicitor, twelve [men] *loco Ballivorum*, in English, '[in] Baliffes places', Coroner, chief Mace-bearer of the aforesaid Mayor and the aforesaid twenty-four Councillors or [men] of the Common Council, or other [134] Officials of the aforesaid City from their respective aforesaid Offices, or after the death or resignation of them or any of them, the remaining [men] of the Common Council of the aforesaid City which exists at the time are instructed or ordered through our Letters Mandatory [135] or those of our heirs or Successors under our Seal and Signature or that of our heirs or Successors, which are addressed or are to be addressed to the same men, to elect, admit and swear in some other person or some other persons [136] of our nomination or [of that] of our heirs or Successors, for and into the separate and respective positions and Offices or the position or Office of any one or more of the persons thus removed from there by death or resignation as is said previously; that on that occasion [137] and as many others it should be permitted now and in the future for the same Common Council of the aforesaid City that is in office at the time – however few in number they may happen to be – or to the greater part of them who upon public notice or summons [138] are willing to be present at that time – to elect and admit – and the same men through the present documents are required to elect and admit – whatsoever such respective person or persons for and to the aforesaid position or Office or positions or Offices of the persons or person respectively thus removed from there by death or resignation, as in that case from time to time hereafter through such Letters Mandatory *[139-40]* should be and shall be nominated or prescribed respectively; [140] And that in such a case, any other election or installation at all that is held or is to be held contrary to the stipulation of these present documents or contrary to the requirement of the aforesaid Letters Mandatory, for all Intents and purposes whatsoever *[140-1]* shall be null and void and have no force; [141] Also through the present documents on behalf of ourselves [and] our heirs and Successors we give and grant to the Common Council of the aforesaid City that is in office at any given time, or to such of them through whom such an election or installation in accordance with the true [142] intent of these present documents is or shall be held and carried out, full power and authority to administer the Oath of Office or Offices to any Mayor, Aldermen, Assistants, Bailiffs, Head Steward, [143] Recorder, Common Clerk, Solicitor, twelve [men] *loco Ballivorum*, in English, '[in] Bayliffes places', Coroner, chief Mace-bearer of the aforesaid Mayor and aforesaid twenty-four Common Councillors or [men] of [144] the Common Council, or [any] other Officer of the aforesaid City, [who is or are] in the way already stated elected or admitted or to be elected or admitted within the same City; also that any Mayor, Aldermen, Assistants, Bailiffs, Head Steward, Recorder, [145] Common Clerk, Solicitor, Coroner, twelve [men] *loco Ballivorum*, in English, '[in] Bayliffes places', chief Mace-bearer of the aforesaid Mayor and the twenty-four Councillors or [men] of the Common Council, or [any] other Officer of the aforesaid City [who is or are] in the way [146] already stated elected, admitted and sworn in or in future to be elected, admitted or sworn in, should be able and authorised to hold, enjoy and exercise his or their separate respective aforesaid Offices or aforesaid Office within the aforesaid City [147] just as fully and completely and in so broad a manner and form for all intents and purposes, as any other Mayor, Aldermen, Assistants, Bailiffs, Head Steward, Recorder, [148] Common Clerk, Solicitor, twelve [men] *loco Ballivorum*, in English, '[in] Bayliffes places', Coroner, chief Mace-bearer of the aforesaid Mayor and the aforesaid twenty-four Common Councillors or [men] of the Common Council, or [any] other Officer [149] within the same City [who is] in any other manner elected, admitted and sworn in or in future to be elected, admitted and sworn in, is able or authorised to do; any other manner or form of election, admission or Swearing-in written down above in the present documents [150] or customary within the aforesaid City prior to this that is contrary to this in some way notwithstanding; AND FURTHERMORE it is our will, and through the present documents on behalf of ourselves [and] our heirs and Successors we grant to the aforementioned Mayor, Bailiffs and Commonalty of the aforesaid City and to their Successors [151] that the Mayor, Bailiffs and Commonalty of that City who are in place at any given time, or the larger part of them, of whom it is our will that the Mayor of that City who is in office at the time should be one, should be able to elect, nominate and appoint from time to time and for all [152] time to come according to their pleasure and will as many Chamberlains, Mace-bearers, Constables, and other Lesser Officers and Ministers within the aforesaid City, as prior to this in the same City were elected, nominated [153] and appointed, or were accustomed to be elected, nominated and appointed, and that the Chamberlains, Mace-bearers, Constables and other Officers and Ministers who are thus to be elected and nominated in the future shall be elected, nominated and sworn in [154] by such persons on the kind of days and times and in such a manner and form as Chamberlains, Mace-bearers, Constables and other Officers and Ministers of the aforesaid City prior to this used to be elected, nominated, appointed and [155] sworn in; AND FURTHERMORE as an act of our [even] wider special grace and from secure knowledge and of our own free will we have granted, and through the present documents on behalf of ourselves [and] our heirs and Successors we grant to the aforementioned Mayor, Bailiffs and Commonalty of the aforesaid City and [156] to their Successors, all and every kind and as many, as great and such of the same kind and similar Coroners, Escheators, Courts of Record, Investigations of pleas, goods and Chattels of Fugitive Felons and outlaws, deodands, abandoned goods, escheated goods, [157] Markets, Festivals, Fairs, Tolls, Tollbooths, Levies, Taxes, Fines, Reliefs, Revenues, Amercements, Forfeits, acquisitions, Law-courts, Gaol-deliveries, Concessions, Franchises, Immunities, Privileges, exemptions, quittances, jurisdictions, [158] Customs Duties, liberties, Customary Tax Duties, Manors, Mills, fishing waters, Fish Traps, land, tenements and hereditaments whatsoever, just as many and as great and of such a kind and which the Mayor, Bailiffs and Commonalty of the aforesaid City currently have, hold, enjoy [159] [and] use, or were accustomed or ought to have, hold, use and enjoy, or [which] one or more of them, or [which] their Predecessors, under whatsoever names or name or through whatsoever Incorporation or by the authority [160] of whatsoever Incorporation prior to this they had, used or enjoyed or ought to have had, held, used and enjoyed [these things], owed to them and to their Successors in perpetuity on account of hereditary title [161] by reason of any Charters, Concessions or Letters Patent [that] prior to this [were] made and confirmed or granted through us or through any of our Forefathers or Ancestors or Predecessors in whatever manner, or by whatever other legal [162] prescripton, usage or custom or by any other legal means, right or title that prior to this was possessed or habitual, even if the same [rights and benefits] or any one or more of them prior to this were not used, or were or was abused or badly used, or discontinued [163] or surrendered, and even if the same [rights and benefits] or any one or more of them are or were forfeited or lost; THEY ARE TO BE HAD, held and enjoyed by the aforementioned Mayor, Bailiffs and Commonalty of the aforesaid City of Oxford and by their Successors [164] in perpetuity, And there are to be Rendered and Paid therefrom annually to us [and] to our heirs and Successors so many, so great and such of the same sort and similar fixed payments, Fees, Revenues, services, cash payments, amounts and claims whatsoever, however many and great and of such a kind [165] as prior to this for the same things were accustomed to be rendered or paid or ought to have been rendered or paid to us, and in the similar manner and form as the same [payments] prior to this were accustomed to be rendered to us or to our Progenitors; IT IS OUR WILL also, and through [166] the present documents on behalf of ourselves [and] our heirs and Successors we grant to the aforementioned Mayor, Bailiffs and Commonalty of the aforesaid City and to their Successors, that they should have, hold, use and enjoy, *[166-7]* and in perpetuity be able [and] authorised fully to have, hold, use and enjoy [167] all the liberties, free customary rights, privileges, quittances, jurisdictions and Hereditaments according to the stipulation and purpose of these Letters Patent of ours without the interference or Hindrance of us or of any of our heirs or Successors [168] whatsoever, IT NOT BEING OUR WILL that the same Mayor, Bailiffs and Commonalty of the aforesaid City and their Successors by reason of the premisses or of any one of them, *[169]* should on that account be interfered with, troubled, plagued or oppressed, [or that any individual should be] troubled, plagued, oppressed or disturbed in any matter *[168]* by us or our heirs, [or by the] Judges, sheriffs, Escheators or other Bailiffs or Ministers of ourselves [169] or of any at all of our heirs or Successors; IT IS OUR WILL in addition, and through the present documents on behalf of ourselves [and] our heirs and Successors [170] we take precautions, and by strong injunctions We Order and command, that the Dissolution of the Body Corporate of the aforesaid City carried out thus as previously said should in no way apply or be arranged to apply so as to result in [171] any loss, prejudice or impairment of the liberties, Franchises, Immunities, Privileges or any hereditaments that through the present documents are given and restored to the aforementioned Mayor, Bailiffs and Commonalty of the aforesaid City of Oxford and [172] to their Successors, nor as giving to the Chancellor, Teachers and Students of our University of Oxford any Privileges, Advantages or Gains at all which they themselves or their Predecessors did not have or by right [173] use or enjoy before the aforesaid Dissolution of the Corporation of the aforesaid City, but that all and every one of the Liberties, Franchises, Immunities, Privileges and Hereditaments of the aforementioned Mayor, Bailiffs and Commonalty of the aforesaid City [174] and of their Successors shall be and shall remain valid, fixed and undamaged and in their full strength for all future times, any affair, case or matter whatsoever in any way contrary to that notwithstanding; [175] PROVIDED always, and we declare our Royal will through the present documents, that no Head Steward, Recorder or Common Clerk of the said City [who is] in future to be elected or appointed for the Exercise [176] of his respective Office should be installed unless the approval of us [or of] our heirs or Successors, under our Seal or Signature [or that] of our heirs or Successors in that area has previously been indicated, anything *[176-7]* mentioned above in the present documents [177] or any other affair, Case or matter whatsoever contrary to that notwithstanding; AND FURTHERMORE because of different Causes and Considerations which move us particularly to this, [178] out of our special grace and from certain knowledge and of our own free will and by virtue of our Royal Prerogative WE HAVE MADE ALLOWANCE, Pardoned, Remitted and Acquitted and [179] through the present documents on behalf of ourselves [and] of our Heirs and Successors We Make Allowance, Pardon, Remit and Acquit the aforesaid Edward Henry [the] Earl of Litchfield, Richard Carter, William [180] Wright senior, Edward Walker, Thomas Eustace, Richard Carter, Tobias Browne, Edward Combes, Richard Hawkins, Alexander Wright, James Pinnell, Richard Tidmarsh, William [181] Greene, John Tomkins, Henry Trinder, William Wright junior, John Weller, John Philipps, Thomas Baker, Abraham White, Timothy Box, Richard Dodwell, William [182] Ayleworth, William Badger, Thomas Neale, Richard Houghton, Richard Keats, Timothy Perry, John Knibb, William Walker, Arthur Madle, John Weller, John Phillips, [183] Thomas Kimber, James Finch, Richard Crouch, Thomas Bliss, William Ryley, Michael Ackland, Edward Salter, Chilton Tubb, William Appleby, Theodore Spencer, Antony [184] Mathews, Robert Hensley, William Stibbs, Richard Carter, Laurence King, William Nicholls, Henry Wildgoose, Daniel Monday, Robert Kenrick, Henry Richardson, [185] Joseph Mayo, William Playter, James Burrowes, John Burrowes, and John Toms, being the aforesaid Mayor, aforesaid Head Steward, Recorder, Deputy Recorder, Aldermen, [186] Assistants, Bailiffs, Coroner, Common Clerk, Solicitor, twelve [men] *loco Ballivorum*, in English, '[in] Bayliffes places', chief Mace-bearer of the Mayor and twenty-four Councillors [187] or [men] of the Common Council of the aforesaid City nominated in the present documents, and any one of them and any other Officer or Officers of this kind and all other Officers or Ministers respectively [188] within the same City [who are] in future to be nominated, elected or installed, from all Taking and Receiving of the *Juramentum Primatie*, in English, the Oath of Supremacy, mentioned [189] in a certain Act of Parliament made in the Parliament of the Lady Elizabeth lately Queen of England, in the first Year of her Reign, or in any other Statute or Act of Parliament; [190] And also from Taking and Receiving of the *Juramentum Ligeantie*, in English, the Oath of Allegiance or Obedience, mentioned or set out in a certain Act of Parliament [191] made in the Parliament of the

Lord James the First, our Grandfather, lately King of England, [that was] held in the Third Year of his Reign, or in any other Statute or Act of Parliament; And also [192] from Taking and Receiving of the Oath mentioned and contained in a certain Statute made in the Parliament of the Lord Charles the Second, lately King of England *[192-3]* [that was] held in the Thirteenth Year of his Reign [193] Entitled an Act for the well governing and Regulating of Corporations; And also from all Receiving of *Sacramentum Cene Dominice*, [194] in English, the Sacrament of the Lord's Supper, according to the rites or usages of the Church of England or According to the rule of any Canons or Statutes or of any Canon or [195] Statute of this Kingdom of ours of England; and also from Taking and Signing of the Declaration mentioned or contained in the aforesaid Statute in the Thirteenth Year of Charles the Second, [196] and also from taking and Signing of the Declaration mentioned and set out in a certain other Statute made in the Parliament of the said Lord King Charles the Second *[196-7]* in the Twenty-Fifth Year of his Reign [197] Entitled an Act for preventing Dangers which may happen from Popish Recusants; And also from Taking and Receiving of any [198] Oaths and Receiving of the Sacrament of the Lord's Supper and Signing of any Declarations or any Declaration mentioned or set out in the aforesaid Statutes [199] or [in] the Acts of Parliament mentioned above or [in] any one of them, or mentioned or contained [in] any other Statute, about and concerning the premisses, and from all Criminal Convictions, [200] Punishments, Penalties, forfeits, losses, Disqualifications and Disabilities incurred or to be incurred in future because of the same [statutes] or any one of them, or to be imputed or charged to the same people or to any one of them, [201] or with which any one or more of them may now be or could hereafter be chargeable on the grounds that they did not take or receive or that [202] any one of them did not take or receive, or [that] hereafter they will not have taken or received or any one of them will not have taken or received the aforementioned Oaths and Sacraments of the Lord's Supper, [203] or [that] they have not signed or made or hereafter they will not have signed or made or some one of them has not or will not have signed or has not or will not have made the aforesaid Declarations [204] mentioned above or any one of them or any other whatsoever that are commanded or prescribed through the aforesaid Statutes or any one of them, or through any other Statute previously [205] made or given out requiring taking of the aforesaid Oaths or of any one of them or receiving of the Sacrament of the Lord's Supper according to the rites and usages of the Church of England or the utterance [206] and signing of the aforesaid Declarations or any one of them; And from all and all kinds of Instructions, Presentations, Indictments, Prosecutions, Disputes, Claims and [207] demands whatsoever, both in the name of ourselves [and] our heirs or Successors and in the name or names of any other person or persons previously [208] had, brought up and now pending, or in the future to be had, brought up or to become pending in any Court of ours [and] of our heirs and Successors or in any other Courts or Places whatsoever, about, because of or [209] concerning any defect, neglect, omission or refusal in taking, performing, receiving or signing the aforesaid Oaths, Sacrament of the Lord's Supper or Declarations in the above-mentioned Acts of Parliament, [210] or demanded or prescribed through them or through any one of them, or because of any other defect in the carrying out of the premisses or of any one of them; AND FURTHERMORE out of our abundant grace and out of [211] certain knowledge and of our own free will, we desire and declare and through the present documents on behalf of ourselves [and] our Heirs and Successors We Grant to the same aforesaid people, to the Mayor, aforesaid Head Steward, [212] Recorder, Deputy Recorder, Aldermen, Assistants, Bailiffs, Coroner, Common Clerk, Solicitor, twelve [men] *loco Ballivorum*, in English, '[in] Bayliffes places', chief Mace-bearer [213] of the Mayor and Twenty-four Councillors or [men] of the Common Council, and to all other Officers or Ministers of the aforesaid City who are in office now or at any other time and to any one of them [214] full and sufficient ability, capacity, power and authority to have, enjoy and exercise their respective aforesaid Offices respectively and all and everything *[214-5]* regarding and pertaining to them respectively, [215] without and apart from the taking of the aforesaid Oaths or any one of them, or the receiving of the Sacrament of the Lord's Supper according to the rites and usages of the Church of England, or the Utterance and [216] Signing of the aforesaid Declarations or any one of them, or the performing of any Order or Request whatsoever that is notified through any aforesaid Statute [217] to be performed or incurred, or becoming Subject to any Charges, Offences, Disabilities, Incapacities, Fines, Prosecutions, Punishments, Penalties, Forfeits, Lawsuits or [218] losses whatsoever; And as fully and freely as if the same Mayor, Head Steward, Recorder, Deputy Recorder, Aldermen, Assistants, Bailiffs, Coroner, Common Clerk, [219] Solicitor, twelve [men] *loco Ballivorum*, in English, '[in] Bayliffes places', chief Mace-bearer of the Mayor and twenty-four Councillors or [men] of the Common Council, and all other Officials [220] or Ministers of the aforesaid City who are in office now and at any other time, had taken, received, made and signed the aforesaid Oaths, Sacrament of the Lord's Supper and Declarations [221] according to the form and purpose of the aforesaid Statutes and the Acts of Parliament mentioned above; the aforesaid Acts and Statutes or any of them, or anything *[221-2]* contained in them or in any one of them [222] or any other Statute, Act of Parliament, Law or Provision contrary to this in any respect notwithstanding; *[222-3]* OF WHICH to serve as evidence we have produced these our Letters Patent [223] as I myself am WITNESS, at Westminster the Fifteenth Day of September in the fourth Year of our Reign. Through the King himself.

[224] PIGOTT

Appendix I: Family Trees of Oxford Dissenters

Family Tree of Richard Tidmarsh

Family Tree of Edward Wyans senior

Family Tree of Thomas Tisdale

Family Tree of Lawrence King

Family Tree of John Toms senior

Family Tree of Roger Hatchman

Family Tree of John Higgins

Family Tree of Ralph Austen

Family Tree of Richard Quelch junior

Family Tree of James Jennings

Family Tree of Thomas Williams

The Family Tree of Richard Tidmarsh

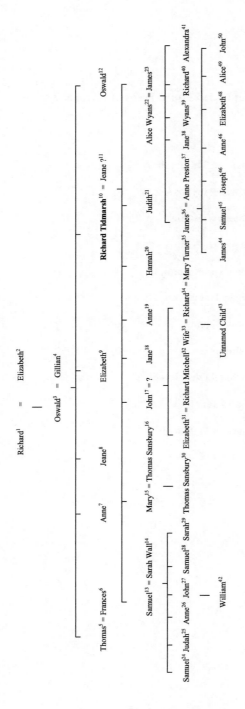

1 Burial – 2 February 1614 – *Adlestrop Parish Register* – *1598-1673* (P5 IN 1/2), folio 64 verso.
2 Burial – 19 July 1626 – *Adlestrop Parish Register* – *1598-1673* (P5 IN 1/2), folio 66 verso.
3 Burial – 7 May 1667 – *Adlestrop Parish Register* – *1598-1673* (P5 IN 1/2), folio 71 recto.
4 Burial – 19 October 1672 – *Adlestrop Parish Register* – *1598-1673* (P5 IN 1/2), folio 71 recto.
5 Burial – 9 June 1690 – *Adlestrop Parish Register* – *1678-1700* (P5 IN 1/3), folio 33 recto; Will of Thomas Tidmarsh – 29 May 1690 – *Adlestrop Wills 1541-1800* (AdWPR 1690/190).
6 Will of Thomas Tidmarsh – 29 May 1690 – *Adlestrop Wills 1541-1800* (AdWPR 1690/190).
7 Burial – 2 May 1660 – *Adlestrop Parish Register* – *1598-1673* (P5 IN 1/2), folio 70 verso.
8 Baptism – 29 September 1639 – *Adlestrop Parish Register* – *1598-1673* (P5 IN 1/2), folio 42 verso.
9 Baptism – 10 March 1632 – *Adlestrop Parish Register* – *1598-1673* (P5 IN 1/2), folio38 verso.
10 Baptism – 13 March 1626 – *Adlestrop Parish Register* – *1598-1673* (P5 IN 1/2), folio 36 verso.
11 Burial – 6 September 1673 – *Parish Register of St Thomas* – *1655-1721* (Par 217/1/R1/1), folio 62 verso.
12 Baptism – 20 October 1629 – *Adlestrop Parish Register* – *1598-1673* (P5 IN 1/2), folio 37 recto.
13 *Poll Tax of 1667* (P.5.7), folio 24 verso; Marriage – Lambeth Palace Library: *Faculty Office Marriage Allegation* – 20 January 1681; Apprenticeship – 7 November 1670 – *Stationers' Company Archives: Apprenticeship Register* – *7 August 1666-6 March 1727*, folio 23 recto; Citizenship – 2 December 1678 – *Stationers' Company Archives: The Register of Freemen* – *2 July 1605-6 March 1703*, folio 122 recto.
14 Marriage – Lambeth Palace Library: *Faculty Office Marriage Allegation* – 20 January 1681.
15 *Poll Tax of 1667* (P.5.7), folio 24 verso; Marriage – 15 November 1685 – *Parish Register of St Aldate's* – *1678-1813* (MS DD Par Oxford – St Aldate's b.1), folio 110 verso.
16 Marriage – 15 November 1685 – *Parish Register of St Aldate's* – *1678-1813* (MS DD Par Oxford – St Aldate's b.1), folio 110 verso; Burial – 24 December 1694 – *Parish Register of St Aldate's* – *1678-1813* (MS DD Par Oxford – St Aldate's b.1), folio 63 verso.
17 Citizenship – 7 February 1678 – *Civic Enrolments 1662-1699* (L.5.4), page 629; Burial – 26 May 1696 –*Parish Register of St Ebbe's* – *1678-1812* (MS DD Par Oxford – St Ebbe's b. 35), folio 54 recto.
18 Baptism – 22 October 1669 – *Parish Register of St Thomas* – *1655-1721* (Par 217/1/R1/1), folio 2 recto.
19 *Poll Tax of 1667* (P.5.7), folio 24 verso; *Taxes* – *1691-1694* (P.5.9), folio 6 verso.
20 Birth – 17 December 1670 – *Parish Register of St Thomas* – *1655-1721* (Par 217/1/R1/1), folio 2 recto; Burial – 3 August 1672 – *Parish Register of St Thomas* – *1655-1721* (Par 217/1/R1/1), folio 62 verso.
21 *Poll Tax of 1667* (P.5.7), folio 7 verso.
22 *Poll Tax of 1667* (P.5.2), folio 8 recto; Marriage – 31 March 1684 – *Parish Register of St Thomas* – *1655-1721* (Par 217/1/R1/1), folio 41 verso; Will of Edward Wyans senior – 13 March 1671 – (OWPR 72/1/9); Will of Edward Wyans junior – 23 May 1687 (OWPR 73/2/3).
23 *Poll Tax of 1667* (P.5.2), folio 24 verso; Marriage – 31 March 1684 – *Parish Register of St Thomas* – *1655-1721* (Par 217/1/R1/1), folio 41 verso; Will of Edward Wyans junior – 23 May 1687 (OWPR 73/2/3); Death before 6 December 1721.
24 Baptism – 11 March 1683 – *Parish Register of St Michael Cornhill* – *1653-1736* (GL MS 4063/1), folio 28 recto; Burial – 6 April 1683 – *Parish Register of St Michael Cornhill* – *1653-1736* (GL MS 4063/1), folio 168 recto.
25 Baptism – 5 June 1684 – *Parish Register of St Michael Cornhill* – *1653-1736* (GL MS 4063/1), folio 29 recto; Burial – 24 July 1684 – *Parish Register of St Michael Cornhill* – *1653-1736* (GL MS 4063/1), folio 169 verso.
26 Baptism – 5 June 1684 – *Parish Register of St Michael Cornhill* – *1653-1736* (GL MS 4063/1), folio 29 recto; Burial – 24 July 1684 – *Parish Register of St Michael Cornhill* – *1653-1736* (GL MS 4063/1), folio 169 verso.

27 Baptism – 17 May 1685 – *Parish Register of St Michael Cornhill* – *1653-1736* (GL MS 4063/1), folio 30 recto; Apprenticeship – 1 April 1701 – *Vintners' Company Apprenticeships* – *1666-1736* (GL MS 15, 220/2), page 494; Will of William Knight – 11 November 1731 (*PCC* – *Will of William Knight* (PROB 11/647), folios 285 recto–287 verso; Burial – 3 January 1752 – *Parish Register of St Botolph-without-Bishopsgate* – *1715-1752* (GL MS 4517/1).

28 Baptism – 1 March 1687 – *Parish Register of St Michael Cornhill* – *1653-1736* (GL MS 4063/1), folio 31 verso.

29 Baptism – 17 June 1688 – *Parish Register of St Michael Cornhill* – *1653-1736* (GL MS 4063/1), folio 33 recto.

30 Burial – 31 May 1694 – *Parish Register of St Aldate's* – *1678-1813* (MS DD Par Oxford – St. Aldate's b.1), folio 63 verso.

31 Marriage – 22 June 1696 – Parish Register of St Peter-in-the-East – *1653-1807* (Par 213/1/R1/3), folio 43.

32 Marriage – 22 June 1696 – Parish Register of St Peter-in-the-East – *1653-1807* (Par 213/1/R1/3), folio 43.

33 Burial – 2 November 1689 – *Parish Register of St Thomas* – *1655-1721* (Par 217/1/R1/1), folio 69 recto.

34 Marriage – 24 April 1692 – *Parish Register of St Thomas* – *1655-1721* (Par 217/1/R1/1), folio 43 recto.

35 Marriage – 24 April 1692 – *Parish Register of St Thomas* – *1655-1721* (Par 217/1/R1/1), folio 43 recto.

36 Marriage Bond – 21 October 1727 – *St Katherine-by-the-Tower* – *1720-1802* (GL (9772/6), folio 80; Will of James Tidmarsh – 4 January 1740 (*PCC* – *Will of James Tidmarsh* (PROB 11/700), folio 205 verso–206 recto.

37 Marriage Bond – 21 October 1727 – *St Katherine-by-the-Tower* – *1720-1802* (GL (9772/6), folio 80; Will of James Tidmarsh – 4 January 1740 (*PCC* – *Will of James Tidmarsh* (PROB 11/700), folio 205 verso–206 recto.

38 Birth – 19 January 1685 – *Parish Register of St Thomas* – *1655-1721* (Par 217/1/R1/1), folio 11 recto; Will of Edward Wyans junior – 23 May 1687 (OWPR 73/2/3); Burial – 16 December 1687 – *Parish Register of St Thomas* – *1655-1721* (Par 217/1/R1/1), folio 68 recto.

39 Apprenticeship – 18 December 1704 – *Feltmakers' Company Apprentices, Volume 1* – *1694-1731* (GL MS 1573/1), folios 11 verso; Will of James Tidmarsh – 4 January 1740 (*PCC* – *Will of James Tidmarsh* (PROB 11/700), folio 205 verso –206 recto.

40 Apprenticeship – 6 December 1721 – *Vintners' Company Apprenticeships* – *1666-1736* (GL MS 15, 220/2), page 667; Will of James Tidmarsh – 4 January 1740 (*PCC* – *Will of James Tidmarsh* (PROB 11/700), folio 205 verso –206 recto.

41 Will of James Tidmarsh – 4 January 1740 (*PCC* – *Will of James Tidmarsh* (PROB 11/700), folio 205 verso–206 recto.

42 Apprenticeship – 7 June 1732 – *Vintners' Company Apprenticeships* – *1666-1736* (GL MS 15, 220/2), page 759; Will of William Knight – 11 November 1731 (*PCC* – *Will of William Knight* (PROB 11/647), folios285 recto–287 verso;.

43 Burial – 29 July 1681 – *Parish Register of St Thomas* – *1655-1721* (Par 217/1/R1/1), folio 66 recto.

44 Will of James Tidmarsh – 4 January 1740 (*PCC* – *Will of James Tidmarsh* (PROB 11/700), folio 205 verso–206 recto.

45 Will of James Tidmarsh – 4 January 1740 (*PCC* – *Will of James Tidmarsh* (PROB 11/700), folio 205 verso–206 recto.

46 Will of James Tidmarsh – 4 January 1740 (*PCC* – *Will of James Tidmarsh* (PROB 11/700), folio 205 verso–206 recto.

47 Will of James Tidmarsh – 4 January 1740 (*PCC* – *Will of James Tidmarsh* (PROB 11/700), folio 205 verso–206 recto.

48 Will of James Tidmarsh – 4 January 1740 (*PCC* – *Will of James Tidmarsh* (PROB 11/700), folio 205 verso–206 recto.

49 Will of James Tidmarsh – 4 January 1740 (*PCC* – *Will of James Tidmarsh* (PROB 11/700), folio 205 verso–206 recto.

50 Will of James Tidmarsh – 4 January 1740 (*PCC* – *Will of James Tidmarsh* (PROB 11/700), folio 205 verso–206 recto.

The Family Tree of Edward Wyans senior

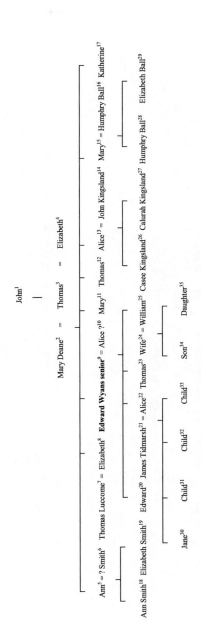

[1] Son's Apprenticeship record – 1 September 1620 – *Civic Enrolments 1613-1640* (L.5.2), folio 347 verso).

[2] Marriage – 19 July 1632 – *Parish Register of St Mary Magdalen – 1602-1662* (Par 208/1/R1/1), folio 43 recto; Burial – 4 May 1657 – *Parish Register of St Mary Magdalen – 1602-1662* (Par 208/1/R1/1), folio 74 verso.

[3] Marriage – 19 July 1632 – *Parish Register of St Mary Magdalen – 1602-1662* (Par 208/1/R1/1), folio 43 recto; Will of Thomas Wyans – 14 April 1664 – (OWPR 71/4/2); Will of Edward Wyans senior – 13 March 1671 (OWPR 72/1/9).

[4] Burial – 20 February 1628 – *Parish Register of St Mary Magdalen – 1602-1662* (Par 208/1/R1/1), folio 56 recto.

[5] Will of Thomas Wyans – 14 April 1664 (OWPR 71/4/2).

[6] Will of Thomas Wyans – 14 April 1664 (OWPR 71/4/2).

[7] Marriage – 28 March 1649 – *Parish Register of St Mary Magdalen – 1602-1662* (Par 208/1/R1/1), folio 46 verso.

[8] Marriage – 28 March 1649 – *Parish Register of St Mary Magdalen – 1602-1662* (Par 208/1/R1/1), folio 46 verso.

[9] Baptism – 20 October 1616 – *Parish Register of St Mary Magdalen – 1602-1662* (Par 208/1/R1/1), folio 3 recto; *Poll Tax of 1667* (P.5.2), folio 8 recto; Burial – 8 February 1672 – *Parish Register of St Martin's – 1569-1705* (Par 207/1/R1/2), folio 60 verso; Will of Edward Wyans senior – 13 March 1671 (OWPR 72/1/9).

[10] *Poll Tax of 1667* (P.5.2), folio 8 recto; Will of Edward Wyans senior – 13 March 1671 – (OWPR 72/1/9); Will of Edward Wyans junior – 23 May 1687 (OWPR 73/2/3); Burial – 9 January 1705 – *Parish Register of St Peter-in-the-Bailey 1684-1742* (Par 214/1/R1/3), folio 62 recto.

[11] Baptism – 10 April 1624 – *Parish Register of St Mary Magdalen – 1602-1662* (Par 208/1/R1/1), folio 54 verso.

[12] Baptism – 29 May 1622 – *Parish Register of St Mary Magdalen – 1602-1662* (Par 208/1/R1/2), folio 62 verso.

[13] Baptism – 12 October 1619 – *Parish Register of St Mary Magdalen – 1602-1662* (Par 208/1/R1/1), folio 4 verso; Will of Thomas Wyans – 14 April 1664 (OWPR 71/4/2).

[14] Will of Thomas Wyans – 14 April 1664 (OWPR 71/4/2).

[15] Baptism – 25 April 1626 – *Parish Register of St Mary Magdalen – 1602-1662* (Par 208/1/R1/1), folios 8 verso; Will of Edward Wyans senior – 13 March 1671 (OWPR 72/1/9).

[16] Will of Thomas Wyans – 14 April 1664 – (OWPR 71/4/2); Will of Edward Wyans senior – 13 March 1671 (OWPR 72/1/9).

[17] Baptism – 9 February 1628 – *Parish Register of St Mary Magdalen – 1602-1662* (Par 208/1/R1/1), folio 9 verso; Burial – 2 September 1628 – *Parish Register of St Mary Magdalen – 1602-1662* (Par 208/1/R1/1), folios 56 verso.

[18] Will of Thomas Wyans – 14 April 1664 (OWPR 71/4/2).

[19] Will of Thomas Wyans – 14 April 1664 (OWPR 71/4/2).

[20] Birth – 28 August 1647 – *Parish Register of St Martin's – 1569-1705* (Par 207/1/R1/2), folio 28 recto; *Poll Tax of 1667* (P.5.2), folio 8 recto; Burial – 22 December 1687 – *Parish Register of St. Martin's – 1678-1789* (Par 207/1/R1/4), folio 8 recto; Will of Thomas Wyans – 14 April 1664 – (OWPR 71/4/2); Will of Edward Wyans senior – 13 March 1671 (OWPR 72/1/9); Will of Edward Wyans junior – 23 May 1687 (OWPR 73/2/3).

[21] *Poll Tax of 1667* (P.5.2), folio 8 recto; *Parish Register of St Thomas – 1655-1721* (Par 217/1/R1/1), folio 41 verso; Will of Edward Wyans junior – 23 May 1687 (OWPR 73/2/3); Marriage – 31 March 1684 – *Parish Register of St Thomas – 1655-1721* (Par 217/1/R1/1), folio 41 verso; Will of Edward Wyans senior – 21 July 1709 – *London Diocese Marriage Allegation – June-December 1709* (MS 10,091/45), Marriage – 21 July 1709 – Allhallows London Wall, London (GL MS 5087); Death before 6 December 1721.

[22] *Poll Tax of 1667* (P.5.2), folio 8 recto; Marriage – 31 March 1684 – *Parish Register of St Thomas – 1655-1721* (Par 217/1/R1/1), folio 41 verso; Will of Edward Wyans senior – March 1671 (OWPR 72/1/9); Will of Edward Wyans junior – 23 May 1687 (OWPR 73/2/3).

[23] Birth – 1 December 1652 – *Parish Register of St Martin's – 1569-1705* (Par 207/1/R1/2), folio 29 recto.

[24] *Poll Tax of 1667* (P.5.2), folio 22 recto.

[25] *Poll Tax of 1667* (P.5.2), folio 22 recto.

[26] Will of Thomas Wyans – 14 April 1664 (OWPR 71/4/2).

[27] Will of Thomas Wyans – 14 April 1664 (OWPR 71/4/2).

[28] Will of Thomas Wyans – 14 April 1664 (OWPR 71/4/2).

[29] Will of Thomas Wyans – 14 April 1664 (OWPR 71/4/2).

[30] Birth – 19 January 1685 – *Parish Register of St Thomas – 1655-1721* (Par 217/1/R1/1), folio 11 recto; Will of Edward Wyans junior – 23 May 1687 (OWPR 73/2/3);
Burial – 16 December 1687 – *Parish Register of St Thomas – 1655-1721* (Par 217/1/R1/1), folio 68 recto.

[31] *Poll Tax of 1692* (P.5.9), folio 5 verso.

[32] *Poll Tax of 1692* (P.5.9), folio 5 verso.

[33] *Poll Tax of 1692* (P.5.9), folio 5 verso.

[34] *Poll Tax of 1667* (P.5.2), folio 22 recto.

[35] *Poll Tax of 1667* (P.5.2), folio 22 recto.

The Family Tree of Thomas Tisdale

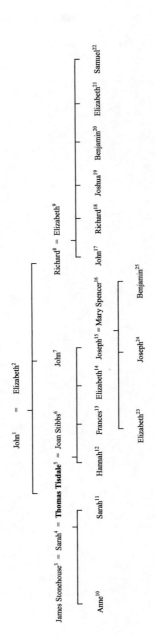

John[1] = Elizabeth[2]

James Stonehouse[3] = Sarah[4] = **Thomas Tisdale**[5] = Joan Stibbs[6]   John[7]   Richard[8] = Elizabeth[9]

Anne[10]   Sarah[11]   Hannah[12]   Frances[13]   Elizabeth[14]   Joseph[15] = Mary Spencer[16]   John[17]   Richard[18]   Joshua[19]   Benjamin[20]   Elizabeth[21]   Samuel[22]

Elizabeth[23]   Joseph[24]   Benjamin[25]

1. Burial – 17 August 1665 – Abingdon, *St Helen Parish Registers - Baptisms 1538-1679 and Burials 1538-1678* (2001), page 201.

2. Probate Record – 26 March 1672 – *Will of Elizabeth Tesdale* (AWPR D/A1/128/92).

3. Probate Bond – 21 February 1721 – *Probate Bond of Sarah Teasdale* (OWPR 175/3/13); Will of Hannah Stonhouse – 3 August 1732 (PCC – *Will of Hannah Stonhouse* (PROB 11/703), folios 190 recto – 191 recto).

4. Probate Bond – 21 February 1721 – *Probate Bond of Sarah Teasdale* (OWPR 175/3/13); Will of Hannah Stonhouse – 3 August 1732 (PCC – *Will of Hannah Stonhouse* (PROB 11/703), folios 190 recto – 191 recto).

5. Apprenticeship – 23 March 1644 – *Civic Enrolments 1639-1662* (L.5.3), folio 39 verso; Marriage – 11 March 1658 – *Parish Register of St. Michael at the North Gate – 1653-1683* (Par 211/1/R1/2), folio 41 verso; Burial – 17 July 1702 – *Abingdon, St Helen Parish Registers - Burials 1688-1812* (2003), page 247.

6. Marriage – 11 March 1658 – *Parish Register of St. Michael at the North Gate – 1653-1683* (Par 211/1/R1/2), folio 41 verso; *Poll Tax of 1667* (P.5.7), folio 6 verso; Burial – 22 July 1677 – *Parish Register of St Martin's – 1569-1705* (Par 207/1/R1/2), folio 62 recto.

7. Burial – 4 September 1644 – *Abingdon, St Helen Parish Registers - Baptisms 1538-1679 and Burials 1538-1678* (2001), page 189.

8. Apprenticeship – 4 July 1639 (*Civic Enrolments 1613-1640* (L.5.2), folio 322 recto); Citizenship – 14 December 1646 (*Civic Enrolments – 1639-1662* (L.5.3), folio 259 recto); Burial – 14 January 1666 – Abingdon, St Helen Parish Registers - Baptisms 1538-1679 and Burials 1538-1678 (2001), page 201; *Will of Richard Tesdale* (AWPR D/A1/128/58).

9. Burial – 22 May 1666 – Abingdon, *St Helen Parish Registers - Baptisms 1538-1679 and Burials 1538-1678* (2001), page 202.

10. Baptism – 22 February 1680 – *Parish Register of St Peter-in-the-Bailey 1659-1689* (Par 214/1/R1/2), folio 28 recto.

11. Burial – 17 May 1695 – *Parish Register of St Ebbe's – 1678-1812* (MS DD Par Oxford – St Ebbe's b. 35), folio 54 recto.

12. *Poll Tax of 1667* (P.5.7), folio 6 verso.

13. Burial – 18 February 1697 – *Abingdon, St Helen Parish Registers - Burials 1688-1812* (2003), page 240.

14. *Poll Tax of 1667* (P.5.7), folio 6 verso.

15. Marriage – 2 March 1690 – *Parish Register of St Cross, Hollywell – 1654-1812* (Par 199/1/R1/1), page 173; Burial – 23 March 1727 – *Abingdon, St Helen Parish Registers - Burials 1688-1812* (2003), page 287.

16. Marriage – 2 March 1690 – *Parish Register of St Cross, Hollywell – 1654-1812* (Par 199/1/R1/1), page 173.

17. Named in Will - *Will of Richard Tesdale* (AWPR D/A1/128/58).

18. Named in Will - *Will of Richard Tesdale* (AWPR D/A1/128/58).

19. Named in Will - *Will of Richard Tesdale* (AWPR D/A1/128/58).

20. Named in Will - *Will of Richard Tesdale* (AWPR D/A1/128/58).

21. Named in Will - *Will of Richard Tesdale* (AWPR D/A1/128/58).

22. Named in Will - *Will of Richard Tesdale* (AWPR D/A1/128/58); Burial – 18 November 1655 – *Abingdon, St Helen Parish Registers - Baptisms 1538-1679 and Burials 1538-1678* (2001), page 198.

23. Burial – 19 February 1696 – *Abingdon, St Helen Parish Registers – Burials 1688-1812* (2003), page 238.

24. Burial – 8 March 1699 – *Abingdon, St Helen Parish Registers – Burials 1688-1812* (2003), page 243.

25. Burial – 7 October 1703 – *Abingdon, St Helen Parish Registers – Burials 1688-1812* (2003), page 250.

The Family Tree of Lawrence King

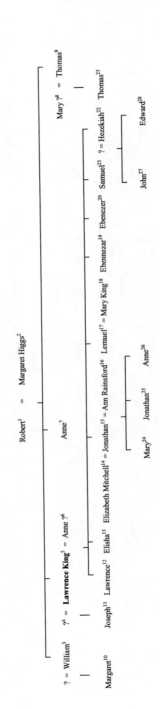

[1] Marriage – 30 October 1624 – *Parish Register of St Mary the Virgin* – *1599-1694* (Par 209/1/R1/1), page 24; Caveat on Will – 4 August 1651 – *Oxford Caveats* – *1643-1677* (MS Wills 307), folio 53.

[2] Marriage – 30 October 1624 – *Parish Register of St Mary the Virgin* – *1599-1694* (Par 209/1/R1/1), page 24; Caveat on Will – 4 August 1651 – *Oxford Caveats* – *1643-1677* (MS Wills 307), folio 53; Burial – 11 May 1680 – *Parish Register of St Peter-in-the-Bailey* – *1659-1689* (Par 214/1/R1/2), folio 56 recto.

[3] Birth – 16 October 1627 – *Parish Register of All Saints* – *1559-1810* (Par 189/1/R1/1), folio 15 verso; Apprenticeship – 31 May 1641 – *Civic Enrolments 1639-1652* (L.5.3), folio 12 verso.

[4] Poll Tax - *Taxes* – *1691-1694* (P.5.9), folios 22 recto and 43 verso.

[5] Birth – 18 November 1629 – *Parish Register of All Saints* – *1559-1810* (Par 189/1/R1/1), folio 16 recto; Burial – 4 January 1710 – *Parish Register of St Michael-at-the-Northgate* – *1683-1736* (Par 211/1/R1/3), page 92.

[6] Burial – 11 June 1681 – *Parish Register of All Saints* – *1678-1812* (Par 189/1/R1/2), folio 5 verso.

[7] Burial – 8 November 1630 – *Parish Register of All Saints* – *1559-1810* (Par 189/1/R1/1), folio 87 recto.

[8] Burial – 9 March 1702 – *Parish Register of St Peter-in-the-Bailey* – *1684-1742* (Par 214/1/R1/3), folio 64 verso.

[9] Baptism – 16 May 1633 – *Parish Register of St Peter-in-the-Bailey* – *1585-1646* (Par 214/1/R1/1), folio 45 recto; Apprenticeship – 23 March 1646 – *Civic Enrolments 1639-1662* (L.5.3), folio 62 verso; Citizenship – 1 April 1660 *Civic Enrolments 1639-1652* (L.5.3), folio 217 verso; Excommunicated – 1 July 1665 – *ODR: Excommunication Schedules* – *1662-1667* (c. 100), folio 149 recto; *ODR: Excommunications: 1633-1791* (c. 99), folio 243 verso; Burial – 28 May 1702 – *Parish Register of St Peter-in-the-Bailey* – *1684-1742* (Par 214/1/R1/3), folio 64 recto.

[10] Baptism – 27 July 1673 – *Parish Register of St Peter-in-the-Bailey* – *1659-1689* (Par 214/1/R1/2), folio 17 verso.

[11] Burial – 28 February 1687 – *Parish Register of St Martin's* – *1678-1789* (Par 207/1/R1/4), folio 3 recto.

[12] Apprenticeship – 7 November 1674 – *Civic Enrolments 1662-1699* (L.5.4), page 236.

[13] Apprenticeship dispute – 17 October 1690 – *Petty Sessions Clerk's Notebook 1687-1701* (O.2.1), folios 39 verso-40 recto; Burial – 22 October 1697 – *Parish Register of St. Martin's* – *1678-1789* (Par 207/1/R1/4), folio 6 verso.

[14] Marriage – 8 July 1699 – *OAR: Marriage Bonds* – *1699* (c. 485), folio 80; Burial – 12 July 1706 – *Parish Register of St Michael-at-the-Northgate* – *1683-1736* (Par 211/1/R1/3), page 48.

[15] Marriage – 8 July 1699 – *OAR: Marriage Bonds* – *1699* (c. 485), folio 80; Marriage – 15 October 1709 – *OAR: Marriage Bonds* – *1709* (c. 495), folio 97; Death – 19 January 1719 – *Probate Records Inventory* (OWPR 169/2/15).

[16] Marriage – 15 October 1709 – *Archdeaconry Marriage Bonds* – *1709* (c. 495), folio 97; Burial – 18 May 1742 – *Parish Register of St Michael-at-the-Northgate* – *1683-1736* (Par 211/1/R1/3), page 159.

[17] Birth – 4 December 1658 – *MS Top Oxon* (b. 40), folio 1 verso; Marriage – 11 November 1681 – *Archdeaconry Marriage Bonds* – *1681* (c. 469), folio 68; Burial – 16 June 1719 – *Parish Register of St James, Clerkenwell, Middlesex* – *Burials 1666-1719*.

[18] Marriage – 11 November 1681 – *Archdeaconry Marriage Bonds* – *1681* (c. 469), folio 68; Burial – 2 September 1690 – *Parish Register of All Saints* – *1678-1812* (Par 189/1/R1/2), folio 13 verso.

[19] Birth – 15 March 1655 – *MS Top Oxon* (b. 40), folio 1 recto.

[20] Birth – 24 July 1656 – *MS Top Oxon* (b. 40), folio 1 recto; and 1 verso (4 December 1658).

[21] Apprenticeship – 14 October 1681 – *Painter-Stainers' Company Apprenticeships* – *1666-1795* (GL MS 5669/1), folio 56 recto.

[22] Burial – 23 July 1713 – *Parish Register of St Peter-in-the-Bailey* – *1684-1742* (Par 214/1/R1/3), folio 53 verso.

[23] Excommunicated – 2 July 1693 - *Diocesan Records* – *Excommunications: 1633-1791* (c. 99), folio 117 recto; Burial – 10 May 1711 – *Parish Register of St Michael-at-the-*

Northgate – 1683-1736 (Par 211/1/R1/3), page 95.

[24] Birth – 16 September 1710 – *Parish Register of St Michael-at-the-Northgate – 1683-1736* (Par 211/1/R1/3), page 305.

[25] Birth – 23 February 1712 – *Parish Register of St Michael-at-the-Northgate – 1683-1736* (Par 211/1/R1/3), page 307; Burial – 26 September 1713 – *Parish Register of St Michael-at-the-Northgate – 1683-1736* (Par 211/1/R1/3), page 99.

[26] Birth – 3 November 1715 – *Parish Register of St Michael-at-the-Northgate – 1683-1736* (Par 211/1/R1/3), page 295; Burial – 26 April 1719 – *Parish Register of St Michael-at-the-Northgate – 1683-1736* (Par 211/1/R1/3), page 108.

[27] Baptism – 9 January 1691 – *Parish Register of St Peter-in-the-Bailey – 1684-1742* (Par 214/1/R1/3), folio 9 verso.

[28] Baptism – 18 May 1692 – *Parish Register of St Peter-in-the-Bailey – 1684-1742* (Par 214/1/R1/3), folio 10 verso.

The Family Tree of John Toms senior

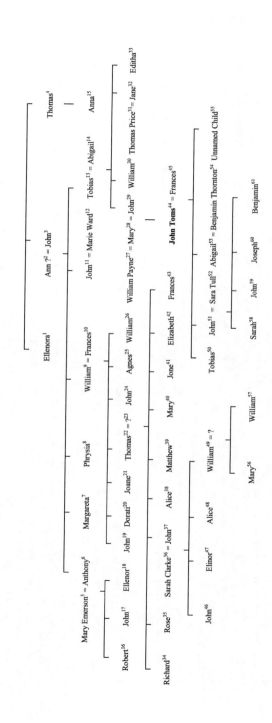

[1] Burial – 17 April 1627 – Parish Register of St Peter-in-the-East – 1559-1653 (Par 213/1/R1/1), folio 58 recto; Inventory of Ellenora Toms – 19 April 1627 (OWPR 14/3/93).

[2] Burial – 11 November 1651 – Parish Register of All Saints – 1559-1810 (Par 189/1/R1/1), folio 94 recto; Will of Ann Toms – 11 November 1651 (OWPR 66/2/64).

[3] Burial – 18 March 1636 – Parish Register of All Saints – 1559-1810 (Par 189/1/R1/1), folio 88 recto.

[4] Burial of child – 17 May 1610 – Parish Register of All Saints – 1559-1810 (Par 189/1/R1/1), folio 85 recto.

[5] Marriage – 20 September 1621 – Parish Register of St Peter-in-the-East – 1559-1653 (Par 213/1/R1/1), folio 32 verso.

[6] Marriage – 20 September 1621 – Parish Register of St Peter-in-the-East – 1559-1653 (Par 213/1/R1/1), folio 32 verso; Burial – 4 April 1635 – Parish Register of All Saints – 1559-1810 (Par 189/1/R1/1), folio 87 verso; Will of Ann Toms – 11 November 1651 (OWPR 66/2/64).

[7] Baptism – 29 September 1608 – Parish Register of All Saints - 1559-1810 (Par 189/1/R1/1), folio 11 verso; Burial – 4 October 1610 – Parish Register of All Saints – 1559-1810 (Par 189/1/R1/1), folio 85 recto.

[8] Baptism – 19 March 1606 – Parish Register of All Saints - 1559-1810 (Par 189/1/R1/1), folio 10 verso.

[9] Burial – 2 November 1669 – Parish Register of St Peter-in-the-Bailey – 1659-1689 (Par 214/1/R1/2), folio 66 verso.

[10] Burial – 3 October 1641 – Parish Register of St Peter-in-the-Bailey – 1585-1646 (Par 214/1/R1/1), folio 65 recto.

[11] Marriage – 26 October 1628 – Parish Register of St Giles – 1576-1680 (MS DD Par Oxford – St Giles b.1), page 91; Inventory of Ellenora Toms – 19 April 1627 (OWPR 14/3/93); Burial – 7 December 1643 – Parish Register of All Saints - 1559-1810 (Par 189/1/R1/1), folio 91 verso; Probate Bond of Tobias Toms – 28 September 1633 (OWPR 66/1/43).

[12] Marriage – 26 October 1628 – Parish Register of St Giles – 1576-1680 (MS DD Par Oxford – St Giles b.1), page 91.

[13] Burial – 29 May 1633 – Parish Register of All Saints – 1559-1810 (Par 189/1/R1/1), folio 87 verso; Will of Tobias Toms – 23 May 1633 (OWPR 66/1/43); Probate Record of Tobias Toms – 28 September 1633 (OWPR 66/1/43).

[14] Will of Tobias Toms – 23 May 1633 (OWPR 66/1/43); Probate Record of Tobias Toms – 28 September 1633 (OWPR 66/1/43).

[15] Burial – 17 May 1610 – Parish Register of All Saints – 1559-1810 (Par 189/1/R1/1), folio 85 recto.

[16] Baptism – 8 September 1622 – Parish Register of All Saints - 1559-1810 (Par 189/1/R1/1), folio 14 verso; Will of Ann Toms – 11 November 1651 (OWPR 66/2/64).

[17] Baptism – 27 July 1624 – Parish Register of All Saints – 1559-1810 (Par 189/1/R1/1), folio 15 recto.

[18] Birth – 29 January 1627 – Parish Register of All Saints – 1559-1810 (Par 189/1/R1/1), folio 15 verso; Baptism – 8 February 1627 – Parish Register of All Saints - 1559-1810 (Par 189/1/R1/1), folio 15 verso.

[19] Baptism – 5 June 1622 – Parish Register of All Saints – 1559-1810 (Par 189/1/R1/1), folio 15 verso.

[20] Baptism – 2 May 1626 – Parish Register of All Saints – 1559-1810 (Par 189/1/R1/1), folio 16 recto.

[21] Baptism – 23 June 1627 – Parish Register of All Saints – 1559-1810 (Par 189/1/R1/1), folio 16 verso.

[22] Baptized – 26 April 1628 – Parish Register of St Peter-in-the-Bailey – 1585-1646 (Par 214/1/R1/1), folio 16 verso; Death before 10 July 1657 - Son's Apprenticeship – Civic Enrolments 1639-1662 (L.5.3), folio 157 verso.

[23] Burial – 19 November 1669 – Parish Register of St Peter-in-the-Bailey – 1659-1689 (Par 214/1/R1/2), folio 66 verso.

[24] Baptism – 31 December 1629 – Parish Register of All Saints - 1559-1810 (Par 189/1/R1/1), folio 17 verso.

[25] Baptism – 2 May 1634 – Parish Register of All Saints – 1559-1810 (Par 189/1/R1/1), folio 45 verso.

[26] Baptism – 12 September 1637 – Parish Register of St Peter-in-the-Bailey – 1659-1689 (Par 214/1/R1/2), folio 47 recto.

[27] Marriage – 1 October 1632 – Parish Register of St Peter-in-the-East – 1559-1653 (Par 213/1/R1/1), folio 33 verso; Probate Record of John Toms – 16 February 1633 (OWPR 87/3/5).

[28] Marriage – 1 October 1632 – Parish Register of St Peter-in-the-East – 1559-1653 (Par 213/1/R1/1), folio 33 verso; Probate Record of John Toms – 16 February 1633 (OWPR 87/3/5).

29 Baptism – 1 November 1605 – *Parish Register of All Saints - 1559-1810* (Par 189/1/R1/1), folio 10 verso; Burial – 7 June 1632 – *Parish Register of All Saints - 1559-1810* (Par 189/1/R1/1), folio 87 verso; Probate Record of John Toms – 16 February 1633 (OWPR 87/3/5); Will of Tobias Toms – 28 September 1633 (OWPR 66/1/43).

30 Will of Tobias Toms – 28 September 1633 (OWPR 66/1/43).

31 Marriage – 17 October 1634 – *Parish Register of St Peter-in-the-East – 1559-1653* (Par 213/1/R1/1), folio 34 recto.

32 Baptism – 2 November 1607 – *Parish Register of All Saints - 1559-1810* (Par 189/1/R1/1), folio 12 verso; Marriage – 17 October 1634 – *Parish Register of St Peter-in-the-East – 1559-1653* (Par 213/1/R1/1), folio 34 recto; Will of Tobias Toms – 28 September 1633 (OWPR 66/1/43).

33 Baptism – 2 January 1613 – *Parish Register of All Saints - 1559-1810* (Par 189/1/R1/1), folio 12 verso.

34 Baptized – 6 April 1629 – *Parish Register of St Peter-in-the-Bailey – 1585-1646* (Par 214/1/R1/1), folio 43 verso.

35 Baptized – 4 September 1631 – *Parish Register of St Peter-in-the-Bailey – 1585-1646* (Par 214/1/R1/1), folio 18 verso.

36 Marriage – 19 February 1666 – OAR: *Marriage Bonds – 1665* (c. 456), folio 234; *Poll Tax of 1667* (P.5.7), folio 46 verso; Burial – 10 July 1716 – *Parish Register of St Peter-in-the-East – 1670-1812* (Par 213/1/R1/5), folio 17 verso.

37 Apprenticeship – 10 July 1657 – *Civic Enrolments 1639-1662* (L.5.3), folio 157 verso; Marriage – 19 February 1666 – OAR: *Marriage Bonds – 1665* (c. 456), folio 234; *Poll Tax of 1667* (P.5.7), folio 46 verso; Burial – 22 December 1708 – *Parish Register of St Peter-in-the-East – 1670-1812* (Par 213/1/R1/5), folio 13 verso.

38 Baptized – 3 June 1639 – *Parish Register of St Peter-in-the-Bailey – 1585-1646* (Par 214/1/R1/1), folio 49 verso; Burial – 8 September 1641 – *Parish Register of St Peter-in-the-Bailey – 1585-1646* (Par 214/1/R1/1), folio 41 recto.

39 Baptized – 4 January 1636 – *Parish Register of St Peter-in-the-Bailey – 1585-1646* (Par 214/1/R1/1), folio 47 verso.

40 Baptized – 15 December 1636 – *Parish Register of St Peter-in-the-Bailey – 1585-1646* (Par 214/1/R1/1), folio 15 verso; Burial – 8 September 1641 – *Parish Register of St Peter-in-the-Bailey – 1585-1646* (Par 214/1/R1/1), folio 41 recto.

41 Baptized – 29 October 1640 – *Parish Register of St Peter-in-the-Bailey – 1585-1646* (Par 214/1/R1/1), folio 50 verso.

42 Baptized – 10 December 1643 – *Parish Register of St Mary Magdalen – 1602-1662* (Par 208/1/R1/1), folio 18 verso.

43 Baptized – 12 July 1628 – *Parish Register of St Mary Magdalen – 1602-1662* (Par 208/1/R1/1), folio 10 recto.

44 Apprenticeship – 17 October 1644 – *Civic Enrolments 1639-1662* (L.5.3), folio 42 verso; *Poll Tax of 1667* (P.5.7), folio 12 recto; Burial – 27 November 1693 – *Parish Register of All Saints – 1678-1812* (Par 189/1/R1/2), folio 14 verso; Probate Record of John Toms – 2 March 1694 (OWPR 175/2/27).

45 *Poll Tax of 1667* (P.5.7), folio 12 recto; Burial – 4 September 1694 – *Parish Register of All Saints – 1678-1812* (Par 189/1/R1/2), folio 14 verso.

46 Baptism – 26 April 1667 – *Parish Register of St Peter-in-the-Bailey – 1659-1689* (Par 214/1/R1/2), folio 8 verso; Death – 1696 - MS Morrell 14 – *Minutes of Meetings of the Guild of Cordwayners (1614-1711)*, folio 138 recto.

47 Baptism – 5 October 1668 – *Parish Register of St Peter-in-the-East – 1670-1812* (Par 213/1/R1/2), folio 17 recto; Burial – 15 November 1687 – *Parish Register of St Peter-in-the-East – 1670-1812* (Par 213/1/R1/2), folio 64 verso.

48 Burial – 20 October 1671 – *Parish Register of St Peter-in-the-Bailey – 1659-1689* (Par 214/1/R1/2), folio 5 recto.

49 Baptism – 24 October 1678 – *Parish Register of St Peter-in-the-East – 1653-1807* (Par 213/1/R1/3), folio 7 verso; Citizenship – 27 April 1705 - *Civic Enrolments – 1697-1780* (L.5.5), folio 22 recto; Burial – 30 December 1711 – *Parish Register of St Peter-in-the-East – 1670-1812* (Par 213/1/R1/5), folio 15 recto.

50 Birth – 11 February 1655 – MS Top Oxon (b. 40), folio 1 recto; *Poll Tax of 1667* (P.5.7), folio 12 recto.

51 Birth – 15 January 1660 – MS Top Oxon (b. 40), folio 1 verso; *Poll Tax of 1667* (P.5.7), folio 12 recto; Marriage – 28 June 1687 – OAR: *Marriage Bonds – 1687* (c. 475), folio 136; Probate Record of John Toms – 2 March 1694 (OWPR 175/2/27).

52 Marriage – 28 June 1687 – *OAR: Marriage Bonds – 1687* (c. 475), folio 136.
53 Baptism – 9 June 1662 – *Parish Register of All Saints – 1559-1810* (Par 189/1/R1/1), folio 25 verso; *Poll Tax of 1667* (P.5.7), folio 12 recto; Probate Record of John Toms – 2 March 1694 (OWPR 175/2/27).
54 Probate Record of John Toms – 2 March 1694 (OWPR 175/2/27).
55 *Poll Tax of 1667* (P.5.7), folio 12 recto.
56 Burial – 20 June 1706 – *Parish Register of St Peter-in-the-East – 1670-1812* (Par 213/1/R1/5), folio 12 recto.
57 Burial – 9 October 1708 – *Parish Register of St Peter-in-the-East – 1670-1812* (Par 213/1/R1/5), folio 13 recto.
58 Birth – 29 March 1690 – *Parish Register of St Thomas – 1655-1721* (Par 217/1/R1/1), folio 16 recto; Burial –17 February 1691 – *Parish Register of St Peter-in-the-East – 1670-1812* (Par 213/1/R1/5), folio 6 recto.
59 Birth – 29 June 1691 – *Parish Register of St Thomas – 1655-1721* (Par 217/1/R1/1), folio 17 recto.
60 Birth – 2 January 1694 – *Parish Register of St Thomas – 1655-1721* (Par 217/1/R1/1), folio 18 verso.
61 Birth – 13 November 1695 – *Parish Register of St Thomas – 1655-1721* (Par 217/1/R1/1), folio 19 verso.

The Family Tree of Roger Hatchman

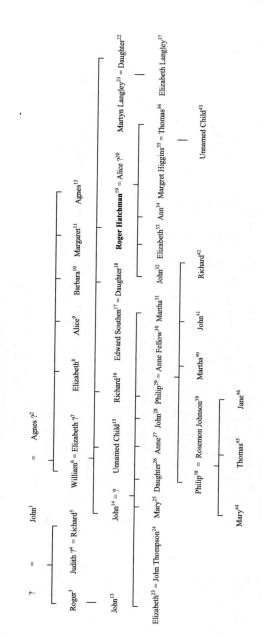

1 Will of John Hatchman – 15 April 1588 (*Dorchester Peculiar* 69/1/2).

2 Will of Agnes Hatchman – 8 November 1610 (*Dorchester Peculiar* 30/1/17).

3 Will of John Hatchman – 15 April 1588 (*Dorchester Peculiar* 69/1/2); Will of Agnes Hatchman – 8 November 1610 (*Dorchester Peculiar* 30/1/17).

4 Will of Richard Hatchman – 7 March 1637 (*Dorchester Peculiar* 69/1/20).

5 Will of John Hatchman – 15 April 1588 (*Dorchester Peculiar* 69/1/2); Will of Agnes Hatchman – 8 November 1610 (*Dorchester Peculiar* 30/1/17); Will of Richard Hatchman – 7 March 1637 (*Dorchester Peculiar* 69/1/20).

6 Will of Agnes Hatchman – 8 November 1610 (*Dorchester Peculiar* 30/1/17); Will of William Hatchman – 1 August 1642 (*Dorchester Peculiar* 69/1/24).

7 Burial – 18 June 1638 – *Dorchester Parish Register* – 1638-1726 (Par 87/1/R1/1), folio 31 recto.

8 Will of Agnes Hatchman – 8 November 1610 (*Dorchester Peculiar* 30/1/17); Will of John Hatchman – 15 April 1588 (*Dorchester Peculiar* 69/1/2).

9 Will of Agnes Hatchman – 8 November 1610 (*Dorchester Peculiar* 30/1/17); Will of John Hatchman – 15 April 1588 (*Dorchester Peculiar* 69/1/2).

10 Will of Agnes Hatchman – 8 November 1610 (*Dorchester Peculiar* 30/1/17); Will of John Hatchman – 15 April 1588 (*Dorchester Peculiar* 69/1/2).

11 Will of Agnes Hatchman – 8 November 1610 (*Dorchester Peculiar* 30/1/17); Will of John Hatchman – 15 April 1588 (*Dorchester Peculiar* 69/1/2).

12 Will of John Hatchman – 15 April 1588 (*Dorchester Peculiar* 69/1/2).

13 Probate Bond of John Hatchman – 11 November 1661 (OWPR 80/4/17); Caveat on the estate of John Hatchman – *Oxford Caveats* – 1643-1677 (MS Wills 307), folio 47 recto.

14 Will of William Hatchman – 1 August 1642 (*Dorchester Peculiar* 69/1/24); Probate Bond of John Hatchman – 11 November 1661 (OWPR 80/4/17); Caveat on the estate of John Hatchman – *Oxford Caveats* – 1643-1677 (MS Wills 307), folio 47 recto.

15 Will of Agnes Hatchman – 8 November 1610 (*Dorchester Peculiar* 30/1/17).

16 Will of William Hatchman – 1 August 1642 (*Dorchester Peculiar* 69/1/24).

17 Will of William Hatchman – 1 August 1642 (*Dorchester Peculiar* 69/1/24).

18 Will of William Hatchman – 1 August 1642 (*Dorchester Peculiar* 69/1/24).

19 Will of William Hatchman – 1 August 1642 (*Dorchester Peculiar* 69/1/24); Baptism of Son – 17 September 1639 – *Dorchester Parish Register* – 1638-1726 (Par 87/1/R1/1), folio 1 verso; Caveat on the estate of John Hatchman – 11 November 1661 (OWPR 80/4/17); Caveat on the estate of John Hatchman – *Oxford Caveats* – 1643-1677 (MS Wills 307), folio 47 recto.

20 *Poll Tax of 1667* (P.5.7), folio 50 recto.

21 Will of William Hatchman – 1 August 1642 (*Dorchester Peculiar* 69/1/24).

22 Will of William Hatchman – 1 August 1642 (*Dorchester Peculiar* 69/1/24).

23 Baptism – 17 July 1638 – *Dorchester Parish Register* – 1638-1726 (Par 87/1/R1/1), folio 1 recto; Will of William Hatchman – 1 August 1642 (*Dorchester Peculiar* 69/1/24); Marriage – October 1666 – *Dorchester Parish Register* – 1638-1726 (Par 87/1/R1/1), folio 25 recto.

24 Marriage – October 1666 – *Dorchester Parish Register* – 1638-1726 (Par 87/1/R1/1), folio 25 recto.

25 Baptism – 4 March 1641 – *Dorchester Parish Register* – 1638-1726 (Par 87/1/R1/1), folio 2 recto.

26 Baptism – 24 June 1645 – *Dorchester Parish Register* – 1638-1726 (Par 87/1/R1/1), folio 4 verso.

27 Baptism – 20 February 1649 – *Dorchester Parish Register* – 1638-1726 (Par 87/1/R1/1), folio 5 recto.

28 Baptism – 20 July 1651 – *Dorchester Parish Register* – 1638-1726 (Par 87/1/R1/1), folio 5 recto.

29 Baptism – 1 May 1654 – *Dorchester Parish Register* – 1638-1726 (Par 87/1/R1/1), folio 5 verso; Marriage – 1 April 1676 – *Dorchester Parish Register* – 1638-1726 (Par 87/1/R1/1), folio 25 verso.

30 Marriage – 1 April 1676 – *Dorchester Parish Register* – 1638-1726 (Par 87/1/R1/1), folio 25 verso.

31 Baptism – 17 December 1657 – *Dorchester Parish Register – 1638-1726* (Par 87/1/R1/1), folio 6 recto.

32 Baptism – 17 September 1639 – *Dorchester Parish Register – 1638-1726* (Par 87/1/R1/1), folio 1 verso; Will of William Hatchman – 1 August 1642 *(Dorchester Peculiar 69/1/24)*.

33 *Poll Tax of 1667* (P.5.7), folio 65 verso.

34 *Poll Tax of 1667* (P.5.7), folio 68 recto.

35 Marriage – 9 November 1657 – *Parish Register of St Michael-at-the-Northgate – 1654-1683* (Par 211//1/R1/2), folio 40 verso.

36 Marriage – 9 November 1657 – *Parish Register of St Michael-at-the-Northgate – 1654-1683* (Par 211//1/R1/2), folio 40 verso.

37 Will of William Hatchman – 1 August 1642 *(Dorchester Peculiar 69/1/24)*.

38 Baptism – 13 February 1678 – *Dorchester Parish Register – 1638-1726* (Par 87/1/R1/1), folio 10 verso; Marriage – 27 June 1703 – *Dorchester Parish Register – 1638-1726* (Par 87/1/R1/1), folio 28 recto.

39 Marriage – 27 June 1703 – *Dorchester Parish Register – 1638-1726* (Par 87/1/R1/1), folio 28 recto.

40 Baptism – 25 November 1680 – *Dorchester Parish Register – 1638-1726* (Par 87/1/R1/1), folio 11 verso.

41 Baptism – 26 February 1683 – *Dorchester Parish Register – 1638-1726* (Par 87/1/R1/1), folio 12 recto

42 Baptism – 12 May 1685 – *Dorchester Parish Register – 1638-1726* (Par 87/1/R1/1), folio 13 recto.

43 Burial – 3 November 1659 – *Parish Register of St Mary Magdalen* (Par 189/1/R1/1), folio 75 recto.

44 Baptism – 11 July 1704 – *Dorchester Parish Register – 1638-1726* (Par 87/1/R1/1), folio 17 recto.

45 Baptism – 25 November 1705 – *Dorchester Parish Register – 1638-1726* (Par 87/1/R1/1), folio 17 recto.

46 Baptism – 17 April 1709 – *Dorchester Parish Register – 1638-1726* (Par 87/1/R1/1), folio 18 recto.

The Family Tree of John Higgins

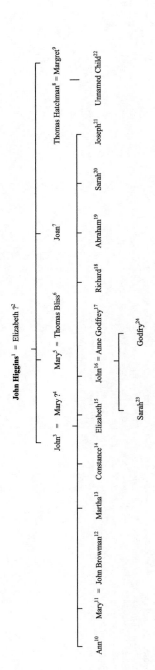

1 Burial – 13 February 1685 – *Parish Register of St Giles – 1679-1768* (MS DD Par Oxford – St Giles c.1), page 184.

2 Burial – 8 August 1691 – *Parish Register of St Giles – 1679-1768* (MS DD Par Oxford – St Giles c.1), page 186.

3 Apprenticeship – 2 April 1652 (*Civic Enrolments – 1639-1662* (L.5.3), folio 109 recto; Will of John Higgins – 6 May 1693 (OWPR 132/4/21); Burial – 20 February 1693 – *Parish Register of St Giles – 1679-1768* (MS DD Par Oxford – St Giles c.1), page 187.

4 Will of John Higgins – 6 May 1693 (OWPR 132/4/21); Will of Mary Higgins – 11 November 1696 (OWPR 34/5/4); Burial – 8 November 1696 – *Parish Register of St Giles – 1679-1768* (MS DD Par Oxford – St Giles c.1), page 188.

5 Baptism – 20 April 1637 – *Parish Register of St Mary Magdalen – 1662-1682* (Par 208/1/R1/2), page 34; Marriage – 30 December 1660 – *Parish Register of St Mary Magdalen – 1602-1662* (Par 208/1/R1/1), folio 48 recto.

6 Marriage – 30 December 1660 – *Parish Register of St Mary Magdalen – 1602-1662* (Par 208/1/R1/1), folio 48 recto.

7 Baptism – 23 February 1640 – *Parish Register of St Giles – 1576-1680* (MS DD Par Oxford – St Giles b.1), page 36.

8 Marriage – 9 November 1657 – *Parish Register of St Michael-at-the-Northgate– 1654-1683* (Par 211/1/1/R1/2), folio 40 verso.

9 Marriage – 9 November 1657 – *Parish Register of St Michael-at-the-Northgate– 1654-1683* (Par 211/1/1/R1/2), folio 40 verso.

10 Birth – 16 November 1660 – *Parish Register of St Giles – 1576-1680* (MS DD Par Oxford – St Giles b.1), page 40.

11 Baptism – 27 January 1663 – *Parish Register of St Mary Magdalen – 1662-1682* (Par 208/1/R1/2), page 3; Marriage – 10 September 1684 – *OAR: Marriage Bonds – 1684* (c. 472), folio 10; Will of John Higgins – 6 May 1693 (OWPR 132/4/21); Will of Mary Higgins – 11 November 1696 (OWPR 34/5/4).

12 Marriage – 10 September 1684 – *OAR: Marriage Bonds – 1684* (c. 472), folio 10; Will of John Higgins – 6 May 1693 (OWPR 132/4/21); Will of Mary Higgins – 11 November 1696 (OWPR 34/5/4).

13 Baptism – 23 June 1675 – *Parish Register of St Giles – 1576-1680* (MS DD Par Oxford – St Giles b.1), page 45; Will of John Higgins – 6 May 1693 (OWPR 132/4/21); Will of Mary Higgins – 11 November 1696 (OWPR 34/5/4).

14 Baptism – 27 May 1677 – *Parish Register of St Giles – 1576-1680* (MS DD Par Oxford – St Giles b.1), page 46; Will of John Higgins – 6 May 1693 (OWPR 132/4/21); Will of Mary Higgins – 11 November 1696 (OWPR 34/5/4).

15 Baptism – 5 November 1664 – *Parish Register of St Mary Magdalen – 1662-1682* (Par 208/1/R1/2), page 8; Burial – 9 January 1696 – *Parish Register of St Giles – 1679-1768* (MS DD Par Oxford – St Giles c.1), page 188.

16 Baptism – 5 February 1667 – *Parish Register of St Mary Magdalen – 1662-1682* (Par 208/1/R1/2), page 14; Marriage – 23 September 1696 – *OAR: Marriage Bonds – 1696* (c. 482), folio 71; Will of John Higgins – 6 May 1693 (OWPR 132/4/21); Will of Mary Higgins – 11 November 1696 (OWPR 34/5/4).

17 Marriage – 23 September 1696 – *OAR: Marriage Bonds – 1696* (c. 482), folio 71.

18 Baptism – 3 February 1669 – *Parish Register of St Mary Magdalen – 1662-1682* (Par 208/1/R1/2), page 18; Burial – 22 March 1671 – *Parish Register of St Giles – 1576-1680* (MS DD Par Oxford – St Giles b.1), page 134.

19 Baptism – 23 February 1671 – *Parish Register of St Mary Magdalen – 1662-1682* (Par 208/1/R1/2), page 23; Burial – 12 November 1674 – *Parish Register of St Giles – 1576-1680* (MS DD Par Oxford – St Giles b.1), page 134.

20 Baptism – 20 May 1673 – *Parish Register of St Mary Magdalen – 1662-1682* (Par 208/1/R1/2), page 28; Will of John Higgins – 6 May 1693 (OWPR 132/4/21); Will of Mary Higgins – 11 November 1696 (OWPR 34/5/4).

21 Baptism – 23 September 1680 – *Parish Register of St Giles – 1576-1680* (MS DD Par Oxford – St Giles b.1), page 48; Burial – 10 May 1681 – *Parish Register of St Giles – 1679-1768* (MS DD Par St Giles c.1), page 180.

22 Burial – 3 November 1659 – *Parish Register of St Mary Magdalen* (Par 189/1/R1/1), folio 75 recto.

23 Baptism – 22 June 1697 – *Parish Register of St Martin's – 1678-1789* (Par 207/1/R1/4), folio 20 recto.

24 Burial – 2 June 1698 – *Parish Register of St Giles – 1679-1768* (MS DD Par Oxford – St Giles c.1), page 189.

The Family Tree of Ralph Austen

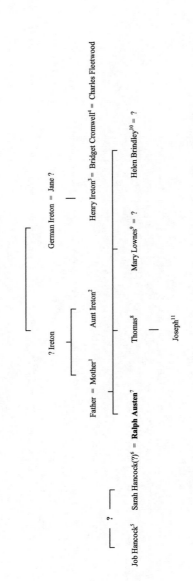

1 Austen Letter to Hartlib – 2 June 1654 (*Hartlib 45/2/5B*).
2 Austen Letter to Hartlib – 2 June 1654 (*Hartlib 45/2/5B*).
3 Marriage – 15 June 1646 – *Parish Register of Holton* – 1633-1794 (Par 135/1/R1/1), folio 13 verso.
4 Marriage – 15 June 1646 – *Parish Register of Holton* – 1633-1794 (Par 135/1/R1/1), folio 13 verso.
5 Austen Letter to Hartlib – 7 October 1658 (*Hartlib 41/1/70A*).
6 Will of Ralph Austen – 24 September 1673 – *Bodleian Wills – Austen, Ralph.*
7 Burial – 26 October 1676 – *Parish Register of St Peter-in-the-Bailey* – 1663-1689 (Par 214/1/R1/2), folio 59 verso.
8 Property Indenture – 30 June 1675 – *MS Ch Oxon c. 50* (#4501); Property Indenture – 10 December 1690 – *MS Ch Oxon c. 50* (#4503a).
9 Property Indenture – 30 June 1675 – *MS Ch Oxon c. 50* (#4501); Austen Letter to Hartlib – 7 October 1658 (*Hartlib 45/2/5B*).
10 Property Indenture – 30 June 1675 – *MS Ch Oxon c. 50* (#4501).
11 Property Indenture – 27 June 1678 – *MS Ch Oxon c. 50* (#4502); Property Indenture – 10 December 1690 – *MS Ch Oxon c. 50* (#4503a).

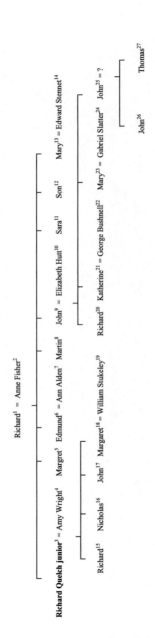

The Family Tree of Richard Quelch junior

[1] Marriage – 11 September 1625 – *Parish Register of St. Martin's – 1569-1705* (Par 207/1/R1/2), folio 68 recto.

[2] Marriage – 11 September 1625 – *Parish Register of St. Martin's – 1569-1705* (Par 207/1/R1/2), folio 68 recto.

[3] Baptism – 1 December 1631 – *Parish Register of St Martin's – 1569-1705* (Par 207/1/R1/2), folio 20 verso; Marriage – 4 February 1656 – *Parish Register of St Michael-at-the-Northgate – 1653-1683* (Par 211/1/R1/2), folio 34 verso.

[4] Marriage – 4 February 1656 – *Parish Register of St Michael-at-the-Northgate – 1653-1683* (Par 211/1/R1/2), folio 34 verso.

[5] Baptism – 16 January 1629 – *Parish Register of St Martin's – 1569-1705* (Par 211/1/R1/1), folio 78 verso.

[6] Marriage – 14 February 1666 – *Parish Register of St Michael-at-the-Northgate – 1558-1666* (Par 211/1/R1/1), folio 52 verso.

[7] Marriage – 14 February 1666 – *Parish Register of St Michael-at-the-Northgate – 1558-1666* (Par 211/1/R1/1), folio 52 verso.

[8] Baptism – 9 April 1634 – *Parish Register of St Martin's – 1569-1705* (Par 207/1/R1/2), folio 21 recto; Apprenticeship – 16 February 1650 – *Civic Enrolments 1639-1662* (L.5.3), folio 90 verso.

[9] Baptism – 28 August 1639 – *Parish Register of St Michael-at-the-Northgate – 1558-1666* (Par 211/1/R1/1), folio 36 verso; Marriage – 12 August 1667 – *ODR: Marriage Bonds* (d. 76), folio 3.

[10] Baptism – 12 August 1667 – *ODR: Marriage Bonds* (d. 76), folio 3.

[11] Baptism – 17 July 1636– *Parish Register of St Michael-at-the-Northgate – 1558-1666* (Par 211/1/R1/1), folio 33 recto; Burial – 3 February 1638– *Parish Register of St Michael-at-the-Northgate – 1558-1666* (Par 211/1/R1/1), folio 79 recto.

[12] Burial – 11 October 1643 – *Parish Register of St Michael-at-the-Northgate – 1558-1666* (Par 211/1/R1/1), folio 71 recto.

[13] Baptism – 2 August 1626 – *Parish Register of St Martin's – 1569-1705* (Par 207/1/R1/2), folio 18 verso; Marriage – 19 July 1654 – *Parish Register of St Michael-at-the-Northgate – 1653-1683* (Par 211/1/R1/2), folio 28 verso.

[14] Marriage – 19 July 1654 – *Parish Register of St Michael-at-the-Northgate – 1653-1683* (Par 211/1/R1/2), folio 28 verso.

[15] Burial – 18 January 1671 – *Parish Register of All Saints – 1559-1810* (Par 189/1/R1/1), folio 97 verso.

[16] Baptism – 26 January 1671 – *Parish Register of St Martin's – 1569-1705* (Par 207/1/R1/2), folio 33 recto.

[17] Birth – 4 February 1658 – *MS Top Oxon* (b. 40), folio 1 verso.

[18] Marriage – 30 December 1693 – *OAR: Marriage Bonds – 1693* (c. 479), folio 84.

[19] Marriage – 30 December 1693 – *OAR: Marriage Bonds – 1693* (c. 479), folio 84.

[20] Baptism – 2 November 1668 – *Parish Register of All Saints – 1559-1810* (Par 189/1/R1/1), folio 27 recto.

[21] Baptism – 23 January 1671 – *Parish Register of All Saints – 1559-1810* (Par 189/1/R1/1), folio 28 recto.

[22] Marriage – 24 January 1696 – *OAR: Marriage Bonds – 1696* (c. 481), folio 23.

[23] Baptism – 9 August 1674 – *Parish Register of All Saints – 1559-1810* (Par 189/1/R1/1), folio 30 recto; Marriage – 21 April 1690 – *OAR: Marriage Bonds – 1690* (c. 477), folio 85.

[24] Marriage – 21 April 1690 – *OAR: Marriage Bonds – 1690* (c. 477), folio 85.

[25] Baptism – 24 March 1678 – *Parish Register of All Saints – 1559-1810* (Par 189/1/R1/1), folio 31 verso.

[26] Apprenticeship – 29 June 1711 – *The Enrolments of Apprentices – 1697-1800* (F.4.9), folio 84 verso.

[27] Apprenticeship – 14 September 1717 – *The Enrolments of Apprentices – 1697-1800* (F.4.9), folio 118 verso.

The Family Tree of James Jennings

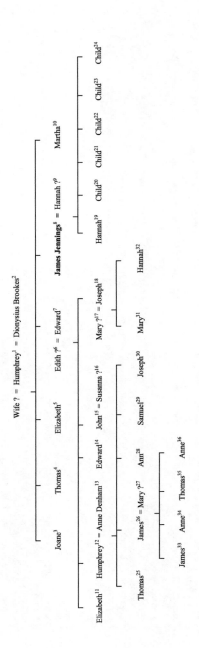

[1] Apprenticeship of son – 19 October 1632 – *Civic Enrolments 1613-1640* (L.5.2), folio 229 verso; Burial – 4 October 1643 – *Parish Register of All Saints – 1559-1810* (Par 189/1/R1/1), folio 91 recto.

[2] Marriage – 15 November 1637 – *Parish Register of St Giles – 1576-1680* (MS DD Par Oxford – St Giles b.1), page 100; Burial – 4 February 1639 – *Parish Register of All Saints – 1559-1810* (Par 189/1/R1/1), folio 88 verso.

[3] Burial – 8 June 1612 – *Parish Register of All Saints – 1559-1810* (Par 189/1/R1/1), folio 85 verso.

[4] Baptism – 25 February 1613 – *Parish Register of All Saints – 1559-1810* (Par 189/1/R1/1), folio 12 verso; Burial – 13 July 1628 – *Parish Register of All Saints – 1559-1810* (Par 189/1/R1/1), folio 88 recto.

[5] Baptism – 18 September 1614 – *Parish Register of All Saints – 1559-1810* (Par 189/1/R1/1), folio 13 recto.

[6] *Poll Tax of 1667* (P.5.7), folio 51 recto; Burial – 26 March 1702 – *Parish Register of St Michael-at-the-Northgate – 1683-1736* (Par 211/1/R1/3), page 77.

[7] Baptism – 25 September 1616 – *Parish Register of All Saints – 1559-1810* (Par 189/1/R1/1), folio 15 verso; Apprenticeship – 19 October 1632 – *Civic Enrolments 1613-1640* (L.5.2), folio 229 verso; Citizenship – 4 September 1639 – *Civic Enrolments 1639-1662* (L.5.3), folio 277 verso; Burial – 24 July 1673 – *Parish Register of St Michael-at-the-Northgate – 1653-1683* (Par 211/1/R1/2), folio 25 verso.

[8] Baptism – 28 September 1618 – *Parish Register of All Saints – 1559-1810* (Par 189/1/R1/1), folio 14 recto; Apprenticeship – 19 October 1632 – *Civic Enrolments 1613-1640* (L.5.2), folio 229 verso; Citizenship – 11 September 1639 – *Civic Enrolments 1639-1662* (L.5.3), folio 277 verso; *Poll Tax of 1667* (P.5.7), folio 13 recto; Burial – 6 June 1679 – *Parish Register of All Saints – 1678-1812* (Par 189/1/R1/2), folio 3 recto.

[9] *Poll Tax of 1667* (P.5.7), folio 13 recto; Listed as Recusant – 1682 – *OAR: Records – Returns of Recusants – 1682-1705* (c. 430), folio 41 recto.

[10] Baptism – 26 June 1623 – *Parish Register of All Saints – 1559-1810* (Par 189/1/R1/1), folio 15 recto.

[11] Baptism – 30 May 1640 – *Parish Register of All Saints – 1559-1810* (Par 189/1/R1/1), folio 18 recto; Burial – 27 August 1641 – *Parish Register of All Saints – 1559-1810* (Par 189/1/R1/1), folio 90 recto.

[12] Baptism – 16 October 1641 – *Parish Register of All Saints – 1559-1810* (Par 189/1/R1/1), folio 18 recto; Citizenship – 1 April 1660 – *Civic Enrolments 1639-1662* (L.5.3), folio 217 verso; Marriage Bond – 5 February 1669 – *ODR: Marriage Bonds* (d. 58), folio 6; Burial – 9 August 1685 – *Parish Register of St Michael-at-the-Northgate – 1683-1736* (Par 211/1/R1/3), page 33; Probate Bond of Humphrey Jennings – 21 August 1685 (OWPR 82/2/6).

[13] Marriage Bond – 5 February 1669 – *ODR: Marriage Bonds* (d. 58), folio 6; Burial – 20 June 1684 – *Parish Register of St Michael-at-the-Northgate – 1683-1736* (Par 211/1/R1/3), page 31.

[14] Baptism – 16 October 1641 – *Parish Register of All Saints – 1559-1810* (Par 189/1/R1/1), folio 18 recto; Burial – 1 November 1641 – *Parish Register of All Saints – 1559-1810* (Par 189/1/R1/1), folio 90 recto.

[15] Baptism – 24 September 1646 – *Parish Register of All Saints 1559-1810* (Par 189/1/R1/3), folio 21 verso; Burial – 27 March 1703 – *Parish Register of St Michael-at-the-Northgate – 1683-1736* (Par 211/1/R1/3), page 80; Will of John Jennings – 3 May 1703 (OWPR 137/1/6); Probate Bond of John Jennings – 30 May 1703 (OWPR 137/1/6).

[16] Burial – 8 September 1679 – *Parish Register of St Michael-at-the-Northgate – 1653-1683* (Par 211/1/R1/2), folio 20 recto.

[17] Burial – 2 September 1698 – *Parish Register of St Michael-at-the-Northgate – 1683-1736* (Par 211/1/R1/3), page 68.

[18] Born – 1658 – *ODR: 27 September 1662-15 April 1665* (c. 4), folio 85 verso; *Poll Tax of 1667* (P.5.7), folio 51 recto; Citizenship – 16 July 1677 – *Civic Enrolments 1662-1699* (L.5.4), page 646; *City Council Proceedings - 1663-1701* (B.5.1), folio 156 recto; Burial – 23 July 1713 – *Parish Register of St Michael-at-the-Northgate – 1683-1736* (Par 211/1/R1/3), page 98; Will of Joseph Jennings – 4 August 1713 (OWPR 137/1/23).

[19] Burial – 14 August 1649 – *Parish Register of All Saints – 1559-1810* (Par 189/1/R1/1), folio 93 recto.

[20] *Poll Tax of 1667* (P.5.7), folio 13 recto.

[21] *Poll Tax of 1667* (P.5.7), folio 13 recto.

[22] *Poll Tax of 1667* (P.5.7), folio 13 recto.

[23] *Poll Tax of 1667* (P.5.7), folio 13 recto.

24 *Poll Tax of 1667* (P.5.7), folio 13 recto.

25 School Entry – 2 July 1694 – *Alderman Nixon's Free School – 1658* (Q.5.1), page 171.

26 Birth – 5 October 1671 – *Parish Register of St Michael-at-the-Northgate – 1653-1683* (Par 211/1/R1/2), folio 3 recto; School Entry - 27 September 1683 – *Alderman Nixon's Free School – 1658* (Q.5.1), page 165; Apprenticeship – 16 July 1686 – *Civic Enrolments 1662-1699* (L.5.4), page 392.

27 Baptism of children – Birth – 24 April 1710 – *Parish Register of St Michael-at-the-Northgate – 1683-1736* (Par 211/1/R1/3), page 306; 21 December 1711 – *Parish Register of St Michael-at-the-Northgate – 1683-1736* (Par 211/1/R1/3), page 301; 9 August 1716 – *Parish Register of St Michael-at-the-Northgate – 1683-1736* (Par 211/1/R1/3), page 293.

28 Baptism – 24 October 1674 – *Parish Register of St Michael-at-the-Northgate – 1653-1683* (Par 211/1/R1/2), folio 5 verso.

29 Baptism – 21 August 1677 – *Parish Register of St Michael-at-the-Northgate – 1653-1683* (Par 211/1/R1/2), folio 8 recto; Apprenticeship – 13 May 1691 – *Civic Enrolments 1662-1699* (L.5.4), page 444; Burial – 3 June 1695 – *Parish Register of St Michael-at-the-Northgate – 1683-1736* (Par 211/1/R1/3), page 58.

30 Baptized – 15 August 1684 – *Parish Register of St Michael-at-the-Northgate – 1683-1736* (Par 211/1/R1/3), page 386; Will of Joseph Jennings – 4 August 1713 (OWPR 137/1/23).

31 Birth – 17 December 1691 – *Parish Register of St Michael-at-the-Northgate – 1683-1736* (Par 211/1/R1/3), page 358; Will of Joseph Jennings – 4 August 1713 (OWPR 137/1/23).

32 Birth – 2 January 1693 – *Parish Register of St Michael-at-the-Northgate – 1683-1736* (Par 211/1/R1/3), page 350; Burial – 2 September 1694 – *Parish Register of St Michael-at-the-Northgate – 1683-1736* (Par 211/1/R1/3), page 53.

33 Citizenship – 27 January 1726 – *Civic Enrolments 1697-1780* (L.5.5), folio 217 verso.

34 Birth – 24 April 1710 – *Parish Register of St Michael-at-the-Northgate – 1683-1736* (Par 211/1/R1/3), page 306.

35 Baptism – 21 December 1711 – *Parish Register of St Michael-at-the-Northgate – 1683-1736* (Par 211/1/R1/3), page 301.

36 Birth – 9 August 1716 – *Parish Register of St Michael-at-the-Northgate – 1683-1736* (Par 211/1/R1/3), page 293.

The Family Tree of Thomas Williams

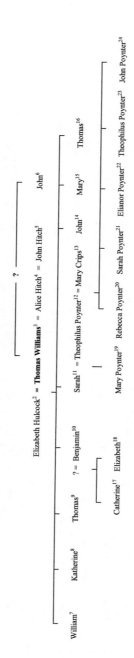

Elizabeth Hulcock[2] = **Thomas Williams**[3] = Alice Hitch[4] = John Hitch[5]

William[7] Katherine[8] Thomas[9] ? = Benjamin[10] Sarah[11] = Theophilus Poynter[12] = Mary Crips[13] John[14] Mary[15] Thomas[16] John[6]

Catherine[17] Elizabeth[18]

Mary Poynter[19] Rebecca Poynter[20] Sarah Poynter[21] Elianor Poynter[22] Theophilus Poynter[23] John Poynter[24]

?

1 Marriage – 28 April 1617 – Parish Register of St Martin's – 1569-1705 (Par 207/1/R1/2), folio 67 verso.

2 Marriage – 2 February 1629 – Parish Register of St Giles – 1576-1680 (MS DD Par St Giles b.1), page 92; Burial – 18 December 1662 – Parish Register of All Saints – 1559-1810 (Par 189/1/R1/1), folio 94 recto.

3 Marriage – 2 February 1629 – Parish Register of St Giles – 1576-1680 (MS DD Par St Giles b.1), page 92; Marriage – 18 August 1664 – ODR: Marriage Records: W 1634-1704 (c. 92/2), folio 4; Will of Thomas Williams – 12 January 1674 – PCC – Will of Thomas Williams (PROB 11/345), pages 318-319); Burial – 5 March 1674 – Parish Register of All Saints - 1559-1810 (Par 189/1/R1/1), folio 98 verso.

4 Will of John Hitch – 16 December 1658 – PCC – Will of John Hitch (PROB 11/285), folio 158 verso; Marriage – 18 August 1664 – ODR: Marriage Records: W 1634-1704 (c. 92/2), folio 4; Will of Thomas Williams – 12 January 1674 – PCC – Will of Thomas Williams (PROB 11/345), pages 318-319; Burial – 5 November 1699 – Parish Register of St Mary the Virgin – 1678-1812 (Par 209/1/R1/4), page 23.

5 Will of John Hitch – 16 December 1658 – PCC – Will of John Hitch (PROB 11/285), folio 158 verso.

6 Burial – 17 January 1634 – Parish Register of All Saints – 1559-1810 (Par 189/1/R1/1), folio 87 verso.

7 Baptism – 30 July 1630 – Parish Register of All Saints – 1559-1810 (Par 189/1/R1/1), folio 16 recto; Burial – 14 November 1631 – Parish Register of All Saints – 1559-1810 (Par 189/1/R1/1), folio 88 recto.

8 Baptism – 12 June 1636 – Parish Register of All Saints – 1559-1810 (Par 189/1/R1/1), folio 17 recto; Burial – 11 December 1636 – Parish Register of All Saints – 1559-1810 (Par 189/1/R1/1), folio 88 recto.

9 Baptism – 5 December 1637 – Parish Register of All Saints – 1559-1810 (Par 189/1/R1/1), folio 17 verso; Burial – 15 July 1646 – Parish Register of St Mary the Virgin – 1599-1694 (Par 209/1/R1/1), page 43.

10 Baptism – 26 January 1640 – Parish Register of All Saints – 1559-1810 (Par 189/1/R1/1), folio 17 verso; Will of Thomas Williams – 12 January 1674 – PCC – Will of Thomas Williams (PROB 11/345), pages 318-319.

11 Baptism – 14 July 1642 – Parish Register of All Saints – 1559-1810 (Par 189/1/R1/1), folio 18 recto; Will of Thomas Williams – 12 January 1674 – PCC – Will of Thomas Williams (PROB 11/345), pages 318-319.

12 Marriage – 2 June 1664 – ODR: Marriage Bonds – 1664 (d. 70), folio 137; Will of Thomas Williams – 12 January 1674 – PCC – Will of Thomas Williams (PROB 11/345), pages 318-319; Burial – 16 September 1709 – Parish Register of St Mary the Virgin – 1678-1812 (Par 209/1/R1/4), page 34; Will of Theophilus Poynter – 21 August 1706 – PCC – Will of Theophilus Poynter (PROB 11/514), folios 225 verso-229 recto.

13 Marriage – 2 June 1664 – ODR: Marriage Bonds – 1664 (d. 70), folio 137; Will of Theophilus Poynter – 21 August 1706 – PCC – Will of Theophilus Poynter (PROB 11/514), folios 225 verso-229 recto; Burial – 10 December 1718 – Parish Register of St Mary the Virgin – 1678-1812 (Par 209/1/R1/4), page 39.

14 Baptism – 24 September 1646 – Parish Register of All Saints – 1559-1810 (Par 189/1/R1/1), folio 20 verso; Apprenticeship – 20 December 1660 – Civic Enrolments 1639-1662 (L.5.3), folio 188 verso; Poll Tax of 1667 (P.5.7), folio 10 recto; Burial – 23 June 1673 – Parish Register of All Saints – 1559-1810 (Par 189/1/R1/1), folio 98 verso.

15 Burial – 3 February 1651 – Parish Register of All Saints – 1559-1810 (Par 189/1/R1/1), folio 93 verso.

16 Baptism – 24 April 1653 – Parish Register of All Saints – 1559-1810 (Par 189/1/R1/1), folio 23 recto; Burial – 12 June 1653 – Parish Register of All Saints – 1559-1810 (Par 189/1/R1/1), folio 94 verso.

17 Baptism – 24 November 1685 – Parish Register of All Saints – 1559-1810 (Par 189/1/R1/1), folio 34 recto.

18 Baptism – 10 April 1687 – Parish Register of All Saints – 1559-1810 (Par 189/1/R1/1), folio 35 recto.

19 Poll Tax entry – Poll Tax of 1667 (P.5.7), folio 54 verso; Death – 3 April 1692 – Memorial inscription in Saint Mary the Virgin Church, Oxford.

20 Will of Theophilus Poynter – 21 August 1706 – PCC – Will of Theophilus Poynter (PROB 11/514), folios 225 verso-229 recto.

21 Birth – 28 March 1672 – Parish Register of St Michael-at-the-Northgate – 1653-1683 (Par 211/1/R1/2), folio 3 verso; Death – 15 September 1702 – Memorial inscription in Saint Mary the Virgin Church, Oxford.

[22] Baptism – 14 September 1675 – *Parish Register of St Mary the Virgin – 1599-1694* (Par 209/1/R1/1), page 76; Death – 14 May 1703 – Memorial inscription in Saint Mary the Virgin Church, Oxford; Burial – 19 May 1703 – *Parish Register of St Mary the Virgin – 1678-1812* (Par 209/1/R1/4), page 28.

[23] Baptism – 23 October 1678 – *Parish Register of St Mary the Virgin – 1599-1694* (Par 209/1/R1/1), page 77; Death – 19 June 1706 – Memorial inscription in Saint Mary the Virgin Church, Oxford; Burial – 22 June 1706 – *Parish Register of St Mary the Virgin – 1678-1812* (Par 209/1/R1/4), page 31.

[24] Baptism – 19 September 1680 – *Parish Register of St Mary the Virgin – 1599-1694* (Par 209/1/R1/1), page 77; Burial – 24 September 1680 – *Parish Register of St Mary the Virgin – 1599-1694* (Par 209/1/R1/1), page 77.

Bibliography

Manuscripts and Documents in the Angus Library, Regent's Park College, Oxford

The Abingdon Association Records Book (D/AA/1)
The Longworth Churchbook (Longworth 1/1)
Records of the Baptist Meetings in Devon (D/DA 1) – mentions Tidmarsh from Oxford
Letter of Joshua Thomas to John Rippon (D/RPN 4/1), page 2 – record of a payment to Richard Tidmarsh for a mission to Devon (17 March 1690)
Baptist Missionary Society – Home Papers: Underhill's Copies of Three 17th-Century Letters (H/13/5/iii) – London Baptists call for a General Assembly in London (28 July 1689)
Stinton, Benjamin *A Journal of the Affairs of ye Antipaedobaptists beginning with ye Reign of King George whose Accession to the Throne was on the first of August1714* (Reg Angus 3.h.30)

Manuscripts and Documents in Christ Church, Oxford

Deanery Papers
    Christ Church Deanery Papers (DP ii.c.1) – letter from Ralph Austen (21 January1656)
Disbursements Books
    Disbursements Book 1641-2 (Ch. Ch. MS xii b 85)
Lease Books and Registers
    Book of Evidences, Part 1 (Ch Ch MS c.2)
    Lease Book 4 – 1635-1658 (Ch.Ch. MS xx.c.4), pages 18-19 and 362-364 – Hatchman leases
Leases
    VIII. St Martin's – 1st Tenement (65 Cornmarket Street)
        #6 – Lease to Richard Shurley (25 October 1658) (Shurley's copy)
        #7 – Lease to Richard Shurley (25 October 1658) (Dean's copy)
        #8 – Lease to Thomas Tesdale (10 December 1672) (Tisdale's copy)
        #9 – Lease to Thomas Tesdale (10 December 1672) with bond of £100 (Dean's copy)
    II. St Thomas – Alley Meads #7 - #19 – Leases mentioning Richard Tidmarsh as occupying a neighbouring property
        #7 – 22 March 1670
        #8 and #9 – 11 July 1672
        #10 and #11 – 28 January 1682
        #12 and #13 – 22 December 1692

#14 and #15 – 6 December 1700
#16 – 1 June 1708
#17, #18 and #19 – 20 August 1715
Christ Church Lease – Roger Hatchman (22 December 1636)
Christ Church Lease – Roger Hatchman (25 April 1654)

Manuscripts and Documents in New College, Oxford

Lease Books, Valuations and Estate Administration Documents
    Lease Book #10 – 1649-1654 (Steer #9765), pages 219 and 222 – Hatchman lease
        from 1654
    New College Archives: Valuations (Steer #1442)
    Estate Administration (Steer #1422)
    New College Archives: Valuations (Steer #1446)
Leases
    New College Archives: Leases (Steer #2244) – Hatchman lease from 1654

Manuscripts and Documents in Worcester College, Oxford

Clarke MS 46 (Monck's Order Book)
Clarke MS 49 (Monck's Order Book)

Manuscripts and Documents in the Bodleian Library, Oxford

Addit. MSS c. 303, folio 45 recto – on John Trask being branded with the letter 'J' as a
    Jewish Christian
Bodleian Wills – Austen, Ralph – Will written and signed on 24 September 1674
Bodleian Wills – Williams, John – 4 June 1641
Gerard Langbaine's Collections Volume 3, (WP γ 26 1) – On the masons' dispute with
    the University
Liber Computus Vicecancellarii Oxon 1547-1666 (WPB/21/4) – The Vice-Chancellor's
    Account Book
Malone 402 – Anotated copy of Thomas Weaver's *Songs and Poems of Love and
    Drollery* (1654)
MS ADD d. 114 – The Siege of Oxford – folio 12 recto refers to Tom Ayres house; folio
    17 is a census of men aged 16-60 in Oxford on 7 June 1643
MS ADD c. 302, folio 250 – Letter from Vice-Chancellor Peter Mews to Archbishop
    Sheldon(?) dated 26 June 1672
MS Ballard 68 – Twayne's description of events from August 1642 – Used by Wood in
    his *History*
MS Bodl 594, folios 157 recto – 159 recto – on Tisdale and the noctivagation
    controversy (folio 158 verso)
MS Bodl 898 – Accounts for the Building of the Sheldonian Theatre
MS Ch Oxon c. 50 (#4501) – Charter on Ralph Austen's property in St Peter-in-the-
    Bailey (30 June 1675)
MS Ch Oxon c. 50 (#4502) – Charter on Ralph Austen's property in St Peter-in-the-
    Bailey (27 June 1678)

MS Ch Oxon c. 50 (#4503a) – Indenture on Ralph Austen's property in St Peter-in-the-Bailey (10 December 1690)

MS Ch Oxon c. 50 (#4503b) – Sale of Ralph Austen's property in St Peter-in-the-Bailey (1691)

MS Clarendon 65, folios 139-140 – Commissioners of Oxford letter to Council of State (5 October 1659)

MSS DD All Souls College – Rentals 21-40 (b. 20)

MSS DD All Souls College – Rent Rolls 1657-1665 (c. 338) – (12 rolls)

MSS DD All Souls College – Rent Rolls 1666-1672 (c. 339) – (14 rolls)

MSS DD All Souls College – Rent Rolls 1673-1679 (c. 340) – (14 rolls)

MS Eng. hist. (c. 53) – Journal of Sir Samuel Luke

MS Morrell 6 – Election and Order Book of the Company of Taylors (1572-1711) – Williams signs order folio 156 recto

MS Morrell 7 - Election and Order Book of the Company of Taylors (1710-1833)

MS Morrell 12 – Gylde of Cordwayners (1648-1758) – Wyans and Toms as Cordwainers

MS Morrell 14 – Minutes of Meetings of the Guild of Cordwayners (1614-1711) – Wyans and Toms as Cordwainers

MS Morrell 20 – Annual Meetings & Accounts (1534-1645) – Wyans' entry into guild

MS Morrell 21 - Company of Taylors Minute Book (1658-1689)

MS Morrell 22 – The Company of Taylors: Enrolling Book (1604-1807) – 1646 – Thomas King – folio 46 – 'The names of those that were not Freemans sonnes of the Company of Taylors'

MS Morrell 23 – List of Cordwainers' Apprentices (1590-1660) – King, Wyans, Toms, Seale as Cordwainers

MS Morrell 24 – Guylde of Cordwayners – Thomas Tomes as a journeyman Cordwayner circa 1632

Ms e Musaeo 77 – Register of the Parliamentary Visitors

MS Rawlinson A 34, folio 40 – General Monck made Commander in Chief of Army in Scotland

MS Rawlinson A 29, page 633 – Testimonials to the character of Thomas Denver of St Michael's Parish dated 24 February 1655 signed by Thomas Williams

MS Rawlinson A 54, folio 225 – on Richard Quelch junior as a Fifth Monarchist agent

MS Rawlinson A 64, folio 141 – on Fifth Monarchists in Abingdon after Pendarves's funeral (September 1656)

MS Rawlinson B 402a, folio 1 recto – Thomas Williams swears in Matthew Jellyman as registrar to five parish churches on 10 October 1653

MS Rawlinson D 859, folio 162 - On John Pendarves's death

MS Rawlinson poet 211, folios 78 recto–80 verso – Thomas Weaver's notebook

MS Tanner 102, Part 1, folio 32 recto = 'Anabaptists come to cut their throats'; folio 89 verso – on All Saints' steeple rocking; folio 121 verso = 'Tom Pun's house' is described as 'Hall's house behind and northward of the schools'

MS Tanner 102, Part 2, folio 80 recto = 'Oxford in a position of defence because of Anabaptists'

MS Tanner 466, folio 64 recto–65 recto – satirical verses by Henry Thomas of University College on the new mace commissioned by John Lambe for Oxford's celebration of the Restoration

MS Top Oxon (b. 40) – Baptismal records of Lemuel and Nebennezar King + Tisdale, Toms + Quelch

MS Top Oxon (d. 44) – All Saints' Oxford – Births 1654-1660 – transcription of *MS Top Oxon b. 40* by Andrew Clark in 1896

MS Twyne-Langbaine IV – Details of a controversy between the University and Stonemasons' Guild

MS Wood D 4, folio 297b – Comment on Richard Croke, Serjeant at Law who wrote the speech for James II when the new mace was delivered

MS Wood D 19 (3), folios 13 recto – 13 verso – Four college leaders expelled by Chancellor Clarendon for keeping conventicles in their colleges

MS Wood Diaries 3 – on Maypole celebrations (folio 16 verso); 1659 on Anabaptist meeting in Abingdon (folio 17 verso); Anabaptists come to cut their throats (folio 19 verso); Wood buys gloves from John Sheene (folio 21 recto)

MS Wood Diaries 4 – folio 7 verso on Hatchman supporting John Belcher at St Peter-in-the-Bailey in January 1660

MS Wood Diaries 5, folio 22 recto – Wood buys a copy of *A Short History of the Anabaptists of High and Low Germany* (1642)

MS Wood Diaries 7, folio 1 verso – on the cheat Robert Bullock (1663); folio 2 recto – Wood witnesses a rental agreement involving Abraham Davies (11 February 1663); folio 18 recto – on conventicle of Davis the bookseller in December 1663; folio 36 – on the discovery of a suspected conventicle

MS Wood Diaries 13, folio 18 recto – Anthony Wood drinks cider at Austen's on 2, 15 & 23 June 1669

MS Wood Diaries 16, folio 14 recto – on Anabaptists' reaction to the publication of the *Act of Toleration* on 15 March 1672

MS Wood Diaries 21 – folios 2 recto and 15 recto – on Ralph Austen's death in 1677(sic)

MS Wood Diaries 25, folios 38 recto–39 recto – on the trial and execution of Stephen Colledge

MS Wood Diaries 27, folio 29 verso – on Lawrence King's house being searched on 25 May 1683; folios 43 recto and verso – on celebrations in Oxford

MS Wood Diaries 29, folio 60 verso – On the repair of the bridge at Castle Mills

MS Wood Diaries 30, folio 42 verso – On Anabaptists glad to receive *Declaration of Indulgence*

MS Wood Diaries 32, page 26 – on Jonas Proast being expelled from All Souls; page 49 – on the receipt of the Charter of Oxford; page 60 – on Thomas Lamplugh

MS Wood Diaries 33, folio 11 recto – on Dancing School; folio 44 verso – on conventiclers

MS Wood Diaries 36, folio 38 recto – on Dissenting meetings held in Tidmarsh house (6 July 1692)

MS Wood E 4 – note on the Parliamentary Visitors and the placement of their *Register* in the Bodleian Library

MS Wood F 1 – Wood's Manuscript for *The Histories and Antiquities of the Universitie of Oxford;* page 1123 – description of Baptists as 'fanatic party'

MS Wood F 4 – page 101 – coat of arms of John Nixon

MS Wood F 29a – Original MS for *Antiquities of the City of Oxford* - Tom Ayres house on folios 78-9

MS Wood F 31 – History of Oxford manuscript – King baptizing (folio 7 verso); Baptists as 'unstable people' (folio 7 verso); Baptists as 'notorious sectaryes' (folio 14 recto); Thomas Lamplugh described (folios 4 verso + 14 verso)

MS Wood F 35 – Collected papers relating to the Parliamentary Visitors to Oxford

Rent Rolls

> *Rent Rolls 1661-1665: MSS DD All Souls College* (c. 338)
> *Rent Rolls 1666-1672: MSS DD All Souls College* (c. 339)
> *Rent Rolls 1673-1677: MSS DD All Souls College 1673-1679* (c. 340)

Wood 276a (331) – *A Letter from a Person of Quality in Edenburgh* (1659)
Wood 401 (198) – *A True Relation of a Notorious Cheater one Robert Bullock* (1663)
Wood 402 (92) – *A True Relation of a Notorious Cheater one Robert Bullock* (1663)
Wood 514 (29) – order from Sir Thomas Fairfax to Colonel Kelsey about Oxford troops supporting the Parliamentary Visitors (31 March 1648)
Wood 515 (14) – *Here followeth a true Relation of Some of the Sufferings inflicted upon the servrnts [sic] of the Lord who are called Quakers Oxford* (1654)

Manuscripts and Documents in The Cambridge University Library, Cambridge

Cambridge University Library MS Add 3976, folio 16a = Newton to Oldenburg (28 November 1676)
Cambridge University Library MS Add 3976, folio 17a = Oldenburg to Newton (2 January 1677)

Manuscripts and Documents in The Guildhall Library, London

Apprenticeship Records
  Feltmakers' Company Apprenticeships – 1692-1708 (GL MS 1570/2), pages 424 and 484 – Apprenticeship of Wyans Tidmarsh (18 December 1704 and 7 April 1707)
  Feltmakers' Company Apprenticeships – 1726-1749 (GL MS 1570/3), Apprenticeship of Spelman Simmons to Wyans Tidmarsh (1 July 1728)
  Painter-Stainers' Company Apprenticeships – 1666-1795 (GL MS 5669/1), folio 56 recto – Apprenticeship of Samuel King (1681-1685)
  Pewterers' Company Apprenticeships – 1675-1691 (GL MS 7090/7), folio 153 verso – Apprenticeship of Samuel Tidmarsh (26 April 1683)
  Pewterers' Company Apprenticeships – 1691-1711 (GL MS 7090/8), folio 34 verso – Apprenticeship of James Tidmarsh (14 December 1693)
  Pewterers' Company Apprenticeships – 1711-1740 (GL MS 7090/9), folios 220 recto and 259 recto – Apprenticeship of John Hawkins to James Tidmarsh (20 December 1734)
  Vintners' Company Apprenticeships – 1666-1736 (GL MS 15, 220/2), pages 667 and 759 – Apprenticeships of Richard Tidmarsh (6 December 1721); William Tidmarsh (7 June 1732)
Diocesan Records
  London Diocese Marriage Allegation – June-December 1709 (MS 10,091/45) – Marriage of James Tidmarsh and Phyllis Harrison on 21 July 1705
Parish Registers
  Parish Register of Allhallows London Wall, London (GL MS 5087) – Marriage of James Tidmarsh and Phyllis Harrison on 21 July 1705
  Parish Register of St Botolph-without-Bishopsgate – 1715-1752 (GL MS 4517/1) – Burial of John Tidmarsh (son of Samuel and Sarah Tidmarsh) on 3 January 1752
  Parish Register of St Dunstan in the West – 1669-1709 (GL MS 10,348) – Baptism of Mary Tidmarsh (daughter of Richard and Elizabeth from Chancery Lane) on 23 November 1686
  Parish Register of St Dunstan in the West – 1669-1709 (GL MS 10,348) – Baptism of Elizabeth Tidmarsh (daughter of Richard and Elizabeth from Chancery Lane) on 8 July 1688

Parish Register of St James, Clerkenwell, Middlesex – Burials 1666-1719 – Burial of
   Lemuel King on 16 June 1719
Parish Register of St Michael Cornhill – 1653-1736 (GL MS 4063/1), folios 28
   recto, 29 recto, 30 recto, 31 verso, 33 recto – Baptisms of Samuel Tidmarsh on
   11 March 1683; Judah and Anne Tidmarsh on 5 June 1684; an unnamed son on
   30 May 1685; Samuel Tidmarsh (son of Samuel and Elizabeth) on 1 March
   1687; and Sarah (daughter of Samuel and Elizabeth) on 17 June 1688
Baptist Church Records
   Devonshire Square (Particular) Baptist Church (GL MS 20 228 1A) – Records of
      John Toms's involvement in the London church from 1698-1727
   Petty France (Particular) Baptist Church (GL MS 20 228 1B) – Records of three
      people who transferred membership to and from Oxford

Manuscripts and Documents of The Stationers' Company, London

Stationers' Company Archives: Apprenticeship Register – 7 August 1666-6 March 1727,
   folios 23 recto and 68 recto – Apprenticeship records of Samuel Tidmarsh and
   Richard Carter
*Stationers' Company Archives: Master and Apprenticeship Calendar – 5 March 1654-7
   September 1685*, folio 32 verso – Apprenticeship record of Samuel Tidmarsh
Stationers' Company Archives: The Register of Freemen – 2 July 1605-6 March 1703,
   folio 122 recto – Citizenship record of Samuel Tidmarsh
*Stationers' Company Archives: Master and Apprenticeship Calendar – 2 May 1670-17
   July 1690*, folio 34 verso – Master record of Samuel Tidmarsh

Manuscripts and Documents in The British Library, London

BL ADD MS 4294, folio 17 recto – Letter from John Beale to Henry Oldenberg about
   Ralph Austen (6 August 1671)
BL ADD MS 4294, folio 12a-d – Letter from Isaac Newton to Henry Oldenberg about
   Ralph Austen (14 November 1676)
BL ADD MS 4459, folio 111 recto and verso – Quelch(?) listed as a 'Brother from
   Oxford' visiting Venner's congregation
BL Additional MS 28929, folio 60 recto – Letter from Humphrey Prideaux to John Ellis
   about Richard Tidmarsh and Stephen Colledge (22 September 1681)

Manuscripts and Documents in The Friends Meeting House Library, London

Manuscripts – First Publishers of Truth: Portfolio 7, folio 64 recto-65 recto – Accounts
   of Quakers in Oxford in 1654
Swarthmore MS, Volume 352/208 – Margaret Fell's account of Elizabeth Levens

Manuscripts and Documents in The Lambeth Palace Library, London

Lambeth MS 951/1, folios 112 recto-113 verso – Bishop Walter Blandford's report about
   conventicles in the Oxford diocese compiled in 1669

Marriage – Lambeth Palace Library: Faculty Office Marriage Allegation – 20 January 1681 – Marriage of Samuel Tidmarsh and Sarah Wall

Manuscripts and Documents in The National Archives, Kew Gardens, London

Association Oath Roll – Oxford – 1696 (c. 213/86)
Association Oath Roll – Tiverton – 1696 (c. 213/86)
Hearth Taxes (E 179)
  Hearth Tax for Michaelmas 1662 (E 179/255/3) – contains 94 membranes and is dated 1662 – *Hearth Tax Documents* for the County of Oxfordshire
  Hearth Tax of August-November 1662 (E 179/255/4) – contains 293 membranes and is dated August-November 1662
  Hearth Tax of Michaelmas 1665 (E 179/164/513) – contains 72 rots and is dated 1665 = Weinstock *Hearth Tax*
  Hearth Tax of 24 April 1666 (E 179/164/514) = contains 67 rots and is dated 24 April 1666 = published in Salter (1923): 183-212 (but wrongly described by him as from Michaelmas rather than Lady Day)
Lay Subsidies (E 179)
  Lay Subsidy of 10-23 December 1640 (E 179/164/477) – contains 1 folio and was collected 20 March 1641
  Lay Subsidy of 10-23 December 1640 (E 179/164/495) – contains 1 folio and was collected 30 April 1641
  Lay Subsidy of 23 June 1647 (E 179/164/497) – contains 6 rots and was collected 27 December 1647
  Lay Subsidy of 23 June 1647 (E 179/164/498) – contains 5 rots and was collected in 1648
  Lay Subsidy of 23 June 1647 (E 179/164/498a) – contains 4 rots and was collected in 1648
  Lay Subsidy of 17 March 1648 (E 179/164/499) – contains 6 folios and was collected in 1648 = published in Salter (1923): 163-182
  Lay Subsidy of 29 December 1660 (E 179/164/501a) – contains 4 folios and was collected 12 July 1661
  Free and Voluntary Present of 8 July 1661 (E 179/255/5/4) – contains 7 rots and is dated to 13 October 1661
  Lay Subsidy of 27 July 1663 (E 179/164/503) – contains 8 folios and is dated to 17 October 1663 = published in Weinstock (1940)
Privy Council Register – 1 October 1669–28 April 1671 (PC 2/62) – page 92 is on Peter Mews and his suppression of conventicles (31 December 1669)
Special Commission of Inquiry – Exchequer (E 178/6906) – on the property damages to Dissenters' meeting houses in Oxford in the riots of 1715
Star Chamber Depositions (STAC 8/114/18) – Roger and Richard Hatchman give evidence in a dispute over enclosures in Dorchester-on-Thames (1612-1614)
State Papers Domestic (SP)
  SP 16/314, folio 79 recto - warrant issued by the Court of High Commission in 1636 about conventiclers
  SP 18/279, folio 76 – a copy of *The Declaration of the County of Oxon to His Excellency the Lord General Monck* (13 February 1660)
  SP 25/66, pages 117-118 – The Council of State orders that letters be written to Oxford's civic and university officials about behaviour of students (25 December 1651)

SP 25/78, pages 213-214 and 516 – Thomas Williams the apothecary appointed as tax collector (October 1657 and March 1658)

SP 25/78, page 276 – Thomas Williams the apothecary petitions Charles II about his failure to meet tax obligations (November 1660)

SP 25/79, pages 428 and 431 – warrant for the arrest of Lord Falkland (12 August 1659)

SP 25/79, page 501 – the Council of State orders the search of Lord Falkland's house (29 August 1659)

SP 25/79, page 513 – Council of State orders Lord Falkland's re-examination over hidden arms (2 September 1659)

SP 25/79, pages 609 and 620 – Council of State discussions of documents captured by the Oxfordshire militia (21 and 26 September 1659)

SP 25/79, page 650 – Council of State receives reports about the capture of arms in Lord Falkland's house (2 October 1659)

SP 25/79, page 661 – Council of State sends thanks to the Commissioners of the Oxfordshire militia (10 October 1659)

SP 25/97), pages 51-52 – The Council of State writes letters to Oxford's civic and university officials about behaviour of students (29 December 1651)

SP 25/98, pages 52 and 105 – Council of State approves Oxford militia commissions (11 August 1659)

SP 25/98, page 217 - Council of State sends thanks to the Commissioners of the Oxfordshire militia (10 October 1659)

SP 29/28, page 109 – letter from Thomas Lamplugh to Joseph Williamson about Dissenters (15 January 1661)

SP 29/42, folios 68 recto-69 verso – letter from William Pestell to Edward Nicholas about John Belcher and the Fifth Monarchists (26 September 1661)

SP 29/44, pages 194-195 – letter from Roger Griffin to Lord Falkland which discusses the threat of Baptist insurrectionists in Oxford (25 November 1661)

SP 29/44, folios 258 recto-259 recto – letter from Captain William Pestell to Edward Nichols about the Fifth Monarchists including John Belcher (28 November 1661)

SP 29/272, folio 76 recto–75 verso – Peter Mews writes to the Privy Council and mentions a conventicle in the house of Lawrence King (13 January 1670)

SP 29/291, page 148 – Informants report about a sermon by John Belcher at Bell Lane, Spitalfields in London (24 June 1671)

SP 29/291, page 149 – Note about John Belcher's imprisonment (1671)

SP/29 320, page 118 – application for licenses for a Baptist meeting house in Oxford (1672)

SP/29 320, page 278 – application for a license for Robert Pawling as a Presbyterian teacher in Oxford (1672)

SP/29 320, page 146 – acknowledgement of the licenses for the Baptist meeting house in Oxford (22 April 1672)

SP/29 320, page 190 – application for a license for Thomas Gilbert as a Congregationalist teacher in Oxford (1672)

SP 29/401, folio 20 - letter from John Nicholls to Sir Joseph Williamson on the noctivagation issue (6 February 1678)

SP 29/416, Part 2, page 52 – Thomas Hyde reports to Sir Leoline Jenkins about the trial of Stephen College (27 August 1681)

SP 44/38A, page 6 – record of the licenses of the Independent meeting house in Chipping Norton (April 1672)

SP/44 38A, page 33 – record of the licenses of the Baptist meeting house in Oxford (19 April 1672)

SP 44/38A, page 191 – application for a license for Henry Cornish as a Presbyterian preacher and teacher in Oxford (29 June 1672)

SP 44/38A, page 228 – record of the license for Henry Cornish (10 August 1672)

SP 44/38A, page 249 – record of the licenses of the Baptist meeting house in Wolvercote (5 September 1672)

SP/44 38A, page 278 – Anthony Hall's home licensed as a Presbyterian meeting-house with Robert Pawlyn as a teacher based there (9 December 1672)

SP 44/337, pages 160-161 – warrant issued by James II preventing legal process against Thomas Tidmarsh (17 December 1686)

SP 44/338, pages 47-49 – warrant for the issuing of the Oxford Charter (9 August 1688)

Prerogative Court of Canterbury and Related Probate Jurisdictions: Will Registers 1384-1858 (PCC)

    Walter Cave (PROB 11/311) – Probated 2 June 1663
    Stephen Ford (PROB 11/431) – Probated 14 May 1696
    Job Hancock (PROB 11/364) – Probated 8 December 1680
    John Hitch (PROB 11/285) – Probated 16 December 1658
    John Hunt (PROB 11/228) – Probated 17 February 1659
    William Knight (PROB 11/647) – Probated 11 November 1731
    John Langley (PROB 11/267) – Probated 20 September 1657
    Joane Nixon (PROB 11/337) – Probated 20 September 1671
    John Nixon (PROB 11/307) – Probated 30 April 1662
    John Poynter (PROB 11/375) – Probated 17 March 1684
    Theophilus Poynter (PROB 11/514) – Probated 13 March 1709
    Hannah Stonhouse (PROB 11/703) – Probated 10 June 1740
    James Tidmarsh (PROB 11/700) – Probated 4 January 1740
    John Tidmarsh (PROB 11/670) – Probated 10 April 1735
    Mary Tidmarsh (PROB 11/813) – Probated 28 January 1755
    Thomas Tidmarsh (PROB 11/622) – Probated 3 June 1728
    Thomas Williams (PROB 11/345) – Probated 8 July 1674

Manuscripts and Documents in the Berkshire Records Office, Reading

Abingdon Wills and Probate Records (AWPR)
    Elizabeth Tesdale (AWPR D/A1/128/92) – Probated 26 March 1672
    John Tesdale (AWPR D/A1/128/57) – Probated 26 December 1665
    John Tesdale (AWPR D/A1/129/24) – Probated 28 March 1696
    Richard Tesdale (AWPR D/A1/128/58) – Probated 9 January 1667

Miscellaneous Quarter Sessions Papers Relating to Nonconformity in Abingdon – 1637-1704 (A/JQz 11), #1-#99

Radley, St James Parish Registers – Burials 1599-1741 (D/P/95/1/1)

Abingdon, St Helen Parish Registers – Baptisms 1538-1679 and Burials 1538-1678 (2001)

Abingdon, St Helen Parish Registers - Burials 1688-1812 (2003)

Manuscripts and Documents in the Devonshire Records Office, Exeter

Tiverton Baptist Church Records (TBCR)
  Church Minute Meeting Book – 1687-1845 – #3958D #1
  Thomas Whinnell Letter – 18 February 1695 – #3958D #2
  Thomas Whinnell Letter – 9 February 1695 – #3958D #3
  License for the Baptist Meeting House – 18 May 1697 – #3958D #4
  Elizabeth Fursdon Donation to the Baptist Ministry – 1687-1802 – #3958D Add #1
  Jane Prowse Trust Deed – 1694-1702 – #3958D Add #5
  Jane Prowse Trust Payments – 1701-1717 – #3958D Add #6
  Elizabeth Fursdon Will – 10 May 1687 – #3958D Add #9

Manuscripts and Documents in the Gloucestershire Records Office, Gloucester

Adlestrop Parish Register 1598-1673 (P5 IN 1/2)
Adlestrop Parish Register 1673-1700 (P5 IN 1/3)
Adlestrop Wills and Probate Records - 1541-1800 (AdWPR)
John Tidmarsh (AdWPR 1698/226)
Thomas Tidmarsh (AdWPR 1690/190)

Manuscripts and Documents in the Oxfordshire Records Office, Oxford

Alderman Nixon's Free School- 1658 (Q.5.1)
Audit Book – Accounts of the Common Chest 1644-1685 (P.4.2)
Audit Book – 1592-1682 (P.5.2)
Benefactions –1630-1824 (E.4.2)
City Council Records
  City Council Minutes – 1635-1657 (A.4.3)
  City Council Minutes – 1657-1668 (A.4.4).
  City Council Proceedings – 1629-1663 (A.5.7)
  City Council Proceedings – 1663-1701 (B.5.1)
  City Council Minutes – 1635-1715 (E.4.5)
Civic Enrolments (Hanister's Lists)
  Civic Enrolments – 1590-1614 (L.5.1)
  Civic Enrolments – 1613-1640 (L.5.2)
  Civic Enrolments – 1639-1662 (L.5.3)
  Civic Enrolments – 1662-1699 (L.5.4)
  Civic Enrolments – 1697-1780 (L.5.5)
The Enrolments of Apprentices – 1697-1800 (F.4.9)
Civil War, Charities & General Minutes – 1645-1695 (E.4.6)
Dorchester Peculiar Wills and Probate Records (DPWPR)
  Agnes Hatchman (DPWPR 30/1/17) – Will probated on 8 November 1610
  John Hatchman (DPWPR 69/1/2) – Will probated on 15 April 1588
  Richard Hatchman (DPWPR 69/1/20) – Will probated on 7 March 1637
  William Hatchman (DPWPR 69/1/24) – Will probated on 1 August 1642
Dorchester Parish Registers
  Dorchester Parish Register – 1638-1726 (Par 87/1/R1/1)
Enrollment Book of Statute Merchants – 1637-1675 (F.4.1)
Holton Parish Registers
  Parish Register of Holton – 1633-1794 (Par 135/1/R1/1), folio 13 verso – marriage
    of Henry Ireton and Bridget Cromwell

Husting and Mayors Courts – (Husting on Mondays, Mayors on Fridays)
Husting and Mayors Courts – *1660-1664* (M.4.4)
Husting and Mayors Courts – *1665-1666* (M.4.5)
Husting and Mayors Courts – *1666-1672* (M.4.6)
Husting and Mayors Courts – *1672-1677* (M.4.7)
Husting and Mayor's Court 1662; Licenses and Overseers (N.4.3)
James II Charter for Oxford – *15 September 1688* (I. 43).
Journeyman Tailors' Company Accounts – *1613-1697* (F.4.2)
Languables – *1668-1737* (P.5.3)
Mercers, Grocers & Linendrapers Guild Book – *1572-1855* (G.5.4)
Old Leases and Counterparts
    Old Leases and Counterparts: All Saints Parish (S 1.1c)
    Old Leases and Counterparts: All Saints Parish (S 1.1d)
Oxford Caveats – *1643-1677* (MS Wills 307) – Book of Caveats on Wills.
Oxford City Ledgers
    Oxford City Ledgers – *1578-1636* (D.5.5)
    Oxford City Ledgers – *1636-1675* (D.5.6)
    Oxford City Ledgers – *1675-1696* (D.5.7)
    Oxford City Ledgers – *1697-1706* (D.5.9)
    Oxford City Records – *1605-1649* (D.5.2), folio 250) – on Martin Seale's attempt to break up a gambling game
Oxford Archdeaconry Records (OAR)
    OAR: 11 May 1667-21 July 1669 (c. 17)
    OAR: 24 July 1669–July 1672 (c. 19)
    OAR: 29 November 1673-20 February 1675 (c. 21)
    OAR: 1 June 1678-30 July 1681 and 4 July 1674-17 October 1674 (c. 22)
    OAR: 15 October 1681-16 December 1693 (c. 23)
    OAR: Excommunications – *1610-1783* (c. 121)
    OAR: Allegations and Depositions – *1621-1672* (c. 175)
    OAR: Returns of Recusants – *1679-1706* (c. 430) – Bishop Fell's List of Recusants and Dissenters = Fell's triennial visitations to the diocese were in June 1679, May 1682 and August 1685
    OAR: Marriage Bonds – *1665* (c. 456)
    OAR: Marriage Bonds – *1668* (c. 458)
    OAR: Marriage Bonds – *1669* (c. 459)
    OAR: Marriage Bonds – *1673* (c. 462)
    OAR: Marriage Bonds – *1676* (c. 464)
    OAR: Marriage Bonds –*1681* (c. 469)
    OAR: Marriage Bonds –*1683* (c. 471)
    OAR: Marriage Bonds – *1684* (c. 472)
    OAR: Marriage Bonds – *1687* (c. 475)
    OAR: Marriage Bonds – *1689* (c. 476)
    OAR: Marriage Bonds – *1693* (c. 479)
    OAR: Marriage Bonds – *1696* (c. 482)
    OAR: Marriage Bonds – *1699* (c. 485)
    OAR: Marriage Bonds – *1709* (c. 495)
Oxford Diocesan Records (ODR)
    ODR: Memorandum from Diocesan Books – *1679-1814* (b. 68)
    ODR: 1 February 1660 – 4 October 1662 (c. 3)
    ODR: 27 September 1662-15 April 1665 (c. 4)
    ODR: 7 October 1665-7 March 1668 (c. 5)

ODR: 4 April 1663-12 December 1663 (c. 6)
ODR: 23 June 1666-22 January 1670 (c. 9)
ODR: 19 November 1670-27 June 1672 (c. 11)
ODR: 28 August 1675-7 July 1677 (c. 13)
ODR: 16 January 1686–13 November 1686 (c. 14)
ODR: Citations – 1662-1664 (c. 39)
ODR: Citations – 1664-1667 (c. 40)
ODR: Citations – 1678-1681 (c. 46)
ODR: Citations – 1688-1691 (c. 49)
ODR: Miscellaneous Citations (c. 62)
ODR: Excommunications – 1633-1791 (c. 99)
ODR: Excommunication Schedules – 1662-1667 (c. 100)
ODR: 1 June 1678–27 November 1680 (c. 2134)
ODR: 15 October 1664 – 30 September 1665 (d. 12)
ODR: Marriage Bonds (d. 58)
ODR: Marriage Bonds (d. 60)
ODR: Marriage Bonds (d. 70)
ODR: Marriage Bonds (d. 76)
ODR: Marriage Records – W 1634-1704 (d. 92/2)
ODR: Bishop Fell's Notes on Dissenters – 1679-1685 (d. 708)
Oxford Parish Records
Parish Register of All Saints – 1559-1810 (Par 189/1/R1/1)
Parish Register of All Saints – 1678-1812 (Par 189/1/R1/2)
Parish Register of St Aldate's – 1678-1813 (MS DD Par Oxford – St Aldate's b.1)
Parish Register of St Cross, Hollywell – 1654-1812 (Par 199/1/R1/1)
Parish Register of St Ebbe's – 1557-1672 (MS DD Par Oxford - St Ebbe's b. 33)
Parish Register of St Ebbe's – 1678-1812 (MS DD Par Oxford – St Ebbe's b. 35)
Parish Register of St Giles – 1576-1680 (MS DD Par Oxford – St Giles b.1)
Parish Register of St Giles – 1679-1768 (MS DD Par Oxford – St Giles c.1)
Parish Register of St Martin's – 1569-1705 (Par 207/1/R1/2)
Parish Register of St Martin's – 1678-1789 (Par 207/1/R1/4)
Parish Register of St Mary Madalene – 1602-1662 (Par 208/1/R1/1)
Parish Register of St Mary the Virgin – 1599-1694 (Par 209/1/R1/1)
Parish Register of St Mary the Virgin – 1678-1812 (Par 209/1/R1/4)
Parish Register of St Michael-at-the-Northgate – 1558-1666 (Par 211/1/R1/1)
Parish Register of St Michael-at-the-Northgate – 1653-1683 (Par 211/1/R1/2)
Parish Register of St Michael-at-the-Northgate – 1683-1736 (Par 211/1/R1/3)
Parish Register of St Peter-in-the-Bailey – 1585-1646 (Par 214/1/R1/1)
Parish Register of St Peter-in-the-Bailey – 1659-1689 (Par 214/1/R1/2)
Parish Register of St Peter-in-the-Bailey – 1684-1742 (Par 214/1/R1/3)
Parish Register of St Peter-in-the-East – 1559-1653 (Par 213/1/R1/1)
Parish Register of St Peter-in-the-East – 1600-1673 (Par 213/1/R1/2)
Parish Register of St Peter-in-the-East – 1653-1807 (Par 213/1/R1/3)
Parish Register of St Peter-in-the-East – 1670-1812 (Par 213/1/R1/5)
Parish Register of St Thomas – 1655-1755 (Par 217/1/R1/1)
Oxford Petty Sessions Records
Oxford Petty Sessions Roll – 1656-1678 (O.5.11)
Oxford Petty Sessions Roll – 1679-1712 (O.5.12)
Oxford Petty Sessions Clerk's Notebook – 1687-1701 (O.2.1)
Oxford Wills and Probate Records (OWPR)
Dorothy Eyers (OWPR 164/5/1) – Bond dated 18 December 1663

John Hatchman (OWPR 80/4/17) – Bond dated 11 November 1661
Frances Higgins (OWPR 134/1/20) – Will probated 25 July 1723
John Higgins (OWPR 132/4/21) – Will probated 6 May 1693
Mary Higgins (OWPR 34/5/4) – Will probated 11 November 1696
John Hitch (OWPR 34/3/26) – Will dated 23 January 1688; Inventory dated 18 April
    1688
Humphrey Jennings (OWPR 82/2/6) – Bond dated 21 August 1685
John Jennings (OWPR 137/1/6) – Will probated 3 May 1703
Joseph Jennings (OWPR 137/1/23) – Will probated 4 August 1713
John Johnson (OWPR 38/1/3) – Will probated 8 October 1677
Jonathan King (OWPR 169/2/15) – Bond dated 10 November 1719
Richard King (OWPR 138/2/35) – Will probated 27 September 1699
Ellinor Seale (OWPR 149/9/19) – Bond dated 19 February 1681
Sarah Teasdale (OWPR 175/3/13) – Bond dated 21 February 1721
John Tombs (OWPR 87/3/5) – Bond dated 16 February 1633
Ann Toms (OWPR 66/2/64) – Will probated 11 November 1651
Ellenora Toms (OWPR 14/3/93) – Inventory dated 19 April 1627
John Toms (OWPR 175/2/27) – Bond dated 2 March 1694
Tobias Toms (OWPR 66/1/43) – Will probated 28 September 1633
Thomas Williams (OWPR 88/2/34) – Bond dayed 27 January 1671
Edward Wyans senior (OWPR 72/1/9) – Will probated 13 March 1671
Edward Wyans junior (OWPR 73/2/3) – Will probated 23 May 1687
Thomas Wyans (OWPR 71/4/2) – Will probated 14 April 1664
Oxfordshire Quarter Sessions – Easter 1701 (QS/1701/EA), folio 76 = Jonathan King
    bond of recognizance
Precedents – 1660-1710 (N.4.6)
Rent Rolls
    Rent Roll for 1658 (A.1.1 – CT.1.E.02).
    Rent Roll for 1660 (A.1.1 – CT.1.E.03).
    Rent Roll for 1663 (A.1.1 – CT.1.E.04).
Suits with the University – 1634-1680 (F.4.3), folios 170-173 – on the coronation of
Charles II on 23 April 1661
Suits with the University: Barbour v. Dodwell – 1979 (N.4.15).
Sundry Documents – Hester's Collections I – 1549-1750 (F.5.2), folio 140 = Petition for
Town Hall.
Taxes and Susidies
    Subsidies granted to the King by Parliament (B.1.4)
    Lay Subsidy of 20 March 1641 (B.1.4c) – contains 1 folio (probably the Oxford
        record of *Lay Subsidy of 10-23 December 1640* (E 179/164/477))
    Lay Subsidy of 6 December 1641 (B.1.4d) – contains 1 folio and was collected 6
        December 1641
    Lay Subsidy of 11 April 1664 (B.1.4f) – contains 1 folio
Poll Tax of 1667 (P.5.7) = published in Salter (1923): 213-336.
    War Taxes – 1667-1668 (P.5.8) = Records for seven assessments for the years 1667-
    1668
        Collection of 24 June 1667 – folios 1-19 = This was for the 10th of 12 quarterly
            assessments of the 'Royal Ayde Act' passed on 9 February 1665, and for the
            6th of 8 quarterly assessments of the 'Additional Act' passed on 31 October
            1665 (published by Salter (1923): 337-353)

Collection of 29 September 1667 – folios 20-39 = This was for the 11th of 12 quarterly assessments of the 'Royal Ayde' Tax, and for the 7th of 8 quarterly assessments of the 'Additional Act'

Collection of 21 December 1667 – folios 40-56 = This was for the 12th of 12 quarterly assessments of the 'Royal Ayde' Tax, and for the 8th of 8 quarterly assessments of the 'Additional Act'

Collection of 26 March 1668 – folios 57-73 = This was for the so-called 'Act for Assessment to the Duke of York', passed by the Cavalier Parliament on 31 October 1665, which was collected together with the taxes levied under the 'Act for Granting £1,256,347 13*s* for the War against the Dutch', passed on 8 February 1668

Collection of 26 June 1668 – folios 74-88 = This was a quarterly tax assessment relating to the 'Act for Granting £1,256,347 13*s* for the War against the Dutch'

Collection of 26 September 1668 – folios 89-103 = This was a quarterly tax assessment relating to the 'Act for Granting £1,256,347 13*s* for the War against the Dutch'

Collection of 26 December 1668 – folios 104-117 = This was a quarterly tax assessment relating to the 'Act for Granting £1,256,347 13*s* for the War against the Dutch'. Lists of Assessors – folios 132-125

Taxes – 1691-1694 (P.5.9) = Records for nine assessments for the years 1692-1695
  Poll Tax of 10 March 1692 – folios 2 recto-30 recto
  Poll Tax of 27 June 1692 - 2nd Quarterly payment – folios 34 recto-62 recto
  Poll Tax of 1693 – folios 63 verso–recto
  1694 – folios 95 verso-125 verso
  2 May 1694 – folios 126 recto-147 recto
  27 August 1694 – folios 148 recto-162 recto
  20 November & 17 December 1694 – folios 162 verso-179 verso
  25 February 1695 – 4th Quarterly payment – folios 180 recto-192 recto
  1692 – Refunds and releases from payment – folios 205 verso-193 recto

Taxes – 1694-1746 (P.5.10)
  Poll Tax of 1694 (P.5.10) – folios 1-15
  Poll Tax of 1695 (P.5.10) – folios 17-25
  Marriage, Birth and Burial Tax of 1695 (P.5.10) – folios 27-28 – 5 parishes only
  Poll Tax of 1696 (P.5.10) – folios 29-46
  Window Tax of 1696 (P.5.10) – folios 48-59 = published in Hobson (1939): 340-372
  Window Tax of 1697 (P.5.10) – folios 60-66
  Marriage, Birth and Burial Tax of 1696 (P.5.10) – folios 159-162

Manuscripts and Documents in Dr. Williams's Library, London

James Penny Letter to Mr. Norton (18 June 1672) - Richard Baxter's *Letters*, Volume 2, No. 51

Church Book of the Francis Bampfield Congregation 1686-1843 – Photograph copy of MSS presented to Dr. Williams Library by the Seventh Day Congregation, Plainfield, New Jersey in 1952

Manuscripts and Documents in the Library of the Royal Society, London

BL. 1.16 – Letter from Ralph Austen to Robert Boyle (14 January 1665)

CL.P. X (iii) 7 – Austen's Proposal for Planting Timber and Fruit-Trees (14 December 1664)

Royal Society MS B 1, no. 90 – Letter from Robert Boyle to Henry Oldenburg (17 September 1665)

Royal Society Letter-Book – Supplement, Volume 2, B-C (1663-1693), pages 31-33 – copy of Boyle's letter to Oldenburg cited above

Seventeenth-Century Newspapers and Journals

A Continuation of certain Speciall and Remarkable passages from both Houses of Parliament, Number 26 (2-9 September 1646)

The Impartial Protestant Mercury

The Impartial Protestant Mercury (No. 37 - 26-30 August 1681)

Journal of the House of Commons (JHC)

    JHC 7: 742 – Parliamentary commission for Roger Hatchman

    JHC 7: 752-3 – Parliament grants military commissions for Oxford (9 August 1659)

    JHC 7: 844 – On Thomas Williams and tax assessments for Oxford

The London Gazette

    The London Gazette #2255 (Monday, 27 June to Thursday, 30 June 1687)

    The London Gazette #2294 (Thursday 10 November to Monday 14 November 1687)

The Loyall Scout

    The Loyall Scout (Friday, July 22 to Friday, July 19, 1659)

    The Loyall Scout (Friday, July 29 to Friday, August 5, 1659)

    The Loyall Scout 28 (4-11 November 1659)

Mercurius Politicus

    Mercurius Politicus #582, page 647 (5 August 1659) – Commissioners appointed for Oxfordshire

    Mercurius Politicus #583, pages 664-665 (11-18 August 1659),– on the arrest of Lord Falkland

The Publick Intelligencer

    The Public Intelligencer, No. 187 (Monday, July 25 to Monday, August 1, 1659):

    The Publick Intelligencer, No. 201 (31 October – 7 November 1659)

Speciall Passages and certain Informations from severall places (Number 5: 6-13 September 1642)

The Weekly Intelligencer of the Common-Wealth, No. 5 (Tuesday, May 31 to Tuesday, June 7, 1659).

The Weekly Post

    The Weekly Post (Tuesday August 2, to Tuesday August 9, 1659)

    The Weekly Post, No. 27 (1-8 November 1659)

Seventeenth-Century Tracts, Broadsheets, Pamphlets and Books

Abingdons and Alisburies Present Miseries (1642).

An Act for An Assessment at the Rate of One hundred and twenty thousand Pounds by the Moneth, for Six Moneths; From the Twenty fifth day of December 1653, to the Twenty fourth day of June then next ensuing (1653).

An Act for An Assessment of One Hundred Thousand Pounds by the Moneth, upon England, Scotland, and Ireland, for six Moneths (1659).

An Act for An Assessment upon England, at the Rate of Sixty thousand Pounds by the Moneth, for Three Moneths; From the Twenty fifth day of March 1657, to the Twenty fourth day of June then next ensuing (1657).

The Act of Toleration (1689).

The Act of Uniformity (1662).

An Act Touching Marriages and the Registring thereof; and also touching Births and Burials (1653).

Allen, William *Killing; No Murder: with some Additions Briefly Discussed in Three Questions* (1657).

The Answer of the Officers at Whitehall to the Letter from the Officers of the Parliaments Army in Scotland from Linlithgow, Oct. 22, with a Return of the General and Officers in Scotland thereunto (1659).

The Arraignment, Tryal and Condemnation of Stephen Colledge for High Treason (1681).

The Arraignment, Tryall, Conviction, and Confession of Francis Deane ... and of John Faulkner ... for the Murther of ... Mr. Daniel (1643).

Austen, Ralph *A Treatise of Fruit-trees Shewing the manner of Grafting, Setting, Pruning and Ordering of them ... With the Alimentall and Physical Use of Fruits* (1653, 1657).

_____ *The Spiritual Use of an Orchard, or Garden of Fruit Trees* (1653, 1657).

_____ *Observations upon some part of Sr Francis Bacons Naturall History as it concernes,Fruit Trees, Fruits, and Flowers: especially the Fifth, Sixth, and Seaventh Centuries, Improving the Experiments mentioned to the best Advantage* (1658) .

_____ *A Treatise of Fruit-Trees, Shewing the manner of Planting, Grafting, Pruning, and ordering of them in all respects according to Rules of Experience Gathered in the space of Thirty-seven Years, whereunto is Annexed Observations Upon Sr. Fran. Bacons Natural History as it concerns Fruit-trees, Fruits, and Flowers, Also, Directions for Planting of Wood for Building, Fuel, and other uses, whereby the Value of Lands may be much improved in a short time, with small Cost and little Labour* (1665).

_____ *A Dialogue, or Familiar Discourse, and conference between the Husbandman, and Fruit-trees in his Nurseries, Orchards, and Gardens* (1676).

_____ *The Strong Man Armed not Cast out, But Removed to a stronger Hold: Viz. From Profaneness to Hypocrisie* (1676).

Bampfield, Francis *The Judgment of Mr. Francis Bamfield ... for the Observation of the Jewish ... Sabboth* (1672).

_____ *All in One* (1677).

_____ *The House of Wisdom* (1681).

_____ *A Name, An After-One* (1681).

_____ *The Holy Scriptures* (1684).

_____ *A Just Appeal from Lower Courts on Earth* (1683).

_____ *The Lord's Free Prisoner* (1683).

Bloody Newes from Dover (1647).

Blount, Thomas *Animadversions upon Sr Richard Baker's Chronicle* (1672).

Boyle, Robert *Free Discourse Against Swearing* (1695).

A Brief Confession or Declaration of Faith set forth by many of us who are (falsely) called Ana-Baptists (1660).

A Brief History of the Rise, Growth, Reign, Supports, and sodain fatal Foyl of Popery during the three Years and an half of James the Second, King of England, Scotland, France and Ireland, together with a description of the Six Popish Pillars (1690).

Burrough, Edward *Declaration of the present Sufferings of above 140 Persons of the people of God ... called Quakers* (1659).
Bunyan, John *The Pilgrim's Progress, The* (1678).
Chillenden, Edmund *The Inhumanity of the Kings Prison Keeper at Oxford* (1643).
A Collection of Several Letters and Declarations Sent by General Monck (1660).
Colledge, Stephen *The Speech and Carriage of Stephen Colledge at Oxford before the Castle on Wednesday, August 31, 1681* (1681).
The Complaining Testimony of Some ... of Sions Children (1656).
The Compton Census (1676)
The Confession of Faith, of those Churches which are commonly (though falsely) called Anabaptists (1644).
A Congratulation of the Protestant Joyner to Anthony King of Poland upon his Arrival in the Lower World (1681).
The Conventicle Act (1664).
Croese, Gerardus *The General History of the Quakers* (1696).
The Declaration of Indulgence (1672).
A Declaration of Several of the Churches of Christ and Godly People in and about the Citie of London (1654).
A Declaration of the Commander in Chief of the Forces in Scotland (1659).
The Declaration of the County of Oxon to His Excellency the Lord General Monck (1660).
A Declaration of the Lords and Commons ... Concerning an insolent Letter sent to M. Clarke ... from Sir John Biron, Knight (1642).
A Defence of the Rights and Priviledges of the University of Oxford (1690).
A Description of the Seige of Basing Castle Kept by the Lord Marquisse of Winchester for the Service of His Majesty: Against, the Forces of the Rebells, under Command of Colonell Norton (1644).
Die Veneris, 21 April 1648 – An Order of the Commons assembled in Parliament enabling the Visitors of Oxford to displace such Fellows, and other Officers and Members of Colledges, as shall contemn the Authority of Parliament (1648).
An Essay Toward Settlement upon a Sure Foundation (1659).
Exceeding Good News from Oxfordshire (1642).
Fairfax, Thomas *A Declaration from His Excellencie Sr Thomas Fairfax and His Councell of War concerning their proceeding in the Proposalls prepared and agreed on by the Councell of the Armie* (1647).
Fanatique Queries, Propos'd to the present Assertors of the Good Old Cause (1660).
Featley, Daniel *The Dippers Dipt, or, the Anabaptist duck'd and plung'd over head and eares* (1645).
Fell, John *Articles of Visitation & Enquiry Exhibited to the Ministers, Churchwardens, and Sidemen of every Parish in the primary Episcopal Visitation of the Right Reverend Father in God John* (1679).
Fiennes, William (Viscount Say and Sele) *Folly and Madnesse Made Manifest* (1659).
Finch, Leopold *The Case of Mr Jonas Proast* (1693).
Fisher, Samuel *The Rustics Alarm to the Rabbires* (1660).
Fletcher, Elizabeth *A Few Words in Season to all the Inhabitants of the Earth* (1660).
Ford, Stephen *An Epistle to the Church of Christ in Chippin-Norton* (1657).
Greenwood, Daniel *Vice-Chancellor's Declaration of 9 January 1651* (1652a).
_____ *Vice-Chancellor's Declaration of 22 March 1651* (1652b) .
_____ *Vice-Chancellor's Declaration of 5 July 1652* (1652c) .
Gumble, Thomas *The Life of General Monck, Duke of Albemarle, &tc. With Remarks Upon His Actions* (1671).

A Happy Victory Obtained by the Trained Band of Oxford (1642).

Hartlib, Samuel *Designe for Plentie by a Universall Planting of Fruit Trees* (1652).

_____ *The Reformed Virginian Silk-Worm, or, a Rare and New Discovery of a speedy way, and easie means, found out by a young Lady in England she having made full proof thereof in May, Anno 1652* (1655)

Hawles, John *Remarks upon the Tryals of Edward Fitzharris, Stephen Colledge, Count Coningsmark, The Lord Russel, Colonel Sidney, Henry Cornish, and Charles Bateman* (1689).

Here followeth a true Relation of Some of the Sufferings inflicted upon the servrnts [sic] of the Lord who are called Quakers (1654).

Hicks, Thomas *Three Dialogues between a Christian and a Quaker* (1674).

Hicks, William *Oxford Drollery, Being New Poems and Songs* (1671).

His Majesties Declaration to All His Loving Subjects Concerning the Treasonable Conspiracy Against His Sacred Person and Government Lately Discovered (1683).

Hubberthorne, Richard *A True Testimony of the Zeal of Oxford-Professors and University-men* (1654).

Hughes, W. *Munster and Abingdon* (1657).

The Humble Apology of some commonly called Anabaptists (1661).

The Humble Petition of the Mayor, Aldermen, Bayliffs and Commonalty of the City of Oxon (1649).

Innocency Vindicated: or, Reproach Wip'd Off (1689).

Ireton, Henry *The Heads of the Proposals* (1947).

_____ *A Remonstrance of His Excellency Thomas Lord Fairfax, Lord Generall of the Parliaments Forces, and of the Generall Councell of Officers Held at St Albans the 16 of November, 1648* (1648).

Jackson, James *The Strong Man armed Cast Out, and his goods spoiled: or, The poorman sitting at Jesus' feet clothed, and in his right mind* (1674).

_____ *The Malice of the Rebellious Husband-men against The True Heir, Plainly discovered in this Brief Reply to the Blasphemies, Lies, and Slanders, of Ra. Austen* (1676).

Jessey, Henry *A Narrative Of the late Proceeds at White-Hall, Concerning the Jews* (1956).

Johnson, Edward *An Examination of the Essay, Or, An Answer to the Fifth Monarchy* (1659).

Kennett, White *Some Remarks on the Life, Death, and Burial of Mr. Henry Cornish, B.D.* (1699).

Kiffen, William *A Glimpse of Sions Glory* (1641).

Lamb, Thomas [?] *The Fountain of Free Grace Opened* (1645).

Langley, John, *Gemitus Columbae: The Mournfull Note of the Dove* (1644).

L'Estrange, Roger *Notes Upon Stephen Colledge* (1681a).

_____ *A Letter from A Gentlemen in London to his Friend in the Countrey on the Occasion of the late Tryal of Stephen Colledge* (1681b).

A Letter from a Person of Quality in Edenburgh to an Officer of the Army, wherein is given a true account of Generall Moncks proceedings (1659).

A Letter from Collonel Barkestead, Collonel Okey, and Miles Corbet, to Their Friends in the Congregated Churches in London (1662).

A Letter from Mr. Edward Whitaker to the Protestant Joyner upon his being sent to Oxford (1681).

A Letter from the Grand-Jury of Oxford to the London Grand-Jury relating to the Case of the Protestant Joyner (1681).

A Letter of the Officers of the Army in Scotland under the Commander in Chief there to the Officers of the Army in England (1659).

A Letter Sent by Col. Cobbet from the General Council of Officers to Gen. Monk (1659).

Lieutenant General Cromwells Letter to the Honourable William Lenthall Esq; Speaker of the House of Commons (1645).

Lluelyn, Martin *Men-Miracles, with Other Poems* (1646).

Locke, John *A Letter Concerning Toleration* (1689).

Loggan, David *Oxonia Illustrata* (1675).

A Memoriall Intended to be delivered to the Lords States, Monday 10 March, Stilo Novo, to the High and Mighty Lords, the States of Holland, by the Forraign Anabaptist Churches, upon the apprehending and giving up Colonel Barkestead, Colonel Okey and Mr. Miles Corbet to the English Resident (1662).

Mews, Peter *The Ex-ale-tation of Ale* (1663).

Milton, John *Paradise Lost* (1668).

A Narrative of the Proceedings of the General Assembly (1689).

A Narrative of the Proceedings of the General Assembly (1690) .

A Narrative of the Proceedings of the General Assembly (1691).

North, Sir Francis *A Letter concerning the Tryal at Oxford of Stephen Colledge, August 17, 1681* (1681a).

_____ *The Arraignment, Tryal and Condemnation of Stephen Colledge for High Treason in Conspiring the Death of the King, the Levying of War, and the Subversion of the Government* (1681b).

The Northern Queries from The Lord Gen: Monck his Quarters; sounding an Allarum to all Loyal Hearts and Freeborn English men (1659).

Nutt, Thomas *The Humble Request of Certain Christians, reproachfully called Anabaptists* (1643).

The Office of the Clerk of Assize (1682).

Ollyffe, John *A Sermon Preach'd at the Funeral of the Revd Mr. Henry Cornish, B.D.* (1699).

An Owl at Athens: Or, A True Relation of the Enterance of the Earle of Pembroke into Oxford, April xi. 1648 (1648).

Pendarves, John *Arrows Against Babylon* (1656).

A Perfect Diurnal of the Passages of the Souldiers that are under the Command of The Lord Say in Oxford (1642).

Plot, Robert *The Natural History of Oxfordshire* (1677).

A Poem (by way of Elegie) upon Mr. Stephen Colledge, Vulgarly known by the Name of the Protestant Joyner (1681).

Price, John *The Mystery and Method of His Majesty's Happy Restauration Laid Open to Publick View* (1680).

The Protestant Joyners Ghost to Hone the Protestant Carpenter in Newgate (1683).

A Remonstrance of the Army (1648).

Resolved upon the question by the Parliament, that all the militias in the respective counties, and the powers given to them, be and are hereby revoked (1660).

Reynolds, Edward *A Sermon Touching the Use of Humane Learning* (1658).

Several Letters from the Lord General Monck (1660).

A Short History of the Anabaptists of High and Low Germany (1642).

The Speeches, Discourses, and Prayers of Col. John Barkstead, Col. John Okey, and Miles Corbet; upon the 19th of April, being the Day of their Suffering at Tyburn (1662).

The Standard of the Lord Lifted Up Against the Kingdom of Satan (1653).

Stennet, Edward *The Seventh Day is the Sabbath of the Lord* (1664).

Stennet, Joseph *The Groans of a Saint under the burden of a mortal body* (1695).

Stubbs, Philip *Christial Glas for Christian Women: contayning a most excellent Discourse of the Godly Life and Christian Death of Mrs. Katherine Stubbs* (1689).

Taylor, John *A Three-fold Discourse Betweene Three Neighbours, Algate, Bishopsgate, and John Heyden the late Cobler of Hounsditch, a Professed Brownist, Whereunto is added a true Relation (by way of Dittie) of a lamentable fire which happened at Oxford two nights before Christ-tide last, in a religious brothers shop, known by the name of John of All-trades* (1642).

A Preter-Pluperfect, Spick and Span New Nocturnall (1643).

A Testimony to truth, agreeing with an Essay for Settlement upon a sure foundation (1659).

A True and Most Sad Relation of the Hard Usage and Extreme Cruelty Used on Captaine Wingate, Captaine Vivers, Captaine Austin etc., (1643).

True and New Newes with an example from Warwick Castle, and also other parts, especially upon the anti-round-heads (1642).

True News from Oxford (1642).

A True Relation of a Notorious Cheater one Robert Bullock (1663).

A True Relation of the Manner of Taking the Earl of Northampton (1642).

University News, or, The Unfortunate Proceedings of the Cavaliers in Oxford (1642).

Vicars, John *A Looking-glass for Malignants, or God's hand against God-haters* (1643).

A Brief Review of the most material Parliamentary Proceedings of this Present Parliament (1652).

A Warning for England, Especially for London in the Famous History of the Frantick Anabaptists, Their Wild Preachings and Practices in Germany (1642).

A Warning-Piece to the General Council of the Army, Being Sundry Concurrent Essaies Towards a Righteous Settlement (1659).

Weaver, Thomas *Songs and Poems of Love and Drollery* (1654).

The Whiggs Lamentation for the Death of their Dear Brother Colledge, The Protestant Joyner (1681).

The Whole Business of Sindercombe from first to last, it being a Perfect Narrative of his Carriage during the time of his imprisonment in the Tower of London (1657).

Wood, Anthony *Athenae Oxonienses*, 2 Volumes (1692).

The Woollen Act (1678).

A Word to the Twenty Essayes towards a Settlement (1659).

Yarranton, Andrew *A Full Discovery of the First Presbyterian Sham-Plot* (1681).

Other Sources

Abernathy, George R, 'Clarendon and the Declaration of Indulgence', *Journal of Ecclesiastical History* 11 (1960): 55-73.

Adair, John *By the Sword Divided: Eyewitness Accounts of the English Civil War* (Stroud: Sutton Publishing, 1998).

Alden, Edward C *The Old Church at New Road: A Contribution to the History of Oxford Nonconformity* (Oxford: Alden & Co. Ltd., Bocardo Press, 1904).

Alden's Oxford Guide (Oxford: Alden & Co. Ltd., Bocardo Press, 1910).

Allott, Stephen *Friends in Oxford: The History of a Quaker Meeting* (Williton, Somerset: Gants Hill Press, 1952).

Ashley, Maurice *Cromwell's Generals* (London: Jonathan Cape, 1954).

_____ *The Glorious Revolution of 1688* (London: Hodder and Stoughton, 1966).

_____ *General Monck* (London: Jonathan Cape, 1977).

Atkin, Malcolm *'Cromwell's Crowning Mercy': The Battle of Worcester, 1651* (Stroud: Sutton Publishing, 1998).

Aylmer, G E *The State's Servants: The Civil Service of the English Republic, 1649 – 1660* (London: Routledge & Kegan Paul, 1973).

Baines, Arnold H J, *'Innocency Vindicated: or, Reproach Wip'd Off*, The Baptist Quarterly 16 (1955-56): 164-170.

Ball, Bryan W *The Seventh-day Men: Sabbatarians and Sabbatarianism in England and Wales, 1600-1800* (Oxford: Clarendon Press, 1994).

Bate, Frank *The Declaration of Indulgence 1672: A Study in the Rise of Organised Dissent* (London: University Press of Liverpool, 1908).

Bauman, Richard *Let Your Words Be Few: Symbolism of Speaking and Silence Among Seventeenth Century Quakers* (Cambridge: Cambridge University Press, 1983).

Beddard, Robert *A Kingdom Without a King: The Journal of the Provisional Government of the Revolution of 1688* (Oxford: Phaidon, 1988).

Beeson, C F C *Clockmaking in Oxfordshire 1400-1850* (Oxford: Museum of the History of Science, 1989 3rd edition).

Bennett, Jim (and Scott Mandelbrote) *The Garden, the Ark, the Tower, the Temple: Biblical metaphors of knowledge in early modern Europe* (Oxford: The Museum of the History of Science, 1998).

Besse Joseph *A Collection of the Sufferings of the People Called Quakers for the Testimony of a Good Conscience,* 2 Volumes (London: Luke Hinde, 1753).

Birch, Thomas (ed) *A Collection of the State Papers of John Thurloe,* 6 Volumes (London, 1742).

_____ (ed) *The History of the Royal Society of London from Improving of Natural Knowledge from its First Rise,* 4 Volumes (London, 1756, 1757).

Bliss, Philip *Athenae Oxonienses, by Anthony Wood,* 4 Volumes (London: 1813, 1815, 1817, 1820, Third Edition).

_____ *Fasti Oxonienses or Annals of the University of Oxford by Anthony Wood, M.A.,* 2 Volumes, (London: Robert Knaplock, Daniel Midwinter, and Jacob Tonson, 1815, 1820, Third edition).

Brailsford, M R *Quaker Women 1650-1690* (London: Duckworth & Co., 1915).

Braithwaite, William C *The Beginnings of Quakerism* (Cambridge: Cambridge University Press, 1970, Second edition).

Brinkworth, E R, 'The Study and Use of Archdeacons' Court Records: Illustrated from the Oxford Records (1566-1759)', *Transactions of the Royal Historical Society* 25 (1943): 93-119.

Brown, John *John Bunyan (1628-1688) His Life, Times and Work* (London: The Hulbert Publishing Company, 1928).

Brown, Louise Fargo *The Political Activities of the Baptists and Fifth Monarchy Men in England During the Interregnum* (Oxford: Oxford University Press, 1912).

Burrage, Champlin, 'The Fifth Monarchy Insurrections', *English Historical Review* 25 (1910): 722-747.

Burrows, Montagu (ed) *The Register of the Visitors of the University of Oxford from A.D. 1647 to A.D. 1658* (London: The Camden Society, 1881).

Calamy, Edmund *Souldier's Pocket Bible* (1643).

Capp, B S *The Fifth Monarchy Men: A Study of Seventeenth-century English Millenarianism* (London: Faber and Faber, 1972).

_____ *Astrology and the Popular Press: English Almanacs 1500-1800* (Ithaca, New York: Cornell University Press, 1979).

_____ 'The Fifth Monarchy and Popular Millenarianism', in J F McGregor and B Reay (eds) *Radical Religion in the English Reformation* (Oxford: Oxford University Press, 1984): 165-189.

_____ *Cromwell's Navy: The Fleet and the English Revolution, 1648-1660* (Oxford: Clarendon Press, 1989).

_____ *The World of John Taylor the Water Poet, 1578-1653* (Oxford: Clarendon Press, 1994).

Carlton, Charles *Going to the Wars: The Experience of the British Civil Wars, 1638-1651* (London: Routledge, 1992).

Carroll, Kenneth L, 'The Early Quakers and "Going Naked as a Sign"', *Quaker History* 67 (1978): 69-87.

Case, H B *The History of the Baptist Church in Tiverton, 1607-1907* (London: The Baptist Union Publication Department, 1907).

Childs, John, 'The Army and the Oxford Parliament of 1681', *English Historical Review* (1979): 580-587.

_____ '1688', *History* 73 (1988): 398-424.

Clapinson, Mary (ed) *Bishop Fell and Nonconformity: Visitation Documents from the Oxford Diocese, 1682-1683* (Oxfordshire Record Society Volume 52; Leeds: W S Maney and Sons, Ltd, 1980).

Clarendon, Edward *State Papers Collected by Edward, Earl of Clarendon, Volume 3* (Oxford: Clarendon Printing House, 1786).

Clark, Andrew *The Life and Times of Anthony Wood, antiquary, of Oxford, 1632-1695, described by Himself*, 5 Volumes (Oxford: Clarendon Press, 1891, 1892, 1894, 1895, 1900).

Clifford, Helen *A Treasured Inheritance: 600 Years of Oxford College Silver* (Oxford: The Ashmolean Library, 2004).

Cole, Catherine, 'Appendix: The Wall Paintings at No. 118 High Street, Oxford: A Possible Attribution', *Oxoniensia* 37 (1972): 205-207.

Colvin, Christina, 'Oxford: Protestant Nonconformity and Other Christian Bodies', in Alan Crossley (ed) *The Victoria History of the Counties of England: Oxfordshire, Volume 4* (Oxford: Oxford University Press, 1979): 415-424.

Cooper, Janet, 'Markets and Fairs', in Alan Crossley (ed) *The Victoria History of the Counties of England: Oxfordshire, Volume 4* (Oxford: Oxford University Press, 1979): 305-312.

Coulton, Barbara, 'Cromwell and the "readmission" of the Jews on England, 1656', *Cromwelliana* (2001): 21-38.

Coward, Barry *The Cromwellian Protectorate* (Manchester: Manchester University Press, 2002).

Crawford, Judith (ed) *The Hartlib Papers Project, 2* CD-Rom set (Ann Arbor, Michigan: The University of Michigan, 1995).

Crawford, Patricia, 'The Challenges to Patriarchalism: How did the Revolution affect Women?', in John Morrill (ed) *Revolution and Restoration: England in the 1650s* (London: Collins & Brown, 1992): 112-128.

Crosby, Thomas *The History of the English Baptists From the Reformation to the Beginning of the Reign of King George I*, 4 Volumes (London: John Robinson, 1738, 1739, 1740 and 1740).

Crossley, Alan, 'Craft Guilds', in Alan Crossley (ed) *The Victoria History of the Counties of England: Oxfordshire, Volume 4* (Oxford: Oxford University Press, 1979): 312-327.

_____ 'City and University', in Nicholas Tyacke (ed) *The History of the University of Oxford IV: Seventeenth-Century Oxford* (Oxford: Oxford University Press, 1997): 105-134.

Cruickshanks, Eveline, 'Attempts to Restore the Stuarts, 1689-96', in Eveline Cruickshanks and Edward Corp (eds) *The Stuart Court in Exile and the Jacobites* (London: The Hambledon Press, 1995): 1-13

Curtis, Mark H *Oxford and Cambridge in Transition 1558-1642* (Oxford: Clarendon Press, 1959).

Davies, Godfrey *The Restoration of Charles II, 1658-1660* (Oxford: Oxford University Press, 1955).

Davis, C A *History of the Baptist Church, King's Road Reading, from its Commencement in 1640* (Reading: *The Reading Observer* Office, 1891).

Dickinson, Michael J *Seventeenth Century Tokens of the British Isles and their Values* (London: Seaby, 1986).

Dorchester-on-Thames Grammar School (Dorchester-on-Thames Archeology & Local History Group: Dorchester-on-Thames, 1976).

Ebsworth, J W, 'College, Stephen', in *Dictionary of National Biography*, Volume IV. Chamber-Craigie (London: Smith, Elder, & Co., 1908): 787-9.

Farrer, A J D, 'The Fifth Monarchy Movement, 1645-1660' *Transactions of the Baptist Historical Society* 2 (1910-11): 166-181.

Fiddes, Paul S, 'Receiving One Another: the History and Theology of the Church Covenant, 1780', in Rosie Chadwick (ed) *A Protestant Catholic Church of Christ: Essays on the History and Life of New Road Baptist Church* (Oxford: New Road Baptist Church, 2003): 65-105.

Firth, Colin H, 'Cromwell and the Expulsion of the Long Parliament in 1653', *English Historical Review* 8 (1893): 526-534.

_____ (ed) *Scotland and the Protectorate: Letters and Papers Relating to the Military Government of Scotland from January 1654 to June 1659* (Edinburgh: Edinburgh University Press, 1899).

_____ (ed) *The Clark Papers, Volume 4* (London: Longmans, Green & Co., 1901).

_____ 'Killing No Murder', *English Historical Review* 17 (1902): 308-311.

_____ *Cromwell's Army: A History of the English Soldier During the Civil Wars, The Commonwealth and the Protectorate* (London: Methuen & Co., 1905).

_____ *The Regimental History of Cromwell's Army*, 2 Volumes (Oxford: Clarendon Press, 1940).

Firth, Colin H (and R S Rait) (eds) *Acts and Ordinances of the Interregnum, 1642-1660*, 2 Volumes, (London: HMSO, 1911).

Fletcher, Carteret J H *A History of the Church and Parish of St Martin's (Carfax), Oxford* (Oxford: B.H. Blackwells, 1896).

Fox, Adam *Oral and Literate Culture in England, 1500-1700* (Oxford Studies in Social History; Oxford: Oxford University Press, 1998).

Fox, John *Holton, Wheatley and Oxford in the Civil War* (Oxford: The Alden Press, 2004).

Fraser, Antonia *The Weaker Vessel: Woman's Lot in Seventeenth-Century England* (London: Methuen, 1985).

Friedman, Jerome *Miracles and the Pulp Press During the English Revolution: The Battle of the Frogs and Fairford's Flies* (London: UCL Press, 1993).

Fulton, John F *A Bibliography of the Honourable Robert Boyle* (Oxford: Clarendon Press, 1961, second edition).

Garrett, Jane *The Triumphs of Providence: The Assassination plot, 1696* (Cambridge: Cambridge University Press, 1980).

Geere Jeremy *Index to Oxfordshire Hearth Tax 1665* (Oxford: Oxfordshire Family History Society, 1985).

Gentles, Ian *The New Model Army in England, Ireland and Scotland, 1645-1653* (Oxford: Blackwell, 1992).

Gill, Catie *Women in the Seventeenth-Century Quaker Community: A Literary Study of Political Identities, 1650-1700* (Ashgate Pulishing Limited: Aldershot, Hampshire 2005).

Goldie, Mark, 'The Theory of Religious Intolerance in Restoration England', in Ole Peter Grell, Jonathan I. Israel and Nicholas Tyacke (eds) *From Persecution to Toleration: The Glorious Revolution and Religion in England* (Oxford: Clarendon Press, 1991): 331-368.

Grainger, John D *Cromwell Against the Scots: The Last Anglo-Scottish War, 1650-1652* (East Linton: Tuckwell Press, 1997).

Greaves, Richard L, 'Belcher, John', in Richard L Greaves and Robert Zaller (eds) *Biographical Dictionary of British Radicals in the Seventeenth Century, Volume I: A-F* (Brighton: The Harvester Press, 1982): 52-3.

_____ 'College, Stephen', in Richard L Greaves and Robert Zaller (eds) *Biographical Dictionary of British Radicals in the Seventeenth Century, Volume I: A-F* (Brighton: The Harvester Press, 1982): 161-2.

_____ 'Kelsey, Thomas', in Richard L Greaves and Robert Zaller (eds) *Biographical Dictionary of British Radicals in the Seventeenth Century, Volume II: G-O* (Brighton: The Harvester Press, 1983): 154-5.

_____ *Saints and Rebels: Seven Nonconformists in Stuart England* (Macon: Mercer University Press, 1985).

_____ *Deliver Us From Evil : The Radical Underground in Britain, 1660-1663* (Oxford: Oxford University Press, 1986).

_____ *Enemies Under His Feet: Radicals and Nonconformists in Britain, 1664-1677* (Stanford, California: Stanford University Press, 1990).

_____ *Glimpses of Glory: John Bunyan and English Dissent* (Palo Alto, California: Stanford University Press, 2002).

Green, Ian *Print and Protestantism in Early Modern England* (Oxford: Oxford University Press, 2000).

Grell, Ole Peter (with Jonathan I Israel and Nicholas Tyacke (eds) *From Persecution to Toleration: The Glorious Revolution and Religion in England* (Oxford: Clarendon Press, 1991).

Griffiths, John *An Index to Wills Proved in the Court of the Chancellor of the University of Oxford* (Oxford: Oxford University Press, 1862).

Gutch, John *The History and Antiquities of the University of Oxford, in two books: by Anthony Wood, 2 Volumes* (Oxford, 1792, 1796).

Hall, A Rupert and Marie Boas Hall (ed) *The Correspondence of Henry Oldenburg, Volume II 1663-1665* (Madison, Wisconsin: The University of Wisconsin Press, 1966).

Hambleton, Michael *A Sweet and Hopeful People: The Story of Abingdon Baptist Church 1649-2000* (Wantage: Wessex Press, 2000).

Hardacre, P H, 'William Allen, Cromwellian Agitator and "Fanatic"', *The Baptist Quarterly* 19 (1961-62): 292-308.

Harris, Tim, 'Introduction: Revising the Restoration', in Tim Harris, Paul Seaward, and Mark Goldie (eds) *The Politics of Religion in Restoration England* (Oxford: Basil Blackwell, 1990): 1-28.

_____ *Politics Under the Later Stuarts* (London, 1993).

Hayden, Philip, 'The Baptists in Oxford, 1656-1819,' *The Baptist Quarterly* 29 (1981-82): 127-136.

Henderson, T F, 'Austen, Ralph', in Leslie Stephen and Sidney Lee (eds) *Dictionary of National Biography, Volume 1* (London: Smith, Elder & Co., 1908): 732-3.

Herspring, Dale R *Soldiers, Commissars, and Chaplains: Civil-Military Relations since Cromwell*(Lanham, Maryland: Rowman & Littlefield, 2001).

Hibbert, Christopher (and Edward Hibbert) (eds) *The Encyclopedia of Oxford* (London: Macmillan, 1988).

Hill, Christopher *Society and Puritanism in Pre-Revolutionary England* (London: Secker and Warburg, 1962a).

_____ *Puritanism and Revolution: Studies in Interpretation of the English Revolution of the 17th Century* (London: Mercury Books, 1962b).

_____ *Reformation to Industrial Revolution* (The Pelican Economic History of Britain, Volume 2; Harmondsworth: Pelican Books, 1969).

_____ *God's Englishmen: Oliver Cromwell and the English Revolution* (London: Penguin, 1970).

_____ 'The Radical Critics of Oxford and Cambridge in the 1650s', on John W Baldwin and Richard A Goldtwaite (eds) *Universities in Politics* (Baltimore: Johns Hopkins University Press, 1972): 107-132.

_____ *The World Turned Upside Down: Radical Ideas During the English Revolution* (Harmondsworth: Penguin Books, 1975).

_____ *The Century of Revolution 1603-1714* (London: Abacus Books, 1978).

_____ *Cavaliers and Roundheads: The English at War 1642-1649* (London: HarperCollins Publishers, 1993).

Hiscock, W G *A Christ Church Miscellany* (Oxford: Oxford University Press, 1946).

Historical Manuscripts Commission (HMC) Series 78 – *MSS of Reginald Rawdon Hastings, Volume 2* (London, 1930): 315-316.

Hoad, Joyce, 'Riot in Oxford 1715', *The Oxfordshire Family Historian* 8 (1994): 105-7.

Hobson, M G *Oxford Council Acts, 1665-1701* (Oxford: Clarendon Press, 1939).

Hobson, M G (and H E Salter) *Oxford Council Acts, 1626-1665* (Oxford: Clarendon Press, 1933).

Horle, Craig W, 'Quakers and Baptists, 1647-1660', *The Baptist Quarterly* 26 (1975-6): 344-362.

Houlbrooke, Ralph *Death, Religion, and the Family in England, 1480-1750* (Oxford Studies in Social History: Oxford, Oxford University Press, 1998).

Hunter, Michael *Establishing the New Science: The Experience of the Early Royal Society* (Woodbridge: Boydell, 1989).

Hutchinson, Lucy *Memoirs of the Life of Colonel Hutchinson* (London: Phoenix Press, 2000).

Hutton, Ronald *The Restoration: A Political and Religious History of England and Wales 1658-1667* (Oxford: Oxford University Press, 1985).

Ivimey, Joseph *A History of the English Baptists*, 4 Volumes (London, 1811, 1814, 1823 and 1830).

Jabez-Smith, A R, 'Joseph Williamson and Thomas Lamplugh', *Transactions of the Cumberlad & Westmorland Antiquarian & Archaeological Society* 86 (1986): 145-161.

Jacob, J R *Robert Boyle and the English Revolution: A Study in Social and Intellectual Change* (New York: Burt Franklin & Co., 1977).

_____ 'Booth's Rising of 1659', *Bulletin of the John Rylands Library* 39 (1956-57): 413-443.

Jurkowski, M (with C L Smith and D Crook) *Lay Taxes in England and Wales, 1188-1688* (Kew, Richmond: PRO Publications, 1998).

Kaplan, L, 'Ireton, Henry (1611-1651)', in Richard L Greaves and Robert Zaller (eds) *Biographical Dictionary of British Radicals in the Seventeenth Century, Volume II: G-O* (Brighton: The Harvester Press, 1983): 130-134.

Katz, David S *Philo-Semiticism and the Readmission of the Jews to England, 1603-55* (Oxford: Oxford University Press, 1982).

_____ 'Menasseh Ben Israel's Christian Connection: Henry Jessey and the Jews', in Yosef Kaplan, Henry Méchoulan and Richard H Popkin (eds) *Menasseh Ben Israel and His World* (Leiden: E.J. Brill, 1989): 117-138.

Kearney, Hugh *Gentlemen and Scholars: Universities and Society in pre-industrial Britain, 1500-1700* (London: Faber and Faber, 1970).

Keeble, N H *The Restoration: England in the 1660s* (Oxford: Blackwell Publishing, 2002).

Kent, Susan Kingsley *Gender and Power in Britain, 1640-1990* (London: Routledge, 1990).

Kenyon, John *The Popish Plot* (London: Phoenix Press, 2000).

Kishlansky, Mark, 'The Case of the Army Truly Stated: The Creation of the New Model Army, *Past & Present* 81 (1978): 51-74.

_____ *The Rise of the New Model Army* (Cambridge: Cambridge University Press, 1979).

Klaiber, Ashley J, 'Early Baptist Movements I Suffolk', *The Baptist Quarterly* 4 (1928-29): 116-120.

_____ *The Story of the Suffolk Baptists* (London: The Kingsgate Press, 1931).

Kreitzer, Larry J 'The Fifth Monarchist John Pendarves (†1656) – A Victim of 'Studious Bastard Consumption'?', *The American Baptist Quarterly* 33 (2004a): 281-289.

_____ 'The Election in the Guildhall: A satirical glimpse of Oxford politics in the seventeenth century,' *The Baptist Quarterly* 40 (2004b): 430-435.

_____ '1653 or 1656: When did Oxford Baptists Join the Abingdon Association?', in Anthony R. Cross (ed) *Recycling History or Researching the Past: Studies in Baptist Historiography and Myths* (2005): 207-219.

_____ 'A "Famous prank" in Oxford: The Jacobite Riots of 1715 and the Charge of Sexual Scandal', (forthcoming)

Lacey, D R *Dissent and Parliamentary Politics in England, 1661-1689* (New Brunswick, New Jersey: Rutgers University Press, 1969).

Langley, Arthur S, 'Seventeenth Century Baptist Disputations', *Transactions of the Baptist Historical Society* 6 (1918-19): 216-243.

Laurence, Anne *Parliamentary Army Chaplains, 1642-1651* (Woodbridge, Suffolk: Royal Historical Society, 1990).

Leeds, E Thurlow, 'Oxford Tradesmen's Tokens', in H E Salter (ed) *Surveys and Tokens* (Oxford: Clarendon Press, 1923): 355-451.

Liu, Tai *Discord in Zion: The Puritan Divines and the Puritan Revolution 1640-1660* (The Hague: Martinus Nijhoff, 1973).

Luttrell, Narcissus *A Brief Historical Relation of State Affairs from September 1678 to April 1714, Volume 1* (Oxford: Oxford University Press, 1857).

MacCulloch, Diarmaid *Suffolk and the Tudors: Politics and Religion in an English County, 1500-1600* (Oxford: Clarendon Press, 1986).

Mackinnon, Daniel *Origins and Services of the Coldstream Guards, 2 Volumes* (London: Richard Bentley, 1833).

Madan, Falconer *Oxford Books: A Bibliography of Printed Works Relating to the University and City of Oxford or Printed or Published There, Volume 3, Oxford Literature 1651-1680* (Oxford: The Clarendon Press, 1931).

Magrath, John Richard (ed) *The Flemings in Oxford, Volume 2 (1680-1690)* (Oxford: Clarendon Press, 1913).

Marsh, Christopher, 'In the Name of God? Will-Making and Faith in Early-Modern England', in G H Martin and M Spufford (eds), *The Records of the Nation* (The British Record Society: The Boydell Press, 1990): 215-249.

Marshall, Alan, 'Sir Joseph Williamson and the Conduct of Administration in Restoration England', *Historical Research* 69 (1996): 18-41.

_____ *The Strange Death of Edmund Godfrey: Plots and Politics in Restoration London* (Stroud: Sutton Publishing Limited, 1999).

_____ 'Killing No Murder', *History Today* (2003): 20-25.

Marshall, Lydia M, 'The Levying of the Hearth Tax, 1662-1688', *English Historical Review* 55 (1936): 628-46.

Matthews, A G *Calamy Revised: Being a Revision of Edmund Calamy's Account of the Ministers and Others Ejected and Silenced, 1660-2* (Oxford: Clarendon Press, 1934).

Mayers, Ruth E *1659: The Crisis of the Commonwealth* (The Royal Historical Society/The Boydell Press: Woodbride, Suffolk, 2004).

McDonald, F M S, 'The Timing of General George Monck's March into England, 1 January 1660', *English Historical Review* 105 (1990): 363-376.

McGregor, J F, 'The Baptists: Fount of All Heresy', in J F McGregor and B Reay (eds) *Radical Religion in the English Reformation* (Oxford: Oxford University Press, 1984): 23-63.

Mendelson, Sara (and Patricia Crawford) *Women in Early Modern England* (Oxford: Oxford University Press, 1998).

Miller, John, 'James II and Toleration', in Eveline Cruickshanks (ed) *By Force or By Default?: The Revolution of 1688-89* (Edinburgh: John Donald Publishers, 1989): 8-27.

Milne, Doreen J, 'The Results of the Rye House Plot and their Influence upon the Revolution of 1688', *Transactions of the Royal Historical Society* (5th Series, Volume 1, 1951): 91-108.

Milne-Tyte, Robert *Bloody Jeffreys: The Hanging Judge* (London: Andre Deutsch, 1989).

Moffatt, Harold Charles *Old Oxford Plate* (London: Archibald Constable & Co. Ltd, 1906).

Moore, James L *Earlier and Later Nonconformity in Oxford* (Oxford: Publisher Unknown, 1875).

Munby, Julian, 'A Note on Building Investigations at 113-119 High Street, Oxford,' *Oxoniensia* 65 (2000): 441-442.

Ogle, Octavius, 'The Oxford Market', in Montagu Burrows (ed) *Collectanea, Second Series* (Oxford: Clarendon Press, 1890): 1-136.

_____ *Royal Letters Addressed to Oxford and Now Existing in the City Archives* (London: James Parker and Co., 1892).

Oxford English Dictionary (1994, second edition)

Paintin, Harry *Souvenir of the Centenary 1813-1913* (Oxford: Alden & Co., Ltd., Bocardo Press, 1913).

Payne, Ernest A *The Baptists of Berkshire Through Three Centuries* (London: Carey Kingsgate Press, 1951).

_____ 'More about the Sabbatarian Baptists', *The Baptist Quarterly* 14 (1951-2): 161-166.

Penney, Norman (ed) *The First Publishers of Truth, Being Early Records of the Introduction of Quakerism into the Counties of England and Wales* (London: Headley Brothers, 1907).

Philip, I G, 'River Navigation at Oxford during the Civil War and Commonwealth', *Oxoniensia* 2 (1937): 152-65.

_____ *Journal of Sir Samuel Luke, 3 Volumes* (Oxford: The Oxfordshire Record Society, 1950a, 1950b, 1953).

Poole, William, 'Two Early Readers of Milton: John Beale and Abraham Hill', *Milton Quarterly* 38 (2004): 76-99.

Porter, Stephen, 'The Oxford Fire of 1644', *Oxoniensia* 49 (1984): 289-300.

_____ 'The Oxford Fire Regulations of 1671', *Bulletin of the Institute of Historical Research* (1985): 251-255.

Preston, Arthur E *The Church and Parish of St Nicholas, Abingdon* (Clarendon Press: Oxford Historical Society, 1935).

Ramsey, Robert W *Henry Ireton* (London: Longmans, Green and Co., 1949).

Ricketts, Carl *Pewterers of London, 1600-1900* (London: The Pewter Society, 2001).

Roberts, Stephen K, 'Erbury [Erbery], William (1604-5–1654)', *Oxford Dictionary of National Biography* (Oxford: Oxford University Press, 2004).

Robinson, Henry Wheeler *The Life and Faith of the Baptists* (London: Methuen, 1927).

Rogers, P G *The Fifth Monarchy Men* (Oxford: Oxford University Press, 1966).

Salter, H E *The Oxford Deeds of Balliol College* (Oxford: Clarendon College, 1913).

_____ (ed) *Surveys and Tokens* (Oxford: Clarendon Press, 1923).

_____ *Snappe's Formulary and Other Records* (Oxford: Clarendon Press, 1924).

_____ *Oxford City Properties* (Oxford: Oxford University Press, 1926).

_____ *Oxford Council Acts 1583-1626* (Oxford: Clarendon Press, 1928).

_____ *Cartulary of Oseney Abbey, 6 Volumes* (Oxford: Clarendon Press, 1929a, 1929b, 1931, 1934, 1935, 1936).

_____ *Survey of Oxford*, 2 Volumes (Oxford: Clarendon Press, 1960, 1969).

Sanford, Don A *A Choosing People: The History of the Seventh Day Baptists* (Nashville, Tennessee: Broadman Press, 1992).

Schochet, Gordon J, 'John Locke and religious toleration,' on Lois G Schwoerer (ed) *The Revolution of 1688-1689: Changing perspectives* (Cambridge: Cambridge University Press, 1992): 147-164.

Schulz, T E, 'The Woodstock Glove Industry', *Oxoniensia* 3 (1938): 139-152.

Scott, Jonathan, 'England's Troubles: Exhuming the Popish Plot', in Tim Harris, Paul Seaward, and Mark Goldie (eds) *The Politics of Religion in Restoration England* (Oxford: Basil Blackwell, 1990): 107-131.

Seaward, Paul *The Restoration, 1660-1688* (London, 1991).

Smith, Nigel *Perfection Proclaimed: Language and Literature in English Radical Religion 1640-1660* (Oxford: Clarendon Press, 1989).

Southern, Antonia *Forlorn Hope: Soldier Radicals of the Seventeenth Century* (Lewes, East Sussex: The Book Guild Ltd., 2001).

Spufford, Margaret, 'The importance of religion in the sixteenth and seventeenth centuries', in Margaret Spufford (ed) *The World of Rural Dissenters, 1520-1725* (Cambridge University Press: Cambridge, 1995): 1-102.

Spurr, John, 'Religion in Restoration England', in Lionel K J Glassey (ed) *The Reigns of Charles II and James VII & II* (London: Macmillan Press Ltd., 1997): 90-124.

Spurrier, Edward *Memorials of the Baptist Church Worshipping in Eld Lane Chapel, Colchester* (Colchester: F. Wright, 1889).

Stevens, Walter, 'The Pioneers and their Successors', in Walter Stevens and Walter W Bottoms *The Baptists of New Road, Oxford* (Oxford: Alden Press, 1948): 3-10.

Stevenson, Bill, 'The Social Integrity of Post-Restoration Dissenters, 1660-1725', in Margaret Spufford (ed) *The World of Rural Dissenters, 1520-1725* (Cambridge University Press: Cambridge, 1995): 360-387.

Tate, W E *The Parish Chest: A Study of the Records of Parochial Administration in England* (Cambridge: Cambridge University Press, 1969, 3rd edition).

Teague, Frances, 'A Voice for Hermaphroditical Education', in Danielle Clarke and Elizabeth Clarke (eds) *'This Double Voice': Gendered Writings in Early Modern England* (Basingstoke: Macmillan Press Ltd., 2000): 249-69.

Thirtle, J W, 'The Fifth-Monarchy Manifesto of 1654', in *Transactions of the Baptist Historical Society* 3 (1912-13): 129-53.

Thomas, Keith, 'Women and the Civil War Sects', *Past & Present* 13 (1958): 42-62.

Thomas, Roger, 'Comprehension and Indulgence', in Geoffrey F Nuttall and Owen Chadwick (eds) *From Uniformity to Unity, 1662-1962* (London: SPCK, 1962): 189-253.

Thompson, Edward Maunde (ed) *Letters of Humphrey Prideaux, Sometime Dean of Norwich, to John Ellis, Sometime Under-Secretary of State, 1674-1722* (London: Camden Society, 1875).

Thompson, R H (and Michael J Dickinson) *Sylloge of Coins of the British Isles 44: The Norweb Collection Cleveland, Ohio, USA. Tokens of the British Isles, 1575-1750. Part IV: Norfolk to Somerset* (London: Spink & Son Limited, 1993).

Thompson, Roger *Women in Stuart England and America: A Comparative Study* (London: Routledge & Kegan Paul, 1974).

Thurloe, John *A Collection of the State Papers of John Thurloe*, 7 Volumes (London: Thomas Woodward and Charles Davis, 1742).

Tolmie, Murray *The Triumph of the Saints: The Separate Churches of London 1616-1649* (Cambridge: Cambridge University Press, 1977).

Tomlinson, Steven, 'Burials in Woollen in Oxfordshire', *Oxfordshire Local History* (1981: Volume 1, Number 3): 2-10.

Toon, Peter (ed) *The Oxford Orations of Dr. John Owen* (Callington: Cornwall: Gospel Communication, 1971).

Torbert, Robert *A History of the Baptists* (Valley Forge: Judson Press, 1963 third edition).

Toynbee, Margaret, 'The City of Oxford and the Restoration of 1660', *Oxoniensia* 25 (1960): 73-95 + Plates VI and VII.

Turnbull, G H *Hartlib, Durt and Comenius: Gleanings from Hartlib's Papers* (London: Hodder & Stoughton, 1947).

Turnbull, H W (ed) *The Correspondence of Isaac Newton, Volume II 1676-1687* (Cambridge: Cambridge University Press, 1960).

Turner, G. Lyon *Original Records of Early Nonconformity Under Persecution and Indulgence*, 3 Volumes (London: T. Fisher Unwin, 1911 and 1914).

Turner, James, 'Ralph Austen, An Oxford Horticulturalist of the Seventeenth Century', *Garden History* 6 (1978): 39-45.

_____ 'Austen, Ralph (c. 1612-1676)', *Oxford Dictionary of National Biography* (Oxford: Oxford University Press, 2004).

Tyacke, Nicholas 'Religious Controversy', in Nicholas Tyacke (ed) *The History of the University of Oxford IV: Seventeenth-Century Oxford* (Oxford: Oxford University Press, 1997): 569-619.

_____ *Aspects of Enlish Protestantism, c. 1530-1700* (Manchester: Manchester University Press, 2001).

Underdown, David *Royalist Conspiracy in England, 1649-1660* (New Haven, Connecticut: Yale University Press, 1960).

_____ *Pride's Purge: Politics in the Puritan Revolution* (Oxford: Clarendon Press, 1971).

_____ *Revel, Riot and Rebellion: Popular Politics and Culture in England 1603-1660* (Oxford: Clarendon Press, 1985).

_____ *A Freeborn People: Politics and the Nation in Seventeenth-Century England* (Oxford: Clarendon Press, 1996).

Underwood, A C *A History of the English Baptists* (London: The Kingsgate Press, 1947).

Underwood, T L *Primitivism, Radicalism, and the Lamb's War: The Baptist-Quaker Conflict in Seventeenth-Century England* (Oxford: Oxford University Press, 1977).

Van der Wall, Ernestine G E, 'A Philo-Semitic Millenarian on the Reconciliation of Jews and Christians: Henry Jessey and His "The Glory and Salvation of Jehudah and Israel" (1650)', in David S Katz and Jonathan I Israel (eds) *Sceptics, Millenarians and Jews* (Leiden: E J Brill, 1990): 161-184.

Varley, Frederick John, 'The Castle at Oxford and Its Prisoners', *The Bodleian Quarterly Record* 7 (1932-34): 420-422.

_____ 'Oxford Army List for 1642-1646', *Oxoniensia* 2 (1937): 141-151.

Vernon, Richard, 'Locke's Antagonist, Jonas Proast', *The Locke Newsletter* 24 (1993): 95-106.

Walker, James, 'The English Exiles in Holland During the Reigns of Charles II and James II', *Transactions of the Royal Historical Society*, 4th Series 30 (1948): 111-125.

Watt, Tessa *Cheap Print and Popular Piety, 1550-1640* (Cambridge: Cambridge University Press, 1991).

Watts, Michael R *The Dissenters: From the Reformation to the French Revolution* (Oxford: Oxford University Press, 1978).

Webster, Charles *The Great Instauration: Science, Medicine and Reform, 1626-1660* (London: Duckworth, 1975).

Wedgwood, C V *Oliver Cromwell* (London: Gerald Duckworth & Co. Ltd, 1939).

Weinstock, Maureen M B *Hearth Tax Returns: Oxfordshire, 1665* (Oxford: Oxfordshire Record Society, 1940).

White, Barrie R, 'The Baptists of Reading 1652-1715', *The Baptist Quarterly* 22 (1967-68): 249-270.

_____ 'John Trask (1585-1636) and London Puritanism', *Transactions* 20 (1968): 223-33.

_____ 'William Erbery (1604-1654) and the Baptists', *The Baptist Quarterly* 23 (1969-70): 114-125.

_____ 'John Pendarves, the Calvinistic Baptists and the Fifth Monarchy', *The Baptist Quarterly* 25 (1973-74): 251-71.

_____ *Association Records of the Particular Baptists of England, Wales and Ireland to 1660: Part 3. The Abingdon Association* (London: The Baptist Historical Society, 1974).

_____ *The English Baptists of the Seventeenth Century* (London: The Baptist Historical Society, 1983, 1996).

Whiteman, Anne (ed) *The Compton Census of 1676: A Critical Edition* (Records of Social and Economic History, New Series 10; Oxford: Oxford University Press, 1986).

_____ 'The Compton Census of 1676', in Kevin Schurer and Tom Arkell (eds) *Surveying the People: The interpretation and use of document sources for the study of population in the later seventeenth century* (Leopard's Head Press: Oxford, 1992): 78-96.

Whitley, William T, 'The Bunyan Christening - 1672', *Transactions of the Baptist Historical Society* 2 (1910-11): 255-263.

_____ 'John Tombes as a Correspondent', *Transactions of the Baptist Historical Society* (1920-21): 13-18.

_____ *A History of British Baptists* (London: Charles Griffin & Co., 1932).

_____ 'The Rev. Colonel Paul Hobson: Fellow of Eton', *The Baptist Quarterly* 9 (1938-39): 307-10.

_____ Seventh Day Baptists in England', *The Baptist Quarterly* 12 (1946-48): 252-258.

_____ *Men of the Seventh Day:, or Sabbath Keepers of the Seventeenth Century* (Unpublished typescript in the Angus Library, Regent's Park College, Oxford, no date).

Whittet, T D, 'A survey of apothecaries' tokens, including some previously unrecognized speciment: Part 14: Norfolk to Rutland', *Pharmaceutical Journal* 237 (1986): 111-113.

Wilson, Charles *England's Apprenticeship 1603-1763* (London: Longmans, 1965).

Wilson, Derek *The King and the Gentleman: Charles Stuart and Oliver Cromwell 1599-1649* (London: Pimlico Books, 2000).

Wood, Anthony *Modius Salium: A Collection of Pieces of Humour As Prevail'd at Oxford* (London: R Clements, 1751).

Woodhouse, A S P *Puritanism and Liberty, Being the Army Debates (1647-9) from the Clarke Manuscripts with Supplementary Documents* (London: J.M. Dent and Sons Limited, 1938).

Woolrych, Austin H, 'The Good Old Cause and the Fall of the Protectorate', *Cambridge Historical Journal* 13 (1957): 133-61.

_____ 'The Calling of the Barebones Parliament', *English Historical Review* 80 (1965): 492-513.

_____ 'The English Revolution: An Introduction', in E W Ives (ed) *The English Revolution 1600-1660* (London: Edward Arnold, 1968): 1-33.

_____ *Commonwealth to Protectorate* (Oxford: Clarendon Press, 1982).

Worms, Lawrence, 'Goddard, John (*fl.*. 1631-1663)', *Oxford Dictionary of National Biography* (Oxford: Oxford University Press, 2004).

Wykes, David L, 'Religious Dissent and the Penal Laws: An Explanation of Business Success?', *History* 75 (1990): 39-62.

Indexes

List of Entries in the
Chronological Source Catalogue

#1: 18 April 1610 – Will of Agnes Hatchman (*Dorchester Peculiar* 30/1/17)

#2: 11 May 1610 – John Bosseley lease on 'the antiquated dancing school' outside the North Gates (*Oxford City Ledgers 1578-1636* (D.5.5), folios 180 recto – 181 recto)

#3: 5 June 1612 – John Bosseley lease on 'the antiquated dancing school' outside the North Gates (*Oxford City Ledgers 1578-1636* (D.5.5), folio 189 recto)

#4: 1 September 1620 – Thomas Wyans granted Oxford Citizenship (the 'Freedom of the City') (*Civic Enrolments 1613-1640* (L.5.2), folio 347 verso)

#5: 22 August 1629 – Apprenticeship contract between Thomas Williams and John Nixon (*Civic Enrolments 1613-1640* (L.5.2), folio 184 verso)

#6: 1 November 1631 – Apprenticeship contract between Edward Wyans and Robert White; amended to a contract between Wyans and Richard Phillips on 6 July 1635 (*Civic Enrolments 1613-1640* (L.5.2), folio 214 verso)

#7: 21 February 1632 – Thomas Williams granted Oxford Citizenship (the 'Freedom of the City') (*Civic Enrolments 1613-1640* (L.5.2), folio 359 verso)

#8: 21 February 1632 – Thomas Williams granted Oxford Citizenship (the 'Freedom of the City') (*City Council Proceedings 1629-1663* (A.5.7), folio 31 verso)

#9: 19 October 1632 – Apprenticeship contract between James Jennings and Humphrey Jennings (*Civic Enrolments 1613-1640* (L.5.2), folio 229 verso)

#10: 22 October 1632 – Edward Wyans presented as an apprentice to the Guild of Cordwainers by Robert White (*MS Morrell 23 – List of Cordwainers' Apprentices (1590-1660)*, folio 72 verso)

#11: 31 August 1635 – Thomas Williams agrees to help sponsor a poor boy from the house of correction (*City Council Proceedings 1629-1663* (A.5.7), folio 58 verso)

#12: 26 September 1636 – William Stokes and John Bosseley lease on 'the antiquated dancing school' outside the North Gates (*Oxford City Ledgers 1636-1675* (D.5.6), folios 5 verso – 6 verso)

#13: 22 December 1636 – Roger Hatchman's lease on a property in the parish of St. Thomas (*Christ Church Lease*)

#14: 22 May 1637 – Apprenticeship contract between William Davis and Thomas Williams (*Civic Enrolments 1613-1640* (L.5.2), folio 296 recto)

#15: 15 June 1638 – Robert King granted Oxford Citizenship (the 'Freedom of the City') (*City Council Proceedings – 1629-1663* (A.5.7), folio 83 recto)

#16: 12 December 1638 – Robert King granted Oxford Citizenship (the 'Freedom of the City') (*Civic Enrolments 1613-1640* (L.5.2), folio 340 verso)

#17: 25 August 1640 – Dispute between the masons and freemasons working in University College (*MS Twyne-Langbaine IV*, folio 87 recto and verso)

#18: 25 August 1640 – Dispute between the masons and freemasons working on University College (*Gerard Langbaine's Collections Volume 3* (WP γ 26 1) page 454)

#19: 11 September 1640 – James Jennings granted Oxford Citizenship (the 'Freedom of the City') (*Civic Enrolments 1639-1662* (L.5.3), folio 277 verso)

#20: 30 September 1640 – Thomas Williams is given a bayliff's place (*City Council Proceedings – 1629-1663* (A.5.7), folio 107 verso)

#21: 16 November 1640 – Robert (Edward) Wyans granted Oxford Citizenship (the 'Freedom of the City') (*Civic Enrolments 1639-1662* (L.5.3), folio 275 verso)

#22: 30 November 1640 – Edward Wyans admitted as a member of the Guild of Cordwainers (*MS Morrell 14 - Order Book of the Guild of Cordwayners (1614-1711)*, folio 39 verso)

#23: 4 December 1640 – Members of the Guild of Cordwainers refuse to attend a breakfast put on by Edward Wyans and are rebuked by the mayor of Oxford (*MS Morrell 14 - Order Book of the Guild of Cordwayners (1614-1711)*, folio 40 recto)

#24: 31 May 1641 – Apprenticeship contract between William King and John Browne; amended to a contract between King and Richard Saintsbury on 20 June 1645 (*Civic Enrolments 1639-1662* (L.5.3), folio 12 verso)

#25: 6 July 1641 – Apprenticeship contract between Lawrence King and Thomas Meares; amended to a contract between King and John Sheene on 11 September 1646 (*Civic Enrolments 1639-1662* (L.5.3), folio 14 verso)

#26: 30 July 1641 – Thomas Ayres granted a forty-year lease for ground in Broken Hayes (*City Council Proceedings – 1629-1663* (A.5.7), folio 115 verso)

#27: 6 September 1641 – Thomas Ayres's lease is sealed with the city seal (*City Council Proceedings – 1629-1663* (A.5.7), folio 117 recto)

#28: 1641 – Anthony Wood notes that Thomas Ayres builds a house in Broken Hayes (*MS Wood F 29a*, folio 79 recto)

#29: 3 January 1642 – The city council orders fire equipment in case of emergencies (*City Council Proceedings – 1629-1663* (A.5.7), folio 121 recto)

#30: 10 June 1642 – An Act of Council regarding the Butchers' trade (*City Council Proceedings 1629-1663* (A.5.7), folio 123 recto)

#31: 30 July 1642 – Tom Ayres lease on a property in Broken Hayes (*Oxford City Ledgers 1636-1675* (D.5.6), folios 48 verso – 50 recto)

#32: 1 August 1642 – Will and inventory of goods of William Hatchman, Roger Hatchman's father (Will of William Hatchman – 1 August 1642 (*Dorchester Peculiar 69/1/24*))

*#33: 28 August 1642 – Brian Twyne's account of the arrival of royalist troops in Oxford (*MS Ballard 68*, page 5)

#34: 28 August 1642 – Anthony Wood's account of the arrival of royalist troops in Oxford and the flight of some townsmen to Abingdon (*MS Wood F 1*, page 900)

#35: 19 September 1642 – Thomas Ayres requests an additional piece of land next to his leasehold on Broken Hayes (*City Council Proceedings – 1629-1663* (A.5.7), folios 123 verso – 124 recto)

#36: 3 October 1642 – Thomas Ayres has his lease renewed and is granted an additional piece of land next to his leasehold on Broken Hayes (*City Council Proceedings – 1629-1663* (A.5.7), folios 125 recto)

#37: 4 October 1642 – Apprenticeship contract between William Baselye and Thomas Ayres (*Civic Enrolments 1639-1662* (L.5.3), folio 28 verso)

#38: 14 February 1643 – Thomas Hitchman employed as a scout for Sir Samuel Luke's army (*MS Eng. hist. c. 53*, folio 133 verso)

#39: 22 February 1643 – Thomas Hitchman reports on a spying mission to Oxford (*MS Eng. hist. c. 53*, folio 12 recto and verso)

#40: 22 May 1643 – Thomas Ayres's tenements in Broken Hayes are considered for demolition (*MS ADD D 114*, folio 12 recto)

#41: 7 August 1643 – Apprenticeship contract between William Thompson and Thomas Wyans (*Civic Enrolments 1639-1662* (L.5.3), folio 32 verso)

#42: 11 August 1643 – Thomas Williams (?) is alluded to in a satirical tract by John Taylor (*A Preter-Pluperfect, Spick and Span New Nocturnall*) (1643), page 10)

#43: 14 September 1643 – Thomas Williams and Roger Hatchman are removed from their civic offices by order of Charles I (*City Council Proceedings – 1629-1633* (A.5.7), folio 130 verso)

#44: 23 March 1644 – Apprenticeship contract between Thomas Tisdale and George Potter (*Civic Enrolments 1639-1662* (L.5.3), folio 39 verso)

#45: 25 March 1644 – Apprenticeship contract between Richard Tidmarsh and John Walter; amended to a contract between Tidmarsh and Matthew Langley on 27 January 1645 (*Civic Enrolments 1639-1662* (L.5.3), folio 39 verso)

#46: 17 October 1644 – Apprenticeship contract between John Toms and Richard Phillipps (*Civic Enrolments 1639-1662* (L.5.3), folio 42 verso)

#46a: 15 June 1646 – Marriage of Henry Ireton and Bridget Cromwell (*Parish Register of Holton – 1633-1794* (Par 135/1/R1/1), folio 13 verso)

#47: 29 June 1646 – Thomas Williams and Roger Hatchman have their places in the city council restored (*City Council Proceedings – 1629-1633* (A.5.7), folio 147 recto)

#48: 29 June 1646 – Thomas Williams and Roger Hatchman have their places in the city council restored (*City Council Minutes – 1635-1657* (A.4.3), folio 161 verso)

#49: 24 December 1646 – Apprenticeship contract between William Bourne and John Teagle; amended to a contract between Bourne and Edward Wyans on 30 June 1651 (*Civic Enrolments 1639-1662* (L.5.3), folio 60 recto)

#50: 23 March 1647 – Apprenticeship contract between Thomas King and John Willgoose (*Civil War Charities and General Minutes 1645-1695* (E.4.6), folio 6 verso)

#51: 23 March 1647 – Apprenticeship contract between Thomas King and John Willgoose (*Civic Enrolments 1639-1662* (L.5.3), folio 62 verso)

#52: 30 July 1647 – Robert King granted a license for the *Flying Horse* inn (*Oxford City Ledgers 1636-1675* (D.5.6), folio 555 verso)

#53: 20 September 1647 – James Jennings, Richard Quelch, Thomas Williams and others sign a petition against the election of anti-parliamentarians to civic offices (*MS Wood F 35*, folios 13 recto and verso)

#54: 23 September 1647 – Apprenticeship contract between George Ryland and Edward Wyans (*Civic Enrolments 1639-1662* (L.5.3), folio 68 verso)

#55: 4 October 1647 – Thomas Williams is named one of the five Keykeepers of the city (*City Council Proceedings – 1629-1633* (A.5.7), folio 162 recto)

#56: 8 November 1647 – Thomas Williams is among those appointed to help reconcile differences in the city council (*City Council Proceedings – 1629-1633* (A.5.7), folio 164 recto)

#56a: 31 March 1648 – Sir Thomas Fairfax orders Colonel Kelsey to use Oxford troops to support the Parliamentary Visitors as needed (*Wood 514* (29))

#57: 27 April 1648 – Ralph Austen as Deputy Registrar of the Parliamentary Visitors orders treasurers and bursars of colleges to turn in their records (*MS Wood F 35*, folio 226 recto)

#58: 9 May 1648 – Ralph Austen as Deputy Registrar of the Parliamentary Visitors orders fellows and members of Brasenose College to appear before them (*MS Wood F 35*, folio 227 recto)

#59: 12 May 1648 – Ralph Austen's order as Deputy Registrar of the Visitors concerning Magdalen College rents (*Ms e Musaeo* 77, (Register of the Visitors), page 82)

#60: 15 May 1648 – Ralph Austen verifies an order sent by from the Parliamentary Committee for the Reformation of the University expelling staff and students (*Ms e Musaeo* 77, (Register of the Visitors), page 127)

#61: 20 May 1648 – Ralph Austen as Deputy Registrar of the Parliamentary Visitors orders fellows and members of Lincoln college to appear before them (*MS Wood F 35*, folio 231 recto)

#62: 22 May 1648 – Ralph Austen verifies an order sent by from the Parliamentary Committee for the Reformation of the University (*Ms e Musaeo* 77, (Register of the Visitors), page 144)

#63: 26 May 1648 – Ralph Austen as Registrar of the Parliamentary Visitors orders that that all professors and lecturers of the university return to Oxford and attend to their duties (*MS Wood F 35*, folio 232 recto)

#64: 26 May 1648 – Ralph Austen as Registrar of the Parliamentary Visitors orders that no member of the university is to leave Oxford without permission (*MS Wood F 35*, folio 233 recto)

#65: 26 May 1648 – Ralph Austen as Registrar of the Parliamentary Visitors orders that that all members of the university must state whether they submit to the authority of Parliament (*MS Wood F 35*, folio 234 recto)

#66: 30 May 1648 – Ralph Austen verifies an order sent by from the Parliamentary Committee for the Reformation of the University (*Ms e Musaeo* 77, (Register of the Visitors), page 144)

#67: 30 May 1648 – Ralph Austen verifies an order sent by from the Parliamentary Committee for the Reformation of the University concerning the incarceration of Dr. Gilbert Sheldon (*MS Wood F 35*, folio 235 recto)

#68: 6 June 1648 – Ralph Austen verifies the testimony of Edward Copley against John Greaves in a matter of dispute at Merton College (*Ms e Musaeo* 77, (Register of the Visitors), page 302)

#69: 6 June 1648 – Ralph Austen as Registrar of the Parliamentary Visitors orders that that all holders of positions of authority or responsibility return to Oxford (*MS Wood F 35*, folio 236 recto)

#70: 14 June 1648 – Ralph Austen verifies an order for expulsions from colleges (*Ms e Musaeo* 77, (Register of the Visitors), page 148)

#71: 27 June 1648 – Ralph Austen as Registrar of the Parliamentary Visitors orders that Mr. Henry Tozer surrender all his keys and documents pertaining to Exeter College (*MS Wood F 35*, folio 239 recto)

#72: 29 June 1648 – Ralph Austen as Registrar of the Parliamentary Visitors conveys an order that six members of Exeter College be expelled from the University (*MS Wood F 35*, folio 240 recto)

#73: 29 June 1648 – Ralph Austen as Registrar of the Parliamentary Visitors conveys an order about the 64 members from sixteen colleges be expelled from the University (*MS Wood F 35*, folio 241 recto and verso)

#74: 5 July 1648 – Ralph Austen as Registrar of the Parliamentary Visitors conveys an order about the new appointments to Exeter College (*MS Wood F 35*, folio 244 recto)

#75: 5 July 1648 – Ralph Austen as Registrar of the Parliamentary Visitors conveys an order about the suspension of Mr. Proctor of Exeter College (*MS Wood F 35*, folio 245 recto)

#76: 7 July 1648 – Ralph Austen as Registrar of the Parliamentary Visitors conveys an order about the 73 members from ten colleges be expelled from the University (*MS Wood F 35*, folio 246 recto)

#77: 18 October 1648 – Ralph Austen as Registrar of the Parliamentary Visitors conveys an order concerning Gilbert Sheldon's alleged theft of horses belonging to All Souls College; the order is countermanded on 18 December 1648 (*MS Wood F 35*, folio 297 recto)

#78: 3 January 1649 – Thomas Kelsey issues orders suppressing soldiers from working as tailors without permission of the guild (*MS Morrell 6 - Election and Order Book of the Company of Taylors (1572-1711)*, folio 142 recto)

#79: 10 April 1649 – Richard Quelch and James Jennings are named among those inhabitants of Oxford to be placed in college positions by the Visitors of the University of Oxford (*Ms e Musaeo 77*, (Register of the Visitors), page 244)

#80: 21 June 1649 – Thomas Williams, as one of the city senior bayiffs, is part of a delegation that meets with the parliamentary Committe for the Regulation of the University in order to air the city's grievances against the university (*City Council Proceedings – 1629-1663 (A.5.7)*, folio 177 verso)

#81: 8 August 1649 – Ralph Austen as Registrar of the Visitors writes to the Provost of Queen's College with instructions about college regulation (*MS Wood F 35*, folio 349 recto)

#82: 17 September 1649 – Thomas Williams hands on his responsibilities as one of the city senior bailiffs (*City Council Proceedings – 1629-1663 (A.5.7)*, folio 180 recto)

#83: 18 October 1649 – Ralph Austen verifies an order sent by from the Parliamentary Committee for the Reformation of the University concerning the subscribing to directives (*MS Wood F 35*, folio 353 recto)

#84: 9 November 1649 – Ralph Austen as Registrar of the Visitors writes to the colleges and halls with details of an engagement required by all members of the university (*MS Wood F 35*, folio 355 recto)

#85: 16 February 1650 – Apprenticeship contract between Martin Quelch and Richard Quelch senior (*Civic Enrolments 1639-1662* (L.5.3), folio 90 verso; amended to a contract with Richard Quelch junior on 18 February 1653)

#86: 16 May 1650 – Thomas Williams verifies a receipt of repayment made by the Mayor and the Thirteen (*City Council Minutes – 1635-1715* (E.4.5), folio 310 verso)

#87: 25 November 1650 – Ralph Austen as Registrar of the Visitors conveys an order for the appointment of George Hitchcock to a fellowship in Lincoln College (*MS Wood F 35*, folio 363 recto)

#88: 22 January 1651 – Ralph Austen verifies an order for expulsions from colleges (*Ms e Musaeo* 77, (Register of the Visitors), page 148)

#89: 14 January 1651 – Ralph Austen is appointed *Registrarius Commissionariorum* (*Ms e Musaeo* 77, (Register of the Visitors), page 334)

#90: 8 April 1651 – Edward Wyans admitted to a warden's place within the Guild of Cordwainers (*MS Morrell 14 - Order Book of the Guild of Cordwayners (1614-1711)*, folio 53 verso)

#91: 1 July 1651 – Roger Hatchman to be granted Oxford Citizenship (the 'Freedom of the City') (*City Council Minutes – 1635-1657* (A.4.3), folio 246 verso)

#92: 1 July 1651 – Robert Hatchman granted Oxford Citizenship (the 'Freedom of the City') (*City Council Proceedings – 1629-1663* (A.5.7), folio 199 recto)

#93: 11 July 1651 – Apprenticeship contract between William Wilder and Edward Wyans (*Civic Enrolments 1639-1662* (L.5.3), folio 103 verso)

#94: 11 July 1651 – Robert Hatchman granted Oxford Citizenship (the 'Freedom of the City') (*Oxford Civic Enrolments – 1639-1662* (L.5.3), folio 33 recto)

#95: July 1651 – Robert Hatchman granted Oxford Citizenship (the 'Freedom of the City') (*Oxford City Audit Book – 1592-1682* (P.5.2), folio 280 recto)

#96: 4 August 1651 – Caveats on the estate of Robert King (*Oxford Caveats 1643-1677* (MS Wills 307), folio 53 recto)

#97: 13 August 1651 – The City Council calls for the establishment of a militia in the face of the invasion of a Scottish army (*City Council Proceedings – 1629-1633* (A.5.7), folio 199 verso)

#98: 16 September 1651 – Apprenticeship contract between William Ford and Thomas Wyans (*Civic Enrolments 1639-1662* (L.5.3), folio 104 verso)

#99: 22 September 1651 – Lawrence King granted Oxford Citizenship (the 'Freedom of the City') (*Civic Enrolments 1639-1662* (L.5.3), folio 244 recto)

#100: 2 December 1651 – John Higgins senior desires to be granted Oxford Citizenship (the 'Freedom of the City') (*City Council Proceedings – 1629-1633* (A.5.7), folio 203 verso)

#101: 2 December 1651 – Thomas Williams is elected one of the Mayor's assistants (*City Council Proceedings 1629-1663* (A.5.7), folio 204 recto)

#102: 25 December 1651 – The Council of State orders that letters be written to Oxford's civic and university officials in response to a petition by Oxford citizens complaining about the riotous behaviour of some students (*State Papers Domestic* (SP 25/66), page 118) (extract)

#103: 29 December 1651 – The Council of State letters to Oxford's civic and university officials in response to a petition by Oxford citizens complaining about the riotous behaviour of some students (*State Papers Domestic* (SP 25/97), pages 51-52)

#103a: 9 January 1652 – Daniel Greenwood issues an order about the conduct of students who were disrupting the worship of Dissenters in their meeting houses (*Vice-Chancellor's Declaration of 9 January 1651* (1652))

#104: 19 January 1652 – Thomas Tisdale granted Oxford Citizenship (the 'Freedom of the City') (*Civic Enrolments 1639-1662* (L.5.3), folio 242 recto)

#105: 19 January 1652 – Richard Tidmarsh granted Oxford Citizenship (the 'Freedom of the City') (*Civic Enrolments 1639-1662* (L.5.3), folio 241 verso)

#106: 26 February 1652 – A letter from Ralph Austen to Benjamin Martin (*Hartlib 41/1/2A-3B*)

#107: 26 February 1652? – An [undated] letter from Ralph Austen to Samuel Hartlib (*Hartlib 41/1/144A-145B*)

#108: 19 March 1652 – William Hodges lease on 'the antiquated dancing school' outside the North Gates (*Oxford City Ledgers 1636-1675* (D.5.6), folios 135 verso-136 verso)

#109: 2 April 1652 – John Higgins senior granted Oxford Citizenship (the 'Freedom of the City') (*Civic Enrolments 1639-1662* (L.5.3), folio 241 verso)

#110: 2 April 1652 – Apprenticeship contract between John Higgins senior and John Higgins junior (*Civic Enrolments 1639-1662* (L.5.3), folio 109 recto)

#111: 8 April 1652 – A letter from Ralph Austen to Samuel Hartlib (*Hartlib 41/1/4A-5B*)

#112: 13 April 1652 – Ralph Austen gives evidence in the case of Mr. Holloway, a royalist who supported Charles II in the battle of Worcester (*Ms e Musaeo* 77, (Register of the Visitors), page 378)

#113: 23 April 1652 – A letter from Ralph Austen to Samuel Hartlib (*Hartlib 41/1/6A-7B*)

#114: 16 May 1652 – Will and probate records of John Tesdale (*Abingdon Wills and Probate Records* (AWPR D/A1/128/57); the will was probated on 26 December 1665 and an inventory of his goods was also submitted on that day.

#115: 20 June 1652 – John Toms granted Oxford Citizenship (the 'Freedom of the City') (*Civic Enrolments 1639-1662* (L.5.3), folio 240 recto)

#116: 5 July 1652 – Daniel Greenwood issues an order about the conduct of students who were disrupting the worship of Dissenters in their meeting houses (*Vice-Chancellor's Declaration of 5 July 1652* (1652))

#117: 12 July 1652 – A letter from Ralph Austen to Samuel Hartlib (*Hartlib 41/1/8A-9B*)

#118: 15 July 1652 – John Toms admitted as a member of the Guild of Cordwainers (*MS Morrell 14 - Order Book of the Guild of Cordwayners (1614-1711)*, folio 53 verso)

#119: 26 July 1652 – A letter from Ralph Austen to Samuel Hartlib (*Hartlib 41/1/10A-11B*)

#120: 1 November 1652 – A letter from Ralph Austen to Samuel Hartlib (*Hartlib 41/1/12A-13B*)

#121: 16 November 1652 – Roger Hatchman lease on a property in the parish of St. Peter-in-the-Bailey (*New College Archives: Leases* (Steer #2244)

#122: 17 November 1652 – Thomas Williams signs an order forbidding the illegal collection of corn toll by the market clerks (*City Council Minutes – 1635-1715* (E.4.5), folio 291 verso)

#123: 18 November 1652? – A letter from Ralph Austen to Samuel Hartlib (*Hartlib 41/1/142A-143B*); together with a scribal copy of a portion of the letter (*Hartlib 41/1/141A-B*)

#124: 26 November 1652 – Richard Quelch granted Oxford Citizenship (the 'Freedom of the City') (*Civic Enrolments 1639-1662* (L.5.3), folio 238 verso)

#125: 29 November 1652 – Apprenticeship contract between John Quelch and Richard Quelch (*Civic Enrolments 1639-1662* (L.5.3), folio 116 recto)

#126: 11 December 1652 – Apprenticeship contract between Francis Smith and Lawrence King (*Civic Enrolments 1639-1662* (L.5.3), folio 116 verso)

#127: 15 December 1652 – Apprenticeship contract between Thomas Ewstace and Thomas Williams (*Civic Enrolments 1639-1662* (L.5.3), folio 117 recto)

#128: 1652 – Ralph Austen mentioned in the Preface of Samuel Hartlib's *Designe for Plentie by a Universall Planting of Fruit Trees* (1652).

#129: 7 January 1653 – A letter from Ralph Austen to Samuel Hartlib (*Hartlib 41/1/14A-15B*)

#130: 17 January 1653 – A letter from Ralph Austen to Samuel Hartlib (*Hartlib 41/1/16A-17B*)

#131: 21 January 1653 – Apprenticeship contract between John Terrell and Richard Tidmarsh (*Civic Enrolments 1639-1662* (L.5.3), folio 117 verso)

#132: 18 March 1653 – A letter from Ralph Austen to Samuel Hartlib (*Hartlib 41/1/18A-19B*)

#133: 1 April 1653 – A letter from Ralph Austen to Samuel Hartlib (*Hartlib 41/1/20A-21B*)

#134: 12 April 1653 – A letter from Ralph Austen to Samuel Hartlib (*Hartlib 41/1/22A-23B*)

#135: 25 April 1653 – A letter from Ralph Austen to Samuel Hartlib (*Hartlib 41/1/24A-25B*)

#136: 6 May 1653 – A letter from Ralph Austen to Samuel Hartlib (*Hartlib 41/1/26A-27B*)

#137: 16 May 1653 – A letter from Ralph Austen to Samuel Hartlib (*Hartlib 41/1/28A-29B*)

#138: 30 May 1653 – A letter from Ralph Austen to Samuel Hartlib (*Hartlib 41/1/30A-31B*)

#139: 6 June 1653 – A letter from Ralph Austen to Samuel Hartlib (*Hartlib 41/1/32A-33B*)

#140: 14 June 1653 – A letter from Ralph Austen to Samuel Hartlib (*Hartlib 41/1/34A-35B*)

#141: 20 June 1653 – Ralph Austen is re-appointed *Registrarius Commissionariorum* (*Ms e Musaeo* 77, (Register of the Visitors), page 393)

#142: 27 June 1653 – A letter from Ralph Austen to Samuel Hartlib (*Hartlib 41/1/36A-37B*)

#143: 8 July 1653 – A letter from Ralph Austen to Samuel Hartlib (*Hartlib 41/1/38A-39B*)

#144: 25 July 1653 – A letter from Ralph Austen to Samuel Hartlib (*Hartlib 41/1/40A-41B*)

#145: 24 August 1653 – Thomas Williams appoints Jeremy Digbie registrar to four parish churches (*Parish Register of St. Mary Magdalene – 1602-1660* (Par 208/1/R1/1), folio 33 verso)

#146: 30 August 1653 – A letter from Ralph Austen to Samuel Hartlib (*Hartlib 41/1/44A-45B*)

#147: 31 August 1653 – A letter from Ralph Austen to Samuel Hartlib (*Hartlib 41/1/46A-47B*)

#148: 5 September 1653 – Ralph Austen acknowledges receipt of a letter from Oliver Cromwell (*Ms e Musaeo* 77, (Register of the Visitors), page 398)

#149: 5 September 1653 – A letter from Ralph Austen to Samuel Hartlib (*Hartlib 41/1/48A-49B*)

#150: 19 September 1653 – Thomas Williams is elected mayor of Oxford (*City Council Proceedings 1629-1663* (A.5.7), folio 215 verso)

#151: 26 September 1653 – A letter from Ralph Austen to Samuel Hartlib (*Hartlib 41/1/52A-53B*)

#152: September 1653[?] – A petition from Ralph Austen to the Barebones Parliament (*Hartlib 41/1/146A-B*)

#153: 30 September 1653 – Richard Tidmarsh is elected to Oxford Common Council (*City Council Proceedings 1629-1663* (A.5.7), folio 217 verso)

#154: 10 October 1653 – Thomas Williams, as a justice of the peace for the city of Oxford, swears in Matthew Jellyman to be the registrar to five church parishes (*MS Rawlinson B 402a*), folio 1 recto)

#155: 21 October 1653 – A letter from Ralph Austen to Samuel Hartlib (*Hartlib 41/1/54A-55B*)

#156: 17 November 1653 – The City Council orders that the Bocardo prison be repaired (*City Council Proceedings 1629-1663* (A.5.7), folio 218 verso)

#157: 24 November 1653 – Thomas Williams appointed as a Commissioner for taxes to be raised in the city of Oxford (*An Act for An Assessment at the Rate of One hundred and twenty thousand Pounds by the Moneth for Six Moneths, From the Twenty fifth day of December 1653, to the Twenty fourth day of June then next ensuing; towards the Maintenance of the Armies and Navies of this Commonwealth* (1654), pages 266 and 292)

#158: 26 November 1653 – As mayor of Oxford Thomas Williams performs a marriage between William Hanmore and Elizabeth Beale (*Parish Register of St. Michael at the North Gate – 1653-1683* (Par 211/1/R1/2), folio 26 recto)

#159: 6 December 1653 – A letter from Ralph Austen to Samuel Hartlib (*Hartlib 41/1/56A-57B*)

#160: 12 December 1653 – A letter from Ralph Austen to Samuel Hartlib (*Hartlib 41/1/58A-59B*)

#161: 26 December 1653 – Edward Wyans signs the revision of the rules of order for the Guild of Cordwainers (*MS Morrell 14 - Order Book of the Guild of Cordwayners (1614-1711)*, folios 58 verso–59 verso)

#162: 17 January 1654 – A letter from Ralph Austen to Samuel Hartlib (*Hartlib 41/1/60A-61B*)

#163: 6 February 1654 – A letter from Ralph Austen to Samuel Hartlib (*Hartlib 41/1/62A-63B*)

#164: 6 February 1654 – A petition from Ralph Austen to Oliver Cromwell (*Hartlib 66/22A-B*)

#165: 8 February 1654 – A letter from Ralph Austen to Samuel Hartlib (*Hartlib 41/1/64A-65B*)

#166: 10 February 1654 – A letter from Ralph Austen to Samuel Hartlib (*Hartlib 41/1/66A-67B*)

#167: 20 February 1654 – A letter from Ralph Austen to Samuel Hartlib (*Hartlib 41/1/68A-69B*)

#168: 27 February 1654 – As mayor Thomas Williams performs the marriage of Robert Jones and Elizabeth Green (*Parish Register of St. Michael at the North Gate – 1653-1683* (Par 211/1/R1/2), folio 27 recto)

#169: 4 March 1654 – Roger Hatchman becomes involved in a property dispute (*New College Archives: Valuations* (Steer #1446)

#170: 23 March 1654 – As mayor Thomas Williams performs the marriage of Baldwin Hodges and Marie Clinch (*Parish Register of St. Michael at the North Gate – 1653-1683* (Par 211/1/R1/2), folio 27 recto)

#171: 25 April 1654 – Roger Hatchman lease on a property in the parish of St. Thomas (*Christ Church Lease*)

#172: 1 May 1654 – Mayor Thomas Williams and the city council send a letter of congratulation to Oliver Cromwell the Lord Protector (*City Council Proceedings 1629-1663* (A.5.7), folio 220 recto)

#173: 1 May 1654 – A letter of congratulation to Oliver Cromwell the Lord Protector (*Civil War Charities and General Minutes 1645-1695* (E.4.6) folios 12 recto and verso):

#174: 29 May 1654 – As mayor Thomas Williams performs the marriage of William Horne and Anne Adams (*Parish Register of St. Michael at the North Gate – 1653-1683* (Par 211/1/R1/2), folio 32 recto)

#175: 2 June 1654 – A letter from Ralph Austen to Samuel Hartlib (*Hartlib 41/1/70A-71B*)

#176: 16 June 1654 – Thomas Hatchman granted Oxford Citizenship (the 'Freedom of the City') (*City Council Proceedings 1629-1663* (A.5.7), folio 220 verso)

#177: 17 June 1654 – As mayor Thomas Williams performs the marriage of Stephen Gilkes and Margaret Basely (*Parish Register of St. Michael at the North Gate – 1653-1683* (Par 211/1/R1/2), folio 27 verso)

#178: 19 June 1654 – As mayor Thomas Williams performs the marriage of John Bishop and Margaret Basely (*Parish Register of St. Michael at the North Gate – 1653-1683* (Par 211/1/R1/2), folio 27 verso)

#179: 22 June 1654 – As mayor Thomas Williams performs the marriage of Thomas Smith and Elizabeth Barksdale (*Parish Register of St. Michael at the North Gate – 1653-1683* (Par 211/1/R1/2), folio 27 verso)

#180: 24 June 1654 – As mayor Thomas Williams performs the marriage of John Godbyheare and Ann Silverside (*Parish Register of St. Michael at the North Gate – 1653-1683* (Par 211/1/R1/2), folio 28 recto)

#181: 25 June 1654 – A letter from Ralph Austen to Samuel Hartlib (*Hartlib 41/1/72A-73B*)

#182: June 1654 – Two Quaker women (Elizabeth Heavens and Elizabeth Fletcher) are mistreated by Oxford students (excerpt from Richard Hubberthorne's *A true Testimony of the zeal of Oxford-professors and University-men* (1654): 1-4)

#183: June 1654 – Two Quaker women are mistreated by Oxford students (excerpt from *Here followeth a true relation of the sufferings inflicted upon the servrnts [sic] of the Lord who are called Quakers* (1654): 1-2)

#184: June 1654 – The Mayor of Oxford (Thomas Williams) intervenes on the part of two Quaker women who were mistreated by Oxford students (cited in Joseph Besse (ed.) *A Collection of the Sufferings of the People Called Quakers for the Testimony of a Good Conscience,* 2 Volumes (London: Luke Hinde, 1753) 1.562-563)

#185: 5 July 1654 – Thomas Williams presides over a meeting of the Company of Taylors in which three members of the guild are charged with breaking rules over the enrolment of apprentices (*MS Morrell 6 - Election and Order Book of the Company of Taylors (1572-1711)*, folio 154 recto)

#186: 19 July 1654 – Edward Stennet and Mary Quelch marry (*Parish Register of St. Michael at the North Gate – 1653-1683* (Par 211/1/R1/2), folio 28 verso)

#187: 7 August 1654 – Thomas Williams proposes that fire engines for the city ordered (*City Council Proceedings – 1629-1663* (A.5.7), folio 221 recto)

#188: 16 August 1654 – Thomas Hatchman granted Oxford Citizenship (the 'Freedom of the City') (*City Council Proceedings 1629-1663* (A.5.7), folio 221 recto)

#189: 16 August 1654 – Thomas Hatchman granted Oxford Citizenship (the 'Freedom of the City') (*Civic Enrolments 1639-1662* (L.5.3), folio 234 verso)

#190: 4 September 1654 – As mayor Thomas Williams performs the marriage of Christopher Brook and Margaret Outridd (*Parish Register of St. Michael at the North Gate – 1653-1683* (Par 211/1/R1/2), folio 29 recto)

#191: 4 September 1654 – The City of Oxford pays for cushions and a pulpit cloth for the church of St Martin's (*City Council Proceedings 1629-1663* (A.5.7), folio 221 verso)

#192: 29 September 1654 – Thomas Williams hands over the keys of his mayoral office (*City Council Proceedings 1629-1663* (A.5.7), folio 222 verso)

#193: 30 September 1654 – Richard Tidmarsh replaced on the Oxford Common Council (*City Council Proceedings 1629-1663* (A.5.7), folio 223 verso)

#194: 26 October 1654 – A letter from Ralph Austen to Samuel Hartlib (*Hartlib 41/1/74A-75B*)

#195: 12 November 1654 – Oliver Cromwell orders the raising of a militia in Oxford and sends commissions (*Civil War Charities and General Minutes 1645-1695* (E.4.6) folio 15 recto)

#196: 23 November 1654 – General Monck's order to Captain Roger Hatchman about a case of military discipline (Monck's Order Book: *MS Clark 46* (23 November 1654)

#197: 26 December 1654 – A letter from Ralph Austen to Samuel Hartlib (*Hartlib 41/1/76A-77B*)

#198: 29 December 1654 – Thomas [Richard?] Tisdale and Elizabeth Stiles marry (*Parish Register of St. Michael at the North Gate – 1653-1683* (Par 211/1/R1/2), folio 30 recto)

#199: 1654 – Accounts of persecutions of Quakers in Oxford (*Manuscripts – First Publishers of Truth: Portfolio 7*, folio 64 recto-65 recto; (the account was probably composed in 1706). (Cited in Norman Penney (ed.) *The First Publishers of Truth, Being Early Records of the Introduction of Quakerism into the Counties of England and Wales* (London: Headley Brothers, 1907)

#200: 1654 – Lawrence King paid for producing gloves for the Quarter Session court judges (*Audit Book 1592-1682* (P.5.2), folio 290 recto and verso)

#200a: 1654 – The Poem about Thomas Williams entitled 'Zeal Overheated' in Thomas Weaver's *Songs and Poems of Love and Drollery* (Oxford, 1654)

#201: 5 January 1655 – A letter from Ralph Austen to Samuel Hartlib (*Hartlib 41/1/78A-79B*)

#202: 1 February 1655 – Thomas Williams is a signatory on a city council order to lend £50 for the paying of soldiers sequestered in the city (*Civil War Charities and General Minutes 1645-1695* (E.4.6) folio 13 recto)

#203: 18 February 1655 – A letter from Ralph Austen to Samuel Hartlib (*Hartlib 41/1/80A-81B*)

#203a: 18 February 1655 – A letter from Ralph Austen to Samuel Hartlib (*Hartlib 41/1/80A-81B*) – published in Samuel Hartlib's *The Reformed Virginian Silk-Worm, or, a Rare and New Discovery of a speedy way, and easie means, found out by a young Lady in England she having made full proof thereof in May, Anno 1652* (1655), pages 7-8)

#204: 24 February 1655 – Thomas Williams signs a testimonial letter for Thomas Denver of St. Michael's parish (*MS Rawlinson A 29*), pages 632-633)

#205: 22 March 1655 – Thomas Ayres has his lease renewed and is granted an additional piece of land next to his leasehold on Broken Hayes (*City Council Proceedings – 1629-1663* (A.5.7), folio 225 verso)

#206: 25 April 1655 – Thomas Williams performs the marriage of Thomas Browne and Elizabeth Dely (*Parish Register of St. Michael at the North Gate – 1653-1683* (Par 211/1/R1/2), folio 31 recto)

#207: 29 April 1655 – A letter from Ralph Austen to Samuel Hartlib (*Hartlib 41/1/82A-83B*)

#208: 8 May 1655 – A letter from Ralph Austen to Samuel Hartlib (*Hartlib 41/1/84A-85B*)

#209: 9 May 1655 – Thomas Williams performs the marriage of Thomas Browne and Elizabeth Dely (*Parish Register of St. Michael at the North Gate – 1653-1683* (Par 211/1/R1/2), folio 32 verso)

#210: 10 May 1655 – Thomas Williams performs the marriage of Thomas Potter and Anne Sky (*Parish Register of St. Michael at the North Gate – 1653-1683* (Par 211/1/R1/2), folio 31 verso)

#211: 14 May 1655 – Thomas Williams performs the marriage of Richard Cadbury and Anne Archer (*Parish Register of St. Michael at the North Gate – 1653-1683* (Par 211/1/R1/2), folio 31 verso)

#212: 5 June 1655 – A letter from Ralph Austen to Samuel Hartlib (*Hartlib 41/1/86A-87B*)

#213: 12 June 1655 – A letter from Ralph Austen to Samuel Hartlib (*Hartlib 41/1/88A-89B*)

#214: 19 June 1655 – A letter from Ralph Austen to Samuel Hartlib (*Hartlib 41/1/90A-91B*)

#215: ? June 1655 – Thomas Williams performs the marriage of William Pule and Anne Alsappe (*Parish Register of St. Michael at the North Gate – 1653-1683* (Par 211/1/R1/2), folio 28 recto)

#216: 5 July 1655 – A letter from Ralph Austen to Samuel Hartlib (*Hartlib 41/1/92A-93B*)

#217: 20 July 1655 – John Ayres granted a forty-year lease on his father's tenement in Broken Hayes (*City Council Proceedings – 1629-1663* (A.5.7), folio 226 recto)

#218: 6 August 1655 – Thomas Williams performs the marriage of Christopher Prudix and Joane Blackwell (*Parish Register of St. Michael at the North Gate – 1653-1683* (Par 211/1/R1/2), folio 31 verso)

#219: 15 August 1655 – Apprenticeship contract between Moses Clark and Lawrence King (*Civic Enrolments 1639-1662* (L.5.3), folio 138 verso)

#220: 20 August 1655 – A letter from Ralph Austen to Samuel Hartlib (*Hartlib 41/1/94A-95B*)

#221: 25 August 1655 – Thomas Williams performs the marriage of Henry Johnson and Elinor Kookoe (*Parish Register of St. Michael at the North Gate – 1653-1683* (Par 211/1/R1/2), folio 33 recto)

#222: 30 August 1655 – John Ayres lease on a tenement in Broken Hayes (*Oxford City Ledgers 1636-1675* (D.5.6), pages 172-174)

#223: 30 August 1655 – A letter from Ralph Austen to Samuel Hartlib (*Hartlib 41/1/96A-97B*)

#224: 6 September 1655 – Maline Hodges lease on 'the antiquated dancing school' outside the North Gates (*Oxford City Ledgers 1636-1675* (D.5.6), pages 177-180)

#225: 7 September 1655 – A letter from Ralph Austen to Samuel Hartlib (*Hartlib 41/1/98A-99B*)

#226: 17 September 1655 – Widow Hedges gives securities for the repair of the 'antiquated dancing school' outside the North Gate (*City Council Proceedings – 1629-1663* (A.5.7), folio 227 recto)

#227: 20 September 1655 – Widow Hedges's lease on the 'antiquated dancing school' outside the North Gate is sealed (*City Council Proceedings – 1629-1663* (A.5.7), folio 227 verso)

#228: 22 November 1655 – George Astin and Margarie Stibbes marry (*Parish Register of St. Michael at the North Gate – 1653-1683* (Par 211/1/R1/2), folio 34 recto)

#229: 28 November 1655 – A letter from Ralph Austen to Samuel Hartlib (*Hartlib 41/1/100A-101B*)

#230: 1 December 1655 – A letter from Ralph Austen to Samuel Hartlib (*Hartlib 41/1/102A-103B*)

#231: 10 December 1655 – A letter from Ralph Austen to Samuel Hartlib (*Hartlib 41/1/104A-105B*)

#232: 21 January 1656 – Ralph Austen as Register of the Visitors conveys an order requiring college officials to verify the religious activities of their students (*Christ Church Deanery Papers* (DP ii.c.1), folio 52 recto)

#233: 4 February 1656 – Richard Quelch and Amy Wright marry (*Parish Register of St. Michael at the North Gate – 1653-1683* (Par 211/1/R1/2), folio 34 verso)

#234: 6 March 1656 – A letter from Ralph Austen to Samuel Hartlib (*Hartlib 41/1/106A-107B*)

#235: 11 April 1656 – George Astin granted Oxford Citizenship (the 'Freedom of the City') (*City Council Proceedings 1629-1663* (A.5.7), folio 231 recto)

#236: 24 April 1656 – A letter from Ralph Austen to Samuel Hartlib (*Hartlib 41/1/108A-109B*)

#237: 27 May 1656 – Oxford messengers raise a question about sabbatarianism at the Abingdon Association meetings (*Abingdon Association Record Book*, (D/AA/1), folio 20 verso)

#238: 1 June 1656 – A letter from Ralph Austen to Samuel Hartlib (*Hartlib 41/1/110A-110B*)

#239: 2 July 1656 – A letter from Ralph Austen to Samuel Hartlib (*Hartlib 41/1/112A-113B*)

#240: 18 September 1656 – Thomas Tisdale is a signatory of a letter sent from the Abingdon Association to churches in Warwick, Tewksbury, Derby, Morton-hinmarsh, Burton-on-the-Water, and Hooke Norton (*Abingdon Association Record Book*, (D/AA/1), folio 25 recto)

#241: 2 October 1656 – A letter from Ralph Austen to Samuel Hartlib (*Hartlib 41/1/114A-115B*)

#242: 3 October 1656 – A letter from Ralph Austen to Samuel Hartlib (*Hartlib 41/1/116A-118B*)

#243: 10 October 1656 – A letter from Ralph Austen to Samuel Hartlib (*Hartlib 41/1/119A-120B*)

#244: 16 December 1656 – An Act of Council regarding the Butchers' trade (*City Council Proceedings 1629-1663* (A.5.7), folio 237 recto and verso)

#245: 17 December 1656 – Apprenticeship contract between Richard Bignell and Edward Wyans (*Civic Enrolments 1639-1662* (L.5.3), folio 151 verso)

#246: January 1657 – Richard Quelch alluded to as 'the brother from Oxford' in minutes from Thomas Venner's congregation in London (*BL ADD MS 4459*), folio 111 recto and verso):

#247: 9 February 1657 – A letter from Ralph Austen to Samuel Hartlib (*Hartlib 41/1/121A-122B*)

#248: 24 March 1657 – An Act of Council regarding the Butchers' trade (*City Council Proceedings 1629-1663* (A.5.7), folio 239 verso)

#249: 25 March 1657 – Thomas Williams appointed as a Commissioner for taxes to be raised in the city of Oxford (*An Act for An Assessment upon England, at the Rate of Sixty thousand Pounds by the Moneth for Three Moneths, From theTwenty fifth day of March 1657, to the Twenty fourth day of June then next ensuing.* (1657), pages 4 and 35)

#250: 7 April 1657 – An Act of Council regarding the Butchers' trade (*City Council Proceedings 1629-1663* (A.5.7), folio 240 recto)

#251: 15 July 1657 – Anthony Wood comments about Dissenters such as Vavasor Powell, who preached against the University of Oxford from the pulpit of All Saints' church (*MS Wood F 1*, page 1099)

#252: 21 July 1657 – Apprenticeship contract between William Goodson and John Toms (*Civic Enrolments 1639-1662* (L.5.3), folio 158 recto)

#253: 3 September 1657 – Apprenticeship contract between Thomas Creed and Richard Quelch (*Civic Enrolments 1639-1662* (L.5.3), folio 159 verso)

#254: 21 September 1657 – City Council orders payment to Richard Tidmarsh (*City Council Proceedings 1629-1663* (A.5.7), folio 243 recto)

#255: 9 November 1657 – Thomas Hatchman and Margret Higgins marry (*Parish Register of St. Michael at the North Gate – 1653-1683* (Par 211/1/R1/2), folio 40 verso)

#255a: 5 January 1658 – Thomas Tisdale witnesses the will of John Hunt (*Will of Hunt – Prerogative Court of Canterbury and Related Probate Jurisdictions: Will Registers 1384-1858* (PROB 11/288), folios 170 recto and verso); the will was probated on 17 February 1659

#256: 11 March 1658 – Thomas Tisdale and Joan Stibbes marry (*Parish Register of St. Michael at the North Gate – 1653-1683* (Par 211/1/R1/2), folio 41 verso)

#257: March 1658 – The question of women speaking publicly in church is discussed at the Abingdon Association meeting (*Abingdon Association Record Book*, (D/AA/1), folio 34 verso)

#258: 19 April 1658 – Apprenticeship contract between Thomas Walter and Richard Tidmarsh (*Civic Enrolments 1639-1662* (L.5.3), folio 164 verso)

#259: 3 May 1658 – A letter from Ralph Austen to Samuel Hartlib (*Hartlib 45/2/1A-2B*)

#260: 4 June 1658 – Thomas Hatchman has the regulations governing the sale of meat read to him (*Civil War Charities and General Minutes – 1645-1695* (E.4.6), folio 21 recto)

#260a: 13 June 1658 – Will of John Hitch (*Prerogative Court of Canterbury and Related Probate Jurisdictions: Will Registers 1384-1858* (PROB 11/285), folio 158 verso); the will was probated on 16 December 1658

#261: 18 June 1658 – Anthony Wood remarks about the Anabaptist uprising in Oxford which was thought to have been planned for 8 May 1658 (*MS Wood F 1*, page 1101)

#262: 28 June 1658 – Thomas Hatchman and others cited for breaking the regulations governing the sale of meat (*Civil War Charities and General Minutes – 1645-1695* (E.4.6), folio 21 verso)

#263: 2 July 1658 – An Act of Council regarding the Butchers' trade (*City Council Proceedings 1629-1663* (A.5.7), folio 250 recto)

#264: 15 July 1658 – An Act of Council regarding the Butchers' trade (*City Council Proceedings 1629-1663* (A.5.7), folio 261 recto)

#265: 30 July 1658 – A letter from Ralph Austen to John Beale, together with John Beale's reply dated 23 August 1658 (a scribal copy corrected by Samuel Hartlib) (*Hartlib 45/2/3A-4B* and *Hartlib 41/1/123A-124B*)

#266: 7 September 1658 – A letter from Ralph Austen to John Beale together with John Beale's reply dated 16 September 1658 (scribal copies corrected by Samuel Hartlib) (*Hartlib 52/169A-172B*)

#267: 14 September 1658 – Lawrence King rebuked for arriving late at the Abingdon Association meetings (*Abingdon Association Record Book*, (D/AA/1), folio 35 recto)

#268: 7 October 1658 – A letter from Ralph Austen to Samuel Hartlib (*Hartlib 45/2/5A-6B*)

#269: 11 October 1658 – Apprenticeship contract between John Bignell and Edward Wyans (*Civic Enrolments 1639-1662* (L.5.3), folio 169 verso)

#270: 25 October 1658 – Thomas Tisdale is named as the occupier of a property in the parish of St. Martin (*Christ Church Leases – VIII. St Martin's – 1st Tenement – #7*)

#271: 8 December 1658 – A letter from Ralph Austen to Samuel Hartlib (*Hartlib 45/2/7A-8B*)

#272: 17 December 1658 – Widow Hedges's lease on the 'antiquated dancing school' tenement outside the North Gate is sealed (*City Council Proceedings – 1629-1663* (A.5.7), folio 256 recto)

#273: December 1658 – A petition from Ralph Austen to Lord Fleetwood (*Hartlib 45/2/9A*)

#274: 10 January 1659 – John Twicrosse is granted a lease on the 'antiquated dancing school' an a tenement (36 Cornmarket) outside the North Gate (*City Council Proceedings – 1629-1663* (A.5.7), folio 256 verso)

#275: 12 January 1659 – John Pitman's lease on a tenement (33-35 Cornmarket) outside the North Gate (*Oxford City Ledgers 1636-1675* (D.5.6), folios 264 recto and 264 verso)

#276: 12 January 1659 – John Twicrosse's lease on the 'antiquated dancing shool' and a tenement (36 Cornmarket) outside the North Gate (*Oxford City Ledgers 1636-1675* (D.5.6), folios 265 recto and 265 verso)

#277: 4 February 1659 – City Council orders payment regarding the Castle Mill bridge (*City Council Proceedings 1629-1663* (A.5.7), folio 257 recto)

#278: 15 February 1659 – Record of the agreement between Oxford City Council and the parish of St. Thomas regarding the Castle Mill bridge (*Civil War Charities and General Minutes – 1645-1695* (E.4.6), folio 23 verso)

#279: 5-7 April 1659 – Richard Tidmarsh reports to the Abingdon Association meeting about the state of the church in Oxford (*Abingdon Association Record Book*, (D/AA/1), folio 38 recto)

#280: 5-7 April 1659 – Richard Tidmarsh is appointed to assist in a controversy over sabbatarianism (*Abingdon Association Record Book*, (D/AA/1), folios 40 recto and 40 verso)

#281: 5-7 April 1659 – The church at Oxford raises a question about church discipline for the Abingdon Association to discuss (*Abingdon Association Record Book*, (D/AA/1), folio 41 recto)

#282: 11 April 1659 – John Higgins junior granted Oxford Citizenship (the 'Freedom of the City') (*Civic Enrolments 1639-1662* (L.5.3), folio 221 verso)

#283: 11 April 1659 – John Higgins junior granted Oxford Citizenship (the 'Freedom of the City') (*Civic Enrolments 1639-1662* (L.5.3), folio 222 recto)

#284: 3 May 1659 – A letter from Ralph Austen to Samuel Hartlib (*Hartlib 41/1/125A-126B*)

#285: 11 May 1659 – A letter from Ralph Austen to Samuel Hartlib (*Hartlib 41/1/129A-130B*)

#286: 15 July 1659 – Ralph Austen's house in the parish of St. Peter-in-the-Bailey is discussed by the City Council (*City Council Proceedings 1629-1663* (A.5.7), folio 260 verso)

#287: 30 July 1659 – Roger Hatchman's military commission to George Monck's Regiment of Foot (*Journal of the House of Commons* 7 (1659), pages 740, 742)

#288: 31 July 1659 – Frightened parishioners of St. Martin's parish church think Anabaptists and Quakers have come to cut their throats (*MS Wood Diaries 3*, folio 19 verso)

#289: 31 July 1659 – Frightened parishioners of St. Martin's parish church think Anabaptists and Quakers have come to cut their throats (*Tanner MS 102, Part 1*, folio 32 recto)

#290: 31 July 1659 – Newspaper report of the great wind storm which frightened parishioners of St Martin's parish church into thinking that Anabaptists and Quakers had come to cut their throats (*The Weekly Post* (Tuesday August 2, to Tuesday August 9, 1659) page 116)

#291: 9 August 1659 – Richard Tidmarsh, Ralph Austen and Thomas Tisdale are commissioned as officers within the Oxfordshire militia (*Journal of the House of Commons* 7 (1659), pages 752-3)

#292: 11 August 1659 – Parliament approves the commissions of officers within the Oxfordshire militia (*State Papers Domestic* (SP 25/98), page 105)

#293: 7 September 1659 – Apprenticeship contract between John Claydon and Lawrence King (*Civic Enrolments 1639-1662* (L.5.3), folio 177 verso)

#294: 30 September 1659 – Richard Tidmarsh Elected as a Chamberlain (*City Council Proceedings 1629-1663* (A.5.7), folio 265 recto)

#295: 1 October 1659 – Apprenticeship contract between Adam Turner and John Higgins senior (*Civic Enrolments 1639-1662* (L.5.3), folio 178 verso)

#296: 5 October 1659 – The Council of State receives a report from the Commissioners of the Oxfordshire Militia about the planned up-rising in Oxfordshire under the leadership of Lord Falkland (*MS Clarendon 65*, folios 139-140)

#297: 5 October 1659 – The Council of State receives reports about the discovery of a cache of arms hidden in Lord Falkland's house (*State Papers Domestic* (SP 25/79), pages 650 and 652-653)

#298: 25 October 1659 – Captain Roger Hatchman named in a published broadsheet describing General Monck's purging of his army (*A Letter from a person of quality in Edenburgh to an Officer of the Army, wherein is given a true account of Generall Moncks proceedings, Dated the 25th. Of October 1659*)

#299: 26 October 1659 – Captain Roger Hatchman named in a newssheet describing General Monck's purging of his army (*The Publick Intelligencer*, No. 201 (31 October – 7 November 1659) 840-842)

#300: 7 November 1659 – Captain Roger Hatchman named in newssheet describing General Monck's purging of his army (*The Loyall Scout,* No. 28 (4-11 November 1659) 223)

#301: 7 November 1659 – Captain Roger Hatchman named in newssheet describing General Monck's purging of his army (*The Weekly Post,* No. 27 (1-8 November 1659) 216)

#302: 7 November 1659 – General Monck writes about Generall Fleetwood about the imprisonment of Captain Roger Hatchman and others (*The Answer of the Officers at Whitehall to the Letter from the Officers of the Parliaments Army in Scotland from Linlithgow, Oct. 22, with a Return of the General and Officers in Scotland thereunto* (Edinburgh, 1659) 8; reissued in *A Collection of Several Letters and Declarations Sent by General Monck* (London, 1660): 22)

#303: 19 November 1659 – Captain Roger Hatchman is discharged from the army by order of General Monck (Monck's Order Book: *MS Clarke 49* (19 November 1659)

#304: 16 December 1659 – A letter from Ralph Austen to Samuel Hartlib (*Hartlib 41/1/131A-132B*)

#305: December 1659 – Anthony Wood records his having witnessed Lawrence King performing public baptisms in the river (*MS Wood F 31*, folio 7 verso)

#306: 16 January 1660 – Roger Hatchman and Ralph Austen support the preaching of John Belcher in the parish church of St. Peter-in-the-Bailey (*MS Wood F 1*, pages 1110-1111)

#307: 16 January 1660 – Roger Hatchman and Ralph Austen support the preaching of John Belcher in the parish church of St. Peter-in-theBailey (*MS Wood Diaries 4*, folio 7 verso)

#308: 16 February 1660 – Thomas Williams appointed as a Commissioner for taxes to be raised in the city of Oxford (*Journal of the House of Commons* 7: 844)

#309: 1 April 1660 – Thomas King granted Oxford Citizenship (the 'Freedom of the City') (*Civic Enrolments 1639-1662* (L.5.3), folio 217 verso)

#309a: 1 April 1660 – Humphry Jennings granted Oxford Citizenship (the 'Freedom of the City') (*Civic Enrolments 1639-1662* (L.5.3), folio 217 verso)

#310: 5 June 1660 – A letter from Ralph Austen to Samuel Hartlib (*Hartlib 41/1/133A-134B*)

#311: 19-20 June 1660 – Roger Hatchman listed among the messengers at the Abingdon Association meeting (*Abingdon Association Record Book*, (D/AA/1), folio 44 recto)

#312: 19-20 June 1660 – Roger Hatchman reports to the Abingdon Association meeting about the state of the church in Oxford (*Abingdon Association Record Book*, (D/AA/1), folio 44 verso)

#313: 20 June 1660 – The censure of John Belcher is discussed at the Abingdon Association meeting (*Abingdon Association Record Book*, (D/AA/1), folios 45 recto and verso)

#314: 22 July 1660 – A letter from Ralph Austen to Samuel Hartlib (*Hartlib 41/1/135A-136B*)

#315: 28 September 1660 – Richard Tidmarsh election as a Chamberlain is voided (*City Council Proceedings 1629-1663* (A.5.7), folio 279 verso)

#316: 4 October 1660 – Richard Tidmarsh and Lawrence King offer securities for William Robins who is accused of sedition (*Oxford Petty Sessions Roll – 1656-1678* (O.5.11), folio 36 verso):

#317: 6 December 1660 – City Council orders repairs of the High bridge (*City Council Proceedings 1629-1663* (A.5.7), folio 282 verso)

#318: 20 December 1660 – Thomas Ewstace granted Oxford Citizenship (the 'Freedom of the City') (*City Council Proceedings 1629-1663* (A.5.7), folio 284 recto)

#319: 20 December 1660 – Apprenticeship contract between John Williams and Thomas Williams (*Civic Enrolments 1639-1662* (L.5.3), folio 188 verso)

#320: 15 January 1661 – Thomas Lamplugh letter about the Baptists meeting in Oxford (*State Papers* (SP 29/28), page 109)

#321: 11 March 1661 – A letter from Ralph Austen to Samuel Hartlib (*Hartlib 41/1/137A-138B*)

#322: 16 April 1661 – Thomas Williams is appointed one of the scrutineers for the parliamentary elections (*City Council Proceedings 1629-1663* (A.5.7), folio 288 recto)

#323: 25 April 1661 – William Stubbes admitted as a member of the Guild of Cordwainers (*MS Morrell 14 - Order Book of the Guild of Cordwayners (1614-1711)*, folio 72 verso)

#324: 3 May 1661 – A letter from Ralph Austen to Samuel Hartlib (*Hartlib 41/1/139A-140B*)

#325: 8 May 1661 – William Stubbes granted Oxford Citizenship (the 'Freedom of the City') (*Civic Enrolments 1639-1662* (L.5.3), folio 215 verso)

#326: 30 June 1661 – Richard Quelch fined for failing to appear before the Quarter Sessions court and explain why he did not appear to serve on a grand inquest (*Oxford Petty Sessions Roll – 1656-1678* (O.5.11), folio 41 verso)

#327: 8 August 1661 – Thomas Williams is a signatory to an agreement made between the mayor and the mayor's council that they will meet regularly (*Civil War Charities and General Minutes 1645-1695* (E.4.6) folio 26 recto)

#328: 16 August 1661 – Thomas Williams to participate in the public ceremonies pertaining to the visit of Charles II to Oxford (*City Council Proceedings 1629-1663* (A.5.7), folio 291 recto)

#329: Summer 1661 – Thomas Williams sponsors a soldier in the Oxford militia (*Civil War Charities and General Minutes 1645-1695* (E.4.6) folios 35 recto and verso)

#330: 26 September 1661 – William Pestell letter about John Belcher and the Fifth Monarchists (*State Papers Domestic* (SP 29/42), pages 68 recto – 69 verso)

#331: 13 October 1661 – Thomas Williams is present at a city meeting in which the musicians who are to receive city fines are appointed (*Civil War Charities and General Minutes 1645-1695* (E.4.6) folio 28 verso)

#332: 8 November 1661 – Caveat on the estate of John Hatchman (*Oxford Caveats – 1643-1677* (MS Wills 307), folio 47 recto)

#333: 11 November 1661 – Probate bond of John Hatchman (*Oxford Wills and Probate Records* 80/4/17); an inventory of his goods was made on 30 December 1661, and a request for probate payments was made on 4 January 1662

#334: 25 November 1661 – Roger Griffin letter and enclosure about Tidmarsh and the Baptists meeting in Oxford (*State Papers Domestic* (SP 29/44), pages 194 recto and verso; 195 recto)

#335: 28 November 1661 – William Pestell letter about John Belcher and the Fifth Monarchists (*State Papers Domestic* (SP 29/44), page 258 recto–259 recto)

#336: November 1661 – A number of Baptists are among those implicated in an insurrection against the monarchy (Andrew Yarranton *A Full Discovery of the First Presbyterian Sham-Plot* (1681), pages 7-12 (excerpt)

#337: 23 December 1661 – Apprenticeship contract between Edward Rawlins and Edward Wyans (*Civic Enrolments 1639-1662* (L.5.3), folio 196 recto)

#338: 1661(?) – Edward Jennings and Humphrey Jennings sign an agreement governing the employment of apprentices and journeymen within the Company of Taylors (*MS Morrell 6 - Election and Order Book of the Company of Taylors (1572-1711)*, folio 174 verso)

#339: 9 January 1662 – Ralph Austin, Lawrence King, Roger Hatchman and Richard Tidmarsh are indicted to appear before the court charged with being seditious sectaryes and disloyal persons (*Oxford Petty Sessions Roll – 1656-1678* (O.5.11), folios 45 verso-46 recto)

#340: 15 March 1662 – Edward Jennings is indicted to appear before the court (*Oxford Diocese Record – 1 February 1660 – 4 October 1662* (c. 3) folio 13 verso)

#341: 5 June 1662 – Apprenticeship contract between Richard Harris and Thomas Tisdale (*Civic Enrolments 1639-1662* (L.5.3), folio 200 verso)

#342: 6 June 1662 – Thomas Williams is replaced as an 'Assistant' (*City Council Proceedings 1629-1663* (A.5.7), folio 299 recto)

#343: 28 June 1662 – Ralph Austen and his wife indicted to appear before the court (*Oxford Diocese Record – 1 February 1660 – 4 October 1662* (c. 3) folio 29 recto)

*#344: 28 June 1662 – Lawrence King and his wife indicted to appear before the court (*Oxford Diocese Record – 1 February 1660 – 4 October 1662* (c. 3) folio 29 verso):

#345: 28 June 1662 – Edward Wyans and his wife indicted to appear before the court (*Oxford Diocese Record – 1 February 1660 – 4 October 1662* (c. 3) folio 30 recto)

#346: 5 July 1662 – Ralph Austen and his wife indicted to appear before the court (*Oxford Diocese Record – 1 February 1660 – 4 October 1662* (c. 3) folio 31 verso)

#347: 12 July 1662 – Edward Wyans and his wife indicted to appear before the court (*Oxford Diocese Record – 1 February 1660 – 4 October 1662* (c. 3) folio 33 verso)

#348: 19 July 1662 – John Belcher is excommunicated (*Diocesan Excommunication Schedules – 1662-1667* (c. 100), folio 3 recto and verso); the order was published in the parish church of Aston Rowant on 3 August 1662)

#349: 26 July 1662 – Edward Wyans and his wife indicted to appear before the Court and are excommunicated (*Oxford Diocese Record – 1 February 1660 – 4 October 1662* (c. 3) folio 39 recto)

#350: 26 July 1662 – Richard Betteris is excommunicated (*Diocesan Records – Excommunications: 1662-1667* (c. 100), folios 2 recto and verso); the order was published in the parish church of Saint Peter-in-the-Bailey on 7 February 1664

#351: 26 July 1662 – Lawrence King and his wife indicted to appear before the court (*Oxford Diocese Record – 1 February 1660 – 4 October 1662* (c. 3) folio 38 verso)

#352: 14 August 1662 – Edward Jennings is admitted into the Company of Taylors (*MS Morrell 21 - Company of Taylors Minute Book (1658-1689)*, folio 84 recto)

#353: 8 November 1662 – Lawrence King indicted for not going to church (*Oxford Diocesan Records – 27 September 1662-15 April 1665* (c. 4), folio 29 recto)

#354: 8 November 1662 – James Jennings indicted for not paying his taxes to the church (*Oxford Diocesan Records – 27 September 1662-15 April 1665* (c. 4), folio 29 recto)

#355: 15 November 1662 – Lawrence King is ordered to consult with ecclesiastical authorities and certify that he has attended his local parish church (*Oxford Diocesan Records – 27 September 1662-15 April 1665* (c. 4), folio 36 recto)

#356: 15 November 1662 – James Jennings indicted for not paying his taxes to the church (*Oxford Diocesan Records – 27 September 1662-15 April 1665* (c. 4), folio 36 recto)

#357: 15 November 1662 – James Jennings is excommunicated (*Diocesan Records – Excommunications: 1662-1667* (c. 100), folio 20 recto and verso)

#358: 6 December 1662 – Roger and Mary [*sic*] Hatchman indicted for not going to their parish church (*Oxford Diocesan Records – 27 September 1662-15 April 1665* (c. 4), folio 51 verso)

#359: 13 December 1662 – Roger Hatchman indicted for not going to his parish church (*Oxford Diocesan Records – 27 September 1662-15 April 1665* (c. 4), folio 57 verso)

#360: 30 December 1662 – John Higgins appeals against his excommunication and promises to conform (*Oxford Diocesan Records – 27 September 1662-15 April 1665* (c. 4), folio 60 verso)

#361: 1662 – Lawrence King is called upon to give reasons for not attending his parish church (*Oxford Archdeaconry Papers: Allegations and Depositions 1621-1672* (c. 175), folios 141 recto & verso, and 142 recto)

#362: 6 January 1663 – Will of Thomas Wyans (*Oxford Wills and Probate Records* 71/4/2)

#363: 8 January 1663 – Matthew Jellyman is indicted to appear before the court (*Oxford Diocese Record – 27 September 1662 – 15 April 1665* (c. 4) folio 61 verso)

#364: 8 January 1663 – Francis Smith completes his apprenticeship with Lawrence King and is granted Oxford Citizenship (the 'Freedom of the City') (*Precedents – 1660-1710* (N.4.6), folios 164 recto-163 verso)

#365: 15 January 1663 – Richard Tidmarsh indicted for Refusing the Oath of Allegiance (*Oxford Petty Sessions Roll – 1656-1678* (O.5.11), folio 49 recto)

#366: 15 January 1663 – Lawrence King, John Toms, Edward Wyans, Richard Quelch, and James Jennings are indicted for attending an illegal conventicle (*Oxford Petty Sessions Roll – 1656-1678* (O.5.11), folio 49 verso)

#367: 15 January 1663 – Lawrence King, Richard Quelch, and James Jennings are indicted for Refusing the Oath of Allegiance (*Oxford Petty Sessions Roll – 1656-1678* (O.5.11), folio 49 verso)

#368: 26 January 1663 – Francis Smith granted Oxford Citizenship (the 'Freedom of the City') (*Civic Enrolments 1662-1699* (L.5.4), page 737)

#369: 21 February 1663 – Edward Jennings indicted over the baptism of his son (*Oxford Diocesan Records – 27 September 1662-15 April 1665* (c. 4), folio 85 verso)

#370: 12 March 1663 – Abraham Davies indicted to appear before the ecclesiastical court (*Oxford Diocesan Records – 27 September 1662-15 April 1665* (c. 4), folio 154 recto)

#371: 19 March 1663 – Abraham Davies indicted for not going to church (*Oxford Diocesan Records – 27 September 1662-15 April 1665* (c. 4), folio 158 recto)

#372: Spring 1663 – Richard Tidmarsh and John Higgins are appointed overseeers of the poor (*Husting and Mayor's Court 1662; Licenses and Overseers* (N.4.3), folio 15 recto)

#373: 11 April 1663 – Humphrey Gillet is excommunicated (*Diocesan Excommunication Schedules – 1662-1667* (c. 100), folio 50 recto)

#374: 30 April 1663 – Roger Hatchman is indicted for being 'a seditious sectarye and a disloyal person' and is fined 5 shillings (*Oxford Petty Sessions Roll – 1656-1678* (O.5.11), folio 52 recto)

#375: 2 May 1663 – Edward Jennings expresses willingness to have his son baptized (*Oxford Diocesan Records – 27 September 1662-15 April 1665* (c. 4), folio 111 recto)

#376: 18 May 1663 – Apprenticeship contract between James Browne and Richard Quelch (*Civic Enrolments 1662-1699* (L.5.4), page 13)

#377: 23 May 1663 – Edward Wyans is indicted indicted for not paying his taxes to the church (*Oxford Diocese Record – 4 April 1663 – 12 December 1663* (c. 6) folio 14 verso)

#378: 30 May 1663 – Edward Wyans is indicted indicted for not paying his taxes to the church (*Oxford Diocese Record – 4 April 1663 – 12 December 1663* (c. 6) folio 19 recto)

#379: 12 June 1663 – City viewers render an opinion about the property of Thomas Tisdale near St Martin's church (*Husting and Mayors Court 1660-1664* (M.4.4), folio 94 verso (Mayors))

#380: 27 June 1663 – Edward Wyans is indicted for not paying his taxes to the church (*Oxford Diocese Record – 27 September 1663 – 15 April 1665* (c. 4) folio 123 recto)

#381: 8 July 1663 – Edward Wyans is indicted indicted for not paying his taxes to the church (*Oxford Diocese Record – 27 September 1663 – 15 April 1665* (c. 4) folio 127 recto)

#382: 18 July 1663 – Edward Wyans is excommunicated (*Diocesan Records - Excommunication Schedules – 1662-1667* (c. 100), folio 58 recto and verso); the order was published in the church of Saint Martin's on 21 February 1664

#383: 7 September 1663 – John Quelch granted Oxford Citizenship (the 'Freedom of the City') (*Civic Enrolments 1662-1699* (L.5.4), page 733)

#384: 30 September 1663 – Four college leaders expelled by Chancelor Clarendon for keeping conventicles in their colleges (*MS Wood D 19 (3)*, folios 13 recto – 13 verso)

#385: 31 October 1663 – Richard Quelch is excommunicated (*Archdeaconry Records – Excommunications: 1610-1783* (c. 121), folio 265 recto and verso); the order was published in the parish church of All Saints' on 17 January 1664

#386: 21 November 1663 – Apprenticeship contract between Thomas Davies and James Ward; amended to a contract with John Higgins senior on 2 April 1666 (*Civic Enrolments 1662-1699* (L.5.4), page 23)

#387: December 1663 – A suspected conventicle is raided (*MS Wood Diaries 7*, folio 36 recto)

#388: 12 December 1663 – Thomas Swan is excommunicated (*Archdeaconry Records – Excommunications: 1610-1783* (c. 121), folio 268 recto and verso); the order was published in the parish church of All Saints' on 17 January 1664

#389: 13 January 1664 – Apprenticeship contract between John Haines and Richard Tidmarsh (*Civic Enrolments 1662-1699* (L.5.4), page 27)

#389a: 14 January 1664 – Conventicles in the city of Oxford are to be oppressed (*Oxford Petty Sessions Roll – 1656-1678* (O.5.11), folio 62 recto)

#390: 30 March 1664 – Apprenticeship contract between Richard Mullis and John Toms (*Civic Enrolments 1662-1699* (L.5.4), page 31)

#391: Spring 1664 – Abraham Davies is appointed an overseeer of the poor (*Husting and Mayor's Court 1662; Licenses and Overseers* (N.4.3), folio 23 recto)

#392: 14 April 1664 – Lawrence King, Richard Quelch and Edward Wyans indicted for not going to church (*Oxford Petty Sessions Roll – 1656-1678* (O.5.11), folio 66 verso)

#393: 9 June 1664 – Richard Tidmarsh is indicted for not going to church (*Oxford Petty Sessions Roll – 1656-1678* (O.5.11), folio 68 recto)

#394: 23 June 1664 – Thomas and Joan Tisdale are indicted for not going to church (*Oxford Diocese Record – 27 September 1662 – 15 April 1665* (c. 4) folio 186 recto)

#395: 4 August 1664 – Apprenticeship contract between Francis Carter and Lawrence King (*Civic Enrolments 1662-1699* (L.5.4), page 39)

#396: 18 August 1664 – Marriage bond between Thomas Williams and Alice Hitch (*Oxford Marriage Records: W 1634-1704* (c. 92/2), folio 4)

#397: 18 August 1664 – Richard Bignall granted Oxford Citizenship (the 'Freedom of the City') (*City Council Proceedings - 1663-1701* (B.5.1), folio 12 recto)

#398: 24 August 1664 – Apprenticeship contract between John Baker and Lawrence King (*Civic Enrolments 1662-1699* (L.5.4), page 40)

#399: 6 October 1664 – Quarter Sessions Court orders payment to Richard Tidmarsh (*Oxford Petty Sessions Roll – 1656-1678* (O.5.11), folio 72 verso)

#400: 10 December 1664 – Katharine Gillet is excommunicated (*Diocesan Excommunication Schedules – 1662-1667* (c. 100), folio 119 recto); the order was published in the parish church of Swerford on 19 February 1665)

#401: 14 January 1665 – Ralph Austen letter to Robert Boyle about the third edition of *A Treatise of Fruit Trees* (*Royal Society Library (BL. 1.16)*

#402: 3 February 1665 – City viewers render an opinion about the property dispute between Roger Hatchman and Richard Betteris in New Inn Hall Street (*Husting and Mayors Court 1665-1666* (M.4.5), folio 93 verso (Mayors))

#403: 20 March 1665 – Property Measurements on Roger Hatchman's house in New Inn Hall Street (*New College Archives: Valuations* (Steer #1442)

#404: Spring 1665 – Ralph Austen is appointed an overseeer of the poor (*Husting and Mayor's Court 1662; Licenses and Overseers* (N.4.3), folio 31 recto)

#405: 10 April 1665 – Roger Hatchman and his wife Alice are involved in a property dispute with the Quaker surgeon Richard Betteris (*New College Archives: Valuations* (Steer #1442)

#406: 29 April 1665 – Lawrence King and his wife indicted for not going to church (*Diocesan Records – 15 October 1664-30 September 1665* (d. 12), folio 144 recto)

#407: 6 May 1665 – Lawrence King and his wife indicted for not going to church (*Diocesan Records – 15 October 1664-30 September 1665* (d. 12), folio 155 recto)

#408: 6 May 1665 – Abraham Davies is indicted for not having his child baptized (*Diocesan Records – 15 October 1664-30 September 1665* (d. 12), folio 155 recto)

#409: 6 May 1665 – Abraham Davies is indicted for not attending his parish church (*Diocesan Records – 15 October 1664-30 September 1665* (d. 12), folio 155 verso)

#410: 10 June 1665 – Lawrence King and his wife indicted for not going to church (*Diocesan Records – 15 October 1664-30 September 1665* (d. 12), folio 182 recto)

#411: 10 June 1665 – Abraham Davies fails to appear before the court and is pronounced contumacious (*Diocesan Records – 15 October 1664-30 September 1665* (d. 12), folio 182 verso)

#412: 10 June 1665 – Thomas Tisdale and his wife indicted for not going to church (*Diocesan Records – 15 October 1664-30 September 1665* (d. 12), folio 185 verso)

#413: 15 June 1665 – James Jennings is excommunicated (*Diocesan Records – Excommunications: 1662-1667* (c. 100), folio 137 recto); the order was published in the church of All Saints' on 7 January 1666

#414: 21 June 1665 – Anne King is indicted for not going to church (*Diocesan Records – 15 October 1664-30 September 1665* (d. 12), folio 198 verso)

#415: 24 June 1665 – Lawrence King is indicted for not going to church (*Diocesan Records – 15 October 1664-30 September 1665* (d. 12), folio 210 verso)

#416: 24 June 1665 – Thomas Tisdale and his wife indicted for not going to church (*Diocesan Records – 15 October 1664-30 September 1665* (d. 12), folio 211 verso)

#417: 29 June 1665 – Apprenticeship contract between Thomas King and William White (*Civic Enrolments 1662-1699* (L.5.4), page 58)

#418: 1 July 1665 – Thomas King and Thomas Mason are excommunicated (*Diocesan Records - Excommunication Schedules – 1662-1667* (c. 100), folio 149 recto); the order was published in the church of Saint Peter-in-the-Bailey on 16 July 1665

#419: 14 July 1665 – Abraham Davies produces a certificate of baptism and is admonished to attend his parish church (*Diocesan Records – 15 October 1664-30 September 1665* (d. 12), folios 244 verso and 245 recto)

#420: 19 July 1665 – Thomas Tisdale is appointed a trustee for Mrs Nixon's charity for Apprenticing Boys out of the Nixon Free School (*Alderman Nixon's Free School- 1658* (Q.5.1), pages 22-24)

#421: 17 September 1665 – Robert Boyle writes to Henry Oldenberg about Ralph Austen's book *A Treatise on Fruit Trees* (1653) (*Royal Society MS B 1*, no. 90) (cited in A. Rupert Hall and Marie Boas Hall (eds.) *The Correspondence of Henry Oldenberg, Volume II 1663-1665* (Madison, Wisconsin: The University of Wisconsin Press, 1966), page 509) (extract)

#422: 26 December 1665 – Will and probate records of Richard Tesdale (*Abingdon Wills and Probate Records* (AWPR D/A1/128/58); the will was probated on 20 January 1666, with an inventory of his goods being compiled on 7 December 1666 and presented to the court on 9 January 1667)

#423: 1661-1665 – Names of the Excommunicants (*Diocesan Records – Excommunications: 1633-1791* (c. 99), folios 237-244)

#424: 9 January 1666 – Apprenticeship contract between John Tompkins and Thomas Tisdale (*Civic Enrolments 1662-1699* (L.5.4), page 658)

#425: Spring 1666 – Thomas King is appointed an overseeer of the poor (*Husting and Mayor's Court 1662; Licenses and Overseers* (N.4.3), folio 39 recto)

#426: 20 April 1666 – Edward Wyans and John Toms assist in the renewing of the orders of the Guild of Cordwainers (*MS Morrell 14 - Order Book of the Guild of Cordwayners (1614-1711)*, folio 80 recto)

#427: 7 May 1666 – Apprenticeship contract between Joshua Jellyman and Edward Wyans (*Civic Enrolments 1662-1699* (L.5.4), page 72)

#428: 7 July 1666 – Thomas and Alice Williams indicted for not receiving the sacrament at Easter; Thomas is accused of being an Anabaptist, but denies it (*Diocesan Records – 23 June 1666-22 January 1670* (c. 9), folio 13 recto)

#429: 21 July 1666 – Richard Tidmarsh indicted for not going to church (*Diocesan Records – 23 June 1666-22 January 1670* (c. 9), folio 39 verso)

#430: 21 July 1666 – Lawrence King indicted for not going to church (*Diocesan Records – 23 June 1666-22 January 1670* (c. 9), folio 40 verso)

#431: 21 July 1666 – Alice Williams is excommunicated (*Diocesan Excommunication Schedules – 1662-1667* (c. 100), folio 157 recto)

#432: 6 August 1666 – City Council orders payment to Richard Tidmarsh (*City Council Proceedings - 1663-1701* (B.5.1), folio 39 verso)

#433: 13 August 1666 – James Jennings petitions the court that the excommunication order against him be lifted (*Diocesan Records – 23 June 1666-22 January 1670* (c. 9), folio 57 verso)

#434: 15 November 1666 – John Toms junior admitted as a member of the Guild of Cordwainers (*MS Morrell 14 - Order Book of the Guild of Cordwayners (1614-1711)*, folio 80 recto)

#435: 10 January 1667 – Richard Tidmarsh explains his absence from the parish church (*Diocesan Records – 7 October 1665-7 March 1668* (c. 5), folios 166 verso-167 recto)

#436: 26 January 1667 – Lawrence King pronounced contumacious for not appearing in court (*Diocesan Records – 7 October 1665–7 March 1668* (c. 5), folio 176 recto)

#437: 22 February 1667 – Edward Jennings petitions the court that the excommunication order against him be lifted (*Diocesan Records – 23 June 1666-22 January 1670* (c. 9), folio 140 verso)

#438: 26 February 1667 – Apprenticeship contract between Nathaniel Lloyd and Lawrence King; amended on 15 October 1669 and 26 September 1670 (*Civic Enrolments 1662-1699* (L.5.4), page 85)

#439: 1 March 1667 – Apprenticeship contract between Henry Miles and John Toms (*Civic Enrolments 1662-1699* (L.5.4), page 86)

#440: 11 March 1667 – Apprenticeship contract between Thomas Powell and Lawrence King (*Civic Enrolments 1662-1699* (L.5.4), page 87)

#441: 30 March 1667 – Lawrence King, Toms and Richard Tidmarsh to certify their attendance at the parish church (*Diocesan Records – 7 October 1665-7 March 1668* (c. 5), folio 266 recto)

#442: 18 April 1667 – Richard Tidmarsh presented to Quarter Sessions court for several offences (*Oxford Petty Sessions Roll – 1656-1678* (O.5.11), folio 93 verso)

#443: 6 June 1667 – Thomas Williams and others indicted for illegal trading practices; the case is qushed by the court (*Oxford Petty Sessions Roll – 1656-1678* (O.5.11), folio 97 verso)

#444: 10 June 1667 – Apprenticeship contract between John Johnson and John Toms (*Civic Enrolments 1662-1699* (L.5.4), page 96)

#445: 2 September 1667 – Richard Tidmarsh to certify his attendance at the parish church (*Oxford Archdeaconry Records – 11 May 1667-21 July 1669* (c. 17), folio 56 recto)

#445a: 7 January 1668 – Apprenticeship contract between Edward Dubber and John Higgins (*Civic Enrolments 1662-1699* (L.5.4), page 108)

#446: 18 January 1668 – Ralph Austen appears before the court (*Oxford Diocese Record – 7 October 1665 – 7 March 1668* (c. 5), folios 263 recto and verso)

#447: 8 February 1668 – Ralph Austen appears before the court (*Oxford Diocese Record – 7October 1665 – 7 March 1668* (c. 5), folios 265 verso)

#448: 7 March 1668 – Will of Edward Wyans senior witnessed by Richard Tidmarsh (*Oxford Wills and Probate Records* 72/1/9)

#449: 14 March 1668 – Ralph Austen appears before the court (*Oxford Archdeaconry Records – 11 May 1667–21 July 1669* (c. 17), folio vii verso)

#450: 16 March 1668 – Apprenticeship contract between Jeffery Hands and Jude Meare; amended to a contract with Lawrence King on 16 May 1673 (*Civic Enrolments 1662-1699* (L.5.4), page 112)

#451: Spring 1668 – Lawrence King and Edward Wyans are appointed overseers of the poor (*Husting and Mayor's Court 1662; Licenses and Overseers* (N.4.3), folio 57 recto)

#452: 14 April 1668 – Apprenticeship contract between James Newman and Jude Meare; amended to a contract with Lawrence King on 22 August 1670 (*Civic Enrolments 1662-1699* (L.5.4), page 114)

#453: 23 April 1668 – Thomas Tisdale and his wife to certify their attendance at their parish church and their receiving of the sacrament (*Oxford Archdeaconry Records – 11 May 1667-21 July 1669* (c. 17), folio 84 verso)

#454: 21 May 1668 – Ralph Austen indicted to appear before the court (*Oxford Petty Sessions Roll – 1656-1678* (O.5.11), folio 104 recto)

#455: 6 June 1668 – John and Elizabeth Higgins appear before the court (*Oxford Archdeaconry Records – 11 May 1667-21 July 1669* (c. 17), folio 108 verso)

#456: 8 September 1668 – Edward Jennings is fined for failing to attend a meeting of the Company of Taylors (*MS Morrell 21 - Company of Taylors Minute Book (1658-1689)*, folio 66 recto)

#457: 25 September 1668 – Edward Wyans junior granted Oxford Citizenship (the 'Freedom of the City') (*Civic Enrolments 1662-1699* (L.5.4), page 704)

#458: 14 October 1668 – Apprenticeship contract between Joseph Jennings and George Blackwell; amended to a contract with Humphrey Jennings on 10 January 1669 (*Civic Enrolments 1662-1699* (L.5.4), page 126)

#459: 12 December 1668 – Lawrence King, John Toms and James Jennings to be excommunicated (*Oxford Archdeaconry Records – 11 May 1667-21 July 1669* (c. 17), folio 240 recto)

#460: 12 December 1668 – Richard Tidmarsh to be excommunicated (*Oxford Archdeaconry Records – 11 May 1667-21 July 1669* (c. 17), folio 240 recto)

#461: 7 January 1669 – Lawrence King is excommunicated (*Archdeaconry Records – Excommunications: 1610-1783* (c. 121), folio 294 recto); the order was published in the church of St. Mary the Virgin on 17 April 1670

#462: 7 January 1669 – Richard Tidmarsh is excommunicated (*Archdeaconry Records – Excommunications: 1610-1783* (c. 121), folio 327 recto); the order was published in his local parish church on 5 June 1670

#463: 5 February 1669 – Humphrey Jennings signs a marriage bond for his marriage to Anne Denham (*Oxford Diocesan Marriage Bonds* (d. 58), folio 6)

#464: 16 February 1669 – Humphrey Jennings admitted to the Company of Taylors (*MS Morrell 6 - Election and Order Book of the Company of Taylors (1572-1711)*, folio 194 recto)

#465: 10 March 1669 – Apprenticeship contract between Samuel Denny and Humphrey Jennings; terminated by mutual consent on 21 November 1673 (*Civic Enrolments 1662-1699* (L.5.4), page 133)

#466: 22 April 1669 – Thomas Williams and others indicted for illegal trading practices (*Oxford Petty Sessions Roll – 1656-1678* (O.5.11), folio 108 recto)

#467: 22 April 1669 – Constables are ordered to suppress conventicles in the city of Oxford (*Oxford Petty Sessions Roll – 1656-1678* (O.5.11), folio 108 verso)

#468: 26 April 1669 – Apprenticeship contract between Daniel Wildgoose and Edward Wyans senior; amended to a contract with Edward Wyans junior on 28 October 1672 (*Civic Enrolments 1662-1699* (L.5.4), page 137)

#469: 10 June 1669 – Documents relating to Thomas Williams and others being indicted for illegal trading practices are returned (*Oxford Petty Sessions Roll – 1656-1678* (O.5.11), folio 110 recto)

#470: 10 June 1669 – Thomas Williams initiates proceedings against John Rutter for illegal trading practices (*Oxford Petty Sessions Roll – 1656-1678* (O.5.11), folio 110 verso)

#471: 22 June 1669 – Lawrence King involved in a civil suit of the glover Thomas Mason (*Oxford Petty Sessions Roll – 1656-1678* (O.5.11), folio 110 verso)

#472: 22 June 1669 – Ralph Austen and others indicted for attending an unlawful conventicle (*Oxford Petty Sessions Roll – 1656-1678* (O.5.11), folio 112 recto)

#473:   21 July 1669 – John Higgins appears before the court (*Oxford Archdeaconry Records – 11 May 1667-21 July 1669* (c. 17), folio 296 verso); the left edge of the page is torn and some of the text missing

#474: 20 August 1669 – Ralph Austen signs an agreement to pay an annual fine for his house in the parish of St Peter-in-the-Bailey (*Languables – 1668-1737* (P.3.9), page 20)

#475: 20 September 1669 – Thomas Tisdale is fined for not performing his duties as bailiff during the mayoral elections (*City Council Proceedings - 1663-1701* (B.5.1), folio 78 verso)

#476: 30 September 1669 – Fines are imposed upon those who refuse to take up or neglect their elected offices (*City Council Proceedings - 1663-1701* (B.5.1), folio 81 recto)

#477: 25 October 1669 – John Toms senior pays his fee to obtain a warden's place within the Guild of Cordwainers (*MS Morrell 14 - Order Book of the Guild of Cordwayners (1614-1711)*, folio 86 verso)

#478: 27 November 1669 – Richard Harris granted Oxford Citizenship (the 'Freedom of the City') (*Civic Enrolments 1662-1699* (L.5.4), page 694)

#479:   31 December 1669 – Peter Mews is sent instructions about suppressing conventicles in Oxford (*Privy Council Register – 1 October 1669 – 28 April 1671* (SP 29/62), page 92)

#480: 13 January 1670 – Abraham Ward, Richard Tidmarsh, John Toms, Lawrence King and John Higgins fined for being at an unlawful conventicle (*Oxford Petty Sessions Roll – 1656-1678* (O.5.11), folio 114 recto)

#481: 13 January 1670 – Thomas Mason is discharged from the civil suit over illegal trading practices (*Oxford Petty Sessions Roll – 1656-1678* (O.5.11), folio 114 recto)

#482: 13 January 1670 – Vice-chancellor Peter Mews is commended for breaking up a conventicle at Lawrence King's house (*State Papers Domestic* (SP 29/272), folios 76 recto and 75 verso)

#483: 7 April 1670 – Ralph Austen and others pay fines and are discharged (*Oxford Petty Sessions Roll – 1656-1678* (O.5.11), folio 115 recto)

#484: 7 April 1670 – Lawrence King fined for not attending his parish church (*Oxford Petty Sessions Roll – 1656-1678* (O.5.11), folio 115 verso)

#485: 25 June 1670 – Apprenticeship contract between Thomas Cooper and Lawrence King (*Civic Enrolments 1662-1699* (L.5.4), page 160)

#486: 23 August 1670 – James Jennings signs an agreement to pay an annual fine for his house in the parish of All Saints' (*Languables – 1668-1737* (P.3.9), page 30)

#487:   29 August 1670 – Apprenticeship contract between Thomas George and John Toms (*Civic Enrolments 1662-1699* (L.5.4), page 162)

#488: 12 September 1670 – John Claydon granted Oxford Citizenship (the 'Freedom of the City') (*Civic Enrolments 1662-1699* (L.5.4), page 690)

#489: 30 September 1670 – A public disturbance over the city elections is condemned and an inquiry set up to determine the ringleaders (*City Council Proceedings - 1663-1701* (B.5.1), folio 91 recto)

#490: 6 October 1670 – Peter Mews hands in the the bayliffes money collected from fines levied against conventiclers (*Oxford Petty Sessions Roll – 1656-1678* (O.5.11), folio 119 verso)

#491: 6 October 1670 – Thomas Williams indicted for 'disturbing the peace' and for 'hissing at the mayor' (*Oxford Petty Sessions Roll – 1656-1678* (O.5.11), folio 119 verso)

#492: 31 October 1670 – Edward Jennings and Humphrey Hennings are fined for failing to attend a meeting of the Company of Taylors (*MS Morrell 21 - Company of Taylors Minute Book (1658-1689)*, folio 58 verso)

#492a: 7 November 1670 – Apprenticeship contract between Samuel Tidmarsh and John Syms (*Stationers' Company Archives: Apprenticeship Register – 7 August 1666-6 March 1727*, folio 23 recto)

#493: 17 January 1671 – Apprenticeship contract between William Stibbs and Richard Tidmarsh (*Civic Enrolments 1662-1699* (L.5.4), page 171)

#493a: 31 March 1671 – Apprenticeship contract between William Milday and John Higgins; amended to a contract between Milday and William Hamblen on 26 July 1672 (*Civic Enrolments 1662-1699* (L.5.4), page 175)

#494: 17 April 1671 – Will and probate records of Elizabeth Tesdale (*Abingdon Wills and Probate Records* (AWPR D/A1/128/92); the will was probated on 26 March 1672 and an inventory of her goods compiled on 24 December 1671 was also submitted on that day

#495: 22 May 1671 – Apprenticeship contract between Robert Stiles and Thomas Tisdale (*Civic Enrolments 1662-1699* (L.5.4), page 178)

#496: 27 May 1671 – Thomas Williams and his wife cited to appear in court (*Diocesan Records – 19 November 1670-27 July 1672* (c. 11), folio 139 recto)

#497: 1 July 1671 – Informants report about John Belcher's preaching at Bell Lane, Spitalfields in London on 24 June 1671 (*State Papers Domestic* (SP 29/291), page 149)

#498: 6 August 1671 – John Beale writes to Henry Oldenberg about Ralph Austen's horticultural activities in Oxford (H. Oldenberg Correspondence - *British Library ADD MS 4294*, folio 17 recto) (cited in A. Rupert Hall and Marie Boas Hall (eds.) *The Correspondence of Henry Oldenberg, Volume II 1663-1665* (Madison, Wisconsin: The University of Wisconsin Press, 1966), pages 187-188) (extract)

#499: 11 September 1671 – Francis Carter granted Oxford Citizenship (the 'Freedom of the City') (*Civic Enrolments 1662-1699* (L.5.4), page 684)

#500: 5 February 1672 – Thomas Davis granted Oxford Citizenship (the 'Freedom of the City') (*Civic Enrolments 1662-1699* (L.5.4), page 679)

#501: 17 February 1672 – Lawrence King indicted for not baptizing his children (*Oxford Archdeaconry Records - 24 July 1669–Michaelmas 1672* (c. 19), folio 195 recto)

#502: 28 February 1672 – Inventory of goods belonging to Edward Wyans senior witnessed by Richard Tidmarsh (*Oxford Wills and Probate Records* 72/1/9 - Inventory)

#503: 15 March 1672 – Anthony Wood comments about Dissenters upon the publication of the *Act of Toleration* (*MS Wood Diaries 16*, folio 14 recto)

#504: 11 April 1672 – Apprenticeship contract between Caleb Tomkins and Lawrence King (*Civic Enrolments 1662-1699* (L.5.4), page 195)

#505: April 1672 – Richard Tidmarsh and Lawrence King apply for a license for the Baptist meeting house in Oxford (*State Papers Domestic* (SP/29 320), page 118)

#506: 19 April 1672 – Richard Tidmarsh and Lawrence King apply for a license for the Baptist meeting house in Oxford (*State Papers Domestic – Entry Book 38A* (SP/44 38A), page 33)

#507: 22 April 1672 – Richard Tidmarsh and Lawrence King apply for a license for the Baptist meeting house in Oxford (*State Papers Domestic* (SP/29 320), page 146)

#508: 18 June 1672 – James Penny writes from Christ Church to William Norton about Richard Tidmarsh (Dr. Williams's Library, Richard Baxter's *Letters*, Volume 2, No. 51, folio 3)

#509: 26 June 1672 – Peter Mews writes to Gilbert Sheldon about the meeting houses in Oxford (*MS ADD* (c. 302), folio 250) (extract)

#510: 28 June 1672 – Edward Wyans junior admitted to the Guild of Cordwainers upon the death of his father (*MS Morrell 14 - Order Book of the Guild of Cordwayners (1614-1711)*, folio 91 verso)

#511: 2 July 1672 – Apprenticeship contract between John Hardwell and Edward Wyans (*Civic Enrolments 1662-1699* (L.5.4), page 199)

#512: 23 August 1672 – Apprenticeship contract between Lemuel King and Daniel Porter (*Civic Enrolments 1662-1699* (L.5.4), page 210)

#513: 3 October 1672 – John Higgins discharged by the Quarter Sessions court (*Oxford Petty Sessions Roll – 1656-1678* (O.5.11), folio 134 verso)

#514: 9 December 1672 – Anthony Hall and Robert Pawlyn apply for a license for a Presbyerian meeting house in Oxford (*State Papers Domestic – Entry Book 38A* (SP/44 38A), page 278)

#515: 10 December 1672 – Thomas Tisdale lease and property bond on a property in the parish of St. Martin (*Christ Church Leases – VIII. St Martin's – 1ˢᵗ Tenement – #9*)

#516: 12 February 1673 – John Pitman's lease on a tenement (33-35 Cornmarket) outside the North Gate is renewed (*Oxford City Ledgers 1636-1675* (D.5.6), folios 503 recto – 504 recto)

#517: 16 April 1673 – Apprenticeship contract between James Leverett and Lawrence King (*Civic Enrolments 1662-1699* (L.5.4), page 208)

#518: 2 May 1673 – John Tompkins granted Oxford Citizenship (the 'Freedom of the City') (*Civic Enrolments 1662-1699* (L.5.4), page 694)

#519: 24 September 1673 – Will of Ralph Austen (*Bodleian Wills – Austen, Ralph*)

#520: 30 September 1673 – Thomas Tisdale is elected to be 'one of the 24ty' on the city council (*City Council Proceedings - 1663-1701* (B.5.1), folio 123 recto)

#521: 3 November 1673 – City viewers render an opinion about the property dispute between Edward Wyans and John Johnson in St Martin's parish (*Husting and Mayors Court 1672-1677* (M.4.7), folio 21 recto (Mayor's Court))

#522: 5 November 1673 – John Higgins senior signs a marriage bond between John Faulkner and Rebecca Atley (*Oxford Archdeaconry Records: Marriage Bonds – 1673* (c. 462), folio 43 recto)

#523: 12 January 1674 – Thomas Tisdale refuses to swear his oath of office (*City Council Proceedings - 1663-1701* (B.5.1), folio 126 recto)

#523a: 12 January 1674 – Will of Thomas Williams (*Prerogative Court of Canterbury and Related Probate Jurisdictions: Will Registers 1384-1858* (PROB 11/345), folios 318 verso-319 recto); the will was probated on 8 July 1674

#524: 28 February 1674 – John Higgins senior appears before the court (*Archdeaconry Records – 29 November 1673-20 February 1675* (c. 21), folio 40 recto)

#525: 6 March 1674 – John Twicrosse's lease on a tenement (36 Cornmarket) outside the North Gate is renewed; the 'antiquated dancing school' is not included (*Oxford City Ledgers 1636-1675* (D.5.6), folios 522 verso–524 recto)

#526: 15 June 1674 – An attempt is made to force Thomas Tisdale to swear his oath of office (*City Council Proceedings - 1663-1701* (B.5.1), folio 128 verso)

#527: 25 August 1674 – The council agrees that Thomas Tisdale is to be brought before Charles II over the matter of refusing to swear his oath of office (*City Council Proceedings - 1663-1701* (B.5.1), folio 129 verso)

#528: 28 August 1674 – Thomas Tisdale takes up his place as a Bailiff and pays a reduced fine for the office (*City Council Proceedings - 1663-1701* (B.5.1), folio 130 verso)

#529: 4 September 1674 – Apprenticeship contract between Joseph Mason and Lawrence King (*Civic Enrolments 1662-1699* (L.5.4), page 232)

#530: 12 October 1674 – John Pittman lease on a tenement (33-35 Cornmarket) and 'the antiquated dancing school' outside the North Gate is renewed (*Oxford City Ledgers 1636-1675* (D.5.6), folios 540 verso – 541 verso)

#531: 7 November 1674 – Apprenticeship contract between Lawrence King junior and Lawrence King (*Civic Enrolments 1662-1699* (L.5.4), page 236)

#532: 7 December 1674 – Edmund Dubber granted Oxford Citizenship (the 'Freedom of the City') (*Civic Enrolments 1662-1699* (L.5.4), page 660)

#533: 7 June 1675 – Jeffery Hands granted Oxford Citizenship (the 'Freedom of the City') (*Civic Enrolments 1662-1699* (L.5.4), page 659)

#534: 8 June 1675 – Thomas Tisdale fined for not attending a council meeting (*City Council Proceedings 1663-1701* (B.5.1), folio 139 recto)

#535: 25 June 1675 – Thomas Tisdale signs a subscription for building a Guild Hall (*Sundry Documents – Hester's Collections I – 1649-1750* (F.5.2), folio 140 recto)

#536: 30 June 1675 – Ralph Austen signs an indenture on his property in the parish of St. Peter-in-the-Bailey (*MS Ch Oxon c. 50* (#4501)

#537: 9 July 1675 – Apprenticeship contract between Thomas Meares and Lawrence King (*Civic Enrolments 1662-1699* (L.5.4), page 245)

#538: 25 October 1675 – John Toms senior is admitted to a master's place within the Guild of Cordwainers (*MS Morrell 14 - Order Book of the Guild of Cordwayners (1614-1711)*, folio 96 verso)

#539: 1675 – The home of Richard Tidmarsh within the parish of St. Thomas (detail from David Loggan's *Oxonia Illustrata* (1675), plate 2)

#540: 1675 – The home of Thomas Williams at 120 High Street within the parish of All Saints' (detail from David Loggan's *Oxonia Illustrata* (1675), plate 2)

#541: 1675 – The home of Lawrence King at 119 High Street within the parish of All Saints' (detail from David Loggan's *Oxonia Illustrata* (1675), plate 2)

#542: 1675 – The home of Edward Wyans at 140 High Street within the parish of St. Martin's (detail from David Loggan's *Oxonia Illustrata* (1675), plate 2)

#543: 1675 – The home of Thomas Tisdale at 65 Cornmarket within the parish of St. Martin's (detail from David Loggan's *Oxonia Illustrata* (1675), plate 2); Tisdale also rented a stable and hayhouse together with a garden plot to the west

#544: 1675 – The home of Thomas King and Thomas Mason within the parish of St. Peter-in-the-Bailey (detail from David Loggan's *Oxonia Illustrata* (1675), plate 2)

#545: 1675 – The home of Roger Hatchman within the parish of St. Thomas (detail from David Loggan's *Oxonia Illustrata* (1675), plate 2)

#546: 1675 – The possible location of Broken Hayes where Thomas (Pun) Ayres built a house in 1642 which was later used as a meeting house for Dissenters (detail from David Loggan's *Oxonia Illustrata* (1675), plate 2)

#547: 1675 – The home of Roger Hatchman within the parish of St. Peter-in-the-Bailey (detail from David Loggan's *Oxonia Illustrata* (1675), plate 2)

#548: 1675 – The home of Ralph Austen within the parish of St. Peter-in-the-Bailey (detail from David Loggan's *Oxonia Illustrata* (1675), plate 2)

#549: 1675 – The home of Jonathan King within the parish of St. Michael's (detail from David Loggan's *Oxonia Illustrata* (1675), plate 2)

#550: 1675 – The home of John Toms within the parish of St. Thomas (detail from David Loggan's *Oxonia Illustrata* (1675), plate 2)

#551: 1675 – The location of the Butcher's Row in St. Peter-in-the-Bailey where Thomas Hatchman had a shop in 1658 (detail from David Loggan's *Oxonia Illustrata* (1675), plate 2)

#552: 1675 – The location of the 'antiquated dancing school' outside the North Gate where Dissenters met for religious worship starting after the issuing of the *Declaration of Indulgence* in 1672 (detail from David Loggan's *Oxonia Illustrata* (1675), plate 2)

#553: 3 April 1676 – Apprenticeship contract between Michael Whately and John Toms (*Civic Enrolments 1662-1699* (L.5.4), page 256)

#554: 14 June 1676 – Apprenticeship contract between William Cannon and John Toms (*Civic Enrolments 1662-1699* (L.5.4), page 259)

#555: 18 August 1676 – Edward Wyans's apprentice Richard Bignall is admitted to the Guild of Cordwainers (*MS Morrell 14 - Order Book of the Guild of Cordwayners (1614-1711)*, folio 98 verso)

#556: 14 November 1676 – Isaac Newton writes to Henry Oldenberg asking for a recommendation to Ralph Austen (H. Oldenburg Correspondence – *British Library ADD MS 4294*, folio 12a-d) (cited in H.W. Turnbull (ed.) *The Correspondence of Isaac Newton, Volume II 1676-1687* (Cambridge: Cambridge University Press, 1960), page 181) (extract)

#557: 28 November 1676 – Inventory of Ralph Austen's goods (*Bodleian Wills – Austen, Ralph*)

#558: 15 December 1676 – The city council takes action against Thomas Tisdale and others for not attending council meetings (*City Council Proceedings 1663-1701* (B.5.1), folio 152 recto)

#559: 2 January 1677 – Henry Oldenberg writes to Isaac Newton about Ralph Austen's death (*Cambridge University Library MS Add 3976*, folio 17a) (cited in H.W. Turnbull (ed.) *The Correspondence of Isaac Newton, Volume II 1676-1687* (Cambridge: Cambridge University Press, 1960), page 187) (extract)

#560: 26 February 1677 – Thomas Tisdale and others are rebuked for not attending council meetings (*City Council Proceedings 1663-1701* (B.5.1), folio 152 verso-153 recto)

#561: 4 March 1677 – John Johnson granted Oxford Citizenship (the 'Freedom of the City') (*Civic Enrolments 1662-1699* (L.5.4), page 636)

#562: 16 March 1677 – Thomas Tisdale is fined for not attending a council meeting (*City Council Proceedings 1663-1701* (B.5.1), folio 154 recto)

#563: 12 April 1677 – Thomas Tisdale is fined for not attending a council meeting (*City Council Proceedings 1663-1701* (B.5.1), folio 154 verso)

#563a: 29 April 1677 – Francis Gibbs from Oxford was received into membership at the Baptist church in Petty France, London (*Petty France (Particular) Baptist Church* (MS 20 228 1B), page 5)

#564: 25 June 1677 – Apprenticeship contract between William Fowler and Richard Quelch (*Civic Enrolments 1662-1699* (L.5.4), page 274)

#565: 16 July 1677 – Thomas Tisdale is fined for not attending a council meeting (*City Council Proceedings 1663-1701* (B.5.1), folio 155 verso)

#566: 27 August 1677 – Thomas Tisdale is admitted to a bailiff's place and has his fines remitted (*City Council Proceedings 1663-1701* (B.5.1), folio 157 recto)

#567: August 1677 – Thomas Tisdale and William Cornish approach George Barbour about his case against Philip Dodwell for noctivagation (MS Bodl 594), folio 158 verso (extract)

#568: 17 September 1677 – Thomas Tisdale is elected to a bailiff's place (*City Council Proceedings 1663-1701* (B.5.1), folio 157 verso)

#569: 21 September 1677 – Daniel Wildgoose granted Oxford Citizenship (the 'Freedom of the City') (*Civic Enrolments 1662-1699* (L.5.4), page 643)

#570: 29 September 1677 – Thomas Tisdale takes up the office of senior bailiff and swears the required oaths of office (*City Council Proceedings 1663-1701* (B.5.1), folio 158 recto)

#571: 9 November 1677 – Edward Wyans junior is admitted to a warden's place within the Guild of Cordwainers (*MS Morrell 14 - Order Book of the Guild of Cordwayners (1614-1711)*, folio 102 recto)

#571a: 16 December 1677 – Sister Hall from Oxford was received into membership at the Baptist church in Petty France, London (*Petty France (Particular) Baptist Church* (MS 20 228 1B), page 7)

#572: 17 January 1678 – Apprenticeship contract between William Burrowes and Thomas Tisdale; amended to a contract between Burrowes and John Tompkins on 6 September 1680 (*Civic Enrolments 1662-1699* (L.5.4), page 281)

#573: 7 February 1678 – John Tidmarsh granted Oxford Citizenship (the 'Freedom of the City') (*Civic Enrolments 1662-1699* (L.5.4), page 629)

#574: 10 February 1678 – Thomas Cooper granted Oxford Citizenship (the 'Freedom of the City') (*Civic Enrolments 1662-1699* (L.5.4), page 626)

#575: 8 April 1678 – Robert Stiles granted Oxford Citizenship (the 'Freedom of the City') (*Civic Enrolments 1662-1699* (L.5.4), page 638)

#576: 12 April 1678 – John Johnson apprentice of John Toms admitted as a member of the Guild of Cordwainers (*MS Morrell 14 - Order Book of the Guild of Cordwayners (1614-1711)*, folio 102 recto)

#577: 27 May 1678 – Apprenticeship contract between William Beck and Edward Wyans (*Civic Enrolments 1662-1699* (L.5.4), page 287)

#578: 31 May 1678 – William Stibbs granted Oxford Citizenship (the 'Freedom of the City') (*Civic Enrolments 1662-1699* (L.5.4), page 637)

#579: 27 June 1678 – Indenture on Ralph Austen's property in the parish of St. Peter-in-the-Bailey guaranteeing Sarah Austen's right to live there until the end of her life (*MS Ch Oxon c. 50* (#4502)

#580: 22 July 1678 – Thomas George granted Oxford Citizenship (the 'Freedom of the City') (*Civic Enrolments 1662-1699* (L.5.4), page 623)

#581: 22 July 1678 – Henry Miles granted Oxford Citizenship (the 'Freedom of the City') (*Civic Enrolments 1662-1699* (L.5.4), page 636)

#582: 13 September 1678 – Thomas Tisdale takes up a the office of senior bailiff and swears the required oaths of office (*City Council Proceedings 1663-1701* (B.5.1), folio 167 verso)

#583: 29 September 1678 – Thomas Tisdale surrenders the office of senior bailiff (*City Council Proceedings 1663-1701* (B.5.1), folio 168 recto)

#584: 14 January 1679 – Edward Wyans's apprentice Daniel Wildgoose is admitted to the Guild of Cordwainers (*MS Morrell 14 - Order Book of the Guild of Cordwayners (1614-1711)*, folio 103 verso)

#585: 14 January 1679 – John Toms fined for not appearing a meeting of the Guild of Cordwainers (*MS Morrell 14 - Order Book of the Guild of Cordwayners (1614-1711)*, folio 104 recto)

#586: 29 January 1679 – Richard Tidmarsh and Ellinor Seale are named among 104 persons excommunicated (*Diocesan Records – Excommunications: 1633-1791* (c. 99), folios 226 recto – 227 recto)

#587: 24 August 1679 – John Hardwell granted Oxford Citizenship (the 'Freedom of the City') (*City Council Proceedings - 1663-1701* (B.5.1), folio 176 recto)

#588: 1679 – Bishop John Fell's list of Dissenters for the parish of All Saints' in the city of Oxford (*Oxford Archdeaconry Records – Returns of Recusants: 1679-1706* (c. 430), folio 41 recto)

#589: 1679 – Bishop John Fell's list of Dissenters for the parishes of Saint Michael's and St Peter-in-the-Bailey in the city of Oxford (*Oxford Archdeaconry Records – Returns of Recusants: 1679-1706* (c. 430), folio 41 verso)

#590: 1679 – John Toms and James Jennings presented by churchwardens of All Saints' parish in the city of Oxford (*Oxford Diocesan Records – Memorandum from Diocesan Books: 1679-1814* (b. 68), folio 4 recto)

#591: 9 March 1680 – Apprenticeship contract between Jonathan King and Lawrence King (*Civic Enrolments 1662-1699* (L.5.4), page 311)

#592: 9 June 1680 – Richard Tidmarsh, Lawrence King and John Toms are cited to appear before the court (*Oxford Diocesan Records – Miscellaneous Citations* (c. 62), folio 39 recto)

#593: 11 June 1680 – Thomas Tisdale is appointed to view a property in a lease renewal application (*City Council Proceedings 1663-1701* (B.5.1), folio 183 recto)

#594: 6 July 1680 – Richard Tidmarsh is named among 17 persons from Oxford parishes cited to appear before the court (*Oxford Diocesan Records – Citations 1678-1681* (c. 46), folio 131)

#595: 31 July 1680 – Lawrence King and Anne King are cited to appear before the ecclesiastical courts (*Diocesan Records – 1 June 1678–27 November 1680* (c. 2134), folio 111 recto)

#596: 3 August 1680 – Thomas Tisdale resigns his position as an 'Assistant' (*City Council Proceedings 1663-1701* (B.5.1), folio 184 recto)

#597: 9 August 1680 – Richard Carter is elected to replace Thomas Tisdale as an 'Assistant' but refuses to serve (*City Council Proceedings 1663-1701* (B.5.1), folio 184 verso)

#598: 30 August 1680 – Richard Tidmarsh and John Higgins senior are among a number excommunicated (*Diocesan Records – Excommunications: 1633-1791* (c. 99), folio 60 recto and verso)

#599: 1 October 1680 – Lawrence King, John Toms and James Jennings are cited to appear before the court (*Oxford Diocesan Records – Miscellaneous Citations* (c. 62), folio 32 recto)

#600: 9 November 1680 – Apprenticeship contract between Timothy Bignell and Edward Wyans (*Civic Enrolments 1662-1699* (L.5.4), page 321); amended to a contract between Bignell and Charles Prince on 11 May 1685

*#601: 15 November 1680 – Lemuel King granted Oxford Citizenship (the 'Freedom of the City') (*Civic Enrolments 1662-1699* (L.5.4), page 610)

#601a: 20 January 1681 – Marriage allegation for the marriage of Samuel Tidmarsh and Sarah Wall (*Lambeth Palace Library: Faculty Office Marriage Allegation – 20 January 1681*)

#602: February 1681(?) – John and Frances Toms and James Jennings are named among 38 persons from Oxfordshire parishes who cited to appear before the court (*Oxford Diocesan Records – Miscellaneous Citations* (c. 62), folio 41)

#603: 4 March 1681 – Apprenticeship contract between Edmund Drinkwater and John Toms (*Civic Enrolments 1662-1699* (L.5.4), page 323)

#604: 11 June 1681 – Anne King buried in All Saints' parish church (*Parish Register of All Saints' -1678-1812* (Par 189/1/R1/2), folio 5 verso)

#605: 29 June 1681 – Roger Cooper is cited to appear before the court (*Oxford Diocesan Records – Citations –1678-1681* (c. 46), folio 149 recto)

#606: 2 July 1681 – Roger Cooper indicted for burying the excommunicated Anne King in the parish church grounds (*Oxford Archdeaconry Acts - 1678-1688* (c. 22), folio 163 recto)

#607: 27 August 1681 – Letter from Thomas Hyde to Leoline Jenkins about Richard Tidmarsh and Stephen College (*State Papers* 29/416, Part 2), page 52)

#608: 22 September 1681 – Letter from Humphrey Prideaux about Richard Tidmarsh and Stephen Colledge (*BL Additional MS 28929*, folio 60 recto) = *Letters of Humphrey Prideaux to John Ellis*, edited by Edward Maunde Thompson (Camden Society, 1875), page 95) (extract)

#608a: 14 October 1681 – Apprenticeship contract between Samuel King and Leonard Cotes (*Painter-Stainers Company Apprenticeships – 1666-1795* (GL MS 5669/1), folio 56 recto)

#609: 11 November 1681 – Marriage bond between Lemuel King and Mary King (*Oxford Archdeaconry Records: Marriage Bonds – 1681* (c. 469), folio 68 recto)

#610: 26 November 1681 – Richard Betteris junior is excommunicated (*Archdeaconry Records – Excommunications: 1610-1783* (c. 121), folio 300 recto)

#611: 25 June 1683 – Lawrence King's house searched for arms (*MS Wood Diaries 27*, folio 29 verso)

#612: 2 December 1683 – Richard Tidmarsh is fined £20 for not going to his parish church (*Precedents – 1660-1710* (N.4.6), folio 197 verso)

#613: 5 May 1684 – Apprenticeship contract between Robert Tewson and Lawrence King (*Civic Enrolments 1662-1699* (L.5.4), page 363)

#614: 1 May 1685 – Edward Wyans's apprentice John Hardwell is admitted to the Guild of Cordwainers (*MS Morrell 14 - Order Book of the Guild of Cordwayners (1614-1711)*, folio 114 recto)

#615: 30 October 1685 – Anthony Wood's entry about the St Thomas bridge (*MS Wood Diaries 29*, folio 60 verso)

#616: 16 July 1686 – Apprenticeship contract between James Jennings and Thomas Day; amended to a contract between Jennings and Robert Books on 7 November 1691, and to a contract between Jennings and John Shelfox on 8 May 1692 (*Civic Enrolments 1662-1699* (L.5.4), page 392)

#617: 21 December 1686 – Will and probate records of Edward Wyans junior (*Oxford Wills and Probate Records 73/2/3*); the will was probated on 23 May 1687 and an inventory of his goods was also submitted on that day

#618: 10 May 1687 – Last will and testament of Elizabeth Fursdon (*Tiverton Baptist Baptist Church Records – Will of Elizabeth Fursdon – 10 May 1687 –* #3958D Add #9)

#619: 28 June 1687 – Marriage bond between John Toms and Sarah Tull (*Oxford Archdeaconry Records: Marriage Bonds – 1687*, (c. 475), folio 136)

#620: 19 October 1687 – Thomas Tisdale lease and property bond on a property in the parish of St. Martin (*Christ Church Leases – VIII. St Martin's – 1ˢᵗ Tenement – #11*)

#621: November 1687– The Anabaptists of Oxford, Abingdon and Wantage send an address to James II – (*The London Gazette* #2294 (Thursday 10 November to Monday 14 November 1687), page 1)

#622: 30 December 1687 – John Toms fined for not appearing a a meeting of the Guild of Cordwainers (*MS Morrell 14 - Order Book of the Guild of Cordwayners (1614-1711)*, folio 121 recto)

#623: 18 January 1688 – John Toms signs an agreement that all members of the Guild of Cordwainers should abide by its regulations (*MS Morrell 14 - Order Book of the Guild of Cordwayners (1614-1711)*, folio 122 recto)

#624: 16 February 1688 – City Council receives orders from King James II to appoint Richard Tidmarsh a Bayliffe (*City Council Proceedings - 1663-1701* (B.5.1), folio 261 recto)

#625: 13 February 1688 – Minutes of a disciplinary case involving the churches of John Belcher and Francis Bampfield (*Church Book of the Francis Bampfield Congregation 1686-1843*, page 11)

#626: 14 May 1688 – Apprenticeship contract between John Charman and John Toms (*Civic Enrolments 1662-1699* (L.5.4), page 413)

#627: 14 May 1688 – William Cannon granted Oxford Citizenship (the 'Freedom of the City') (*Civic Enrolments 1662-1699* (L.5.4), page 566)

#628: 9 August 1688 – Warrant for the Oxford Charter includes civic appointments for Richard Tidmarsh, Lawrence King and John Toms (*State Papers Domestic* (SP 44/338), pages 47-49)

#629: 28 September 1688 – Lawrence King appointed to the Common Council (*City Council Proceedings 1663-1701* (B.5.1), folio 266 verso)

#630: 15 April 1689 – Clerk's note about Lawrence King and Richard Tidmarsh certifying to the court of the existence of a Baptist church meeting at Tidmarsh's house (*Oxford Petty Sessions Clerk's Notebook – 1687-1701* (O.2.1), folio 18 verso)

#631: 7 June 1689 – Frances Higgins is cited to appear before the court (*Oxford Diocesan Records – Citations –1688-1691* (c. 49), folio 38 recto)

#632: 8 June 1689 – A dispute between Frances Higgins and Mary Jennings is brought before the ecclesiastical court (*Archdeaconry Records – 15 October 1681-16 December 1693* (c. 23), folio 120 recto)

#633: 15 July 1689 – Lawrence King and Richard Tidmarsh certify to the court the existence of a Baptist church meeting at Tidmarsh's house (*Oxford Petty Sessions Roll – 1679-1712* (O.5.12), folio 66 verso)

#633a: 28 July 1689 – London Baptists call for a General Assembly in London (*Baptist Missionary Society – Home Papers: Underhill's Copies of Three Seventeenth-Century Letters* (H/13/5/iii), pages 1-2)

#634: 3-12 September 1689 – General Assembly of Baptists plan a mission to eastern counties (*Narrative of the Proceedings of the General Assembly* (1690), pages 4-5)

#635: 13 September 1689 – Jonathan King granted Oxford Citizenship (the 'Freedom of the City') (*Civic Enrolments – 1663-1669* (L.5.4), page 554)

#636: 27 September 1689 – Jonathan King granted Oxford Citizenship (the 'Freedom of the City') (*City Council Proceedings - 1663-1701* (B.5.1), folio 275 verso)

#637 27 September 1689 – John Toms junior is admitted into the Guild of Cordwainers (*MS Morrell 14 - Order Book of the Guild of Cordwayners (1614-1711)*, folio 123 verso)

#638: 1689 – Richard Tidmarsh's preaching tour in Essex, Suffolk and Norfolk (Edward Spurrier *Memorials of the Baptist Church Worshipping in Eld Lane Chapel, Colchester* (Colchester: F. Wright, 1889), pages 10-11)

#639: 26 December 1689 – Richard Tidmarsh serves on the panel of ministers adjudicating the controversy between the churches of John Belcher and Francis Bampfield (*Church Book of the Francis Bampfield Congregation 1686-1843*, page 16)

#640: 2 January 1690 – John Toms fined for not appearing a a meeting of the Guild of Cordwainers (*MS Morrell 14 - Order Book of the Guild of Cordwayners (1614-1711)*, folio 128 recto)

#641: 9 February 1690 – William Burrowes granted Oxford Citizenship (the 'Freedom of the City') (*Civic Enrolments 1662-1699* (L.5.4), page 545)

#642: 27 February 1690 – Joseph Tisdale signs a marriage bond between Joseph Tisdale and Mary Spencer (*Oxford Archdeaconry Records: Marriage Bonds – 1689* (c. 476), folio 133 recto)

#643: 17 March 1690 – Richard Tidmarsh receives financial gift for his preaching in Devon (Letter of Joshua Thomas to John Rippon (Rippon Collection in Angus Library (D/RPN 4/1), page 2)

#644: 17 October 1690 – Lawrence King is mentioned within an apprenticeship dispute between Elisha King and Lemuel King (*Oxford Petty Sessions Clerk's Notebook – 1687-1701* (O.2.1), folios 39 verso–40 recto)

#645: 10 December 1690 – Ralph Austen's property in the parish of St. Peter-in-the-Bailey is sold to John Greeneway (*MS Ch Oxon c. 50* (#4503a)

#646: 16 April 1691 – Thomas Tisdale attends a trustees' meeting for Mrs Nixon's charity for Apprenticing Boys out of the Nixon Free School (*Alderman Nixon's Free School- 1658* (Q.5.1), page 25)

#647: 2 May 1691 – John Pittman lease on a tenement (33-35 Cornmarket) and 'the antiquated dancing school' outside the North Gate is renewed (*Oxford City Ledgers 1675-1696* (D.5.7), folios 268 verso and 269 recto)

#648: 1691(?) – Ralph Austen's property in the parish of St. Peter-in-the-Bailey is sold to John Greeneway (*MS Ch Oxon c. 50* (#4503b)

#649: 12 November 1691 – Richard Tidmarsh is ordained to ministry in Tiverton, Devon (*Tiverton Baptist Church Records – Church Minute Meeting Book – 1687-1845 – #3958 #1*, folio 3 verso); (cited in Joseph Ivimey *A History of the English Baptists*, Volume 2 (London, 1814), page 138)

#650: 6 July 1692 – Anthony Wood's entry about Richard Claridge and Richard Tidmarsh's meeting house (*MS Wood Diaries 36*, folio 38 recto)

#651: 1692 – Anthony Wood's entry about Thomas Weaver and his publication of the ballad *Zeal observed* in 1654 – (*Athenae Oxonienses, Volume 2* (1692), pages 212-213)

#652: 1692 – Anthony Wood's note about John Troughton and the meetings held in Tom Pun's house in Broken Hayes (*Athenae Oxonienses, Volume 2* (1692), page 511)

#653: 1692 – Anthony Wood's note about Henry Cornish in *Fasti Oxonienses* entry for 1649 – (*Athenae Oxonienses, Volume 2* (1692), page 771)

#654: 1692 – Anthony Wood's note about Ralph Austen in *Fasti Oxonienses* entry for 1652 – (*Athenae Oxonienses, Volume 2* (1692), page 780)

#655: 2 July 1693 – Thomas King is excommunicated (*Diocesan Records – Excommunications: 1633-1791* (c. 99), folio 117 recto)

#656: 3 January 1694 – Jane Prowse sets up a trust to benefit the work of Baptists (*Tiverton Baptist Church Records – Prowse Trust Deed – 1694-1702 –* #3958D Add #5, folio 2 recto-2 verso)

#567: 27 February 1694 – Inventory record of John Toms (*Oxford Wills and Probate Records* 175/2/27)

#658: 2 March 1694 – Probate record of John Toms (*Oxford Wills and Probate Records* 175/2/27)

#659: 13 April 1694 – Edward Drinkwater granted Oxford Citizenship (the 'Freedom of the City') (*Civic Enrolments 1662-1699* (L.5.4), page 524)

#660: 4 January 1695 – John Toms fined for not appearing a a meeting of the Guild of Cordwainers (*MS Morrell 14 - Order Book of the Guild of Cordwayners (1614-1711)*, folio 135 recto)

#661: 11 January 1695 – Apprenticeship contract between Richard Meares and Jonathan King (*Civic Enrolments 1662-1699* (L.5.4), page 480)

#662: 9 February 1695 – Thomas Whinnell letter to Tristram Trurin which mentions Richard Tidmarsh (*Tiverton Baptist Church Records – Thomas Whinnell Letter – 9 February 1695 –* #3958 #3)

*#663: 18 February 1695 – Thomas Whinnell letter to Robert Stone which mentions Richard Tidmarsh (*Tiverton Baptist Church Records – Thomas Whinnell Letter – 18 February 1695 –* #3958 #2)

#664: 13 September 1695 – Thomas Meares granted Oxford Citizenship (the 'Freedom of the City') (*Civic Enrolments 1662-1699* (L.5.4), page 523)

#665: 23 September 1695 – John Charman granted Oxford Citizenship (the 'Freedom of the City') (*Civic Enrolments 1662-1699* (L.5.4), page 523)

#666: 9 January 1696 – Elisha King indicted for mistreating his apprentice (*Oxford Petty Sessions Roll – 1679-1712* (O.5.12), folio 86 verso)

#667: 12 July 1696 – John Charman admitted as a member of the Guild of Cordwainers (*MS Morrell 14 - Order Book of the Guild of Cordwayners (1614-1711)*, folio 137 recto)

#668: 1696 – 1825 Oxford citizens sign an Association Oath supporting William III (*Association Oath Roll – Oxford – 1696* (c. 213/208))

#669: 1696 – 434 Tiverton citizens sign an Association Oath supporting William III (*Association Oath Roll – Tiverton – 1696* (c. 213/86))

#670: 18 May 1697 – License granted to the Baptist church in Tiverton by William III lists Richard Tidmarsh as one of the ministers (*Tiverton Baptist Church Records* #3958D #4)

#670a: 2 March 1698 – John Toms involved in a case of church discipline of Sarah Kiffin (*Devonshire Square (Particular) Baptist Church* (MS 20 228 1A), folios 13 recto-verso)

#671: 9 January 1699 – Richard Tidmarsh involved in a case of church discipline (*Tiverton Baptist Church Records – Church Minute Meeting Book – 1687-1845 – #3958 #1*, folio 7 recto)

*#672: 2 April 1699 – Richard Tidmarsh involved in a case of church discipline (*Tiverton Baptist Church Records – Church Minute Meeting Book – 1687-1845 – #3958 #1*, folios 7 verso-8 recto)

#673: 2 May 1700 – Richard Tidmarsh involved in a case of church discipline (*Tiverton Baptist Church Records – Church Minute Meeting Book – 1687-1845 – #3958 #1*, folios 9 recto-9 verso)

#674: 24 September 1701 – Apprenticeship contract between John Sheppard and Jonathan King (*The Enrolments of Apprentices 1697-1800* (F.4.9), folio 26 recto)

#675: 23 October 1701 – Thomas Tisdale lease and property bond on a property in the parish of St. Martin (*Christ Church Leases – VIII. St Martin's – 1ˢᵗ Tenement – #13*)

#676: 5 November 1701 – The church appoints another minister to support the ageing Richard Tidmarsh (*Tiverton Baptist Church Records – Church Minute Meeting Book – 1687-1845 – #3958 #1*, folio 13 verso)

#677: 12 July 1702 – Richard Tidmarsh involved in a case of church discipline (*Tiverton Baptist Church Records – Church Minute Meeting Book – 1687-1845 – #3958 #1*, folios 12 verso-13 recto)

#678: 21 February 1703 – Richard Tidmarsh involved in a case of church discipline (*Tiverton Baptist Church Records – Church Minute Meeting Book – 1687-1845 – #3958 #1*, folio 15 recto)

#679: 13 June 1704 – Apprenticeship contract between William Carter and Jonathan King (*The Enrolments of Apprentices 1697-1800* (F.4.9), folio 44 recto)

#680: 14 February 1705 – Apprenticeship contract between John Brooker and Jonathan King (*The Enrolments of Apprentices 1697-1800* (F.4.9), folio 48 recto)

#681: 1 March 1705 – Trust of Elizabeth Fursdon is established to benefit the Baptist ministry (*Tiverton Baptist Baptist Church Records – Will of Elizabeth Fursdon – 10 May 1687* – #3958D Add #9, folio 9 verso)

#682: 27 April 1705 – William Toms granted Oxford Citizenship (the 'Freedom of the City') (*Civic Enrolments 1697-1780* (L.5.5), folio 22 recto)

#682a: 22 September 1709 – Memorial plaque for Theophilus Poynter and his family (Memorial inscription in Saint Mary the Virgin Church, Oxford)

#683: 5 May 1712 – Apprenticeship contract between John Wills and Jonathan King (*The Enrolments of Apprentices 1697-1800* (F.4.9), folio 88 recto)

#684: 1 July 1719 – James and Hannah Stonehouse lease and property bond on a property in the parish of St. Martin (*Christ Church Leases – VIII. St Martin's – 1st Tenement – #15*)

#685: 10 November 1719 – Probate records of Jonathan King (*Oxford Wills and Probate Records* 169/2/15); an inventory of his goods was compiled on 9 November 1719

#686: 21 February 1721 – Probate bond of Sarah Tisdale (*Oxford Wills & Probate Records* 175/3/13)

#687: 25 May 1733 – Hannah Stonehouse surrenders her lease on a property in the parish of St. Martin (*Christ Church Leases – VIII. St Martin's – 1st Tenement – #16*)

#687a: 1 January 1740 – Will of James Tidmarsh (*Prerogative Court of Canterbury and Related Probate Jurisdictions: Will Registers 1384-1858* (PROB 11/700), folios 205 verso-206 recto); the will was probated on 4 January 1740

#688: 1820 – Anthony Wood's note about Thomas Gilbert (*Athenae Oxonienses*, 3rd edition, revised by Philip Bliss, Volume 4 (London: 1820), page 407

Studies in Baptist History and Thought

(All titles uniform with this volume)
Dates in bold are of projected publication
Volumes in this series are not always published in sequence

David Bebbington and Anthony R. Cross (eds)
Global Baptist History
(SBHT vol. 14)

This book brings together studies from the Second International Conference on Baptist Studies which explore different facets of Baptist life and work especially during the twentieth century.

2006 / 1-84227-214-4 / approx. 350pp

David Bebbington (ed.)
The Gospel in the World
International Baptist Studies
(SBHT vol. 1)

This volume of essays from the First International Conference on Baptist Studies deals with a range of subjects spanning Britain, North America, Europe, Asia and the Antipodes. Topics include studies on religious tolerance, the communion controversy and the development of the international Baptist community, and concludes with two important essays on the future of Baptist life that pay special attention to the United States.

2002 / 1-84227-118-0 / xiv + 362pp

John H.Y. Briggs (ed.)
Pulpit and People
Studies in Eighteenth-Century English Baptist Life and Thought
(SBHT vol. 28)

The eighteenth century was a crucial time in Baptist history. The denomination had its roots in seventeenth-century English Puritanism and Separatism and the persecution of the Stuart kings with only a limited measure of freedom after 1689. Worse, however, was to follow for with toleration came doctrinal conflict, a move away from central Christian understandings and a loss of evangelistic urgency. Both spiritual and numerical decline ensued, to the extent that the denomination was virtually reborn as rather belatedly it came to benefit from the Evangelical Revival which brought new life to both Arminian and Calvinistic Baptists. The papers in this volume study a denomination in transition, and relate to theology, their views of the church and its mission, Baptist spirituality, and engagements with radical politics.

2007 / 1-84227-403-1 / approx. 350pp

July 2005

Damian Brot
Church of the Baptized or Church of Believers?
A Contribution to the Dialogue between the Catholic Church and the Free Churches with Special Reference to Baptists
(SBHT vol. 26)
The dialogue between the Catholic Church and the Free Churches in Europe has hardly taken place. This book pleads for a commencement of such a conversation. It offers, among other things, an introduction to the American and the international dialogues between Baptists and the Catholic Church and strives to allow these conversations to become fruitful in the European context as well.

2006 / 1-84227-334-5 / approx. 364pp

Dennis Bustin
Paradox and Perseverence
Hanserd Knollys, Particular Baptist Pioneer in Seventeenth-Century England
(SBHT vol. 23)
The seventeenth century was a significant period in English history during which the people of England experienced unprecedented change and tumult in all spheres of life. At the same time, the importance of order and the traditional institutions of society were being reinforced. Hanserd Knollys, born during this pivotal period, personified in his life the ambiguity, tension and paradox of it, openly seeking change while at the same time cautiously embracing order. As a founder and leader of the Particular Baptists in London and despite persecution and personal hardship, he played a pivotal role in helping shape their identity externally in society and, internally, as they moved toward becoming more formalised by the end of the century.

2006 / 1-84227-259-4 / approx. 324pp

Anthony R. Cross
Baptism and the Baptists
Theology and Practice in Twentieth-Century Britain
(SBHT vol. 3)
At a time of renewed interest in baptism, *Baptism and the Baptists* is a detailed study of twentieth-century baptismal theology and practice and the factors which have influenced its development.

2000 / 0-85364-959-6 / xx + 530pp

Anthony R. Cross and Philip E. Thompson (eds)
Baptist Sacramentalism
(SBHT vol. 5)
This collection of essays includes biblical, historical and theological studies in the theology of the sacraments from a Baptist perspective. Subjects explored include the physical side of being spiritual, baptism, the Lord's supper, the church, ordination, preaching, worship, religious liberty and the issue of disestablishment.

2003 / 1-84227-119-9 / xvi + 278pp

Anthony R. Cross and Philip E. Thompson (eds)
Baptist Sacramentalism 2
(SBHT vol. 25)
This second collection of essays exploring various dimensions of sacramental theology from a Baptist perspective includes biblical, historical and theological studies from scholars from around the world.

2006 / 1-84227-325-6 / approx. 350pp

Paul S. Fiddes
Tracks and Traces
Baptist Identity in Church and Theology
(SBHT vol. 13)
This is a comprehensive, yet unusual, book on the faith and life of Baptist Christians. It explores the understanding of the church, ministry, sacraments and mission from a thoroughly theological perspective. In a series of interlinked essays, the author relates Baptist identity consistently to a theology of covenant and to participation in the triune communion of God.

2003 / 1-84227-120-2 / xvi + 304pp

Stanley K. Fowler
More Than a Symbol
The British Baptist Recovery of Baptismal Sacramentalism
(SBHT vol. 2)
Fowler surveys the entire scope of British Baptist literature from the seventeenth-century pioneers onwards. He shows that in the twentieth century leading British Baptist pastors and theologians recovered an understanding of baptism that connected experience with soteriology and that in doing so they were recovering what many of their forebears had taught.

2002 / 1-84227-052-4 / xvi + 276pp

Steven R. Harmon
Towards Baptist Catholicity
Essays on Tradition and the Baptist Vision
(SBHT vol. 27)

This series of essays contends that the reconstruction of the Baptist vision in the wake of modernity's dissolution requires a retrieval of the ancient ecumenical tradition that forms Christian identity through rehearsal and practice. Themes explored include catholic identity as an emerging trend in Baptist theology, tradition as a theological category in Baptist perspective, Baptist confessions and the patristic tradition, worship as a principal bearer of tradition, and the role of Baptist higher education in shaping the Christian vision.

2006 / 1-84227-362-0 / approx. 210pp

Michael A.G. Haykin (ed.)
'At the Pure Fountain of Thy Word'
Andrew Fuller as an Apologist
(SBHT vol. 6)

One of the greatest Baptist theologians of the eighteenth and early nineteenth centuries, Andrew Fuller has not had justice done to him. There is little doubt that Fuller's theology lay behind the revitalization of the Baptists in the late eighteenth century and the first few decades of the nineteenth. This collection of essays fills a much needed gap by examining a major area of Fuller's thought, his work as an apologist.

2004 / 1-84227-171-7 / xxii + 276pp

Michael A.G. Haykin
Studies in Calvinistic Baptist Spirituality
(SBHT vol. 15)

In a day when spirituality is in vogue and Christian communities are looking for guidance in this whole area, there is wisdom in looking to the past to find untapped wells. The Calvinistic Baptists, heirs of the rich ecclesial experience in the Puritan era of the seventeenth century, but, by the end of the eighteenth century, also passionately engaged in the catholicity of the Evangelical Revivals, are such a well. This collection of essays, covering such things as the Lord's Supper, friendship and hymnody, seeks to draw out the spiritual riches of this community for reflection and imitation in the present day.

2006 / 1-84227-149-0 / approx. 350pp

Brian Haymes, Anthony R. Cross and Ruth Gouldbourne
On Being the Church
Revisioning Baptist Identity
(SBHT vol. 21)
The aim of the book is to re-examine Baptist theology and practice in the light of the contemporary biblical, theological, ecumenical and missiological context drawing on historical and contemporary writings and issues. It is not a study in denominationalism but rather seeks to revision historical insights from the believers' church tradition for the sake of Baptists and other Christians in the context of the modern–postmodern context.
2006 / 1-84227-121-0 / approx. 350pp

Ken R. Manley
From Woolloomooloo to 'Eternity': A History of Australian Baptists
Volume 1: Growing an Australian Church (1831–1914)
Volume 2: A National Church in a Global Community (1914–2005)
(SBHT vols 16.1 and 16.2)
From their beginnings in Australia in 1831 with the first baptisms in Woolloomoolloo Bay in 1832, this pioneering study describes the quest of Baptists in the different colonies (states) to discover their identity as Australians and Baptists. Although institutional developments are analyzed and the roles of significant individuals traced, the major focus is on the social and theological dimensions of the Baptist movement.
2 vol. set 2006 / 1-84227-405-8 / approx. 900pp

Ken R. Manley
'Redeeming Love Proclaim'
John Rippon and the Baptists
(SBHT vol. 12)
A leading exponent of the new moderate Calvinism which brought new life to many Baptists, John Rippon (1751–1836) helped unite the Baptists at this significant time. His many writings expressed the denomination's growing maturity and mutual awareness of Baptists in Britain and America, and exerted a long-lasting influence on Baptist worship and devotion. In his various activities, Rippon helped conserve the heritage of Old Dissent and promoted the evangelicalism of the New Dissent
2004 / 1-84227-193-8 / xviii + 340pp

Peter J. Morden
Offering Christ to the World
Andrew Fuller and the Revival of English Particular Baptist Life
(SBHT vol. 8)
Andrew Fuller (1754–1815) was one of the foremost English Baptist ministers of his day. His career as an Evangelical Baptist pastor, theologian, apologist and missionary statesman coincided with the profound revitalization of the Particular Baptist denomination to which he belonged. This study examines the key aspects of the life and thought of this hugely significant figure, and gives insights into the revival in which he played such a central part.
2003 / 1-84227-141-5 / xx + 202pp

Peter Naylor
Calvinism, Communion and the Baptists
A Study of English Calvinistic Baptists from the Late 1600s to the Early 1800s
(SBHT vol. 7)
Dr Naylor argues that the traditional link between 'high-Calvinism' and 'restricted communion' is in need of revision. He examines Baptist communion controversies from the late 1600s to the early 1800s and also the theologies of John Gill and Andrew Fuller.
2003 / 1-84227-142-3 / xx + 266pp

Ian M. Randall, Toivo Pilli and Anthony R. Cross (eds)
Baptist Identities
International Studies from the Seventeenth to the Twentieth Centuries
(SBHT vol. 19)
These papers represent the contributions of scholars from various parts of the world as they consider the factors that have contributed to Baptist distinctiveness in different countries and at different times. The volume includes specific case studies as well as broader examinations of Baptist life in a particular country or region. Together they represent an outstanding resource for understanding Baptist identities.
2005 / 1-84227-215-2 / approx. 350pp

James M. Renihan
Edification and Beauty
The Practical Ecclesiology of the English Particular Baptists, 1675–1705
(SBHT vol. 17)
Edification and Beauty describes the practices of the Particular Baptist churches at the end of the seventeenth century in terms of three concentric circles: at the centre is the ecclesiological material in the Second London Confession, which is then fleshed out in the various published writings of the men associated with these churches, and, finally, expressed in the church books of the era.
2005 / 1-84227-251-9 / approx. 230pp

Frank Rinaldi
'The Tribe of Dan'
A Study of the New Connexion of General Baptists 1770–1891
(SBHT vol. 10)
'The Tribe of Dan' is a thematic study which explores the theology, organizational structure, evangelistic strategy, ministry and leadership of the New Connexion of General Baptists as it experienced the process of institutionalization in the transition from a revival movement to an established denomination.
2006 / 1-84227-143-1 / approx. 350pp

Peter Shepherd
The Making of a Modern Denomination
John Howard Shakespeare and the English Baptists 1898–1924
(SBHT vol. 4)
John Howard Shakespeare introduced revolutionary change to the Baptist denomination. The Baptist Union was transformed into a strong central institution and Baptist ministers were brought under its control. Further, Shakespeare's pursuit of church unity reveals him as one of the pioneering ecumenists of the twentieth century.
2001 / 1-84227-046-X / xviii + 220pp

Karen Smith
The Community and the Believers
A Study of Calvinistic Baptist Spirituality in Some Towns and Villages of Hampshire and the Borders of Wiltshire, c.1730–1830
(SBHT vol. 22)

The period from 1730 to 1830 was one of transition for Calvinistic Baptists. Confronted by the enthusiasm of the Evangelical Revival, congregations within the denomination as a whole were challenged to find a way to take account of the revival experience. This study examines the life and devotion of Calvinistic Baptists in Hampshire and Wiltshire during this period. Among this group of Baptists was the hymn writer, Anne Steele.

2005 / 1-84227-326-4 / approx. 280pp

Martin Sutherland
Dissenters in a 'Free Land'
Baptist Thought in New Zealand 1850–2000
(SBHT vol. 24)

Baptists in New Zealand were forced to recast their identity. Conventions of communication and association, state and ecumenical relations, even historical divisions and controversies had to be revised in the face of new topographies and constraints. As Baptists formed themselves in a fluid society they drew heavily on both international movements and local dynamics. This book traces the development of ideas which shaped institutions and styles in sometimes surprising ways.

2006 / 1-84227-327-2 / approx. 230pp

Brian Talbot
The Search for a Common Identity
The Origins of the Baptist Union of Scotland 1800–1870
(SBHT vol. 9)

In the period 1800 to 1827 there were three streams of Baptists in Scotland: Scotch, Haldaneite and 'English' Baptist. A strong commitment to home evangelization brought these three bodies closer together, leading to a merger of their home missionary societies in 1827. However, the first three attempts to form a union of churches failed, but by the 1860s a common understanding of their corporate identity was attained leading to the establishment of the Baptist Union of Scotland.

2003 / 1-84227-123-7 / xviii + 402pp

Philip E. Thompson
The Freedom of God
Towards Baptist Theology in Pneumatological Perspective
(SBHT vol. 20)

This study contends that the range of theological commitments of the early Baptists are best understood in relation to their distinctive emphasis on the freedom of God. Thompson traces how this was recast anthropocentrically, leading to an emphasis upon human freedom from the nineteenth century onwards. He seeks to recover the dynamism of the early vision via a pneumatologically-oriented ecclesiology defining the church in terms of the memory of God.

2006 / 1-84227-125-3 / approx. 350pp

Philip E. Thompson and Anthony R. Cross (eds)
Recycling the Past or Researching History?
Studies in Baptist Historiography and Myths
(SBHT vol. 11)

In this volume an international group of Baptist scholars examine and re-examine areas of Baptist life and thought about which little is known or the received wisdom is in need of revision. Historiographical studies include the date Oxford Baptists joined the Abingdon Association, the death of the Fifth Monarchist John Pendarves, eighteenth-century Calvinistic Baptists and the political realm, confessional identity and denominational institutions, Baptist community, ecclesiology, the priesthood of all believers, soteriology, Baptist spirituality, Strict and Reformed Baptists, the role of women among British Baptists, while various 'myths' challenged include the nature of high-Calvinism in eighteenth-century England, baptismal anti-sacramentalism, episcopacy, and Baptists and change.

2005 / 1-84227-122-9 / approx. 330pp

Linda Wilson
Marianne Farningham
A Plain Working Woman
(SBHT vol. 18)

Marianne Farningham, of College Street Baptist Chapel, Northampton, was a household name in evangelical circles in the later nineteenth century. For over fifty years she produced comment, poetry, biography and fiction for the popular Christian press. This investigation uses her writings to explore the beliefs and behaviour of evangelical Nonconformists, including Baptists, during these years.

2006 / 1-84227-124-5 / approx. 250pp

Other Paternoster titles
relating to Baptist history and thought

George R. Beasley-Murray
Baptism in the New Testament
(Paternoster Digital Library)

This is a welcome reprint of a classic text on baptism originally published in 1962 by one of the leading Baptist New Testament scholars of the twentieth century. Dr Beasley-Murray's comprehensive study begins by investigating the antecedents of Christian baptism. It then surveys the foundation of Christian baptism in the Gospels, its emergence in the Acts of the Apostles and development in the apostolic writings. Following a section relating baptism to New Testament doctrine, a substantial discussion of the origin and significance of infant baptism leads to a briefer consideration of baptismal reform and ecumenism.

2005 / 1-84227-300-0 / x + 422pp

Paul Beasley-Murray
Fearless for Truth
A Personal Portrait of the Life of George Beasley-Murray

Without a doubt George Beasley-Murray was one of the greatest Baptists of the twentieth century. A long-standing Principal of Spurgeon's College, he wrote more than twenty books and made significant contributions in the study of areas as diverse as baptism and eschatology, as well as writing highly respected commentaries on the Book of Revelation and John's Gospel.

2002 / 1-84227-134-2 / xii + 244pp

David Bebbington
Holiness in Nineteenth-Century England
(Studies in Christian History and Thought)

David Bebbington stresses the relationship of movements of spirituality to changes in their cultural setting, especially the legacies of the Enlightenment and Romanticism. He shows that these broad shifts in ideological mood had a profound effect on the ways in which piety was conceptualized and practised. Holiness was intimately bound up with the spirit of the age.

2000 / 0-85364-981-2 / viii + 98pp

Clyde Binfield
Victorian Nonconformity in Eastern England 1840–1885
(Studies in Evangelical History and Thought)

Studies of Victorian religion and society often concentrate on cities, suburbs, and industrialisation. This study provides a contrast. Victorian Eastern England—Essex, Suffolk, Norfolk, Cambridgeshire, and Huntingdonshire—was rural, traditional, relatively unchanging. That is nonetheless a caricature which discounts the industry in Norwich and Ipswich (as well as in Haverhill, Stowmarket and Leiston) and ignores the impact of London on Essex, of railways throughout the region, and of an ancient but changing university (Cambridge) on the county town which housed it. It also entirely ignores the political implications of such changes in a region noted for the variety of its religious Dissent since the seventeenth century. This book explores Victorian Eastern England and its Nonconformity. It brings to a wider readership a pioneering thesis which has made a major contribution to a fresh evolution of English religion and society.

2006 / 1-84227-216-0 / approx. 274pp

Edward W. Burrows
'To Me To Live Is Christ'
A Biography of Peter H. Barber

This book is about a remarkably gifted and energetic man of God. Peter H. Barber was born into a Brethren family in Edinburgh in 1930. In his youth he joined Charlotte Baptist Chapel and followed the call into Baptist ministry. For eighteen years he was the pioneer minister of the new congregation in the New Town of East Kilbride, which planted two further congregations. At the age of thirty-nine he served as Centenary President of the Baptist Union of Scotland and then exercised an influential ministry for over seven years in the well-known Upton Vale Baptist Church, Torquay. From 1980 until his death in 1994 he was General Secretary of the Baptist Union of Scotland. Through his work for the European Baptist Federation and the Baptist World Alliance he became a world Baptist statesman. He was President of the EBF during the upheaval that followed the collapse of Communism.

2005 / 1-84227-324-8 / xxii + 236pp

Christopher J. Clement
Religious Radicalism in England 1535–1565
(Rutherford Studies in Historical Theology)

In this valuable study Christopher Clement draws our attention to a varied assemblage of people who sought Christian faithfulness in the underworld of mid-Tudor England. Sympathetically and yet critically he assess their place in the history of English Protestantism, and by attentive listening he gives them a voice.

1997 / 0-946068-44-5 / xxii + 426pp

July 2005

Anthony R. Cross (ed.)
Ecumenism and History
Studies in Honour of John H.Y. Briggs
(Studies in Christian History and Thought)
This collection of essays examines the inter-relationships between the two fields in which Professor Briggs has contributed so much: history—particularly Baptist and Nonconformist—and the ecumenical movement. With contributions from colleagues and former research students from Britain, Europe and North America, *Ecumenism and History* provides wide-ranging studies in important aspects of Christian history, theology and ecumenical studies.
2002 / 1-84227-135-0 / xx + 362pp

Keith E. Eitel
Paradigm Wars
The Southern Baptist International Mission Board
Faces the Third Millennium
(Regnum Studies in Mission)
The International Mission Board of the Southern Baptist Convention is the largest denominational mission agency in North America. This volume chronicles the historic and contemporary forces that led to the IMB's recent extensive reorganization, providing the most comprehensive case study to date of a historic mission agency restructuring to continue its mission purpose into the twenty-first century more effectively.
2000 / 1-870345-12-6 / x + 140pp

Ruth Gouldbourne
The Flesh and the Feminine
Gender and Theology in the Writings of Caspar Schwenckfeld
(Studies in Christian History and Thought)
Caspar Schwenckfeld and his movement exemplify one of the radical communities of the sixteenth century. Challenging theological and liturgical norms, they also found themselves challenging social and particularly gender assumptions. In this book, the issues of the relationship between radical theology and the understanding of gender are considered.
2005 / 1-84227-048-6 / approx. 304pp

David Hilborn
The Words of our Lips
Language-Use in Free Church Worship
(Paternoster Theological Monographs)
Studies of liturgical language have tended to focus on the written canons of
Roman Catholic and Anglican communities. By contrast, David Hilborn
analyses the more extemporary approach of English Nonconformity. Drawing
on recent developments in linguistic pragmatics, he explores similarities and
differences between 'fixed' and 'free' worship, and argues for the
interdependence of each.
2006 / 0-85364-977-4

Stephen R. Holmes
Listening to the Past
The Place of Tradition in Theology
Beginning with the question 'Why can't we just read the Bible?' Stephen
Holmes considers the place of tradition in theology, showing how the doctrine
of creation leads to an account of historical location and creaturely limitations as
essential aspects of our existence. For we cannot claim unmediated access to the
Scriptures without acknowledging the place of tradition: theology is an
irreducibly communal task. *Listening to the Past* is a sustained attempt to show
what listening to tradition involves, and how it can be used to aid theological
work today.
2002 / 1-84227-155-5 / xiv + 168pp

Mark Hopkins
Nonconformity's Romantic Generation
Evangelical and Liberal Theologies in Victorian England
(Studies in Evangelical History and Thought)
A study of the theological development of key leaders of the Baptist and
Congregational denominations at their period of greatest influence, including
C.H. Spurgeon and R.W. Dale, and of the controversies in which those among
them who embraced and rejected the liberal transformation of their evangelical
heritage opposed each other.
2004 / 1-84227-150-4 / xvi + 284pp

Galen K. Johnson
Prisoner of Conscience
John Bunyan on Self, Community and Christian Faith
(Studies in Christian History and Thought)
This is an interdisciplinary study of John Bunyan's understanding of conscience across his autobiographical, theological and fictional writings, investigating whether conscience always deserves fidelity, and how Bunyan's view of conscience affects his relationship both to modern Western individualism and historic Christianity.

2003 / 1-84227- 151-2 / xvi + 236pp

R.T. Kendall
Calvin and English Calvinism to 1649
(Studies in Christian History and Thought)
The author's thesis is that those who formed the Westminster Confession of Faith, which is regarded as Calvinism, in fact departed from John Calvin on two points: (1) the extent of the atonement and (2) the ground of assurance of salvation.

1997 / 0-85364-827-1 / xii + 264pp

Timothy Larsen
Friends of Religious Equality
Nonconformist Politics in Mid-Victorian England
During the middle decades of the nineteenth century the English Nonconformist community developed a coherent political philosophy of its own, of which a central tenet was the principle of religious equality (in contrast to the stereotype of Evangelical Dissenters). The Dissenting community fought for the civil rights of Roman Catholics, non-Christians and even atheists, on an issue of principle which had its flowering in the enthusiastic and undivided support which Nonconformity gave to the campaign for Jewish emancipation. This reissued study examines the political efforts and ideas of English Nonconformists during the period, covering the whole range of national issues raised, from state education to the Crimean War. It offers a case study of a theologically conservative group defending religious pluralism in the civic sphere, showing that the concept of religious equality was a grand vision at the centre of the political philosophy of the Dissenters.

2007 / 1-84227-402-3 / x + 300pp

Donald M. Lewis
Lighten Their Darkness
The Evangelical Mission to Working-Class London, 1828–1860
(Studies in Evangelical History and Thought)
This is a comprehensive and compelling study of the Church and the complexities of nineteenth-century London. Challenging our understanding of the culture in working London at this time, Lewis presents a well-structured and illustrated work that contributes substantially to the study of evangelicalism and mission in nineteenth-century Britain.

2001 / 1-84227-074-5 / xviii + 372pp

Stanley E. Porter and Anthony R. Cross (eds)
Semper Reformandum
Studies in Honour of Clark H. Pinnock
Clark Pinnock has clearly been one of the most important evangelical theologians of the last forty years in North America. Always provocative, especially in the wide range of opinions he has held and considered, Pinnock, himself a Baptist, has recently retired after twenty-five years of teaching at McMaster Divinity College. His colleagues and associates honour him in this volume by responding to his important theological work which has dealt with the essential topics of evangelical theology. These include Christian apologetics, biblical inspiration, the Holy Spirit and, perhaps most importantly in recent years, openness theology.

2003 / 1-84227-206-3 / xiv + 414pp

Meic Pearse
The Great Restoration
The Religious Radicals of the 16th and 17th Centuries
Pearse charts the rise and progress of continental Anabaptism – both evangelical and heretical – through the sixteenth century. He then follows the story of those English people who became impatient with Puritanism and separated – first from the Church of England and then from one another – to form the antecedents of later Congregationalists, Baptists and Quakers.

1998 / 0-85364-800-X / xii + 320pp

Charles Price and Ian M. Randall
Transforming Keswick
Transforming Keswick is a thorough, readable and detailed history of the convention. It will be of interest to those who know and love Keswick, those who are only just discovering it, and serious scholars eager to learn more about the history of God's dealings with his people.

2000 / 1-85078-350-0 / 288pp

Jim Purves
The Triune God and the Charismatic Movement
A Critical Appraisal from a Scottish Perspective
(Paternoster Theological Monographs)

All emotion and no theology? Or a fundamental challenge to reappraise and realign our trinitarian theology in the light of Christian experience? This study of charismatic renewal as it found expression within Scotland at the end of the twentieth century evaluates the use of Patristic, Reformed and contemporary models (including those of the Baptist Union of Scotland) of the Trinity in explaining the workings of the Holy Spirit.

2004 / 1-84227-321-3 / xxiv + 246pp

Ian M. Randall
Evangelical Experiences
A Study in the Spirituality of English Evangelicalism 1918–1939
(Studies in Evangelical History and Thought)

This book makes a detailed historical examination of evangelical spirituality between the First and Second World Wars. It shows how patterns of devotion led to tensions and divisions. In a wide-ranging study, Anglican, Wesleyan, Reformed and Pentecostal-charismatic spiritualities are analysed.

1999 / 0-85364-919-7 / xii + 310pp

Ian M. Randall
One Body in Christ
The History and Significance of the Evangelical Alliance

In 1846 the Evangelical Alliance was founded with the aim of bringing together evangelicals for common action. This book uses material not previously utilized to examine the history and significance of the Evangelical Alliance, a movement which has remained a powerful force for unity. At a time when evangelicals are growing world-wide, this book offers insights into the past which are relevant to contemporary issues.

2001 / 1-84227-089-3 / xii + 394pp

Ian M. Randall
Spirituality and Social Change
The Contribution of F.B. Meyer (1847–1929)
(Studies in Evangelical History and Thought)

This is a fresh appraisal of F.B. Meyer (1847–1929), a leading Free Church minister. Having been deeply affected by holiness spirituality, Meyer became the Keswick Convention's foremost international speaker. He combined spirituality with effective evangelism and socio-political activity. This study shows Meyer's significant contribution to spiritual renewal and social change.

2003 / 1-84227-195-4 / xx + 184pp

Geoffrey Robson
Dark Satanic Mills?
Religion and Irreligion in Birmingham and the Black Country
(Studies in Evangelical History and Thought)
This book analyses and interprets the nature and extent of popular Christian belief and practice in Birmingham and the Black Country during the first half of the nineteenth century, with particular reference to the impact of cholera epidemics and evangelism on church extension programmes.
2002 / 1-84227-102-4 / xiv + 294pp

Alan P.F. Sell
Enlightenment, Ecumenism, Evangel
Theological Themes and Thinkers 1550–2000
(Studies in Christian History and Thought)
This book consists of papers in which such interlocking topics as the Enlightenment, the problem of authority, the development of doctrine, spirituality, ecumenism, theological method and the heart of the gospel are discussed. Issues of significance to the church at large are explored with special reference to writers from the Reformed and Dissenting traditions.
2005 / 1-84227330-2 / xviii + 422pp

Alan P.F. Sell
Hinterland Theology
Some Reformed and Dissenting Adjustments
(Studies in Christian History and Thought)
Many books have been written on theology's 'giants' and significant trends, but what of those lesser-known writers who adjusted to them? In this book some hinterland theologians of the British Reformed and Dissenting traditions, who followed in the wake of toleration, the Evangelical Revival, the rise of modern biblical criticism and Karl Barth, are allowed to have their say. They include Thomas Ridgley, Ralph Wardlaw, T.V. Tymms and N.H.G. Robinson.
2006 / 1-84227-331-0

Alan P.F. Sell and Anthony R. Cross (eds)
Protestant Nonconformity in the Twentieth Century
(Studies in Christian History and Thought)
In this collection of essays scholars representative of a number of Nonconformist traditions reflect thematically on Nonconformists' life and witness during the twentieth century. Among the subjects reviewed are biblical studies, theology, worship, evangelism and spirituality, and ecumenism. Over and above its immediate interest, this collection provides a marker to future scholars and others wishing to know how some of their forebears assessed Nonconformity's contribution to a variety of fields during the century leading up to Christianity's third millennium.

2003 / 1-84227-221-7 / x + 398pp

Mark Smith
Religion in Industrial Society
Oldham and Saddleworth 1740–1865
(Studies in Christian History and Thought)
This book analyses the way British churches sought to meet the challenge of industrialization and urbanization during the period 1740–1865. Working from a case-study of Oldham and Saddleworth, Mark Smith challenges the received view that the Anglican Church in the eighteenth century was characterized by complacency and inertia, and reveals Anglicanism's vigorous and creative response to the new conditions. He reassesses the significance of the centrally directed church reforms of the mid-nineteenth century, and emphasizes the importance of local energy and enthusiasm. Charting the growth of denominational pluralism in Oldham and Saddleworth, Dr Smith compares the strengths and weaknesses of the various Anglican and Nonconformist approaches to promoting church growth. He also demonstrates the extent to which all the churches participated in a common culture shaped by the influence of evangelicalism, and shows that active co-operation between the churches rather than denominational conflict dominated. This revised and updated edition of Dr Smith's challenging and original study makes an important contribution both to the social history of religion and to urban studies.

2006 / 1-84227-335-3 / approx. 300pp

July 2005

David M. Thompson
Baptism, Church and Society in Britain from the Evangelical Revival to
Baptism, Eucharist and Ministry

The theology and practice of baptism have not received the attention they deserve. How important is faith? What does baptismal regeneration mean? Is baptism a bond of unity between Christians? This book discusses the theology of baptism and popular belief and practice in England and Wales from the Evangelical Revival to the publication of the World Council of Churches' consensus statement on *Baptism, Eucharist and Ministry* (1982).

2005 / 1-84227-393-0 / approx. 224pp

Martin Sutherland
Peace, Toleration and Decay
The Ecclesiology of Later Stuart Dissent
(Studies in Christian History and Thought)

This fresh analysis brings to light the complexity and fragility of the later Stuart Nonconformist consensus. Recent findings on wider seventeenth-century thought are incorporated into a new picture of the dynamics of Dissent and the roots of evangelicalism.

2003 / 1-84227-152-0 / xxii + 216pp

Haddon Willmer
Evangelicalism 1785–1835: An Essay (1962) and Reflections (2004)
(Studies in Evangelical History and Thought)

Awarded the Hulsean Prize in the University of Cambridge in 1962, this interpretation of a classic period of English Evangelicalism, by a young church historian, is now supplemented by reflections on Evangelicalism from the vantage point of a retired Professor of Theology.

2006 / 1-84227-219-5

Linda Wilson
Constrained by Zeal
Female Spirituality amongst Nonconformists 1825–1875
(Studies in Evangelical History and Thought)

Constrained by Zeal investigates the neglected area of Nonconformist female spirituality. Against the background of separate spheres, it analyses the experience of women from four denominations, and argues that the churches provided a 'third sphere' in which they could find opportunities for participation.

2000 / 0-85364-972-3 / xvi + 294pp

Nigel G. Wright
Disavowing Constantine
Mission, Church and the Social Order in the Theologies of
John Howard Yoder and Jürgen Moltmann
(Paternoster Theological Monographs)
This book is a timely restatement of a radical theology of church and state in the
Anabaptist and Baptist tradition. Dr Wright constructs his argument in dialogue
and debate with Yoder and Moltmann, major contributors to a free church
perspective.
2000 / 0-85364-978-2 / xvi + 252pp

Nigel G. Wright
Free Church, Free State
The Positive Baptist Vision
Free Church, Free State is a textbook on baptist ways of being church and a
proposal for the future of baptist churches in an ecumenical context. Nigel
Wright argues that both baptist (small 'b') and catholic (small 'c') church
traditions should seek to enrich and support each other as valid expressions of
the body of Christ without sacrificing what they hold dear. Written for pastors,
church planters, evangelists and preachers, Nigel Wright offers frameworks of
thought for baptists and non-baptists in their journey together following Christ.
2005 / 1-84227-353-1 / xxviii + 292

Nigel G. Wright
New Baptists, New Agenda
New Baptists, New Agenda is a timely contribution to the growing debate about
the health, shape and future of the Baptists. It considers the steady changes that
have taken place among Baptists in the last decade – changes of mood, style,
practice and structure – and encourages us to align these current movements and
questions with God's upward and future call. He contends that the true church
has yet to come: the church that currently exists is an anticipation of the joyful
gathering of all who have been called by the Spirit through Christ to the Father.
2002 / 1-84227-157-1 / x + 162pp

Paternoster:
thinking faith

Paternoster
9 Holdom Avenue,
Bletchley,
Milton Keynes MK1 1QR,
United Kingdom
Web: www.authenticmedia.co.uk/paternoster

July 2005